THE CARAVAN & CAMPING GUIDE 2016

AA Lifestyle Guides

Published by AA Publishing, a trading name of AA Media Limited, whose registered office is Fanum House, Basing View, Basingstoke RG21 4EA. Registered number 06112600

48th edition November 2015

Assessments of the AA campsites are based on the experience of the AA Caravan & Camping Inspectors on the occasion(s) of their visit(s) and therefore descriptions given in this guide necessarily contain an element of subjective opinion which may not reflect or dictate a reader's own opinion on another occasion. See pages 10-11 for a clear explanation of how, based on our Inspectors' inspection experiences, campsites are graded.

AA Media Limited strives to ensure accuracy of the information in this guide at the time of printing. Nevertheless, the Publisher cannot be held responsible for any errors or omissions, or for changes in the details given in this guide, or for the consequences of any reliance on the information provided by the same. This does not affect your statutory rights. Due to the constantly evolving nature of the subject matter the information is subject to change. AA Media Limited gratefully receives advice from readers regarding any necessary update.

Please contact:
Advertising Sales Department: advertisingsales@theAA.com
Editorial Department: lifestyleguides@theAA.com

Website addresses are included in some entries as specified by the respective establishment. Such websites are not under the control of AA Media Limited and as such AA Media Limited has no control over them and will not accept any responsibility or liability in respect of any and all matters whatsoever relating to such websites including access, content, material and functionality. By including the addresses of third party websites the AA does not intend to solicit business or offer any security to any person in any country, directly or indirectly.

Photographs in the gazetteer are provided by the establishments.

Typeset/Repro by Servis Filmsetting Ltd, Stockport
Printed and bound by Printer Trento SRL, Trento

Directory compiled by the AA Lifestyle Guides Department and managed in the Librios Information Management System.

Country and county opening pages: Nick Channer

Maps prepared by the Mapping Services Department of AA Publishing.

Information on National Parks in England provided by the Countryside Agency (Natural England).

Information on National Parks in Scotland provided by Scottish Natural Heritage.

Information on National Parks in Wales provided by The Countryside Council for Wales.

A CIP catalogue for this book is available from the British Library.

ISBN: 978-0-7495-7727-8

A05324

Contents

VOYAGER

Welcome to the AA Caravan & Camping Guide 2016

Welcome to the 48th edition of the AA's bestselling Caravan & Camping Guide featuring over 860 fully inspected and independently graded camping parks across England, Scotland, Wales, Northern Ireland and the Republic of Ireland

Who's in the guide?

Within these pages you'll find simple rural campsites, beautifully landscaped parks with top quality toilet facilities and excellent customer care, and self-contained Holiday Centres that offer a wide range of sport, leisure and entertainment facilities. We also include Holiday Home Parks offering holiday caravans, chalets and lodges for hire and glamping sites with different types of 'outdoor' accommodation. The sites pay an annual fee for the inspection, recognition and rating.

AA Pennant classification

Campsites apply for AA recognition and they receive an unannounced visit each year by one of the AA's qualified Campsite Inspectors. Touring pitches, facilities and hospitality are fully checked and campsites are graded from 1 to 5 Pennants, or rated as a Holiday Centre or Holiday Home Park, using fixed criteria for each Pennant rating. A qualitative assessment score is also given to each campsite. Gold Pennants identify the top quality parks that score 90% and above within the 2 to 5 Pennant ratings and Green Pennants signify glamping-only sites.

AA Campsites of the Year

Following nominations by our inspectors we award an overall winner from three national finalists; five regional winners and a Holiday Centre winner – all are selected for their outstanding overall quality and high levels of customer care. Our two special awards recognise the best small campsite, and the most improved campsite.

South Lytchett Manor Caravan & Camping Park, Poole, Dorset is the worthy overall winner for 2016 (see page 14 for details).

An in-depth look

This year we're highlighting glamorous camping and what you can expect to find at several such sites around the country. Having booked, you just arrive to find a ready-made shelter in the form of a basic wooden pod or, for an even grander experience a stylish yurt, tipi or shepherd's hut. Many have mod cons that wouldn't look out of place in an interior design magazine (see page 20). The AA now inspects sites that specialise in glamping accommodation and you can find details of these throughout the guide (look for the Green Pennant symbols). For a list of all AA-rated sites that offer glamping see pages 487-490.

In our second feature (see page 24) we offer some handy tips and encouragement for anyone who is new to holidaying with a caravan, motorhome or tent.

The best sites for...

Our quick reference list (pages 28-29) details the AA inspectors' favourite campsites for stunning views, waterside pitches, on-site fishing, great places to stay with your children, good restaurants on site, those that are eco-friendly and even where the toilets are really top-notch.

How to use the AA Caravan & Camping Guide

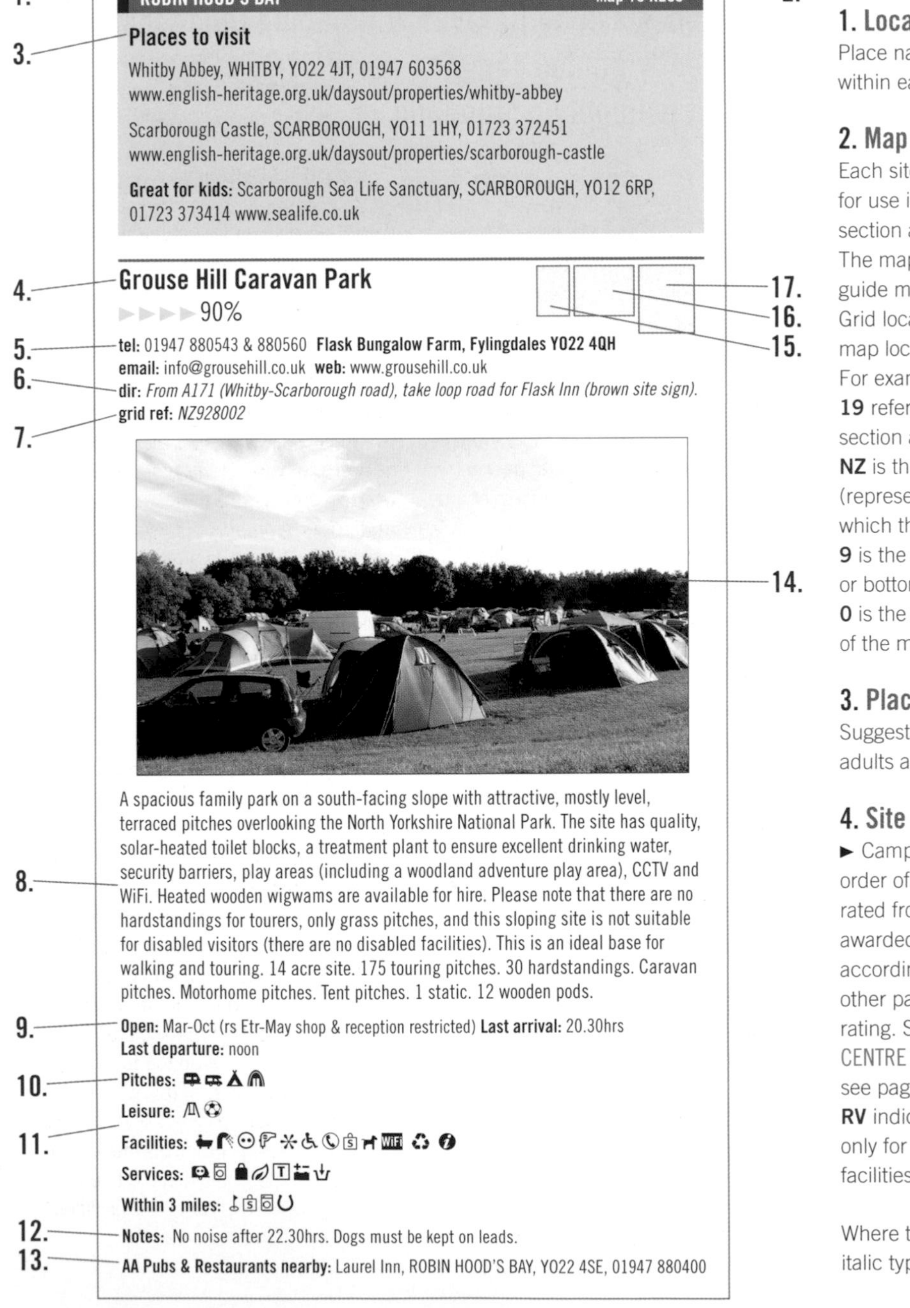

1. **ROBIN HOOD'S BAY** — **Map 19 NZ90** 2.

3. **Places to visit**

Whitby Abbey, WHITBY, YO22 4JT, 01947 603568
www.english-heritage.org.uk/daysout/properties/whitby-abbey

Scarborough Castle, SCARBOROUGH, YO11 1HY, 01723 372451
www.english-heritage.org.uk/daysout/properties/scarborough-castle

Great for kids: Scarborough Sea Life Sanctuary, SCARBOROUGH, YO12 6RP, 01723 373414 www.sealife.co.uk

4. **Grouse Hill Caravan Park** 17. 16. 15.

90%

5. **tel:** 01947 880543 & 880560 **Flask Bungalow Farm, Fylingdales YO22 4QH**
email: info@grousehill.co.uk **web:** www.grousehill.co.uk

6. **dir:** *From A171 (Whitby-Scarborough road), take loop road for Flask Inn (brown site sign).*

7. **grid ref:** *NZ928002*

14.

8. A spacious family park on a south-facing slope with attractive, mostly level, terraced pitches overlooking the North Yorkshire National Park. The site has quality, solar-heated toilet blocks, a treatment plant to ensure excellent drinking water, security barriers, play areas (including a woodland adventure play area), CCTV and WiFi. Heated wooden wigwams are available for hire. Please note that there are no hardstandings for tourers, only grass pitches, and this sloping site is not suitable for disabled visitors (there are no disabled facilities). This is an ideal base for walking and touring. 14 acre site. 175 touring pitches. 30 hardstandings. Caravan pitches. Motorhome pitches. Tent pitches. 1 static. 12 wooden pods.

9. **Open:** Mar-Oct (rs Etr-May shop & reception restricted) **Last arrival:** 20.30hrs
Last departure: noon

10. **Pitches:**

Leisure:

11. **Facilities:**

Services:

Within 3 miles:

12. **Notes:** No noise after 22.30hrs. Dogs must be kept on leads.

13. **AA Pubs & Restaurants nearby:** Laurel Inn, ROBIN HOOD'S BAY, YO22 4SE, 01947 880400

1. Location

Place names are listed alphabetically within each county.

2. Map reference

Each site is given a map reference for use in conjunction with the atlas section at the back of the guide.
The map reference comprises the guide map page number, the National Grid location square and a two-figure map location reference.
For example: **Map 19 NZ90**.
19 refers to the page number of the map section at the back of the guide.
NZ is the National Grid lettered square (representing 100,000sq metres) in which the location will be found.
9 is the figure reading across the top or bottom of the map page.
0 is the figure reading down each side of the map page.

3. Places to visit

Suggestions of nearby places to visit for adults and children.

4. Site name and rating

► Campsites are listed in descending order of their Pennant rating. Sites are rated from 1 to 5 Pennants and are also awarded a score ranging from 50–100% according to how they compare with other parks within the same Pennant rating. Some sites are given a HOLIDAY CENTRE grading. For a fuller explanation see pages 10-11.
RV indicates a category of park catering only for recreational vehicles (no toilet facilities are provided at these sites).

Where the name of the site appears in italic type, the information that follows

has not been confirmed by the campsite for the 2016 edition.
NEW indicates that the site is new in the guide this year.

5. Contact details

6. Directions

Brief directions from a recognisable point, such as a main road, are included in each entry. Please contact the individual site for more detailed directions or use the AA Route Planner at **theAA.com**, and enter the site's postcode.

7. Grid reference

Each entry includes a six-figure National Grid reference as many sites are in remote locations. Use the reference alongside the relevant Ordnance Survey map and in conjunction with the atlas at the back of this guide to help you find the precise location.

8. Description

Descriptions are based on information supplied by the AA inspector at the time of the last visit.
Please note: The AA Pennant classification is based on the touring pitches and the facilities only. AA inspectors do not visit or report on statics or chalets for hire under the AA Caravan & Camping quality standards scheme. However, the AA has a category of HOLIDAY HOME PARK and these static caravan, chalet or lodge-only parks are inspected.
For sites other than those listed as HOLIDAY HOME PARK we only include the number of static caravan pitches in order to give an indication of the nature and size of the site.

9. Opening, arrival and departure times

Parks are not necessarily open all year and while most sites permit arrivals at any time, checking beforehand is advised (see page 12).

10. Pitches

Rates given after each appropriate symbol (caravan), (motorhome), (tent) are the overnight cost for one unit. The prices can vary according to the number of people in the party, but some parks have a fixed fee per pitch regardless of the number of people. Please note that some sites charge separately for certain facilities, including showers; and some sites charge a different rate for pitches with or without electricity. Prices are supplied to us in good faith by the site operators and are as accurate as possible. They are, however, only a guide and are subject to change during the currency of this publication. indicates that the campsite offers one or more types of glamping accommodation (see point 15, below).
* If this symbol appears before the prices, it indicates that the site has not advised us of the prices for 2016; they relate to 2015.

11. Symbols and abbreviations

These are divided into Pitches, Leisure, Facilities, Services and Within 3 miles sections. A guide to abbreviations and symbols can be found on page 9 and on pages throughout the guide.

12. Notes

This includes information about additional facilities and any restrictions the site would like their visitors to be aware of. () As most sites now accept credit and debit cards, we have only indicated those that don't accept cards.

13. AA pubs and restaurants

An entry may include suggestions for nearby pubs and/or restaurants recognised by the AA. Some of these establishments will have been awarded Rosettes for food excellence. To find out the distance by road between the campsite and the pub or restaurant, enter both postcodes into a Sat Nav or the AA Route Planner at **theAA.com**.

14. Photograph

Optional photograph/s supplied by the campsite.

15. Glamping

The campsite offers one or more types of 'glamorous camping' accommodation, i.e. wooden pods, tipis, yurts, bell tents, safari tents, shepherd's huts, Airstream caravans, vintage caravans etc. Check with the site to see what type of glamping experience they offer.

16. Best of British

A group of over 50 parks, both large and small, which focus on high quality facilities and amenities. www.bob.org.uk

17. David Bellamy Awards

Many AA recognised sites are also recipients of a David Bellamy Award for Conservation. The awards are graded Gold, Silver and Bronze. The symbols we show indicate the 2014/15 winners as this was the most up-to-date information at the time of going to press. For the 2015/16 winners please contact: British Holiday & Homes Parks Association Tel: 01452 526911 www.bellamyparks.co.uk

Facilities for disabled guests

The Equality Act 2010 provides legal rights for disabled people including access to goods, services and facilities, and means that service providers may have to consider making adjustments to their premises. For more information about the Act see: www.gov.uk/definition-of-disability-under-equality-act-2010

If a site has told us that they provide facilities for disabled visitors their entry in the guide will include the following symbol: . The sites in this guide should be aware of their responsibilities under the Act. However, we recommend that you always phone in advance to ensure the site you have chosen has facilities to suit your needs.

Symbols and abbreviations

Pitches

Caravan

Motorhome

Tent

Glamping-style accommodation

Leisure

Indoor swimming pool

Outdoor swimming pool

Tennis court

Games room

Children's playground

Kid's club

Stables & horse riding

Golf course (on site or within 3 miles)

Boats for hire

Cinema

Entertainment

Fishing

Mini golf

Watersports

Gym

Sports field

Spa Spa

Separate TV room

Facilities

Bath

Shower

Electric shaver

Hairdryer

Ice pack facility

Disabled facilities

Public telephone

Shop on site or within 200yds

Mobile shop (calling at least 5 days per week)

BBQ area

Picnic area

WiFi access

Internet access

Recycling facilities

Tourist information

Dog exercise area

Services

Toilet fluid

Café or restaurant

Fast food/Takeaway

Baby care

Electric hook up

Motorvan service point

Launderette

Licensed bar

Calor Gas

Camping Gaz

Battery charging

Other

No dogs

No credit or debit cards

Children of all ages accepted

Abbreviations

BH/BHs Bank Holiday/s

Etr Easter

Spring BH Spring Bank Holiday (late May)

fr from

hrs hours

m mile

mdnt midnight

rdbt roundabout

rs restricted service

RV Recreational vehicles

U rating not confirmed

wk week

wknd weekend

The AA classification scheme

AA parks are classified on a 5-point scale according to their style and the range of facilities they offer. As the number of Pennants increases, so the quality and variety of facilities is generally greater.

What can you expect at an AA-rated park?

All AA parks must meet a minimum standard: they should be clean, well maintained and welcoming. In addition they must have a local authority site licence (unless specially exempt), and satisfy local authority fire regulations.

The AA inspection

Each campsite that applies for AA recognition receives an unannounced visit each year by one of the AA's highly qualified team of inspectors. They make a thorough check of the site's touring pitches, facilities and hospitality. The sites pay an annual fee for the inspection, recognition and rating, and receive a text entry in the *AA Caravan & Camping Guide*.

AA inspectors pay when they stay overnight on a site. The criteria used by the inspectors in awarding the AA Pennant rating is shown on this and the opposite page.

AA Quality percentage score

AA rated Campsites, Caravan Parks, Holiday Centres and Holiday Home Parks are awarded a percentage score alongside their Pennant rating, Holiday Centre or Holiday Home Park status. This is a qualitative assessment of various factors including customer care and hospitality, toilet facilities and park landscaping. The % score runs from 50% to 100% and indicates the relative quality of parks with the same number of Pennants. For example, one 3-Pennant park may score 70%, while another 3-Pennant park may achieve 90%.
Holiday Centres and Holiday Home Parks also receive a percentage score between 50% and 100% to differentiate between quality levels within this grading. Like the Pennant rating, the percentage is reassessed annually.

The Pennant Criteria

One Pennant Parks

These parks offer a fairly simple standard of facilities including:

- No more than 30 pitches per acre
- At least 5% of the total pitches allocated to touring caravans
- An adequate drinking water supply and reasonable drainage
- Washroom with flush toilets and toilet paper provided, unless no sanitary facilities are provided in which case this should be clearly stated
- Chemical disposal arrangements, ideally with running water, unless tents only
- Adequate refuse disposal that is clearly signed
- Well-drained ground and some level pitches
- Entrance and access roads of adequate width and surface
- Location of emergency phone clearly signed
- Emergency phone numbers fully displayed

Two Pennant Parks

Parks in this category should meet all of the above requirements, but offer an increased level of facilities, services, customer care, security and ground maintenance. They should include the following:

- Separate washrooms, including at least two male and two female WCs and washbasins per 30 pitches
- Hot and cold water direct to each basin
- Externally lit toilet blocks
- Warden available during day, times to be indicated
- Whereabouts of shop/chemist is clearly signed
- Dish-washing facilities, covered and lit
- Basic security (i.e. lockable gate and/or CCTV)
- Reception area

Three Pennant Parks

Many parks come within this rating and the range of facilities is wide. All parks will be of a very good standard and will meet the following minimum criteria:

- Facilities, services and park grounds are clean and well maintained, with buildings in good repair and attention paid to customer care and park security
- Evenly surfaced roads and paths

- Clean modern toilet blocks with all-night lighting and containing toilet seats in good condition, soap and hand dryers or paper towels, mirrors, shelves and hooks, shaver and hairdryer points, and lidded waste bins in female toilets
- Modern shower cubicles with sufficient hot water and attached, private changing space
- Electric hook-ups
- Some hardstanding/wheel runs/firm, level ground
- Laundry with automatic washing and drying facilities, separate from toilets
- Children's playground with safe equipment
- 24-hour public phone on site or nearby where mobile reception is poor
- Warden availability and 24-hour contact number clearly signed

Four Pennant Parks

These parks have achieved an excellent standard in all areas, including landscaping of grounds, natural screening and attractive park buildings, and customer care and park security. Toilets are smart, modern and immaculately maintained, and generally offer the following facilities:

- Spacious vanitory-style washbasins, at least two male and two female per 25 pitches
- Fully-tiled shower cubicles with doors, dry areas, shelves and hooks, at least one male and one female per 30 pitches
- Availability of washbasins in lockable cubicles, or combined toilet/washing cubicles, or a private/family room with shower/toilet/washbasin

Other requirements are:

- Baby changing facilities
- A shop on site, or within reasonable distance
- Warden available 24 hours
- Reception area open during the day, with tourist information available
- Internal roads, paths and toilet blocks lit at night
- Maximum 25 pitches per campable acre
- Toilet blocks heated October to Easter
- Approximately 50% of pitches with electric hook-ups
- Approximately 10% of pitches have hardstandings
- Late arrivals enclosure
- Security barrier and/or CCTV

Five Pennant Premier Parks

Premier parks are of an extremely high standard, set in attractive surroundings with superb mature landscaping. Facilities, security and customer care are of an exceptional quality. As well as the above they will also offer:

- First-class toilet facilities including several designated self-contained cubicles, ideally with WC, washbasin and shower
- Ideally electric hook-ups to 75% of pitches
- Approximately 20% of pitches have hardstandings
- Some fully-serviced 'super' pitches: of larger size, with water and electricity supplies connected
- A motorhome service point
- Toilet block/s should be heated
- Excellent security – coded barrier or number plate recognition and CCTV

Many Premier Parks will also provide:

- Heated swimming pool
- Well-equipped shop
- Café or restaurant and bar
- A designated walking area for dogs (if accepted)

Gold Pennants

AA Gold Pennants are awarded to the very best camping parks scoring 90% and above within the 2, 3, 4 and 5 Pennant ratings.

Green Pennants

AA Green Pennants (3, 4 and 5 Pennants) are awarded to sites that specialise in glamping-style accommodation (they may also offer a small number of touring pitches).

Holiday Centres and Holiday Home Parks

There are separate categories for Holiday Centres and Holiday Home Parks. The AA inspects these sites and awards an appropriate quality percentage score.

HOLIDAY CENTRES

In this category we distinguish parks that cater for all holiday needs including cooked meals and entertainment. They provide:

- A wide range of on-site sports, leisure and recreational facilities
- Supervision and security at a very high level
- A choice of eating outlets
- Facilities for touring caravans that equal those available to rented holiday accommodation
- A maximum density of 25 pitches per acre
- Clubhouse with entertainment
- Laundry with automatic washing machines

HOLIDAY HOME PARKS

Parks in this category are static – only parks offering holiday caravans, chalets or lodges for hire and catering for all holiday needs. They provide:

- Quality holiday hire caravans and chalets or luxurious lodges
- A wide range of on-site sports, leisure and recreational facilities
- Supervision and security at a very high level
- A choice of eating outlets
- Clubhouse with entertainment

Useful information

Booking information

It is advisable to book in advance during peak holiday seasons and in school or public holidays. It is also wise to check whether or not a reservation entitles you to a particular pitch. It does not necessarily follow that an early booking will secure the best pitch; you may simply have the choice of what is available at the time you check in.

Some parks may require a deposit on booking which may be non-returnable if you have to cancel your holiday. If you do have to cancel, notify the proprietor at once because you may be held legally responsible for partial or full payment unless the pitch can be re-let. Consider taking out insurance such as AA Travel Insurance, tel: 0800 912 5002 or visit theAA.com for details to cover a lost deposit or compensation. Some parks will not accept overnight bookings unless payment for the full minimum period (e.g. two or three days) is made.

Last arrival Unless otherwise stated, parks will usually accept arrivals at any time of the day or night, but some have a special 'late arrivals' enclosure where you have to make temporary camp to avoid disturbing other people on the park. Please note that on some parks access to the toilet block is by key or pass card only, so if you know you will be late, do check what arrangements can be made.

Last departure Most parks will specify their overnight period e.g. noon to noon. If you overstay the departure time you can be charged for an extra day.

Chemical closet disposal point

You will usually find one on every park, except those catering only for tents. It must be a specially constructed unit, or a WC permanently set aside for the purpose of chemical disposal and with adjacent rinsing and soak-away facilities. However, some local authorities are concerned about the effect of chemicals on bacteria in cesspools etc, and may prohibit or restrict provision of chemical closet disposal points in their areas.

Complaints

If you have any complaints speak to the park proprietor or supervisor immediately, so that the matter can be sorted out on the spot. If this personal approach fails you may decide, if the matter is serious, to approach the local authority or tourist board. AA guide users may also write to:

The Editor, AA Caravan & Camping Guide,
AA Lifestyle Guides, 13th floor, Fanum House,
Basing View, Basingstoke, RG21 4EA

The AA may at its sole discretion investigate any complaints received from guide users for the purpose of making any necessary amendments to the guide. The AA will not in any circumstances act as representative or negotiator or undertake to obtain compensation or enter into further correspondence or deal with the matter in any other way whatsoever. The AA will not guarantee to take any specific action.

Dogs

Dogs may or may not be accepted at parks; this is entirely at the owner's or warden's discretion (assistance dogs should be accepted). Even when the park states that they accept dogs, it is still discretionary, and certain breeds may not be considered as suitable, so we strongly advise that you check when you book. Some sites have told us they do not accept dangerous breeds. (The following breeds are covered under the Dangerous Dogs Act 1991 – Pit Bull Terrier, Japanese Tosa, Dogo Argentino and Fila Brazilerio). Dogs should always be kept on a lead and under control, and letting them sleep in cars is not encouraged.

Electric hook-up

Many parks now have electric hook-ups available on some of their pitches, however if you need electric you should request it when making your booking. Generally the voltage is 240v AC, 50 cycles, although this can vary slightly according to the location. The supply however can vary considerably from 5 amps to 16 amps although 16 amps is becoming the norm – again you should check with the campsite if this is important to you. Remember, if your consumption is greater than the supply the electricity will trip out and need resetting.

Electric hook-up connections are now standardised in the UK with the blue coloured safety connectors. However, it is good practice to always connect your cable to your caravan, motorhome or tent electric distribution unit before connecting to the hook-up supply.

It is also important that tents or trailer tents have a Residual Circuit Device (RCD) for safety reasons and to avoid overloading the circuit. Caravans and motorhomes have RCDs built in. You should remember that if your RCD trips out at 16 amps and the campsite supply is say 10 amps you can easily overload the supply and cause the hook-up to trip out.

It is quite easy to check what demands your appliances can place on the supply at any one time. Details are normally available in the caravan or motorhome handbooks which show the wattage of appliances fitted.

The amperage used is based on the wattage of appliance divided by the supply voltage.

The following table is a quick check of electrical consumption, depending what is switched on.

Average amperage (based on a 240v supply)

Caravan fridge (125 watts)	0.5 amps
Caravan heater set at (500 watts)	2.1 amps
Caravan heater set at (1000 watts)	4.2 amps
Caravan heater set at (2000 watts)	8.4 amps
Caravan water heater (850 watts)	3.5 amps
Kettle (domestic type) (1500 watts)	6.3 amps
Kettle (low wattage type) (750 watts)	3.1 amps
Hairdryer (2100 watts)	8.8 amps
Microwave (750 watts)	3.1 amps
Colour TV (flat-screen LED type) (30 watts)	0.13 amps
Battery charger (built-in type) (200 watts)	0.8 amps

Motorhomes
At some parks motorhomes are only accepted if they remain static throughout the stay. Also check that there are suitable level pitches at the parks where you plan to stay.

Overflow pitches
Campsites are legally entitled to use an overflow field which is not a normal part of their camping area for up to 28 days in any one year as an emergency method of coping with additional numbers at busy periods. When this 28-day rule is being invoked site owners should increase the numbers of sanitary facilities accordingly. In these circumstances the extra facilities are sometimes no more than temporary portacabins.

Parking
Some park operators insist that cars are left in a parking area separate from the pitches; others will not allow more than one car to be parked beside each caravan, tent or glamping unit.

Park restrictions
Many parks in our guide are selective about the categories of people they will accept on their parks. In the caravan and camping world there are many restrictions and some categories of visitor are banned altogether. Where a park has told us of a restriction/s this is included in notes in their entry.

On many parks in this guide, unaccompanied young people, single-sex groups, single adults, and motorcycle groups will not be accepted. The AA takes no stance in this matter, basing its Pennant classification on facilities, quality and maintenance. On the other hand, some parks cater well for teenagers and offer magnificent sporting and leisure facilities as well as discos; others have only very simple amenities. A small number of parks in our guide exclude all children in order to create an environment aimed at holiday makers in search of total peace and quiet (see page 39).

Pets
The importation of animals into the UK is subject to strict controls. Penalties for trying to avoid these controls are severe. However, the Pet Travel Scheme (PETS) allows cats, dogs, ferrets and certain other pets coming from the EU and certain other countries to enter the UK without quarantine provided the appropriate conditions are met.
For more details: www.gov.uk/take-pet-abroad/overview
PETS Helpline: 0370 241 1710

Pets resident in the British Isles (UK, Republic of Ireland, Isle of Man and Channel Islands) are not subject to any quarantine or PETS rules when travelling within the British Isles.

Seasonal touring pitches
Some park operators allocate a number of their hardstanding pitches for long-term seasonal caravans. These pitches can be reserved for the whole period the campsite is open, generally between Easter and September, and a fixed fee is charged for keeping the caravan on the park for the season. These pitches are in great demand, especially in popular tourist areas, so enquire well in advance if you wish to book one.

Shops
The range of provisions in shops is usually in proportion to the park's size. As far as AA Pennant requirements are concerned, a mobile shop calling several times a week, or a general store within easy walking distance of the park is acceptable.

AA Campsites of the Year

Following nominations by our inspectors we award an overall winner from three national finalists, five regional winners and a Holiday Centre winner – all are selected for their outstanding overall quality and high levels of customer care. Our two special awards recognise the best small campsite, and the most improved campsite.

ENGLAND & OVERALL WINNER OF THE AA CAMPSITE OF THE YEAR

SOUTH LYTCHETT MANOR CARAVAN & CAMPING PARK

►►►►► **96%** POOLE, DORSET page 196

Set in 20 acres of tranquil parkland, South Lytchett Manor Caravan and Camping Park is in a perfect location on the outskirts of Poole, and within easy reach of the region's most popular areas and beaches, namely Bournemouth, Swanage and Studland. It is very much a family-run park and David, Joanne and Matthew Bridgen, and their dedicated team, have developed the park to its current superb standard – all facilities are well thought out, modern and spotlessly clean. Their ethos is very much 'customer is king' and everyone connected with the park goes out of their way to ensure their guests are looked after from arrival to departure – nothing is too much trouble. The pitches are spacious and varied and many are fully serviced. This very high level of customer care really sets South Lytchett Manor apart and many of their guests return time after time because of it. The regular Jurassic X53 bus (Exeter to Poole) stops right outside the park entrance and is very popular with motorhome owners. The Bridgens have now introduced glamping to the park in the form of a luxury, modern 'Twaggon' (a Gypsy caravan). This is a very worthy winner of the AA's overall award, which recognises the dedication and hard work the family owners have put into making such a stunning park.

SCOTLAND

CRAIGTOUN MEADOWS HOLIDAY PARK

►►►►► **94%** ST ANDREWS, FIFE page 393

Craigtoun Meadows is a traditional, well-managed Holiday Park in a peaceful location on the edge of Craigtoun Country Park and close to the busy tourist town of St Andrews. Set in secluded woodland, which has been divided into smaller areas with mature trees and exceptionally well-managed borders, grass and buildings, it feels like you are arriving at a stately home as you approach along the drive to the reception. Your first impression will be one of quality, which carries through to the holiday homes area. When you enter the touring area the sense of openness with its large pitches – some with summerhouses and great landscaping – will confirm that you were right to choose a stay at this park. There is an outstandingly well-maintained amenity block, a café serving good quality traditional fare, two games rooms and a large fenced play area for children (that includes a zip wire), an all-weather ball pitch and climbing frames to suit all ages. Expect to find good, old-fashioned quality at this site where the staff provide the very highest standards of service. The park makes a great base for touring this lovely area and is also perfect for just sitting back and relaxing. It certainly deserves the AA Campsite of the Year for Scotland award.

WALES

PONT KEMYS CARAVAN & CAMPING PARK

►►►►► **86%** USK, MONMOUTHSHIRE page 438

With the River Usk meandering through it and the surrounding trees creating a wonderful habitat for wildlife, the only distractions at Pont Kemys are the pleasant ones of running water and birdsong. Hands-on owners Bryan and Rosy Jones have been welcoming guests to their immaculately maintained holiday destination for many years. It has the benefit of separate family and adults-only enclosed areas, the latter providing fully-serviced and very spacious all-level pitches. Indigenous wild flowers and shrubs are complemented by stunning displays of pretty seasonal flowers and at the time of our last inspection, it was a joy to observe happy families enjoying the many attractions provided. The centrally located modern amenities block is tastefully decorated, equipped with top-notch modern fixtures and fittings, including air-conditioning and central heating for the cooler months. There is low-level lighting around the park to avoid light pollution, and the CCTV and barrier system ensure good safety and security at all times. Many historical attractions and the pretty market town of Usk are within easy travelling distance. This excellent, well-run park is an obvious choice to receive the AA Campsite of the Year for Wales award.

AA Campsites of the Year *continued*

SOUTH WEST ENGLAND

DORNAFIELD ►►►►► 95%
NEWTON ABBOT, DEVON page 168

The Dewhirst family's immaculately kept park is set in a tranquil wooded valley between Dartmoor and Torbay. At the heart of the 30-acre site is Dornafield, a beautifully restored 14th-century farmhouse, adapted for campers' use. Peter and Simon Dewhirst's passion for the park, lovingly developed over 25 years, is clearly evident with year-on-year improvements; the general attention to detail and high levels of customer care results in many people returning time and again. The park comprises three stunning areas, including the charming Orchard with 16 spacious tent pitches, and the very impressive Blackrock Copse with 60 fully-serviced, all-weather gravel pitches, and there's a stone console housing drinking and waste water, TV and electric hook-up, a chemical disposal point, refuse bin and low-level lighting. There are also two ultra-modern toilet blocks, an excellent licensed shop, a fully-equipped games room, and the Quarry Café. Following his 2015 inspection visit our inspector commented: 'To me this park is the ultimate in camping and caravanning, it blends peace and tranquillity with a friendly family atmosphere, and the hard work the Dewhirsts have put in over the years is certainly paying off, as it's now one of the best parks in the country.'

SOUTH EAST ENGLAND

CONCIERGE CAMPING ►►►►► 87%
CHICHESTER, WEST SUSSEX page 323

Developing this stunning new park in a field adjoining their house has been a labour of love for Tracey and Guy Hodgkin who have invested £350k to create a first-class small park for 15 units. Opening in June 2015, it has been an immediate hit with those who seek a touch of luxury while staying close to Chichester, Goodwood, West Wittering beach and the South Downs. Everything is top spec, from very spacious, fully-serviced pitches and the reception (replete with a shop stocking local produce, coffee and drinks, late-arrival and breakfast hampers) to the state-of-the-art amenities block painted in a smart Farrow & Ball green and displaying the Concierge Camping logo on the glass doors. Even electric cars can be hired. The hotel-standard toilets have the 'wow' factor – Ratham Estate toiletries, piped radio, full-length mirrors, smart partitioning, ultra-efficient rain showers, air-blade hand driers, stylish washbasins with top-spec temperature controls, and an excellent family/disabled room. The block is heated in winter and air-conditioned in summer. Excellent decking with LED lighting, smart seating and barbecues complete the picture here. It may be new but this exciting and very impressive park really deserves the AA's campsite award for the South East.

HEART OF ENGLAND

CLOVER FIELDS TOURING CAMPING PARK ►►► 95%

BUXTON, DERBYSHIRE page 146

This developing and spacious adults-only park is located just over a mile from Buxton and provides the perfect base for exploring the Peak District, with the Castleton Caverns, Haddon Hall, Chatsworth House and excellent walking country all just a short drive away. Owners Jan and Stephen Redfern and daughter Jody go the extra mile to ensure that every visitor is made to feel 'special' and 'part of the family' when they arrive – that's what sets Clover Fields, a beautifully maintained park, apart from other parks with a similar three Pennant rating. Designed as a continual loop, pitches are fully serviced and have individual barbecues, and are laid out on terraces, each with extensive views over the countryside. Swathes of natural meadow grasses and flowers cloak the terraces and surrounding fields – it is a truly peaceful rural oasis for a relaxing break away. The Redferns continue to invest year on year, with the addition of the excellent Teapots Café for 2015, which has proved a real hit with campers, especially for weekend breakfasts and suppers. In addition, a new ultra-modern facilities block is due to be completed for the 2016 season. The family are very proud of their achievements at Clover Fields and the Heart of England Campsite of the Year award is well deserved.

NORTH WEST ENGLAND

HOLLINS FARM CAMPING & CARAVANNING ►►►► 90%

FAR ARNSIDE, LANCASHIRE page 240

Enjoying a tranquil country setting with extensive views across the Cheshire Plain to the Welsh hills, this secluded landscaped park has experienced major investment in recent years, which has lifted the overall quality at this notable holiday destination. Improvements include the superb new amenities block that provides excellent privacy options combined with first-class interior fixtures and fittings and underfloor heating. Additionally, the grounds are immaculately maintained, with a wide variety of seasonal and indigenous trees, colourful foliage and stunning floral displays that create an air of peace and tranquillity. Generous pitch density provides optimum privacy; some super pitches have hardstandings and full services, and additional facilities include a heated outdoor swimming pool, an all-weather tennis court and coarse fishing on several lakes. Avid anglers should consider booking the holiday home that overlooks the adult-only fishing lake as they can cast a line from the decked balcony. Campers here can simply relax and enjoy the many varieties of wildlife, which is encouraged on the site – there are bird tables, bat and owl boxes, and informative nature signs that detail the flora and fauna. Happy memories are sure to be made following a stay at this park.

AA Campsites of the Year *continued*

NORTH EAST ENGLAND

NABURN LOCK CARAVAN PARK ►►►► **90%**
NABURN, NORTH YORKSHIRE page 354

Naburn Lock Caravan Park is located beside the River Ouse, just four miles south of York. It provides an excellent and very tranquil base for exploring the city, the coastal resort of Whitby and the North York Moors. In fact, the river bus to York leaves from a jetty beside the park, which is very popular with motorhome visitors. Hands-on owners Peter and Catherine Wilkinson have a deep passion for their beautifully manicured park and personally run it on a day-to-day basis, and they are steadily upgrading the facilities. From conception to actual building, they throw themselves 100% into improving the site year-on-year ensuring that visitors experience good quality amenities, a high degree of customer care, and a home-from-home feel. Following the 2015 inspection, the park was awarded an increased Quality Score of 90%, so achieving Gold Pennants, which reflected the improvements and the general attention to detail across the park; for example extending pitches to accommodate large units, adding hardstanding pitches, re-designing the area at the front of reception, and a full redecoration of the very modern toilet blocks and the reception and shop. As such, this riverside gem is the North East Campsite of the Year winner.

HOLIDAY CENTRE OF THE YEAR

CRAIG TARA HOLIDAY PARK
HOLIDAY CENTRE **85%** AYR, SOUTH AYRSHIRE page 383

Craig Tara Holiday Park is a lovely holiday centre on the outskirts of Ayr that has been carefully developed over the years to maximise the views across the bay towards Ayr, Troon and the Isle of Arran. It would be fair to say it is actually a small self-contained village, geared towards providing a great family-orientated holiday whilst also catering for those who just wish to sit and relax in a safe and pleasant environment. A large park, it is a testament to the commitment of all the staff that every visitor feels welcomed, and the wide-ranging facilities are truly excellent. The centre has various large complexes with show bars, restaurants, takeaways and entertainment centres to suit all ages. In 2015 the pool complex was completely refurbished and now boasts flumes, slides, splash zones and pools for different levels of swimming competence – it must be one of the best of its kind in Scotland, if not the UK. There are good shops on site, a large soft play area and a members' club for sole use of holiday-home owners with a pool, gym, club and restaurant. The park has steadily improved over the years and to sum up, it provides exemplary service combined with excellent modern facilities in an outstanding location. It deserves to receive the AA Holiday Centre of the Year award.

ROGER ALMOND MOST IMPROVED CAMPSITE

TREVALGAN TOURING PARK ►►►►► 83%

ST IVES, CORNWALL page 112

Serious investment by hands-on owners, Annette and Neil Osborne, has totally transformed this park over the past two seasons. Situated between St Ives and Zennor on the wild and rugged Penwith peninsula, it has become a top-notch and very welcoming touring destination. When our inspector arrived in 2014 he thought he was at the wrong park – the entrance had new electronic security barriers, there was a smart, new reception building, a fully refurbished facility block (which boasts under-floor heating, family rooms and top-notch fittings), a new play area, beautiful planting and improvements to the pitches (with more space and privacy). In 2015, he found 27 new electric hook-ups, a new motorhome service point, high-speed WiFi across the park, new water and grey waste stations, and upgrades in the facility block. Annette and Neil enthusiastically promote Cornwall, not just by offering local produce in their excellent shop, but also through their beautifully landscaped park – they work hard to ensure that visitors leave them having thoroughly enjoyed their holiday. It's been a stunning transformation in just two years, so fully deserves the upgrade to five Pennants and The AA's Roger Almond Award for the Most Improved Campsite.

SMALL CAMPSITE OF THE YEAR

LONG ACRES TOURING PARK ►►►► 90%

BOSTON, LINCOLNSHIRE page 246

Long Acres Touring Park is a small adults-only site in an attractive rural setting within easy reach of Boston, Spalding and Skegness. Tardis-like, the site extends back from John and Tracey Plant's beautiful bungalow and gardens. New arrivals are amazed when they see the well-designed and very tranquil camping area opening up as they drive through the gate. John and Tracey have worked hard to ensure that the pristine landscaping is maintained to a very high standard, with mature high hedging providing shelter from the wind. This is matched by the very modern toilet block, a home-from-home, with upmarket fittings, piped music, freshly laundered shower curtains, mops and cloths, and everything is spotlessly clean. The lawns are beautifully manicured and the gravel hardstandings well weeded. Improvements for 2015 included a fully operational CCTV system, super-fast broadband, a new biodegradable 'doggy waste facility', and the addition of a purpose-built and very welcoming and professional reception area. The hands-on owners are to be commended for transforming the long patch of land behind their property into a stunning park, one that deserves its new Gold Pennant status and the accolade of Small Campsite of the Year.

Glamping comes of age

A look at how the luxury camping market has blossomed

Everyone knows what glamping means these days – it's glamorous camping, it's boutique camping, it's luxury camping, it's all about experiencing life in the great outdoors without having to rough it. It's meant that thousands of people have discovered there's no more setting up camp or feeling the chill. AA inspector Colin Church has been out and about looking at three different glamping sites.

The word 'glamping' was widely adopted around 2007, but perhaps back then it just meant staying in a basic wooden pod or a carpeted tent and bringing along your own bed rolls and sleeping bags. Today, those beehive-like pods can still be hired in their basic form, but now the imagination of the glamping entrepreneur knows no bounds, it seems. The wide variety of accommodation is intriguing – African savannah safari tents, North American tipis, Mongolian yurts, Iranian alachighs, tree houses, shepherd's huts, gypsy vardos, double decker buses – the list goes on and on.

Glamping enthusiasts can realistically expect their chosen little haven of luxury to feature electricity, en suite bathrooms, kitchens, wood-burning stoves, king size beds, Egyptian cotton bed linen, cookers, fridges and a TV, and on arrival they step into a scene straight out of a glossy interior design magazine.

Everland, Wight Glamping Holidays

Newport, Isle of Wight

Newcomers to the glamping scene, Dawn and Duncan Fidler, moved to the Isle of Wight in the 1990s with the idea of some day running their own campsite. However, it took them 20 years to fulfil their dream, waiting until their children had left the nest. Purchasing two acres of gently sloping land at Everland, they knew their new business would follow the luxury camping route.

Opposite: Durrell Wildlife Camp Below: Everland, Wight Glamping

"Guests were encouraged to give feedback and it became clear that apart from well-equipped glamping units they also expected top quality facilities."

In 2014 they set up and opened Everland, Wight Glamping Holidays. They decided that they would start with just three units and chose Lotus Belle tents as they were a little different to the usual yurts or bell tents. The organic and stylish shape appealed to them and the inside space was ideal for their interior decoration ideas.

Dawn and Duncan's concept was to provide very comfortable accommodation with an individual cooking area plus nearby high-quality toilet and shower facilities. Lotus Belle tents offer plenty of height, and space to accommodate a king-size bed plus sofa bed, which can be converted to a large double or two singles, making the tent suitable for a family or two couples. Top quality bed linen and covers are provided and the tent has heating and lighting plus plenty of clothes storage. The table and four chairs are ideal on inclement days when eating under cover is essential. At the rear is a spacious utility tent with a cooking unit that includes all cutlery and crockery that will be required. There is a very high-spec and stylish toilet and shower block with two shower rooms and two toilet rooms.

Each of the tents is on its own decked area with a picnic table and chairs as well as a barbecue. A welcome pack is provided containing local produce, information on the Isle of Wight and essential contact numbers.

However, the crowning glory at Everland is its countryside setting with beautiful views over a valley, making it a great place to sit outside on the decking and just chill. Dawn and Duncan plan to add one or two more glamping units in the future, including some with their own facilities.

Dorset Country Holidays

Blackmore Vale Caravan & Camping Park, Shaftesbury, Dorset

Dorset Country Holidays is run by Rob Farrow. The glamping accommodation is set on the family-owned and well-established Blackmore Vale Caravan & Camping Park, which has seen some significant changes over the years. The Farrow family initially noticed that young families in tents or caravans were no longer choosing the campsite as often as they once had, and seeing a gap in the market, Rob decided to start with tipis, then a bell tent. Having drawn on all their business experience, the new glamping units went down a storm.

Rob made this side of the business his focus. Wishing to widen the range of upmarket camping units, he soon added more bell tents, pods, cabins, shepherd's huts and an iconic vintage caravan. Each, he quickly learnt, has its own foibles and maintenance issues.

Guests were encouraged to give feedback and it became clear that apart from well-equipped glamping units they also expected top quality facilities. After the site's new toilet and shower block was built in 2012 it was realised that the glamping units were just not close enough. Not a problem…six months later they had all been relocated to take advantage of the modern facilities.

Next came another rethink. In order to improve the levels of service to customers, it was decided to scale back on the type of accommodation offered. Now there's a choice of British made, fully insulated yurts that have heating and lighting, one family tent, two bell tents, a vintage caravan and a two-room 'Country Kabin'. The levels of service that Rob and his team offer their guests is excellent and as Rob says, he no longer greets his guests in shorts and a sports shirt, but in a jacket, tie and trousers – the standards and market expectations are certainly changing it seems.

Durrell Wildlife Camp

Trinity, Jersey

This site provides something quite different yet again, and is perhaps setting the standards for the future of glamping holidays. Durrell Wildlife Camp in the Channel Islands is part of the Durrell Wildlife Conservation Trust, an international charity founded by author and naturalist Gerald Durrell, and home to some of the most threatened animal species in the world.

The concept of this camp is to provide sympathetic accommodation adjacent to the Wildlife Park so guests can experience an outdoor luxury holiday close to the animals. Ashley Mullins and his team were responsible for setting up the camp and continue to run it.

There are 12 spacious canvas 'geo' pods, each with a king-size bed plus two singles, bed linen, a wood-burning stove, electric lighting and storage for clothes. Everything is of the highest quality and wouldn't look out of place in a top hotel. Adjacent to each is a separate and very spacious pod housing not only a stylish bathroom with shower, toilet and washbasin but also a very well-equipped kitchen. For larger families a smaller tipi can be added – just right for two children or teenagers to stay in by themselves.

The glamping area is beautifully landscaped in keeping with the ambience of the wildlife park. You can even see the lemurs in the trees on their own island. Lemur Lodge, a large safari tent, serves as a reception, meeting place and function area.

What sets this camp apart however, is the remarkable level of customer care and service demonstrated by Ashley and his team. The attention to detail is quite extraordinary. From arrival to departure their only objective is to make your stay as enjoyable and memorable as possible.

Anyone staying at the camp has complimentary access to the Wildlife Park, and its top quality restaurant serves breakfasts, lunches and main meals. The camp can even organise behind-the-scenes experiences such as 'keeper for a day' packages.

Give it a go

Glamping has certainly changed over the last few years and has evolved into an exciting sector of the leisure market. If you're looking for something different, you must give it a try – families will love it and the levels of comfort and customer service can rival sophisticated hotels. Glamping has certainly come of age.

Opposite: Everland, Wight Glamping

Above and right: Durrell Wildlife Camp

Glamping and the AA

For some years now we have seen many of our traditional caravan and camping sites introducing glamping units. Some just started in a small way with a few yurts, pods or safari tents in order to test the market. In virtually all cases they have proved very popular. Even large Holiday Centres are offering fully-equipped safari tents now.

The AA has incorporated these glamping sites into their Pennant Grading scheme. The grading will be on a similar basis to existing sites, ranging from 1 Pennant to 5 Pennants, but they will be green, instead of black or gold, to differentiate them. From 2016 we intend to add a Quality Score expressed as a percentage which will bring glamping sites in line with the AA ratings for touring campsites and holiday home sites.

A beginner's guide to camping

It's always a little daunting trying something new, but camping expert Nick Harding outlines how to get started so you can make the most of your camping adventures.

The adventure really starts as soon as you sit down and decide to make that first campsite stay.

If you've just invested in your first caravan or motorhome, do find out whether your supplying dealer has any links with local campsites. Many do, and may even offer discounts for those making their first such visit. An initial night or two away is perfect for getting to know your new leisure vehicle or tent – and for it to get to know you!

Also, there's no reason to feel you have to travel long distances initially, and actually it's probably not the best idea. That initial 'fact-finding mission' to a local site will definitely pay dividends in the longer term. There are as many as 3,000 authorised places to camp throughout the UK. This guide lists over 860 – all are independently visited and graded by qualified AA inspectors every year. Each of these sites will have a slightly different protocol for accepting guests.

Here are a few guidelines for making sure your first visit to a campsite starts off on exactly the right foot.

What kind of site?

There is, indeed, plenty of choice of campsite out there – adults-only, pet-friendly, those offering day-time activities and evening entertainments... there's everything from large holiday centres through to the quietest countryside get-away to consider. Browse through this guide – you'll soon get a flavour of the very best that's out there.

Use this guide to narrow down your choices – depending on what part of the country you wish to visit, when, and what type of site you prefer. Comprehensive details for each AA-rated site are given but it's always a good idea to visit a specific site's own website.

Many offer some kind of online booking facility. However, if this really is your first time, we recommend making phone contact and explaining your circumstances. That gives site staff a chance to get some idea of your requirements as well as prepare themselves a bit more for your arrival. Also, if you visit a campsite outside its busiest periods the staff may just have a bit more time to spend with you.

Before you set off

A bit of preparation is key of course. Don't forget any paperwork, such as a booking confirmation. Get a weather report for your destination. It might just give you some clues as to what clothing and equipment to take.

But also, do investigate further the type of ground you're likely to be camping on – grass or hardstanding? What pegs might you need for your tent or awning? How is the ground for drainage purposes? And how level is it likely to be?

A bit of journey planning, including allowing for an en route stop-off or two if you're travelling any distance, will mean you're more relaxed when you arrive. You're on holiday now, after all.

So, take one final check that all is OK and it's time to go.

Finding your campsite

Don't be tempted to rely totally on putting just a postcode into your Sat Nav to get you to your campsite, especially if you're towing or have a larger-than-average size vehicle. Most campsite locations are out in the countryside, where postcodes can cover wide areas. Your chosen campsite will always be happy to advise on the best routes to their door, including information on any narrow lanes that might be encountered on your approach.

As part of the directions for each entry in this guide, a six-figure National Grid map reference is given. This can be used in conjunction with the atlas section at the back of the guide and with the relevant larger-scale Ordnance Survey map to pinpoint your destination.

Get your timing right

Be aware of opening and closing dates for any site you're considering – a lot close in the winter, for example. They may also have minimum booking periods at peak periods like Bank Holiday weekends. Any campsite can expect to be busy at certain times such as when popular local events are taking place – so do book as soon as you have made your mind up where you want to stay.

Just as important, take note of arrival and departure times. Nearly every site will set a deadline for arriving so that existing guests aren't disturbed by late-night noises and movements.

Likewise, in the mornings there will probably be an official time before which traffic cannot move on site and one for when you have to leave. The key here is that everyone has a fair chance of a good night's sleep. If you intend to arrive particularly late or especially early – maybe to meet ferry timings, for instance – let the campsite know in advance. They will be able to help you.

Arriving on site

A friendly welcome awaits... as long as you've arrived at the right time! Seriously, if there's nobody at reception, there's usually a good reason – and a bell to ring or number to call might be your first contact. Actually, if you do get held up and are running late, a phone call ahead can save a bit of embarrassment.

The best site staff will soon become invaluable friends. Not only will they happily offer advice relating to any aspect of the site, you'll soon realise they are the experts on local attractions including the best places for meals out.

Pitching

Some sites will let you choose your own pitch, others prefer to allocate a pitch to you (although there will always be the offer to change). If it's a big site, you may be given a map with numbered pitches that also shows the locations of toilet blocks, chemical toilet disposal points and other facilities.

Don't forget, if you are choosing your own pitch, you'll need to go back to reception to let them know where you've ended up.

There will be different ways of getting you to your pitch, too. Some sites are happy to escort you personally, others will let you do your own thing – again, if it's all a bit new and bewildering, do ask for assistance.

Something to consider is whether or not to pitch near a toilet block – it might mean easier access to the essential amenities, but do bear in mind 'traffic' around locations such as this is likely to be heavier, and therefore it will be a bit noisier.

Also, make yourself aware of any other essentials, such as fire-fighting equipment.

Gas, electrics, water... all at your service

Gas – If you use gas, make sure you have sufficient supplies for your stay away. Most campsites will sell small gas cartridges (for camping gear) and/or offer larger gas cylinder refills/replacements. When your new caravan or motorhome was handed over, its interior gas isolator taps will have been shown to you – now's the time to make sure they're in the 'on' position.

Electrics – When you booked your pitch, you will have been asked if you want mains electricity. Plug your lead into your unit first, before connecting up to the site's supply and checking any trip switches (at the electric hook-up point as well as inside your unit) are in the 'on' position.

Typically, you'll have a 10amp or 16amp mains electricity supply. Just be careful how many appliances you use at any time – domestic hair dryers, kettles, toasters, microwave ovens etc draw a lot of power (see page 13 for further information).

Water – All campsites provide fresh water. If you have booked a Super Pitch for your caravan or motorhome, you can connect directly to a fresh water supply as well as grey water drainage. There could also be a TV aerial plug-in point. Separate to the fresh and waste water supplies – for obvious reasons – will be the disposal point for chemical toilet waste.

Time to make a move...

A little bit of preparation and you'll have got the most out of your first visit to a campsite. Having said that, experience is a great thing, and you can only build that up by learning from a few mistakes.

One last thing to remember as you pack up to go. Before you leave the campsite, have one final and careful check over your pitch, and under the caravan. You'll be surprised how easy it is to leave things behind. You really don't want to hear "where's teddy?" as you're pull into your drive back at home.

First-time campers: a checklist of Dos, and a couple of Don'ts

Key: C = caravans M = motorhomes T = tents

Before you leave home or the site (hitching)

- Before you go away for the first time practise putting up your tent; hitching and unhitching your caravan; reversing your motorhome or towed van into an enclosed space. **(CMT)**
- Make a list of all the essentials you need to take with you. Mains lead, gas cylinder, levelling ramps and/or chocks... all the way through to small essentials like a box of matches, spare fuses, and a torch (check batteries). **(CMT)**
- Check all interior items are safely stored, cupboards closed, all interior electrics are set correctly, turn off gas bottles, make sure roof lights and windows are closed and the external door is locked. **(CM)**
- Empty fresh and waste water containers and toilet cassettes. **(CM)**
- Check that corner steadies are raised tightly, and chocks and steps stowed. **(C)**
- Connect tow bracket electric plugs, check that the breakaway safety cable is connected and, if used, that the anti-snake device is fitted correctly. **(C)**
- Check the caravan's noseweight. **(C)**
- Adjust the hitch height – i.e. above the car's towball. **(C)**
- Secure the hitch on the towball. **(C)**
- Use the jockey wheel to raise the car about 2.5cm to ensure the caravan and car are properly coupled. If fitted, also check the tow hitch indicator (green = correctly coupled). **(C)**
- Raise the jockey wheel and lock in position. **(C)**
- Check that the caravan number plate is secure (and that it replicates the towing vehicle's number plate). **(C)**
- Ask another person to stand behind the caravan or motorhome to check all the lights and indicators work. **(CM)**
- On leaving a site disconnect the hook-ups and make that final check of the empty pitch. **(CM)**

Arriving at your destination (unhitching)

- Tell the site this is your first time. They're more likely to go out of their way to help. **(CMT)**
- Listen to what the site staff tell you when you arrive (if you're a family, it's a good idea for you all to step into reception – that way you all understand the same message). **(CMT)**
- Check caravan handbrake is on, chocks are in place and corner steadies are lowered. **(C)**
- Lower jockey wheel and level the caravan and then lock in place. **(C)**
- Give everyone in the family designated tasks when you arrive on site (finding the way to the toilet block, locating the nearest fresh water point etc). **(CMT)**
- Get to know your surroundings. An early-evening stroll around any campsite is a great opportunity to check out the facilities. **(CMT)**
- Say hello to your neighbours. They might just come in handy, and who knows you might a make a lot of new friends. **(CMT)**

DON'T churn up the grass. You're only ruining things for subsequent visitors. If you have a bit of a mishap, let the staff know so they can rectify things as soon as possible.

And finally **DON'T** be afraid to ask. All the campsites in this guide are adept at helping first-timers – most will happily guide you to your pitch if you ask. Although you'll soon find your fellow campers are happy to chip in and help out, too.

There's even more useful information on www.theaa.com/motoring_advice/general-advice/towingadvice-what-you-need-to-know

The best sites for...

...WATERSIDE PITCHES

ENGLAND

South End Caravan Park,
Barrow-in-Furness, Cumbria
River Dart Country Park,
Ashburton, Devon
Riverside C&C Park,
South Molton, Devon
Sleningford Watermill CC Park,
North Stainley, North Yorkshire
Howgill Lodge,
Bolton Abbey, North Yorkshire
Wolds Way Caravan and Camping,
West Knapton, North Yorkshire

CHANNEL ISLANDS

Rozel Camping Park,
St Martin, Jersey

SCOTLAND

Banff Links Caravan Park,
Banff, Aberdeenshire
Inver Mill Farm Caravan Park,
Dunkeld, Perth & Kinross
Skye C&C Club Site,
Edinbane, Isle of Skye

WALES

Riverside Camping,
Caernarfon, Gwynedd

NORTHERN IRELAND

Drumaheglis Marina & Caravan Park,
Ballymoney, County Antrim

...STUNNING VIEWS

ENGLAND

Tristram C&C Park,
Polzeath, Cornwall
Troutbeck C&C Club Site,
Troutbeck, Cumbria
Sykeside Camping Park,
Patterdale, Cumbria
Warcombe Farm C&C Park
Woolacombe, Devon
Highlands End Holiday Park,
Bridport, Dorset
Sea Barn Farm
Weymouth, Dorset
New Hall Farm Touring Park,
Southwell, Nottinghamshire
Wimbleball Lake,
Dulverton, Somerset

SCOTLAND

Oban C&C Park,
Oban, Argyll & Bute
Linnhe Lochside Holidays,
Corpach, Highland
Invercoe C&C Park,
Glencoe, Highland
John O'Groats Caravan Site,
John O'Groats, Highland
Strathfillan Wigwam Village
Tyndrum, Stirling

WALES

St David's Park,
Red Wharf Bay, Isle of Anglesey
Bron-Y-Wendon Caravan Park,
Llanddulas, Conwy
Bodnant Caravan Park,
Llanwrst, Conwy
Beach View Caravan Park,
Abersoch, Gwynedd
Tyn-y-Mur Touring & Camping,
Abersoch, Gwynedd
Trawsdir Touring C&C Park,
Barmouth, Gwynedd
Eisteddfa, Criccieth, Gwynedd
Barcdy Touring C&C Park,
Talsarnau, Gwynedd
Fishguard Bay Resort,
Fishguard, Pembrokeshire
Carreglwyd C&C Park,
Port Eynon, Swansea

...GOOD ON-SITE RESTAURANTS

ENGLAND

Stroud Hill Park,
St Ives, Cambridgeshire
Tristram C&C Park,
Polzeath, Cornwall
Cofton Country Holidays
Dawlish, Devon
Bingham Grange T&C Park,
Bridport, Dorset
Highlands End Holiday Park,
Bridport, Dorset
Bay View Holiday Park,
Bolton-le-Sands, Lancashire
The Old Brick Kilns,
Barney, Norfolk
Beaconsfield Farm Caravan Park,
Shrewsbury, Shropshire

CHANNEL ISLANDS

Beuvelande Camp Site,
St Martin, Jersey

SCOTLAND

Glen Nevis C&C Park,
Fort William, Highland

WALES

St David's Park,
Red Wharf Bay, Isle of Anglesey

...TOP TOILETS

ENGLAND

Carnon Downs C&C Park,
Truro, Cornwall
Beech Croft Farm,
Buxton, Derbyshire
Crealy Meadows C&C Park
Clyst St Mary, Devon
Riverside C&C Park,
South Molton, Devon
Meadowbank Holidays
Christchurch, Dorset
Shamba Holidays,
St Leonards, Dorset
Teversal C&C Club Site,
Teversal, Nottinghamshire
Dell Touring Park,
Bury St Edmunds, Suffolk
Moon & Sixpence,
Woodbridge, Suffolk
Riverside Caravan Park,
High Bentham, North Yorkshire

Wayside Holiday Park,
Pickering, North Yorkshire
Moor Lodge Park,
Leeds, West Yorkshire

SCOTLAND

Beecraigs C&C Site,
Linlithgow, West Lothian
Skye C&C Club Site,
Edinbane, Isle of Skye

...ON-SITE FISHING

ENGLAND

Fields End Water CP & Fishery,
Doddington, Cambridgeshire
Upper Tamar Lake
Kilkhampton, Cornwall
Back of Beyond Touring Park,
St Leonards, Dorset
Blackmore Vale C&C Park,
Shaftesbury, Dorset
Woodland Waters,
Ancaster, Lincolnshire
Lakeside Caravan Park & Fisheries,
Downham Market, Norfolk
Northam Farm Caravan & Touring Park,
Brean, Somerset
Thorney Lakes Caravan Park,
Langport, Somerset
Carlton Meres Country Park,
Saxmundham, Suffolk
Marsh Farm Caravan Site,
Saxmundham, Suffolk
Sumners Ponds Fishery & Campsite,
Barns Green, West Sussex

SCOTLAND

Hoddom Castle Caravan Park,
Ecclefechan, Dumfries & Galloway
Milton of Fonab Caravan Park,
Pitlochry, Perth & Kinross
Gart Caravan Park,
Callander, Stirling

WALES

Afon Teifi C&C Park,
Newcastle Emlyn, Carmarthenshire
Ynysymaengwyn Caravan Park,
Tywyn, Gwynedd

...THE KIDS

ENGLAND

Trevornick Holiday Park,
Holywell Bay, Cornwall
Eden Valley Holiday Park,
Lostwithiel, Cornwall
Golden Valley C&C Park,
Ripley, Derbyshire
Freshwater Beach Holiday Park,
Bridport, Dorset
Sandy Balls Holiday Village,
Fordingbridge, Hampshire
Heathland Beach Caravan Park,
Kessingland, Suffolk
Golden Square C&C Park,
Helmsley, North Yorkshire
Riverside Caravan Park,
High Bentham, North Yorkshire
Goosewood Caravan Park,
Sutton-on-the-Forest, North Yorkshire

SCOTLAND

Blair Castle Caravan Park,
Blair Atholl, Perth & Kinross
Beecraigs C&C Site
Linlithgow, West Lothian

WALES

Home Farm Caravan Park,
Marian-Glas, Isle of Anglesey
Hendre Mynach Touring C&C Park,
Barmouth, Gwynedd
Trawsdir Touring C&C Park,
Barmouth, Gwynedd

...BEING ECO-FRIENDLY

ENGLAND

South Penquite Farm,
Blisland, Cornwall
Lowarth Glamping
Wadebridge, Devon
River Dart Country Park,
Ashburton, Devon
Brook Lodge Farm C&C Park (Bristol),
Cowslip Green, Somerset

SCOTLAND

Carradale Bay Caravan Site
Carradale, Argyll & Bute
Shieling Holidays,
Craignure, Isle of Mull

WALES

Caerfai Bay Caravan & Tent Park,
St Davids, Pembrokeshire

►►►►► Premier Parks

5 GOLD PENNANTS

►►►►►

ENGLAND

CAMBRIDGESHIRE

ST IVES
Stroud Hill Park

CHESHIRE

CODDINGTON
Manor Wood Country Caravan Park

WHITEGATE
Lamb Cottage Caravan Park

CORNWALL

BUDE
Wooda Farm Holiday Park

CARLYON BAY
Carlyon Bay Caravan & Camping Park

CRANTOCK
Trevella Holiday Park

MEVAGISSEY
Seaview International Holiday Park

PADSTOW
Padstow Touring Park

REDRUTH
Globe Vale Holiday Park

REJERRAH
Newperran Holiday Park

ST IVES
Polmanter Touring Park

ST JUST-IN-ROSELAND
Trethem Mill Touring Park

TRURO
Carnon Downs Caravan & Camping Park

CUMBRIA

AMBLESIDE
Skelwith Fold Caravan Park

WINDERMERE
Park Cliffe Camping & Caravan Estate

DEVON

DARTMOUTH
Woodlands Grove Caravan & Camping Park

NEWTON ABBOT
Dornafield
Ross Park

SIDMOUTH
Oakdown Country Holiday Park

DORSET

BRIDPORT
Bingham Grange Touring & Camping Park
Highlands End Holiday Park

CHARMOUTH
Wood Farm Caravan & Camping Park

POOLE
South Lytchett Manor Caravan & Camping Park

WAREHAM
Wareham Forest Tourist Park

WEYMOUTH
East Fleet Farm Touring Park

HAMPSHIRE

FORDINGBRIDGE
Sandy Balls Holiday Village

HEREFORDSHIRE

PEMBRIDGE
Townsend Touring Park

ISLE OF WIGHT

NEWBRIDGE
The Orchards Holiday Caravan Park

RYDE
Whitefield Forest Touring Park

WROXALL
Appuldurcombe Gardens Holiday Park

LANCASHIRE

SILVERDALE
Silverdale Caravan Park

LINCOLNSHIRE

WOODHALL SPA
Woodhall Country Park

NORFOLK

BARNEY
The Old Brick Kilns

CLIPPESBY
Clippesby Hall

NORTHUMBERLAND

BELFORD
South Meadows Caravan Park

NOTTINGHAMSHIRE

TEVERSAL
Teversal Camping & Caravanning Club Site

OXFORDSHIRE

HENLEY-ON-THAMES
Swiss Farm Touring & Camping

STANDLAKE
Lincoln Farm Park

SHROPSHIRE

SHREWSBURY
Beaconsfield Farm Caravan Park

SOMERSET

BISHOP SUTTON
Bath Chew Valley Caravan Park

GLASTONBURY
The Old Oaks Touring Park

STAFFORDSHIRE

LONGNOR
Longnor Wood Holiday Park

SUFFOLK

WOODBRIDGE
Moon & Sixpence

YORKSHIRE, NORTH

ALLERSTON
Vale of Pickering Caravan Park

HIGH BENTHAM
Riverside Caravan Park

SCOTLAND

ABERDEENSHIRE

HUNTLY
Huntly Castle Caravan Park

FIFE

ST ANDREWS
Cairnsmill Holiday Park
Craigtoun Meadows Holiday Park

LOTHIAN, EAST

DUNBAR
Thurston Manor Leisure Park

PERTH & KINROSS

BLAIR ATHOLL
Blair Castle Caravan Park

WALES

ANGLESEY, ISLE OF

DULAS
Tyddyn Isaf Caravan Park

MARIAN-GLAS
Home Farm Caravan Park

GWYNEDD

BARMOUTH
Trawsdir Touring Caravans & Camping Park

TAL-Y-BONT
Islawrffordd Caravan Park

PEMBROKESHIRE

ST DAVIDS
Caerfai Bay Caravan & Tent Park

POWYS

BRECON
Pencelli Castle Caravan & Camping Park

WREXHAM

EYTON
Plassey Holiday Park

NORTHERN IRELAND

COUNTY ANTRIM

BUSHMILLS
Ballyness Caravan Park

5 BLACK PENNANTS

►►►►►

ENGLAND

BERKSHIRE

HURLEY
Hurley Riverside Park

CAMBRIDGESHIRE

DODDINGTON
Fields End Water Caravan Park & Fishery

CORNWALL

GOONHAVERN
Silverbow Park

HOLYWELL BAY
Trevornick Holiday Park

LANDRAKE
Dolbeare Park Caravan and Camping

LEEDSTOWN
Calloose Caravan & Camping Park

LOSTWITHIEL
Eden Valley Holiday Park

NEWQUAY
Hendra Holiday Park

PENTEWAN
Sun Valley Resort

ST AUSTELL
River Valley Holiday Park

ST IVES
Ayr Holiday Park
Trevalgan Touring Park

ST MERRYN
Atlantic Bays Holiday Park

ST MINVER
Gunvenna Holiday Park

TRURO
Cosawes Park
Truro Caravan and Camping Park

WATERGATE BAY
Watergate Bay Touring Park

CUMBRIA

APPLEBY-IN-WESTMORLAND
Wild Rose Park

BOOT
Eskdale Camping & Caravanning Club Site

KESWICK
Castlerigg Hall Caravan & Camping Park

KIRKBY LONSDALE
Woodclose Caravan Park

PENRITH
Lowther Holiday Park

TROUTBECK (NEAR KESWICK)
Troutbeck Camping and Caravanning Club Site

ULVERSTON
Bardsea Leisure Park

WINDERMERE
Hill of Oaks & Blakeholme

DERBYSHIRE

BIRCHOVER
Barn Farm Campsite

DEVON

BRAUNTON
Hidden Valley Park

CLYST ST MARY
Crealy Meadows Caravan and Camping Park

COMBE MARTIN
Newberry Valley Park

DAWLISH
Cofton Country Holidays
Lady's Mile Holiday Park

DREWSTEIGNTON
Woodland Springs Adult Touring Park

KINGSBRIDGE
Island Lodge Carvan & Camping Site
Parkland Caravan and Camping Site

PAIGNTON
Beverley Parks Caravan & Camping Park

SAMPFORD PEVERELL
Minnows Touring Park

TAVISTOCK
Langstone Manor Camping & Caravan Park
Woodovis Park

WOOLACOMBE
Warcombe Farm Caravan & Camping Park

DORSET

ALDERHOLT
Hill Cottage Farm Camping and Caravan Park

CHARMOUTH
Newlands Caravan & Camping Park

CHRISTCHURCH
Meadowbank Holidays

ST LEONARDS
Shamba Holidays

SWANAGE
Ulwell Cottage Caravan Park

WIMBORNE MINSTER
Merley Court
Wilksworth Farm Caravan Park

HAMPSHIRE

ROMSEY
Hill Farm Caravan Park

KENT

ASHFORD
Broadhembury Caravan & Camping Park

MARDEN
Tanner Farm Touring Caravan & Camping Park

LANCASHIRE

THORNTON
Kneps Farm Holiday Park

NORFOLK

BELTON
Rose Farm Touring & Camping Park

KING'S LYNN
King's Lynn Caravan and Camping Park

NORTH WALSHAM
Two Mills Touring Park

NORTHUMBERLAND

BELLINGHAM
Bellingham Camping & Caravanning Club Site

BERWICK-UPON-TWEED
Ord House Country Park

HALTWHISTLE
Herding Hill Farm

RUTLAND

GREETHAM
Rutland Caravan & Camping

▶▶▶▶▶ Premier Parks *continued*

SHROPSHIRE

BRIDGNORTH
Stanmore Hall Touring Park

SHREWSBURY
Oxon Hall Touring Park

TELFORD
Severn Gorge Park

WHEATHILL
Wheathill Touring Park

SOMERSET

CROWCOMBE
Quantock Orchard Caravan Park

PORLOCK
Porlock Caravan Park

WELLS
Wells Touring Park

WIVELISCOMBE
Waterrow Touring Park

SUFFOLK

LEISTON
Cakes & Ale

SAXMUNDHAM
Carlton Meres Country Park

SUSSEX, WEST

CHICHESTER
Concierge Camping

WARWICKSHIRE

HARBURY
Harbury Fields

WILTSHIRE

LANDFORD
Greenhill Farm Caravan & Camping Park

WORCESTERSHIRE

HONEYBOURNE
Ranch Caravan Park

YORKSHIRE, NORTH

ALNE
Alders Caravan Park

HARROGATE
Ripley Caravan Park
Rudding Holiday Park

HELMSLEY
Golden Square Caravan & Camping Park

OSMOTHERLEY
Cote Ghyll Caravan & Camping Park

RIPON
Riverside Meadows Country Caravan Park

SCARBOROUGH
Jacobs Mount Caravan Park

SUTTON-ON-THE-FOREST
Goosewood Caravan Park

WYKEHAM
St Helens Caravan Park

CHANNEL ISLANDS

GUERNSEY

CASTEL
Fauxquets Valley Campsite

JERSEY

ST MARTIN
Beuvelande Camp Site

SCOTLAND

DUMFRIES & GALLOWAY

BRIGHOUSE BAY
Brighouse Bay Holiday Park

ECCLEFECHAN
Hoddom Castle Caravan Park

KIRKCUDBRIGHT
Seaward Caravan Park

DUNBARTONSHIRE, WEST

BALLOCH
Lomond Woods Holiday Park

HIGHLAND

CORPACH
Linnhe Lochside Holidays

MORAY

LOSSIEMOUTH
Silver Sands Holiday Park

PERTH & KINROSS

BLAIR ATHOLL
River Tilt Caravan Park

STIRLING

ABERFOYLE
Trossachs Holiday Park

WALES

CARMARTHENSHIRE

LLANDOVERY
Erwlon Caravan & Camping Park

NEWCASTLE EMLYN
Cenarth Falls Holiday Park

CONWY

LLANDDULAS
Bron-Y-Wendon Caravan Park

LLANRWST
Bron Derw Touring Caravan Park

GWYNEDD

BARMOUTH
Hendre Mynach Touring Caravan & Camping Park

DINAS DINLLE
Dinlle Caravan Park

MONMOUTHSHIRE

USK
Pont Kemys Caravan & Camping Park

POWYS

BUILTH WELLS
Fforest Fields Caravan & Camping Park

CHURCHSTOKE
Daisy Bank Caravan Park

NORTHERN IRELAND

COUNTY ANTRIM

BALLYMONEY
Drumaheglis Marina & Caravan Park

COUNTY FERMANAGH

BELCOO
Rushin House Caravan Park

5 GREEN PENNANTS

▶▶▶▶▶

ENGLAND

DORSET

SHAFTESBURY
Dorset Country Holidays

CHANNEL ISLANDS

JERSEY

TRINITY
Durrell Wildlife Camp

SCOTLAND

STIRLING

TYNDRUM
Strathfillan Wigwam Village

WALES

MONMOUTHSHIRE

LLANVAIR DISCOED
Penhein Glamping

Gold Pennant parks

ENGLAND

CAMBRIDGESHIRE

COMBERTON
Highfield Farm Touring Park

ST IVES
Stroud Hill Park

CHESHIRE

CODDINGTON
Manor Wood Country Caravan Park

WHITEGATE
Lamb Cottage Caravan Park

CORNWALL

BUDE
Wooda Farm Holiday Park

CARLYON BAY
Carlyon Bay Caravan & Camping Park

CRANTOCK
Trevella Holiday Park

GWITHIAN
Gwithian Farm Campsite

KENNACK SANDS
Chy Carne Holiday Park

MEVAGISSEY
Seaview International Holiday Park

NEWQUAY
Treloy Touring Park

PADSTOW
Padstow Touring Park

POLRUAN
Polruan Holidays-Camping & Caravanning

PORTHTOWAN
Porthtowan Tourist Park

REDRUTH
Globe Vale Holiday Park

REJERRAH
Newperran Holiday Park

ROSUDGEON
Kenneggy Cove Holiday Park

ST IVES
Polmanter Touring Park

ST JUST-IN-ROSELAND
Trethem Mill Touring Park

SUMMERCOURT
Carvynick Country Club

TRURO
Carnon Downs Caravan & Camping Park

WADEBRIDGE
The Laurels Holiday Park
St Mabyn Holiday Park

CUMBRIA

AMBLESIDE
Skelwith Fold Caravan Park

WINDERMERE
Park Cliffe Camping & Caravan Estate

DERBYSHIRE

BUXTON
Clover Fields Touring Caravan Park

MATLOCK
Lickpenny Caravan Site

DEVON

BUCKFASTLEIGH
Churchill Farm Campsite

COMBE MARTIN
Stowford Farm Meadows

DARTMOUTH
Woodlands Grove Caravan & Camping Park

NEWTON ABBOT
Dornafield
Ross Park

SIDMOUTH
Oakdown Country Holiday Park

SOUTH MOLTON
Riverside Caravan & Camping Park

DORSET

BRIDPORT
Bingham Grange Touring & Camping Park
Highlands End Holiday Park

CHARMOUTH
Wood Farm Caravan & Camping Park

CORFE CASTLE
Corfe Castle Camping & Caravanning Club Site

POOLE
South Lytchett Manor Caravan & Camping Park

WAREHAM
Wareham Forest Tourist Park

WEYMOUTH
East Fleet Farm Touring Park
West Fleet Holiday Farm

HAMPSHIRE

FORDINGBRIDGE
Sandy Balls Holiday Village

HEREFORDSHIRE

PEMBRIDGE
Townsend Touring Park

ISLE OF WIGHT

NEWBRIDGE
The Orchards Holiday Caravan Park

RYDE
Whitefield Forest Touring Park

WROXALL
Appuldurcombe Gardens Holiday Park

LANCASHIRE

FAR ARNSIDE
Hollins Farm Camping & Caravanning

SILVERDALE
Silverdale Caravan Park

LINCOLNSHIRE

BOSTON
Long Acres Touring Park

MARSTON
Wagtail Country Park

WOODHALL SPA
Woodhall Country Park

NORFOLK

BARNEY
The Old Brick Kilns

CLIPPESBY
Clippesby Hall

NORTHUMBERLAND

BELFORD
South Meadows Caravan Park

NOTTINGHAMSHIRE

TEVERSAL
Teversal Camping & Caravanning Club Site

TUXFORD
Orchard Park Touring Caravan & Camping Park

OXFORDSHIRE

BLETCHINGDON
►►►► Greenhill Leisure Park

HENLEY-ON-THAMES
►►►►► Swiss Farm Touring & Camping

STANDLAKE
►►►►► Lincoln Farm Park

SHROPSHIRE

SHREWSBURY
►►►►► Beaconsfield Farm Caravan Park

SOMERSET

BISHOP SUTTON
►►►►► Bath Chew Valley Caravan Park

BREAN
►►►► Northam Farm Caravan & Touring Park

BRIDGETOWN
►►►► Exe Valley Caravan Site

GLASTONBURY
►►►►► The Old Oaks Touring Park

PORLOCK
►►►► Burrowhayes Farm Caravan & Camping Site & Riding Stables

SHEPTON MALLET
►► Greenacres Camping

STAFFORDSHIRE

LONGNOR
►►►►► Longnor Wood Holiday Park

SUFFOLK

WOODBRIDGE
►►►►► Moon & Sixpence

WEST MIDLANDS

MERIDEN
►►►► Somers Wood Caravan Park

WILTSHIRE

SALISBURY
►►►► Coombe Touring Park

YORKSHIRE, EAST RIDING OF

BRANDESBURTON
►►►► Blue Rose Caravan Country Park

YORKSHIRE, NORTH

ALLERSTON
►►►►► Vale of Pickering Caravan Park

FILEY
►►►► Lebberston Touring Park

HIGH BENTHAM
►►►►► Riverside Caravan Park

NABURN
►►►► Naburn Lock Caravan Park

ROBIN HOOD'S BAY
►►►► Grouse Hill Caravan Park

SNAINTON
►►►► Jasmine Caravan Park

WHITBY
►►►► Ladycross Plantation Caravan Park

CHANNEL ISLANDS

JERSEY

ST MARTIN
►►►► Rozel Camping Park

SCOTLAND

ABERDEENSHIRE

HUNTLY
►►►►► Huntly Castle Caravan Park

ARGYLL & BUTE

CARRADALE
►►► Carradale Bay Caravan Park

DUMFRIES & GALLOWAY

WIGTOWN
►►► Drumroamin Farm Camping & Touring Site

FIFE

ST ANDREWS
►►►►► Cairnsmill Holiday Park
►►►►► Craigtoun Meadows Holiday Park

HIGHLAND

FORT WILLIAM
►►►► Glen Nevis Caravan & Camping Park

LOTHIAN, EAST

DUNBAR
►►►►► Thurston Manor Leisure Park

PERTH & KINROSS

BLAIR ATHOLL
►►►►► Blair Castle Caravan Park

STIRLING

BLAIRLOGIE
►►►► Witches Craig Caravan & Camping Park

SCOTTISH ISLANDS

ISLE OF SKYE

EDINBANE
►►►► Skye Camping & Caravanning Club Site

WALES

ANGLESEY, ISLE OF

DULAS
►►►►► Tyddyn Isaf Caravan Park

MARIAN-GLAS
►►►►► Home Farm Caravan Park

CARMARTHENSHIRE

LLANGENNECH
►►► South Wales Caravan Park

CEREDIGION

ABERAERON
►►► Aeron Coast Caravan Park

DENBIGHSHIRE

RHUALLT
►►►► Penisar Mynydd Caravan Park

GWYNEDD

BARMOUTH
►►►►► Trawsdir Touring Caravans & Camping Park

TAL-Y-BONT
►►►►► Islawrffordd Caravan Park

PEMBROKESHIRE

FISHGUARD
►►► Fishguard Bay Resort

ST DAVIDS
►►►►► Caerfai Bay Caravan & Tent Park

POWYS

BRECON
►►►►► Pencelli Castle Caravan & Camping Park

SWANSEA

RHOSSILI
►►► Pitton Cross Caravan & Camping Park

WREXHAM

EYTON
►►►►► Plassey Holiday Park

NORTHERN IRELAND

COUNTY ANTRIM

BUSHMILLS
►►►►► Ballyness Caravan Park

AA Holiday Centres

These parks cater for all holiday needs. See page 11 for further information.

ENGLAND

CORNWALL

HAYLE
St Ives Bay Holiday Park

LOOE
Tencreek Holiday Park

PERRANPORTH
Perran Sands Holiday Park

WIDEMOUTH BAY
Widemouth Bay Caravan Park

CUMBRIA

FLOOKBURGH
Lakeland Leisure Park

POOLEY BRIDGE
Park Foot Caravan & Camping Park

SILLOTH
Solway Holiday Village
Stanwix Park Holiday Centre

DEVON

EXMOUTH
Devon Cliffs Holiday Park

WOOLACOMBE
Golden Coast Holiday Park
Twitchen House Holiday Park
Woolacombe Bay Holiday Park

DORSET

BRIDPORT
Freshwater Beach Holiday Park

POOLE
Rockley Park

WEYMOUTH
Littlesea Holiday Park
Seaview Holiday Park

DURHAM, COUNTY

BLACKHALL COLLIERY
Crimdon Dene

ESSEX

CLACTON-ON-SEA
Highfield Grange
Martello Beach Holiday Park

MERSEA ISLAND
Waldegraves Holiday Park

ST LAWRENCE
Waterside St Lawrence Bay

ST OSYTH
The Orchards Holiday Park

WALTON ON THE NAZE
Naze Marine

ISLE OF WIGHT

COWES
Thorness Bay Holiday Park

ST HELENS
Nodes Point Holiday Park

SHANKLIN
Lower Hyde Holiday Park

WHITECLIFF BAY
Whitecliff Bay Holiday Park

KENT

EASTCHURCH
Warden Springs Caravan Park

LANCASHIRE

BLACKPOOL
Marton Mere Holiday Village

LONGRIDGE
Beacon Fell View Holiday Park

LINCOLNSHIRE

CLEETHORPES
Thorpe Park Holiday Centre

MABLETHORPE
Golden Sands Holiday Park

SALTFLEET
Sunnydale

SKEGNESS
Southview Leisure Park

MERSEYSIDE

SOUTHPORT
Riverside Holiday Park

NORFOLK

BELTON
Wild Duck Holiday Park

BURGH CASTLE
Breydon Water

CAISTER-ON-SEA
Caister-on-Sea Holiday Park

GREAT YARMOUTH
Vauxhall Holiday Park

HUNSTANTON
Manor Park Holiday Village
Searles Leisure Resort

NORTHUMBERLAND

BERWICK-UPON-TWEED
Haggerston Castle Holiday Park

NORTH SEATON
Sandy Bay

SOMERSET

BREAN
Holiday Resort Unity
Warren Farm Holiday Centre

BRIDGWATER
Mill Farm Caravan & Camping Park

BURNHAM-ON-SEA
Burnham-on-Sea Holiday Village

SUFFOLK

KESSINGLAND
Kessingland Beach Holiday Park

SUSSEX, EAST

CAMBER
Camber Sands

SUSSEX, WEST

SELSEY
Warner Farm Touring Park

YORKSHIRE, EAST RIDING OF

SKIPSEA
Skipsea Sands
Skirlington Leisure Park

TUNSTALL
Sand le Mere Holiday Village

WITHERNSEA
Withernsea Sands Holiday Park

YORKSHIRE, NORTH

FILEY
Blue Dolphin Holiday Park
Flower of May Holiday Park
Primrose Valley Holiday Park
Reighton Sands Holiday Park

SCOTLAND

AYRSHIRE, NORTH

SALTCOATS
Sandylands

AYRSHIRE, SOUTH

AYR
Craig Tara Holiday Park

DUMFRIES & GALLOWAY

GATEHOUSE OF FLEET
Auchenlarie Holiday Park

LOTHIAN, EAST

LONGNIDDRY
Seton Sands Holiday Village

SCOTTISH BORDERS

EYEMOUTH
Eyemouth

WALES

CEREDIGION

BORTH
Brynowen Holiday Park

CONWY

TOWYN
Ty Mawr Holiday Park

DENBIGHSHIRE

PRESTATYN
Presthaven Sands Holiday Park

GWYNEDD

PORTHMADOG
Greenacres Holiday Park

PWLLHELI
Hafan y Mor Holiday Park

PEMBROKESHIRE

TENBY
Kiln Park Holiday Centre

SWANSEA

SWANSEA
Riverside Caravan Park

NORTHERN IRELAND

COUNTY ANTRIM

BALLYCASTLE
Causeway Coast Holiday Park

Green Pennant parks

5 GREEN PENNANTS

▶▶▶▶▶

ENGLAND

DORSET

SHAFTESBURY
Dorset Country Holidays

CHANNEL ISLANDS

JERSEY

TRINITY
Durrell Wildlife Camp

SCOTLAND

STIRLING

TYNDRUM
Strathfillan Wigwam Village

WALES

MONMOUTHSHIRE

LLANVAIR DISCOED
Penhein Glamping

4 GREEN PENNANTS

▶▶▶▶

ENGLAND

CORNWALL

WADEBRIDGE
Lowarth Glamping

DEVON

OTTERY ST MARY
Cuckoo Down Farm Glamping

ISLE OF WIGHT

NEWPORT
Wight Glamping Holidays

NORFOLK

BELTON
Swallow Park Leisure

SOMERSET

GLASTONBURY
Middlewick Farm

YORKSHIRE, NORTH

KIRKLINGTON
Camp Kátur

SCOTLAND

HIGHLAND

AVIEMORE
Aviemore Glamping

WALES

SWANSEA

OLDWALLS
Oldwalls Gower Glamping

WREXHAM

BRONINGTON
The Little Yurt Meadow

3 GREEN PENNANTS

▶▶▶

ENGLAND

CORNWALL

LISKEARD
Luxury Cornish Yurts

DEVON

KENN
Glebe Farm Shepherd's Huts

Adults only – no children parks

ENGLAND

CAMBRIDGESHIRE

BURWELL
Stanford Park

DODDINGTON
Fields End Water Caravan Park & Fishery

ST IVES
Stroud Hill Park

CHESHIRE

WETTENHALL
New Farm Caravan Park

WHITEGATE
Lamb Cottage Caravan Park

CORNWALL

CHACEWATER
Killiwerris Touring Park

ST HILARY
Wayfarers Caravan & Camping Park

CUMBRIA

CARLISLE
Green Acres Caravan Park

MEALSGATE
Larches Caravan Park

DERBYSHIRE

BUXTON
Clover Fields Touring Caravan Park

DEVON

DREWSTEIGNTON
Woodland Springs Adult Touring Park

EAST ANSTEY
Zeacombe House Caravan Park

TORQUAY
Widdicombe Farm Touring Park

DORSET

BRIDPORT
Bingham Grange Touring & Camping Park

HURN
Fillybrook Farm Touring Park

ST LEONARDS
Back of Beyond Touring Park

GLOUCESTERSHIRE

CHELTENHAM
Briarfields Motel & Touring Park

HEREFORDSHIRE

MORETON ON LUGG
Cuckoo's Corner Campsite

LANCASHIRE

BLACKPOOL
Manor House Caravan Park

LINCOLNSHIRE

BOSTON
Long Acres Touring Park
Orchard Park

NORFOLK

NORTH WALSHAM
Two Mills Touring Park

STANHOE
The Rickels Caravan & Camping Park

SWAFFHAM
Breckland Meadows Touring Park

THREE HOLES
Lode Hall Holiday Park

NORTHAMPTONSHIRE

BULWICK
New Lodge Farm Caravan & Camping Site

NORTHUMBERLAND

SEAHOUSES
Westfield Paddock

NOTTINGHAMSHIRE

SOUTHWELL
New Hall Farm Touring Park

OXFORDSHIRE

BURFORD
Wysdom Touring Park

SHROPSHIRE

SHREWSBURY
Beaconsfield Farm Caravan Park

TELFORD
Severn Gorge Park

WHEATHILL
Wheathill Touring Park

SOMERSET

BISHOP SUTTON
Bath Chew Valley Caravan Park

BRIDGETOWN
Exe Valley Caravan Site

GLASTONBURY
The Old Oaks Touring Park

SPARKFORD
Long Hazel Park

WELLINGTON
Greenacres Touring Park

WELLS
Homestead Park
Wells Touring Park

WIVELISCOMBE
Waterrow Touring Park

STAFFORDSHIRE

LONGNOR
Longnor Wood Holiday Park

SUFFOLK

THEBERTON
Sycamore Park

WOODBRIDGE
Moat Barn Touring Caravan Park

WEST MIDLANDS

MERIDEN
Somers Wood Caravan Park

YORKSHIRE, EAST RIDING OF

BRANDESBURTON
Blue Rose Caravan Country Park

YORKSHIRE, NORTH

HARROGATE
Shaws Trailer Park

HELMSLEY
Foxholme Caravan Park

YORK
Rawcliffe Manor Caravan Park

YORKSHIRE, WEST

LEEDS
Moor Lodge Park
St Helena's Caravan Park

WALES

CARMARTHENSHIRE

LLANGENNECH
South Wales Caravan Park

MONMOUTHSHIRE

ABERGAVENNY
Wernddu Caravan Park

POWYS

CHURCHSTOKE
Daisy Bank Caravan Park

CRICKHOWELL
Riverside Caravan & Camping Park

LLANDRINDOD WELLS
Dalmore Camping & Caravanning Park

WREXHAM

OVERTON
The Trotting Mare Caravan Park

the Best of British

Quality family owned Touring and Holiday Parks to suit all tastes, with a warm and friendly welcome

PO Box 28249, Edinburgh, EH9 2YZ

www.bob.org.u

Island camping

Channel Islands

Tight controls are operated because of the narrow width of the mainly rural roads. On all of the islands tents can be hired on recognised campsites and some sites offer luxury glamping units. Early booking is strongly recommended during July and August.

Alderney

Neither caravans nor motorhomes are allowed, and campers must have a confirmed booking on the one official campsite before they arrive on the island.

Guernsey

Only islanders may own and use towed caravans, but a limited number of motorhomes are permitted on the island. The motorhome, used for overnight accommodation, must be not more than 6.9mtrs long and 2.3mtrs wide, must be booked into an authorised site (Fauxquets Valley Campsite, La Bailloterie or Le Vaugrat Camp Site) and a permit must be obtained from the site operator before embarking on a ferry for Guernsey – Condor Ferries will not accept motorhomes without this permit. The permit must be displayed in the window at all times, motorhomes must return to the site each night, and permits are valid for a maximum of one month. Permission is not required to bring a trailer tent to the island. (See www.visitguernsey.com).

Herm and Sark

These two small islands are traffic free. Herm has a small campsite for tents, and these can also be hired. Sark has two campsites. New arrivals are met from the boat by a tractor which carries people and luggage up the steep hill from the harbour. All travel is on foot, by bike, or by horse and cart.

Jersey

Visiting caravans and motorhomes (size restrictions apply) require a permit (maximum one month) that must be displayed at all times and they are restricted to one journey to, and one journey from, the campsite and the port. Caravans must remain on the designated campsites for the period of the permit. Motorhomes can travel around the island on a daily basis but must return to the designated campsite each night. Many roads on the island are narrow and may have limited access (see www.jersey.com).

Bookings should be made through the chosen campsite and they will also arrange a permit.

Isle of Man

Permits can be obtained by contacting The Secretary, Planning Committee, Department of Local Government and the Environment, Murray House, Mount Havelock, Douglas, Isle of Man, IM1 2SF. Tel: 01624 685911 Email: planning@gov.im

A copy of each issued permit is sent directly to the ferry company.

Isles of Scilly

Caravans and motorhomes are not allowed on the islands, and campers must stay at official sites. Booking is advisable on all sites, especially during school holidays.

Scotland

For advice on wild camping in Scotland see the Scottish Outdoor Access Code website (http://outdooraccess-scotland.com/practical-guide/public/camping)

Inner Hebrides

Arran, Coll, Islay & Mull – all have official campsites and welcome caravans, motorhomes and tents; wild camping is also permitted but access rights apply (check each island's website for details). **Colonsay and Cumbrae** – prior arrangements must be made if you wish to camp with a motor vehicle or go wild camping (see www.colonsay.org.uk). **Great Cumbrae** – caravanning or camping is not permitted. **Iona** – a backpackers' paradise and non-residents' vehicles are not permitted; tents are only permitted on the campsite. **Isle of Bute** – camping is only permitted on the official site. **Jura and Gigha** – both have small, designated areas. Prior arrangements are required. **Lismore** – caravans and motorhomes are banned but tents are permitted (there are no official sites and few suitable places). **Rùm and Eigg** – the ferries only take foot passengers and there are no campsites. **Skye** – caravans, motorhomes and tents are permitted and there are official campsites. **Tiree** – caravans, motorhomes and tents are permitted. Wild camping is permitted but check the island's website for details (www.isleoftiree.com).

Orkney

There are no camping and caravanning restrictions, and there are plenty of beauty spots where you can pitch camp.

Shetland Islands

There are official campsites on some of the Shetland Islands, and wild camping is possible with landowner's permission. Caravans and motorhomes must keep to the main roads. Camping 'böds' offer basic accommodation for campers with their own bed rolls and sleeping bags. **Fetlar** – there is no longer a dedicated campsite but wild camping is permitted with the landowner's permission (see www.fetlar.org). **Noss, Bressay and Fair Isle** – camping and caravanning is not permitted.

Western Isles (Outer Hebrides)

Harris, Lewis, North & South Uist – there are official campsites on these islands, and wild camping is allowed with the landowner's prior permission.

Ireland

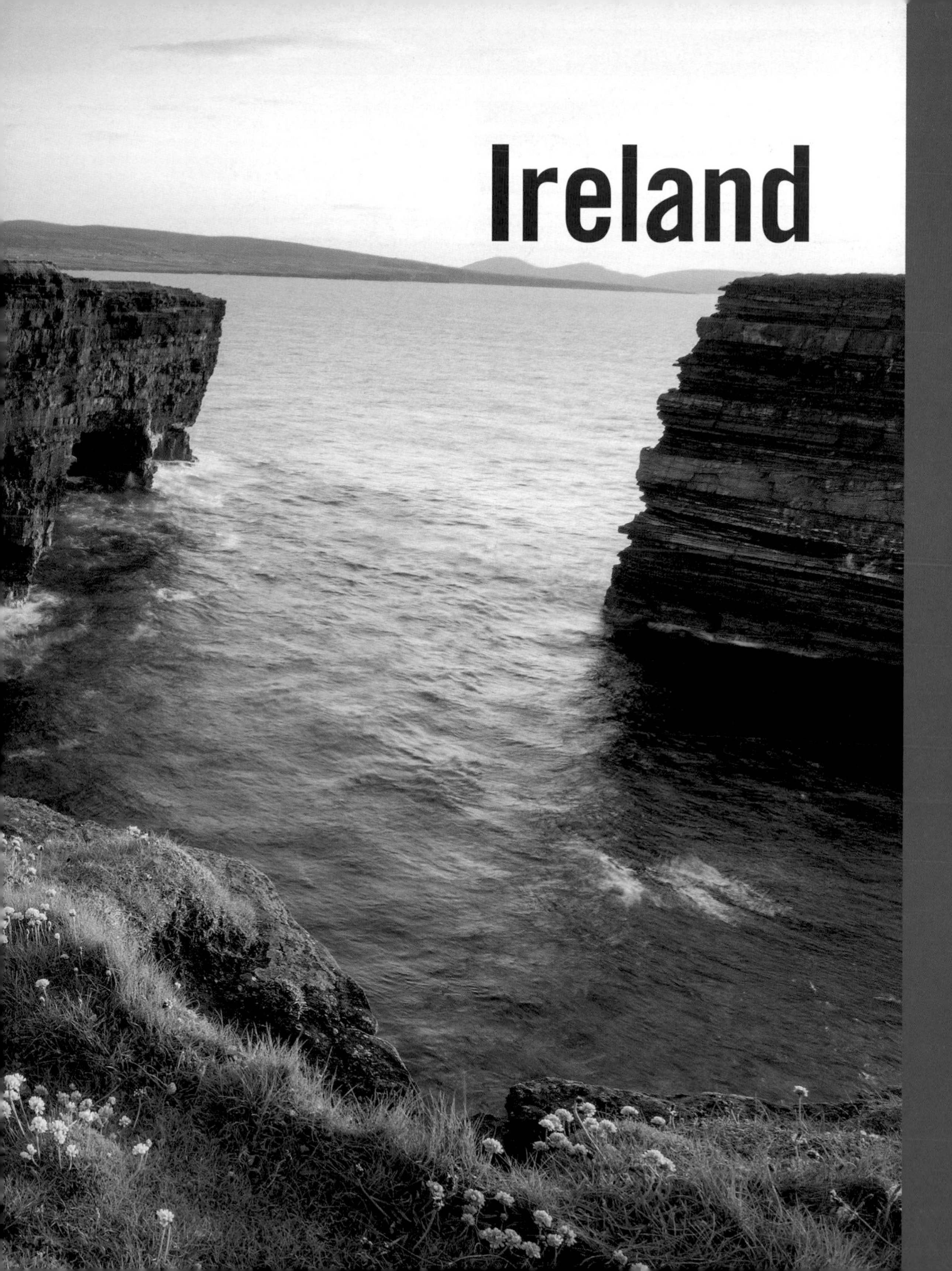

NORTHERN IRELAND

COUNTY ANTRIM

ANTRIM

Map 1 D5

Places to visit

Antrim Round Tower, ANTRIM, BT41 1BJ, 028 9023 5000 www.discovernorthernireland.com/Antrim-Round-Tower-Antrim-P2813

Great for kids: Belfast Zoological Gardens, BELFAST, BT36 7PN, 028 9077 6277 www.belfastzoo.co.uk

Six Mile Water Caravan Park

►►►► 81%

tel: 028 9446 4963 & 9446 3113 **Lough Rd BT41 4DG**
email: sixmilewater@antrim.gov.uk
dir: *From A6, Dublin road into Lough Rd signed Antrim Forum & Loughshore Park. Site at end of road on right.* **grid ref:** *J137870*

A pretty tree-lined site in a large municipal park, within walking distance of Antrim and the Antrim Forum leisure complex, yet very much in the countryside. The modern toilet block is well equipped, and other facilities include a laundry and electric hook-ups, and a new restaurant for the 2016 season. All the pitches are precisely set on generous plots. 9.61 acre site. 45 touring pitches. 37 hardstandings. Caravan pitches. Motorhome pitches. Tent pitches.

Open: Mar-Oct (rs Feb & Nov wknds only) **Last arrival:** 21.00hrs **Last departure:** noon

Pitches: * £21-£23 £21-£23 £15-£18

Leisure:

Facilities:

Services:

Within 3 miles:

Notes: Max stay 7 nights, no noise between 22.00hrs-08.00hrs. Dogs must be kept on leads. Watersports, angling stands.

AA Pubs & Restaurants nearby: Galgorm Resort & Spa, BALLYMENA, BT42 1EA, 028 2588 1001

BALLYCASTLE

Places to visit

Carrick-a-Rede Rope Bridge and Larrybane Visitor Centre, CARRICK-A-REDE, BT54 6LS, 028 2076 9839 www.nationaltrust.org.uk

Old Bushmills Distillery, BUSHMILLS, BT57 8XH, 028 2073 1521 www.bushmills.com

Causeway Coast Holiday Park

NEW HOLIDAY CENTRE 73%

tel: 028 2076 2550 & 07720 464465 **21 Clare Rd BT54 5DB**
email: causewaycoast@hagansleisure.co.uk
dir: *From A44 in Ballycastle follow Portrush sign (A2). 1st right into Moyle Rd. At T-junct right into Clare Rd.* **grid ref:** *NW298987*

In an elevated location close to the seafront with views of Ballycastle Bay and Rathlin Island, this bustling holiday park is ideally located for visiting the many attractions along this unspoilt coastline including the Giant's Causeway just 15 minutes away. Facilities include a pub, refurbished for 2015, a well-equipped indoor swimming pool with slide and an outdoor play area. Most of the grassed touring pitches have an electric supply. Please note that the site does not have hardstandings and tents are not accepted. 28 acre site. 38 touring pitches. 20 hardstandings. Caravan pitches. Motorhome pitches. 176 statics.

Open: Mar-Oct **Last arrival:** 23.00hrs **Last departure:** 10.00hrs

Pitches: * £24.74-£30.90 £24.74-£30.90

Leisure:

Facilities:

Services:

Within 3 miles:

Notes: Quiet time 22.00hrs-07.00hrs, no children out after 23.00hrs. Dogs must be kept on leads.

BALLYMONEY

Map 1 C6

Places to visit

Bonamargy Friary, BALLYCASTLE, 028 2076 2225 www.discovernorthernireland.com/Bonamargy-Friary-Ballycastle-P2818

Great for kids: Dunluce Castle, PORTBALLINTRAE, BT57 8UY, 028 2073 1938 www.discovernorthernireland.com/Dunluce-Castle-P15619

PREMIER PARK

Drumaheglis Marina & Caravan Park

►►►►► 83%

tel: 028 2766 0280 & 2766 0200 **36 Glenstall Rd BT53 7QN**
email: drumaheglis@causewaycoastandglens.gov.uk
web: www.causewaycoastandglens.gov.uk
dir: *Signed from A26, approx 1.5m from Ballymoney towards Coleraine. Also accessed from B66, S of Ballymoney.* **grid ref:** *C901254*

An exceptionally well-designed and laid out park beside the Lower Bann River that has seen serious investment and improvements over the past two years. It has 55 very spacious pitches (all fully serviced), two quality toilet blocks, a stylish reception building, which also houses a games room, IT suite, and the Slipway Café serving fresh pastries and meals. There's table tennis, picnic and BBQ areas, a grass volleyball court and a nature walk. This makes an ideal base for watersport enthusiasts and for those touring County Antrim. Five camping pods are available. 16 acre site. 54 touring pitches. 54 hardstandings. 20 seasonal pitches. Caravan pitches. Motorhome pitches. Tent pitches. 5 wooden pods.

Open: 17 Mar-Oct **Last arrival:** 20.00hrs **Last departure:** 13.00hrs

Pitches: * £24-£25 £24-£25 £17

Leisure:

Facilities:

Services:

Within 3 miles:

Notes: Dogs must be kept on leads. Marina berths, outdoor gym.

BUSHMILLS

Map 1 C6

Places to visit

Old Bushmills Distillery, BUSHMILLS, BT57 8XH, 028 2073 1521
www.bushmills.com

PREMIER PARK

Ballyness Caravan Park

►►►►► 92%

GOLD

tel: 028 2073 2393 **40 Castlecatt Rd BT57 8TN**
email: info@ballynesscaravanpark.com
dir: *0.5m S of Bushmills on B66, follow signs.* **grid ref:** *C944397*

A quality park with superb toilet and other facilities, on farmland beside St Columb's Rill, the stream that supplies the famous nearby Bushmills Distillery. The friendly owners created this park with the discerning camper in mind and continue to invest year on year to enhance the customer experience; the stylish new amenities block interior for 2015 is just one example. There is a pleasant walk around several ponds, and the park is peacefully located close to the beautiful north Antrim coast. There is a spacious play barn and a holiday cottage to let. 16 acre site. 50 touring pitches. 50 hardstandings. Caravan pitches. Motorhome pitches. 65 statics.

Open: 17 Mar-Oct **Last arrival:** 21.00hrs **Last departure:** noon

Pitches: * £25 £25

Leisure:

Facilities:

Services:

Within 3 miles:

Notes: No skateboards or rollerblades. Dogs must be kept on leads. Library.

AA Pubs & Restaurants nearby: Bushmills Inn Hotel, BUSHMILLS, BT57 8QG, 028 2073 3000

BELFAST

DUNDONALD

Map 1 D5

Places to visit

Mount Stewart, NEWTOWNARDS, BT22 2AD, 028 4278 8387
www.nationaltrust.org.uk/mount-stewart

Giant's Ring, BELFAST, 028 9023 5000
www.discovernorthernireland.com/Giants-Ring-Belfast-P2791

Great for kids: Belfast Zoological Gardens, BELFAST, BT36 7PN, 028 9077 6277
www.belfastzoo.co.uk

Dundonald Touring Caravan Park

►►►► 80%

tel: 028 9080 9123 & 9080 9129 **111 Old Dundonald Rd BT16 1XT**
email: sales@castlereagh.gov.uk **web:** www.theicebowl.com
dir: *From Belfast city centre follow M3 & A20 to City Airport. Then A20 to Newtownards, follow signs to Dundonald & Ulster Hospital. At hospital right at sign for Dundonald Ice Bowl. Follow to end, turn right, Ice Bowl on left.* **grid ref:** *J410731*

A purpose-built park in a quiet corner of Dundonald Leisure Park on the outskirts of Belfast. This peaceful park is ideally located for touring County Down and exploring the capital. In the winter it offers an 'Aire de Service' for motorhomes. 1.5 acre site. 22 touring pitches. 22 hardstandings. Caravan pitches. Motorhome pitches. Tent pitches.

Open: 14 Mar-Oct (rs Nov-Mar Aire de Service restricted to motorhomes/caravans with own bathroom facilities) **Last arrival:** 23.00hrs **Last departure:** noon

continued

DUNDONALD *continued*

Pitches: * £8.50-£23.50 £8.50-£23.50 £15.50-£17

Facilities: **Services:**

Within 3 miles:

Notes: No commercial vehicles. Dogs must be kept on leads. Bowling, indoor play area, olympic-size ice rink (additional charges apply).

See advert below

COUNTY FERMANAGH

BELCOO Map 1 C5

Places to visit

Florence Court, ENNISKILLEN, BT92 1DB, 028 6634 8249 www.nationaltrust.org.uk

PREMIER PARK

Rushin House Caravan Park

►►►►► 84%

tel: 028 6638 6519 **Holywell BT93 5DY**
email: enquiries@rushinhousecaravanpark.com
dir: *From Enniskillen take A4 W for 13m to Belcoo. Right onto B52 towards Garrison for 1m. Site signed.* **grid ref:** *H835047*

This park occupies a scenic location overlooking Lough MacNean, close to the picturesque village of Belcoo, and is the product of meticulous planning and execution. There are 24 very generous, fully serviced pitches standing on a terrace overlooking the lough, with additional tenting pitches below; all are accessed via well-kept, wide tarmac roads. Facilities include a lovely, well-equipped play area and a hard surface, fenced five-a-side football pitch. There is a slipway providing boat access to the lough and, of course, fishing; an access path to the lake for less able visitors was added in 2015. The excellent toilet facilities are purpose-built and include family rooms. 5 acre site. 38 touring pitches. 38 hardstandings. Caravan pitches. Motorhome pitches. Tent pitches.

Open: mid Mar-Oct (rs Nov-Mar Aire de Service facilities available)
Last arrival: 21.00hrs **Last departure:** 13.00hrs

Pitches: **Leisure:**

Facilities:

Services: **Within 3 miles:**

Notes: No cars by tents. Dogs must be kept on leads. Lakeside walk.

IRVINESTOWN Map 1 C5

Places to visit

Castle Coole, ENNISKILLEN, BT74 6JY, 028 6632 2690 www.nationaltrust.org.uk

Great for kids: Castle Balfour, LISNASKEA, 028 9023 5000 www.discovernorthernireland.com/Castle-Balfour-Lisnaskea-Enniskillen-P2901

Castle Archdale Caravan Park & Camping Site

►►►► 82%

tel: 028 6862 1333 **Lisnarick BT94 1PP**
email: info@castlearchdale.com **web:** www.castlearchdale.com
dir: *From Irvinestown take B534 signed Lisnarick. Left onto B82 signed Enniskillen. Approx 1m right by church, signed.* **grid ref:** *H176588*

This park is located within the grounds of Castle Archdale Country Park on the shores of Lough Erne which boasts stunning scenery, forest walks and also war and wildlife museums. The site is ideal for watersport enthusiasts with its marina and launching facilities. Also on site are a shop, licenced restaurant, takeaway and play park. There are 56 fully serviced, hardstanding pitches. 11 acre site. 158 touring pitches. 120 hardstandings. Caravan pitches. Motorhome pitches. Tent pitches. 144 statics.

Open: Apr-Oct (rs Apr-Jun & Sep-Oct shop & bar open wknds only) **Last departure:** noon

Pitches: * £25-£30 £25-£30 £10-£40

Leisure:

Facilities:

Services:

Within 3 miles:

Notes: No open fires. Dogs must be kept on leads.

AA Pubs & Restaurants nearby: Lough Erne Resort, ENNISKILLEN, BT93 7ED, 028 6632 3230

LISNASKEA Map 1 C5

Places to visit

Castle Balfour, LISNASKEA, 028 9023 5000 www.discovernorthernireland.com/Castle-Balfour-Lisnaskea-Enniskillen-P2901

Florence Court, ENNISKILLEN, BT92 1DB, 028 6634 8249 www.nationaltrust.org.uk

Great for kids: Castle Coole, ENNISKILLEN, BT74 6JY, 028 6632 2690 www.nationaltrust.org.uk

Lisnaskea Caravan Park

►►► 81%

tel: 028 6772 1040 **BT92 0NZ**
dir: *From Lisnaskea take B514 signed Carry Bridge, site signed.* **grid ref:** *H297373*

A pretty riverside site set in peaceful countryside, with well-kept facilities and friendly owners. Fishing is available on the river, and this quiet area is an ideal location for touring the lakes of Fermanagh. 6 acre site. 43 touring pitches. 43 hardstandings. Caravan pitches. Motorhome pitches. Tent pitches. 8 statics.

Open: Mar-Sep **Last arrival:** 21.00hrs **Last departure:** 14.00hrs

Pitches:

Leisure:

Facilities:

Services:

Within 3 miles:

Notes: Dogs must be kept on leads.

AA Pubs & Restaurants nearby: Lough Erne Resort, ENNISKILLEN, BT93 7ED, 028 6632 3230

COUNTY TYRONE

DUNGANNON Map 1 C5

Places to visit

The Argory, MOY, BT71 6NA, 028 8778 4753 www.nationaltrust.org.uk

U S Grant Ancestral Homestead, BALLYGAWLEY, BT70 1TW, 028 8555 7133 www.dungannon.gov.uk

Great for kids: Mountjoy Castle, MOUNTJOY, 028 9023 5000 www.ehsni.gov.uk

Dungannon Park

►►►► 85%

tel: 028 8772 8690 & 03000 132132 **Moy Rd BT71 6DY**
email: parks@midulstercouncil.org
dir: *M1 junct 15, A29 towards Dungannon, left at 2nd lights.* **grid ref:** *H805612*

A modern caravan park in a quiet area of a stunning public park with fishing lake and excellent facilities, especially for disabled visitors. Additional fully serviced pitches, a new amenities block and coffee shop are features planned for 2016. 4 acre site. 37 touring pitches. 24 hardstandings. Caravan pitches. Motorhome pitches. Tent pitches.

Open: Mar-Oct **Last arrival:** 20.30hrs **Last departure:** 13.00hrs

Pitches: * £16.50-£20.50 £16.50-£20.50 £12.50-£20.50

Leisure:

Facilities:

Services:

Within 3 miles:

Notes: No noise between 22.00hrs-08.00hrs, no generators. Dogs must be kept on leads.

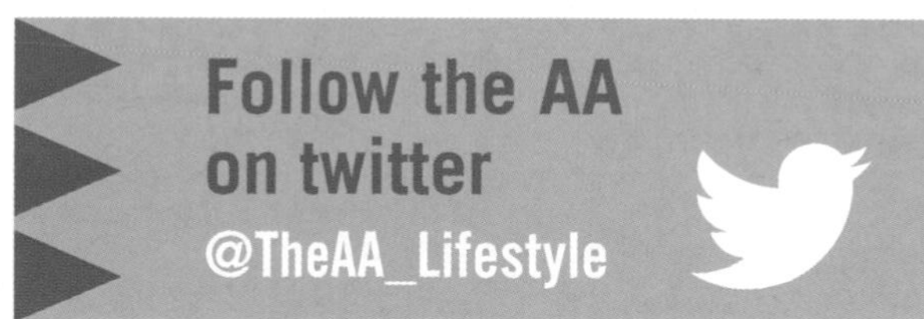

REPUBLIC OF IRELAND

COUNTY CORK

BALLINSPITTLE — Map 1 B2

Garrettstown House Holiday Park

►►►► 80%

tel: 021 4778156 & 4775286
email: reception@garrettstownhouse.com
dir: *6m from Kinsale, through Ballinspittle, past school & football pitch on main road to beach. Beside stone estate entrance.* **grid ref:** *W588445*

Elevated holiday park with tiered camping areas and superb panoramic views. Plenty of on-site amenities, and close to beach and forest park. 7 acre site. 60 touring pitches. 20 hardstandings. Caravan pitches. Motorhome pitches. Tent pitches. 80 statics.

Open: 4 May-9 Sep (rs Early season-1 Jun shop closed) **Last arrival:** 22.00hrs **Last departure:** noon

Pitches:

Leisure:

Facilities:

Services:

Within 3 miles:

Notes: Dogs must be kept on leads. Crazy golf, video shows, snooker, adult reading lounge, tots' playroom.

BALLYLICKEY — Map 1 B2

Eagle Point Caravan and Camping Park

►►►► 85%

tel: 027 50630
email: info@eaglepointcamping.com
dir: *From Cork: N71 to Bandon, R586 to Bantry, then N71, 4m to Glengarriff, opposite petrol station. From Killarney: N22 to Macroom, R584 to Ballickey Bridge, N71 to Glengarriff.* **grid ref:** *V995535*

An immaculate park set in an idyllic position on a headland overlooking the rugged Bantry Bay and the mountains of West Cork. There are boat launching facilities, small and safe pebble beaches, a football field, tennis court, a small playground, and TV rooms for children and adults on the park. There is an internet café in the reception and a shop and petrol station across from the park entrance. Nearby are two golf courses, riding stables, a sailing centre and cycle hire facilities. 20 acre site. 125 touring pitches. 20 hardstandings. 60 seasonal pitches. Caravan pitches. Motorhome pitches. Tent pitches.

Open: 15 Apr-19 Sep **Last arrival:** 21.00hrs **Last departure:** noon

Pitches: * €26-€29 €26-€29 €26-€29

Leisure:

Facilities:

Services:

Within 3 miles:

Notes: No commercial vehicles, skates, scooters or jet skis. Children not permitted to ride bikes.

AA Pubs & Restaurants nearby: Seaview House Hotel, BALLYLICKEY, 027 50073

COUNTY DONEGAL

PORTNOO — Map 1 B5

Places to visit

Glebe House & Gallery, LETTERKENNY, 074 9137071 www.heritageireland.ie/en/glebehouseandgallery/

Tower Museum, LONDONDERRY, BT48 6LU, 028 7137 2411 www.derrycity.gov.uk/museums

Boyle's Caravan Park

►► 70%

tel: 074 9545131 & 086 8523131
email: pboylecaravans@gmail.com
dir: *Exit N56 at Ardra onto R261, 6m. Follow signs for Santa Anna Drive.*
grid ref: *G702990*

This open park sits among the sand dunes overlooking Narin Beach and close to a huge selection of water activities, including wind surfing, fishing, scuba diving and kayaking on a magnificent stretch of the Atlantic on the Donegal coast. There is an 18-hole golf links, and a café and shop at the entrance to the site. The park is very well maintained by the Boyle family. 1.5 acre site. 20 touring pitches. Caravan pitches. Motorhome pitches. Tent pitches. 80 statics.

Open: 18 Mar-Oct **Last arrival:** 23.00hrs **Last departure:** 11.00hrs

Pitches:

Leisure:

Facilities:

Services:

Within 3 miles:

Notes: No skateboards. 1.5m Blue Flag beach.

COUNTY DUBLIN

CLONDALKIN — Map 1 D4

Places to visit

Castletown, CELBRIDGE, 01 6288252 www.heritageireland.ie/en/castletown/

Irish Museum of Modern Art, DUBLIN, 01 6129900 www.imma.ie

Great for kids: Dublin Zoo, DUBLIN, 01 4748900 www.dublinzoo.ie

Camac Valley Tourist Caravan & Camping Park

►►►► 81%

tel: 01 4640644 **Naas Rd, Clondalkin**
email: info@camacvalley.com
dir: *M50 junct 9, N7 (South), exit 2, follow signs for Corkagh Park.* **grid ref:** *O056300*

A pleasant, lightly wooded park with good facilities, security and layout, situated within an hour's drive, or a bus ride, from the city centre. 15 acre site. 163 touring pitches. 113 hardstandings. Caravan pitches. Motorhome pitches. Tent pitches.

Open: all year **Last arrival:** 22.00hrs **Last departure:** noon

Pitches:

Leisure:

Facilities:

Services:

Within 3 miles:

Notes: Lights must be out by 23.00hrs. Dogs must be kept on leads.

AA Pubs & Restaurants nearby: Ashling Hotel, DUBLIN, 01 6772324

COUNTY MAYO

CASTLEBAR — Map 1 B4

Lough Lannagh Caravan Park

►►►► 80%

tel: 094 9027111 **Old Westport Rd**
email: info@loughlannagh.ie **web:** www.loughlannagh.ie
dir: *N5, N60, N84 to Castlebar. At ring road follow signs for Westport. Signs for Lough Lannagh Village on all approach roads to Westport rdbt.* **grid ref:** *M140890*

This park is part of the Lough Lannagh Village which is situated in a wooded area a short walk from Castlebar. Leisure facilities include tennis courts, boules, children's play area and café. 2.5 acre site. 20 touring pitches. 20 hardstandings. Caravan pitches. Motorhome pitches. Tent pitches.

Open: 25 Mar-Aug **Last arrival:** 18.00hrs **Last departure:** 10.00hrs

Pitches: €25 €25 €25

Leisure:

Facilities:

Services:

Within 3 miles:

Notes: Pets accepted by prior arrangement only, no pets allowed Jun-Aug. Dogs must be kept on leads. Bike hire.

AA Pubs & Restaurants nearby: Knockranny House Hotel, WESTPORT, 098 28600

KNOCK — Map 1 B4

Knock Caravan and Camping Park

►►►► 76%

tel: 094 9388100 **Claremorris Rd**
email: caravanpark@knock-shrine.ie
dir: *From rdbt in Knock, through town. Site on left in 1km, opposite petrol station.*
grid ref: *M408828*

A pleasant, very well maintained camping park within the grounds of Knock Shrine, offering spacious terraced pitches and excellent facilities. 10 acre site. 88 touring pitches. 88 hardstandings. Caravan pitches. Motorhome pitches. Tent pitches. 12 statics.

Open: last Sun Mar-1st Sun Oct **Last arrival:** 22.00hrs **Last departure:** noon

Pitches: * €20-€22 €22-€24 €16-€17

Leisure:

Facilities:

Services:

Within 3 miles:

Notes: Dogs must be kept on leads.

COUNTY ROSCOMMON

BOYLE — Map 1 B4

Places to visit

King House - Georgian Mansion & Military Barracks, BOYLE, 071 9663242 www.kinghouse.ie

Lough Key Caravan & Camping Park

►►► 74%

tel: 071 9662212 **Lough Key Forest Park**
email: info@loughkey.ie
dir: *3km E of Boyle on N4. Follow Lough Key Forest Park signs, site within grounds. Approx 0.5km from entrance.* **grid ref:** *G846039*

Peaceful and very secluded site within the extensive grounds of a beautiful forest park. Lough Key offers boat trips and waterside walks, and there is a viewing tower. 15 acre site. 72 touring pitches. 52 hardstandings. Caravan pitches. Motorhome pitches. Tent pitches.

Open: Apr-20 Sep **Last arrival:** 18.00hrs **Last departure:** noon

Pitches:

Leisure:

Facilities:

Services:

Within 3 miles:

Notes: No cars by tents.

COUNTY MAPS

England

1 Bedfordshire
2 Berkshire
3 Bristol
4 Buckinghamshire
5 Cambridgeshire
6 Greater Manchester
7 Herefordshire
8 Hertfordshire
9 Leicestershire
10 Northamptonshire
11 Nottinghamshire
12 Rutland
13 Staffordshire
14 Warwickshire
15 West Midlands
16 Worcestershire

Scotland

17 City of Glasgow
18 Clackmannanshire
19 East Ayrshire
20 East Dunbartonshire
21 East Renfrewshire
22 Perth & Kinross
23 Renfrewshire
24 South Lanarkshire
25 West Dunbartonshire

Wales

26 Blaenau Gwent
27 Bridgend
28 Caerphilly
29 Denbighshire
30 Flintshire
31 Merthyr Tydfil
32 Monmouthshire
33 Neath Port Talbot
34 Newport
35 Rhondda Cynon Taff
36 Torfaen
37 Vale of Glamorgan
38 Wrexham

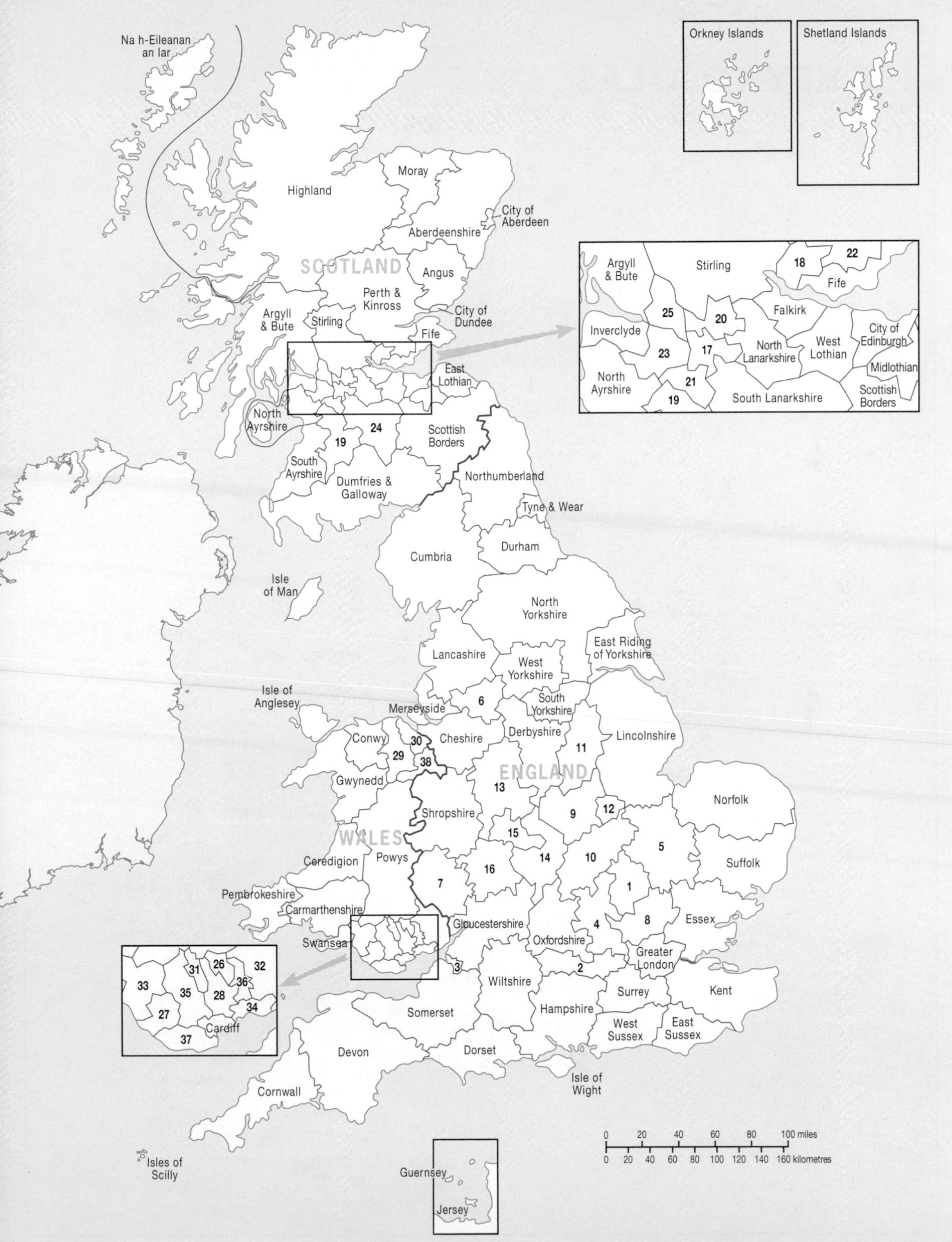

Na h-Eileanan an Iar
Orkney Islands
Shetland Islands
Highland
Moray
City of Aberdeen
Aberdeenshire
SCOTLAND
Angus
Perth & Kinross
Argyll & Bute
Stirling
City of Dundee
Fife
East Lothian
North Ayrshire
24
19
Scottish Borders
South Ayrshire
Dumfries & Galloway
Northumberland
Tyne & Wear
Durham
Cumbria
Isle of Man
North Yorkshire
East Riding of Yorkshire
Lancashire
West Yorkshire
Isle of Anglesey
Merseyside
6
South Yorkshire
Conwy
30
Cheshire
Derbyshire
Lincolnshire
29
11
38
Gwynedd
ENGLAND
13
Norfolk
12
Shropshire
9
WALES
15
Ceredigion
Powys
14
10
5
16
Suffolk
7
1
Pembrokeshire
Carmarthenshire
8
Essex
Gloucestershire
4
Swansea
Oxfordshire
Greater London
3
2
Wiltshire
Surrey
Kent
Hampshire
Somerset
West Sussex
East Sussex
Devon
Dorset
Isle of Wight
Cornwall
Isles of Scilly
Guernsey
Jersey
Argyll & Bute
Stirling
18
22
Fife
25
20
Falkirk
Inverclyde
North Lanarkshire
West Lothian
City of Edinburgh
23
17
North Ayrshire
21
Midlothian
19
South Lanarkshire
Scottish Borders
33
31
26
32
35
28
36
34
27
Cardiff
37
0 20 40 60 80 100 miles
0 20 40 60 80 100 120 140 160 kilometres

KEY TO ATLAS

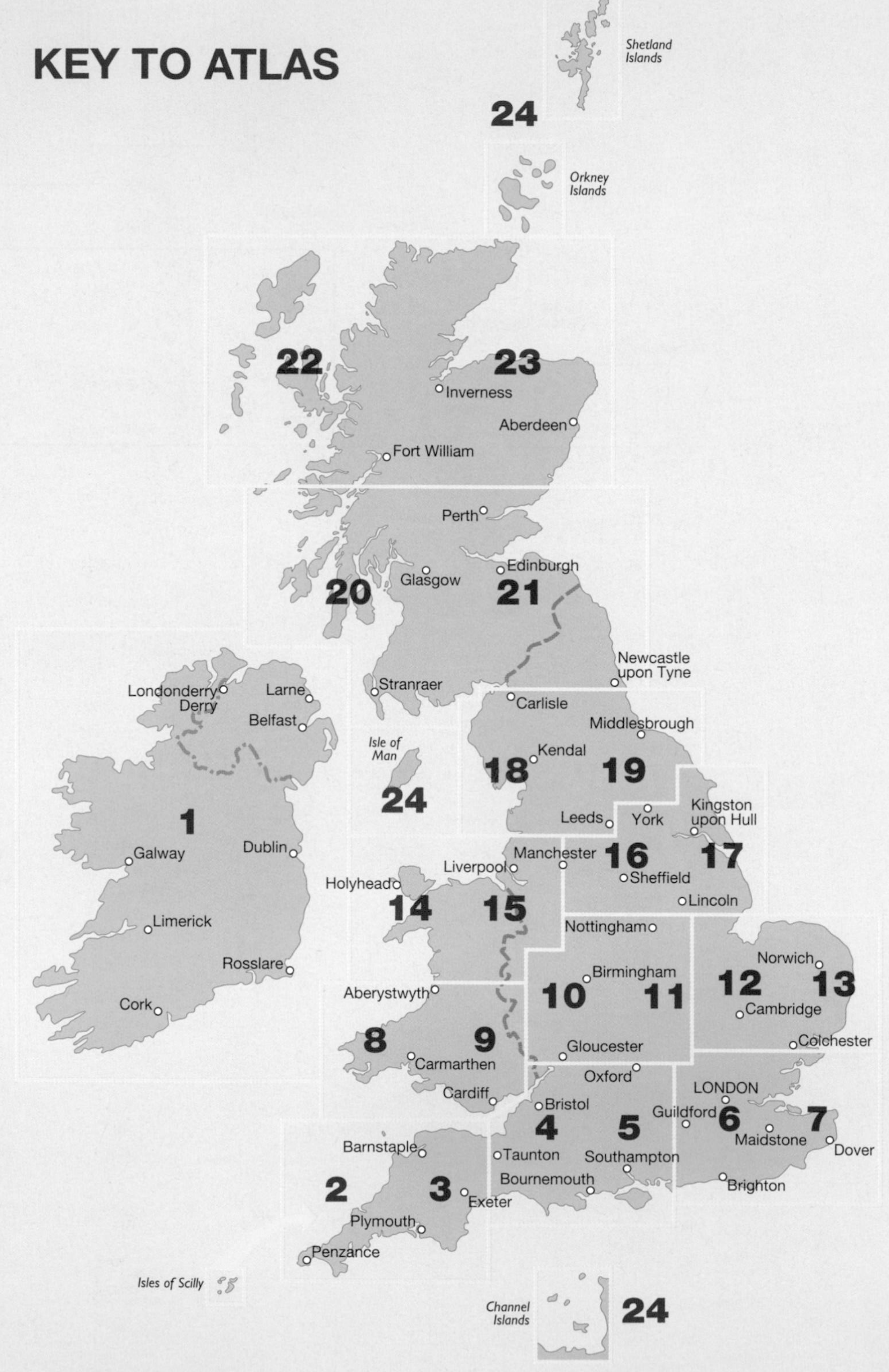

Shetland Islands
24
Orkney Islands
22
23
Inverness
Aberdeen
Fort William
Perth
Edinburgh
Glasgow
20
21
Newcastle upon Tyne
Stranraer
Londonderry Derry
Larne
Belfast
Carlisle
Middlesbrough
Isle of Man
Kendal
18
19
24
1
Leeds
York
Kingston upon Hull
Galway
Dublin
Manchester
16
17
Liverpool
Sheffield
Holyhead
14
15
Lincoln
Limerick
Nottingham
Norwich
Rosslare
Birmingham
12
13
Aberystwyth
10
11
Cork
Cambridge
8
9
Gloucester
Colchester
Carmarthen
Oxford
LONDON
Cardiff
Bristol
Guildford
6
7
4
5
Maidstone
Barnstaple
Taunton
Southampton
Dover
Bournemouth
Brighton
2
3
Exeter
Plymouth
Penzance
Isles of Scilly
Channel Islands
24

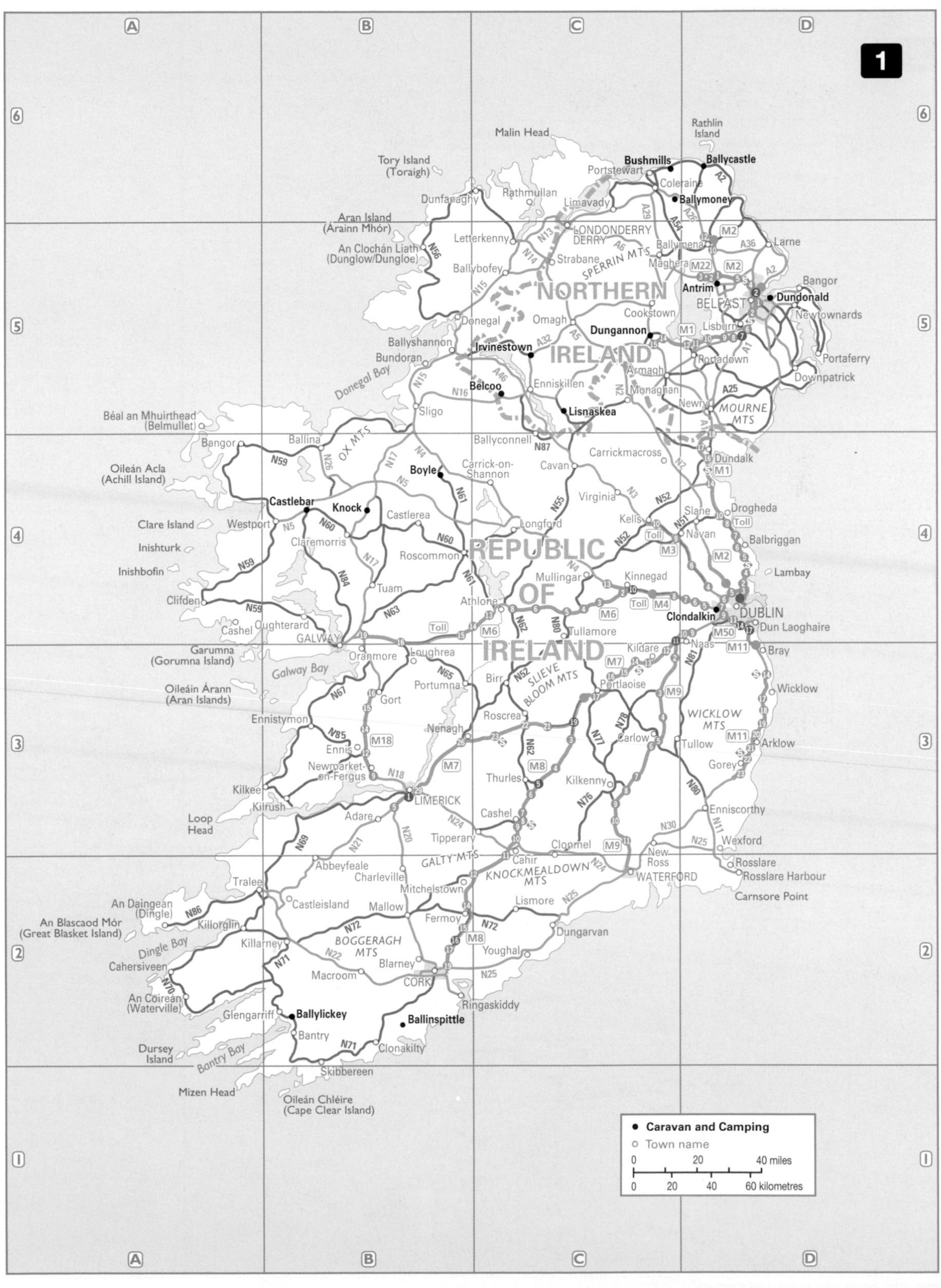

1
A
B
C
D
6
5
4
3
2
1
Malin Head
Rathlin Island
Tory Island (Toraigh)
Bushmills
Ballycastle
Portstewart
Coleraine
Ballymoney
Dunfanaghy
Rathmullan
Limavady
Aran Island (Árainn Mhór)
Letterkenny
LONDONDERRY DERRY
An Clochán Liath (Dunglow/Dungloe)
Ballymena
Larne
Strabane
SPERRIN MTS
Maghera
Ballybofey
Antrim
Bangor
NORTHERN
BELFAST
Dundonald
Newtownards
Donegal
Omagh
Cookstown
Dungannon
Lisburn
Ballyshannon
Irvinestown
IRELAND
Portaferry
Bundoran
Armagh
Portadown
Downpatrick
Donegal Bay
Belcoo
Enniskillen
Monaghan
Newry
MOURNE MTS
Béal an Mhuirthead (Belmullet)
Sligo
Lisnaskea
Bangor
Ballina
OX MTS
Ballyconnell
Carrickmacross
Dundalk
Oileán Acla (Achill Island)
Boyle
Carrick-on-Shannon
Cavan
Castlebar
Knock
Virginia
Drogheda
Clare Island
Westport
Castlerea
Kells
Slane
Balbriggan
Claremorris
Longford
Navan
Inishturk
REPUBLIC
Roscommon
Inishbofin
Lambay
Tuam
Mullingar
Kinnegad
Clifden
OF
Athlone
Clondalkin
DUBLIN
Cashel
Oughterard
Dun Laoghaire
GALWAY
Tullamore
Garumna (Gorumna Island)
Oranmore
Loughrea
IRELAND
Kildare
Naas
Bray
Galway Bay
Birr
SLIEVE BLOOM MTS
Oileáin Árann (Aran Islands)
Portumna
Portlaoise
Wicklow
Gort
Ennistymon
WICKLOW MTS
Roscrea
Nenagh
Carlow
Tullow
Arklow
Ennis
Newmarket-on-Fergus
Gorey
Kilkee
Thurles
Kilkenny
Kilrush
LIMERICK
Loop Head
Adare
Cashel
Enniscorthy
Tipperary
Clonmel
Wexford
New Ross
Tralee
Abbeyfeale
GALTY MTS
Cahir
Rosslare
Charleville
KNOCKMEALDOWN MTS
WATERFORD
Rosslare Harbour
Mitchelstown
An Daingean (Dingle)
Castleisland
Mallow
Lismore
Carnsore Point
An Blascaod Mór (Great Blasket Island)
Killorglin
Fermoy
Dungarvan
Dingle Bay
Killarney
BOGGERAGH MTS
Youghal
Cahersiveen
Blarney
Macroom
CORK
An Coireán (Waterville)
Ringaskiddy
Glengarriff
Ballylickey
Ballinspittle
Bantry
Dursey Island
Clonakilty
Bantry Bay
Skibbereen
Mizen Head
Oileán Chléire (Cape Clear Island)
Caravan and Camping
Town name
0 20 40 miles
0 20 40 60 kilometres

For continuation pages refer to numbered arrows

3
9
4
SUPER-MARE
BRISTOL CHANNEL
Brean
Bleadon
Biddisham
Cheddar
Draycott
Berrow
Burnham-on-Sea
Brent Knoll
Mark
Wedmore
Highbridge
West Huntspill
Bleadney
Meare
Glastonbury
Ashcott
Bridgwater Bay
Lynmouth
Lynton
Ilfracombe
Combe Martin
Lee
Mortehoe
Woolacombe
Porlock Weir
Brendon
Oare
Porlock
Minehead
Parracombe
EXMOOR
Wootton Courtenay
Dunster
Blue Anchor
Watchet
Kilve
Stogursey
Challacombe
NATIONAL
PARK
Carhampton
Sampford Brett
Cannington
Georgeham
Croyde
Saunton
Braunton
Bratton Fleming
Muddiford
Simonsbath
Exford
Wheddon Cross
Crowcombe
Nether Stowey
Bridgwater
QUANTOCK HILLS
Barnstaple
Bideford Bay
Appledore
Instow
Northam
Westward Ho!
Bideford
Brayford
Withypool
Winsford
Bridgetown
Brompton Regis
Elworthy
Goathurst
North Petherton
Middlezoy
Othery
Walton
SOMERSET
Bishops Lydeard
North Molton
Dulverton
Wiveliscombe
Fitzhead
Milverton
Lyng
Somerton
Clovelly
Horns Cross
South Molton
East Anstey
Exebridge
Petton
Taunton
North Curry
Curry Rivel
Langport
Long Sutton
SS
ST
SX
SY
Monkleigh
Umberleigh
Bampton
Sampford Arundel
Wellington
Taunton Deane
Corfe
Hatch Beauchamp
Ilchester
Martock
Great Torrington
Chittlehamholt
Rackenford
Staple Fitzpaine
South Petherton
Montacute
Little Torrington
Burrington
Beaford
Chulmleigh
East Worlington
Witheridge
Sampford Peverell
Culmstock
Hemyock
Horton
Ilminster
Bradworthy
Stibb Cross
Merton
Dolton
Chawleigh
Tiverton
Halberton
Uffculme
Willand
Cullompton
Kentisbeare
Upottery
Chard
Crewkerne
Milton Damerel
Shebbear
Meeth
Eggesford
Winkleigh
Lapford
Cheriton Fitzpaine
Bickleigh
Yarcombe
Winsham
Misterton
Black Torrington
Sheepwash
Morchard Bishop
Drimpton
Mosterton
Holsworthy
Highampton
Hatherleigh
Copplestone
Silverton
Tytherleigh
Broadwindsor
Halwill Junction
Beaworthy
Crediton
Stoke Canon
Honiton
Wilmington
Beaminster
Clawton
DEVON
Newton St Cyres
Feniton
Whimple
Shute
Axminster
Okehampton
Tedburn St Mary
Broadclyst
Ottery St Mary
Colyton
Charmouth
North Chideock
Ashwater
South Zeal
Crockernwell
EXETER
Clyst St Mary
Colyford
Uplyme
Chideock
Bratton Clovelly
Whiddon Down
Drewsteignton
Axmouth
Lyme Regis
West Bay
Bridport
Broadwoodwidger
Sourton Cross
Sourton
Bridestowe
Dunsford
Topsham
Seaton
Beer
Branscombe
Burton Bradstock
Chagford
DARTMOOR
Kennford
Exminster
Sidmouth
Lifton
Lydford
Moretonhampstead
Kenn
Kenton
Otterton
Lyme Bay
Milton Abbot
Postbridge
Bovey Tracey
Chudleigh
Budleigh Salterton
Exmouth
Lamerton
Mary Tavy
Widecombe in the Moor
Ideford
Dawlish
Tavistock
Princetown
Chudleigh Knighton
Kingsteignton
Bishopsteignton
Teignmouth
Gunnislake
Hexworthy
Bickington
Calstock
Callington
Horrabridge
Ashburton
Newton Abbot
Dousland
Holne
Kingskerswell
Maidencombe
Bere Alston
Yelverton
PARK
Buckfastleigh
Ipplepen
Pillaton
Bere Ferrers
Shaugh Prior
Dartington
TORQUAY
Landrake
South Brent
Cornwood
Totnes
Paignton
Saltash
Plympton
Wrangaton
Stoke Gabriel
Tor Bay
Ivybridge
Harbertonford
Churston Ferrers
Torpoint
PLYMOUTH
Ugborough
Dittisham
Brixham
Crafthole
Halwell
Millbrook
Heybrook Bay
Brixton
Yealmpton
Modbury
Kingswear
Cawsand
Dartmouth
Holbeton
Aveton Gifford
East Allington
Wembury
Newton Ferrers
Stoke Fleming
Strete
Bigbury-on-Sea
Kingsbridge
Slapton
Bigbury Bay
Start Bay
Thurlestone
Chillington
Torcross
Hope
Malborough
Salcombe
Beesands
Start Point
East Prawle
0
10 miles
10
20 kilometres

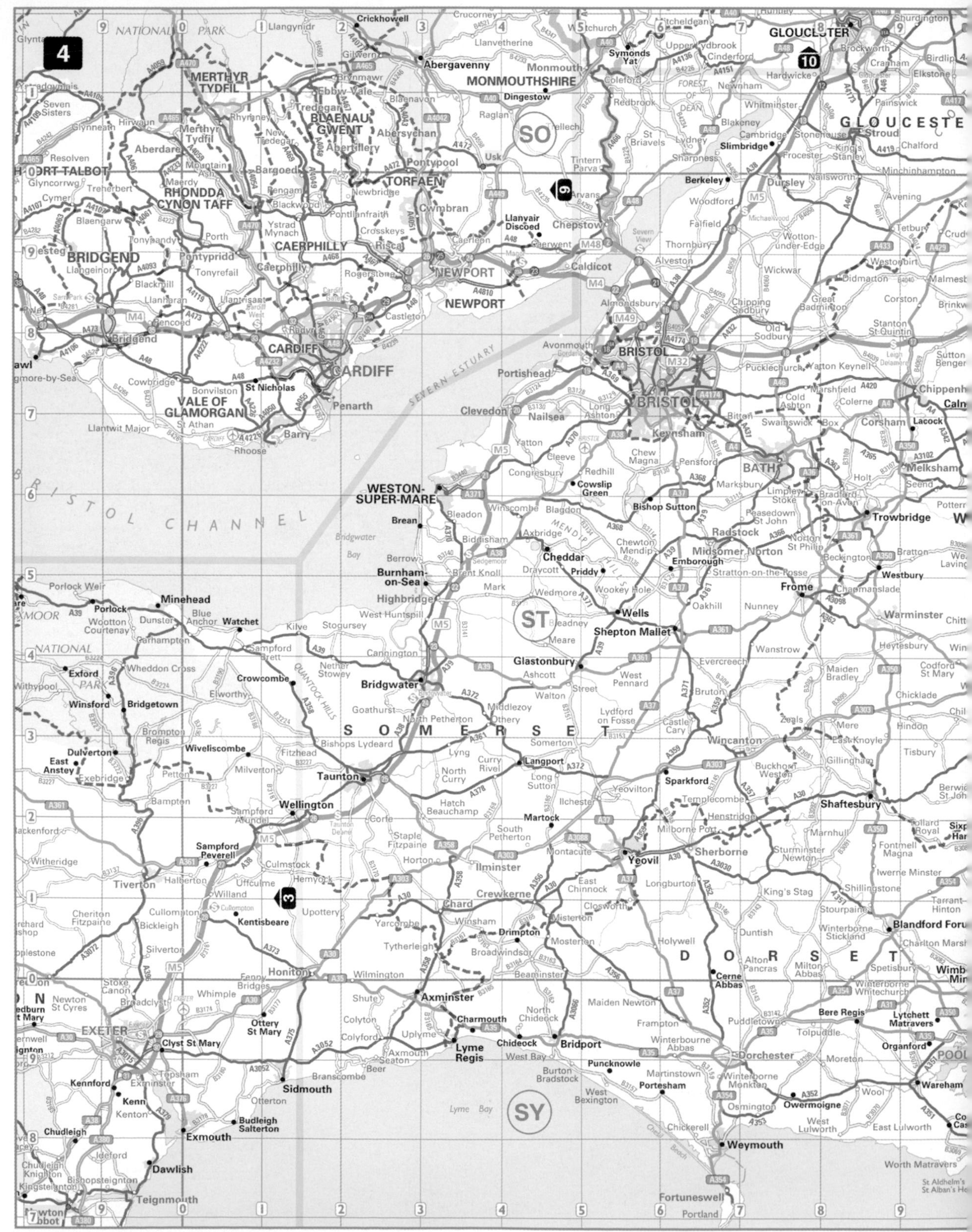

For continuation pages refer to numbered arrows

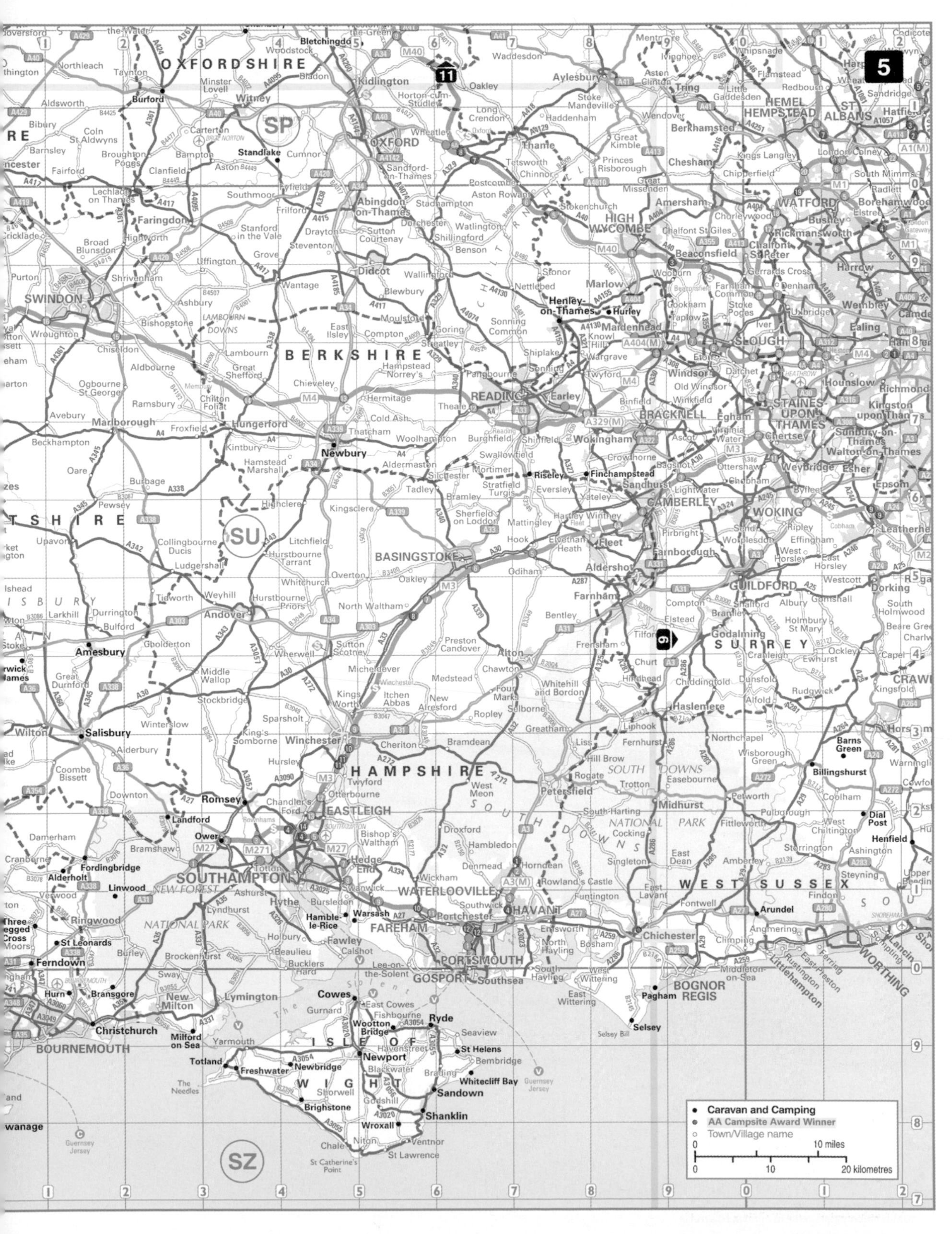
5
OXFORDSHIRE
BERKSHIRE
HAMPSHIRE
SURREY
WEST SUSSEX
ISLE OF WIGHT
SP
SU
SZ
OXFORD
Kidlington
Witney
Burford
Carterton
Standlake
Abingdon-on-Thames
Faringdon
Didcot
Wallingford
Wantage
SWINDON
Marlborough
Hungerford
Newbury
READING
Henley-on-Thames
Hurley
Maidenhead
SLOUGH
Windsor
BRACKNELL
Wokingham
Finchampstead
Riseley
CAMBERLEY
WOKING
GUILDFORD
Farnham
Aldershot
Fleet
Farnborough
BASINGSTOKE
Andover
Amesbury
Salisbury
Winchester
Romsey
EASTLEIGH
SOUTHAMPTON
Ower
Landford
Fordingbridge
Alderholt
Linwood
Ringwood
St Leonards
Ferndown
BOURNEMOUTH
Christchurch
Hurn
Bransgore
Milford on Sea
Lymington
New Milton
NEW FOREST NATIONAL PARK
Hamble-le-Rice
Warsash
FAREHAM
PORTSMOUTH
GOSPORT
Southsea
HAVANT
WATERLOOVILLE
Horndean
Petersfield
SOUTH DOWNS NATIONAL PARK
Midhurst
Chichester
BOGNOR REGIS
Pagham
Selsey
Arundel
WORTHING
Billingshurst
Henfield
Dial Post
Barns Green
Haslemere
Godalming
Alton
Cowes
Ryde
Newport
Totland
Freshwater
Newbridge
St Helens
Whitecliff Bay
Sandown
Shanklin
Brighstone
Wroxall
HIGH WYCOMBE
Beaconsfield
Marlow
Aylesbury
Tring
HEMEL HEMPSTEAD
ST ALBANS
WATFORD
Rickmansworth
STAINES-UPON-THAMES
Aston Clinton
Bletchingdon
Waddesdon
Oakley
Caravan and Camping
AA Campsite Award Winner
Town/Village name
10 miles
20 kilometres

For continuation pages refer to numbered arrows

7
TM
TR
Engaine
Earls Colne
Aldham
COLCHESTER
Ardleigh
Wix
Harwi
Thorpe-le-Soken
Walton on the Naze
Marks Tey
Coggeshall
Copford Green
Wivenhoe
Elmstead Market
Thorrington
Little Clacton
Frinton-on-Sea
Silver End
Kelvedon
Tiptree
Brightlingsea
St Osyth
CLACTON-ON-SEA
Witham
Mersea Island
Tolleshunt D'Arcy
West Mersea
Goldhanger
Tollesbury
Maldon
River Blackwater
Bradwell-on-Sea
Steeple
St Lawrence
Cold Norton
Latchingdon
Southminster
South Woodham Ferrers
Burnham-on-Crouch
Hockley
Rayleigh
Rochford
SOUTHEND
Great Wakering
SOUTHEND-ON-SEA
Canvey Island
Grain
Sheerness
Minster
Eastchurch
Leysdown-on-Sea
Hoo St Werburgh
Isle of Sheppey
Iwade
GILLINGHAM
Herne Bay
Reculver
MARGATE
Broadstairs
Whitstable
St Nicholas at Wade
Ramsgate
Sarre
Minster
Sittingbourne
Faversham
Upstreet
Teynham
Sturry
Hersden
Bredhurst
Ospringe
Blean
Ash
Sandwich
Detling
Boughton Street
Fordwich
Canterbury
Wingham
Maidstone
Hollingbourne
Doddington
Chilham
Chartham
Bridge
Eastry
Lenham
Challock
Aylesham
Deal
Charing
KENT
Kingsdown
Sutton Valence
Wye
Pluckley
St Margaret's at Cliffe
Headcorn
Elham
Alkham
Smarden
Densole
DOVER
Staplehurst
Ashford
Lyminge
Bethersden
Hawkinge
Biddenden
High Halden
Kingsnorth
Sellindge
Sissinghurst
Cranbrook
Woodchurch
Lympne
FOLKESTONE
Benenden
Hythe
Tenterden
Hamstreet
Rolvenden
Wittersham
Appledore
Dymchurch
Brookland
Brenzett
St Mary's Bay
Northiam
New Romney
Peasmarsh
Lydd
LYDD
Rye
Camber
Brede
Winchelsea
Dungeness
STRAIT OF DOVER
Guestling Green
Westfield
Fairlight
HASTINGS
M2
M20
A2
A20
A28
A12
A120
A133
A13
A127
A249
A299
A256
A258
A257
A259
A268
A2070
A251
A290
A291
A228
A414
A274
Caravan and Camping
AA Campsite Award Winner
Town/Village name
0
10 miles
10
20 kilometres

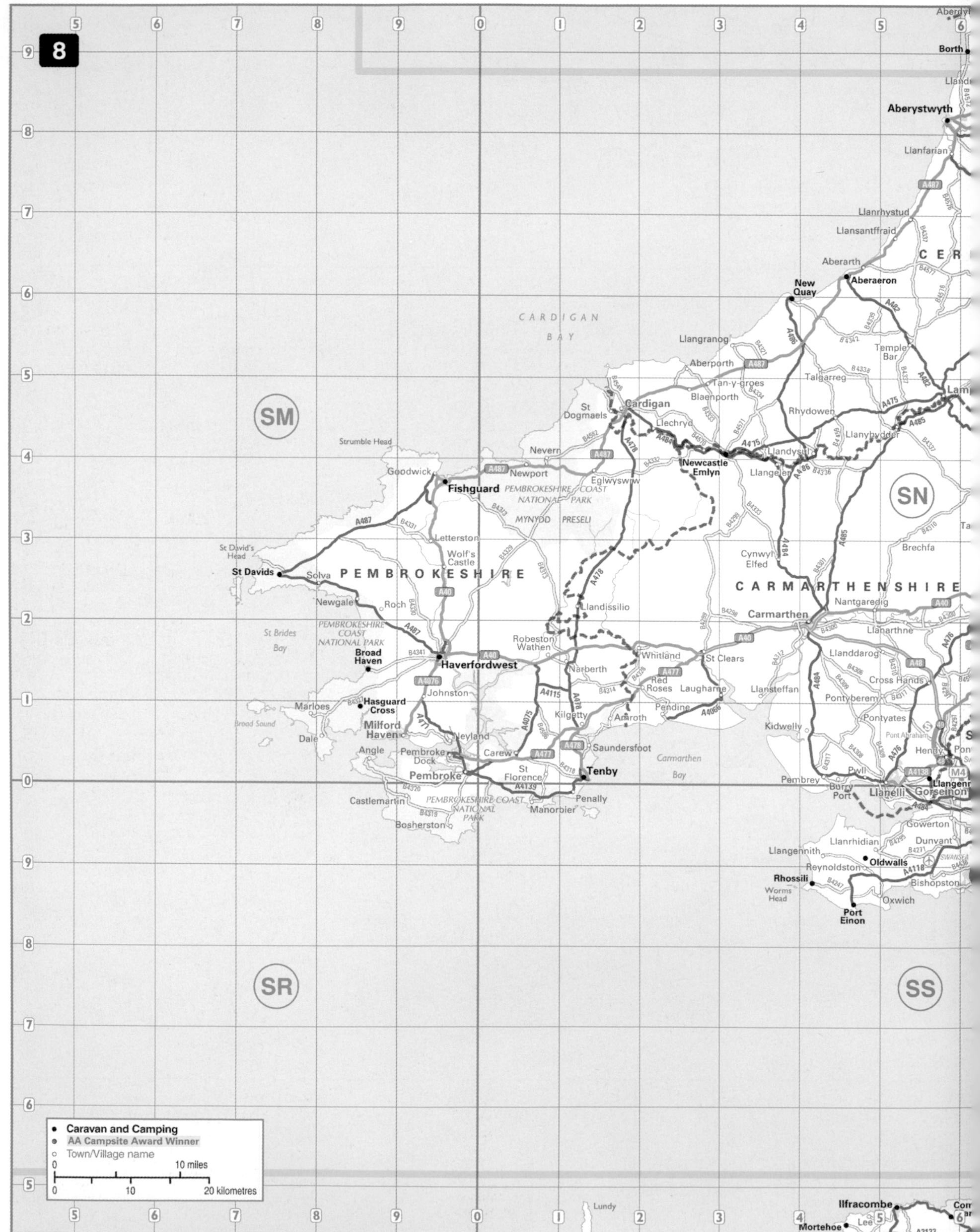

For continuation pages refer to numbered arrows

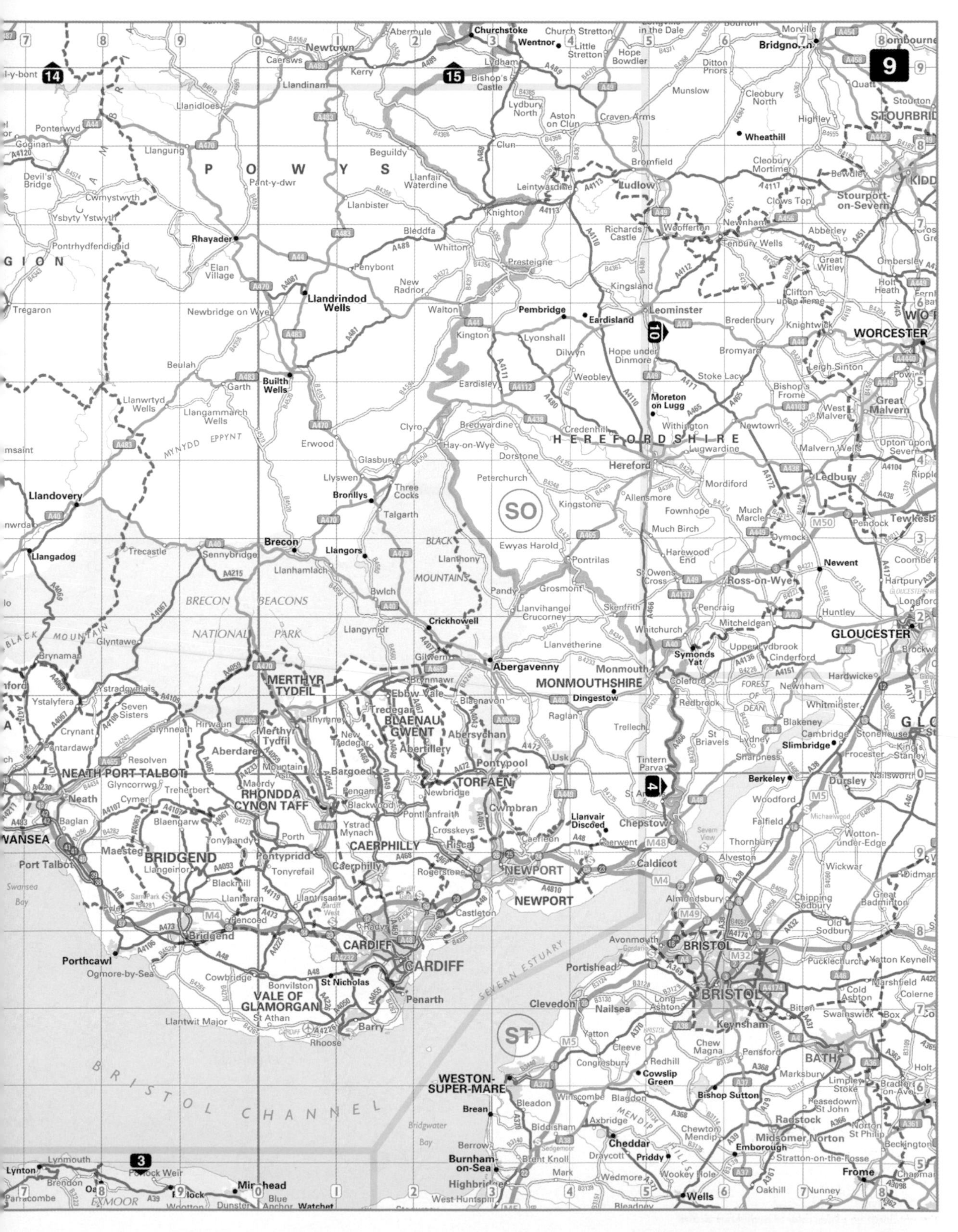

9
14
15
10
4
3
POWYS
CAMBRIAN
GION
HEREFORDSHIRE
MONMOUTHSHIRE
BLAENAU GWENT
TORFAEN
CAERPHILLY
MERTHYR TYDFIL
RHONDDA CYNON TAFF
NEATH PORT TALBOT
BRIDGEND
VALE OF GLAMORGAN
CARDIFF
NEWPORT
BRISTOL
BRECON BEACONS NATIONAL PARK
BLACK MOUNTAINS
BLACK MOUNTAIN
MYNYDD EPPYNT
SEVERN ESTUARY
BRISTOL CHANNEL
MENDIP HILLS
EXMOOR
SO
ST
Swansea Bay
Bridgwater Bay
Abermule
Churchstoke
Church Stretton
Wentnor
Little Stretton
Hope Bowdler
Longville in the Dale
Morville
Bridgnorth
Bourton
Newtown
Caersws
Kerry
Llandinam
Lydham
Bishop's Castle
Ditton Priors
Munslow
Cleobury North
Quatt
Stourton
STOURBRIDGE
Llanidloes
Lydbury North
Aston on Clun
Craven Arms
Highley
Wheathill
Ponterwyd
Goginan
Llangurig
Beguildy
Clun
Bromfield
Cleobury Mortimer
Bewdley
Devil's Bridge
Cwmystwyth
Pant-y-dwr
Llanfair Waterdine
Leintwardine
Ludlow
Clows Top
Stourport-on-Severn
Ysbyty Ystwyth
Llanbister
Knighton
Richards Castle
Woofferton
Newnham
Abberley
Pontrhydfendigaid
Rhayader
Bleddfa
Whitton
Presteigne
Tenbury Wells
Great Witley
Ombersley
Elan Village
Penybont
New Radnor
Kingsland
Clifton upon Teme
Holt Heath
Tregaron
Newbridge on Wye
Llandrindod Wells
Walton
Pembridge
Eardisland
Leominster
Bredenbury
Knightwick
WORCESTER
Kington
Lyonshall
Dilwyn
Hope under Dinmore
Bromyard
Leigh Sinton
Beulah
Builth Wells
Garth
Weobley
Stoke Lacy
Bishop's Frome
Eardisley
Moreton on Lugg
Great Malvern
Llanwrtyd Wells
Llangammarch Wells
Clyro
Bredwardine
Credenhill
Withington
West Malvern
Newtown
Erwood
Hay-on-Wye
Dorstone
Lugwardine
Malvern Wells
Upton upon Severn
Glasbury
Hereford
Ledbury
Llyswen
Peterchurch
Mordiford
Llandovery
Bronllys
Three Cocks
Kingstone
Allensmore
Fownhope
Much Marcle
Talgarth
Much Birch
Pendock
Tewkesbury
Dymock
Ewyas Harold
Llangadog
Trecastle
Sennybridge
Brecon
Llangors
Llanthony
Pontrilas
Harewood End
Newent
Coombe Hill
Llanhamlach
St Owens Cross
Ross-on-Wye
Hartpury
Grosmont
Pandy
Longford
Bwlch
Llanvihangel Crucorney
Skenfrith
Pencraig
Huntley
Crickhowell
Mitcheldean
GLOUCESTER
Glyntawe
Llangynidr
Llanvetherine
Whitchurch
Upper Lydbrook
Brockworth
Brynaman
Gilwern
Abergavenny
Symonds Yat
Cinderford
Monmouth
Hardwicke
Ystradgynlais
Brynmawr
Coleford
Newnham
Ystalyfera
Seven Sisters
Ebbw Vale
Blaenavon
Dingestow
FOREST OF DEAN
Tredegar
Whitminster
Crynant
Glynneath
Hirwaun
Rhymney
Raglan
Redbrook
Pontardawe
Merthyr Tydfil
New Tredegar
Abersychan
Trellech
Blakeney
Cambridge
Stonehouse
Aberdare
Abertillery
St Briavels
Lydney
Slimbridge
Kings Stanley
Resolven
Mountain Ash
Bargoed
Pontypool
Usk
Frocester
Sharpness
Tintern Parva
Berkeley
Dursley
Nailsworth
Glyncorrwg
Treherbert
Maerdy
Pengam
Neath
Cymer
Blackwood
Newbridge
Woodford
Baglan
Blaengarw
Ystrad Mynach
Pontllanfraith
Cwmbran
Llanvair Discoed
Chepstow
Falfield
SWANSEA
Tonypandy
Porth
Crosskeys
Caerleon
Caerwent
Thornbury
Wotton-under-Edge
Maesteg
Risca
Alveston
Port Talbot
Llangeinor
Pontypridd
Tonyrefail
Caerphilly
Rogerstone
Caldicot
Wickwar
Blackmill
Llanharan
Llantrisant
Castleton
Almondsbury
Chipping Sodbury
Great Badminton
Pyle
Pencoed
Radyr
Old Sodbury
Bridgend
Avonmouth
Porthcawl
Ogmore-by-Sea
Portishead
Pucklechurch
Yatton Keynell
Cowbridge
Bonvilston
St Nicholas
Marshfield
Cold Ashton
Colerne
Clevedon
Nailsea
Long Ashton
Penarth
Bitton
Swainswick
Box
Llantwit Major
St Athan
Barry
Rhoose
Keynsham
Yatton
Cleeve
Chew Magna
Pensford
BATH
Congresbury
Redhill
Cowslip Green
Marksbury
WESTON-SUPER-MARE
Bleadon
Winscombe
Blagdon
Bishop Sutton
Limpley Stoke
Bradford-on-Avon
Brean
Biddisham
Axbridge
Chewton Mendip
Radstock
Peasedown St John
Norton St Philip
Berrow
Cheddar
Draycott
Priddy
Midsomer Norton
Emborough
Beckington
Burnham-on-Sea
Brent Knoll
Wookey Hole
Stratton-on-the-Fosse
Frome
Highbridge
Mark
Wedmore
Oakhill
Nunney
West Huntspill
Wells
Chapmanslade
Lynton
Lynmouth
Brendon
Porlock Weir
Porlock
Minehead
Blue Anchor
Watchet
Dunster
Parracombe
Wootton
Bleadney

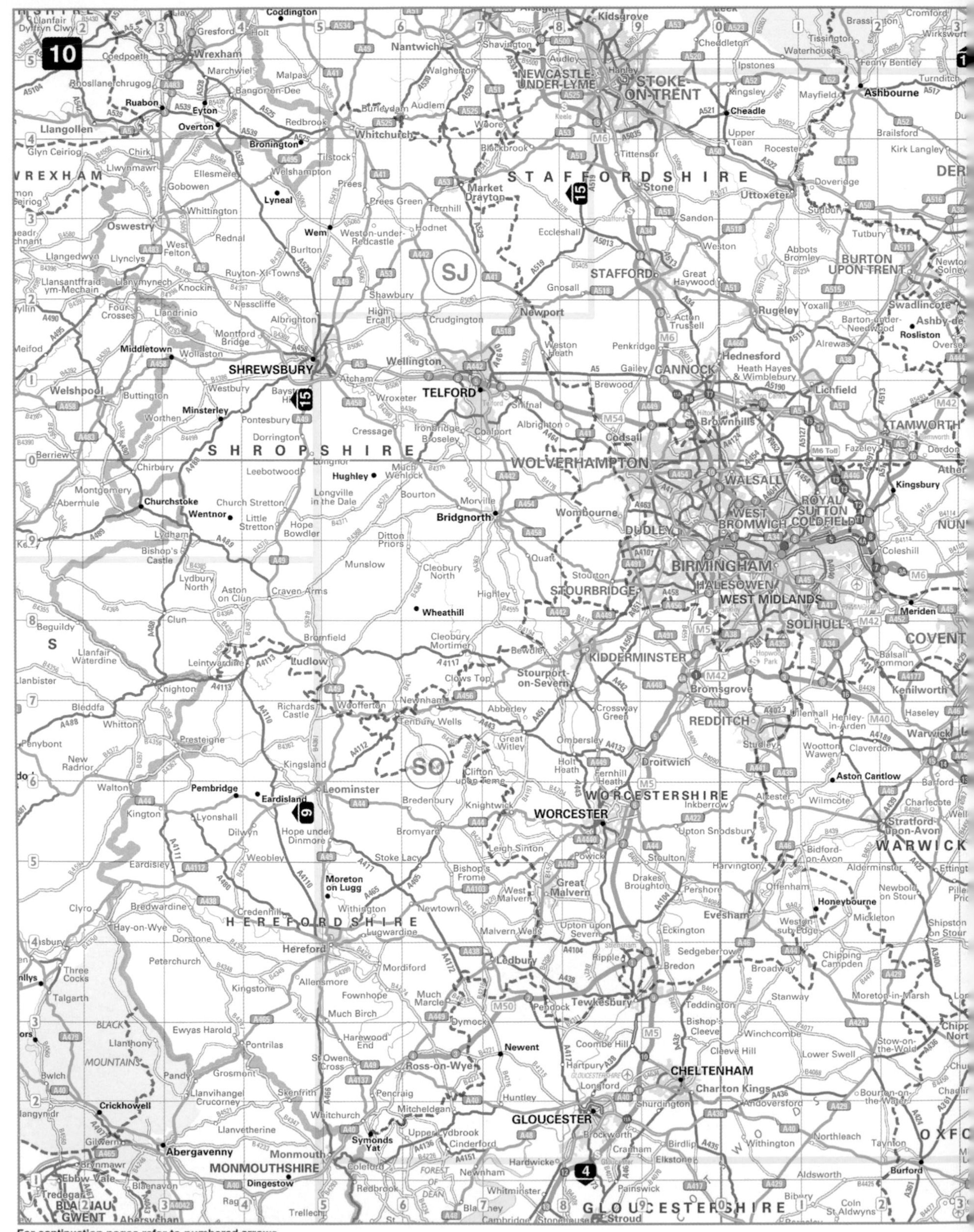

For continuation pages refer to numbered arrows

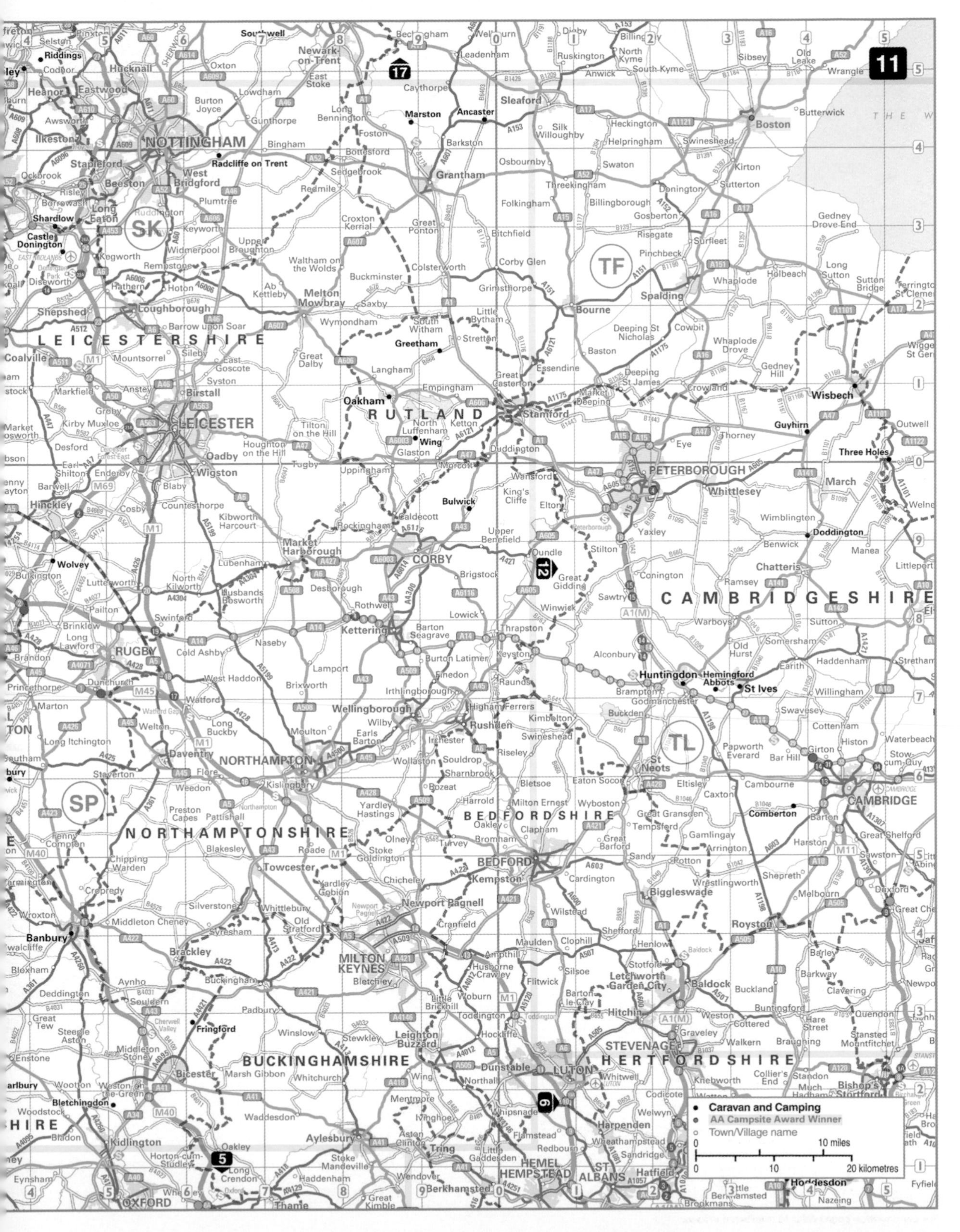
Caravan and Camping
AA Campsite Award Winner
Town/Village name
0
10 miles
0
10
20 kilometres
LEICESTERSHIRE
RUTLAND
CAMBRIDGESHIRE
NORTHAMPTONSHIRE
BEDFORDSHIRE
BUCKINGHAMSHIRE
HERTFORDSHIRE
SK
TF
SP
TL
NOTTINGHAM
LEICESTER
PETERBOROUGH
NORTHAMPTON
CAMBRIDGE
BEDFORD
LUTON
MILTON KEYNES
OXFORD
Southwell
Newark-on-Trent
Riddings
Hucknall
Heanor
Eastwood
Ilkeston
Stapleford
Beeston
West Bridgford
Radcliffe on Trent
Long Eaton
Shardlow
Castle Donington
Kegworth
Loughborough
Shepshed
Coalville
Melton Mowbray
Sleaford
Ancaster
Marston
Grantham
Boston
Butterwick
Wrangle
Spalding
Bourne
Stamford
Oakham
Wing
Greetham
Uppingham
Bulwick
Corby
Kettering
Market Harborough
Wellingborough
Rushden
Oundle
Huntingdon
Hemingford Abbots
St Ives
St Neots
Wisbech
Guyhirn
Three Holes
March
Whittlesey
Doddington
Chatteris
Comberton
Biggleswade
Royston
Stevenage
Letchworth Garden City
Baldock
Hitchin
Harpenden
St Albans
Hemel Hempstead
Hatfield
Hoddesdon
Dunstable
Leighton Buzzard
Aylesbury
Tring
Berkhamsted
Bicester
Fringford
Banbury
Bletchingdon
Kidlington
Brackley
Towcester
Daventry
Rugby
Hinckley
Wolvey
Oadby
Wigston
Newport Pagnell
Kempston
Bishop's Stortford
Thame
Oakley
Long Crendon

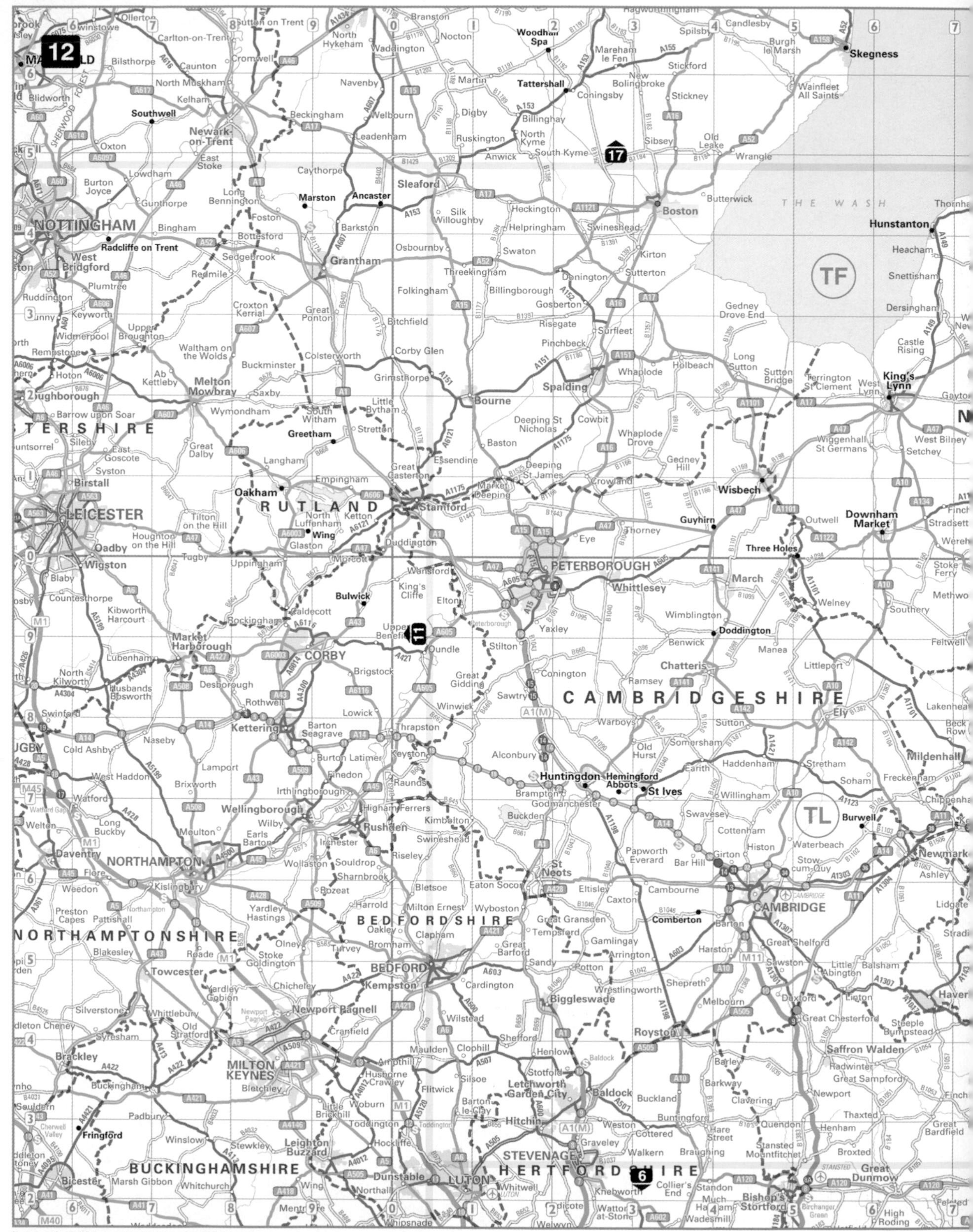

For continuation pages refer to numbered arrows

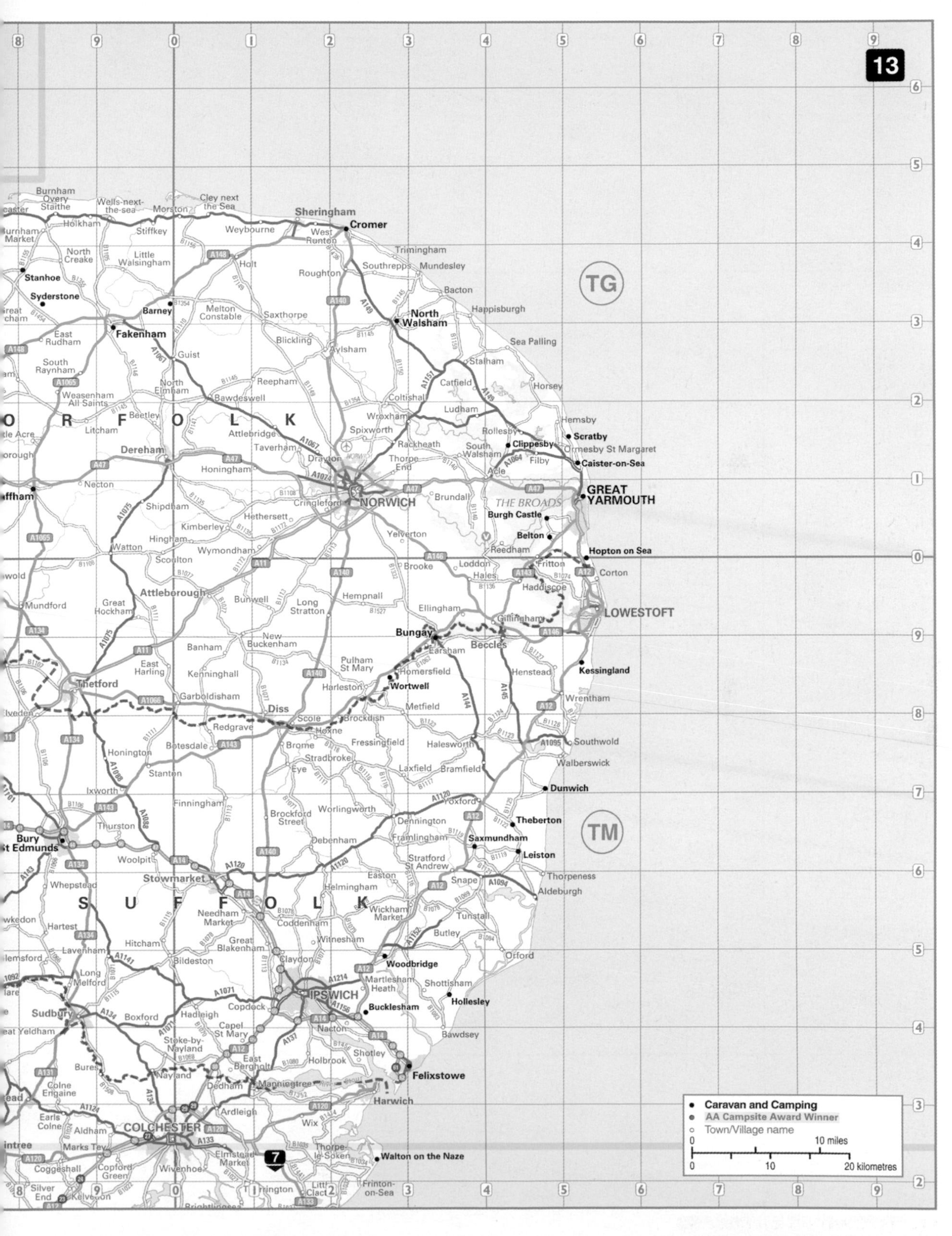
TG
TM
Burnham Overy Staithe
Wells-next-the-sea
Morston
Cley next the Sea
Sheringham
Cromer
Holkham
Stiffkey
Weybourne
West Runton
Trimingham
North Creake
Little Walsingham
Holt
Southrepps
Mundesley
Stanhoe
Roughton
Bacton
Syderstone
Barney
Melton Constable
Saxthorpe
North Walsham
Happisburgh
Fakenham
East Rudham
Guist
Blickling
Aylsham
Sea Palling
South Raynham
Stalham
Catfield
Horsey
North Elmham
Reepham
Weasenham All Saints
Bawdeswell
Coltishall
Ludham
Hemsby
Beetley
Wroxham
Scratby
NORFOLK
Litcham
Attlebridge
Spixworth
Rollesby
Clippesby
Ormesby St Margaret
Dereham
Taverham
Rackheath
South Walsham
Filby
Caister-on-Sea
Honingham
Drayton
Thorpe End
Acle
Necton
NORWICH
Brundall
GREAT YARMOUTH
THE BROADS
Shipdham
Cringleford
Burgh Castle
Hethersett
Kimberley
Yelverton
Belton
Hingham
Watton
Wymondham
Reedham
Hopton on Sea
Scoulton
Brooke
Loddon
Fritton
Hales
Corton
Haddiscoe
Attleborough
Bunwell
Long Stratton
Hempnall
Mundford
Great Hockham
Ellingham
Gillingham
LOWESTOFT
New Buckenham
Bungay
Banham
Earsham
Beccles
East Harling
Pulham St Mary
Homersfield
Henstead
Kessingland
Kenninghall
Thetford
Harleston
Wortwell
Garboldisham
Wrentham
Diss
Metfield
Scole
Brockdish
Redgrave
Hoxne
Botesdale
Brome
Fressingfield
Halesworth
Southwold
Honington
Stradbroke
Walberswick
Stanton
Eye
Laxfield
Bramfield
Ixworth
Dunwich
Finningham
Yoxford
Brockford Street
Worlingworth
Thurston
Dennington
Theberton
Bury St Edmunds
Framlingham
Saxmundham
Debenham
Leiston
Woolpit
Stratford St Andrew
Stowmarket
Easton
Thorpeness
Whepstead
Snape
Aldeburgh
Helmingham
SUFFOLK
Needham Market
Wickham Market
Tunstall
Hartest
Coddenham
Butley
Witnesham
Hitcham
Great Blakenham
Orford
Lavenham
Claydon
Bildeston
Woodbridge
Long Melford
Martlesham Heath
Shottisham
IPSWICH
Hollesley
Copdock
Sudbury
Bucklesham
Boxford
Hadleigh
Capel St Mary
Nacton
Bawdsey
Stoke-by-Nayland
East Bergholt
Shotley
Holbrook
Bures
Nayland
Felixstowe
Colne Engaine
Dedham
Manningtree
Harwich
Ardleigh
Earls Colne
Aldham
COLCHESTER
Wix
Marks Tey
Elmstead Market
Thorpe-le-Soken
Walton on the Naze
Coggeshall
Copford Green
Wivenhoe
Silver End
Kelvedon
Frinton-on-Sea
Caravan and Camping
AA Campsite Award Winner
Town/Village name
0
10 miles
0
10
20 kilometres

For continuation pages refer to numbered arrows

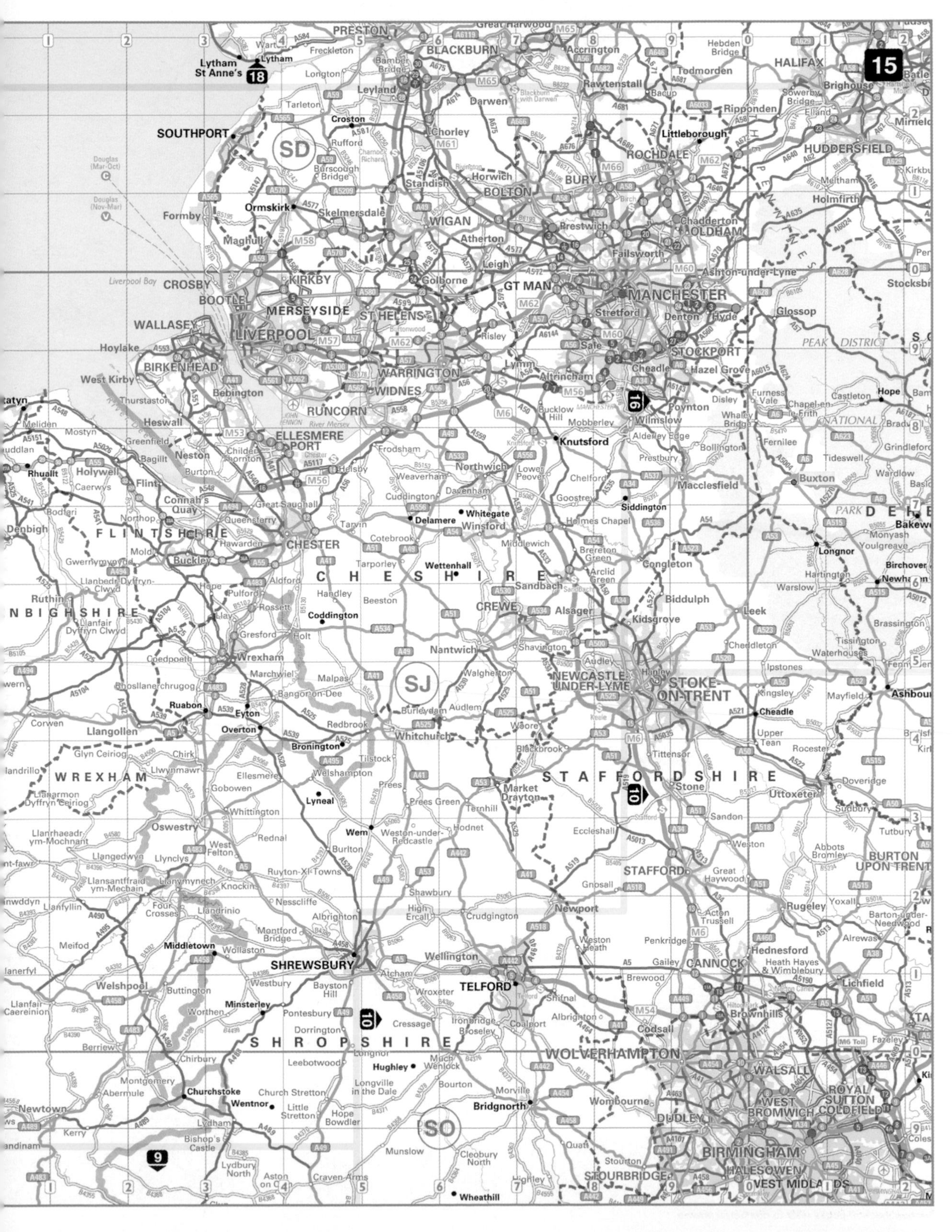

15
PRESTON
BLACKBURN
Accrington
Hebden Bridge
HALIFAX
Lytham St Anne's
Lytham
18
Freckleton
Longton
Leyland
Bamber Bridge
Darwen
Rawtenstall
Todmorden
Brighouse
Tarleton
Croston
Chorley
Littleborough
Ripponden
Sowerby Bridge
Elland
SOUTHPORT
SD
Rufford
ROCHDALE
HUDDERSFIELD
Douglas (Mar-Oct)
Douglas (Nov-Mar)
Burscough Bridge
Standish
Horwich
BURY
BOLTON
Meltham
Holmfirth
Formby
Ormskirk
Skelmersdale
WIGAN
Prestwich
Chadderton
OLDHAM
Maghull
Atherton
Failsworth
Leigh
Liverpool Bay
CROSBY
KIRKBY
Golborne
GT MAN
MANCHESTER
Ashton-under-Lyne
Stocksbridge
BOOTLE
MERSEYSIDE
ST HELENS
Stretford
Denton
Hyde
Glossop
WALLASEY
LIVERPOOL
Risley
Sale
STOCKPORT
PEAK DISTRICT
Hoylake
BIRKENHEAD
WARRINGTON
Lymm
Cheadle
Hazel Grove
West Kirby
WIDNES
Altrincham
16
Poynton
Disley
Furness Vale
Chapel-en-le-Frith
Castleton
Hope
Bebington
Thurstaston
RUNCORN
Bucklow Hill
Mobberley
Wilmslow
Whaley Bridge
NATIONAL
Bradwell
Heswall
Meliden
Mostyn
Greenfield
ELLESMERE PORT
Knutsford
Alderley Edge
Fernilee
Grindleford
Neston
Childer Thornton
Frodsham
Bollington
Prestbury
Tideswell
Rhuallt
Holywell
Bagillt
Burton
Helsby
Northwich
Lower Peover
Chelford
Buxton
Wardlow
Flint
Caerwys
Weaverham
Davenham
Macclesfield
Connah's Quay
Great Saughall
Cuddington
Goostrey
Siddington
Bodfari
Northop
Queensferry
Whitegate
Delamere
Winsford
Holmes Chapel
PARK
Bakewell
Denbigh
FLINTSHIRE
Hawarden
CHESTER
Tarvin
Cotebrook
Middlewich
Monyash
Youlgreave
Longnor
Mold
Buckley
Gwernymynydd
Tarporley
Wettenhall
Brereton Green
Congleton
Birchover
Newhaven
CHESHIRE
Arclid Green
Sandbach
Hartington
Llanbedr Dyffryn-Clwyd
Ruthin
Hope
Pulford
Alford
Handley
Beeston
Warslow
Biddulph
DENBIGHSHIRE
Rossett
Coddington
CREWE
Alsager
Leek
Llanfair Dyffryn Clwyd
Llay
Kidsgrove
Brassington
Gresford
Holt
Nantwich
Shavington
Cheddleton
Tissington
Coedpoeth
Wrexham
Audley
Waterhouses
Marchwiel
Malpas
Walgherton
NEWCASTLE-UNDER-LYME
Hanley
STOKE-ON-TRENT
Ipstones
Fenny Bentley
Rhosllanerchrugog
SJ
Kingsley
Mayfield
Ashbourne
Bangor-on-Dee
Audlem
Ruabon
Eyton
Burleydam
Cheadle
Corwen
Llangollen
Overton
Redbrook
Woore
Upper Tean
Whitchurch
Bronington
Keele
Rocester
Glyn Ceiriog
Chirk
Tilstock
Blackbrook
Tittensor
Llandrillo
WREXHAM
Llwynmawr
Ellesmere
Welshampton
STAFFORDSHIRE
Stone
Doveridge
Llanarmon Dyffryn Ceiriog
Gobowen
Prees
Market Drayton
10
Uttoxeter
Whittington
Lyneal
Prees Green
Tern Hill
Sudbury
Llanrhaeadr-ym-Mochnant
Oswestry
Rednal
Wem
Weston-under-Redcastle
Hodnet
Eccleshall
Sandon
Tutbury
West Felton
Llangedwyn
Llynclys
Burlton
Weston
Abbots Bromley
BURTON UPON TRENT
Ruyton-XI-Towns
STAFFORD
Great Haywood
Llansantffraid-ym-Mechain
Llanymynech
Knockin
Gnosall
Llanfyllin
Nesscliffe
Shawbury
Rugeley
Yoxall
Four Crosses
Llandrinio
High Ercall
Albrighton
Crudgington
Newport
Acton Trussell
Barton-under-Needwood
Meifod
Montford Bridge
Weston Heath
Penkridge
Alrewas
Middletown
Wollaston
Wellington
Hednesford
SHREWSBURY
Gailey
CANNOCK
Heath Hayes & Wimblebury
Llanerfyl
Atcham
TELFORD
Brewood
Lichfield
Welshpool
Westbury
Bayston Hill
Wroxeter
Shifnal
Buttington
Llanfair Caereinion
Minsterley
Pontesbury
Albrighton
Brownhills
Worthen
Cressage
Ironbridge
Broseley
Coalport
Codsall
Dorrington
Berriew
SHROPSHIRE
WOLVERHAMPTON
Fazeley
Longnor
Chirbury
Leebotwood
Much Wenlock
WALSALL
Hughley
Montgomery
Bourton
ROYAL SUTTON COLDFIELD
Abermule
Churchstoke
Church Stretton
Longville in the Dale
Morville
Wombourne
WEST BROMWICH
Newtown
Wentnor
Little Stretton
Hope Bowdler
Bridgnorth
DUDLEY
Kerry
Lydham
SO
Bishop's Castle
Quatt
BIRMINGHAM
9
Munslow
Cleobury North
Lydbury North
Stourton
HALESOWEN
Aston on Clun
Craven Arms
Highley
STOURBRIDGE
WEST MIDLANDS
Wheathill
M6 Toll

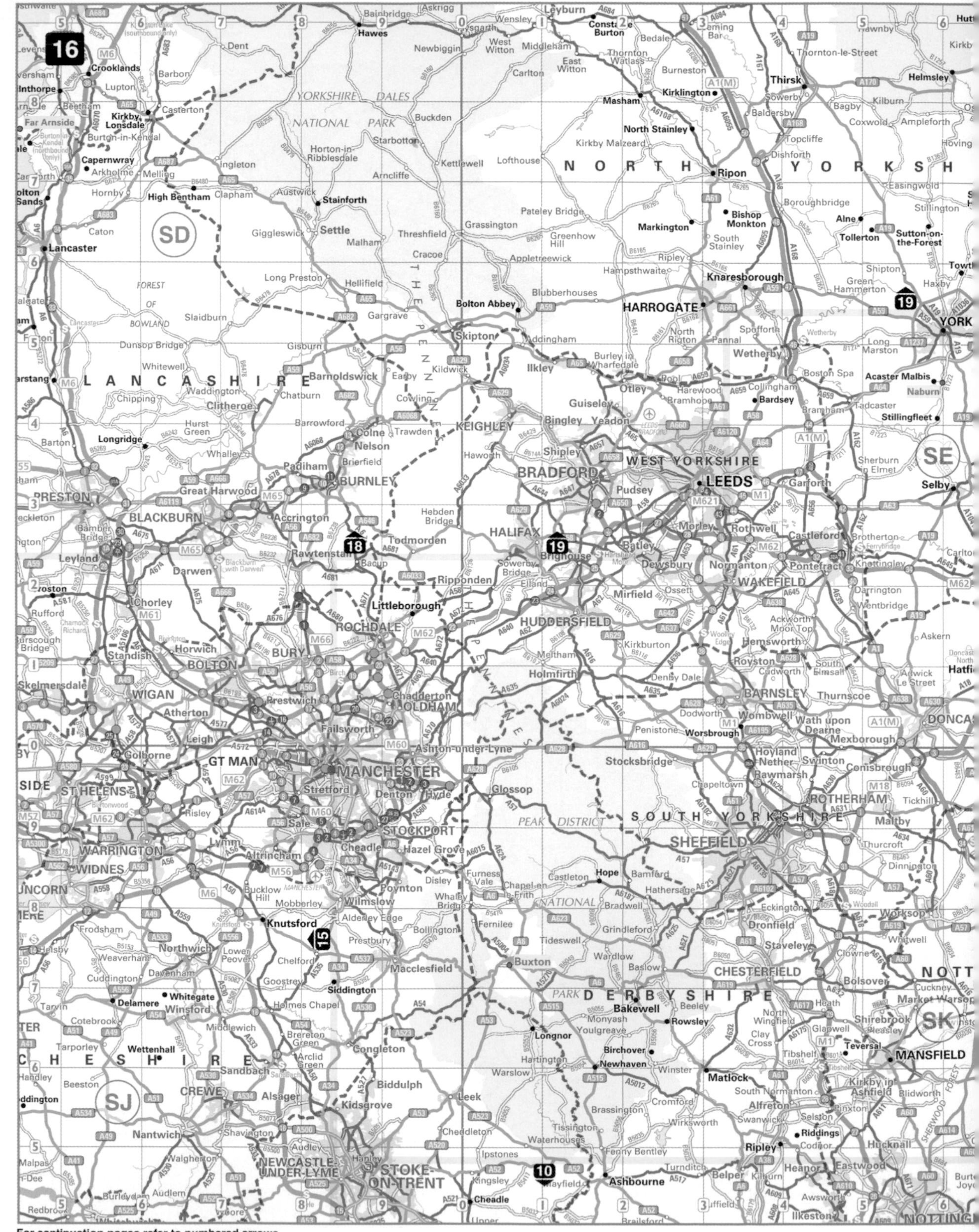

For continuation pages refer to numbered arrows

17
Caravan and Camping
AA Campsite Award Winner
Town/Village name
0
10 miles
0
10
20 kilometres
TA
TF
Lastingham
Cropton
Lockton
Hackness
Scarborough
Wrelton
Thornton-le-Dale
East Ayton
Pickering
Wykeham
Allerston
Snainton
Seamer
Cayton
Brompton-by-Sawdon
Flixton
Filey
Kirby Misperton
Staxton
Sherburn
Hunmanby
Reighton
West Knapton
Rillington
Bempton
Malton
Norton-on-Derwent
Burton Fleming
Flamborough Head
Flamborough
North Grimston
Rudston
Sledmere
Langtoft
Carnaby
Bridlington
Kilham
Burton Agnes
Fridaythorpe
Wetwang
Driffield
Barmston
Skipsea
Stamford Bridge
North Dalton
Bainton
North Frodingham
Beeford
Wilberfoss
Atwick
EAST RIDING
OF YORKSHIRE
Pocklington
Middleton on the Wolds
Brandesburton
Barmby Moor
Hornsea
Leven
Shiptonthorpe
Market Weighton
Holme upon Spalding Moor
Beverley
Walkington
Aldbrough
North Cave
Sproatley
South Cave
Tunstall
Cottingham
Ellougton
Hessle
KINGSTON UPON HULL
Hedon
Withernsea
Goole
Melton
North Ferriby
New Holland
Winteringham
Patrington
Barton upon Humber
Goxhill
Burton upon Stather
Winterton
Easington
Immingham Dock
River Humber
Wootton
Ulceby
Immingham
Crowle
Gunness
SCUNTHORPE
Keelby
GRIMSBY
Spurn Head
Broughton
Wrawby
Cleethorpes
Althorpe
Barnetby le Wold
Belton
Brigg
Laceby
Humberston
Scawby
Waltham
Epworth
Messingham
Hibaldstow
Caistor
Holton le Clay
Swallow
Tetney
Scotter
North Cotes
Haxey
Kirton in Lindsey
Grainthorpe
North Somercotes
Ludborough
Misterton
Waddingham
Saltfleet
Blyton
Binbrook
Gringley on the Hill
Gainsborough
Middle Rasen
Glentham
Saundby
Market Rasen
Louth
Great Carlton
Mablethorpe
Ingham
Faldingworth
Lissington
Legbourne
Sutton on Sea
Retford
Sturton by Stow
East Barkwith
Withern
Church Laneham
Torksey
Wragby
Scamblesby
Alford
Gamston
Newton on Trent
Saxilby
Huttoft
Bilsby
Langworth
Tetford
Markham Moor
Baumber
Chapel St Leonards
NOTTINGHAMSHIRE
Skellingthorpe
LINCOLN
LINCOLNSHIRE
Hogsthorpe
Tuxford
Edlington
Washingborough
Bardney
Horncastle
Ingoldmells
Hagworthingham
Branston
Sutton on Trent
Candlesby
Spilsby
Carlton-on-Trent
North Hykeham
Nocton
Woodhall Spa
Burgh le Marsh
Skegness
Waddington
Mareham le Fen
Caunton
Cromwell
Stickford
North Muskham
Navenby
Martin
New Bolingbroke
Tattershall
Wainfleet All Saints
Kelham
Coningsby
Stickney
Digby
Billinghay
Beckingham
Welbourn
Newark-on-Trent
Leadenham
North Kyme
Sibsey
Ruskington
Old Leake
Anwick
South Kyme
Wrangle
East Stoke
Caythorpe
Sleaford
Long Bennington
Marston
Ancaster
Butterwick
Boston
THE WASH
Thornham
Brancaster
Burnham Overy Staithe
Foston
Silk Willoughby
Heckington
Helpringham
Swineshead
Hunstanton
Burnham Market
Holkham
Barkston
19
11
12

For continuation pages refer to numbered arrows

19
Caravan and Camping
AA Campsite Award Winner
Town/Village name
0
10 miles
0
10
20 kilometres
NZ
SE
TA
21
16
17
NEWCASTLE UPON TYNE
SOUTH SHIELDS
GATESHEAD
TYNE AND WEAR
SUNDERLAND
WASHINGTON
Jarrow
Blaydon
Whickham
Prudhoe
Horsley
Rowland's Gill
Birtley
Burnopfield
Ebchester
Stanley
Beamish
Leadgate
Annfield Plain
Consett
Chester-le-Street
Houghton-le-Spring
Seaham
Lanchester
Castleside
Easington
Durham
Brandon
Peterlee
Thornley
Blackhall Colliery
Tow Law
Wingate
Crook
Trimdon
Spennymoor
HARTLEPOOL
Ferryhill
Witton le Wear
Bishop Auckland
Toft Hill
Sedgefield
Rushyford
Shildon
West Auckland
Copley
Newton Aycliffe
Wolviston
Billingham
Redcar
Marske-by-the-Sea
Saltburn-by-the-Sea
Brotton
STOCKTON-ON-TEES
MIDDLESBROUGH
Staindrop
Gainford
Skelton
Staithes
Eston
Loftus
Hinderwell
Barnard Castle
Piercebridge
DARLINGTON
Guisborough
Lythe
Greta Bridge
Hurworth-on-Tees
Yarm
Sandsend
Whitby
Newsham
Great Ayton
Stokesley
Kildale
Castleton
Ruswarp
Barton
Crathorne
Egton Bridge
Sleights
Gilling West
Scotch Corner
Great Smeaton
West Runton
Robin Hood's Bay
Richmond
Seave Green
NORTH YORK MOORS NATIONAL PARK
Goathland
Ravenscar
Hipswell
Catterick
Chop Gate
Osmotherley
Rosedale Abbey
Scotton
Ainderby Steeple
Northallerton
Cloughton
Leyburn
Wensley
Constable Burton
Leeming Bar
Hutton-le-Hole
Lastingham
Hackness
Scalby
West Witton
Middleham
Bedale
Hawnby
Cropton
Lockton
Scarborough
Thornton Watlass
Kirkbymoorside
Wrelton
East Ayton
East Witton
Thornton-le-Street
Thornton-le-Dale
Wykeham
Carlton
Burneston
Thirsk
Helmsley
Pickering
Seamer
Cayton
Allerston
Snainton
Brompton-by-Sawdon
Masham
Kirklington
Sowerby
Kilburn
Bagby
Oswaldkirk
Kirby Misperton
Flixton
Filey
Staxton
Baldersby
Coxwold
Ampleforth
Sherburn
North Stainley
Topcliffe
Hunmanby
Slingsby
West Knapton
Reighton
Kirkby Malzeard
Hovingham
Rillington
Dishforth
Lofthouse
NORTH YORKSHIRE
Ripon
Malton
Norton-on-Derwent
Burton Fleming
Easingwold
North Grimston
Sheriff Hutton
Rudston
Boroughbridge
Stillington
Carnaby
Pateley Bridge
Bishop Monkton
Alne
Sledmere
Langtoft
Markington
Tollerton
Sutton-on-the-Forest
Kilham
Greenhow Hill
South Stainley
Strensall
Burton Agnes
Appletreewick
Ripley
Hampsthwaite
Shipton
Towthorpe
Fridaythorpe
Driffield
Barmston
Knaresborough
Green Hammerton
Haxby
Wetwang
Blubberhouses
HARROGATE
Stamford Bridge
Skipsea
YORK
North Dalton
Bainton
North Frodingham
Beeford
Addingham
Spofforth
North Rigton
Pannal
Long Marston
Wilberfoss
EAST RIDING OF YORKSHIRE
Wetherby
Pocklington
Middleton on the Wolds
Brandesburton
Ilkley
Burley in Wharfedale
Boston Spa
Elvington
Barmby Moor
Otley
Pool
Harewood
Collingham
Acaster Malbis
Naburn
Leven
Guiseley
Bramhope
Bardsey
Tadcaster
Bramham
Shiptonthorpe
Market Weighton
Bingley
Yeadon
Stillingfleet
Holme upon Spalding Moor
Beverley
Shipley
Walkington
WEST YORKSHIRE
Sherburn in Elmet
BRADFORD
LEEDS
Garforth
Bubwith
North Cave
Pudsey
Selby
Cliffe
South Cave
Cottingham
HALIFAX
Morley
Rothwell
Howden
Ellougton
Hessle
KINGSTON UPON HULL
Batley
Castleford
Brotherton
Brighouse
Dewsbury
Normanton
Carlton
Goole
Melton
North Ferriby
Sowerby Bridge
Pontefract
Knottingley
Winteringham
New Holland
Elland
WAKEFIELD
Barton-upon-Humber
Goxhill
Mirfield
Ossett
Darrington
Burton upon Stather
Winterton
Immingham Dock
Wootton

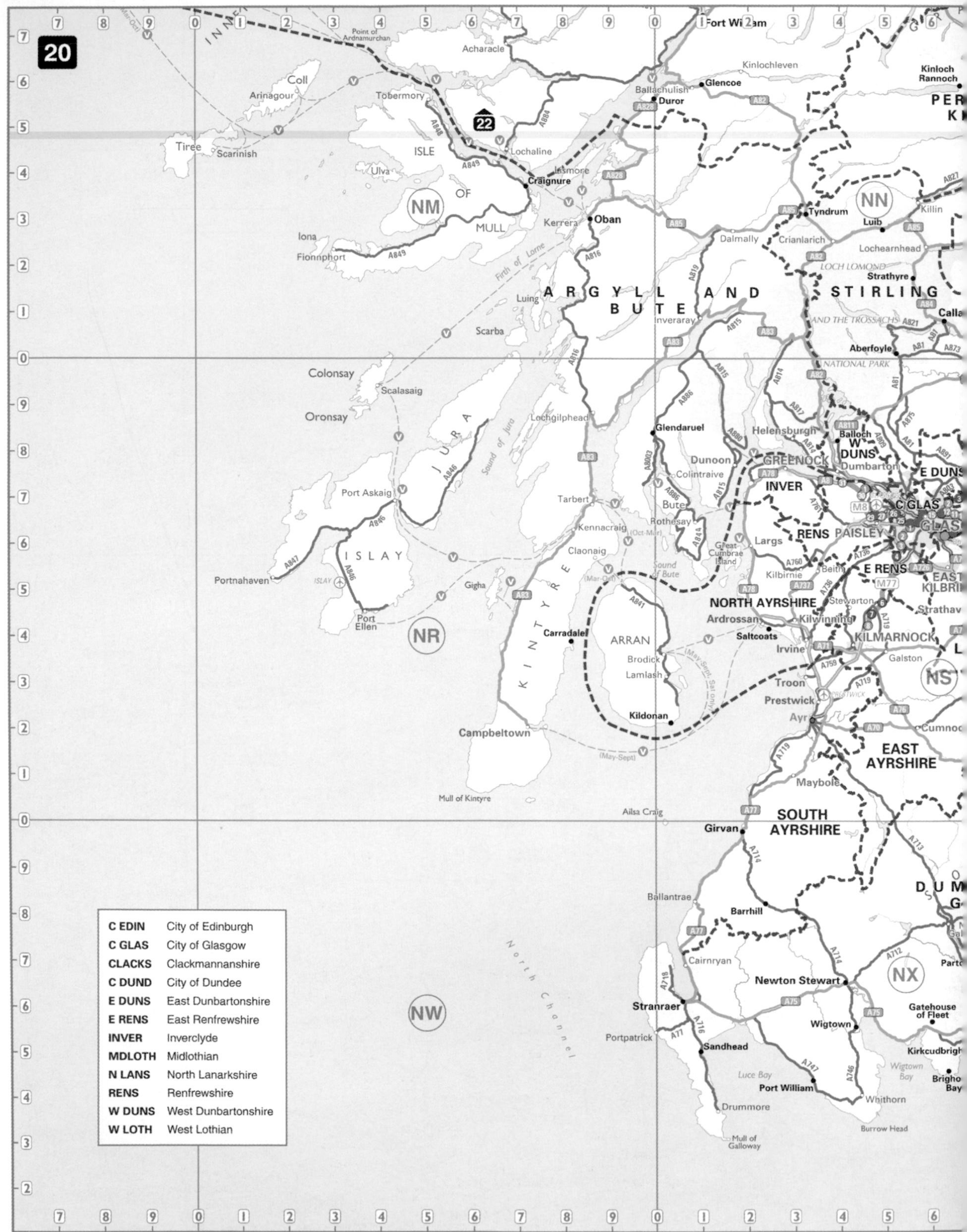

For continuation pages refer to numbered arrows

21
Caravan and Camping
AA Campsite Award Winner
Town/Village name
0
10
20 miles
0
10
20
30 kilometres
ANGUS
Blair Atholl
Pitlochry
Kirriemuir
North Water Bridge
Brechin
Montrose
Inverbervie
Forfar
Blairgowrie
Dunkeld
Coupar Angus
SIDLAW HILLS
NO
Arbroath
Carnoustie
C DUND
Monifieth
DUNDEE
Newport-on-Tay
St Andrews Bay
Perth
Crieff
Newburgh
St Andrews
Auchterarder
Auchtermuchty
Cupar
FIFE
Fife Ness
Crail
Falkland
Kinross
Glenrothes
Anstruther
Leven
CLACKS
Alloa
Kincardine
Kirkcaldy
DUNFERMLINE
NORTH SEA
North Berwick
Aberlady
East Linton
Dunbar
FIRTH OF FORTH
Longniddry
Falkirk
FALKIRK
Linlithgow
EDINBURGH
C EDIN
W LOTH
Musselburgh
Haddington
East Calder
LIVINGSTON
EAST LOTHIAN
Dalkeith
St Abb's Head
Eyemouth
LAMMERMUIR HILLS
PENTLAND HILLS
Penicuik
MDLOTH
Berwick-upon-Tweed
NT
Duns
NU
Lauder
Greenlaw
Holy Island
Peebles
Coldstream
Lanark
Biggar
Bamburgh
Seahouses
Belford
Innerleithen
Galashiels
Melrose
Kelso
Wooler
Abington
Selkirk
SCOTTISH BORDERS
Jedburgh
Hawick
CHEVIOT HILLS
Alnwick
UPLANDS
NORTHUMBERLAND NATIONAL PARK
Amble
Moffat
Thornhill
NORTHUMBERLAND
Ashington
North Seaton
Morpeth
Langholm
Bedlington
Blyth
Lochmaben
Lockerbie
NZ
Penton
Dumfries
NY
Ecclefechan
Longtown
Tynemouth
SOUTH SHIELDS
NEWCASTLE UPON TYNE
Haltwhistle
Corbridge
Hexham
Annan
Gretna
Brampton
GATESHEAD
TYNE AND WEAR
SUNDERLAND
Dalbeattie
18
CARLISLE
19
WASHINGTON
Sandyhills
Silloth
Cumwhitton
Consett
Beamish
Seaham
Wigton
Chester-le-Street
Solway Firth
Alston
Mealsgate
Durham
Peterlee
Blackhall Colliery
Maryport
CUMBRIA
Crook
HARTLEPOOL
Cockermouth
DURHAM
Penrith
Bishop Auckland
Workington
Troutbeck
Penruddock
Pooley Bridge
Redcar
Newton Aycliffe
STOCKTON-ON-TEES
Keswick
Watermillock
Appleby-in-Westmorland
Barnard Castle
MIDDLESBROUGH
Whitehaven
LAKE DISTRICT
DARLINGTON
St Bees Head
Egremont
Brough

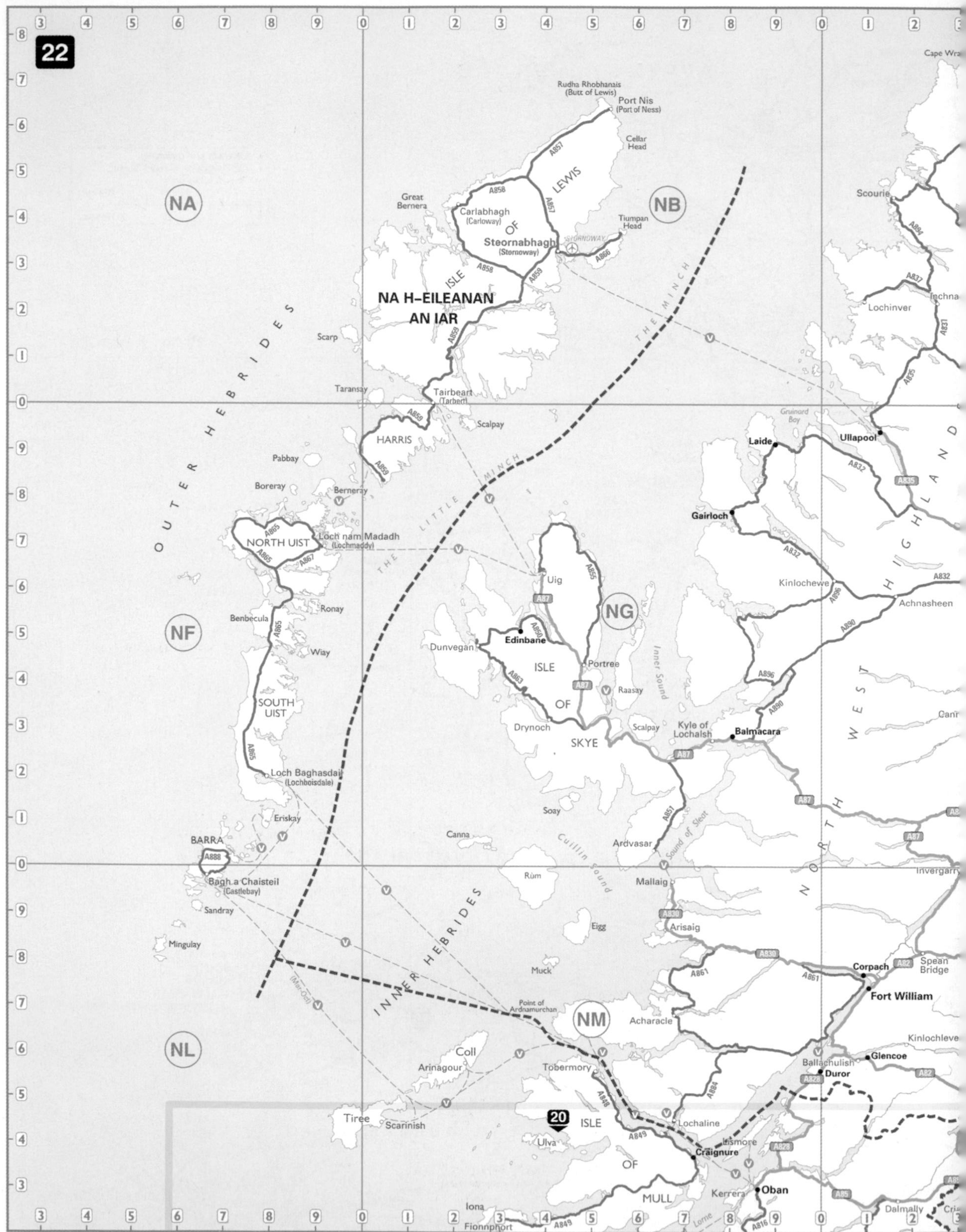

For continuation pages refer to numbered arrows

Caravan and Camping
AA Campsite Award Winner
Town/Village name
0 10 20 miles
0 10 20 30 kilometres
PENTLAND FIRTH
Stromness
Dunnet Head
St Margaret's Hope
Duncansby Head
John o' Groats
Gills
Scrabster
Strathy Point
Thurso
Melvich
Bettyhill
Tongue
Wick
Lybster
Dunbeath
Altnaharra
Helmsdale
Lairg
Golspie
Brora
Bonar Bridge
Dornoch
Tain
HIGHLAND
Alness
Invergordon
Cromarty
MORAY FIRTH
Dingwall
Fortrose
Nairn
Muir of Ord
INVERNESS
Lossiemouth
Buckie
Cullen
Portsoy
Banff
Macduff
Fraserburgh
Elgin
Forres
Fochabers
MORAY
Rothes
Keith
Aberchirder
Turriff
Mintlaw
Peterhead
Aberlour
Huntly
Dufftown
Ellon
Oldmeldrum
Grantown-on-Spey
Carrbridge
Tomintoul
Inverurie
Kintore
Alford
Dyce
CITY OF ABERDEEN
ABERDEEN
Aviemore
Monadhliath Mountains
CAIRNGORMS
CAIRNGORM MOUNTAINS
NATIONAL PARK
ABERDEENSHIRE
Peterculter
Kingussie
Newtonmore
Ballater
Aboyne
Banchory
Braemar
Strachan
Stonehaven
GRAMPIAN MOUNTAINS
Laurencekirk
Inverbervie
North Water Bridge
ANGUS
Blair Atholl
Kinloch Rannoch
Pitlochry
Brechin
Montrose
PERTH AND KINROSS
Kirriemuir
Aberfeldy
Forfar
Blairgowrie
Dunkeld
Coupar Angus
SIDLAW HILLS
Arbroath
Carnoustie
Monifieth
C DUND
DUNDEE
Newport-on-Tay
Killin
Luib
Lochearnhead
Perth
Crieff
St Andrews Bay
NC
ND
NH
NJ
NK
NN
NO
21

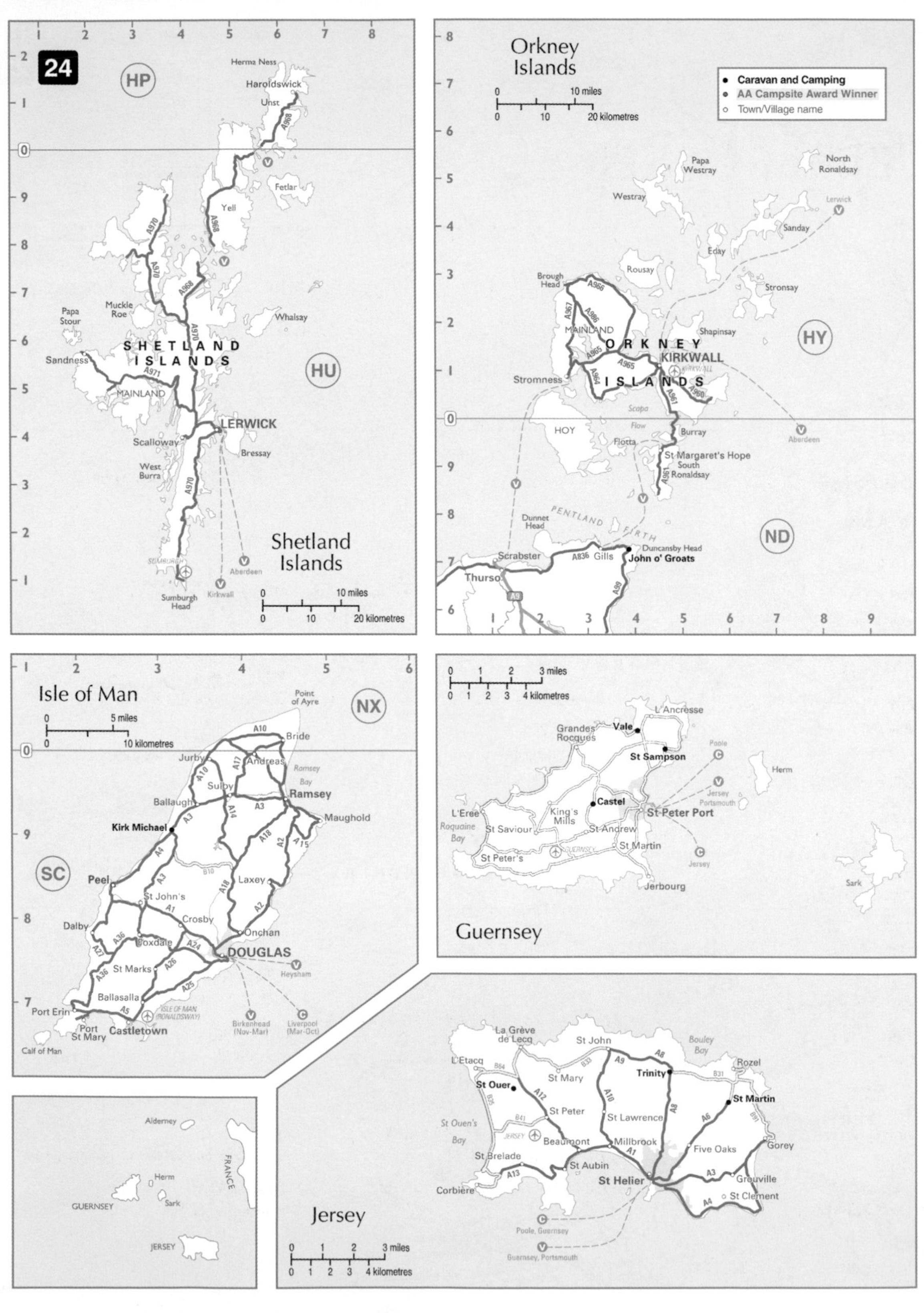
24
Shetland Islands
Orkney Islands
Isle of Man
Guernsey
Jersey
Caravan and Camping
AA Campsite Award Winner
Town/Village name
SHETLAND ISLANDS
LERWICK
ORKNEY ISLANDS
KIRKWALL
DOUGLAS
Herma Ness
Haroldswick
Unst
Fetlar
Yell
Whalsay
Papa Stour
Muckle Roe
Sandness
MAINLAND
Scalloway
Bressay
West Burra
Sumburgh Head
Aberdeen
Kirkwall
Papa Westray
North Ronaldsay
Westray
Sanday
Eday
Rousay
Stronsay
Brough Head
Shapinsay
Stromness
HOY
Flotta
Burray
St Margaret's Hope
South Ronaldsay
Dunnet Head
PENTLAND FIRTH
Scrabster
Thurso
Gills
Duncansby Head
John o' Groats
Point of Ayre
Bride
Jurby
Andreas
Sulby
Ramsey
Ballaugh
Maughold
Kirk Michael
Peel
St John's
Laxey
Crosby
Onchan
Dalby
Foxdale
St Marks
Ballasalla
Port Erin
Port St Mary
Castletown
Calf of Man
Heysham
Birkenhead (Nov-Mar)
Liverpool (Mar-Oct)
L'Ancresse
Grandes Rocques
Vale
St Sampson
Castel
King's Mills
St Peter Port
L'Eree
St Saviour
St Andrew
St Martin
St Peter's
Jerbourg
Herm
Sark
Poole
Jersey Portsmouth
La Grève de Lecq
St John
Bouley Bay
L'Etacq
St Mary
Trinity
Rozel
St Ouen
St Peter
St Martin
St Lawrence
St Ouen's Bay
Beaumont
Millbrook
Five Oaks
Gorey
St Brelade
St Aubin
St Helier
Grouville
St Clement
Corbière
Poole, Guernsey
Guernsey, Portsmouth
Alderney
FRANCE
GUERNSEY
JERSEY

Glamping sites

These campsites offer one or more types of glamping accommodation, i.e. wooden pods, tipis, yurts, bell tents, safari tents, shepherd's huts, Airstream caravans and vintage caravans.

ENGLAND

BERKSHIRE

FINCHAMPSTEAD
California Chalet & Touring Park

CORNWALL & ISLES OF SCILLY

BLISLAND
South Penquite Farm

CARLYON BAY
East Crinnis Camping & Caravan Park

CRANTOCK (NEAR NEWQUAY)
Trevella Holiday Park

GOONHAVERN
Silverbow Park

HAYLE
St Ives Bay Holiday Park

HELSTON
Poldown Caravan Park

HOLYWELL BAY
Trevornick Holiday Park

KILKHAMPTON
Upper Tamar Lake

LANDRAKE
Dolbeare Park Caravan and Camping

LISKEARD
Luxury Cornish Yurts

LOOE
Looe Country Park
Tregoad Park

NEWQUAY
Hendra Holiday Park
Porth Beach Holiday Park

PERRANPORTH
Tollgate Farm Caravan & Camping Park

PORTREATH
Tehidy Holiday Park

RUTHERNBRIDGE
Ruthern Valley Holidays

ST AUSTELL
Meadow Lakes

ST MARY'S (ISLES OF SCILLY)
Garrison Campsite

ST MINVER
Gunvenna Holiday Park

WADEBRIDGE
Lowarth Glamping
St Mabyn Holiday Park

WIDEMOUTH BAY
Widemouth Bay Caravan Park

CUMBRIA

AMBLESIDE
Low Wray National Trust Campsite

APPLEBY-IN-WESTMORLAND
Wild Rose Park

BOOT
Eskdale Camping & Caravanning Club Site

GREAT LANGDALE
Great Langdale National Trust Campsite

KESWICK
Castlerigg Hall Caravan & Camping Park

KIRKBY LONSDALE
Woodclose Caravan Park

MILNTHORPE
Hall More Caravan Park

NETHER WASDALE
Church Stile Farm & Holiday Park

PATTERDALE
Sykeside Camping Park

PENRITH
Lowther Holiday Park

PENTON
Twin Willows

POOLEY BRIDGE
Waterfoot Caravan Park

SANTON BRIDGE
The Old Post Office Campsite

SILLOTH
Stanwix Park Holiday Centre

WASDALE HEAD
Wasdale Head National Trust Campsite

WATERMILLOCK
The Quiet Site
Ullswater Holiday Park

WINDERMERE
Park Cliffe Camping & Caravan Estate

DERBYSHIRE

ROSLISTON
Beehive Woodland Lakes

DEVON

CLYST ST MARY
Crealy Meadows Caravan and Camping Park

COMBE MARTIN
Newberry Valley Park

Glamping sites *continued*

CROYDE
Bay View Farm Caravan & Camping Park

DAWLISH
Lady's Mile Holiday Park

ILFRACOMBE
Hele Valley Holiday Park

KENN
Glebe Farm Shepherd's Huts

KENTISBEARE
Forest Glade Holiday Park

OTTERY ST MARY
Cuckoo Down Farm Glamping

PAIGNTON
Whitehill Country Park

SIDMOUTH
Kings Down Tail Caravan & Camping Park
Oakdown Country Holiday Park

TAVISTOCK
Harford Bridge Holiday Park
Langstone Manor Camping & Caravan Park
Woodovis Park

WOOLACOMBE
Europa Park

DORSET

ALDERHOLT
Hill Cottage Farm Camping and Caravan Park

BERE REGIS
Rowlands Wait Touring Park

BRIDPORT
Graston Copse Holiday Park
Highlands End Holiday Park

CHARMOUTH
Newlands Caravan & Camping Park

CHIDEOCK
Golden Cap Holiday Park

FERNDOWN
St Leonards Farm Caravan & Camping Park

POOLE
South Lytchett Manor Caravan & Camping Park

SHAFTESBURY
Blackmore Vale Caravan & Camping Park
Dorset Country Holidays

SWANAGE
Herston Caravan & Camping Park
Ulwell Cottage Caravan Park

THREE LEGGED CROSS
Woolsbridge Manor Farm Caravan Park

WAREHAM
Lookout Holiday Park

WEYMOUTH
Seaview Holiday Park

DURHAM, COUNTY

BEAMISH
Bobby Shafto Caravan Park

HAMPSHIRE

BRANSGORE
Harrow Wood Farm Caravan Park

FORDINGBRIDGE
Sandy Balls Holiday Village

HEREFORDSHIRE

PEMBRIDGE
Townsend Touring Park

HERTFORDSHIRE

HODDESDON
Lee Valley Caravan Park Dobbs Weir

ISLE OF WIGHT

BRIGHSTONE
Grange Farm

COWES
Thorness Bay Holiday Park

NEWPORT
Wight Glamping Holidays

RYDE
Roebeck Country Park

ST HELENS
Nodes Point Holiday Park

SANDOWN
Old Barn Touring Park

WHITECLIFF BAY
Whitecliff Bay Holiday Park

KENT

MARDEN
Tanner Farm Touring Caravan & Camping Park

WHITSTABLE
Homing Park

LANCASHIRE

BOLTON-LE-SANDS
Bay View Holiday Park

CROSTON
Royal Umpire Caravan Park

FAR ARNSIDE
Hollins Farm Camping & Caravanning

SILVERDALE
Silverdale Caravan Park

THORNTON
Kneps Farm Holiday Park

LINCOLNSHIRE

TATTERSHALL
Tattershall Lakes Country Park

WOODHALL SPA
Woodhall Country Park

LONDON

E4 CHINGFORD
Lee Valley Campsite

NORFOLK

BELTON
Swallow Park Leisure
Wild Duck Holiday Park

GREAT YARMOUTH
Vauxhall Holiday Park

KING'S LYNN
King's Lynn Caravan and Camping Park

NORTHUMBERLAND

BAMBURGH
Waren Caravan & Camping Park

BELLINGHAM
Bellingham Camping & Caravanning Club Site

BERWICK-UPON-TWEED
Ord House Country Park

HALTWHISTLE
Herding Hill Farm

WOOLER
Riverside Leisure Park

NOTTINGHAMSHIRE

TEVERSAL
Teversal Camping & Caravanning Club Site

OXFORDSHIRE

CHARLBURY
Cotswold View Touring Park

FRINGFORD
Glebe Leisure

SHROPSHIRE

WEM
Lower Lacon Caravan Park

SOMERSET

BREAN
Holiday Resort Unity

BURNHAM-ON-SEA
Burnham-on-Sea Holiday Village

DULVERTON
Wimbleball Lake

GLASTONBURY
Middlewick Farm
The Old Oaks Touring Park

STAFFORDSHIRE

LONGNOR
Longnor Wood Holiday Park

SUFFOLK

HOLLESLEY
Run Cottage Touring Park

SUSSEX, WEST

BARNS GREEN
Sumners Ponds Fishery & Campsite

WILTSHIRE

BERWICK ST JAMES
Stonehenge Campsite & Glamping Pods

YORKSHIRE, EAST RIDING OF

BRANDESBURTON
Dacre Lakeside Park

SPROATLEY
Burton Constable Holiday Park & Arboretum

TUNSTALL
Sand le Mere Holiday Village

YORKSHIRE, NORTH

ALNE
Alders Caravan Park

CHOP GATE
Lordstones Country Park

FILEY
Flower of May Holiday Park

KIRKLINGTON
Camp Kátur

MASHAM
Old Station Holiday Park

NORTHALLERTON
Otterington Park

RICHMOND
Brompton Caravan Park

ROBIN HOOD'S BAY
Grouse Hill Caravan Park
Middlewood Farm Holiday Park

ROSEDALE ABBEY
Rosedale Caravan & Camping Park

WYKEHAM
St Helens Caravan Park

CHANNEL ISLANDS

GUERNSEY

VALE
La Bailloterie Camping

JERSEY

ST MARTIN
Beuvelande Camp Site

ST OUEN
Daisy Cottage Campsite

TRINITY
Durrell Wildlife Camp

SCOTLAND

ANGUS

MONIFIETH
Riverview Caravan Park

ARGYLL & BUTE

GLENDARUEL
Glendaruel Caravan Park

OBAN
Oban Caravan & Camping Park

Glamping sites *continued*

DUMFRIES & GALLOWAY

BRIGHOUSE BAY
Brighouse Bay Holiday Park

ECCLEFECHAN
Hoddom Castle Caravan Park

KIRKCUDBRIGHT
Seaward Caravan Park

PALNACKIE
Barlochan Caravan Park

PARTON
Loch Ken Holiday Park

SANDYHILLS
Sandyhills Bay Leisure Park

DUNBARTONSHIRE, WEST

BALLOCH
Lomond Woods Holiday Park

HIGHLAND

AVIEMORE
Aviemore Glamping

DUROR
Achindarroch Touring Park

GLENCOE
Invercoe Caravan & Camping Park

LOTHIAN, EAST

ABERLADY
Aberlady Caravan Park

DUNBAR
Belhaven Bay Caravan & Camping Park

MUSSELBURGH
Drum Mohr Caravan Park

LOTHIAN, WEST

EAST CALDER
Linwater Caravan Park

SCOTTISH BORDERS

PEEBLES
Crossburn Caravan Park

STIRLING

TYNDRUM
Strathfillan Wigwam Village

SCOTTISH ISLANDS

ISLE OF ARRAN

KILDONAN
Sealshore Camping and Touring Site

ISLE OF MULL

CRAIGNURE
Shieling Holidays

ISLE OF SKYE

EDINBANE
Skye Camping & Caravanning Club Site

WALES

CONWY

LLANRWST
Bron Derw Touring Caravan Park

GWYNEDD

BALA
Pen-y-Bont Touring Park

BARMOUTH
Trawsdir Touring Caravans & Camping Park

CAERNARFON
Plas Gwyn Caravan & Camping Park
Ty'n yr Onnen Caravan Park

CRICCIETH
Eisteddfa

DINAS DINLLE
Dinlle Caravan Park

PORTHMADOG
Greenacres Holiday Park

MONMOUTHSHIRE

LLANVAIR DISCOED
Penhein Glamping

PEMBROKESHIRE

FISHGUARD
Fishguard Bay Resort

TENBY
Kiln Park Holiday Centre

POWYS

BUILTH WELLS
Fforest Fields Caravan & Camping Park

CHURCHSTOKE
Daisy Bank Caravan Park

LLANDRINDOD WELLS
Disserth Caravan & Camping Park

SWANSEA

OLDWALLS
Oldwalls Gower Glamping

WREXHAM

BRONINGTON
The Little Yurt Meadow

NORTHERN IRELAND

COUNTY ANTRIM

BALLYMONEY
Drumaheglis Marina & Caravan Park

Index

Entries are listed alphabetically by town name, then campsite name. The following abbreviations have been used: C&C – Caravan & Camping; HP – Holiday Park; CP – Caravan Park; C&C Club – Camping & Caravanning Club Site

C

U

V

W

Y

Acknowledgments

AA Media would like to thank the following photographers, companies and picture libraries for their assistance in the preparation of this book.

Abbreviations for the picture credits are as follows – (t) top; (b) bottom; (c) centre; (l) left; (r) right; (b/g) background; (AA) AA World Travel Library.

Cover

Background Derek Croucher/Alamy.

Interior

3 AA/J Tims; 4 AA/J Tims; 6 courtesy of Grouse Hill Caravan Park; 14-15 bg AA/A Burton; 14l courtesy of South Lytchett Manor Caravan & Camping Park; 14r courtesy of South Lytchett Manor Caravan & Camping Park; 15l courtesy of Craigtoun Meadows Holiday Park; 15r courtesy of Pont Kemys Caravan & Camping Park; 16-17 bg AA/A Burton; 16l courtesy of Dornafield; 16r courtesy of Concierge Camping; 17l courtesy of Clover Fields Touring Camping Park; 17r courtesy of Hollins Farm Camping & Caravanning; 18-19 bg AA/A Burton; 18l courtesy of Naburn Lock Caravan Park; 18r courtesy of Craig Tara Holiday Park; 19l courtesy of Trevalgan Touring Park; 19r courtesy of Long Acres Touring Park; 20 courtesy of Durrell Wildlife Camp; 21 courtesy of Everland; 22 courtesy of Everland; 23l courtesy of Durrell Wildlife Camp; 23r courtesy of Durrell Wildlife Camp; 24 AA/J Tims; 26 AA/J Tims; 29 AA/J Tims; 37 AA/J Tims; 38 courtesy of Eskdale Caravan & Camping; 42 ceredigionpix/Alamy; 44-45 John Potter/Alamy; 54 AA/A Burton; 118 AA/A Burton; 125 AA/J Wood; 127 AA/T Mackie; 136 AA/T Mackie; 148 AA/T Mackie; 150 AA/G Edwardes; 164 AA/G Edwardes; 169 AA/A Burton; 182 AA/A Newey; 202 AA/A Newey; 216 AA/N Setchfield; 225 AA/A Newey; 235 AA/L Noble; 255 AA/D Clapp; 256 AA/T Mackie; 270 AA/J Hunt; 287 AA/M Hayward; 288 AA/J Tims; 308 AA/T Mackie; 313 AA/T Mackie; 317 AA/T Mackie; 319 AA/J Miller; 333 AA/M Moody; 335 AA/J Tims; 337 AA/D Clapp; 350 AA/T Mackie; 368 steven gillis hd9 imaging/Alamy; 369 AA/J Tims; 373 parkerphotography/Alamy; 377 scottishcreative/Alamy; 385 AA/M Alexander; 412 David Angel/Alamy; 417 AA/J Gravell; 449 AA/H Williams; 451 AA/M Bauer; 491 AA/J Tims; 507 AA/A Burton.

Country openers

ENGLAND (44-45) John Potter/Alamy; SCOTLAND (374-375) Angus Alexander Chisholm/Alamy; WALES (410-411) AA/M Bauer; IRELAND (452-453) Gareth McCormack/Alamy.

Every effort has been made to trace the copyright holders, and we apologise in advance for any unintentional omissions or errors. We would be pleased to apply any corrections in a following edition of this publication.

England

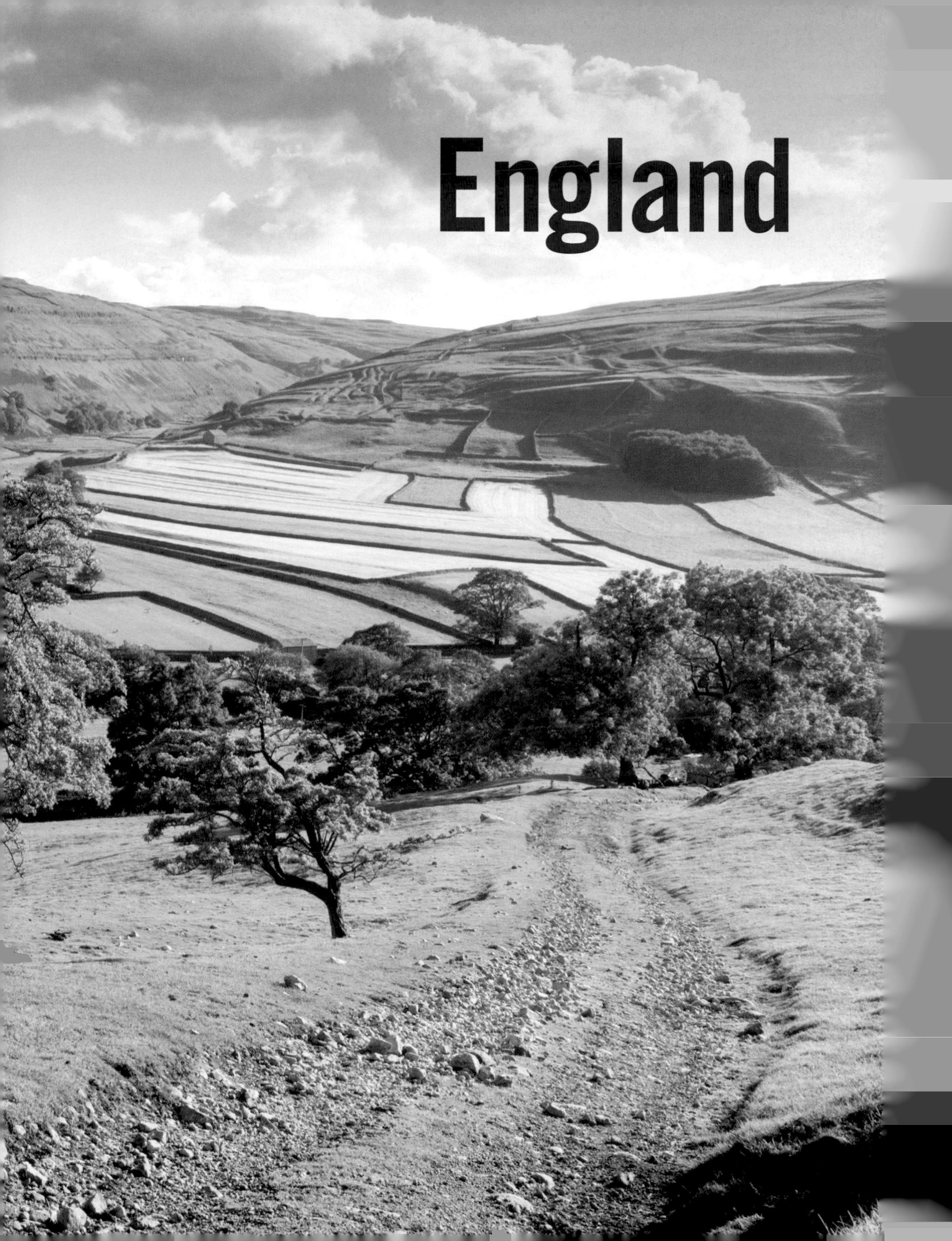

BERKSHIRE

FINCHAMPSTEAD Map 5 SU76

Places to visit

West Green House Gardens, HARTLEY WINTNEY, RG27 8JB, 01252 844611 www.westgreenhouse.co.uk

Museum of English Rural Life, READING, RG1 5EX, 0118 378 8660 www.merl.org.uk

Great for kids: The Look Out Discovery Centre, BRACKNELL, RG12 7QW, 01344 354400 www.bracknell-forest.gov.uk/be

California Chalet & Touring Park

►►► 80%

tel: 0118 973 3928 & 07447 475833 **Nine Mile Ride RG40 4HU**
email: enquiries@californiapark.co.uk
dir: *From A321 (S of Wokingham), right onto B3016 to Finchampstead. Follow Country Park signs on Nine Mile Ride.* **grid ref:** *SU788651*

A simple, peaceful woodland site with secluded pitches among the trees, adjacent to the country park. Several pitches occupy a prime position beside the lake with their own fishing area. The site has large hardstandings, with more planned in the future; the toilet block has quality vanity units and fully tiled showers. The sparsley planted trees allow sunshine onto pitches. Future investment plans remain very positive for this well located park. 5.5 acre site. 44 touring pitches. 44 hardstandings. Caravan pitches. Motorhome pitches. Tent pitches. 2 wooden pods.

Open: all year **Last arrival:** flexible **Last departure:** noon

Pitches: * £22-£29 £22-£29 £18-£45

Facilities:

Services:

Within 3 miles:

Notes: No ground fires, no washing of caravans. Dogs must be kept on leads.

AA Pubs & Restaurants nearby: The Broad Street Tavern, WOKINGHAM, RG40 1AU, 0118 977 3706

L'Ortolan, SHINFIELD, RG2 9BY, 0118 988 8500

HURLEY

Places to visit

Cliveden, CLIVEDEN, SL6 0JA, 01628 605069 www.nationaltrust.org.uk/cliveden

The Hell-Fire Caves, WEST WYCOMBE, HP14 3AJ, 01494 524411 (office) www.hellfirecaves.co.uk

Great for kids: Bekonscot Model Village and Railway, BEACONSFIELD, HP9 2PL, 01494 672919 www.bekonscot.co.uk

HURLEY Map 5 SU88

PREMIER PARK

Hurley Riverside Park

►►►►► 84%

GOLD

tel: 01628 824493 & 823501 **Park Office SL6 5NE**
email: info@hurleyriversidepark.co.uk **web:** www.hurleyriversidepark.co.uk
dir: *Signed on A4130 (Henley to Maidenhead rd), just W of Hurley.* **grid ref:** *SU826839*

A large Thames-side site with a good touring area close to the river. A quality park with three beautifully appointed toilet blocks, one of which houses excellent, fully serviced unisex facilities. Level grassy pitches are sited in small, sectioned areas, and this is a generally peaceful setting. There are furnished tents for hire. 15 acre site. 200 touring pitches. 36 hardstandings. Caravan pitches. Motorhome pitches. Tent pitches. 290 statics.

Open: Mar-Oct **Last arrival:** 20.00hrs **Last departure:** noon

Pitches: * £15-£31 £15-£31 £13-£27 **Leisure:**

Facilities:

Services:

Within 3 miles:

Notes: No unsupervised groups of young people, no commercial vehicles, no fires or fire pits, quiet-park policy applies. Max 2 dogs per pitch. Dogs must be kept on leads. Fishing in season, slipway, nature trail, riverside picnic grounds.

AA Pubs & Restaurants nearby: The Olde Bell Inn, HURLEY, SL6 5LX, 01628 825881

Hotel du Vin Henley-on-Thames, HENLEY-ON-THAMES, RG9 2BP, 01491 848400

See advert on opposite page

NEWBURY — Map 5 SU46

Places to visit

Highclere Castle & Gardens, HIGHCLERE, RG20 9RN, 01635 253210 www.highclerecastle.co.uk

Great for kids: The Living Rainforest, HAMPSTEAD NORREYS, RG18 0TN, 01635 202444 www.livingrainforest.org

Bishops Green Farm Camp Site

►►► 81%

tel: 01635 268365 **Bishops Green RG20 4JP**
dir: *Exit A339 (opposite New Greenham Park) towards Bishops Green & Ecchinswell. Site on left, approx 0.5m by barn.* **grid ref:** *SU502630*

A sheltered and secluded meadowland park close to the Hampshire/Berkshire border, offering very clean and well-maintained facilities, including a toilet block with a disabled/family room. There are woodland and riverside walks to be enjoyed around the farm, and coarse fishing is also available. The site is very convenient for visiting the nearby market town of Newbury with its attractive canal in the town centre. 1.5 acre site. 30 touring pitches. 6 hardstandings. Caravan pitches. Motorhome pitches. Tent pitches.

Open: Apr-Oct **Last arrival:** 21.30hrs

Pitches:

Facilities:

Services:

Within 3 miles:

Notes: Dogs must be kept on leads.

RISELEY — Map 5 SU76

Places to visit

Basildon Park, LOWER BASILDON, RG8 9NR, 0118 984 3040 www.nationaltrust.org.uk/basildonpark

Mapledurham House, MAPLEDURHAM, RG4 7TR, 0118 972 3350 www.mapledurham.co.uk

Great for kids: Beale Park, LOWER BASILDON, RG8 9NH, 0844 826 1761 *(Calls cost 7p per minute plus your phone company's access charge)* www.bealepark.co.uk

Wellington Country Park

►►► 86%

tel: 0118 932 6444 **Odiham Rd RG7 1SP**
email: info@wellington-country-park.co.uk **web:** www.wellington-country-park.co.uk
dir: *M4 junct 11, A33 S towards Basingstoke. Or M3 junct 5, B3349 N towards Reading.*
grid ref: *SU728628*

A peaceful woodland site, popular with families, set within an extensive country park, which comes complete with lakes and nature trails, accessible to campers

continued

RISELEY *continued*

after the country park closes. The park offers good facilities that include a laundry and a good motorhome service point. There's also a herd of Red and Fallow deer that roam the meadow area. This site is ideal for those travelling on the M4 but it is advised not to follow Sat Nav as it takes you to a central point of the post code, which is not the entrance. 80 acre site. 87 touring pitches. 18 hardstandings. Caravan pitches. Motorhome pitches. Tent pitches.

Open: Mar-Nov **Last arrival:** 17.30hrs **Last departure:** noon

Pitches: **Leisure:**

Facilities:

Services: **Within 3 miles:**

Notes: No open fires, last arrival time 16.30hrs in low season. Dogs must be kept on leads. Miniature railway, crazy golf, animal farm, access to Wellington Country Park.

AA Pubs & Restaurants nearby: The George & Dragon, SWALLOWFIELD, RG7 1TJ, 0118 988 4432

BRISTOL

BRISTOL

See Cowslip Green (Somerset)

CAMBRIDGESHIRE

BURWELL Map 12 TL56

Places to visit

National Horseracing Museum and Tours, NEWMARKET, CB8 8JH, 01638 667333 www.nhrm.co.uk

Wicken Fen National Nature Reserve, WICKEN, CB7 5XP, 01353 720274 www.nationaltrust.org.uk/main

Stanford Park

NEW ►►► 81%

tel: 01638 741547 & 07802 439997 **Weirs Drove CB25 0BP**
email: enquirires@stanfordcaravanpark.co.uk
dir: *From A14 junct 37, A142, left signed Burwell. Or from A14 junct 35, B1102 to Burwell (site approx 4m from Newmarket; 8m from Cambridge).* **grid ref:** *TL580665*

Set on the edge of the fens and within walking distance of the historic village of Burwell, this park is an attractive tranquil adults-only site. It is ideally placed for visiting the Wicken Fen National Nature Reserve, Ely Cathedral, Newmarket races and Cambridge. The park is expertly maintained with clean, modern facilities and four open paddocks sheltered by mature deciduous trees. There is an exclusive area for seasonal pitches where winter storage is also available. It is advisable to book for Bank Holidays (minimum three night stay) and for peak periods. 20 acre site. 103 touring pitches. 20 hardstandings. Caravan pitches. Motorhome pitches. Tent pitches.

Open: all year **Last arrival:** 21.00hrs **Last departure:** 11.00hrs

Pitches: * £14-£16 £14-£16 £14-£16

Facilities: **Services:**

Within 3 miles:

Notes: Adults only. Dogs must be kept on leads.

COMBERTON Map 12 TL35

Places to visit

IWM Duxford, DUXFORD, CB22 4QR, 01223 835000 www.iwm.org.uk

Chilford Hall Vineyard, LINTON, CB21 4LE, 01223 895600 www.chilfordhall.co.uk

Great for kids: Linton Zoological Gardens, LINTON, CB21 4NT, 01223 891308 www.lintonzoo.com

Highfield Farm Touring Park

Best of British

►►►► 91%

tel: 01223 262308 **Long Rd CB23 7DG**
email: enquiries@highfieldfarmtouringpark.co.uk
web: www.highfieldfarmtouringpark.co.uk
dir: *M11 junct 12, A603 (Sandy). 0.5m, right onto B1046 to Comberton.*
grid ref: *TL389572*

Run by a very efficient and friendly family, the park is on a well-sheltered hilltop, with spacious pitches including a cosy backpackers/cyclists' area, and separate sections for couples and families. Around the family farm there is a one and a half mile marked walk that has stunning views. 8 acre site. 120 touring pitches. 52 hardstandings. Caravan pitches. Motorhome pitches. Tent pitches.

Open: Apr-Oct **Last arrival:** 20.00hrs **Last departure:** 14.00hrs

Pitches: * £20-£25 £20-£25 £15-£25

Facilities:

Services:

Within 3 miles:

Notes: Max 2 dogs. Dogs must be kept on leads. Postbox.

AA Pubs & Restaurants nearby: The Three Horseshoes, MADINGLEY, CB23 8AB, 01954 210221

Restaurant 22, CAMBRIDGE, CB4 3AX, 01223 351880

DODDINGTON Map 12 TL49

Places to visit

WWT Welney Wetland Centre, WELNEY, PE14 9TN, 01353 860711 www.wwt.org.uk

Flag Fen Archaeology Park, PETERBOROUGH, PE6 7QJ, 01733 313414 www.vivacity-peterborough.com/museums-and-heritage/flag-fen

PREMIER PARK

Fields End Water Caravan Park & Fishery

Best of British

►►►►► 84%

tel: 01354 740199 **Benwick Rd PE15 0TY**
email: info@fieldsendfishing.co.uk
dir: *Exit A141, follow signs to Doddington. At clock tower in Doddington turn right into Benwick Rd. Site 1.5m on right after sharp bends.* **grid ref:** *TL378908*

This meticulously planned and executed park makes excellent use of its slightly elevated position in The Fens. The 33 fully serviced pitches, all with very generous hardstandings, are on smart terraces with sweeping views of the countryside. The two toilet blocks contain several combined cubicle spaces, and there are shady walks through mature deciduous woodland adjacent to two large and appealingly landscaped fishing lakes. High quality pine lodges are available as holiday lets. 20 acre site. 52 touring pitches. 17 hardstandings. Caravan pitches. Motorhome pitches. Tent pitches.

Open: all year **Last arrival:** 20.30hrs **Last departure:** noon

Pitches: * £18-£20 £18-£20 £17

Facilities: WiFi

Services: T

Within 3 miles:

Notes: Adults only. No large groups. Dogs must be kept on leads.

AA Pubs & Restaurants nearby: The Crown Inn, BROUGHTON, PE28 3AY, 01487 824428

The Old Bridge Hotel, HUNTINGDON, PE29 3TQ, 01480 424300

GUYHIRN Map 12 TF40

Places to visit

Peckover House & Garden, WISBECH, PE13 1JR, 01945 583463 www.nationaltrust.org.uk/peckover

Great for kids: WWT Welney Wetland Centre, WELNEY, PE14 9TN, 01353 860711 www.wwt.org.uk

Tall Trees Leisure Park

►►► 87%

tel: 01945 450952 & 450131 **Gull Rd PE13 4ER**
email: enquiries@talltreesleisurepark.co.uk
dir: *A47 from Peterborough towards Wisbech. Left onto B1187 signed Guyhirn.*
grid ref: *TF393035*

Tall Trees Leisure Park is a family-run caravan site set in 35 acres of a former commercial fruit farm. There are 59 electric pitches, each with its own water tap, set out in two perfectly level and maturely landscaped fields. There is also a separate, large rally field. Toilets are provided in well-maintained raised buildings, and the reception also houses a small shop and café. Security is given a high priority with an entrance barrier and CCTV. 35 acre site. 94 touring pitches. 6 seasonal pitches. Caravan pitches. Motorhome pitches. Tent pitches.

Open: all year **Last arrival:** 17.00hrs **Last departure:** noon

Pitches:

Facilities:

Services:

Within 3 miles:

Notes: Dogs must be kept on leads.

HEMINGFORD ABBOTS Map 12 TL27

Quiet Waters Caravan Park

►►► 80%

tel: 01480 463405 **PE28 9AJ**
email: quietwaters.park@btopenworld.com **web:** www.quietwaterscaravanpark.co.uk
dir: *Follow village signs from A14 junct 25, E of Huntingdon. Site in village centre.*
grid ref: *TL283712*

This is an attractive little site on the banks of the Great Ouse that has been in the same family ownership for over 80 years. It is found in a really charming village just a mile from the A14, making an ideal centre from which to tour the Cambridgeshire area. There are fishing opportunities, rowing boats for hire and many walks and cycling routes directly from the park. There are holiday statics for hire. 1 acre site. 20 touring pitches. 18 hardstandings. Caravan pitches. Motorhome pitches. Tent pitches. 40 statics.

Open: Apr-Oct **Last arrival:** 20.00hrs **Last departure:** noon

Pitches: * £18-£22 £18-£22 £18-£22

Facilities: WiFi

Services:

Within 3 miles:

Notes: Dogs must be kept on leads.

AA Pubs & Restaurants nearby: The Cock Pub and Restaurant, HEMINGFORD GREY, PE28 9BJ, 01480 463609

The Old Bridge Hotel, HUNTINGDON, PE29 3TQ, 01480 424300

HUNTINGDON Map 12 TL27

Places to visit

Ramsey Abbey Gatehouse, RAMSEY, PE26 1DG, 01480 301494 www.nationaltrust.org.uk

WWT Welney Wetland Centre, WELNEY, PE14 9TN, 01353 860711 www.wwt.org.uk

Great for kids: The Raptor Foundation, WOODHURST, PE28 3BT, 01487 741140 www.raptorfoundation.org.uk

Huntingdon Boathaven & Caravan Park

►►► 80%

tel: 01480 411977 **The Avenue, Godmanchester PE29 2AF**
email: boathaven.hunts@virgin.net
dir: *S of town. Exit A14 at Godmanchester junct, through Godmanchester on B1043 to site (on left by River Ouse).* **grid ref:** *TL249706*

A small, well laid out site overlooking a boat marina and the River Ouse, set close to the A14 and within walking distance of Huntingdon town centre. The toilets are clean and well kept. A pretty area has been created for tents beside the marina, with wide views across the Ouse Valley. Weekend family activities are organised throughout the season. 2 acre site. 24 touring pitches. 18 hardstandings. Caravan pitches. Motorhome pitches. Tent pitches.

Open: all year (rs Winter open subject to weather conditions) **Last arrival:** 21.00hrs **Last departure:** variable

Pitches: * £16-£21 £16-£21 £11-£20

Facilities:

Services:

Within 3 miles:

Notes: No cars by tents. Dogs must be kept on leads.

AA Pubs & Restaurants nearby: The Old Bridge Hotel, HUNTINGDON, PE29 3TQ, 01480 424300

King William IV, FENSTANTON, PE28 9JF, 01480 462467

The Willows Caravan Park

►►► 80%

tel: 01480 437566 **Bromholme Ln, Brampton PE28 4NE**
email: willows@willows33.freeserve.co.uk
dir: *A1 junct 21 onto A14 (signed Cambridge). Follow Brampton & Huntingdon signs onto B1514. Straight on at 2 rdbts. Right into Bromholme Ln. Site on right (near Brampton Mill pub).* **grid ref:** *TL224708*

A small, friendly site in a pleasant setting beside the River Ouse, on the Ouse Valley Walk. Bay areas have been provided for caravans and motorhomes, and planting for screening is gradually maturing. There are launching facilities and free river fishing. 4 acre site. 50 touring pitches. 10 hardstandings. 10 seasonal pitches. Caravan pitches. Motorhome pitches. Tent pitches.

Open: all year **Last arrival:** 20.00hrs **Last departure:** noon

Pitches:

Leisure:

Facilities:

Services:

Within 3 miles:

Notes: No cars by tents. 5mph one-way system, no generators, no groundsheets, ball games permitted on field only. Dogs must be kept on leads. Free book lending & exchange.

AA Pubs & Restaurants nearby: The Old Bridge Hotel, HUNTINGDON, PE29 3TQ, 01480 424300

ST IVES Map 12 TL37

Places to visit

The Farmland Museum and Denny Abbey, WATERBEACH, CB25 9PQ, 01223 860988 www.english-heritage.org.uk/daysout/properties/denny-abbey-and-the-farmland-museum

Oliver Cromwell's House, ELY, CB7 4HF, 01353 662062 www.visitely.org.uk

PREMIER PARK

Stroud Hill Park

Best of British

►►►►► 93%

tel: 01487 741333 **Fen Rd, Pidley PE28 3DE**
email: stroudhillpark@btconnect.com
dir: *Exit B1040 in Pidley follow signs for Lakeside Lodge Complex, into Fen Rd, site on right.* **grid ref:** *TL335787*

A superb adults-only caravan park designed to a very high specification in a secluded and sheltered spot not far from St Ives. A modern timber-framed barn houses the exceptional facilities. These include the beautifully tiled toilets with spacious cubicles, each containing a shower, washbasin and toilet. A bar and café, and restaurant (The Barn), small licensed shop, tennis court and coarse fishing are among the attractions. There are three pay-as-you-go golf courses plus ten-pin bowling nearby. 6 acre site. 60 touring pitches. 44 hardstandings. Caravan pitches. Motorhome pitches. Tent pitches.

Open: all year **Last arrival:** 20.00hrs **Last departure:** noon

Pitches: * £25-£27 £25-£27 £17

Leisure:

Facilities: Wi-Fi

Services:

Within 3 miles:

Notes: Adults only. No large motorhomes. Dogs must be kept on leads.

AA Pubs & Restaurants nearby: The Crown Inn, BROUGHTON, PE28 3AY, 01487 824428

The Lazy Otter, STRETHAM, CB6 3LU, 01353 649780

WISBECH Map 12 TF40

Places to visit

Peckover House & Garden, WISBECH, PE13 1JR, 01945 583463 www.nationaltrust.org.uk/peckover

Great for kids: WWT Welney Wetland Centre, WELNEY, PE14 9TN, 01353 860711 www.wwt.org.uk

Little Ranch Leisure

►►► 85%

tel: 01945 860066 **Begdale, Elm PE14 0AZ**
email: littleranchleisure@begdalecambs.wanadoo.co.uk
web: www.littleranchleisure.co.uk
dir: *From rdbt on A47 (SW of Wisbech), take Redmoor Lane to Begdale.* **grid ref:** *TF456062*

A friendly family site set in an apple orchard, with 25 fully serviced pitches and a beautifully designed, spacious toilet block. The site overlooks two fishing lakes and pitches are available by the water; the famous horticultural auctions at Wisbech are nearby. 10 acre site. 40 touring pitches. 40 hardstandings. Caravan pitches. Motorhome pitches. Tent pitches.

Open: all year

Pitches: £12-£17 £12-£17 £12-£17

Facilities:

Services:

Within 3 miles:

Notes: Dogs must be kept on leads.

AA Pubs & Restaurants nearby: Crown Lodge Hotel, WISBECH, PE14 8SE, 01945 773391

The Hare Arms, STOW BARDOLPH, PE34 3HT, 01366 382229

CHESHIRE

CODDINGTON Map 15 SJ45

Places to visit

Cholmondeley Castle Gardens, CHOLMONDELEY, SY14 8AH, 01829 720383 www.cholmondeleycastle.com

Hack Green Secret Nuclear Bunker, NANTWICH, CW5 8AP, 01270 629219 www.hackgreen.co.uk

Great for kids: Dewa Roman Experience, CHESTER, CH1 1NL, 01244 343407 www.dewaromanexperience.co.uk

Chester Zoo, CHESTER, CH2 1LH, 01244 380280 www.chesterzoo.org

PREMIER PARK

Manor Wood Country Caravan Park

►►►►► 90%

tel: 01829 782990 & 07762 817827 **Manor Wood CH3 9EN**
email: info@manorwoodcaravans.co.uk
dir: *From A534 at Barton, turn opposite Cock O'Barton pub signed Coddington. Left in 100yds. Site 0.5m on left.* **grid ref:** *SJ453553*

A secluded landscaped park in a tranquil country setting with extensive views towards the Welsh Hills across the Cheshire Plain. The park offers fully serviced pitches, a heated outdoor swimming pool and all-weather tennis courts. The generous pitch density provides optimum privacy and the superb amenities block has excellent decor, under-floor heating and smart modern facilities with very good privacy options. Wildlife is encouraged and there is a fishing lake; country walks and nearby pubs are added attractions. 8 acre site. 45 touring pitches. 38 hardstandings. 30 seasonal pitches. Caravan pitches. Motorhome pitches. Tent pitches. 21 statics.

Open: all year (rs Oct-Mar swimming pool closed) **Last arrival:** 19.00hrs
Last departure: 11.00hrs

Pitches: * £13.50-£25 £13.50-£25 £13.50-£25 **Leisure:**

Facilities: WiFi

Services: **Within 3 miles:**

Notes: No cars by caravans. No noise after 23.00hrs. Dogs must be kept on leads.

AA Pubs & Restaurants nearby: The Calveley Arms, HANDLEY, CH3 9DT, 01829 770619

1851 Restaurant at Peckforton Castle, PECKFORTON, CW6 9TN, 01829 260930

DELAMERE Map 15 SJ56

Places to visit

Jodrell Bank Discovery Centre, JODRELL BANK, SK11 9DL, 01477 571766 www.jodrellbank.net

Little Moreton Hall, CONGLETON, CW12 4SD, 01260 272018 www.nationaltrust.org.uk

Great for kids: Chester Zoo, CHESTER, CH2 1LH, 01244 380280 www.chesterzoo.org

Fishpool Farm Caravan Park

►►►► 85%

tel: 01606 883970 & 07501 506583 **Fishpool Rd CW8 2HP**
email: enquiries@fishpoolfarmcaravanpark.co.uk
dir: *From A49 (Tarporley to Cuddington road), onto A54 signed Chester. At Fishpool Inn left onto B5152 (Fishpool Rd). Site on right.* **grid ref:** *SJ567672*

Developed on a former hay field on the owner's farm, this excellent park has a shop/reception, a superb purpose-built toilet block with laundry facilities, a picnic area, and 50 spacious pitches, all with electric hook-up. There is a lakeside lodge, coarse fishing and a nature walk. 5.5 acre site. 50 touring pitches. 14 hardstandings. Caravan pitches. Motorhome pitches. Tent pitches. 1 static.

Open: 15 Feb-15 Jan **Last arrival:** 19.00hrs **Last departure:** noon

Pitches:

Leisure:

Facilities:

Services:

Within 3 miles:

Notes: No noise after 23.00hrs. Dogs must be kept on leads. Dog walks, fresh eggs from own hens.

AA Pubs & Restaurants nearby: The Fishpool Inn, DELAMARE, CW8 2HP, 01606 883277

Alvanley Arms Inn, TARPORLEY, CW6 9DS, 01829 760200

KNUTSFORD Map 15 SJ77

Places to visit

The Tabley House Collection, KNUTSFORD, WA16 0HB, 01565 750151 www.tableyhouse.co.uk

Great for kids: Jodrell Bank Discovery Centre, JODRELL BANK, SK11 9DL, 01477 571766 www.jodrellbank.net

Woodlands Park

►►► 78%

tel: 01565 723429 & 01332 810818 **Wash Ln, Allostock WA16 9LG**
dir: *M6 junct 18 take A50 N to Holmes Chapel for 3m, turn into Wash Ln by Boundary Water Park. Site 0.25m on left.* **grid ref:** *SJ743710*

A very tranquil and attractive park in the heart of rural Cheshire, and set in 16 acres of mature woodland where in spring the rhododendrons look stunning. Tourers are located in three separate wooded areas that teem with wildlife and you will wake up to the sound of birdsong. This park is just five miles from Jodrell Bank. 16 acre site. 40 touring pitches. Caravan pitches. Motorhome pitches. Tent pitches. 140 statics.

Open: Mar-6 Jan **Last arrival:** 21.00hrs **Last departure:** 11.00hrs

Pitches:

Facilities:

Services:

Within 3 miles:

Notes: No skateboards or rollerblades. Dogs must be kept on leads.

AA Pubs & Restaurants nearby: The Dog Inn, KNUTSFORD, WA16 8UP, 01625 861421

The Duke of Portland, LACH DENNIS, CW9 7SY, 01606 46264

LEISURE: Indoor swimming pool · Outdoor swimming pool · Children's playground · Kid's club · Tennis court · Games room · Separate TV room · golf course · Boats for hire · Cinema · Entertainment · Fishing · Mini golf · Watersports · Gym · Sports field · Spa · Stables
FACILITIES: Bath · Shower · Electric shaver · Hairdryer · Ice Pack Facility · Disabled facilities · Public telephone · Shop on site or within 200yds · Mobile shop (calls at least 5 days a week) · BBQ area · Picnic area · Wi-fi · Internet access · Recycling · Tourist info · Dog exercise area

SIDDINGTON Map 15 SJ87

Places to visit

Capesthorne Hall, CAPESTHORNE, SK11 9JY, 01625 861221 www.capesthorne.com

Gawsworth Hall, GAWSWORTH, SK11 9RN, 01260 223456 www.gawsworthhall.com

Great for kids: Jodrell Bank Discovery Centre, JODRELL BANK, SK11 9DL, 01477 571766 www.jodrellbank.net

Capesthorne Hall

►►►► 88%

tel: 01625 861221 **Congleton Rd SK11 9JY**
email: info@capesthorne.com
dir: *Access to site from A34 between Congleton to Wilmslow. Phone for detailed directions.*
grid ref: *SJ841727*

Located within the grounds of the notable Jacobean Capesthorne Hall, this lush, all level site provides generously sized pitches, all with electricity and most with hardstandings. The Scandanavian-style amenities block has a smart, quality, modern interior and very good privacy levels. Guests also have the opportunity to visit the award-winning gardens on certain days and there are many extensive walking opportunities directly from the camping areas. 5 acre site. 50 touring pitches. 30 hardstandings. Caravan pitches. Motorhome pitches.

Open: Apr-Oct **Last arrival:** 22.00hrs **Last departure:** noon

Pitches: * £25-£30 £25-£30

Facilities:

Services:

Within 3 miles:

Notes: Minimum 3 night stay on BH wknds. No motorised scooters or skateboards. Gas BBQs only. Touring area may close if large events take place (contact site for details). Dogs must be kept on leads. Access to Capesthorne Hall & Gardens – additional cost for hall only.

AA Pubs & Restaurants nearby: The Davenport Arms, MARTON, SK11 9HF, 01260 224269

Egerton Arms, CHELFORD, SK11 9BB, 01625 861366

WETTENHALL Map 15 SJ66

New Farm Caravan Park

►►► 87%

tel: 01270 528213 & 07970 221112 **Long Ln CW7 4DW**
email: info@newfarmcheshire.com
dir: *M6 junct 16, A500 towards Nantwich, right onto Nantwich bypass A51. At lights turn right, follow A51 Caster & Tarporely signs. After Calveley right into Long Ln, follow site sign. Site in 2m.* **grid ref:** *SJ613608*

Diversification at New Farm led to the development of four fishing lakes and the creation of a peaceful small touring park. The proprietors provide a very welcome touring destination within this peaceful part of Cheshire. Expect good landscaping, generous hardstanding pitches, a spotless toilet block, and good attention to detail throughout. Nearly all pitches are very spacious and fully serviced. Please note there is no laundry. 40 acre site. 24 touring pitches. 17 hardstandings. 6 seasonal pitches. Caravan pitches. Motorhome pitches.

Open: all year **Last arrival:** 20.00hrs **Last departure:** noon

Pitches:

Facilities:

Services:

Within 3 miles:

Notes: Adults only. Dogs must be kept on leads.

AA Pubs & Restaurants nearby: The Nags Head, HAUGHTON MOSS, CW6 9RN, 01829 260265

Crewe Hall, CREWE, CW1 6UZ, 01270 253333

WHITEGATE Map 15 SJ66

Places to visit

Beeston Castle, BEESTON, CW6 9TX, 01829 260464 www.english-heritage.org.uk/daysout/properties/beeston-castle-and-woodland-park

Chester Cathedral, CHESTER, CH1 2HU, 01244 500961 www.chestercathedral.com

Great for kids: Blue Planet Aquarium, ELLESMERE PORT, CH65 9LF, 0151 357 8800 www.blueplanetaquarium.com

PREMIER PARK

Lamb Cottage Caravan Park

►►►►► 92%

tel: 01606 882302 **Dalefords Ln CW8 2BN**
email: info@lambcottage.co.uk
dir: *From A556 turn at Sandiway lights into Dalefords Ln, signed Winsford. Site 1m on right.* **grid ref:** *SJ613692*

A secluded and attractively landscaped adults-only park in a glorious location where the emphasis is on peace and relaxation. The serviced pitches are spacious with wide grass borders for sitting out and the high quality toilet block is spotlessly clean and immaculately maintained. A good central base for exploring this area, with access to nearby woodland walks and cycle trails. 6 acre site. 45 touring pitches. 45 hardstandings. 14 seasonal pitches. Caravan pitches. Motorhome pitches. 26 statics.

Open: Mar-Oct **Last arrival:** 20.00hrs **Last departure:** noon

Pitches:

Facilities:

Services:

Within 3 miles:

Notes: Adults only. No tents (except trailer tents), no commercial vehicles. Dogs must be kept on leads.

AA Pubs & Restaurants nearby: The Fishpool Inn, DELAMARE, CW8 2HP, 01606 883277

Fox & Barrel, COTEBROOK, CW6 9DZ, 01829 760529

Cornwall

It's not hard to see why thousands of tourists and holidaymakers flock to Cornwall every year. It has just about everything – wild moorland landscapes, glorious river valley scenery, picturesque villages and miles of breathtaking coastline. It has long been acknowledged as one of Britain's top holiday destinations.

Cornwall's southerly latitude and the influence of the Gulf Stream make the county the mildest and sunniest climate in Britain. It's not surprising therefore that one of its greatest and most popular pursuits is surfing. With more than 80 surfing spots, and plenty of sporting enthusiasts who make their way here to enjoy other similar coastal activities, such as wave-surfing, kite surfing and blokarting, the county is an internationally famous surfing hot spot. Blessed with wonderful surf beaches, Newquay is Cornwall's surfing capital. Nearby Watergate Bay is renowned for its glassy waves and Sennen, near Land's End, is where you might even get to surf with dolphins. Certainly the sea is strikingly blue here and the sands dazzlingly white.

A long-running TV series, filmed in a scenic location, is often a guaranteed way to boost tourism and that is certainly the case at Port Isaac on the north Cornwall coast. The village doubles as Portwenn in the drama *Doc Martin*, starring Martin Clunes as the irascible local GP. Much of Port Isaac has been used for location shooting over the years and it's quite common to bump into actors from the series at different points in the village when filming is taking place. Many films and TV series have been shot in Cornwall – including productions of Daphne du Maurier's *Jamaica Inn* and *Rebecca*, though the original version of the latter, made in 1940, was Alfred Hitchcock's first film in Hollywood and shot entirely in California.

In the book, the setting is a large house on the Cornish coast where the atmosphere is decidedly gothic. Daphne du Maurier modelled the house – which she called Manderley – and its location on the Menabilly estate, near Fowey. *Rebecca* was published in 1938 and five years later the writer made Menabilly her home. The house is not open to the public, but it is possible to explore the setting for the story on foot, following a leafy path from the car park at Menabilly Barton Farm to Polridmouth Bay where there are two secluded and remote coves. A bird's eye view of the entire area is possible from the path to Gribben Head, though Menabilly, at the heart of the story, is hidden by trees, thus preserving the mystery of the book.

The Cornish coastline offers breathtakingly beautiful scenery. The north coast is open and exposed; the 735-ft High Cliff, between Boscastle and St Gennys, represents the highest sheer drop cliff in the county. The Lizard, at Cornwall's most southerly point, is a geological masterpiece of awesome cliffs, stacks and arches.

In recent years new or restored visitor attractions have helped to increase tourism in the region – Tim Smit has been the inspiration and driving force behind two of the county's most visited attractions. The Eden Project is famous for its giant geodesic domes housing exotic plants from different parts of the globe, while nearby the Lost Gardens of Heligan at Pentewan has impressive kitchen gardens and a wildlife hide.

Perhaps the last word on this magical corner of Britain should go to Daphne du Maurier. In her book *Vanishing Cornwall*, published in 1967, she wrote: 'A county known and loved in all its moods becomes woven into the pattern of life, something to be shared. As one who sought to know it long ago…in a quest for freedom, and later put down roots and found content, I have come a small way up the path. The beauty and the mystery beckon still.'

◁ Wheal Coates Tin Mine, St Agnes

CORNWALL & ISLES OF SCILLY

ASHTON Map 2 SW62

Places to visit

Godolphin House, GODOLPHIN CROSS, TR13 9RE, 01736 763194 www.nationaltrust.org.uk/godolphin

Poldark Mine and Heritage Complex, WENDRON, TR13 0ER, 01326 573173 www.poldark-mine.co.uk

Great for kids: The Flambards Theme Park, HELSTON, TR13 0QA, 01326 573404 www.flambards.co.uk

Boscrege Caravan & Camping Park

►►► 79%

tel: 01736 762231 **TR13 9TG**
email: enquiries@caravanparkcornwall.com **web:** www.caravanparkcornwall.com
dir: *A394 from Helston signed Penzance. In Ashton (Lion & Lamb pub on right) right into Higher Lane, approx 1.5m (thatched cottage on right) left at site sign. (NB for recommended towing route contact the park).* **grid ref:** *SW595305*

A quiet and bright little touring park divided into small paddocks with hedges, that offers plenty of open spaces for children to play in. This family-owned park has clean, well-painted toilet facilities and neatly trimmed grass. By an Area of Outstanding Natural Beauty at the foot of Tregonning Hill, this site makes an ideal base for touring the southern tip of Cornwall; Penzance, Land's End, St Ives and the beaches in between are all within easy reach. 14 acre site. 50 touring pitches. 10 seasonal pitches. Caravan pitches. Motorhome pitches. Tent pitches. 38 statics.

Open: Mar-Nov (rs Jan-Dec statics open) **Last arrival:** 22.00hrs **Last departure:** 11.00hrs

Pitches:

Leisure:

Facilities:

Services:

Within 3 miles:

Notes: No fires, no noise after 23.00hrs. Dogs must be kept on leads. Microwave & freezer available, nature trail.

AA Pubs & Restaurants nearby: The Victoria Inn, PERRANUTHNOE, TR20 9NP, 01736 710309

New Yard Restaurant, HELSTON, TR12 6AF, 01326 221595

BLACKWATER

Places to visit

Royal Cornwall Museum, TRURO, TR1 2SJ, 01872 272205 www.royalcornwallmuseum.org.uk

East Pool Mine, POOL, TR15 3NP, 01209 315027 www.nationaltrust.org.uk

Great for kids: National Maritime Museum Cornwall, FALMOUTH, TR11 3QY, 01326 313388 www.nmmc.co.uk

BLACKWATER Map 2 SW74

Trevarth Holiday Park

►►►► 84%

tel: 01872 560266 **TR4 8HR**
email: trevarth@btconnect.com **web:** www.trevarth.co.uk
dir: *Exit A30 at Chiverton rdbt onto B3277 signed St Agnes. At next rdbt take road signed Blackwater. Site on right in 200mtrs.* **grid ref:** *SW744468*

A neat and compact park with touring pitches laid out on attractive, well-screened high ground adjacent to the A30 and A39 junction. This pleasant little park is centrally located for touring, and is maintained to a very good standard. There is a large grassed area for children to play on which is away from all tents. 4 acre site. 30 touring pitches. 14 hardstandings. 6 seasonal pitches. Caravan pitches. Motorhome pitches. Tent pitches. 20 statics.

Open: Apr-Oct **Last arrival:** 21.30hrs **Last departure:** 11.30hrs

Pitches: * £13.50-£21 £13.50-£21 £13.50-£21

Leisure:

Facilities:

Services:

Within 3 miles:

Notes: Dogs must be kept on leads.

AA Pubs & Restaurants nearby: Driftwood Spars, ST AGNES, TR5 0RT, 01872 552428

The Miners Arms, MITHIAN, TR5 0QF, 01872 552375

Chiverton Park

►►►► 83%

tel: 01872 560667 & 07789 377169 **East Hill TR4 8HS**
email: chivertonpark@btopenworld.com **web:** www.chivertonpark.co.uk
dir: *Exit A30 at Chiverton rdbt (Starbucks) onto unclassified road signed Blackwater (3rd exit). 1st right, site 300mtrs on right.* **grid ref:** *SW743468*

A small, well-maintained site with some mature hedges dividing pitches, sited midway between Truro and St Agnes. Facilities include a good toilet block and a steam room, sauna and gym. All touring pitches are fully serviced. There is a games room with pool table, and the children's outside play equipment proves popular with families. 4 acre site. 12 touring pitches. 10 hardstandings. Caravan pitches. Motorhome pitches. Tent pitches. 50 statics.

Open: Mar-end Oct **Last arrival:** 19.00hrs **Last departure:** noon

Pitches:

Leisure: Spa

Facilities:

Services:

Within 3 miles:

Notes: No ball games. Dogs must be kept on leads. Drying lines.

AA Pubs & Restaurants nearby: Driftwood Spars, ST AGNES, TR5 0RT, 01872 552428

The Miners Arms, MITHIAN, TR5 0QF, 01872 552375

BLISLAND Map 2 SX17

Places to visit

Lanhydrock, LANHYDROCK, PL30 5AD, 01208 265950 www.nationaltrust.org.uk

Tintagel Old Post Office, TINTAGEL, PL34 0DB, 01840 770024 www.nationaltrust.org.uk/main/w-tintageloldpostoffice

South Penquite Farm

►►► 85%

tel: 01208 850491 **South Penquite PL30 4LH**
email: thefarm@bodminmoor.co.uk
dir: *From Exeter on A30 exit at 1st sign to St Breward on right, (from Bodmin 2nd sign on left). Follow narrow road across Bodmin Moor. Ignore left & right turns until South Penquite Farm Lane on right in 2m.* **grid ref:** *SX108751*

This genuine 'back to nature' site is situated high on Bodmin Moor on a farm committed to organic agriculture. As well as camping there are facilities for adults and children to learn about conservation, organic farming and the local environment, including a fascinating and informative farm trail (pick up a leaflet); there is also a Geocaching trail. Toilet facilities are enhanced by a timber building with quality showers and a good disabled facility. The site has designated areas where fires may be lit. Organic home-reared lamb burgers and sausages are for sale, and one field contains four Mongolian yurts, available for holiday let. 4 acre site. 40 touring pitches. Motorhome pitches. Tent pitches. 4 yurts.

Open: Apr-Oct **Last arrival:** dusk **Last departure:** 14.00hrs

Pitches: * £17

Leisure:

Facilities:

Services:

Within 3 miles:

Notes: No caravans, no pets.

AA Pubs & Restaurants nearby: St Tudy Inn, ST TUDY, PL30 3NN, 01208 850656

The Old Inn & Restaurant, ST BREWARD, PL30 4PP, 01208 850711

BODMIN Map 2 SX06

Places to visit

Restormel Castle, RESTORMEL, PL22 0EE, 01208 872687 www.english-heritage.org.uk/daysout/properties/restormel-castle

Great for kids: Eden Project, ST AUSTELL, PL24 2SG, 01726 811911 www.edenproject.com

Mena Caravan & Camping Park

►►►► 80%

tel: 01208 831845 **PL30 5HW**
email: mena@campsitesincornwall.co.uk **web:** www.campsitesincornwall.co.uk
dir: *Exit A30 onto A389 N signed Lanivet & Wadebridge. In 0.5m 1st right & pass under A30. 1st left signed Lostwithiel & Fowey. In 0.25m right at top of hill. 0.5m then 1st right. Entrance 100yds on right.* **grid ref:** *SW041626*

This grassy site is about four miles from the Eden Project and midway between the north and south Cornish coasts. Set in a secluded, elevated position with high hedges for shelter, it offers plenty of peace and quiet. There is a small coarse fishing lake on site, hardstanding pitches, a shop and a café, with an alfresco decking area, where breakfasts, cream teas and takeaway food can be purchased. The site is on the Saint's Way, and nearby is the neolithic hill fort of Helman Tor, the highest point on Bodmin Moor. There is a fish and chip restaurant in Lanivet (approximately one mile) – from here there is a bus service to Bodmin. 15 acre site. 25 touring pitches. 4 hardstandings. Caravan pitches. Motorhome pitches. Tent pitches. 2 statics.

Open: all year **Last arrival:** 22.00hrs **Last departure:** noon

Pitches:

Leisure:

Facilities:

Services:

Within 3 miles:

AA Pubs & Restaurants nearby: The Borough Arms, DUNMERE, PL31 2RD, 01208 73118

Trehellas House Hotel & Restaurant, BODMIN, PL30 3AD, 01208 72700

BRYHER (ISLES OF SCILLY) Map 2 SV81

Bryher Camp Site

►►► 82%

tel: 01720 422886 **TR23 0PR**
email: relax@bryhercampsite.co.uk
dir: *Accessed by boat from main island of St Mary's.* **grid ref:** *SV880155*

Set on the smallest inhabited Scilly Isle with spectacular scenery and white beaches, this tent-only site is in a sheltered valley surrounded by hedges. Pitches are located in paddocks at the northern end of the island which is only a short walk from the quay. There is a good, modern toilet block, and plenty of peace and quiet. Although located in a very quiet area, the Fraggle Rock Bar and Restaurant and a well-equipped shop are within easy reach. There is easy boat access to all the other islands. 2.25 acre site. 38 touring pitches. Tent pitches.

Open: Apr-Oct

Pitches: * ▲ fr £20.50

Leisure:

Facilities:

Services:

Within 3 miles:

Notes: No cars by tents. No pets.

AA Pubs & Restaurants nearby: Hell Bay, BRYHER, TR23 0PR, 01720 422947

BUDE Map 2 SS20

See also Kilkhampton, Bridgerule (Devon) & Holsworthy (Devon)

PREMIER PARK

Wooda Farm Holiday Park

►►►►► 93%

Best of British · David Bellamy Conservation Award GOLD

tel: 01288 352069 **Poughill EX23 9HJ**
email: enquiries@wooda.co.uk **web:** www.wooda.co.uk
dir: *2m E. From A39 at outskirts of Stratton follow unclassified road signed Poughill.*
grid ref: *SS229080*

An attractive park set on raised ground overlooking Bude Bay, with lovely sea views. The park is divided into paddocks by hedges and mature trees, and offers high quality facilities in extensive colourful gardens. A variety of activities is provided by way of the large sports hall and hard tennis court, and there's a super children's playground. There are holiday static caravans for hire. An interactive information screen in the reception area is for customer use. 50 acre site. 200 touring pitches. 80 hardstandings. 10 seasonal pitches. Caravan pitches. Motorhome pitches. Tent pitches. 55 statics.

Wooda Farm Holiday Park

Open: Apr-Oct (rs Apr-May & mid Sep-Oct shop hours limited, bar & takeaway) **Last arrival:** 20.00hrs **Last departure:** 10.30hrs

Pitches: * £20-£35 £14-£35 ▲ £14-£30

Leisure:

Facilities:

Services:

Within 3 miles:

Notes: Restrictions on certain dog breeds, no skateboards, rollerblades or scooters. Dogs must be kept on leads. Coarse fishing, clay pigeon shooting, woodland walks, farmyard animals.

AA Pubs & Restaurants nearby: Bay View Inn, WIDEMOUTH BAY, EX23 0AW, 01288 361273

See advert on opposite page

See which sites have been awarded Gold Pennants on page 34

Budemeadows Touring Park

►►►► 89%

tel: 01288 361646 **Widemouth Bay EX23 0NA**
email: holiday@budemeadows.com **web:** www.budemeadows.com
dir: *3m S of Bude on A39. Follow signs after turn to Widemouth Bay. Site accessed via layby from A39.* **grid ref:** *SS215012*

This is a very well-kept site of distinction, with good quality facilities, hardstandings and eight fully serviced pitches. Budemeadows is set on a gentle sheltered slope in nine acres of naturally landscaped parkland, surrounded by mature hedges. The internal doors in the facility block have all been painted in pastel colours to resemble beach huts. The site is just one mile from Widemouth Bay, and three miles from the unspoilt resort of Bude. 9 acre site. 145 touring pitches. 34 hardstandings. 4 seasonal pitches. Caravan pitches. Motorhome pitches. Tent pitches.

Budemeadows Touring Park

Open: all year (rs Sep-late May shop, bar & pool closed, takeaway summer only)
Last arrival: 21.00hrs **Last departure:** 11.00hrs

Pitches: * 🚐 £12.50-£30.50 🚌 £12.50-£30.50 ⛺ £12.50-£29.50

Leisure: [symbols]

Facilities: [symbols]

Services: [symbols]

Within 3 miles: [symbols]

Notes: No noise after 23.00hrs, breatheable groundsheets only. Dogs must be kept on leads. Table tennis, giant chess, baby changing facility.

AA Pubs & Restaurants nearby: Bay View Inn, WIDEMOUTH BAY, EX23 0AW, 01288 361273

BUDE *continued*

Pentire Haven Holiday Park

►►►► 89%

tel: 01288 321601 **Stibb Rd, Kilkhampton EX23 9QY**
email: holidays@pentirehaven.co.uk **web:** www.pentirehaven.co.uk
dir: *A39 from Bude towards Bideford, in 3m turn left signed Sandymouth Bay.*
grid ref: *SS246111*

A very open grass site handy for many beautiful beaches, but in particular the surfing beach of Bude only four miles away. The management and enthusiastic staff continue to make a real impression on this improving park. There are excellent toilet facilities in addition to a very good children's playground and a small swimming pool, which is open during the busy season. There is a rally field and holiday static caravans are available for hire or to buy. 23 acre site. 120 touring pitches. 46 hardstandings. 40 seasonal pitches. Caravan pitches. Motorhome pitches. Tent pitches. 18 statics.

Open: all year **Last arrival:** 23.30hrs **Last departure:** 10.30hrs

Pitches: * £9.95-£25 £9.95-£25 £9.95-£25

Leisure:

Facilities:

Services:

Within 3 miles:

Notes: No fires. Dogs must be kept on leads.

AA Pubs & Restaurants nearby: Bay View Inn, WIDEMOUTH BAY, EX23 0AW, 01288 361273

See advert on opposite page

Widemouth Fields Caravan & Camping Park

►►►► 86%

tel: 01288 361351 & 01489 781256 **Park Farm, Poundstock EX23 0NA**
email: enquiries@widemouthbaytouring.co.uk **web:** www.widemouthbaytouring.co.uk
dir: *M5 junct 27 (signed Barnstaple). A361 to rdbt before Barnstaple. Take A39 signed Bideford & Bude. (NB do not exit A39 at Stratton). S for 3m, follow sign just past x-rds to Widemouth Bay. Into layby, entrance on left.* **grid ref:** *SS215010*

In a quiet location with far reaching views over rolling countryside, this site is only one mile from the golden beach at Widemouth Bay, and just three miles from the resort of Bude. The park has a well-stocked shop, many hardstanding pitches and a cosy bar that offers takeaway breakfasts. The toilets are of outstanding quality with many combined fully serviced cubicles. All the buildings resemble log cabins which certainly adds to the appeal of the site. There is a courtesy shuttle bus into Bude and to the Widemouth Bay Holiday Village, where the facilities can be used by the touring campers. 15 acre site. 156 touring pitches. 156 hardstandings. 40 seasonal pitches. Caravan pitches. Motorhome pitches. Tent pitches. 5 statics.

Open: Apr-Sep **Last arrival:** 21.00hrs **Last departure:** noon

Pitches:

Leisure:

Facilities:

Services:

Within 3 miles:

Notes: Entry to site by swipecard only, deposit taken at time of check in. Bus service to beaches & into Bude (Spring BH-Aug only), access to indoor heated pool.

AA Pubs & Restaurants nearby: Bay View Inn, WIDEMOUTH BAY, EX23 0AW, 01288 361273

See advert on opposite page

PITCHES: Caravans Motorhomes Tents Glamping-style accommodation **SERVICES:** Electric hook up Launderette Licensed bar Calor Gas Camping Gaz Toilet fluid Café/Restaurant Fast Food/Takeaway Battery charging Baby care Motorvan service point
ABBREVIATIONS: BH/bank hols – bank holidays Etr – Easter Spring BH – Spring Bank Holiday fr – from hrs – hours m – mile mdnt – midnight rdbt – roundabout rs – restricted service wk – week wknd – weekend x-rds – cross roads No credit or debit cards No dogs Children of all ages accepted

BUDE *continued*

Willow Valley Holiday Park

►►►► 83%

tel: 01288 353104 **Bush EX23 9LB**
email: willowvalley@talk21.com
dir: *On A39, 0.5m N of junct with A3072 at Stratton.* **grid ref:** *SS236078*

A small sheltered park in the Strat Valley with level grassy pitches and a stream running through it. The friendly family owners have improved all areas of this attractive park, including a smart toilet block and an excellent reception/shop. The park has direct access from the A39, and is only two miles from the sandy beaches at Bude. There are four pine lodges for holiday hire. 4 acre site. 41 touring pitches. Caravan pitches. Motorhome pitches. Tent pitches. 4 statics.

Open: Mar-end Oct **Last arrival:** 21.00hrs **Last departure:** 11.00hrs

Pitches: * £13-£18 £13-£18 £13-£18

Leisure:

Facilities:

Services:

Within 3 miles:

Notes: Dogs must be kept on leads.

Upper Lynstone Caravan Park

►►► 87%

tel: 01288 352017 **Lynstone EX23 0LP**
email: reception@upperlynstone.co.uk
dir: *0.75m S of Bude on coastal road to Widemouth Bay.* **grid ref:** *SS205053*

There are extensive views over Bude to be enjoyed from this quiet, sheltered family-run park, a terraced grass site suitable for all units. There's a spotlessly clean and top quality toilet block, plus a children's playground and a reception with a shop that sells basic food supplies and camping spares. Static caravans for holiday hire. A path leads directly to the coastal footpath with its stunning sea views, and the old Bude Canal is just a stroll away. 6 acre site. 65 touring pitches. Caravan pitches. Motorhome pitches. Tent pitches. 41 statics.

Open: Apr-Oct **Last arrival:** 22.00hrs **Last departure:** 10.00hrs

Pitches: * £17.50-£24 £17.50-£24 £15-£22

Leisure:

Facilities:

Services:

Within 3 miles:

Notes: No groups. Dogs must be kept on leads. Baby changing room.

AA Pubs & Restaurants nearby: Bay View Inn, WIDEMOUTH BAY, EX23 0AW, 01288 361273

CAMELFORD Map 2 SX18

Places to visit

Tintagel Castle, TINTAGEL, PL34 0HE, 01840 770328
www.english-heritage.org.uk/daysout/properties/tintagel-castle

Tintagel Old Post Office, TINTAGEL, PL34 0DB, 01840 770024
www.nationaltrust.org.uk/main/w-tintageloldpostoffice

Juliot's Well Holiday Park

►►►► 87%

SILVER

tel: 01840 213302 **PL32 9RF**
email: holidays@juliotswell.com
dir: *From A39 (SW of Camelford) at Valley Truckle follow B3266 & Boscastle signs. 1st left signed Lanteglos, site 300yds on right.* **grid ref:** *SX095829*

Set in the wooded grounds of an old manor house, this quiet site enjoys lovely and extensive views across the countryside. A rustic inn on site occasionally offers entertainment, and there is plenty to do, both on the park and in the vicinity. The superb, fully serviced toilet facilities are very impressive. There are also self-catering pine lodges, static caravans and five cottages for hire. 33 acre site. 39 touring pitches. Caravan pitches. Motorhome pitches. Tent pitches. 82 statics.

Open: all year **Last arrival:** 20.00hrs **Last departure:** 11.00hrs

Pitches:

Leisure:

Facilities:

Services:

Within 3 miles:

Notes: Complimentary use of cots & high chairs.

AA Pubs & Restaurants nearby: The Mill House Inn, TREBARWITH, PL34 0HD, 01840 770200

The Old Inn & Restaurant, ST BREWARD, PL30 4PP, 01208 850711

Lakefield Caravan Park

►►► 80%

tel: 01840 213279 **Lower Pendavey Farm PL32 9TX**
email: lakefieldcaravanpark@btconnect.com
dir: *From A39 in Camelford onto B3266, right at T-junct, site 1.5m on left.*
grid ref: *SX095853*

Set in a rural location, this friendly park is part of a specialist equestrian centre, and offers good quality services. All the facilities are immaculate and spotlessly clean. Riding lessons and hacks are always available, with a BHS qualified instructor. Newquay, Padstow and Bude are all easily accessed from this site. 5 acre site. 40 touring pitches. Caravan pitches. Motorhome pitches. Tent pitches.

Open: Etr or Apr-Sep **Last arrival:** 22.00hrs **Last departure:** 11.00hrs

Pitches:

Facilities:

Services:

Within 3 miles:

Notes: Dogs must be kept on leads. On-site lake.

AA Pubs & Restaurants nearby: The Port William, TREBARWITH, PL34 0HB, 01840 770230

LEISURE: Indoor swimming pool, Outdoor swimming pool, Children's playground, Kid's club, Tennis court, Games room, Separate TV room, golf course, Boats for hire, Cinema, Entertainment, Fishing, Mini golf, Watersports, Gym, Sports field, Spa, Stables
FACILITIES: Bath, Shower, Electric shaver, Hairdryer, Ice Pack Facility, Disabled facilities, Public telephone, Shop on site or within 200yds, Mobile shop (calls at least 5 days a week), BBQ area, Picnic area, Wi-fi, Internet access, Recycling, Tourist info, Dog exercise area

CARLYON BAY Map 2 SX05

Places to visit

Charlestown Shipwreck & Heritage Centre, ST AUSTELL, PL25 3NJ, 01726 69897 www.shipwreckcharlestown.com

The Lost Gardens of Heligan, PENTEWAN, PL26 6EN, 01726 845100 www.heligan.com

Great for kids: Wheal Martyn, ST AUSTELL, PL26 8XG, 01726 850362 www.wheal-martyn.com

Eden Project, ST AUSTELL, PL24 2SG, 01726 811911 www.edenproject.com

PREMIER PARK

Carlyon Bay Caravan & Camping Park

►►►►► 90%

tel: 01726 812735 **Bethesda, Cypress Av PL25 3RE**
email: holidays@carlyonbay.net **web:** www.carlyonbay.net
dir: *Exit A390 W of St Blazey, left onto A3092 for Par, right in 0.5m. Cypress Ave to Carlyon Bay.* **grid ref:** *SX052526*

An attractive, secluded site set amongst a belt of trees with background woodland. The spacious grassy park is beautifully landscaped and offers quality toilet and shower facilities and plenty of on-site attractions, including a well-equipped games room, TV room, café, an inviting swimming pool, and occasional family entertainment. It is less than half a mile from a sandy beach and the Eden Project is only two miles away. 35 acre site. 180 touring pitches. 12 hardstandings. Caravan pitches. Motorhome pitches. Tent pitches.

Carlyon Bay Caravan & Camping Park

Open: Etr-28 Sep (rs Etr-mid May & mid-end Sep swimming pool, takeaway & shop closed) **Last arrival:** 21.00hrs **Last departure:** 11.00hrs

Pitches:

Leisure:

Facilities:

Services:

Within 3 miles:

Notes: No noise after 23.00hrs. Dogs must be kept on leads. Crazy golf. Children's entertainment Jul-Aug only.

AA Pubs & Restaurants nearby: Austell's, ST AUSTELL, PL25 3PH, 01726 813888

The Britannia Inn & Restaurant, PAR, PL24 2SL, 01726 812889

See advert below

CARLYON BAY *continued*

East Crinnis Camping & Caravan Park

►►►► 82%

tel: 01726 813023 & 07435 974961 **Lantyan, East Crinnis PL24 2SQ**
email: info@eastcrinnis.com
dir: *From A390 (Lostwithiel to St Austell), take A3082 signed Fowey at rdbt by Britannia Inn, site on left.* **grid ref:** *SX062528*

A small rural park with spacious pitches set in individual bays about one mile from the beaches at Carlyon Bay, and just two miles from the Eden Project. The friendly owners keep the site very clean and well maintained, and also offer three self-catering holiday lodges, two yurts and one geo dome for hire. It is a short walk to Par where restaurant food can be found. 2 acre site. 38 touring pitches. 9 hardstandings. 18 seasonal pitches. Caravan pitches. Motorhome pitches. Tent pitches. 2 yurts. 1 geo dome

Open: Etr-Oct **Last arrival:** 21.00hrs **Last departure:** 11.00hrs

Pitches: * £11-£23 fr £11 £11-£23

Leisure:

Facilities:

Services:

Within 3 miles:

Notes: No noise after 23.00hrs. Dogs must be kept on leads. Coarse fishing, wildlife & pond area with dog walk.

AA Pubs & Restaurants nearby: The Britannia Inn & Restaurant, PAR, PL24 2SL, 01726 812889

The Rashleigh Inn, POLKERRIS, PL24 2TL, 01726 813991

Austell's, ST AUSTELL, PL25 3PH, 01726 813888

CHACEWATER Map 2 SW74

Places to visit

Royal Cornwall Museum, TRURO, TR1 2SJ, 01872 272205 www.royalcornwallmuseum.org.uk

Trelissick Garden, TRELISSICK GARDEN, TR3 6QL, 01872 862090 www.nationaltrust.org.uk/trelissick

Killiwerris Touring Park

►►►► 81%

tel: 01872 561356 & 07734 053593 **Penstraze TR4 8PF**
email: killiwerris@aol.com
dir: *Take A30 towards Penzance, at Chiverton Cross rdbt take 3rd exit signed St Agnes. At next mini rdbt take Blackwater exit, in 500yds left into Kea Downs Rd, park 1m on right.* **grid ref:** *SW753454*

A small, adults-only, family-run touring park, just five miles from Truro and four miles from the coastal village of St Agnes, making it an ideal base for exploring west Cornwall. The site has a sunny aspect yet is sheltered by mature trees giving it a very private feel. The facilities are of an exceptionally high standard and include a modern and smart amenities block. It is a peaceful spot in which to relax and get away from the crowds. 2.2 acre site. 17 touring pitches. 17 hardstandings. 3 seasonal pitches. Caravan pitches. Motorhome pitches.

Open: all year **Last arrival:** 21.00hrs **Last departure:** 11.00hrs

Pitches: * £20-£24 £20-£24

Facilities:

Services:

Within 3 miles:

Notes: Adults only. Dogs must be kept on leads.

COVERACK Map 2 SW71

Places to visit

Great for kids: Cornish Seal Sanctuary, GWEEK, TR12 6UG, 01326 221361 www.sealsanctuaries.com

The Flambards Theme Park, HELSTON, TR13 0QA, 01326 573404 www.flambards.co.uk

Little Trevothan Caravan & Camping Park

►►► 80%

tel: 01326 280260 **Trevothan TR12 6SD**
email: sales@littletrevothan.co.uk
dir: *A3083 onto B3293 signed Coverack, approx 2m after Goonhilly Earth Station, right at petrol station onto unclassified road. Approx 1m, 3rd left. Site 0.5m on left.*
grid ref: *SW772179*

A secluded site, with excellent facilities, near the unspoilt fishing village of Coverack, with a large recreation area and good play equipment for children. The nearby sandy beach has lots of rock pools for children to play in, and the many walks both from the park and the village offer stunning scenery. 10.5 acre site. 70 touring pitches. 10 hardstandings. 10 seasonal pitches. Caravan pitches. Motorhome pitches. Tent pitches. 22 statics.

Open: Mar-Oct **Last arrival:** 21.00hrs **Last departure:** noon

Pitches:

Leisure:

Facilities:

Services:

Within 3 miles:

Notes: No noise between 22.00hrs-08.30hrs. Dogs must be kept on leads.

CRANTOCK (NEAR NEWQUAY) Map 2 SW76

PREMIER PARK

Trevella Holiday Park

92%

GOLD

tel: 01637 830308 **TR8 5EW**
email: holidays@trevella.co.uk **web:** www.trevella.co.uk
dir: *Between Crantock & A3075.* **grid ref:** *SW801599*

A well-established and very well-run family site, with outstanding floral displays. Set in a rural area close to Newquay, this stunning park boasts three teeming fishing lakes for both the experienced and novice angler, and a superb outdoor swimming pool and paddling area. The spotlessly clean toilet facilities include excellent en suite wet rooms. All areas are neat and clean and the whole park looks stunning. Yurts, eurotents and safari tents are available for hire. 15 acre site. 171 touring pitches. 73 hardstandings. Caravan pitches. Motorhome pitches. Tent pitches. 142 statics. 2 yurts. Safari tents. Eurotents.

Open: Etr-Oct (rs Etr-mid May & mid Sep-Oct pool closed) **Last arrival:** 21.00hrs **Last departure:** 10.00hrs

Pitches: **Leisure:**

Facilities:

Services: **Within 3 miles:**

Notes: Families & couples. Dogs must be kept on leads. Crazy golf, charge for WiFi.

AA Pubs & Restaurants nearby: The Smugglers' Den Inn, CUBERT, TR8 5PY, 01637 830209

The Lewinnick Lodge Bar & Restaurant, NEWQUAY, TR7 1NX, 01637 878117

See advert on page 66

Treago Farm Caravan Site

86%

tel: 01637 830277 **TR8 5QS**
email: info@treagofarm.co.uk
dir: *From A3075 (W of Newquay), turn right for Crantock. Site signed beyond village.*
grid ref: *SW782601*

A grass site in open farmland in a south-facing sheltered valley with a fishing lake. This friendly family park has spotless toilet facilities, which include three excellent heated family rooms, a good shop and bar with takeaway food, and it has direct access to Crantock and Polly Joke beaches, National Trust land and many natural beauty spots. 5 acre site. 90 touring pitches. Caravan pitches. Motorhome pitches. Tent pitches. 10 statics.

Open: mid May-mid Sep **Last arrival:** 22.00hrs **Last departure:** 18.00hrs

Pitches:

Leisure:

Facilities:

Services:

Within 3 miles:

Notes: Dogs must be kept on leads.

AA Pubs & Restaurants nearby: The Smugglers' Den Inn, CUBERT, TR8 5PY, 01637 830209

The Lewinnick Lodge Bar & Restaurant, NEWQUAY, TR7 1NX, 01637 878117

Quarryfield Holiday Park

83%

tel: 01637 872792 & 830338 **TR8 5RJ**
email: quarryfield@crantockcaravans.orangehome.co.uk **web:** www.quarryfield.co.uk
dir: *From A3075 Newquay-Redruth road follow Crantock signs. Site signed.*
grid ref: *SW793608*

This park has a private path down to the dunes and golden sands of Crantock Beach, about 10 minutes away, and it is within easy reach of all that Newquay has to offer, particularly for families. The park has very modern facilities, and provides plenty of amenities including a great swimming pool. 10 acre site. 145 touring pitches. 12 seasonal pitches. Caravan pitches. Motorhome pitches. Tent pitches. 43 statics.

Open: Etr-Oct **Last arrival:** 23.00hrs **Last departure:** 10.00hrs

Pitches: **Leisure:**

Facilities:

CRANTOCK (NEAR NEWQUAY) *continued*

Services: **Within 3 miles:**

Notes: No campfires, quiet after 22.30hrs. Dogs must be kept on leads.

AA Pubs & Restaurants nearby: The Smugglers' Den Inn, CUBERT, TR8 5PY, 01637 830209

The Lewinnick Lodge Bar & Restaurant, NEWQUAY, TR7 1NX, 01637 878117

Crantock Plains Touring Park

►►►81%

DAVID BELLAMY CONSERVATION AWARD GOLD

tel: 01637 830955 & 07837 534964 **TR8 5PH**
email: crantockp@btconnect.com
dir: *Exit Newquay on A3075, 2nd right signed to park & Crantock. Site on left in 0.75m on narrow road.* **grid ref:** *SW805589*

A small rural park with pitches on either side of a narrow lane, surrounded by mature trees for shelter. This spacious, family-run park has good modern toilet facilities and is ideal for campers who appreciate peace and quiet; it is situated approximately 1.2 miles from pretty Crantock, and Newquay is within easy reach. 6 acre site. 60 touring pitches. 20 seasonal pitches. Caravan pitches. Motorhome pitches. Tent pitches.

Open: mid Apr-end Sep **Last arrival:** 22.00hrs **Last departure:** noon

Pitches: **Leisure:** **Facilities:**

Services: **Within 3 miles:**

Notes: No skateboards. Dogs must be kept on leads.

AA Pubs & Restaurants nearby: The Smugglers' Den Inn, CUBERT, TR8 5PY, 01637 830209

The Lewinnick Lodge Bar & Restaurant, NEWQUAY, TR7 1NX, 01637 878117

CUBERT — Map 2 SW75

Places to visit

Trerice, TRERICE, TR8 4PG, 01637 875404 www.nationaltrust.org.uk/trerice/

Great for kids: Dairy Land Farm World, NEWQUAY, TR8 5AA, 01872 510246 www.dairylandfarmworld.com

Cottage Farm Touring Park

►►►83%

tel: 01637 831083 **Treworgans TR8 5HH**
email: info@cottagefarmpark.co.uk
dir: *From A392 towards Newquay, left onto A3075 towards Redruth. In 2m right signed Cubert, right again in 1.5m signed Crantock, left in 0.5m.* **grid ref:** *SW786589*

A small grassy touring park situated in the tiny hamlet of Treworgans, in sheltered open countryside close to a lovely beach at Holywell Bay. This quiet family-run park boasts very good quality facilities including a fenced playground for children, with a climbing frame, swings, slides etc. 2 acre site. 45 touring pitches. 2 hardstandings. Caravan pitches. Motorhome pitches. Tent pitches. 1 static.

Open: Apr-Sep **Last arrival:** 22.30hrs **Last departure:** noon

Pitches: £12-£18 £12-£18 £12-£18

LEISURE: Indoor swimming pool Outdoor swimming pool Children's playground Kid's club Tennis court Games room Separate TV room golf course Boats for hire Cinema Entertainment Fishing Mini golf Watersports Gym Sports field Spa Stables
FACILITIES: Bath Shower Electric shaver Hairdryer Ice Pack Facility Disabled facilities Public telephone Shop on site or within 200yds Mobile shop (calls at least 5 days a week) BBQ area Picnic area Wi-fi Internet access Recycling Tourist info Dog exercise area

Facilities:

Services:

Within 3 miles:

Notes: No noise after 23.00hrs. Dogs must be kept on leads.

AA Pubs & Restaurants nearby: The Smugglers' Den Inn, CUBERT, TR8 5PY, 01637 830209

The Plume of Feathers, MITCHELL, TR8 5AX, 01872 510387

EDGCUMBE — Map 2 SW73

Places to visit

Poldark Mine and Heritage Complex, WENDRON, TR13 0ER, 01326 573173 www.poldark-mine.co.uk

Great for kids: Cornish Seal Sanctuary, GWEEK, TR12 6UG, 01326 221361 www.sealsanctuaries.com

The Flambards Theme Park, HELSTON, TR13 0QA, 01326 573404 www.flambards.co.uk

Retanna Holiday Park

►►► 81%

tel: 01326 340643 **TR13 0EJ**
email: retannaholpark@btconnect.com
dir: *On A394 towards Helston, site signed on right. Site in 100mtrs.* **grid ref:** *SW711327*

A small family-owned and run park in a rural location midway between Falmouth and Helston, and only about eight miles from Redruth. Its well-sheltered grassy pitches make this an ideal location for visiting the lovely beaches and towns nearby. For a fun day out the Flambards Theme Park is only a short drive away, and for sailing enthusiasts, Stithians Lake is on the doorstep. 8 acre site. 24 touring pitches. Caravan pitches. Tent pitches. 23 statics.

Open: Apr-Oct **Last arrival:** 21.00hrs **Last departure:** noon

Pitches: * £16.50-£25.00 £16.50-£25.00

Leisure:

Facilities:

Services:

Within 3 miles:

Notes: No pets, no disposable BBQs, no open fires. Free use of fridge-freezer in laundry room, free air bed inflation, free mobile phone charging.

AA Pubs & Restaurants nearby: Trengilly Wartha Inn, CONSTANTINE, TR11 5RP, 01326 340332

FALMOUTH

Places to visit

Pendennis Castle, FALMOUTH, TR11 4LP, 01326 316594 www.english-heritage.org.uk/daysout/properties/pendennis-castle

Trebah Garden, MAWNAN SMITH, TR11 5JZ, 01326 252200 www.trebah-garden.co.uk

Great for kids: National Maritime Museum Cornwall, FALMOUTH, TR11 3QY, 01326 313388 www.nmmc.co.uk

FALMOUTH — Map 2 SW83

Tregedna Farm Touring Caravan & Tent Park

►►► 80%

tel: 01326 250529 **Maenporth TR11 5HL**
email: enquiries@tregednafarmholidays.co.uk
dir: *Take A39 from Truro to Falmouth. Turn right at Hill Head rdbt. Site 2.5m on right.*
grid ref: *SW785305*

Set in the picturesque Maen Valley, this gently-sloping, south-facing park is part of a 100-acre farm. It is surrounded by beautiful wooded countryside just minutes from the beach, with spacious pitches and well-kept facilities. 12 acre site. 40 touring pitches. 6 hardstandings. Caravan pitches. Motorhome pitches. Tent pitches.

Open: Apr-Sep **Last arrival:** 22.00hrs **Last departure:** 13.00hrs

Pitches:

Leisure:

Facilities:

Services:

Within 3 miles:

Notes: 1 dog only per pitch. Dogs must be kept on leads.

AA Pubs & Restaurants nearby: Trengilly Wartha Inn, CONSTANTINE, TR11 5RP, 01326 340332

Budock Vean - The Hotel on the River, MAWNAN SMITH, TR11 5LG, 01326 252100

Pennance Mill Farm Touring Park

►►► 76%

tel: 01326 317431 **Maenporth TR11 5HJ**
email: jewell5hj@btinternet.com
dir: *From A39 (Truro to Falmouth road) follow brown camping signs towards Maenporth Beach. At Hill Head rdbt take 2nd exit for Maenporth Beach.* **grid ref:** *SW792307*

The safe, sandy bay at Maenporth, just half a mile away, can be accessed via a private woodland walk and cycle ride directly from this park. It is a mainly level, grassy park in a rural location sheltered by mature trees and shrubs and divided into three meadows. It has a modern toilet block. 6 acre site. 75 touring pitches. 12 hardstandings. Caravan pitches. Motorhome pitches. Tent pitches. 4 statics.

Open: Etr-Nov **Last arrival:** 22.00hrs **Last departure:** 10.00hrs

Pitches:

Leisure:

Facilities:

Services:

Within 3 miles:

Notes: No noise after 23.00hrs.

AA Pubs & Restaurants nearby: Trengilly Wartha Inn, CONSTANTINE, TR11 5RP, 01326 340332

Budock Vean - The Hotel on the River, MAWNAN SMITH, TR11 5LG, 01326 252100

GORRAN Map 2 SW94

Places to visit

Caerhays Castle Gardens, GORRAN, PL26 6LY, 01872 501310
www.caerhays.co.uk

The Lost Gardens of Heligan, PENTEWAN, PL26 6EN, 01726 845100
www.heligan.com

Great for kids: Wheal Martyn, ST AUSTELL, PL26 8XG, 01726 850362
www.wheal-martyn.com

Treveor Farm Caravan & Camping Site

►►► 84%

tel: 01726 842387 **PL26 6LW**
email: info@treveorfarm.co.uk **web:** www.treveorfarm.co.uk
dir: *From St Austell bypass left onto B3273 for Mevagissey. On hilltop before descent to village turn right onto unclassified road for Gorran. Right in 5m, site on right.*
grid ref: *SW988418*

A small family-run camping park set on a working farm, with grassy pitches backing onto mature hedging. This quiet site, with good facilities, is close to beaches and offers a large coarse fishing lake. 4 acre site. 47 touring pitches. Caravan pitches. Motorhome pitches. Tent pitches.

Open: Apr-Oct **Last arrival:** 21.00hrs **Last departure:** 11.00hrs

Pitches: * £6-£20 £6-£20 £6-£20

Leisure:

Facilities:

Services:

Within 3 miles:

Notes: Dogs must be kept on leads.

AA Pubs & Restaurants nearby: The Ship Inn, MEVAGISSEY, PL26 6UQ, 01726 843324

The Crown Inn, ST EWE, PL26 6EY, 01726 843322

Treveague Farm Caravan & Camping Site

►►► 82%

tel: 01726 842295 **PL26 6NY**
email: treveague@btconnect.com
dir: *B3273 from St Austell towards Mevagissey, pass Pentewan at top of hill, right signed Gorran. Past Heligan Gardens towards Gorran Churchtown. Follow brown tourist signs from fork in road. (NB roads to site are single lane & very narrow. It is advisable to follow guide directions & not Sat Nav).* **grid ref:** *SX002410*

Spectacular panoramic coastal views can be enjoyed from this rural park, which is set on an organic farm and well equipped with modern facilities. A stone-faced toilet block with a Cornish slate roof is an attractive feature, as is the building that houses the smart reception, café and shop, which sells meat produced on the farm. There is an aviary with exotic birds, and also chinchillas. A footpath leads to the fishing village of Gorran Haven in one direction, and the secluded sandy Vault Beach in the other. The site is close to a bus route. 4 acre site. 46 touring pitches. Caravan pitches. Motorhome pitches. Tent pitches.

Open: Apr-Sep **Last arrival:** 21.00hrs **Last departure:** noon

Pitches: * £10-£28 £10-£28 £8-£24

Leisure:

Facilities:

Services:

Within 3 miles:

Notes: Bird & animal hide.

AA Pubs & Restaurants nearby: The Ship Inn, MEVAGISSEY, PL26 6UQ, 01726 843324

The Crown Inn, ST EWE, PL26 6EY, 01726 843322

GORRAN HAVEN Map 2 SX04

Places to visit

Caerhays Castle Gardens, GORRAN, PL26 6LY, 01872 501310
www.caerhays.co.uk

The Lost Gardens of Heligan, PENTEWAN, PL26 6EN, 01726 845100
www.heligan.com

Great for kids: Wheal Martyn, ST AUSTELL, PL26 8XG, 01726 850362
www.wheal-martyn.com

Trelispen Caravan & Camping Park

► 74%

tel: 01726 843501 **PL26 6NT**
email: trelispen@care4free.net
dir: *B3273 from St Austell towards Mevagissey, on hilltop at x-rds before descent into Mevagissey turn right on unclassified road to Gorran. Through village, 2nd right towards Gorran Haven, site signed on left in 250mtrs. (NB it is advisable to use guide directions not Sat Nav).* **grid ref:** *SX008421*

A quiet rural site set in three paddocks, and sheltered by mature trees and hedges. The simple toilets have plenty of hot water, and there is a small laundry. Sandy beaches, pubs and shops are nearby, and Mevagissey is two miles away. There is a bus stop 100yds from the site with a regular service to Mevagissey and St Austell. 2 acre site. 40 touring pitches. Caravan pitches. Motorhome pitches. Tent pitches.

Open: Etr & Apr-Oct **Last arrival:** 22.00hrs **Last departure:** noon

Pitches:

Leisure:

Facilities:

Services:

Within 3 miles:

Notes: 30-acre nature reserve.

AA Pubs & Restaurants nearby: The Ship Inn, MEVAGISSEY, PL26 6UQ, 01726 843324

The Crown Inn, ST EWE, PL26 6EY, 01726 843322

GWITHIAN Map 2 SW54

Places to visit

East Pool Mine, POOL, TR15 3NP, 01209 315027 www.nationaltrust.org.uk

Gwithian Farm Campsite

92%

tel: 01736 753127 **Gwithian Farm TR27 5BX**
email: camping@gwithianfarm.co.uk
dir: *Exit A30 at Hayle rdbt, 4th exit signed Hayle, 100mtrs. At 1st mini-rdbt right onto B3301 signed Portreath. Site 2m on left on entering village.* **grid ref:** *SW586412*

An unspoilt site located behind the sand dunes of Gwithian's golden beach, which can be reached by footpath directly from the site, making this an ideal location for surfers. The site boasts stunning floral displays, a superb toilet block with excellent facilities, including a bathroom and baby-changing unit, and first-class hardstanding pitches. Each attractive pitch has been screened by hedge planting. 7.5 acre site. 87 touring pitches. 32 hardstandings. Caravan pitches. Motorhome pitches. Tent pitches.

Open: 31 Mar-1 Oct **Last arrival:** 21.00hrs **Last departure:** 17.00hrs

Pitches:

Leisure:

Facilities:

Services:

Within 3 miles:

Notes: No ball games after 21.00hrs, no noise after 22.30hrs, debit cards accepted (no credit cards). Dogs must be kept on leads. Surf board & wet suit hire, table tennis.

AA Pubs & Restaurants nearby: Basset Arms, PORTREATH, TR16 4NG, 01209 842077

Porthminster Beach Restaurant, ST IVES, TR26 2EB, 01736 795352

HAYLE

Places to visit

Tate St Ives, ST IVES, TR26 1TG, 01736 796226 www.tate.org.uk/stives

Barbara Hepworth Museum & Sculpture Garden, ST IVES, TR26 1AD, 01736 796226 www.tate.org.uk/stives

HAYLE Map 2 SW53

St Ives Bay Holiday Park

HOLIDAY CENTRE 91%

tel: 01736 752274 **73 Loggans Rd, Upton Towans TR27 5BH**
email: enquiries@stivesbay.co.uk
dir: *Exit A30 at Hayle then immediate right onto B3301 at mini-rdbts. Site entrance 0.5m on left.* **grid ref:** *SW577398*

An extremely well-maintained holiday park with a relaxed atmosphere situated adjacent to a three mile beach. The various camping fields are set in hollows amongst the sand dunes and are very tastefully laid out, with the high camping fields enjoying stunning views over St Ives Bay. The touring sections are in a number of separate locations around the extensive site. The park is specially geared for families and couples, and as well as the large indoor swimming pool there are two pubs with seasonal entertainment. There are 17 camping pods for hire. 90 acre site. 240 touring pitches. Caravan pitches. Motorhome pitches. Tent pitches. 250 statics. 17 wooden pods.

Open: Etr-30 Oct **Last arrival:** 21.00hrs **Last departure:** 09.00hrs

Pitches: **Leisure:**

Facilities:

Services:

Within 3 miles:

Notes: No pets. Crazy golf, video room.

AA Pubs & Restaurants nearby: The Red River Inn, GWITHIAN, TR27 5BW, 01736 753223

Porthminster Beach Restaurant, ST IVES, TR26 2EB, 01736 795352

See advert on page 72

HAYLE ***continued***

Atlantic Coast Holiday Park

►►►► 82%

GOLD

tel: 01736 752071 **53 Upton Towans, Gwithian TR27 5BL**
email: enquiries@atlanticcoastpark.co.uk
dir: *From A30 into Hayle, turn right at double rdbt. Site 1.5m on left.* **grid ref:** *NW580400*

Fringed by the sand dunes of St Ives Bay and close to the golden sands of Gwithian Beach, the small, friendly touring area continues to improve year on year and offers fully serviced pitches. There's freshly baked bread, a takeaway and a bar next door. This park is ideally situated for visitors to enjoy the natural coastal beauty and attractions of south-west Cornwall. There is superb landscaping and planting, and campers have the use of facilities such as a kettle and microwave. Static caravans are available for holiday hire. 4.5 acre site. 15 touring pitches. 2 hardstandings. 5 seasonal pitches. Caravan pitches. Motorhome pitches. Tent pitches. 50 statics.

Atlantic Coast Holiday Park

Open: Mar-early Jan **Last arrival:** 20.00hrs **Last departure:** 11.00hrs

Pitches: * £25-£35 £25-£35 £25-£35

Facilities:

Services:

Within 3 miles:

Notes: No commercial vehicles, gazebos or day tents. Dogs must be kept on leads.

AA Pubs & Restaurants nearby: The Red River Inn, GWITHIAN, TR27 5BW, 01736 753223

Porthminster Beach Restaurant, ST IVES, TR26 2EB, 01736 795352

See advert on opposite page

HAYLE *continued*

Higher Trevaskis Caravan & Camping Park

►►► 84%

tel: 01209 831736 **Gwinear Rd, Connor Downs TR27 5JQ**
web: www.highertrevaskiscaravanpark.co.uk
dir: *On A30 at Hayle rdbt take exit signed Connor Downs, in 1m right signed Carnhell Green. Site 0.75m just after level crossing.* **grid ref:** *SW611381*

An attractive paddocked and terraced park in a sheltered rural position on a valley side with views towards St Ives. The terrace areas are divided by hedges. This secluded park is personally run by owners who keep it quiet and welcoming. Three unisex showers are a big hit with visitors. Fluent German is spoken. 6.5 acre site. 82 touring pitches. 4 hardstandings. Caravan pitches. Motorhome pitches. Tent pitches.

Open: mid Apr-Sep **Last arrival:** 20.00hrs **Last departure:** 10.30hrs

Pitches: * £14-£22 £14-£22 £14-£22

Leisure:

Facilities:

Services:

Within 3 miles:

Notes: 5mph speed limit on site, balls games permitted on designated field only, max 2 dogs per pitch, no dangerous dogs. Dogs must be kept on leads.

AA Pubs & Restaurants nearby: The Red River Inn, GWITHIAN, TR27 5BW, 01736 753223

Porthminster Beach Restaurant, ST IVES, TR26 2EB, 01736 795352

Treglisson Touring Park

►►► 81%

tel: 01736 753141 **Wheal Alfred Rd TR27 5JT**
email: treglisson@hotmail.co.uk
dir: *From A30 (Camborne towards Penzance) take 4th exit at rdbt signed Hayle. Left at next mini rdbt, follow site signs. Approx 1.5m past golf course, site sign on left.*
grid ref: *SW581367*

A small secluded site in a peaceful wooded meadow and a former apple and pear orchard. This quiet rural site has level grass pitches and a well-planned modern toilet block, and is just two miles from the glorious beach at Hayle with its vast stretch of golden sand. 3 acre site. 26 touring pitches. 6 hardstandings. Caravan pitches. Motorhome pitches. Tent pitches.

Open: Etr-Sep **Last arrival:** 20.00hrs **Last departure:** 11.00hrs

Pitches: * £14.50-£19 £14.50-£19 £11-£19

Leisure:

Facilities: WiFi

Services:

Within 3 miles:

Notes: Max 6 people per pitch. Dogs must be kept on leads.

AA Pubs & Restaurants nearby: The Red River Inn, GWITHIAN, TR27 5BW, 01736 753223

Porthminster Beach Restaurant, ST IVES, TR26 2EB, 01736 795352

Riviere Sands Holiday Park

HOLIDAY HOME PARK 86%

tel: 01736 752132 **Riviere Towans TR27 5AX**
email: rivieresands@haven.com **web:** www.haven.com/rivieresands
dir: *A30 towards Redruth. Follow signs into Hayle, cross double mini rdbt. Turn right opposite petrol station towards Towans and beaches. Park 1m on right.*
grid ref: *SW556386*

Close to St Ives and with direct access to a safe, white-sand beach, Riviere Sands is an exciting holiday park with much to offer families. Children can enjoy the crazy golf, amusements, swimming pool complex, and the beach of course; evening entertainment for adults is extensive and lively. There is a good range of holiday caravans and apartments.

Open: Mar-Oct

Change over day: Mon, Fri, Sat

Arrival and departure times: Please contact the site

Statics: 295 Sleeps 6-8 Bedrms 2-3 Bathrms 1-2 Toilets 1-2 Microwave Freezer TV Sky/FTV Elec inc Gas inc Grass area

Children: Cots Highchair

Leisure: Cycle hire

HELSTON Map 2 SW62

See also Ashton

Places to visit

Great for kids: The Flambards Theme Park, HELSTON, TR13 0QA, 01326 573404 www.flambards.co.uk

Cornish Seal Sanctuary, GWEEK, TR12 6UG, 01326 221361 www.sealsanctuaries.com

Lower Polladras Touring Park

►►►► 87%

GOLD

tel: 01736 762220 **Carleen, Breage TR13 9NX**
email: lowerpolladras@btinternet.com **web:** www.lower-polladras.co.uk
dir: *From Helston take A394 then B3302 (Hayle road) at Ward Garage, 2nd left to Carleen, site 2m on right.* **grid ref:** *SW617308*

An attractive rural park with extensive views of surrounding fields, appealing to families who enjoy the countryside. The planted trees and shrubs are maturing, and help to divide the area into paddocks with spacious grassy pitches. The site has a dish-washing area, a games room, a dog and nature walk, two fully serviced family rooms and WiFi. 4 acre site. 39 touring pitches. 23 hardstandings. Caravan pitches. Motorhome pitches. Tent pitches. 3 statics.

Open: Apr-Jan **Last arrival:** 22.00hrs **Last departure:** noon

Pitches:

Leisure:

Facilities: WiFi

Services:

Within 3 miles:

Notes: Caravan storage area.

AA Pubs & Restaurants nearby: The Ship Inn, PORTHLEVEN, TR13 9JS, 01326 564204

Kota Restaurant with Rooms, PORTHLEVEN, TR13 9JA, 01326 562407

New Yard Restaurant, HELSTON, TR12 6AF, 01326 221595

Skyburriowe Farm

►►► 82%

tel: 01326 221646 **Garras TR12 6LR**
email: bkbenney@hotmail.co.uk **web:** www.skyburriowefarm.co.uk
dir: *From Helston take A3083 to The Lizard. After Culdrose Naval Airbase continue straight on at rdbt, in 1m left at Skyburriowe Ln sign. In 0.5m right at Skyburriowe B&B/Campsite sign. Pass bungalow to farmhouse. Site on left.* **grid ref:** *SW698227*

A leafy no-through road leads to this picturesque farm park in a rural location on the Lizard Peninsula. The toilet block offers excellent quality facilities, and most pitches have electric hook-ups. There are some beautiful coves and beaches nearby, and for a great day out Flambards Theme Park is also close by. Under the supervision of the owner, children are permitted to watch his herd of Friesian cows being milked. 4 acre site. 30 touring pitches. 4 hardstandings. Caravan pitches. Motorhome pitches. Tent pitches.

Open: Apr-Oct **Last arrival:** 22.00hrs **Last departure:** 11.00hrs

Pitches: * £15-£20 £15-£20 £13-£20

Facilities:

Services:

Within 3 miles:

Notes: Quiet after 23.00hrs. Dogs must be kept on leads.

AA Pubs & Restaurants nearby: The Ship Inn, PORTHLEVEN, TR13 9JS, 01326 564204

Kota Restaurant with Rooms, PORTHLEVEN, TR13 9JA, 01326 562407

New Yard Restaurant, HELSTON, TR12 6AF, 01326 221595

HELSTON *continued*

Poldown Caravan Park

►►► 79%

tel: 01326 574560 **Poldown, Carleen TR13 9NN**
email: stay@poldown.co.uk
dir: *From Helston follow Penzance signs for 1m, right onto B3302 to Hayle, 2nd left to Carleen, 0.5m to site.* **grid ref:** *SW629298*

Ideally located for visiting the towns of Helston, Penzance and St Ives, this small, quiet site is set in attractive countryside. The park is sheltered by mature trees and shrubs. All the level grass pitches have electricity, and there are toilet facilities. Two safari tents are available for hire. 2 acre site. 13 touring pitches. 2 hardstandings. Caravan pitches. Motorhome pitches. Tent pitches. 7 statics. 2 safari tents.

Open: Apr-Sep **Last arrival:** 21.00hrs **Last departure:** noon

Pitches: * £16.50-£21.75 £16.50-£21.75 £12.50-£17.75

Leisure: **Facilities:**

Services: **Within 3 miles:**

Notes: Debit cards accepted (no credit cards). Dogs must be kept on leads. Table tennis.

AA Pubs & Restaurants nearby: The Ship Inn, PORTHLEVEN, TR13 9JS, 01326 564204

Kota Restaurant with Rooms, PORTHLEVEN, TR13 9JA, 01326 562407

New Yard Restaurant, HELSTON, TR12 6AF, 01326 221595

HOLYWELL BAY

Places to visit

Trerice, TRERICE, TR8 4PG, 01637 875404 www.nationaltrust.org.uk/trerice/

Blue Reef Aquarium, NEWQUAY, TR7 1DU, 01637 878134 www.bluereefaquarium.co.uk

Great for kids: Newquay Zoo, NEWQUAY, TR7 2LZ, 0844 474 2244 *(Calls cost 7p per minute plus your phone company's access charge)* www.newquayzoo.org.uk

HOLYWELL BAY

Map 2 SW75

PREMIER PARK

Trevornick Holiday Park

►►►►► 86%

tel: 01637 830531 & 832905 **TR8 5PW**
email: info@trevornick.co.uk
dir: *3m from Newquay exit A3075 towards Redruth. Follow Cubert & Holywell Bay signs.* **grid ref:** *SW776586*

A large seaside holiday complex with excellent facilities and amenities. There is plenty of entertainment including a children's club and an evening cabaret, adding up to a full holiday experience for all the family. A sandy beach is just a 15-minute footpath walk away. The park has 55 Euro tents for hire. 20 acre site. 688 touring pitches. 53 hardstandings. 8 seasonal pitches. Caravan pitches. Motorhome pitches. Tent pitches.

Open: Etr & mid May-mid Sep **Last arrival:** 21.00hrs **Last departure:** 10.00hrs

Pitches:

Leisure: Spa

Facilities:

Services:

Within 3 miles:

Notes: Families & couples only. Dogs must be kept on leads. Fishing, golf course, entertainment, fun park, nature trail, segways.

AA Pubs & Restaurants nearby: The Smugglers' Den Inn, CUBERT, TR8 5PY, 01637 830209

LEISURE: Indoor swimming pool Outdoor swimming pool Children's playground Kid's club Tennis court Games room Separate TV room golf course Boats for hire Cinema Entertainment Fishing Mini golf Watersports Gym Sports field Spa Stables
FACILITIES: Bath Shower Electric shaver Hairdryer Ice Pack Facility Disabled facilities Public telephone Shop on site or within 200yds Mobile shop (calls at least 5 days a week) BBQ area Picnic area Wi-fi Internet access Recycling Tourist info Dog exercise area

INDIAN QUEENS
Map 2 SW95

Places to visit

Wheal Martyn, ST AUSTELL, PL26 8XG, 01726 850362 www.wheal-martyn.com

Trerice, TRERICE, TR8 4PG, 01637 875404 www.nationaltrust.org.uk/trerice/

Gnome World Caravan & Camping Park

►►► 80%

tel: 01726 860812 & 860101 **Moorland Rd TR9 6HN**
email: gnomesworld@btconnect.com
dir: *Signed from slip road at A30 & A39 rdbt in village of Indian Queens – site on old A30, now unclassified road.* **grid ref:** *SW890599*

Set in open countryside, this spacious park is set on level grassy land only half a mile from the A30 (Cornwall's main arterial route) and in a central holiday location for touring the county, and accessing the sandy beaches on the north Cornwall coast. Ablaze with summer flowering plants, it offers spotless facilities, an exciting children's playgound, and a new shop that opened in 2015. 4.5 acre site. 50 touring pitches. 25 hardstandings. Caravan pitches. Motorhome pitches. Tent pitches. 60 statics.

Open: Mar-Dec **Last arrival:** 22.00hrs **Last departure:** noon

Pitches: **Leisure:** **Facilities:**

Services: **Within 3 miles:**

Notes: Dogs must be kept on leads. Nature trail.

AA Pubs & Restaurants nearby: The Plume of Feathers, MITCHELL, TR8 5AX, 01872 510387

See advert on opposite page

ISLES OF SCILLY

See St Mary's and Bryher

JACOBSTOW
Map 2 SX19

Places to visit

Launceston Castle, LAUNCESTON, PL15 7DR, 01566 772365 www.english-heritage.org.uk/daysout/properties/launceston-castle

Tamar Otter & Wildlife Centre, LAUNCESTON, PL15 8GW, 01566 785646 www.tamarotters.co.uk

Great for kids: Launceston Steam Railway, LAUNCESTON, PL15 8DA, 01566 775665 www.launcestonsr.co.uk

Edmore Tourist Park

►►► 80%

tel: 01840 230467 **Edgar Rd, Wainhouse Corner EX23 0BJ**
email: enquiries@cornwallvisited.co.uk
dir: *Exit A39 at Wainhouse Corner onto Edgar Rd, site signed on right in 200yds.*
grid ref: *SX184955*

A quiet family-owned site in a rural location with extensive views, set close to the sandy surfing beaches of Bude, and the unspoilt sandy beach and rock pools at Crackington Haven. The friendly owners keep all facilities in a very good condition including the lovely grounds, and the site has hardstanding pitches and gravel access roads. There is an excellent children's play area. The site is handy for bus routes as it is close to the A39. 3 acre site. 24 touring pitches. 5 hardstandings. 2 seasonal pitches. Caravan pitches. Motorhome pitches. Tent pitches. 3 statics.

Open: 1 wk before Etr-Oct **Last arrival:** 21.00hrs **Last departure:** noon

Pitches: * £16-£21.50 £16-£21.50 £10-£21.50

Leisure:

Facilities:

Services:

Within 3 miles:

Notes: Dogs must be kept on leads.

AA Pubs & Restaurants nearby: Bay View Inn, WIDEMOUTH BAY, EX23 0AW, 01288 361273

KENNACK SANDS Map 2 SW71

Places to visit

Cornish Seal Sanctuary, GWEEK, TR12 6UG, 01326 221361
www.sealsanctuaries.com

Great for kids: The Flambards Theme Park, HELSTON, TR13 0QA, 01326 573404
www.flambards.co.uk

Chy Carne Holiday Park

90%

tel: 01326 290200 & 291161 **Kuggar, Ruan Minor TR12 7LX**
email: enquiries@camping-cornwall.com
dir: *From A3083 onto B3293 after Culdrose Naval Air Station. At Goonhilly ESS right onto unclassified road signed Kennack Sands. Left in 3m at junct.* **grid ref:** *SW725164*

This spacious, beautifully maintained, 12-acre park is in a quiet rural location and has excellent family facilities and will boast a stunning new toilet block for the 2016 season. There are extensive sea and coastal views over the sand at Kennack Sands, less than half a mile away. Food is available from the site's takeaway, and the local hostelry is not far away in the village. 12 acre site. 30 touring pitches. 4 hardstandings. Caravan pitches. Motorhome pitches. Tent pitches. 18 statics.

Open: Etr-Oct **Last arrival:** dusk

Pitches:

Leisure:

Facilities:

Services:

Within 3 miles:

AA Pubs & Restaurants nearby: Cadgwith Cove Inn, CADGWITH, TR12 7JX, 01326 290513

Silver Sands Holiday Park

►►► 86%

GOLD

tel: 01326 290631 **Gwendreath TR12 7LZ**
email: info@silversandsholidaypark.co.uk **web:** www.silversandsholidaypark.co.uk
dir: *From Helston follow signs to St Keverne. After BT Goonhilly Station turn right at x-rds signed Kennack Sands, 1.5m, left at Gwendreath sign, site 1m. (NB it is recommended that guide directions are followed not Sat Nav).* **grid ref:** *SW727166*

A small, family-owned park in a remote location, with individually screened pitches providing sheltered suntraps. The owners continue to upgrade the park, improving the landscaping, access roads and toilets; lovely floral displays greet you on arrival. A footpath through the woods leads to the beach and the local pub. One of the nearby beaches is the historic Mullion Cove, and for the children a short car ride will ensure a great day out at the Flambards Theme Park. 9 acre site. 35 touring pitches. Caravan pitches. Motorhome pitches. Tent pitches. 16 statics.

Open: 21 Mar-2 Nov **Last arrival:** 21.00hrs **Last departure:** 11.00hrs

Pitches: * £15-£23 £15-£23 £12.50-£22.50

Leisure: **Facilities:**

Services:

Within 3 miles:

Notes: No noise after 23.00hrs. Dogs must be kept on leads.

AA Pubs & Restaurants nearby: Cadgwith Cove Inn, CADGWITH, TR12 7JX, 01326 290513

KILKHAMPTON Map 2 SS21

Places to visit

Hartland Abbey, BIDEFORD, EX39 6DT, 01237 441234
www.hartlandabbey.com

Great for kids: The Milky Way Adventure Park, CLOVELLY, EX39 5RY, 01237 431255 www.themilkyway.co.uk

Upper Tamar Lake

►► 75%

tel: 01288 321712 **Upper Tamar Lake EX23 9SB**
email: info@swlakestrust.org.uk
dir: *From A39 at Kilkhampton onto B3254, left in 0.5m onto unclassified road, follow signs approx 4m to site.* **grid ref:** *SS288118*

A well-trimmed, slightly sloping site overlooking the lake and surrounding countryside, with several signed walks. The site benefits from the excellent facilities provided for the watersports centre and coarse anglers, with a rescue launch on the lake when the flags are flying. A good family site, with Bude's beaches and surfing waves only eight miles away. 1 acre site. 28 touring pitches. 2 hardstandings. Caravan pitches. Motorhome pitches. Tent pitches. 1 wooden pod.

Open: Apr-Oct **Last departure:** 11.00hrs

Pitches: **Leisure:**

Facilities:

Services:

Within 3 miles:

Notes: No open fires, off-ground BBQs only, no swimming in lake. Dogs must be kept on leads. Canoeing, sailing, windsurfing, cycle hire.

LANDRAKE

Places to visit

Cotehele, CALSTOCK, PL12 6TA, 01579 351346
www.nationaltrust.org.uk/cotehele

Mount Edgcumbe House & Country Park, TORPOINT, PL10 1HZ, 01752 822236
www.mountedgcumbe.gov.uk

Great for kids: Wild Futures' Monkey Sanctuary, LOOE, PL13 1NZ, 0844 2721271 *(Calls cost 7p per minute plus your phone company's access charge)*
www.monkeysanctuary.org

LANDRAKE Map 3 SX36

PREMIER PARK

Dolbeare Park Caravan and Camping

►►►►► 87%

tel: 01752 851332 **St Ive Rd PL12 5AF**
email: reception@dolbeare.co.uk **web:** www.dolbeare.co.uk
dir: *A38 to Landrake, 4m W of Saltash. At footbridge over A38 turn right, follow signs to site (0.75m from A38).* **grid ref:** *SX363616*

Set in meadowland close to the A38 and the Devon/Cornwall border, this attractive touring park is run by innovative, forward-thinking owners who have adopted a very 'green' approach to running the park. The smart toilet block is very eco-friendly – electronic sensor showers, an on-demand boiler system, flow control valves on the taps, and low-energy lighting, as well as an impressive family room. The park is extremely well presented, with excellent hardstanding pitches, a good tenting field that offers spacious pitches, and good provision for children with a separate ball games paddock and nature trail. Expect high levels of customer care and cleanliness. The on-site shop sells fresh bread and local produce. One pre-erected, fully equipped Eurotent is available for hire. 9 acre site. 60 touring pitches. 54 hardstandings. 12 seasonal pitches. Caravan pitches. Motorhome pitches. Tent pitches. 1 Eurotent.

Dolbeare Park Caravan and Camping

Open: all year **Last arrival:** 18.00hrs **Last departure:** noon

Pitches:

Leisure:

Facilities:

Services:

Within 3 miles:

Notes: No cycling, no kite flying, late arrival fee payable after 18.00hrs. Dogs must be kept on leads. Off-licence, free use of fridge & freezer.

AA Pubs & Restaurants nearby: The Crooked Inn, SALTASH, PL12 4RZ, 01752 848177

See advert below

LEEDSTOWN (NEAR HAYLE) — Map 2 SW63

Places to visit

East Pool Mine, POOL, TR15 3NP, 01209 315027 www.nationaltrust.org.uk

Godolphin House, GODOLPHIN CROSS, TR13 9RE, 01736 763194 www.nationaltrust.org.uk/godolphin

PREMIER PARK

Calloose Caravan & Camping Park

►►►►► 85%

tel: 01736 850431 & 0800 328 7589 **TR27 5ET**
email: calloose@hotmail.com
dir: *From Hayle take B3302 to Leedstown, turn left opposite village hall before entering village. Site 0.5m on left at bottom of hill.* **grid ref:** *SW597352*

A comprehensively equipped leisure park in a remote rural setting in a small river valley. This very good park is busy and bustling, and offers bright, clean toilet facilities, an excellent games room, an inviting pool, a good children's play area, and log cabins and static caravans for holiday hire. 12.5 acre site. 109 touring pitches. 29 hardstandings. Caravan pitches. Motorhome pitches. Tent pitches. 25 statics.

Open: all year **Last arrival:** 22.00hrs **Last departure:** 11.00hrs

Pitches:

Leisure:

Facilities:

Services:

Within 3 miles:

Notes: No noise after mdnt, no pets in statics or log cabins. Crazy golf, skittle alley.

AA Pubs & Restaurants nearby: Mount Haven Hotel & Restaurant, MARAZION, TR17 0DQ, 01736 710249

LISKEARD — Map 2 SX26

Luxury Cornish Yurts

NEW ►►►

tel: 01579 343896 **Little Fursdon Farm, Merrymeet PL14 5AG**
email: fearfursdon@hotmail.com
dir: *From Liskeard take B3254 towards Pensilva. In approx 3m turn right for site.*
grid ref: *SX279675*

Luxury Cornish Yurts is located on a small farm on the edge of Bodmin Moor, not far from Liskeard, and consists of three yurts set in a large field with shrubs, trees and well-cut grass. Each yurt has its own decking area with table and chairs. Inside, there is a king-size bed and two futons, excellent storage space and a wood-burning stove for chilly nights. The separate Cowshed Kitchen makes a great meeting place and has a fully-equipped kitchen area for each group of guests, plus three toilet and shower rooms. A washing machine, drier, toys and games can be found here too. The site also has a hot tub, fire pit and barbecue for guests' use. 2 acre site. 3 yurts.

Open: Apr-mid Sep **Last arrival:** mdnt **Last departure:** 10.00hrs

Pitches: £90-£135

LOOE — Map 2 SX25

Places to visit

Antony House, TORPOINT, PL11 2QA, 01752 812191 www.nationaltrust.org.uk/antony

Mount Edgcumbe House & Country Park, TORPOINT, PL10 1HZ, 01752 822236 www.mountedgcumbe.gov.uk

Great for kids: Wild Futures' Monkey Sanctuary, LOOE, PL13 1NZ, 0844 2721271 *(Calls cost 7p per minute plus your phone company's access charge)* www.monkeysanctuary.org

Tencreek Holiday Park

HOLIDAY CENTRE 82%

tel: 01503 262447 **Polperro Rd PL13 2JR**
email: reception@tencreek.co.uk **web:** www.dolphinholidays.co.uk
dir: *Take A387, 1.25m from Looe. Site on left.* **grid ref:** *SX233525*

Occupying a lovely position with extensive countryside and sea views, this holiday centre is in a rural spot but close to Looe and Polperro. There is a full family entertainment programme, with indoor and outdoor swimming pools, an adventure playground and an exciting children's club. The superb amenities blocks include several private family shower rooms with toilet and washbasin. 24 acre site. 254 touring pitches. 12 hardstandings. 120 seasonal pitches. Caravan pitches. Motorhome pitches. Tent pitches. 101 statics.

Open: all year **Last arrival:** 22.00hrs **Last departure:** 10.00hrs

Pitches: * £13.25-£22 £13.25-£22 £5.25-£11

Leisure:

Facilities:

Services:

Within 3 miles:

Notes: Families & couples only. Dogs must be kept on leads. Multi-sports pitch.

AA Pubs & Restaurants nearby: Trelaske Hotel & Restaurant, LOOE, PL13 2JS, 01503 262159

See advert below

Looe Country Park

►►►► 85%

tel: 01503 240265 **Bucklawren Rd, St Martin PL13 1QS**
email: info@looecountrypark.co.uk
dir: *Follow A38 to Trerulefoot rdbt, turn left at A374 signed Looe & Torpoint, then A387 towards Looe. Through Hessenford & onto Widegates, then stay left onto the B3253 turning left for No Mans Land after 1m. At the top of lane turn left into Bucklawren Rd. Site entrance on right.* **grid ref:** *SX283557*

A very neat and well-kept small grassy site on high ground above Looe in a peaceful rural setting. Friendly and enthusiastic owners continue to invest in the park. The toilet facilities have upmarket fittings (note the infra-red operated taps and under floor heating). A bus stops at the bottom of the lane, but you must flag down the driver. A coastal walk runs by the site, and it is a 20-minute walk to the beach at Looe. 3.3 acre site. 31 touring pitches. 19 hardstandings. Caravan pitches. Motorhome pitches. Tent pitches. 5 statics. 2 wooden pods.

Open: all year **Last arrival:** 22.00hrs **Last departure:** 11.00hrs

Pitches:

Leisure:

Facilities:

Services:

Within 3 miles:

Notes: Dogs must be kept on leads.

AA Pubs & Restaurants nearby: Trelaske Hotel & Restaurant, LOOE, PL13 2JS, 01503 262159

Camping Caradon Touring Park

►►►► 84%

tel: 01503 272388 **Trelawne PL13 2NA**
email: enquiries@campingcaradon.co.uk
dir: *Site signed from junct of A387 & B3359, between Looe & Polperro. Take B3359 towards Pelynt then 1st right. 250mtr on the left.* **grid ref:** *SX218539*

Set in a quiet rural location between the popular coastal resorts of Looe and Polperro, this family-run and developing eco-friendly park is just one and half miles from the beach at Talland Bay. The site caters for both families and couples. The owners take great pride in the site and offer some quality facilities and service to their campers throughout their stay; their constant aim is to provide a carefree and relaxing holiday. The local bus stops inside the park entrance. 3.5 acre site. 75 touring pitches. 23 hardstandings. Caravan pitches. Motorhome pitches. Tent pitches.

Open: all year (rs Nov-Mar prior booking only) **Last arrival:** 21.00hrs **Last departure:** 11.00hrs

Pitches:

Leisure:

Facilities:

Services:

Within 3 miles:

Notes: Quiet from 23.00hrs-07.00hrs & barrier not operational. Dogs must be kept on leads. Family room with TV, undercover washing-up area, RCD lead hire, rallies welcome.

AA Pubs & Restaurants nearby: The Ship Inn, LOOE, PL13 1AD, 01503 263124

Barclay House, LOOE, PL13 1LP, 01503 262929

PITCHES: Caravans Motorhomes Tents Glamping-style accommodation **SERVICES:** Electric hook up Launderette Licensed bar Calor Gas Camping Gaz Toilet fluid Café/Restaurant Fast Food/Takeaway Battery charging Baby care Motorvan service point
ABBREVIATIONS: BH/bank hols – bank holidays Etr – Easter Spring BH – Spring Bank Holiday fr – from hrs – hours m – mile mdnt – midnight rdbt – roundabout rs – restricted service wk – week wknd – weekend x-rds – cross roads No credit or debit cards No dogs Children of all ages accepted

LOOE *continued*

Tregoad Park

►►►► 84%

tel: 01503 262718 **St Martin PL13 1PB**
email: info@tregoadpark.co.uk
dir: *Signed with direct access from B3253, or from E on A387 follow B3253 for 1.75m towards Looe. Site on left.* **grid ref:** *SX272560*

Investment continues at this smart, terraced park with extensive sea and rural views, about a mile and a half from Looe. All pitches are level. The facilities are well maintained and spotlessly clean, and there is a swimming pool with adjacent jacuzzi and sun patio, and a licensed bar where bar meals are served in the conservatory. The site has fishing lakes stocked with carp, tench and roach. There is a bus stop at the bottom of the drive for the Plymouth and Truro routes. Static caravans, holiday cottages and two camping pods are available for holiday hire. 55 acre site. 200 touring pitches. 60 hardstandings. Caravan pitches. Motorhome pitches. Tent pitches. 7 statics. 2 wooden pods.

Open: all year (rs Low season bistro closed) **Last arrival:** 20.00hrs
Last departure: 11.00hrs

Pitches: £21-£38 £21-£38 £9-£35

Leisure:

Facilities:

Services:

Within 3 miles:

Notes: Dogs must be kept on leads. Crazy golf, ball sports area.

AA Pubs & Restaurants nearby: Trelaske Hotel & Restaurant, LOOE, PL13 2JS, 01503 262159

Trelay Farmpark

►►► 82%

tel: 01503 220900 **Pelynt PL13 2JX**
email: stay@trelay.co.uk
dir: *From A390 at East Taphouse, take B3359 S towards Looe. After Pelynt, site 0.5m on left. (NB due to single track roads it is advisable to follow guide directions not Sat Nav).*
grid ref: *SX210544*

A small site with a friendly atmosphere set in a pretty rural area with extensive views. The good-size grass pitches are on slightly-sloping ground, and the toilets are immaculately kept, as is the excellent washing-up room. Looe and Polperro are just three miles away. 6.5 acre site. 75 touring pitches. 75 hardstandings. 7 seasonal pitches. Caravan pitches. Motorhome pitches. Tent pitches. 60 statics.

Open: Dec-Oct **Last arrival:** 21.00hrs **Last departure:** 11.00hrs

Pitches:

Leisure:

Facilities:

Services:

Within 3 miles:

Notes: No skateboards, ball games or kites. Dogs must be kept on leads. Fridge & freezer.

AA Pubs & Restaurants nearby: The Ship Inn, LOOE, PL13 1AD, 01503 263124

Barclay House, LOOE, PL13 1LP, 01503 262929

LOSTWITHIEL Map 2 SX15

Places to visit

Restormel Castle, RESTORMEL, PL22 0EE, 01208 872687

www.english-heritage.org.uk/daysout/properties/restormel-castle

Lanhydrock, LANHYDROCK, PL30 5AD, 01208 265950 www.nationaltrust.org.uk

Great for kids: Eden Project, ST AUSTELL, PL24 2SG, 01726 811911 www.edenproject.com

PREMIER PARK

Eden Valley Holiday Park

►►►►► 84%

GOLD

tel: 01208 872277 **PL30 5BU**
email: enquiries@edenvalleyholidaypark.co.uk
dir: *1.5m SW of Lostwithiel on A390 turn right at brown/white sign in 400mtrs. (NB it is advisable to follow guide directions not Sat Nav).* **grid ref:** *SX083593*

A grassy park set in attractive paddocks with mature trees. A gradual upgrading of facilities continues, and both buildings and grounds are carefully maintained and contain an impressive children's play area. This park is ideally located for visiting the Eden Project, the nearby golden beaches and sailing at Fowey. There are also two self-catering lodges. 12 acre site. 56 touring pitches. 40 hardstandings. 20 seasonal pitches. Caravan pitches. Motorhome pitches. Tent pitches. 38 statics.

Open: Etr or Apr-Oct **Last arrival:** 22.00hrs **Last departure:** 11.30hrs

Pitches: £14-£18 £14-£18 £14-£18

Leisure:

Facilities:

Services:

Within 3 miles:

Notes: No large dogs. Dogs must be kept on leads. Table football, pool, table tennis, football, environmental room.

AA Pubs & Restaurants nearby: The Crown Inn, LANLIVERY, PL30 5BT, 01208 872707

LUXULYAN

Places to visit

Restormel Castle, RESTORMEL, PL22 0EE, 01208 872687
www.english-heritage.org.uk/daysout/properties/restormel-castle

Eden Project, ST AUSTELL, PL24 2SG, 01726 811911 www.edenproject.com

Great for kids: Wheal Martyn, ST AUSTELL, PL26 8XG, 01726 850362 www.wheal-martyn.com

LUXULYAN Map 2 SX05

Croft Farm Holiday Park

►►► 78%

tel: 01726 850228 **PL30 5EQ**
email: enquiries@croftfarm.co.uk
dir: *Exit A30 at Bodmin onto A391 towards St Austell. In 7m left at double rdbt onto unclassified road towards Luxulyan/Eden Project, continue to rdbt at Eden, left signed Luxulyan. Site 1m on left. (NB do not approach any other way as roads are very narrow).* **grid ref:** *SX044568*

A peaceful, picturesque setting at the edge of a wooded valley, and only one mile from The Eden Project. Facilities include a well-maintained toilet block, a well-equipped dishwashing area, replete with freezer and microwave, and a revamped children's play area reached via an attractive woodland trail. There is a good bus service to St Austell and Luxulyan (the bus stop is at the site's entrance) and trains run to Newquay. 10.5 acre site. 22 touring pitches. 18 hardstandings. 10 seasonal pitches. Caravan pitches. Motorhome pitches. Tent pitches. 63 statics.

Open: 21 Mar-21 Jan **Last arrival:** 18.00hrs **Last departure:** 11.00hrs

Pitches: **Leisure:** **Facilities:**

Services: **Within 3 miles:**

Notes: No skateboarding, ball games only in playing field, quiet between 23.00hrs-07.00hrs. Dogs must be kept on leads. Woodland walk, information room.

AA Pubs & Restaurants nearby: The Crown Inn, LANLIVERY, PL30 5BT, 01208 872707

MARAZION Map 2 SW53

See also St Hilary

Places to visit

St Michael's Mount, MARAZION, TR17 0HT, 01736 710507
www.stmichaelsmount.co.uk

Trengwainton Garden, PENZANCE, TR20 8RZ, 01736 363148
www.nationaltrust.org.uk/trengwainton

Wheal Rodney Holiday Park

►►► 82%

tel: 01736 710605 **Gwallon Ln TR17 0HL**
email: reception@whealrodney.co.uk **web:** www.whealrodney.co.uk
dir: *Exit A30 at Crowlas, signed Rospeath. Site 1.5m on right. From Marazion centre turn opposite Fire Engine Inn, site 500mtrs on left.* **grid ref:** *SW525315*

Set in a quiet rural location surrounded by farmland, with level grass pitches and well-kept facilities. Within half a mile are the beach at Marazion and the causeway or ferry to St Michael's Mount. A cycle route is within 400 yards; Penzance is only a short car or cycle ride away. 2.5 acre site. 30 touring pitches. Caravan pitches. Motorhome pitches. Tent pitches.

Open: Etr-Oct **Last arrival:** 20.00hrs **Last departure:** 11.00hrs

Pitches: **Leisure:** **Facilities:**

Services: **Within 3 miles:**

Notes: Quiet after 22.00hrs. Dogs must be kept on leads.

AA Pubs & Restaurants nearby: The Victoria Inn, PERRANUTHNOE, TR20 9NP, 01736 710309

Mount Haven Hotel & Restaurant, MARAZION, TR17 0DQ, 01736 710249

MAWGAN PORTH Map 2 SW86

Sun Haven Valley Country Holiday Park

►►►► 84%

SILVER

tel: 01637 860373 & 0800 634 6744 **TR8 4BQ**
email: sunhaven@sunhavenvalley.com
dir: *Exit A30 at Highgate Hill junct for Newquay; follow signs for airport. At T-junct turn right. At beach level in Mawgan Porth take only road inland, then 0.25m. Site 0.5m beyond 'S' bend.* **grid ref:** *SW861669*

An attractive site with level pitches on the side of a river valley; being just off the B3276 this makes an ideal base for touring the Padstow and Newquay areas. The very high quality facilities include a TV lounge and a games room in a Swedish-style chalet, and a well-kept adventure playground. Trees and hedges fringe the park, and the ground is well drained. 5 acre site. 109 touring pitches. 11 hardstandings. Caravan pitches. Motorhome pitches. Tent pitches. 38 statics.

Open: Apr-Oct **Last arrival:** 22.00hrs **Last departure:** 10.30hrs

Pitches: * £19-£36.50 £19-£36.50 £14.50-£36.50

Leisure: **Facilities:**

Services: **Within 3 miles:**

Notes: Families & couples only, no noise after 22.30hrs. Dogs must be kept on leads. Microwave available, pizza ovens.

AA Pubs & Restaurants nearby: The Falcon Inn, ST MAWGAN, TR8 4EP, 01637 860225

The Scarlet Hotel, MAWGAN PORTH, TR8 4DQ, 01637 861800

See advert on page 84

MAWGAN PORTH *continued*

Trevarrian Holiday Park

►►► 83%

tel: 01637 860381 & 0845 225 5910 *(Calls cost 7p per minute plus your phone company's access charge)* **TR8 4AQ**
email: holiday@trevarrian.co.uk
dir: *From A39 at St Columb rdbt turn right onto A3059 towards Newquay. Fork right in approx 2m for St Mawgan onto B3276. Turn right, site on left.* **grid ref:** *SW853661*

A well-established and well-run holiday park overlooking Mawgan Porth beach. This park has a wide range of attractions including a free entertainment programme in peak season and a 10-pin bowling alley with licensed bar. It is only a short drive to Newquay and approximately 20 minutes to Padstow. 7 acre site. 185 touring pitches. 10 hardstandings. Caravan pitches. Motorhome pitches. Tent pitches.

Open: all year **Last arrival:** 22.00hrs **Last departure:** 11.00hrs

Pitches:

Leisure:

Facilities:

Services:

Within 3 miles:

Notes: No noise after mdnt. Dogs must be kept on leads. Crazy golf.

AA Pubs & Restaurants nearby: The Falcon Inn, ST MAWGAN, TR8 4EP, 01637 860225

MEVAGISSEY

Map 2 SX04

See also Gorran & Pentewan

PREMIER PARK

Seaview International Holiday Park

►►►►► 93%

tel: 01726 843425 **Boswinger PL26 6LL**
email: seaview@swholidayparks.co.uk **web:** www.seaviewinternational.com
dir: *From St Austell take B3273 signed Mevagissey. Turn right before entering village. Follow brown tourist signs to site. (NB very narrow lanes to this site; it is advisable to follow guide directions not Sat Nav).* **grid ref:** *SW990412*

An attractive holiday park set in a beautiful environment overlooking Veryan Bay, with colourful landscaping, including attractive flowers and shrubs. It continues to offer an outstanding holiday experience, with its luxury family pitches, super toilet facilities, takeaway, shop and an alfresco eating area complete with a TV screen. The beach is just half a mile away. There is also an 'off the lead' dog walk, and a 'ring and ride' bus service to Truro, St Austell and Plymouth stops at the park gate. Static caravans are available for holiday hire. 28 acre site. 201 touring pitches. 29 hardstandings. 15 seasonal pitches. Caravan pitches. Motorhome pitches. Tent pitches. 39 statics.

Seaview International Holiday Park

Open: Mar-end Sep (rs mid Sep-end May swimming pool closed) **Last arrival:** 20.00hrs **Last departure:** 10.00hrs

Pitches: * £12-£53 £12-£53 £12-£53

Leisure:

Facilities:

Services:

Within 3 miles:

Notes: Restrictions on certain dog breeds. Dogs must be kept on leads. Crazy golf, volleyball, badminton, scuba diving, boules, tennis.

AA Pubs & Restaurants nearby: The Ship Inn, MEVAGISSEY, PL26 6UQ, 01726 843324

See advert below

MULLION — Map 2 SW61

Places to visit

Great for kids: Cornish Seal Sanctuary, GWEEK, TR12 6UG, 01326 221361 www.sealsanctuaries.com

The Flambards Theme Park, HELSTON, TR13 0QA, 01326 573404 www.flambards.co.uk

Franchis Holiday Park

►►►78%

tel: 01326 240301 **Cury Cross Lanes TR12 7AZ**
email: enquiries@franchis.co.uk **web:** www.franchis.co.uk
dir: *Exit A3083 on left 0.5m past Wheel Inn PH, between Helston & The Lizard.*
grid ref: *SW698203*

A mainly grassy site surrounded by hedges and trees, located on Goonhilly Downs and in an ideal position for exploring the Lizard Peninsula. The site is divided into

continued

NEWQUAY *continued*

Trencreek Holiday Park

►►►► 87%

tel: 01637 874210 **Hillcrest, Higher Trencreek TR8 4NS**
email: trencreek@btconnect.com
dir: *A392 to Quintrell Downs, right towards Newquay, left at 2 mini-rdbts into Trevenson Rd to site.* **grid ref:** *SW828609*

An attractively landscaped park in the village of Trencreek, with modern toilet facilities of a very high standard. Two well-stocked fishing lakes, and evening entertainment in the licensed clubhouse, are extra draws. Located about two miles from Newquay with its beaches and surfing opportunities. 10 acre site. 194 touring pitches. 8 hardstandings. Caravan pitches. Motorhome pitches. Tent pitches. 6 statics.

Open: Spring BH-mid Sep **Last arrival:** 22.00hrs **Last departure:** noon

Pitches: * £11.90-£19.50 £11.90-£19.50 £11.90-£19.50

Leisure:

Facilities:

Services:

Within 3 miles:

Notes: Families & couples only.

AA Pubs & Restaurants nearby: The Lewinnick Lodge Bar & Restaurant, NEWQUAY, TR7 1NX, 01637 878117

Porth Beach Holiday Park

BRONZE

►►►► 82%

tel: 01637 876531 **Porth TR7 3NH**
email: info@porthbeach.co.uk **web:** www.porthbeach.co.uk
dir: *From Newquay take A3058 towards St Columb Major. At rdbt left onto B3276 signed Padstow. Site on right.* **grid ref:** *SW834629*

This attractive, popular park offers level, grassy pitches in neat and tidy surroundings. It is a well-run site set in meadowland in a glorious location adjacent to excellent sands of Porth Beach. The site offers two fully-equipped camping pods positioned on a raised terrace. 6 acre site. 185 touring pitches. 19 hardstandings. Caravan pitches. Motorhome pitches. Tent pitches. 30 statics. 2 wooden pods.

Porth Beach Holiday Park

Open: Mar-Nov **Last arrival:** 18.00hrs **Last departure:** 10.00hrs

Pitches: * £16-£34 £16-£34 £13-£38

Facilities: **Services:**

Within 3 miles:

Notes: Families & couples only. Dogs must be kept on leads.

AA Pubs & Restaurants nearby: The Lewinnick Lodge Bar & Restaurant, NEWQUAY, TR7 1NX, 01637 878117

See advert on page 92

Trethiggey Holiday Park

GOLD

►►►► 82%

tel: 01637 877672 **Quintrell Downs TR8 4QR**
email: enquiries@trethiggey.co.uk **web:** www.trethiggey.co.uk
dir: *A30 onto A392 signed Newquay at Quintrell Downs rdbt, left onto A3058, pass Newquay Pearl centre. Site 0.5m on left.* **grid ref:** *SW846596*

A family-owned park in a rural setting that is ideal for touring this part of Cornwall. It is pleasantly divided into paddocks with maturing trees and shrubs, and offers coarse fishing and tackle hire. This site has a car park for campers as the camping fields are set in a car-free zone for children's safety. 15 acre site. 200 touring pitches. 35 hardstandings. 12 seasonal pitches. Caravan pitches. Motorhome pitches. Tent pitches. 12 statics.

Trethiggey Holiday Park

Open: Mar-Dec **Last arrival:** 22.00hrs **Last departure:** 10.30hrs

Pitches: * £10.20-£17.10 £10.20-£17.10 £10.20-£17.10

Leisure:

Facilities:

Services:

Within 3 miles:

Notes: No noise after mdnt. Dogs must be kept on leads. Off-licence, recreation field.

AA Pubs & Restaurants nearby: The Lewinnick Lodge Bar & Restaurant, NEWQUAY, TR7 1NX, 01637 878117

See advert below

Trenance Holiday Park

►►►► 81%

tel: 01637 873447 **Edgcumbe Av TR7 2JY**
email: enquiries@trenanceholidaypark.co.uk
dir: *Exit A3075 near viaduct. Site by boating lake rdbt.* **grid ref:** *SW818612*

A mainly static park popular with tenters, close to Newquay's vibrant nightlife, and with a newly refurbished café serving excellent breakfasts and takeaways. Set on high ground in an urban area of town, with cheerful owners and clean facilities; a new motorhome service point and an additional games room were added for the 2015 season. The local bus stops at the site entrance. 12 acre site. 50 touring pitches. Caravan pitches. Motorhome pitches. Tent pitches. 190 statics.

Open: 21 Apr-22 Sep **Last arrival:** 22.00hrs **Last departure:** 10.00hrs

Pitches: * £16-£19 £16-£19 £16-£19

Leisure:

Facilities:

Services:

Within 3 miles:

Notes: No pets.

AA Pubs & Restaurants nearby: The Lewinnick Lodge Bar & Restaurant, NEWQUAY, TR7 1NX, 01637 878117

NEWQUAY *continued*

Trebellan Park

►►► 84%

tel: 01637 830522 **Cubert TR8 5PY**
email: enquiries@trebellan.co.uk
dir: *S of Newquay from A392 onto A3075 towards Rejerrah. In approx. 4m, turn right signed Cubert. Left in 0.75m onto unclassified road.* **grid ref:** *SW790571*

A terraced grassy rural park within a picturesque valley with views of Cubert Common, and adjacent to the Smuggler's Den, a 16th-century thatched inn. This park has a very inviting swimming pool and three well-stocked coarse fishing lakes. 8 acre site. 150 touring pitches. Caravan pitches. Motorhome pitches. Tent pitches. 7 statics.

Open: May-Oct **Last arrival:** 21.00hrs **Last departure:** 10.00hrs

Pitches: * £20-£26 £20-£26 £15-£21

Leisure:

Facilities:

Services:

Within 3 miles:

Notes: Families & couples only. Dogs must be kept on leads.

AA Pubs & Restaurants nearby: The Smugglers' Den Inn, CUBERT, TR8 5PY, 01637 830209

The Lewinnick Lodge Bar & Restaurant, NEWQUAY, TR7 1NX, 01637 878117

Riverside Holiday Park

►►► 80%

tel: 01637 873617 **Gwills Ln TR8 4PE**
email: info@riversideholidaypark.co.uk **web:** www.riversideholidaypark.co.uk
dir: *A30 onto A392 signed Newquay. At Quintrell Downs cross rdbt signed Lane. 2nd left in 0.5m onto unclassified road signed Gwills. Site in 400yds.* **grid ref:** *SW829592*

A sheltered valley beside a river in a quiet location is the idyllic setting for this lightly wooded park that caters for families and couples only; the site is well placed for exploring Newquay and Padstow. There is a lovely swimming pool. The site is close to the wide variety of attractions offered by this major resort. Self-catering lodges, cabins and static vans are for hire. 11 acre site. 65 touring pitches. Caravan pitches. Motorhome pitches. Tent pitches. 65 statics.

Open: Mar-Oct **Last arrival:** 22.00hrs **Last departure:** 10.00hrs

Pitches:

Leisure:

Facilities:

Services:

Within 3 miles:

Notes: Families & couples only. Dogs must be kept on leads.

AA Pubs & Restaurants nearby: The Lewinnick Lodge Bar & Restaurant, NEWQUAY, TR7 1NX, 01637 878117

PADSTOW — Map 2 SW97

See also Rumford

Places to visit

Prideaux Place, PADSTOW, PL28 8RP, 01841 532411 www.prideauxplace.co.uk

Great for kids: Devon's Crealy Great Adventure Park, CLYST ST MARY, EX5 1DR, 01395 233200 www.crealy.co.uk

PREMIER PARK

Padstow Touring Park

97%

DAVID BELLAMY CONSERVATION AWARD GOLD

tel: 01841 532061 **PL28 8LE**
email: bookings@padstowtouringpark.co.uk
dir: *1m S of Padstow, on E side of A389 Padstow to Wadebridge rd.*
grid ref: *SW913738*

Improvements continue at this top quality park set in open countryside above the quaint fishing town of Padstow, which can be approached via a footpath directly from the park. This site is divided into paddocks by maturing bushes and hedges that create a peaceful and relaxing holiday atmosphere. The main facility blocks, both now extended and upgraded, have been designed and decorated to a very high standard, plus there is a good children's play area, a well-stocked shop and an excellent coffee lounge with a decked terrace offering country views. 13.5 acre site. 150 touring pitches. 39 hardstandings. Caravan pitches. Motorhome pitches. Tent pitches. 12 statics.

Open: all year **Last arrival:** 21.00hrs **Last departure:** 11.00hrs

Pitches: * £18-£35 £17-£35 £12.50-£35

Leisure:

Facilities:

Services:

Within 3 miles:

Notes: No groups, no noise after 22.00hrs. Dogs must be kept on leads.

AA Pubs & Restaurants nearby: The Seafood Restaurant, PADSTOW, PL28 8BY, 01841 532700

Paul Ainsworth at No. 6, PADSTOW, PL28 8AP, 01841 532093

cornwall's finest parks
independent, top graded parks, offering fabulous facilities, superb locations and superior service - especially for families and couples - choose a great holiday from cornwall's finest quality parks
www.cornwallfinestparks.co.uk

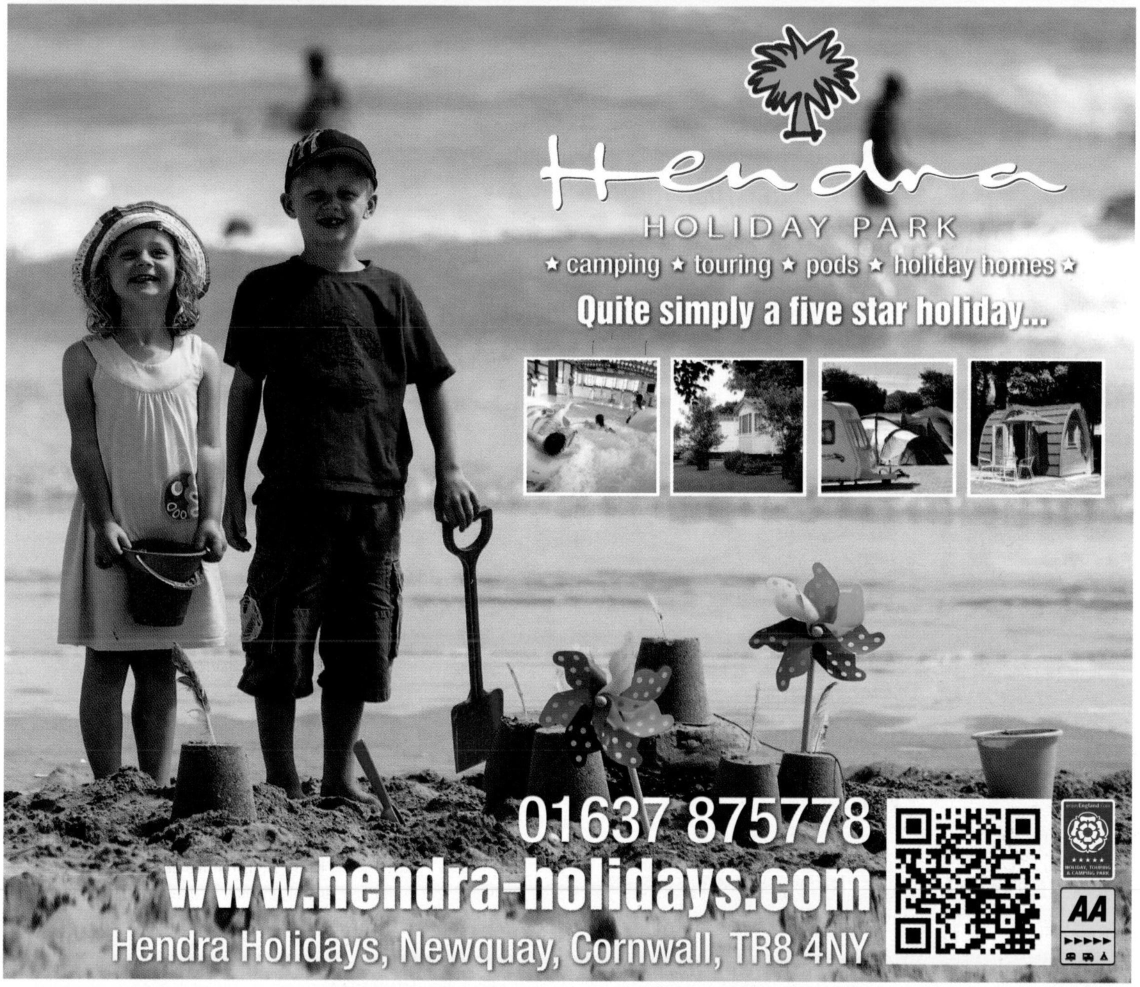

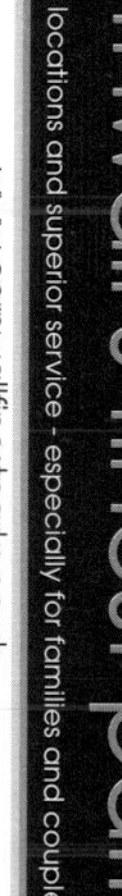

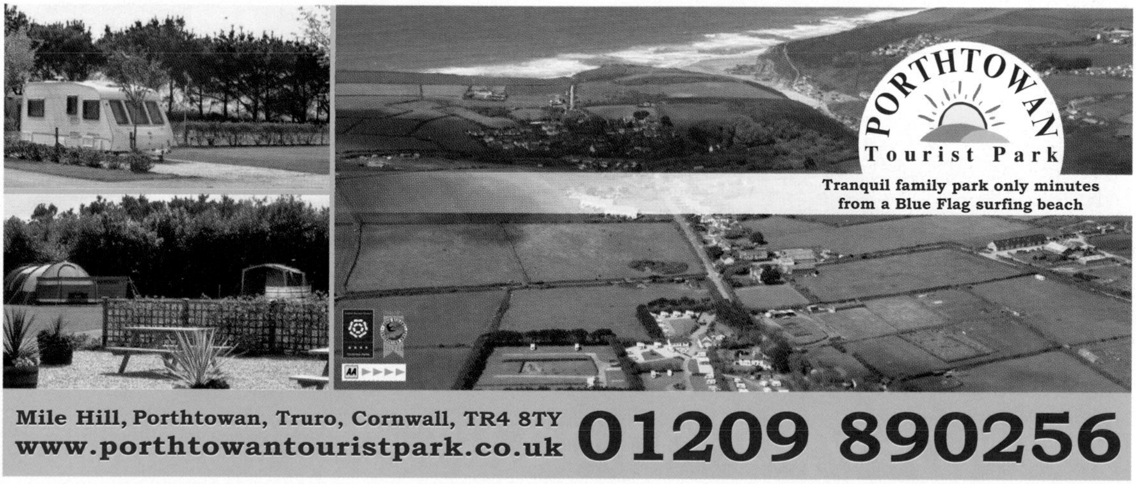

PITCHES: Caravans Motorhomes Tents Glamping-style accommodation **SERVICES:** Electric hook up Launderette Licensed bar Calor Gas Camping Gaz Toilet fluid Café/Restaurant Fast Food/Takeaway Battery charging Baby care Motorvan service point
ABBREVIATIONS: BH/bank hols – bank holidays Etr – Easter Spring BH – Spring Bank Holiday fr – from hrs – hours m – mile mdnt – midnight rdbt – roundabout rs – restricted service wk – week wknd – weekend x-rds – cross roads No credit or debit cards No dogs Children of all ages accepted

LEISURE: Indoor swimming pool · Outdoor swimming pool · Children's playground · Kid's club · Tennis court · Games room · Separate TV room · golf course · Boats for hire · Cinema · Entertainment · Fishing · Mini golf · Watersports · Gym · Sports field · Spa · Stables
FACILITIES: Bath · Shower · Electric shaver · Hairdryer · Ice Pack Facility · Disabled facilities · Public telephone · Shop on site or within 200yds · Mobile shop (calls at least 5 days a week) · BBQ area · Picnic area · Wi-fi · Internet access · Recycling · Tourist info · Dog exercise area

PADSTOW *continued*

Padstow Holiday Park

HOLIDAY HOME PARK 78%

BRONZE

tel: 01841 532289 **Cliffdowne PL28 8LB**
email: mail@padstowholidaypark.co.uk
dir: *Exit A39 onto either A389 or B3274 to Padstow. Site signed 1.5m before Padstow.*
grid ref: *SW009073*

In an Area of Outstanding Natural Beauty and within a mile of the historic fishing village of Padstow, which can be reached via a footpath, this static-only park with 12 well-equipped units for hire aims to provide comfortable relaxing accommodation in a quiet and peaceful atmosphere. With no clubhouse or pool on site, it is ideal for families and couples who want a quiet base that is convenient for all the attractions Cornwall has to offer.

Open: 6 Feb-6 Jan

Statics: 12 Sleeps 4 Bedrms 2 Bathrms 1 (inc en suite) Toilets 2 Microwave Freezer TV Sky/FTV DVD Modem/Wi-fi Elec inc Gas inc Grass area Garden/patio furniture Low season £200-£220 High season £520-£690

Children: Cots Highchair Child gate

Leisure:

Within 3 miles:

PENTEWAN

Places to visit

The Lost Gardens of Heligan, PENTEWAN, PL26 6EN, 01726 845100
www.heligan.com

Charlestown Shipwreck & Heritage Centre, ST AUSTELL, PL25 3NJ, 01726 69897
www.shipwreckcharlestown.com

Great for kids: Eden Project, ST AUSTELL, PL24 2SG, 01726 811911
www.edenproject.com

PENTEWAN — Map 2 SX04

PREMIER PARK

Sun Valley Resort

►►►►► 85%

tel: 01726 843266 & 844393 **Pentewan Rd PL26 6DJ**
email: hello@sunvalleyresort.co.uk **web:** www.sunvalleyresort.co.uk
dir: *From St Austell take B3273 towards Mevagissey. Site 2m on right.*
grid ref: *SX005486*

In a picturesque wooded valley, this neat park has experienced owners who maintain high standards throughout. The extensive amenities include tennis courts, indoor swimming pool, takeaway, licensed clubhouse and restaurant. The sea is just a mile away, and can be accessed via a footpath and cycle path along the river bank. Bikes can be hired on site. A public bus stops at the site entrance. 20 acre site. 29 touring pitches. 13 hardstandings. Caravan pitches. Motorhome pitches. Tent pitches. 75 statics.

Open: all year (rs Winter pool, restaurant & touring field) **Last arrival:** 22.00hrs **Last departure:** 10.30hrs

Pitches: * £10-£32 £10-£32 £10-£32

Leisure:

Facilities:

Services:

Within 3 miles:

Notes: No motorised scooters, skateboards or bikes at night, certain pet restrictions apply (contact site for details). Dogs must be kept on leads. Pets' corner, outdoor & indoor play areas.

AA Pubs & Restaurants nearby: The Crown Inn, ST EWE, PL26 6EY, 01726 843322

Heligan Woods

►►►► 82%

tel: 01726 842714 & 844414 **PL26 6BT**
email: info@pentewan.co.uk
dir: *From A390 take B3273 for Mevagissey at x-rds signed 'No caravans beyond this point'. Right onto unclassified road towards Gorran, site 0.75m on left.*
grid ref: *SW998470*

A pleasant peaceful park adjacent to the Lost Gardens of Heligan, with views over St Austell Bay and well-maintained facilities, including newly refurbished toilets and a smart new disabled/family room. Guests can also use the extensive amenities at the sister park, Pentewan Sands, and there's a footpath with direct access to Heligan Gardens. 12 acre site. 89 touring pitches. 24 hardstandings. 12 seasonal pitches. Caravan pitches. Motorhome pitches. Tent pitches. 17 statics.

Open: 16 Jan-26 Nov (rs 0900hrs-1100hrs & 1700hrs-1800hrs reception open)
Last arrival: 22.00hrs **Last departure:** 10.30hrs

Pitches:

Leisure:

Facilities:

Services:

Within 3 miles:

AA Pubs & Restaurants nearby: Austell's, ST AUSTELL, PL25 3PH, 01726 813888

PENTEWAN *continued*

Little Winnick Touring Park

►►►► 81%

tel: 01726 843687 **PL26 6DL**
email: mail@littlewinnick.co.uk **web:** www.littlewinnick.co.uk
dir: *A390 to St Austell, then B3273 towards Mevagissey, site in 3m on left.*
grid ref: *SX007482*

A small, well maintained rural site within walking distance of Pentewan and its beautiful beach. It has neat level pitches, including some hardstanding pitches, an excellent children's play area, and an ultra-modern toilet block which opened in 2015. It borders the River Winnick and also the Pentewan cycle trail from St Austell to Pentewan, and The Lost Gardens of Heligan and Mevagissey are nearby. There is a bus stop outside the park to Mevagissey and Gorran Haven or St Austell (Asda), Charlestown and Fowey. 14 acre site. 90 touring pitches. 28 hardstandings. 6 seasonal pitches. Caravan pitches. Motorhome pitches. Tent pitches.

Open: Etr-early Oct **Last arrival:** 20.00hrs **Last departure:** noon

Pitches: * £10-£28 £10-£28 £8-£26

Leisure:

Facilities:

Services:

Within 3 miles:

Notes: No noise 22.00hrs-07.00hrs. Dogs must be kept on leads.

AA Pubs & Restaurants nearby: The Ship Inn, MEVAGISSEY, PL26 6UQ, 01726 843324

The Crown Inn, ST EWE, PL26 6EY, 01726 843322

PENZANCE

Map 2 SW43

See also Rosudgeon

Places to visit

Trengwainton Garden, PENZANCE, TR20 8RZ, 01736 363148
www.nationaltrust.org.uk/trengwainton

St Michael's Mount, MARAZION, TR17 0HT, 01736 710507
www.stmichaelsmount.co.uk

Bone Valley Caravan & Camping Park

►►► 80%

tel: 01736 360313 **Heamoor TR20 8UJ**
email: wardmandie@yahoo.co.uk
dir: *Exit A30 at Heamoor/Madron rdbt. 4th on right into Josephs Ln. 800yds left into Bone Valley. Entrance 200yds on left.* **grid ref:** *SW472316*

A compact grassy park on the outskirts of Penzance with well-maintained facilities. It is divided into paddocks by mature hedges, and a small stream runs alongside. 1 acre site. 17 touring pitches. 6 hardstandings. Caravan pitches. Motorhome pitches. Tent pitches. 3 statics.

Open: all year **Last arrival:** 22.00hrs **Last departure:** 10.00hrs

Pitches:

Leisure:

Facilities:

Services:

Within 3 miles:

Notes: No noise after mdnt. Dogs must be kept on leads. Campers' lounge, kitchen & laundry room.

AA Pubs & Restaurants nearby: Dolphin Tavern, PENZANCE, TR18 4BD, 01736 364106

Harris's Restaurant, PENZANCE, TR18 2LZ, 01736 364408

PERRANPORTH

See also Rejerrah

Places to visit

Royal Cornwall Museum, TRURO, TR1 2SJ, 01872 272205
www.royalcornwallmuseum.org.uk

Trerice, TRERICE, TR8 4PG, 01637 875404 www.nationaltrust.org.uk/trerice/

Great for kids: Blue Reef Aquarium, NEWQUAY, TR7 1DU, 01637 878134
www.bluereefaquarium.co.uk

PERRANPORTH

Map 2 SW75

Perran Sands Holiday Park

HOLIDAY CENTRE 90%

tel: 0871 231 0871 *(Calls cost 10p per minute plus your phone company's access charge)* **TR6 0AQ**
email: perransands@haven.com **web:** www.haven.com/perransands
dir: *A30 onto B3285 towards Perranporth. Site on right before descent on hill into Perranporth.* **grid ref:** *SW767554*

Situated amid 500 acres of protected dune grassland, and with a footpath through to the surf and three miles of golden sandy beach, this lively park is set in a large village-style complex. It offers a complete range of on-site facilities and entertainment for all the family, which makes it an extremely popular park. There are two top-of-the-range facility blocks. 550 acre site. 363 touring pitches. 28 hardstandings. Caravan pitches. Motorhome pitches. Tent pitches. 600 statics.

Open: mid Mar-end Oct (rs mid Mar-May & Sep-Oct some facilities may be reduced) **Last arrival:** 22.00hrs **Last departure:** 10.00hrs

Pitches: **Leisure:**

Facilities:

Services:

Within 3 miles:

Notes: No commercial vehicles, no bookings by persons under 21yrs unless a family booking. Max 2 dogs per booking, certain dog breeds banned. Dogs must be kept on leads.

AA Pubs & Restaurants nearby: Driftwood Spars, ST AGNES, TR5 0RT, 01872 552428

See advert on page 96

Tollgate Farm Caravan & Camping Park

►►►► 82%

tel: 01872 572130 **Budnick Hill TR6 0AD**
email: enquiries@tollgatefarm.co.uk **web:** www.tollgatefarm.co.uk
dir: *Exit A30 onto B3285 to Perranporth. Site on right 1.5m after Goonhavern.*
grid ref: *SW768547*

A quiet site in a rural location with spectacular coastal views. Pitches are divided into four paddocks sheltered and screened by mature hedges. Children will like the play equipment and pets' corner, while adults can enjoy the food at the Farm Kitchen, which is open daily. The three miles of sand at Perran Bay are just a walk away through the sand dunes, or by car it is a three-quarter mile drive. There are now five camping pods for hire. 10 acre site. 102 touring pitches. 10 hardstandings. 12 seasonal pitches. Caravan pitches. Motorhome pitches. Tent pitches. 5 wooden pods.

Open: Etr-Sep **Last arrival:** 20.00hrs **Last departure:** 10.30hrs

Pitches: * £15.50-£26 £15.50-£26 £15.50-£26

Leisure:

Facilities:

Services:

Within 3 miles:

Notes: No large groups. Dogs must be kept on leads.

AA Pubs & Restaurants nearby: Driftwood Spars, ST AGNES, TR5 0RT, 01872 552428

See advert on page 96

Perranporth Camping & Touring Park

The park, within easy walking distance (approx. 5 minutes) of beach and town, comprises seven acres of well drained sheltered grass land with tarmacadam access roads and all modern facilities.

Mini Supermarket • Swimming Pool • Launderette • Showers and Washrooms • Six berth luxury vans • Adjacent 'Failte Club' with licensed bar, overlooking heated swimming pool and children's paddling pool

Budnick Road, Perranporth, Cornwall

Tel: Perranporth 01872 572174

AA, Camping Club, Caravan Club

British Tourist Authority listed site

Holiday Park, Perranporth, Cornwall

Save up to 50%* on 2016 holidays

Haven touring + camping

Our favourite bits

- Indoor pool with flume and an outdoor pool and terrace
- Family entertainment and kids' club
- Surf Bay Café serving delicious Cornish cream teas
- Newquay is only 20 minute drive away
- 343 grassy and hard standing pitches

For more information visit

haventouring.com/aaps or call 0333 202 1500 Quote: AAPS

Calls to 0333 numbers are charged at standard UK rates and will be included in any inclusive minute bundles

Terms and conditions: *Save up to 50% discount is available on selected spring and autumn dates in 2016. Full booking terms and conditions apply. Haven Holidays is a trading name of Bourne Leisure Limited, registered in England and Wales, no 04011660. Registered office 1 Park Lane, Hemel Hempstead, Hertfordshire, HP2 4YL.

LEISURE: Indoor swimming pool · Outdoor swimming pool · Children's playground · Kid's club · Tennis court · Games room · Separate TV room · golf course · Boats for hire · Cinema · Entertainment · Fishing · Mini golf · Watersports · Gym · Sports field · Spa · Stables
FACILITIES: Bath · Shower · Electric shaver · Hairdryer · Ice Pack Facility · Disabled facilities · Public telephone · Shop on site or within 200yds · Mobile shop (calls at least 5 days a week) · BBQ area · Picnic area · Wi-fi · Internet access · Recycling · Tourist info · Dog exercise area

PERRANPORTH *continued*

Higher Golla Touring & Caravan Park

►►► 82%

tel: 01872 573963 & 07800 558407 **Penhallow TR4 9LZ**
email: trevor.knibb@gmail.com **web:** www.highergollatouringpark.co.uk
dir: *A30 onto B3284 towards Perranporth (straight on at junct with A3075). Approx 2m. Site signed on right.* **grid ref:** *SW756514*

This peacefully located park is just two miles from Perranporth and its stunning beach, and extensive country views can be enjoyed from all pitches. It has high quality and immaculate toilet facilities, and every pitch has electricity and a water tap. 3 acre site. 30 touring pitches. 2 hardstandings. 4 seasonal pitches. Caravan pitches. Motorhome pitches. Tent pitches. 2 statics.

Open: 10 May-20 Sep (rs Spring BH wk & peak season shop open) **Last arrival:** 20.00hrs **Last departure:** 10.30hrs

Pitches:

Facilities: WiFi

Services: T

Within 3 miles:

Notes: No kite flying, quiet between 21.00hrs-08.00hrs. Dogs must be kept on leads.

AA Pubs & Restaurants nearby: Driftwood Spars, ST AGNES, TR5 0RT, 01872 552428

Why go glamping?
See pages 20-23 to find out

Perranporth Camping & Touring Park

►►► 71%

tel: 01872 572174 **Budnick Rd TR6 0DB**
email: info@perranporthcamping.co.uk
dir: *At mini rdbt in Perranporth take B3285 towards Newquay. 0.5m to site.*
grid ref: *SW768542*

A pleasant site, great for families and just a five-minute, easy walk to Perranporth's beautiful beach and less than 10 minutes to the shops and restaurants in the town centre. There is a clubhouse/bar and heated swimming pool for the sole use of those staying on the site. There is also a takeaway food outlet and small shop. Nine static caravans are available for holiday hire. 6 acre site. 120 touring pitches. 4 hardstandings. Caravan pitches. Motorhome pitches. Tent pitches. 9 statics.

Open: Spring BH-Sep (rs Etr & end Sep shop, swimming pool & club facilities closed) **Last arrival:** 23.00hrs **Last departure:** noon

Pitches:

Leisure:

Facilities:

Services: T

Within 3 miles:

Notes: No noise after 23.00hrs. Dogs must be kept on leads.

AA Pubs & Restaurants nearby: Driftwood Spars, ST AGNES, TR5 0RT, 01872 552428

See advert on opposite page

POLPERRO Map 2 SX25

Places to visit

Restormel Castle, RESTORMEL, PL22 0EE, 01208 872687
www.english-heritage.org.uk/daysout/properties/restormel-castle

Great for kids: Wild Futures' Monkey Sanctuary, LOOE, PL13 1NZ, 0844 2721271 *(Calls cost 7p per minute plus your phone company's access charge)*
www.monkeysanctuary.org

Great Kellow Farm Caravan & Camping Site

►► 78%

tel: 01503 272387 **Lansallos PL13 2QL**
email: enquiries@greatkellowfarm.co.uk
dir: *From Looe to Pelynt. In Pelynt left at church follow Lansallos sign. Left at x-rds, 0.75m. At staggered x-rds left, follow site signs. (NB access is via single track lanes. It is advisable to follow guide directions not Sat Nav).* **grid ref:** *SX201522*

Set on a high level grassy paddock with extensive views of Polperro Bay, this attractive site is on a working dairy and beef farm, and close to National Trust properties and gardens. It is situated in a very peaceful location close to the fishing village of Polperro. 3 acre site. 30 touring pitches. 20 seasonal pitches. Caravan pitches. Motorhome pitches. Tent pitches. 10 statics.

Open: Mar-3 Jan **Last arrival:** 22.00hrs **Last departure:** noon

Pitches:

Facilities:

Services:

Within 3 miles:

Notes: No noise after 23.00hrs. Dogs must be kept on leads.

AA Pubs & Restaurants nearby: Talland Bay Hotel, TALLAND BAY, PL13 2JB, 01503 272667

Barclay House, LOOE, PL13 1LP, 01503 262929

POLRUAN Map 2 SX15

Places to visit

Restormel Castle, RESTORMEL, PL22 0EE, 01208 872687
www.english-heritage.org.uk/daysout/properties/restormel-castle

Great for kids: Wild Futures' Monkey Sanctuary, LOOE, PL13 1NZ, 0844 2721271 *(Calls cost 7p per minute plus your phone company's access charge)*
www.monkeysanctuary.org

Polruan Holidays-Camping & Caravanning

►►► 90%

tel: 01726 870263 **Polruan-by-Fowey PL23 1QH**
email: polholiday@aol.com
dir: *A38 to Dobwalls, left onto A390 to East Taphouse. Left onto B3359. Right in 4.5m signed Polruan.* **grid ref:** *SX133509*

A very rural and quiet site in a lovely elevated position above the village, with good views of the sea. The River Fowey passenger ferry is close by, and the site has a good shop, and barbecues to borrow. The bus for Polperro and Looe stops outside the gate, and the foot ferry to Fowey, which runs until 11pm, is only a 10-minute walk away. 3 acre site. 35 touring pitches. 7 hardstandings. Caravan pitches. Motorhome pitches. Tent pitches. 10 statics.

Open: Etr-Oct **Last arrival:** 21.00hrs **Last departure:** 11.00hrs

Pitches:

Leisure:

Facilities:

Services:

Within 3 miles:

Notes: No skateboards, rollerskates, bikes, water pistols or water bombs. Dogs must be kept on leads.

AA Pubs & Restaurants nearby: The Ship Inn, FOWEY, PL23 1AZ, 01726 832230

The Fowey Hotel, FOWEY, PL23 1HX, 01726 832551

POLZEATH Map 2 SW97

South Winds Caravan & Camping Park

►►► 87%

tel: 01208 863267 & 862215 **Polzeath Rd PL27 6QU**
email: info@southwindscamping.co.uk **web:** www.polzeathcamping.co.uk
dir: *Exit B3314 onto unclassified road signed Polzeath, site on right just past turn to New Polzeath.* **grid ref:** *SW948790*

A peaceful site with beautiful sea and panoramic rural views, within walking distance of a golf complex, and just three quarters of a mile from beach and village. There's an impressive reception building, replete with tourist information, TV, settees and a range of camping spares. 16 acre site. 165 touring pitches. Caravan pitches. Motorhome pitches. Tent pitches.

Open: May-mid Sep **Last arrival:** 21.00hrs **Last departure:** 10.30hrs

Pitches: * £16-£35 £16-£35 £16-£35

Facilities:

Services:

Within 3 miles:

Notes: Families & couples only, no disposable BBQs, no noise 23.00hrs-07.00hrs. Dogs must be kept on leads. Restaurant & farm shop adjacent, Stepper Field open mid Jul-Aug.

AA Pubs & Restaurants nearby: The Maltsters Arms, CHAPEL AMBLE, PL27 6EU, 01208 812473

See advert on opposite page

LEISURE: Indoor swimming pool · Outdoor swimming pool · Children's playground · Kid's club · Tennis court · Games room · Separate TV room · golf course · Boats for hire · Cinema · Entertainment · Fishing · Mini golf · Watersports · Gym · Sports field · Spa · Stables
FACILITIES: Bath · Shower · Electric shaver · Hairdryer · Ice Pack Facility · Disabled facilities · Public telephone · Shop on site or within 200yds · Mobile shop (calls at least 5 days a week) · BBQ area · Picnic area · Wi-fi · Internet access · Recycling · Tourist info · Dog exercise area

Tristram Caravan & Camping Park

►►► 87%

tel: 01208 862215 **PL27 6TP**
email: info@tristramcampsite.co.uk **web:** www.polzeathcamping.co.uk
dir: *From B3314 onto unclassified road signed Polzeath. Through village, up hill, site 2nd right.* **grid ref:** *SW936790*

An ideal family site, positioned on a gently sloping cliff with grassy pitches and glorious sea views, which are best enjoyed from the terraced premier pitches, or over lunch or dinner at the Café India adjacent to the reception overlooking the beach. There is direct, gated access to the beach, where surfing is very popular, and the park has a holiday bungalow for rent. The local amenities of the village are only a few hundred yards away. 10 acre site. 100 touring pitches. Caravan pitches. Motorhome pitches. Tent pitches.

Open: Mar-Nov (rs mid Sep reseeding the site) **Last arrival:** 21.00hrs
Last departure: 10.00hrs

Pitches: * £30-£70 £30-£70 £22-£70

Facilities:

Services:

Within 3 miles:

Notes: No ball games, no disposable BBQs, no noise between 23.00hrs-07.00hrs. Dogs must be kept on leads. Surf equipment hire.

AA Pubs & Restaurants nearby: The Maltsters Arms, CHAPEL AMBLE, PL27 6EU, 01208 812473

See advert below

PORTHTOWAN Map 2 SW64

Porthtowan Tourist Park

96%

tel: 01209 890256 **Mile Hill TR4 8TY**
email: admin@porthtowantouristpark.co.uk **web:** www.porthtowantouristpark.co.uk
dir: *Exit A30 at Avers Junct signed Redruth & Porthtowan. At rdbt follow Portreath, B3300 & brown camping signs. Approx 2m, right at T-junct, follow site sign. Site on left at top of hill.* **grid ref:** *SW693473*

A neat, level grassy site on high ground above Porthtowan, with plenty of shelter from mature trees and shrubs. The superb toilet facilities considerably enhance the appeal of this peaceful rural park, which is almost midway between the small seaside resorts of Portreath and Porthtowan, with their beaches and surfing. There is a purpose-built games and meeting room with a good library where tourist information leaflets are available. A tearoom, adjacent to the campsite, serves takeaway meals during the peak season (limited opening hours at other times of the year). 5 acre site. 80 touring pitches. 11 hardstandings. 8 seasonal pitches. Caravan pitches. Motorhome pitches. Tent pitches.

Open: Apr-Sep **Last arrival:** 21.30hrs **Last departure:** 11.00hrs

Pitches: * £11-£19.50 £11-£19.50 £11-£19.50

Leisure: **Facilities:**

Services: **Within 3 miles:**

Notes: No bikes or skateboards in Jul & Aug. Dogs must be kept on leads.

AA Pubs & Restaurants nearby: Driftwood Spars, ST AGNES, TR5 0RT, 01872 552428

See advert on page 91

Wheal Rose Caravan & Camping Park

75%

tel: 01209 891496 **Wheal Rose TR16 5DD**
email: whealrose@aol.com **web:** www.whealrosecaravanpark.co.uk
dir: *Exit A30 at Scorrier sign, follow signs to Wheal Rose. Site 0.5m on left on the Wheal Rose to Porthtowan road.* **grid ref:** *SW717449*

A quiet, peaceful park in a secluded valley setting, which is well placed for visiting both the lovely countryside and the surfing beaches of Porthtowan (two miles away). The friendly owner works hard to keep this park in immaculate condition, with a bright toilet block and well-trimmed pitches. There is a swimming pool and a games room. 6 acre site. 50 touring pitches. 6 hardstandings. Caravan pitches. Motorhome pitches. Tent pitches. 3 statics.

Open: Mar-Dec **Last arrival:** 21.00hrs **Last departure:** 11.00hrs

Pitches:

Leisure:

Facilities:

Services:

Within 3 miles:

Notes: 5mph speed limit, minimum noise after 23.00hrs, gates locked 23.00hrs. Dogs must be kept on leads.

AA Pubs & Restaurants nearby: Basset Arms, PORTREATH, TR16 4NG, 01209 842077

New to camping?
See pages 24-27 for helpful advice

LEISURE: Indoor swimming pool Outdoor swimming pool Children's playground Kid's club Tennis court Games room Separate TV room golf course Boats for hire Cinema Entertainment Fishing Mini golf Watersports Gym Sports field Spa Stables
FACILITIES: Bath Shower Electric shaver Hairdryer Ice Pack Facility Disabled facilities Public telephone Shop on site or within 200yds Mobile shop (calls at least 5 days a week) BBQ area Picnic area Wi-fi Internet access Recycling Tourist info Dog exercise area

PORTREATH Map 2 SW64

Places to visit

East Pool Mine, POOL, TR15 3NP, 01209 315027 www.nationaltrust.org.uk

Tehidy Holiday Park

►►►► 88%

tel: 01209 216489 **Harris Mill, Illogan TR16 4JQ**
email: holiday@tehidy.co.uk **web:** www.tehidy.co.uk
dir: *Exit A30 at Redruth/Portreath junct onto A3047 to 1st rdbt. Left onto B3300. At junct straight over signed Tehidy Holiday Park. Past Cornish Arms pub, site 800yds at bottom of hill on left.* **grid ref:** *SW682432*

An attractive wooded location in a quiet rural area only two and a half miles from popular beaches. Mostly level pitches on tiered ground, and the toilet facilities are bright and modern. Holiday static caravans and wooden pods are available for hire.

4.5 acre site. 18 touring pitches. 11 hardstandings. 4 seasonal pitches. Caravan pitches. Motorhome pitches. Tent pitches. 32 statics. 2 wooden pods.

Tehidy Holiday Park

Open: all year (rs Nov-Mar part of shower block & shop closed) **Last arrival:** 20.00hrs **Last departure:** 10.00hrs

Pitches: * £14-£23 £14-£23 £14-£23

Leisure:

Facilities:

Services:

Within 3 miles:

Notes: No pets, no noise after 23.00hrs. Pre-booking required for large motorhomes & caravans. Trampoline, off-licence, cooking shelter.

AA Pubs & Restaurants nearby: Basset Arms, PORTREATH, TR16 4NG, 01209 842077

See advert below

PITCHES: Caravans Motorhomes Tents Glamping-style accommodation **SERVICES:** Electric hook up Launderette Licensed bar Calor Gas Camping Gaz Toilet fluid Café/Restaurant Fast Food/Takeaway Battery charging Baby care Motorvan service point
ABBREVIATIONS: BH/bank hols – bank holidays Etr – Easter Spring BH – Spring Bank Holiday fr – from hrs – hours m – mile mdnt – midnight rdbt – roundabout rs – restricted service wk – week wknd – weekend x-rds – cross roads No credit or debit cards No dogs Children of all ages accepted

PORTSCATHO — Map 2 SW83

Places to visit

St Mawes Castle, ST MAWES, TR2 3AA, 01326 270526
www.english-heritage.org.uk/daysout/properties/st-mawes-castle

Trelissick Garden, TRELISSICK GARDEN, TR3 6QL, 01872 862090
www.nationaltrust.org.uk/trelissick

Trewince Farm Touring Park

►►► 80%

tel: 01872 580430 **TR2 5ET**
email: info@trewincefarm.co.uk
dir: *From St Austell take A390 towards Truro. Left on B3287 to Tregony, following signs to St Mawes. At Trewithian, turn left to St Anthony. Site 0.75m past church.*
grid ref: *SW868339*

A site on a working farm with spectacular sea views from its elevated position. There are many quiet golden sandy beaches close by, and boat launching facilities and mooring can be arranged at the nearby Percuil River Boatyard. The village of Portscatho with shops and pubs and attractive harbour is approximately one mile away. 3 acre site. 25 touring pitches. Caravan pitches. Motorhome pitches. Tent pitches.

Open: May-Sep **Last arrival:** 23.00hrs **Last departure:** 11.00hrs

Pitches:

Facilities:

Services:

Within 3 miles:

Notes: Dogs must be kept on leads.

AA Pubs & Restaurants nearby: The New Inn, VERYAN, TR2 5QA, 01872 501362

The Victory Inn, ST MAWES, TR2 5DQ, 01326 270324

Find out about the AA's Pennant rating scheme on pages 10-11

REDRUTH

Places to visit

East Pool Mine, POOL, TR15 3NP, 01209 315027 www.nationaltrust.org.uk

Pendennis Castle, FALMOUTH, TR11 4LP, 01326 316594
www.english-heritage.org.uk/daysout/properties/pendennis-castle

Great for kids: National Maritime Museum Cornwall, FALMOUTH, TR11 3QY, 01326 313388 www.nmmc.co.uk

REDRUTH — Map 2 SW64

PREMIER PARK

Globe Vale Holiday Park

►►►►► 90%

tel: 01209 891183 **Radnor TR16 4BH**
email: info@globevale.co.uk **web:** www.globevale.co.uk
dir: *A30 take Redruth/Porthtowan exit then Portreath/North Country exit from rdbt, right at x-rds into Radnor Rd, left after 0.5m, site on left after 0.5m.*
grid ref: *SW708447*

A family owned and run park set in a quiet rural location yet close to some stunning beaches and coastline. The park's touring area has a number of full facility hardstanding pitches, a high quality toilet block, a comfortable lounge bar serving bar meals, and holiday static caravans. 13 acre site. 138 touring pitches. 25 hardstandings. Caravan pitches. Motorhome pitches. Tent pitches. 10 statics.

Open: all year **Last arrival:** 20.00hrs **Last departure:** 10.00hrs

Pitches: * £15-£25 £15-£25 £15-£25

Leisure:

Facilities:

Services:

Within 3 miles:

Notes: Dogs must be kept on leads. Shower block heated in winter.

AA Pubs & Restaurants nearby: Basset Arms, PORTREATH, TR16 4NG, 01209 842077

See advert on opposite page

LEISURE: Indoor swimming pool Outdoor swimming pool Children's playground Kid's club Tennis court Games room Separate TV room golf course Boats for hire Cinema Entertainment Fishing Mini golf Watersports Gym Sports field Spa Stables
FACILITIES: Bath Shower Electric shaver Hairdryer Ice Pack Facility Disabled facilities Public telephone Shop on site or within 200yds Mobile shop (calls at least 5 days a week) BBQ area Picnic area Wi-fi Internet access Recycling Tourist info Dog exercise area

Lanyon Holiday Park

►►►► 85%

tel: 01209 313474 **Loscombe Ln, Four Lanes TR16 6LP**
email: info@lanyonholidaypark.co.uk **web:** www.lanyonholidaypark.co.uk
dir: *Exit A30 signed Camborne & Pool onto A3047. Straight on at next two lights. Pass Tesco Extra on left. Right signed Four Lanes, over rail bridge. In Four Lanes right at staggered x-rds onto B2397, 2nd right at Pencoys Hall into Loscombe Ln. Site on left in approx 400mtrs.* **grid ref:** *SW684387*

A small, friendly rural park in an elevated position with fine views to distant St Ives Bay. This family owned and run park continues to be upgraded in all areas; a smart new toilet block and two new family rooms will be available for the 2016 season. There is a well-stocked bar and a very inviting swimming pool. Stithians Reservoir for fishing, sailing and windsurfing is two miles away, and the site is close to a cycling trail. Two holiday cottages are available for hire. 14 acre site. 25 touring pitches. 5 seasonal pitches. Caravan pitches. Motorhome pitches. Tent pitches. 49 statics.

Lanyon Holiday Park

Open: Mar-Oct **Last arrival:** 21.00hrs **Last departure:** 11.00hrs

Pitches: * £18-£26 £18-£26 £14-£22

Leisure:

Facilities:

Services:

Within 3 miles:

Notes: Families only. Dogs must be kept on leads.

AA Pubs & Restaurants nearby: Basset Arms, PORTREATH, TR16 4NG, 01209 842077

See advert on page 104

REDRUTH *continued*

Cambrose Touring Park

►►► 79%

tel: 01209 890747 **Portreath Rd TR16 4HT**
email: cambrosetouringpark@gmail.com
dir: *A30 onto B3300 towards Portreath. Approx 0.75m at 1st rdbt right onto B3300. Take unclassified road on right signed Porthtowan. Site 200yds on left.* **grid ref:** *SW684453*

Situated in a rural setting surrounded by trees and shrubs, this park is divided into grassy paddocks. It is about two miles from the harbour village of Portreath. The site has an excellent swimming pool with a sunbathing area. 6 acre site. 60 touring pitches. 6 seasonal pitches. Caravan pitches. Motorhome pitches. Tent pitches.

Open: Apr-Oct **Last arrival:** 22.00hrs **Last departure:** 11.30hrs

Pitches: * £11-£18.50 £11-£18.50 £11-£18.50

Leisure:

Facilities:

Services:

Within 3 miles:

Notes: No noise after 23.30hrs. Dogs must be kept on leads. Mini football pitch.

AA Pubs & Restaurants nearby: Basset Arms, PORTREATH, TR16 4NG, 01209 842077

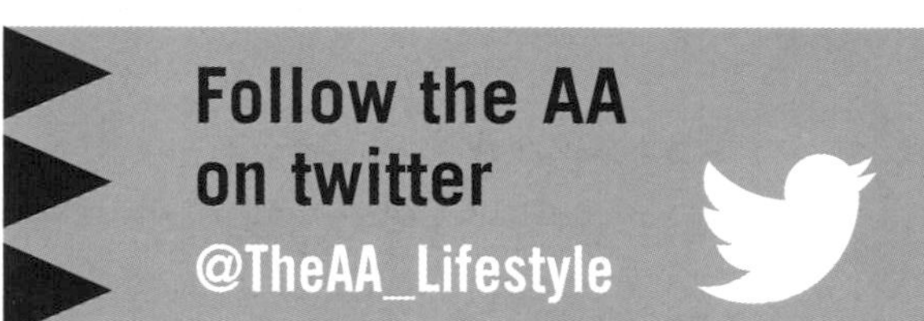

Stithians Lake Country Park

►►► 72%

tel: 01209 860301 **Stithians Lake, Menherion TR16 6NW**
email: stithianswatersports@swlakestrust.org.uk
dir: *From Redruth take B3297 towards Helston. Follow brown tourist signs to Stithians Lake, entrance by Golden Lion Inn.* **grid ref:** *SW705369*

This simple campsite is a two-acre field situated adjacent to the Watersports Centre, which forms part of a large activity complex beside Stithians Lake. Campers are required to use the functional toilet and shower facilities at the centre, and there is an excellent waterside café that also serves breakfasts. This is the perfect campsite for watersport enthusiasts. 2.1 acre site. 40 touring pitches. Caravan pitches. Motorhome pitches. Tent pitches.

Open: 3 Apr-Oct **Last arrival:** 17.30hrs **Last departure:** noon

Pitches: * £14-£22 £14-£22 £14-£22

Leisure:

Facilities:

Services:

Within 3 miles:

Notes: No noise after mdnt, no swimming in lake. Dogs must be kept on leads.

AA Pubs & Restaurants nearby: Basset Arms, PORTREATH, TR16 4NG, 01209 842077

REJERRAH

Places to visit

Trerice, TRERICE, TR8 4PG, 01637 875404 www.nationaltrust.org.uk/trerice/

Blue Reef Aquarium, NEWQUAY, TR7 1DU, 01637 878134 www.bluereefaquarium.co.uk

Great for kids: Newquay Zoo, NEWQUAY, TR7 2LZ, 0844 474 2244 *(Calls cost 7p per minute plus your phone company's access charge)* www.newquayzoo.org.uk

LEISURE: Indoor swimming pool · Outdoor swimming pool · Children's playground · Kid's club · Tennis court · Games room · Separate TV room · golf course · Boats for hire · Cinema · Entertainment · Fishing · Mini golf · Watersports · Gym · Sports field · Spa · Stables
FACILITIES: Bath · Shower · Electric shaver · Hairdryer · Ice Pack Facility · Disabled facilities · Public telephone · Shop on site or within 200yds · Mobile shop (calls at least 5 days a week) · BBQ area · Picnic area · Wi-fi · Internet access · Recycling · Tourist info · Dog exercise area

REJERRAH Map 2 SW75

PREMIER PARK

Newperran Holiday Park

90%

tel: 01872 572407 **TR8 5QJ**
email: holidays@newperran.co.uk **web:** www.newperran.co.uk
dir: *4m SE of Newquay & 1m S of Rejerrah on A3075. Or A30 (Redruth), exit B3275 Perranporth, at 1st T-junct right onto A3075 towards Newquay, site 300mtrs on left.*
grid ref: *SW801555*

A family site in a lovely rural position near several beaches and bays. This airy park offers screening on some pitches, which are set in paddocks on level ground. High season entertainment is available in the park's top quality country inn, and the café has an extensive menu. There is also a swimming pool with a separate toddlers' paddling area, and a skateboard park has now been created. 25 acre site. 357 touring pitches. 34 hardstandings. 15 seasonal pitches. Caravan pitches. Motorhome pitches. Tent pitches. 30 statics.

Open: Etr-Oct **Last arrival:** mdnt **Last departure:** 10.00hrs

Pitches: **Leisure:**

Facilities:

Services:

Within 3 miles:

Notes: Families & couples only. Dogs must be kept on leads.

AA Pubs & Restaurants nearby: The Smugglers' Den Inn, CUBERT, TR8 5PY, 01637 830209

See advert on page 92

ROSUDGEON Map 2 SW52

Places to visit

Trengwainton Garden, PENZANCE, TR20 8RZ, 01736 363148
www.nationaltrust.org.uk/trengwainton

Great for kids: The Flambards Theme Park, HELSTON, TR13 0QA, 01326 573404
www.flambards.co.uk

Kenneggy Cove Holiday Park

90%

tel: 01736 763453 **Higher Kenneggy TR20 9AU**
email: enquiries@kenneggycove.co.uk **web:** www.kenneggycove.co.uk
dir: *On A394 between Penzance & Helston, turn S into signed lane to site & Higher Kenneggy.* **grid ref:** *SW562287*

Set in an Area of Outstanding Natural Beauty with spectacular sea views, this family-owned park is quiet and well kept. There is a well-equipped children's play area, superb toilets, and, in addition to a variety of meals available in the excellent site café, takeaway pizzas are baked on site. A short walk along a country footpath leads to the Cornish Coastal Path, and onto the golden sandy beach at Kenneggy Cove. It's a half mile walk to the main road to pick up the local bus which goes to Penzance or Helston, with many pretty Cornish coves en route. There is also a fish and chip shop and Chinese restaurant with takeaway a short drive away. 4 acre site. 45 touring pitches. Caravan pitches. Motorhome pitches. Tent pitches. 7 statics.

Open: 10 May-Sep **Last arrival:** 21.00hrs **Last departure:** 11.00hrs

Pitches: * £18-£29 £18-£29 £18-£29

Leisure:

Facilities:

Services:

Within 3 miles:

Notes: No large groups, no noise after 22.00hrs. Dogs must be kept on leads. Fresh bakery items, breakfasts, home-made evening meals.

AA Pubs & Restaurants nearby: The Victoria Inn, PERRANUTHNOE, TR20 9NP, 01736 710309

The Ship Inn, PORTHLEVEN, TR13 9JS, 01326 564204

ST IVES *continued*

PREMIER PARK

Ayr Holiday Park

►►►►► 87%

GOLD

tel: 01736 795855 **TR26 1EJ**
email: recept@ayrholidaypark.co.uk **web:** www.ayrholidaypark.co.uk
dir: *From A30 follow St Ives 'large vehicles' route via B3311 through Halsetown onto B3306. Site signed towards St Ives town centre.* **grid ref:** *SW509408*

A well-established park on a cliff side overlooking St Ives Bay, with a heated toilet block that makes winter holidaying more attractive. There are stunning views from most pitches, and the town centre, harbour and beach are only half a mile away, with direct access to the coastal footpath. This makes an excellent base for surfing enthusiasts. Please note that it is advisable not to follow Sat Nav; use guide directions and avoid the town centre. 4 acre site. 40 touring pitches. 20 hardstandings. Caravan pitches. Motorhome pitches. Tent pitches.

Open: all year **Last arrival:** 22.00hrs **Last departure:** 11.00hrs

Pitches: * £24-£43.75 £24-£43.75 £18.50-£38.25

Leisure: **Facilities:**

Services: **Within 3 miles:**

Notes: No disposable BBQs. Dogs must be kept on leads.

AA Pubs & Restaurants nearby: The Sloop Inn, ST IVES, TR26 1LP, 01736 796584
The Queens, ST IVES, TR26 1RR, 01736 796468

ROGER ALMOND AWARD FOR THE MOST IMPROVED CAMPSITE OF THE YEAR 2016

PREMIER PARK

Trevalgan Touring Park

►►►►► 83%

Best of British

tel: 01736 791892 **Trevalgan TR26 3BJ**
email: reception@trevalgantouringpark.co.uk **web:** www.trevalgantouringpark.co.uk
dir: *From A30 follow holiday route to St Ives. B3311 through Halsetown to B3306. Left towards Land's End. Site signed 0.5m on right.* **grid ref:** *SW490402*

Serious investment by the hands-on owners has taken place over the last few years at this welcoming park, which is set in a rural area on the coastal road from St Ives to Zennor. The park is surrounded by mature hedges but there are still extensive views over the sea. There is a smart wood-clad reception and shop (daily-baked bread and pastries are available), excellent upmarket toilet facilities which have family rooms and underfloor heating, and extensive landscaping across the park that has resulted in more spacious pitches which offer both privacy and shelter. A regular bus service connects the park with St Ives from late May to September. A good base for motorhomes. 9 acre site. 120 touring pitches. Caravan pitches. Motorhome pitches. Tent pitches.

Open: May-Sep **Last arrival:** 22.00hrs **Last departure:** 11.00hrs

Pitches: * £16-£35 £16-£35 £16-£35

Leisure: **Facilities:**

Services: **Within 3 miles:**

Notes: Dogs must be kept on leads. Fresh bread, pastries, coffee.

AA Pubs & Restaurants nearby: The Queens, ST IVES, TR26 1RR, 01736 796468
The Sloop Inn, ST IVES, TR26 1LP, 01736 796584

LEISURE: Indoor swimming pool · Outdoor swimming pool · Children's playground · Kid's club · Tennis court · Games room · Separate TV room · golf course · Boats for hire · Cinema · Entertainment · Fishing · Mini golf · Watersports · Gym · Sports field · Spa · Stables
FACILITIES: Bath · Shower · Electric shaver · Hairdryer · Ice Pack Facility · Disabled facilities · Public telephone · Shop on site or within 200yds · Mobile shop (calls at least 5 days a week) · BBQ area · Picnic area · Wi-fi · Internet access · Recycling · Tourist info · Dog exercise area

Higher Penderleath Caravan & Camping Park

►►►► 81%

tel: 01736 798403 & 07840 208542 **Towednack TR26 3AF**
email: holidays@penderleath.co.uk **web:** www.penderleath.co.uk
dir: *From A30 take A3074 towards St Ives. Left at 2nd mini-rdbt, approx 3m to T-junct. Left then immediately right. Next left.* **grid ref:** *SW496375*

Set in a rugged rural location, this tranquil park has extensive views towards St Ives Bay and the north coast. Facilities are all housed in modernised granite barns, and include spotless toilets with fully serviced shower rooms, and there's a quiet licensed bar with beer garden, a food takeaway, breakfast room and bar meals. The owners are welcoming and helpful. There is a bus service to St Ives available in high season. 10 acre site. 75 touring pitches. Caravan pitches. Motorhome pitches. Tent pitches.

Open: Etr-Oct **Last arrival:** 21.30hrs **Last departure:** 10.30hrs

Pitches:

Leisure:

Facilities:

Services:

Within 3 miles:

Notes: No campfires, no noise after 23.00hrs. Dogs must be well behaved & kept on leads.

AA Pubs & Restaurants nearby: The Watermill, ST IVES, TR27 6LQ, 01736 757912

Balnoon Camping Site

►► 88%

tel: 01736 795431 & 07751 600555 **Halsetown TR26 3JA**
email: nat@balnoon.fsnet.co.uk
dir: *From A30 take A3074, at 2nd mini-rdbt 1st left signed Tate/St Ives. In 3m turn right after The Lodge at Balnoon.* **grid ref:** *SW509382*

Small, quiet and friendly, this sheltered site offers superb views of the adjacent rolling hills. The two paddocks are surrounded by mature hedges, and the toilet facilities are kept spotlessly clean. The beaches of Carbis Bay and St Ives are about two miles away. 1 acre site. 23 touring pitches. Caravan pitches. Motorhome pitches. Tent pitches.

Open: Etr-Oct **Last arrival:** 20.00hrs **Last departure:** 11.00hrs

Pitches: * £13-£17 £13-£17 £13-£17

Facilities:

Services:

Within 3 miles:

Notes: No noise between 23.00hrs-07.30hrs. Dogs must be kept on leads. Provisions for sale (peak season).

AA Pubs & Restaurants nearby: The Watermill, ST IVES, TR27 6LQ, 01736 757912

ST JUST (NEAR LAND'S END) Map 2 SW33

Places to visit

Geevor Tin Mine, PENDEEN, TR19 7EW, 01736 788662 www.geevor.com

Carn Euny Ancient Village, SANCREED, 0370 333 1181 www.english-heritage.org.uk/daysout/properties/carn-euny-ancient-village

Roselands Caravan and Camping Park

►►► 87%

tel: 01736 788571 & 07718 745065 **Dowran TR19 7RS**
email: info@roselands.co.uk
dir: *From A30 Penzance bypass onto A3071 for St Just. 5m, left at sign after tin mine chimney, follow signs to site.* **grid ref:** *SW387305*

A small, friendly park in a sheltered rural setting, an ideal location for a quiet family holiday. The owners continue to upgrade the park, and in addition to the attractive little bar there is an indoor games room, children's playground and good toilet facilities. 4 acre site. 25 touring pitches. Caravan pitches. Motorhome pitches. Tent pitches. 19 statics.

Open: Mar-Oct **Last arrival:** 21.00hrs **Last departure:** 11.00hrs

Pitches: £13.50-£19.50 £13.50-£19.50 £12-£19.50

Leisure:

Facilities:

Services:

Within 3 miles:

Notes: Dogs must be kept on leads.

AA Pubs & Restaurants nearby: Harris's Restaurant, PENZANCE, TR18 2LZ, 01736 364408

The Navy Inn, PENZANCE, TR18 4DE, 01736 333232

Who are the AA's award-winning campsites this year? See pages 14-19

ST MERRYN (NEAR PADSTOW) Map 2 SW87

Places to visit

Prideaux Place, PADSTOW, PL28 8RP, 01841 532411 www.prideauxplace.co.uk

Great for kids: Devon's Crealy Great Adventure Park, CLYST ST MARY, EX5 1DR, 01395 233200 www.crealy.co.uk

PREMIER PARK

Atlantic Bays Holiday Park

►►►►► 87%

tel: 01841 520855 **St Merryn PL28 8PY**
email: info@atlanticbaysholidaypark.co.uk **web:** www.atlanticbaysholidaypark.co.uk
dir: *From A30 SW of Bodmin take exit signed Victoria & Roche, 1st exit at rdbt. At Trekenning rdbt 4th exit signed A39 & Wadebridge. At Winnards Perch rdbt left B3274 signed Padstow. Left in 3m, follow signs.* **grid ref:** *SW890717*

Atlantic Bays has a mix of hardstanding and grass pitches, a high quality toilet and shower block and a comfortable bar and restaurant. The park is set in a rural area yet only two miles from the coast and beautiful sandy beaches, and within easy reach of the quaint fishing village of Padstow, and Newquay for fantastic surfing. 27 acre site. 70 touring pitches. 50 hardstandings. 6 seasonal pitches. Caravan pitches. Motorhome pitches. Tent pitches. 171 statics.

Atlantic Bays Holiday Park

Open: Mar-2 Jan **Last arrival:** 21.00hrs **Last departure:** noon

Pitches:

Leisure:

Facilities:

Services:

Within 3 miles:

Notes: Dogs must be kept on leads.

AA Pubs & Restaurants nearby: The Seafood Restaurant, PADSTOW, PL28 8BY, 01841 532700

See advert below

Carnevas Holiday Park & Farm Cottages

►►►► 83%

tel: 01841 520230 & 521209 **Carnevas Farm PL28 8PN**
email: carnevascampsite@aol.com **web:** www.carnevasholidaypark.com
dir: *From St Merryn on B3276 towards Porthcothan Bay. Approx 2m turn right at site sign onto unclassified road opposite Tredrea Inn. Site 0.25m on right.* **grid ref:** *SW862728*

A family-run park on a working farm, divided into four paddocks on slightly sloping grass. The toilets are central to all areas, and there is a small licensed bar serving bar meals. An ideal base for exploring the fishing town of Padstow or the surfing beach at Newquay. 8 acre site. 195 touring pitches. Caravan pitches. Motorhome pitches. Tent pitches. 14 statics.

Carnevas Holiday Park & Farm Cottages

Open: Apr-Oct (rs Apr-Spring BH & mid Sep-Oct shop, bar & restaurant closed)

Pitches: * £11-£22.50 £11-£22.50 £11-£22.50

Leisure: **Facilities:**

Services: **Within 3 miles:**

Notes: No skateboards, no supermarket deliveries. Dogs must be kept on leads.

AA Pubs & Restaurants nearby: The Seafood Restaurant, PADSTOW, PL28 8BY, 01841 532700

See advert below

ST MERRYN (NEAR PADSTOW) *continued*

Tregavone Touring Park

►►► 76%

tel: 01841 520148 **Tregavone Farm PL28 8JZ**
email: info@tregavone.co.uk
dir: *From A389 towards Padstow, right after Little Petherick. In 1m just beyond Padstow Holiday Park turn left onto unclassified road signed Tregavone. Site on left, approx 1m.*
grid ref: *SW898732*

Situated on a working farm with unspoilt country views, this spacious grassy park, run by friendly family owners, makes an ideal base for exploring the north Cornish coast and the seven local golden beaches with surfing areas, or for enjoying quiet country walks from the park. 3 acre site. 40 touring pitches. Caravan pitches. Motorhome pitches. Tent pitches. 1 static.

Open: Mar-Oct

Pitches:

Facilities:

Services:

Within 3 miles:

Notes: Dogs must be kept on leads.

AA Pubs & Restaurants nearby: The Seafood Restaurant, PADSTOW, PL28 8BY, 01841 532700

ST MINVER Map 2 SW97

PREMIER PARK

Gunvenna Holiday Park

►►►►► 85%

tel: 01208 862405 **PL27 6QN**
email: gunvenna.bookings@gmail.com **web:** www.gunvenna.com
dir: *From A39 N of Wadebridge take B3314 (Port Isaac road), site 4m on right.*
grid ref: *SW969782*

An attractive park with extensive rural views in a quiet country location, yet within three miles of Polzeath. This popular park is family owned and run, and provides good facilities in an ideal position for touring north Cornwall. The park has excellent hardstanding pitches, maturing landscaping and a beautiful indoor swimming pool with a glass roof. Two wooden mini glamping lodges, a holiday cottage and static caravans are for hire. The beach at Polzeath is very popular with the surfers. 10 acre site. 75 touring pitches. 24 hardstandings. 15 seasonal pitches. Caravan pitches. Motorhome pitches. Tent pitches. 44 statics. 2 wooden pods.

Open: Etr-Oct **Last arrival:** 20.30hrs **Last departure:** 11.00hrs

Pitches: **Leisure:**

Facilities: WiFi

Services: **Within 3 miles:**

Notes: Children under 16yrs must be accompanied by an adult in pool, owners must clear up after their dogs. Dogs must be kept on leads.

AA Pubs & Restaurants nearby: The Maltsters Arms, CHAPEL AMBLE, PL27 6EU, 01208 812473

Restaurant Nathan Outlaw, ROCK, PL27 6LA, 01208 862737

See advert on opposite page

SENNEN Map 2 SW32

Places to visit

Carn Euny Ancient Village, SANCREED, 0370 333 1181 www.english-heritage.org.uk/daysout/properties/carn-euny-ancient-village

Chysauster Ancient Village, TR20 8XA, 07831 757934 www.english-heritage.org.uk/daysout/properties/chysauster-ancient-village

Great for kids: Geevor Tin Mine, PENDEEN, TR19 7EW, 01736 788662 www.geevor.com

Trevedra Farm Caravan & Camping Site

►►► 88%

tel: 01736 871818 & 871835 **TR19 7BE**
email: trevedra@btconnect.com
dir: *Take A30 towards Land's End. After junct with B3306 turn right into farm lane. (NB Sat Nav directs beyond site entrance to next lane which is unsuitable for caravans).* **grid ref:** *SW368276*

A working farm with dramatic sea views over to the Scilly Isles, just a mile from Land's End. This popular campsite offers well-appointed toilets, a well-stocked shop, and a cooked breakfast or evening meal from the food bar. There is direct access to the coastal footpath, and two beautiful beaches are a short walk away. 8 acre site. 100 touring pitches. Caravan pitches. Motorhome pitches. Tent pitches.

Open: Etr or Apr-Oct **Last arrival:** 19.00hrs **Last departure:** 10.30hrs

Pitches: £15.50-£19.50 £15.50-£19.50 £14.50-£16.50

Facilities:

Services:

Within 3 miles:

Notes: No open fires, no noise 22.00hrs-08.00hrs. Dogs must be kept on leads.

SUMMERCOURT Map 2 SW85

Places to visit

Trerice, TRERICE, TR8 4PG, 01637 875404 www.nationaltrust.org.uk/trerice/

Blue Reef Aquarium, NEWQUAY, TR7 1DU, 01637 878134 www.bluereefaquarium.co.uk

Great for kids: Dairy Land Farm World, NEWQUAY, TR8 5AA, 01872 510246 www.dairylandfarmworld.com

Carvynick Country Club

RV ►►►► 93%

tel: 01872 510716 **TR8 5AF**
email: info@carvynick.co.uk
dir: *Accessed from A3058.* **grid ref:** *SW878564*

Set within the gardens of an attractive country estate, this spacious, dedicated American RV Park (also home to the 'Itchy Feet' retail company) provides full facility pitches on hardstandings. The extensive on-site amenities, shared by the high-quality time share village, include an indoor leisure area with swimming pool, fitness suite, badminton court and a bar and restaurant serving good food. 47 touring pitches. Caravan pitches. Motorhome pitches.

Open: all year (rs Jan-early Feb restricted leisure facilities)

Pitches:

Leisure:

Facilities:

Services:

Within 3 miles:

Notes: Dogs must be kept on leads & exercised off site. 5-hole golf course.

AA Pubs & Restaurants nearby: The Plume of Feathers, MITCHELL, TR8 5AX, 01872 510387

TINTAGEL Map 2 SX08

See also Camelford

Places to visit

Tintagel Castle, TINTAGEL, PL34 0HE, 01840 770328
www.english-heritage.org.uk/daysout/properties/tintagel-castle

Tintagel Old Post Office, TINTAGEL, PL34 0DB, 01840 770024
www.nationaltrust.org.uk/main/w-tintageloldpostoffice

Great for kids: Tamar Otter & Wildlife Centre, LAUNCESTON, PL15 8GW, 01566 785646 www.tamarotters.co.uk

Headland Caravan & Camping Park

►►► 76%

tel: 01840 770239 **Atlantic Rd PL34 0DE**
email: headland.caravan@talktalkbusiness.net **web:** www.headlandcaravanpark.co.uk
dir: *From B3263 follow brown tourist signs through village to Headland.*
grid ref: *SX056887*

A peaceful family-run site in the mystical village of Tintagel, close to the ruins of King Arthur's Castle. There are two well-terraced camping areas with sea and countryside views, immaculately clean toilet facilities, and good, colourful planting across the park. The Cornish Coastal Path and the spectacular scenery are just two of the attractions here, and there are safe bathing beaches nearby. There are holiday statics for hire. 5 acre site. 62 touring pitches. Caravan pitches. Motorhome pitches. Tent pitches. 28 statics.

Open: Etr-Oct **Last arrival:** 21.00hrs

Pitches:

Leisure:

Facilities:

Services:

Within 3 miles:

Notes: Quiet after 23.00hrs. Dogs must be kept on leads & exercised off site.

AA Pubs & Restaurants nearby: The Port William, TREBARWITH, PL34 0HB, 01840 770230

TORPOINT Map 3 SX45

Places to visit

Antony House, TORPOINT, PL11 2QA, 01752 812191
www.nationaltrust.org.uk/antony

Mount Edgcumbe House & Country Park, TORPOINT, PL10 1HZ, 01752 822236
www.mountedgcumbe.gov.uk

Great for kids: Wild Futures' Monkey Sanctuary, LOOE, PL13 1NZ, 0844 2721271 *(Calls cost 7p per minute plus your phone company's access charge)*
www.monkeysanctuary.org

Whitsand Bay Lodge & Touring Park

►►►► 82%

tel: 01752 822597 **Millbrook PL10 1JZ**
email: enquiries@whitsandbayholidays.co.uk
dir: *From Torpoint take A374, left at Anthony onto B3247 for 1.25m to T-junct. Turn left, 0.25m, right into Cliff Rd. Site 2m on left.* **grid ref:** *SX410515*

A very well-equipped park with panoramic coastal, sea and countryside views from its terraced pitches. A quality park with upmarket toilet facilities and other amenities. There is a guided historic walk around The Battery most Sundays, and a bus stop close by. 27 acre site. 49 touring pitches. 30 hardstandings. 15 seasonal pitches. Caravan pitches. Motorhome pitches. Tent pitches. 5 statics.

Open: all year (rs Sep-Mar opening hours at bar restricted) **Last arrival:** 19.00hrs
Last departure: 10.00hrs

Pitches:

Leisure:

Facilities: WiFi

Services:

Within 3 miles:

Notes: Families & couples only. Dogs must be kept on leads. Chapel, library, heritage centre.

AA Pubs & Restaurants nearby: The Finnygook Inn, CRAFTHOLE, PL11 3BQ, 01503 230338

TRURO

See also Portscatho

Places to visit

Royal Cornwall Museum, TRURO, TR1 2SJ, 01872 272205
www.royalcornwallmuseum.org.uk

Trelissick Garden, TRELISSICK GARDEN, TR3 6QL, 01872 862090
www.nationaltrust.org.uk/trelissick

TRURO
Map 2 SW84

PREMIER PARK

Carnon Downs Caravan & Camping Park
►►►►► 95%

GOLD

tel: 01872 862283 **Carnon Downs TR3 6JJ**
email: info@carnon-downs-caravanpark.co.uk
dir: *Take A39 from Truro towards Falmouth. 1st left at Carnon Downs rdbt, site signed.* **grid ref:** *SW805406*

A beautifully mature park set in meadowland and woodland close to the village amenities of Carnon Downs. The four toilet blocks provide exceptional facilities in bright modern surroundings. An extensive landscaping programme has been carried out to give more spacious pitch sizes, and there is an exciting children's playground with modern equipment, plus a football pitch. 33 acre site. 150 touring pitches. 80 hardstandings. Caravan pitches. Motorhome pitches. Tent pitches. 2 statics.

Open: all year **Last arrival:** 22.00hrs **Last departure:** 11.00hrs

Pitches: * £23-£33 £23-£33 £20-£30

Leisure:

Facilities:

Services:

Within 3 miles:

Notes: No children's bikes in Jul & Aug. Baby & child bathroom.

AA Pubs & Restaurants nearby: The Pandora Inn, MYLOR BRIDGE, TR11 5ST, 01326 372678

Tabb's, TRURO, TR1 3BZ, 01872 262110

PREMIER PARK

Cosawes Park
►►►►► 84%

GOLD

tel: 01872 863724 **Perranarworthal TR3 7QS**
email: info@cosawes.com
dir: *Exit A39 midway between Truro & Falmouth. Direct access at site sign after Perranarworthal.* **grid ref:** *SW768376*

A small touring park, close to Perranarworthal, in a peaceful wooded valley, midway between Truro and Falmouth, with a two-acre touring area. There are spotless toilet facilities (with underfloor heating) that include two smart family rooms. Its stunning location is ideal for visiting the many nearby hamlets and villages close to the Carrick Roads, a stretch of tidal water, which is a centre for sailing and other boats. 2 acre site. 59 touring pitches. 25 hardstandings. 15 seasonal pitches. Caravan pitches. Motorhome pitches. Tent pitches.

Open: all year **Last arrival:** 21.00hrs **Last departure:** 10.00hrs

Pitches: * £15.50-£23.50 £15.50-£23.50 £13.50-£23.50

Facilities:

Services:

Within 3 miles:

Notes: Dogs must be kept on leads. Fish & chips Thu-Sat.

AA Pubs & Restaurants nearby: The Pandora Inn, MYLOR BRIDGE, TR11 5ST, 01326 372678

PREMIER PARK

Truro Caravan and Camping Park
►►►►► 82%

tel: 01872 560274 **TR4 8QN**
email: info@trurocaravanandcampingpark.co.uk
dir: *Exit A390 at Threemilestone rdbt onto unclassified road towards Chacewater. Site signed on right in 0.5m.* **grid ref:** *SW772452*

An attractive south-facing and well-laid out park with spacious pitches, including good hardstandings, and quality modern toilets that are kept spotlessly clean. It is situated on the edge of Truro yet close to many beaches, with St Agnes just 10 minutes away by car. It is equidistant from both the rugged north coast and the calmer south coastal areas. There is a good bus service from the gate of the park to Truro. 8.5 acre site. 51 touring pitches. 26 hardstandings. Caravan pitches. Motorhome pitches. Tent pitches. 49 statics.

Open: all year **Last arrival:** 18.00hrs **Last departure:** 10.30hrs

Pitches:

Facilities:

Services:

Within 3 miles:

Notes: Dogs must be kept on leads.

AA Pubs & Restaurants nearby: The Wig & Pen, TRURO, TR1 3DP, 01872 273028

Old Ale House, TRURO, TR1 2HD, 01872 271122

Summer Valley
►►► 82%

tel: 01872 277878 **Shortlanesend TR4 9DW**
email: sv@summervalley.co.uk
dir: *From Truro take B3284 to Shortlanesend (approx. 3m). Through village, site on left.* **grid ref:** *SW800479*

A very attractive and secluded site in a rural setting midway between the A30 and the cathedral city of Truro. The keen owners maintain the facilities to a good standard. 3 acre site. 60 touring pitches. Caravan pitches. Motorhome pitches. Tent pitches.

Open: Apr-Oct **Last arrival:** 20.00hrs **Last departure:** 11.00hrs

Pitches:

Leisure:

Facilities:

Services:

Within 3 miles:

Notes: Dogs must be kept on leads. Campers' lounge.

AA Pubs & Restaurants nearby: Old Ale House, TRURO, TR1 2HD, 01872 271122

Bustophers Bar Bistro, TRURO, TR1 2PN, 01872 279029

WHITE CROSS Map 2 SW96

Places to visit

Trerice, TRERICE, TR8 4PG, 01637 875404 www.nationaltrust.org.uk/trerice/

Great for kids: Dairy Land Farm World, NEWQUAY, TR8 5AA, 01872 510246 www.dairylandfarmworld.com

Piran Meadows Resort and Spa

HOLIDAY HOME PARK 94%

tel: 01726 860415 **TR8 4LW**
email: enquiries@piranmeadows.co.uk
dir: *From A30 take A392 toward Newquay. At x-rds in White Cross left, under rail bridge, site on right.* **grid ref:** *SW889597*

A stunning development that provides excellent standards and facilities for couples and families. Generously spaced, superbly equipped lodges and static holiday homes are equipped with both practical and thoughtful extras and have unrivalled countryside views. The stylish main building with a welcoming reception is decorated and furnished with quality and comfort, and the many facilities include a modern swimming pool, special areas and attractions for children, and the excellent Serenity Spa offering a wide range of treatments. The 'Go Active' sports programme has its own instructors and the restaurant with bar has a spacious exterior area for alfresco dining.

Open: 9 Feb-9 Jan

Change over day: Mon, Fri & Sat

Arrival and departure times: Please contact the site

Statics: 104 Sleeps 6 Bedrms 2-3 Bathrms 1-2 (inc en suite) Toilets 1-2 Dishwasher Microwave Freezer TV Sky/FTV DVD Modem/Wi-fi Linen inc Towels inc Elec inc Gas inc Grass area Garden/patio furniture BBQ

Lodges: 11 Sleeps 8

Bedrms 3-4 Bathrms 2-3 (inc en suite) Toilets 2-3 Dishwasher Wash Machine T/drier Freezer TV Sky/FTV DVD Modem/Wi-fi Linen inc Towels inc Elec inc Gas inc Grass area Garden/patio furniture BBQ

Children: Cots Highchair **Dogs:** 1 on lead

Leisure: Spa

Within 3 miles:

WIDEMOUTH BAY Map 2 SS20

Widemouth Bay Caravan Park

HOLIDAY CENTRE 72%

tel: 01271 866766 **EX23 0DF**
email: bookings@jfhols.co.uk
dir: *From A39 take Widemouth Bay coastal road, turn left. Site on left.* **grid ref:** *SS199008*

A partly sloping rural site set in countryside overlooking the sea and one of Cornwall's finest beaches. There's nightly entertainment in the high season with an emphasis on children's and family club programmes. This park is located less than half a mile from the sandy beaches of Widemouth Bay. A superb base for surfing. One wooden pod and three safari tents are available for hire. 58 acre site. 220 touring pitches. 90 hardstandings. 4 seasonal pitches. Caravan pitches. Motorhome pitches. Tent pitches. 200 statics. 1 wooden pod. 3 safari tents.

Open: Etr-Oct (rs Etr week pools & clubhouse closed) **Last arrival:** dusk **Last departure:** 10.00hrs

Pitches:

Leisure:

Facilities:

Services:

Within 3 miles:

Notes: No noise after 23.00hrs. Dogs must be kept on leads. Crazy golf.

AA Pubs & Restaurants nearby: Bay View Inn, WIDEMOUTH BAY, EX23 0AW, 01288 361273

Cornish Coasts Caravan & Camping Park

►►► 82%

tel: 01288 361380 **Middle Penlean, Poundstock, Bude EX23 0EE**
email: admin@cornishcoasts.co.uk **web:** www.cornishcoasts.co.uk
dir: *5m S of Bude on A39, 0.5m S of Rebel Cinema on right.* **grid ref:** *SS202981*

Situated on the A39 midway between Padstow and the beautiful surfing beaches of Bude and Widemouth Bay, this is a quiet park with lovely terraced pitches that make the most of the stunning views over the countryside to the sea. The reception is in a 13th-century cottage, and the park is well equipped and tidy, with the well maintained and quirky toilet facilities (note the mosaic vanity units) housed in a freshly painted older-style building. 3.5 acre site. 46 touring pitches. 8 hardstandings. Caravan pitches. Motorhome pitches. Tent pitches. 4 statics.

Open: Apr-Oct **Last arrival:** 22.00hrs **Last departure:** 10.30hrs

Pitches: * £12.50-£20 £12.50-£20 £12.50-£20

Leisure:

Facilities:

Services:

Within 3 miles:

Notes: Quiet after 22.00hrs. Dogs must be kept on leads. Post office.

AA Pubs & Restaurants nearby: Bay View Inn, WIDEMOUTH BAY, EX23 0AW, 01288 361273

Penhalt Farm Holiday Park

►►► 75%

tel: 01288 361210 **EX23 0DG**
email: info@penhaltfarm.co.uk **web:** www.penhaltfarm.co.uk
dir: *From Bude on A39 take 2nd right to Widemouth Bay road, left at end by Widemouth Manor signed Millook onto coastal road. Site 0.75m on left.* **grid ref:** *SS194003*

Splendid views of the sea and coast can be enjoyed from all pitches on this sloping but partly level site, set in a lovely rural area on a working farm. About one mile away is one of Cornwall's finest beaches which proves popular with all the family as well as surfers. 8 acre site. 100 touring pitches. 12 hardstandings. Caravan pitches. Motorhome pitches. Tent pitches. 1 static.

Open: Etr-Oct

Pitches:

Leisure:

Facilities:

Services:

Within 3 miles:

Notes: No rollerblades, no noise after mdnt. Dogs must be kept on leads. Pool table, netball & football posts, air hockey & table tennis.

AA Pubs & Restaurants nearby: Bay View Inn, WIDEMOUTH BAY, EX23 0AW, 01288 361273

Cumbria

Cumbria means the Lake District really – a rumpled, rugged landscape that is hard to beat for sheer natural beauty and grandeur. It is almost certainly England's best known and most scenic national park, famous for Lake Windermere, the country's largest lake, and Derwentwater, described as the 'Queen of the English Lakes.'

The Lake District is a region of Britain that leaves some visitors relaxed, others completely exhausted. The list of activities and places to visit is endless. The old adage 'always leave something to come back for' is certainly apt in this remote corner of the country.

This region has long been inextricably associated with poets, artists and writers. Not surprisingly, it was this beautiful countryside that inspired William Wordsworth, Samuel Taylor Coleridge, Arthur Ransome and Robert Southey. Born in the Cumbrian town of Cockermouth, Wordsworth and his sister Dorothy moved to Dove Cottage in Grasmere in 1799. Their annual rent was £5. The poet later moved to Rydal Mount in Ambleside, a family home with a 4-acre garden and a charming setting on the banks of Rydal Water. Today, both Dove Cottage and Rydal Mount are among the most visited of all the Lake District attractions. Another house with strong literary links is Hill Top, the 17th-century farmhouse home of Beatrix Potter who moved here in 1905. Located near Windermere, Hill Top and its surroundings sparked Potter's imagination and she painstakingly reproduced much of what she saw and cherished in her charming book illustrations. Tom Kitten, Samuel Whiskers and Jemima Puddleduck were all created here and the outstanding success of the recent film about Potter's life has introduced her extraordinary work to new audiences.

Walkers are spoilt for choice in Cumbria and the Lake District. The 70-mile Cumbria Way follows the valley floors rather than the mountain summits, while the 190-mile Coast to Coast has just about every kind of landscape and terrain imaginable. The route, pioneered by the well-known fell walker and writer Alfred Wainwright, cuts across the Lake District, the Yorkshire Dales and the North York Moors, spanning the width of England between St Bees on the Cumbrian west coast, and Robin Hood's Bay on the North Yorkshire and Cleveland Heritage Coast. The region is also popular with cyclists and there are a great many cycle hire outlets and plenty of routes available.

As with any popular scenic region of the country, the Lake District has an abundance of attractions but there are plenty of places within its boundaries and outside them where you can experience peace, tranquillity and a true sense of solitude. The southern half of Cumbria is often overlooked in favour of the more obvious attractions of the region. The Lune Valley, for example, remains as lovely as it was when Turner came here to paint. In the 19th century, writer John Ruskin described the view from 'The Brow', a walk running behind Kirkby Lonsdale's parish church, as 'one of the loveliest scenes in England.'

The Cumbrian coast is also one of the county's secret gems. Overlooking the Solway Firth and noted in the area for its wide cobbled streets and spacious green, the town of Silloth is one of the finest examples of a Victorian seaside resort in the north of England and yet outside Cumbria few people know its name. There are other historic towns along this coastline, including Whitehaven, Workington and Maryport. The Roman defences at Ravenglass are a reminder of the occupation, as is the Cumbrian section of Hadrian's Wall where it follows the county's northern coast. Well worth a visit is the ancient and historic city of Carlisle. Once a Roman camp – its wall still runs north of the city – it was captured during the Jacobean rising of 1745. The cathedral dates back to the early 12th century.

Little Langdale, Lake District National Park ▷

CUMBRIA

AMBLESIDE Map 18 NY30

Places to visit

The Armitt Museum & Library, AMBLESIDE, LA22 9BL, 015394 31212
www.armitt.com

Beatrix Potter Gallery, HAWKSHEAD, LA22 0NS, 015394 36269
www.nationaltrust.org.uk

PREMIER PARK

Skelwith Fold Caravan Park

90%

GOLD

tel: 015394 32277 **LA22 0HX**
email: info@skelwith.com
dir: *From Ambleside on A593 towards Coniston, left at Clappersgate onto B5286 (Hawkshead road). Site 1m on right.* **grid ref:** *NY355029*

In the grounds of a former mansion, this park is in a beautiful setting close to Lake Windermere. Touring areas are dotted in paddocks around the extensively wooded grounds, and the all-weather pitches are set close to the many facility buildings. The premium pitches are quite superb. There is a five-acre family recreation area, which has spectacular views of Loughrigg Fell. 130 acre site. 150 touring pitches. 130 hardstandings. 30 seasonal pitches. Caravan pitches. Motorhome pitches. 320 statics.

Open: Mar-15 Nov **Last arrival:** dusk **Last departure:** noon

Pitches:

Leisure:

Facilities:

Services:

Within 3 miles:

Notes: Dogs must be kept on leads.

AA Pubs & Restaurants nearby: Wateredge Inn, AMBLESIDE, LA22 0EP, 015394 32332

Drunken Duck Inn, AMBLESIDE, LA22 0NG, 015394 36347

The Croft Caravan & Campsite

80%

GOLD

tel: 015394 36374 **North Lonsdale Rd, Hawkshead LA22 0NX**
email: enquiries@hawkshead-croft.com
dir: *From B5285 in Hawkshead turn into site opposite main public car & coach park.*
grid ref: *SD352981*

In the historic village of Hawkshead, which is now a popular destination for Beatrix Potter fans, this former working farm has a large tent and touring field, bordering a beck and the sound of running water and birdsong are welcome distractions. Most pitches are fully serviced with water, electricity, TV hook-up and waste water disposal. The smart amenities block provides family bathrooms. In an adjoining field there are stylish wood-clad lodges. 5 acre site. 54 touring pitches. 26 hardstandings. Caravan pitches. Motorhome pitches. Tent pitches. 20 statics.

Open: Mar-Jan **Last arrival:** 20.30hrs **Last departure:** noon

Pitches: **Leisure:** **Facilities:**

Services: **Within 3 miles:**

Notes: No noise 23.00hrs-07.00hrs. Dogs must be kept on leads.

AA Pubs & Restaurants nearby: The Queen's Head Inn & Restaurant, HAWKSHEAD, LA22 0NS, 015394 36271

Kings Arms, HAWKSHEAD, LA22 0NZ, 015394 36372

Hawkshead Hall Farm

79%

tel: 015394 36221 **Hawkshead LA22 0NN**
email: enquiries@hawksheadhall-campsite.com
dir: *From Ambleside take A593 signed Coniston, then B5286 signed Hawkshead. Site signed on left just before Hawkshead. Or from Coniston take B5285 to T-junct. Left, then 1st right into site.* **grid ref:** *SD349988*

A mainly camping site a few minutes' walk from village centre in a landscape of gentle rolling hills. The pitch sizes are generous and there's a very well-equipped, purpose-built amenities block. Surrounded by unspoiled countryside, the adjoining fields are a delight for families, especially during the lambing season. 3 acre site. 55 touring pitches. Caravan pitches. Motorhome pitches. Tent pitches.

Open: Mar-Oct **Last arrival:** 21.00hrs **Last departure:** noon

Pitches: **Facilities:**

Services: **Within 3 miles:**

Notes: No noise 23.00hrs-07.00hrs. Dogs must be kept on leads.

AA Pubs & Restaurants nearby: The Queen's Head Inn & Restaurant, HAWKSHEAD, LA22 0NS, 015394 36271

Kings Arms, HAWKSHEAD, LA22 0NZ, 015394 36372

Low Wray National Trust Campsite

79%

tel: 015394 32733 & 32039 **Low Wray LA22 0JA**
email: campsite.bookings@nationaltrust.org.uk
dir: *3m SW of Ambleside on A593 to Clappersgate, then B5286. Approx 1m left at Wray sign. Site approx 1m on left.* **grid ref:** *NY372013*

Picturesquely set on the wooded shores of Lake Windermere, this site is a favourite with tenters and watersport enthusiasts. The toilet facilities are housed in wooden cabins, and tents can be pitched in wooded glades with lake views or open grassland; here there are wooden camping pods and a mini-reservation of tipis and solar-heated bell tents. In partnership with Quest 4 Adventure, many outdoor activities are available for families (bookable during school holidays). Fresh bread is now baked daily on site, and opposite reception there is a rustic covered area with a pizza oven; there are also visits from the hot-food van in high season. 10 acre site. 140 touring pitches. Motorhome pitches. Tent pitches. 10 wooden pods. Bell tents. Tipis.

Open: wk before Etr-Oct **Last arrival:** variable **Last departure:** 11.00hrs

Pitches: **Leisure:** **Facilities:**

Services: **Within 3 miles:**

Notes: No cars by tents. No groups larger than 4 unless a family group with children, no noise between 23.00hrs-07.00hrs. Dogs must be kept on leads. Launching area for sailing craft, orienteering course, bike hire.

AA Pubs & Restaurants nearby: Wateredge Inn, AMBLESIDE, LA22 0EP, 015394 32332

Drunken Duck Inn, AMBLESIDE, LA22 0NG, 015394 36347

Kings Arms, HAWKSHEAD, LA22 0NZ, 015394 36372

APPLEBY-IN-WESTMORLAND

Map 18 NY62

Places to visit

Acorn Bank Garden and Watermill, TEMPLE SOWERBY, CA10 1SP, 017683 61893 www.nationaltrust.org.uk

Great for kids: Wetheriggs Animal Rescue & Conservation Centre, PENRITH, CA10 2DH, 01768 866657 www.wetheriggsanimalrescue.co.uk

PREMIER PARK

Wild Rose Park

►►►►► 88%

tel: 017683 51077 **Ormside CA16 6EJ**
email: reception@wildrose.co.uk
dir: *In Burrells on B6260 (between Appleby & Hoff) follow site signs. Left, site signed.*
grid ref: *NY698165*

Situated in the Eden Valley, this large leisure group-run park has been carefully landscaped and offers superb facilities maintained to an extremely high standard, including four wooden wigwams for hire. There are several individual pitches, and extensive views from most areas of the park. Traditional stone walls and the planting of lots of indigenous trees help the site to blend into the environment; wildlife is actively encouraged.There is a stylish reception with adjacent internet café, the Cock-a-Hoop bar with slate floor and pub games (and where dogs are welcome) and a choice of adults-only and family entertainment rooms have all been added. Please note, tents are no longer accepted. 85 acre site. 226 touring pitches. 140 hardstandings. Caravan pitches. Motorhome pitches. 273 statics. 4 wooden wigwams.

Open: all year (rs Nov-Mar shop closed, restaurant restricted hours, pool closed 6 Sep-27 May) **Last arrival:** 22.00hrs **Last departure:** noon

Pitches: * fr £24 fr £24

Leisure:

Facilities:

Services:

Within 3 miles:

Notes: No unaccompanied teenagers, no group bookings, no noise after 22.30hrs, no dangerous dogs. Dogs must be kept on leads.

AA Pubs & Restaurants nearby: Tufton Arms Hotel, APPLEBY-IN-WESTMORLAND, CA16 6XA, 017683 51593

Appleby Manor Country House Hotel, APPLEBY-IN-WESTMORLAND, CA16 6JB, 017683 51571

BARROW-IN-FURNESS

Places to visit

The Dock Museum, BARROW-IN-FURNESS, LA14 2PW, 01229 876400 www.dockmuseum.org.uk

Furness Abbey, BARROW-IN-FURNESS, LA13 0PJ, 01229 823420 www.english-heritage.org.uk/daysout/properties/furness-abbey

Great for kids: South Lakes Safari Zoo, DALTON-IN-FURNESS, LA15 8JR, 01229 466086 www.safarizoo.co.uk

BARROW-IN-FURNESS

Map 18 SD26

South End Caravan Park

►►► 85%

tel: 01229 472823 & 471556 **Walney Island LA14 3YQ**
email: enquiries@secp.co.uk **web:** www.walneyislandcaravanpark.co.uk
dir: *M6 junct 36, A590 to Barrow, follow signs for Walney Island. Cross bridge, turn left. Site 6m south.* **grid ref:** *SD208628*

A friendly family-owned and run park next to the sea and close to a nature reserve, on the southern end of Walney Island. It offers an extensive range of quality amenities including an adult lounge, and high standards of cleanliness and maintenance. 7 acre site. 50 touring pitches. 15 hardstandings. 34 seasonal pitches. Caravan pitches. Motorhome pitches. 250 statics.

Open: Mar-Oct (rs Mar-Etr & Oct pool closed) **Last arrival:** 22.00hrs **Last departure:** noon

Pitches: * £18-£26 £18-£26 **Leisure:**

Facilities:

Services: **Within 3 miles:**

Notes: Dogs must be kept on leads. Bowling green, snooker table.

AA Pubs & Restaurants nearby: The Stan Laurel Inn, ULVERSTON, LA12 0AB, 01229 582814

BOOT
Map 18 NY10

Places to visit

Great for kids: Ravenglass & Eskdale Railway, RAVENGLASS, CA18 1SW, 01229 717171 www.ravenglass-railway.co.uk

PREMIER PARK

Eskdale Camping & Caravanning Club Site

►►►►► 85%

tel: 019467 23253 & 0845 130 7633 *(Calls cost 7p per minute plus your phone company's access charge)* **CA19 1TH**
email: eskdale.site@thefriendlyclub.co.uk
dir: *Exit A595 at Gosforth or Holmrook to Eskdale Green, then signs for Boot. Site on left towards Hardknott Pass after railway, 150mtrs after Brook House Inn.*
grid ref: *NY179011*

Stunningly located in Eskdale, a feeling of peace and tranquillity prevails at this top quality campsite, with the sounds of running water and birdsong the only welcome distractions. Although mainly geared to campers, the facilities here are very impressive, with a smart amenities block, equipped with efficient modern facilities including an excellent fully serviced wet room-style, family room with power shower. The surrounding mountains, and the mature trees and shrubs create a wonderful 'back to nature' feeling. There's a nest of camping pods under the trees, with gravel access paths and barbecues, a super backpackers' field and a self-catering camping barn for up to 8 people. Expect great attention to detail and a high level of customer care. The park is only a quarter of a mile from Boot station on the Ravenglass/Eskdale railway (La'al Ratty). 8 acre site. 100 touring pitches. Motorhome pitches. Tent pitches. 10 wooden pods.

Open: Mar-14 Jan **Last arrival:** 20.00hrs **Last departure:** noon

Pitches:

Leisure:

Facilities:

Services:

Within 3 miles:

Notes: Site gates closed & no noise 23.00hrs-07.00hrs, no open fires. Dogs must be kept on leads. Free drying room, hot & cold drinks station, toast & hot snacks.

AA Pubs & Restaurants nearby: Brook House Inn, BOOT, CA19 1TG, 019467 23288

BOWNESS-ON-WINDERMERE

Sites are listed under Windermere

CARLISLE
Map 18 NY35

Places to visit

Lanercost Priory, BRAMPTON, CA8 2HQ, 01697 73030 www.english-heritage.org.uk/daysout/properties/lanercost-priory

Tullie House Museum & Art Gallery Trust, CARLISLE, CA3 8TP, 01228 618718 www.tulliehouse.co.uk

Great for kids: Carlisle Castle, CARLISLE, CA3 8UR, 01228 591922 www.english-heritage.org.uk/daysout/properties/carlisle-castle

Green Acres Caravan Park

►►►► 86%

tel: 01228 675418 & 07720 343820 **High Knells, Houghton CA6 4JW**
email: info@caravanpark-cumbria.com
dir: *M6 junct 44, A689 E towards Brampton for 1m. Left at Scaleby sign. Site 1m on left.*
grid ref: *NY416614*

A small, adults-only touring park in rural surroundings close to the M6 with distant views of the fells. A convenient stopover, this pretty park is run by keen, friendly owners who maintain high standards throughout. The site has a caravan and motorhome pressure-washer area, a field and woodland dog walk and two superb unisex shower rooms which include toilet and wash basin. 3 acre site. 30 touring pitches. 30 hardstandings. 12 seasonal pitches. Caravan pitches. Motorhome pitches. Tent pitches.

Open: Apr-Oct **Last arrival:** 21.00hrs **Last departure:** noon

Pitches: * £17-£21 £17-£21 £12-£16

Leisure:

Facilities:

Services:

Within 3 miles:

Notes: Adults only. Dogs must be kept on leads.

Dandy Dinmont Caravan & Camping Park

►►► 87%

tel: 01228 674611 **Blackford CA6 4EA**
email: dandydinmont@btopenworld.com
dir: *M6 junct 44, A7 N. Site 1.5m on right after Blackford sign.* **grid ref:** *NY399620*

A sheltered, rural site, screened on two sides by hedgerows and only one mile from the M6 and Carlisle. The grass pitches are immaculately kept, and there are some larger hardstandings for motorhomes. This park attracts mainly adults; please note that cycling and ball games are not allowed. Touring customers are invited to view the private award-winning garden. 4.5 acre site. 47 touring pitches. 14 hardstandings. Caravan pitches. Motorhome pitches. Tent pitches. 15 statics.

Open: Mar-Oct **Last arrival:** 21.00hrs **Last departure:** noon

Pitches: * £17 £17 £14-£16

Facilities:

Services:

Within 3 miles:

Notes: Children's activities are restricted. Dogs must be kept on leads & exercised off site. Covered dishwashing area.

CARTMEL Map 18 SD37

Places to visit

Holker Hall & Gardens, HOLKER, LA11 7PL, 015395 58328 www.holker.co.uk

Hill Top, NEAR SAWREY, LA22 0LF, 015394 36269 www.nationaltrust.org.uk/hilltop

Great for kids: Lakes Aquarium, LAKESIDE, LA12 8AS, 015395 30153 www.lakesaquarium.co.uk

Greaves Farm Caravan Park

►►► 80%

tel: 015395 36587 & 36329 **Field Broughton LA11 6HR**
email: info@greavesfarmcaravanpark.co.uk
dir: *M6 junct 36, A590 signed Barrow. Approx 1m before Newby Bridge, turn left at end of dual carriageway signed Cartmel & Holker. Site 2m on left just before church.*
grid ref: *SD391823*

A small family-owned park close to a working farm in a peaceful rural area. Motorhomes are parked in a paddock which has spacious hardstandings, and there is a large field for tents and caravans. This simple park is carefully maintained, offers electric pitches (6amp), and there is always a sparkle to the toilet facilities. Static holiday caravans for hire. 3 acre site. 20 touring pitches. 9 hardstandings. Caravan pitches. Motorhome pitches. Tent pitches. 20 statics.

Open: Mar-Oct **Last arrival:** 21.00hrs **Last departure:** noon

Pitches: * £17-£20 £17-£20 £15-£19

Facilities:

Services:

Within 3 miles:

Notes: Couples & families only. No open fires, no noise after 23.00hrs. Dogs must be kept on leads. Separate chalet for dishwashing, small freezer & fridge available.

AA Pubs & Restaurants nearby: The Cavendish Arms, CARTMEL, LA11 6QA, 015395 36240

The Masons Arms, CARTMEL, LA11 6NW, 015395 68486

Rogan & Company Restaurant, CARTMEL, LA11 6QD, 015395 35917

CROOKLANDS Map 18 SD58

Places to visit

Levens Hall, LEVENS, LA8 0PD, 015395 60321 www.levenshall.co.uk

RSPB Leighton Moss & Morecambe Bay Nature Reserve, SILVERDALE, LA5 0SW, 01524 701601 www.rspb.org.uk/leightonmoss

Waters Edge Caravan Park

►►►► 82%

tel: 015395 67708 & 67527 **LA7 7NN**
email: stay@watersedgecaravanpark.co.uk
dir: *M6 junct 36, A65 towards Kirkby Lonsdale, at 2nd rdbt follow signs for Crooklands/Endmoor. Site 1m on right at Crooklands garage, just beyond 40mph limit.*
grid ref: *SD533838*

A peaceful, well-run park close to the M6, pleasantly bordered by streams and woodland. A Lakeland-style building houses a shop and bar, and the attractive toilet block is clean and modern. This is ideal either as a stopover or for longer stays. 3 acre site. 26 touring pitches. 26 hardstandings. 8 seasonal pitches. Caravan pitches. Motorhome pitches. Tent pitches. 20 statics.

Open: Mar-14 Nov (rs Low season bar not always open on wkdays) **Last arrival:** 22.00hrs **Last departure:** noon

Pitches: **Leisure:**

Facilities:

Services:

Within 3 miles:

Notes: No cars by tents. Dogs must be kept on leads.

AA Pubs & Restaurants nearby: Plough Inn, LUPTON, LA6 1PJ, 015395 67700

CUMWHITTON Map 18 NY55

Places to visit

Lanercost Priory, BRAMPTON, CA8 2HQ, 01697 73030 www.english-heritage.org.uk/daysout/properties/lanercost-priory

Cairndale Caravan Park

►►► 69%

tel: 01768 896280 **CA8 9BZ**
dir: *Exit A69 at Warwick Bridge on unclassified road through Great Corby to Cumwhitton, left at village sign, site 1m.* **grid ref:** *NY518523*

Lovely grass site set in the tranquil Eden Valley with good views to distant hills. The all-weather touring pitches have electricity, and are located close to the immaculately maintained toilet facilities. Static holiday caravans for hire. 2 acre site. 5 touring pitches. 5 hardstandings. Caravan pitches. Motorhome pitches. 15 statics.

Open: Mar-Oct **Last arrival:** 22.00hrs

Pitches: * £12-£15 £12-£15

Facilities: **Services:**

Within 3 miles: **Notes:**

AA Pubs & Restaurants nearby: The String of Horses Inn, FAUGH, CA8 9EG, 01228 670297

FLOOKBURGH

Map 18 SD37

Places to visit

Holker Hall & Gardens, HOLKER, LA11 7PL, 015395 58328 www.holker.co.uk

Lakeland Leisure Park

HOLIDAY CENTRE 85%

GOLD

tel: 0800 197 2080 **Moor Ln LA11 7LT**
email: lakeland@haven.com **web:** www.haven.com/lakeland
dir: *On B5277 through Grange-over-Sands to Flookburgh. Left at village square, site 1m.*
grid ref: *SD372743*

A complete leisure park with full range of activities and entertainment, making this flat, grassy site ideal for families. The touring area, which includes 24 fully serviced pitches, is quietly situated away from the main amenities, but the swimming pools, all-weather bowling green and evening entertainment are just a short stroll away. There is a lake offering water sporting opportunities. 105 acre site. 185 touring pitches. 24 hardstandings. Caravan pitches. Motorhome pitches. Tent pitches. 800 statics.

Open: mid Mar-end Oct (rs mid Mar-May & Sep-Oct reduced activities, outdoor pool closed) **Last arrival:** anytime **Last departure:** 10.00hrs

Pitches:

Leisure:

Facilities:

Services:

Within 3 miles:

Notes: No cars by caravans or tents. No commercial vehicles, no bookings by persons under 21yrs unless a family booking, max 2 dogs per booking, certain dog breeds banned. Dogs must be kept on leads.

AA Pubs & Restaurants nearby: The Cavendish Arms, CARTMEL, LA11 6QA, 015395 36240

The Masons Arms, CARTMEL, LA11 6NW, 015395 68486

Rogan & Company Restaurant, CARTMEL, LA11 6QD, 015395 35917

See advert on opposite page

GRANGE-OVER-SANDS

Map 18 SD47

See also Cartmel

Oak Head Caravan Park

►►► 80%

tel: 015395 31475 **Ayside LA11 6JA**
email: oakheadcaravanpark@btconnect.com
dir: *M6 junct 36, A590 towards Newby Bridge, 14m. From A590 bypass follow signs for Ayside.* **grid ref:** *SD389839*

Three miles from Grange-over-Sands and with direct access from A590 south of Newby Bridge, this is a pleasant terraced site with two separate areas – grass for tents and all gravel pitches for caravans and motorhomes. The site is enclosed within mature woodland and surrounded by hills; it is located in a less busy area but convenient for all the Lake District attractions. 10 acre site. 60 touring pitches. 30 hardstandings. Caravan pitches. Motorhome pitches. Tent pitches. 71 statics.

Open: Mar-Oct **Last arrival:** 20.00hrs **Last departure:** noon

Pitches:

Leisure:

Facilities:

Services:

Within 3 miles:

Notes: No open fires, no noise after 23.00hrs. Dogs must be kept on leads.

AA Pubs & Restaurants nearby: The Cavendish Arms, CARTMEL, LA11 6QA, 015395 36240

The Masons Arms, CARTMEL, LA11 6NW, 015395 68486

Rogan & Company Restaurant, CARTMEL, LA11 6QD, 015395 35917

GREAT LANGDALE — Map 18 NY20

Great Langdale National Trust Campsite

►►► 77%

tel: 015394 63862 & 32733 **LA22 9JU**
email: campsite.bookings@nationaltrust.org.uk
dir: *From Ambleside, A593 to Skelwith Bridge, right onto B5343, approx 5m to New Dungeon Ghyll Hotel. Site on left 500mtrs after hotel.* **grid ref:** *NY286059*

Situated in a green valley, sheltered by mature trees and surrounded by stunning fell views, this site is an ideal base for campers, climbers and fell walkers. The large grass tent area has some gravel parking for cars, and there is a separate area for groups, and one for families with a children's play area. Attractive wooden cabins house the toilets, the reception and shop (selling fresh baked bread and pastries), and drying rooms, and there are wooden camping pods and two yurts for hire. Additionally, it is a gentle 10 minute walk to The Sticklebarn Tavern, the only National Trust run pub. 9 acre site. 220 touring pitches. Motorhome pitches. Tent pitches. 9 wooden pods.Yurts.

Open: all year **Last departure:** 11.00hrs

Pitches:

Leisure:

Facilities:

Services:

Within 3 miles:

Notes: No cars by tents. No noise between 23.00hrs-07.00hrs, no groups of 4 or more unless a family with children. Dogs must be kept on leads.

AA Pubs & Restaurants nearby: The Britannia Inn, ELTERWATER, LA22 9HP, 015394 37210

Langdale Hotel & Spa, ELTERWATER, LA22 9JD, 015394 37302

HOLMROOK — Map 18 SD09

Places to visit

Great for kids: Ravenglass & Eskdale Railway, RAVENGLASS, CA18 1SW, 01229 717171 www.ravenglass-railway.co.uk

Seven Acres Caravan Park

►►► 77%

tel: 01946 822777 **CA19 1YD**
email: reception@seacote.com
dir: *Site signed on A595 between Holmrook & Gosforth.* **grid ref:** *NY078014*

This sheltered park is close to quiet west Cumbrian coastal villages and beaches, and also handy for Eskdale and Wasdale. There is a good choice of pitches, some with hedged bays for privacy and some with coastal views. The park has a heated toilet block. 7 acre site. 37 touring pitches. 20 hardstandings. Caravan pitches. Motorhome pitches. Tent pitches. 16 statics.

Open: Mar-15 Jan **Last arrival:** 21.00hrs **Last departure:** 10.30hrs

Pitches: * £18-£21 £18-£21 £10-£24

Facilities:

Services:

Within 3 miles:

Notes: Dogs must be kept on leads.

AA Pubs & Restaurants nearby: Brook House Inn, BOOT, CA19 1TG, 019467 23288

Bridge Inn, SANTON BRIDGE, CA19 1UX, 019467 26221

KESWICK Map 18 NY22

Places to visit

The Pencil Museum, KESWICK, CA12 5NG, 017687 73626
www.pencilmuseum.co.uk

Honister Slate Mine, BORROWDALE, CA12 5XN, 01768 777230
www.honister-slate-mine.co.uk

Great for kids: Mirehouse, KESWICK, CA12 4QE, 017687 72287
www.mirehouse.com

PREMIER PARK

Castlerigg Hall Caravan & Camping Park

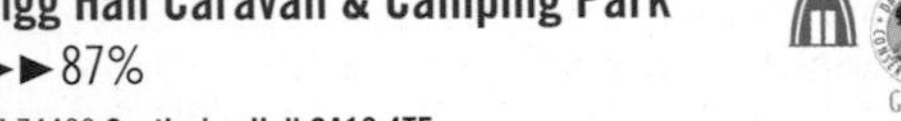

►►►►► 87%

GOLD

tel: 017687 74499 **Castlerigg Hall CA12 4TE**
email: info@castlerigg.co.uk **web:** www.castlerigg.co.uk
dir: *1.5m SE of Keswick on A591, turn right at sign. Site 200mtrs on right past Heights Hotel.* **grid ref:** *NY282227*

Spectacular views over Derwent Water to the mountains beyond are among the many attractions at this lovely Lakeland park. Old farm buildings have been tastefully converted into excellent toilets with private washing cubicles and a family bathroom, reception and a well-equipped shop, and there is a kitchen/dining area for campers, and a restaurant/takeaway. There is a superb toilet block, and wooden camping pods and a further ten all-weather pitches are located in the tent field. 8 acre site. 48 touring pitches. 48 hardstandings. Caravan pitches. Motorhome pitches. Tent pitches. 30 statics. 2 wooden pods.

Castlerigg Hall Caravan & Camping Park

Open: mid Mar-7 Nov **Last arrival:** 21.00hrs **Last departure:** 11.30hrs

Pitches: * £19.75-£35 £19.75-£35 £17-£25

Leisure:

Facilities:

Services:

Within 3 miles:

Notes: Dogs must be kept on leads & not be left unattended, no noise after 22.30hrs. Campers' kitchen, sitting room, gallery.

AA Pubs & Restaurants nearby: The Kings Head, KESWICK, CA12 4TN, 017687 72393

See advert below

Burns Farm Caravan Park

►►► 77%

tel: 017687 79225 & 79112 **St Johns in the Vale CA12 4RR**
email: linda@burns-farm.co.uk **web:** www.burns-farm.co.uk
dir: *Exit A66 signed Castlerigg Stone Circle, Youth Centre & Burns Farm. Site on right in 0.5m.* **grid ref:** *NY307244*

Lovely views of Blencathra and Skiddaw can be enjoyed from this secluded park, set on a working farm which extends a warm welcome to families. This is a good choice for exploring the beautiful and interesting countryside. Pub food available in Threlkeld. 2.5 acre site. 32 touring pitches. Caravan pitches. Motorhome pitches. Tent pitches.

Open: Mar-4 Nov **Last departure:** noon (peak season)

Pitches:

Facilities:

Services:

Within 3 miles:

Notes: No noise after mdnt. Dogs must be kept on leads.

AA Pubs & Restaurants nearby: The Horse & Farrier Inn, KESWICK, CA12 4SQ, 017687 79688

KIRKBY LONSDALE — Map 18 SD67

Places to visit

Sizergh, SIZERGH, LA8 8AE, 015395 60951 www.nationaltrust.org.uk

PREMIER PARK

Woodclose Caravan Park

►►►►► 86%

tel: 015242 71597 **High Casterton LA6 2SE**
email: info@woodclosepark.com **web:** www.woodclosepark.com
dir: *On A65, 0.25m after Kirkby Lonsdale towards Skipton, park on left.*
grid ref: *SD618786*

A peaceful, well-managed park set in idyllic countryside within the beautiful Lune Valley, and centrally located for exploring the Lakes and Dales. Ideal for that 'back to nature' experience, with riverside walks, on-site woodland walks for both families and dogs, and top notch amenities blocks with fully serviced cubicles with one allocated for the wigwam pod village and camping field. The generous pitches are surrounded by mature trees and seasonal planting. Parts of the site are havens for wildlife. 9 acre site. 22 touring pitches. 18 hardstandings. 22 seasonal pitches. Caravan pitches. Motorhome pitches. Tent pitches (see Notes below). 75 statics. 10 wooden pods.

Open: Mar-Oct **Last arrival:** 21.00hrs **Last departure:** noon

Pitches: * £15-£27 £15-£27

Leisure:

Facilities:

Services:

Within 3 miles:

Notes: Tents only allowed certain dates from Apr-Sep - please contact site for further details. No cars by tents. No arrivals before 13.00hrs. Dogs must be kept on leads. Cycle hire, crock boxes for hire.

AA Pubs & Restaurants nearby: The Sun Inn, KIRKBY LONSDALE, LA6 2AU, 015242 71965

The Whoop Hall, KIRKBY LONSDALE, LA6 2GY, 015242 71284

The Pheasant Inn, KIRKBY LONSDALE, LA6 2RX, 01524 271230

KIRKBY LONSDALE *continued*

New House Caravan Park

►►►► 81%

tel: 015242 71590 **LA6 2HR**
email: colinpreece9@aol.com
dir: *1m SE of Kirkby Lonsdale on A65, turn right into site entrance 300yds past Whoop Hall Inn.* **grid ref:** *SD628774*

Colourful floral displays greet new arrivals, creating an excellent first impression at this former farm, which has been carefully changed to provide well-spaced pitches, with hardstandings sheltered by surrounding mature trees and shrubs. An ideal base for exploring the Yorkshire Dales and the Lake District. 3 acre site. 50 touring pitches. 50 hardstandings. Caravan pitches. Motorhome pitches.

Open: Mar-Oct **Last arrival:** 21.00hrs **Last departure:** noon

Pitches: * £18 £18

Facilities:

Services:

Within 3 miles:

Notes: No cycling. Dogs must be kept on leads.

AA Pubs & Restaurants nearby: The Sun Inn, KIRKBY LONSDALE, LA6 2AU, 015242 71965

The Whoop Hall, KIRKBY LONSDALE, LA6 2GY, 015242 71284

The Pheasant Inn, KIRKBY LONSDALE, LA6 2RX, 01524 271230

LONGTOWN — Map 21 NY36

See also Penton

Places to visit

Carlisle Castle, CARLISLE, CA3 8UR, 01228 591922
www.english-heritage.org.uk/daysout/properties/carlisle-castle

Tullie House Museum & Art Gallery Trust, CARLISLE, CA3 8TP, 01228 618718
www.tulliehouse.co.uk

Camelot Caravan Park

►► 75%

tel: 01228 791248 **CA6 5SZ**
email: info@camelotcaravanpark.co.uk
dir: *M6 junct 44, A7, site 5m N & 1m S of Longtown.* **grid ref:** *NY391666*

A very pleasant level grassy site in a wooded setting near the M6, with direct access from the A7, and simple, clean toilet facilities. The park is an ideal stopover site. 1.5 acre site. 20 touring pitches. Caravan pitches. Motorhome pitches. Tent pitches. 2 statics.

Open: Mar-Oct **Last arrival:** 20.00hrs **Last departure:** noon

Pitches:

Facilities:

Services:

Within 3 miles:

Notes: Dogs must be kept on leads.

MEALSGATE — Map 18 NY24

Places to visit

Jennings Brewery Tour and Shop, COCKERMOUTH, CA13 9NE, 01900 820362
www.jenningsbrewery.co.uk

Wordsworth House and Garden, COCKERMOUTH, CA13 9RX, 01900 824805
www.nationaltrust.org.uk/wordsworthhouse

Larches Caravan Park

►►►► 83%

tel: 016973 71379 **CA7 1LQ**
dir: *On A595 (Carlisle to Cockermouth road).* **grid ref:** *NY205415*

This over 18s-only park is set in wooded rural surroundings on the fringe of the Lake District National Park. Touring units are spread out over two sections. The friendly family-run park offers constantly improving facilities, including a well-stocked shop that also provides a very good range of camping and caravanning spares. 20 acre site. 35 touring pitches. 30 hardstandings. Caravan pitches. Motorhome pitches. Tent pitches.

Open: Mar-Oct (rs Early & late season) **Last arrival:** 21.30hrs **Last departure:** noon

Pitches:

Facilities:

Services:

Within 3 miles:

Notes: Adults only.

AA Pubs & Restaurants nearby: Oddfellows Arms, CALDBECK, CA7 8EA, 016974 78227

MILNTHORPE Map 18 SD48

Places to visit

RSPB Leighton Moss & Morecambe Bay Nature Reserve, SILVERDALE, LA5 0SW, 01524 701601 www.rspb.org.uk/leightonmoss

Levens Hall, LEVENS, LA8 0PD, 015395 60321 www.levenshall.co.uk

Hall More Caravan Park

►►►► 77%

GOLD

tel: 01524 781453 & 784221 **Hale LA7 7BP**
email: enquiries@pureleisure-holidays.co.uk
dir: *M6 junct 35, A6 towards Milnthorpe for 4m. Left at Lakeland Wildlife Oasis, follow brown signs.* **grid ref:** *SD502771*

Set on former meadowland and surrounded by mature trees, this constantly improving rural park provides neat, well-spaced pitches with colourful hedged areas enhanced by pretty seasonal flowers. The site is adjacent to a fishery where fly fishing for trout is possible, and near a farm with stables offering pony trekking. There are seven wooden camping pods for hire. 4 acre site. 44 touring pitches. 7 hardstandings. Caravan pitches. Motorhome pitches. Tent pitches. 60 statics. 7 wooden pods.

Open: Mar-Jan **Last arrival:** 22.00hrs **Last departure:** 10.00hrs

Pitches:

Leisure:

Facilities:

Services:

Within 3 miles:

AA Pubs & Restaurants nearby: The Wheatsheaf at Beetham, BEETHAM, LA7 7AL, 015395 62123

Who has won England Campsite of the Year?
See page 14

NETHER WASDALE

Places to visit

Ravenglass & Eskdale Railway, RAVENGLASS, CA18 1SW, 01229 717171 www.ravenglass-railway.co.uk

Hardknott Roman Fort, BOOT www.english-heritage.org.uk/daysout/properties/hardknott-roman-fort

NETHER WASDALE Map 18 NY10

Church Stile Farm & Holiday Park

NEW ►►►► 78%

GOLD

tel: 01946 726252 & 726028 **Church Stile CA20 1ET**
email: info@churchstile.com
dir: *M6 junct 36, (follow signs for Western Lakes) A590, A5092, A595 (towards Whitehaven). In Gosforth follow Nether Wasdale signs. Pass 2 pubs. Site immediately after church.* **grid ref:** *NY125040*

A superb secluded park surrounded by mature trees, hedging and Lakeland stone walling in a peaceful valley setting. The combination of indigenous trees, flora and fauna creates stunning displays to complement the beauty of the surrounding hills. A renowned farm shop with a wide range of local produce is situated within the stylish reception and café. The site offers shepherd's huts for hire. 10 acre site. 50 touring pitches. 13 hardstandings. Motorhome pitches. Tent pitches. 47 statics. 2 shepherd's huts.

Open: Mar-15 Nov **Last arrival:** 21.00hrs **Last departure:** 11.00hrs

Pitches: * £17-£20.50 £15-£24.50

Leisure:

Facilities:

Services:

Within 3 miles:

Notes: No noise after 23.30hrs. Dogs must be kept on leads. Picnic tables.

AA Pubs & Restaurants nearby: Wasdale Head Inn, WASDALE HEAD, CA20 1EX, 019467 26229

Bridge Inn, SANTON BRIDGE, CA19 1UX, 019467 26221

PATTERDALE Map 18 NY31

Sykeside Camping Park

►►► 80%

tel: 017684 82239 **Brotherswater CA11 0NZ**
email: info@sykeside.co.uk
dir: *Direct access from A592 (Windermere to Ullswater road) at foot of Kirkstone Pass.* **grid ref:** *NY403119*

A camper's delight, this family-run park is sited at the foot of Kirkstone Pass, under the 2,000ft Hartsop Dodd in a spectacular area with breathtaking views. The park has mainly grass pitches with a few hardstandings, an area with tipis for hire, and for those campers without a tent there is bunkhouse accommodation. There's a small campers' kitchen and the bar serves breakfast and bar meals. There is abundant wildlife. 10 acre site. 86 touring pitches. 25 hardstandings. Caravan pitches. Motorhome pitches. Tent pitches. 2 tipis.

Open: all year **Last arrival:** 22.30hrs **Last departure:** 14.00hrs

Pitches: * £17.50-£25 £17.50-£25 £13.50-£23

Leisure:

Facilities:

Services:

Within 3 miles:

Notes: No noise after 23.00hrs. Laundry & drying room.

PENRITH

Map 18 NY53

Places to visit

Dalemain Mansion & Historic Gardens, DALEMAIN, CA11 0HB, 017684 86450
www.dalemain.com

Shap Abbey, SHAP, CA10 3NB, 0370 333 1181
www.english-heritage.org.uk/daysout/properties/shap-abbey

Great for kids: The Rheged Centre, PENRITH, CA11 0DQ, 01768 868000
www.rheged.com

PREMIER PARK

Lowther Holiday Park

►►►►► 86%

tel: 01768 863631 **Eamont Bridge CA10 2JB**
email: alan@lowther-holidaypark.co.uk **web:** www.lowther-holidaypark.co.uk
dir: *3m S of Penrith on A6.* **grid ref:** *NY527265*

A secluded natural woodland site with lovely riverside walks and glorious countryside surroundings. The park is home to a rare colony of red squirrels, and trout fishing is available on the two-mile stretch of the River Lowther which runs through it. A birdwatch scheme with a coloured brochure has been introduced, inviting guests to spot some of the 30 different species that can be seen on the park. Fully serviced pitches are now available. 50 acre site. 180 touring pitches. 50 hardstandings. 80 seasonal pitches. Caravan pitches. Motorhome pitches. Tent pitches. 403 statics. 2 wooden pods.

Open: mid Mar-mid Nov **Last arrival:** 22.00hrs **Last departure:** 22.00hrs

Pitches: * £26-£35 £26-£35 £26-£35

Leisure:

Facilities:

Services:

Within 3 miles:

Notes: Families only, no commercial vehicles, rollerblades or skateboards, no cats. Dogs must be kept on leads.

AA Pubs & Restaurants nearby: The Yanwath Gate Inn, YANWATH, CA10 2LF, 01768 862386

Cross Keys Inn, PENRITH, CA11 8TP, 01768 865588

Flusco Wood

►►►► 87%

tel: 017684 80020 & 07818 552931 **Flusco CA11 0JB**
email: info@fluscowood.co.uk
dir: *From Penrith to Keswick on A66 turn right signed Flusco. Approx 800mtrs, up short incline to right. Site on left.* **grid ref:** *NY345529*

Flusco Wood is set in mixed woodland with outstanding views towards Blencathra and the fells around Keswick. It combines two distinct areas, one of which has been designed specifically for touring caravans in neat glades with hardstandings, all within close proximity of the excellent log cabin-style toilet facilities. 24 acre site. 36 touring pitches. 36 hardstandings. 20 seasonal pitches. Caravan pitches. Motorhome pitches.

Open: 22 Mar-Oct **Last arrival:** 20.00hrs **Last departure:** noon

Pitches:

Leisure:

Facilities:

Services:

Within 3 miles:

Notes: Quiet site, not suitable for large groups. Dogs must be kept on leads.

AA Pubs & Restaurants nearby: The Yanwath Gate Inn, YANWATH, CA10 2LF, 01768 862386

Cross Keys Inn, PENRITH, CA11 8TP, 01768 865588

PENRUDDOCK

Map 18 NY42

Beckses Caravan Park

►►► 80%

tel: 01768 483224 **CA11 0RX**
email: contact@becksescaravanpark.co.uk
dir: *M6 junct 40, A66 towards Keswick. Approx 6m, at caravan park sign turn right onto B5288. Site on right in 0.25m.* **grid ref:** *NY419278*

A small, pleasant site on sloping ground with level pitches and views of distant fells, on the edge of the National Park. This sheltered park is in a good location for touring the north lakes. 4 acre site. 25 touring pitches. 25 hardstandings. Caravan pitches. Motorhome pitches. Tent pitches. 18 statics.

Open: Etr-Oct **Last arrival:** 20.00hrs **Last departure:** 11.00hrs

Pitches: * £17-£23 £17-£23 £14-£20

Facilities:

Services:

Within 3 miles:

Notes: No noise after 22.00hrs. Dogs must be kept on leads.

AA Pubs & Restaurants nearby: Rampsbeck Country House Hotel, WATERMILLOCK, CA11 0LP, 017684 86442

Macdonald Leeming House, WATERMILLOCK, CA11 0JJ, 01768 486674

PENTON Map 21 NY47

Twin Willows

►►► 78%

tel: 01228 577313 & 07850 713958 **The Beeches CA6 5QD**
email: davidson_b@btconnect.com
dir: *M6 junct 44, A7 signed Longtown, right into Netherby St, 6m to Bridge Inn pub. Right then 1st left, site 300yds on right.* **grid ref:** *NY449771*

Located close to Longtown, Twin Willows is a spacious park in a rural location on a ridge overlooking the Scottish border. All facilities, including all-weather pitches, are of a high quality. The park is suited to those who enjoy being away-from-it-all yet at the same time like to explore the area's rich history. A seasonal marquee is erected to hold regular barbecue and hog roast parties. 3 acre site. 16 touring pitches. 16 hardstandings. 10 seasonal pitches. Caravan pitches. Motorhome pitches. Tent pitches. 1 static. 1 tipi. 1 wooden pod.

Open: all year **Last arrival:** 22.00hrs **Last departure:** 10.00hrs

Pitches:

Leisure:

Facilities:

Services:

Within 3 miles:

Notes: Dogs must be kept on leads.

POOLEY BRIDGE Map 18 NY42

Park Foot Caravan & Camping Park

HOLIDAY CENTRE 87%

tel: 017684 86309 **Howtown Rd CA10 2NA**
email: holidays@parkfootullswater.co.uk **web:** www.parkfootullswater.co.uk
dir: *M6 junct 40, A66 towards Keswick, then A592 to Ullswater. Turn left for Pooley Bridge, right at church, right at x-rds signed Howtown.* **grid ref:** *NY469235*

A lively park with good outdoor sports facilities, and boats can be launched directly onto Lake Ullswater. The attractive, mainly tenting, park has many mature trees, lovely views across the lake, and a superb amenities block in the family-only field. The Country Club bar and restaurant provides good meals, as well as discos, live music and entertainment in a glorious location. There are lodges and static caravans for holiday hire. 40 acre site. 323 touring pitches. 32 hardstandings. Caravan pitches. Motorhome pitches. Tent pitches. 131 statics.

Open: Mar-Oct (rs Mar-Apr & mid Sep-Oct clubhouse open wknds only)
Last arrival: 22.00hrs **Last departure:** noon

Pitches: * £22-£39.50 £14-£39.50 £14-£36.50

Leisure: **Facilities:**

Services:

Within 3 miles:

Notes: Families & couples only. Dogs must be kept on leads. Boat launch, pony trekking, pool table, table tennis, bike hire, kids' club in summer holidays.

AA Pubs & Restaurants nearby: The Yanwath Gate Inn, YANWATH, CA10 2LF, 01768 862386

Waterfoot Caravan Park

►►► 87%

GOLD

tel: 017684 86302 **CA11 0JF**
email: enquiries@waterfootpark.co.uk **web:** www.waterfootpark.co.uk
dir: *M6 junct 40, A66 for 1m, A592 for 4m, site on right before lake. (NB do not leave A592 until site entrance; Sat Nav not compatible).* **grid ref:** *NY462246*

A quality touring park with neat, hardstanding pitches (most are fully serviced) in a grassy glade within the wooded grounds of an elegant Georgian mansion. The toilet facilities are clean and well maintained, and the lounge bar, with a separate family room, enjoys lake views. A path leads to Ullswater, and Aira Force waterfall, Dalemain House and Gardens and Pooley Bridge are all close by. Wooden wigwam pods for two adults and two children are available for hire. Please note that there is no access via Dacre. 22 acre site. 34 touring pitches. 30 hardstandings. Caravan pitches. Motorhome pitches. 146 statics. Wooden wigwams.

Open: Mar-14 Nov **Last arrival:** 21.30hrs **Last departure:** noon

Pitches: * £15.50-£28.50 £15.50-£28.50

Leisure: **Facilities:**

Services:

Within 3 miles:

Notes: No tents. Dogs must be kept on leads. Coffee lounge.

AA Pubs & Restaurants nearby: The Yanwath Gate Inn, YANWATH, CA10 2LF, 01768 862386

SANTON BRIDGE Map 18 NY10

The Old Post Office Campsite

78%

tel: 01946 726286 & 01785 822866 **CA19 1UY**
email: enquiries@theoldpostofficecampsite.co.uk
dir: *From A595 at Holmrook follow Santon Bridge signs, at T-junct left, site on right before river (NB Sat Nav may suggest a route via Wrynose & Hardknott Passes which may not be suitable for your vehicle at night or in bad weather).* **grid ref:** *NY110016*

A family-run campsite in a delightful riverside setting, beside an attractive stone bridge, that has very pretty pitches. The enthusiastic owner continues to upgrade the park. Permits for salmon, sea and brown trout fishing are available, and there is an adjacent pub. Camping pods are available for hire. 2.2 acre site. 40 touring pitches. 5 hardstandings. Caravan pitches. Motorhome pitches. Tent pitches. 5 wooden pods.

Open: all year **Last departure:** noon

Pitches:

Leisure:

Facilities:

Services:

Within 3 miles:

Notes: Dogs must be kept on leads.

AA Pubs & Restaurants nearby: Bridge Inn, SANTON BRIDGE, CA19 1UX, 019467 26221

Bower House Inn, ESKDALE GREEN, CA19 1TD, 019467 23244

Wasdale Head Inn, WASDALE HEAD, CA20 1EX, 019467 26229

SILLOTH Map 18 NY15

Stanwix Park Holiday Centre

HOLIDAY CENTRE 90%

tel: 016973 32666 **Greenrow CA7 4HH**
email: enquiries@stanwix.com **web:** www.stanwix.com
dir: *1m SW on B5300. From A596 (Wigton bypass), follow signs to Silloth on B5302. In Silloth follow signs to site, approx 1m on B5300.* **grid ref:** *NY108527*

A large well-run family park within easy reach of the Lake District. Attractively laid out, with lots of amenities to ensure a lively holiday, including a 4-lane automatic, 10-pin bowling alley. Excellent touring areas with hardstandings, one in a peaceful glade well away from the main leisure complex, and there's a campers' kitchen and clean, well-maintained toilet facilities. Four camping pods are now available to hire in Skiddaw touring field. 4 acre site. 121 touring pitches. 100 hardstandings. Caravan pitches. Motorhome pitches. Tent pitches. 212 statics. 4 wooden pods.

Stanwix Park Holiday Centre

Open: all year ex 25-26 Dec (rs Nov-Feb (ex New Year) no entertainment, shop closed) **Last arrival:** 21.00hrs **Last departure:** 11.00hrs

Pitches:

Leisure: Spa

Facilities:

Services:

Within 3 miles:

Notes: Families only. Dogs must be kept on leads. Amusement arcade.

See advert on opposite page

Solway Holiday Village

NEW HOLIDAY CENTRE 78%

tel: 016973 31236 **Skinburness Dr CA7 4QN**
email: solway@hagansleisure.co.uk
dir: *From B5302 in Silloth (junct of Criffel St & Petteril St) follow brown signs.*
grid ref: *NY114544*

A long established holiday destination set on a former wartime airfield with a wide range of indoor and outdoor activities. The touring and camping areas are located in a peaceful tree surrounded area with a dedicated warden on hand. For food, in addition to a stylish bistro, there is also The Nags Head bar and Harley's entertainment bar. Children benefit from a wide range of activities including an indoor swimming pool, a soft ball room, great outdoor play equipment and the adjacent Silverstone Open (animal) Farm. 140 acre site. 151 touring pitches. 1 hardstanding. 30 seasonal pitches. Caravan pitches. Motorhome pitches. Tent pitches. 310 statics.

Open: Mar-11 Nov **Last arrival:** 22.00hrs **Last departure:** 11.00hrs

Pitches:

Leisure:

Facilities:

Services:

Within 3 miles:

Notes: Dogs must be kept on leads. Mini farm & tourist train.

LEISURE: Indoor swimming pool Outdoor swimming pool Children's playground Kid's club Tennis court Games room Separate TV room golf course Boats for hire Cinema Entertainment Fishing Mini golf Watersports Gym Sports field Spa Stables
FACILITIES: Bath Shower Electric shaver Hairdryer Ice Pack Facility Disabled facilities Public telephone Shop on site or within 200yds Mobile shop (calls at least 5 days a week) BBQ area Picnic area Wi-fi Internet access Recycling Tourist info Dog exercise area

Hylton Caravan Park

►►►► 88%

tel: 016973 31707 & 32666 **Eden St CA7 4AY**
email: enquiries@stanwix.com **web:** www.stanwix.com
dir: *On entering Silloth on B5302 follow signs for site, approx 0.5m on left, at end of Eden St.* **grid ref:** *NY113533*

A smart, modern touring park with excellent toilet facilities including several bathrooms. This high quality park is a sister site to Stanwix Park, which is just a mile away and offers all the amenities of a holiday centre, which are available to Hylton tourers. 18 acre site. 90 touring pitches. Caravan pitches. Motorhome pitches. Tent pitches. 213 statics.

Open: Mar-15 Nov **Last arrival:** 21.00hrs **Last departure:** 11.00hrs

Pitches:

Leisure:

Facilities:

Services:

Within 3 miles:

Notes: Families only. Dogs must be kept on leads. Use of facilities at Stanwix Park Holiday Centre.

TEBAY Map 18 NY60

Tebay Services Caravan Site

►►► 79%

tel: 01539 711322 **Orton CA10 3SB**
email: caravans@westmorland.com **web:** www.westmorland.com/caravan
dir: *Exit M6 at Westmorland Services, 1m from junct 38. Site accessed through service area from either N'bound or S'bound carriageways. Follow site signs.* **grid ref:** *NY609060*

An ideal stopover site adjacent to the Tebay service station on the M6, and handy for touring the Lake District. The park is screened by high grass banks, bushes and trees, and is within walking distance of the excellent farm shop and restaurant within the services complex, where caravan park customers enjoy a 10% discount. 4 acre site. 80 touring pitches. 80 hardstandings. 43 seasonal pitches. Caravan pitches. Motorhome pitches. 7 statics.

Open: Mar-Nov **Last arrival:** anytime **Last departure:** noon

Pitches: **Facilities:**

Services: **Within 3 miles:**

AA Pubs & Restaurants nearby: The Fat Lamb Country Inn, RAVENSTONEDALE, CA17 4LL, 015396 23242

The Black Swan, RAVENSTONEDALE, CA17 4NG, 015396 23204

TROUTBECK (NEAR KESWICK) Map 18 NY32

PREMIER PARK

Troutbeck Camping and Caravanning Club Site

►►►►► 81%

tel: 017687 79149 **Hutton Moor End CA11 0SX**
dir: *M6 junct 40, A66 towards Keswick. In 9.5m sharp left for Wallthwaite. Site 0.5m on left.* **grid ref:** *NY365271*

Beautifully situated between Penrith and Keswick, this quiet, well-managed Lakeland campsite offers two immaculate touring areas, one a sheltered paddock for caravans and motorhomes, with serviced hardstanding pitches, and a maturing lower field, which has spacious hardstanding pitches and a superb and very popular small tenting area that enjoys stunning and extensive views of the surrounding fells. The toilet block is appointed to a very high standard and includes two family cubicles, and the log cabin reception/shop stocks local and organic produce. A luxury caravan, sleeping six, is available for hire. The enthusiastic franchisees offer high levels of customer care and are constantly improving the park, which is well-placed for visited Keswick, Ullswater and the north lakes. Non-members are also very welcome. 5 acre site. 54 touring pitches. 36 hardstandings. Caravan pitches. Motorhome pitches. Tent pitches. 20 statics.

Open: 9 Mar-11 Nov & 26 Dec-2 Jan **Last arrival:** 20.00hrs **Last departure:** noon

Pitches: **Leisure:**

Facilities:

Services: **Within 3 miles:**

Notes: Site gates closed 23.00hrs-07.00hrs. Dogs must be kept on leads. Dog walk.

ULVERSTON Map 18 SD27

Places to visit

The Dock Museum, BARROW-IN-FURNESS, LA14 2PW, 01229 876400 www.dockmuseum.org.uk

Furness Abbey, BARROW-IN-FURNESS, LA13 0PJ, 01229 823420 www.english-heritage.org.uk/daysout/properties/furness-abbey

Great for kids: South Lakes Safari Zoo, DALTON-IN-FURNESS, LA15 8JR, 01229 466086 www.safarizoo.co.uk

PREMIER PARK

Bardsea Leisure Park

►►►►► 88%

tel: 01229 584712 & 484363 **Priory Rd LA12 9QE**
email: reception@bardsealeisure.co.uk
dir: *M6 junct 36, A590 towards Barrow. At Ulverston take A5087, site 1m on right.*
grid ref: *SD292765*

An attractively landscaped former quarry creates a quiet and very sheltered site; set on the southern edge of the town, it is convenient for both the coast and the Lake District. Many of the generously-sized pitches offer all-weather full facilities. The refurbished and superb amenities blocks providing excellent privacy standards will be ready for the 2016 season. The site has an excellent caravan accessories shop. Please note that this site does not accept tents. 5 acre site. 83 touring pitches. 83 hardstandings. 50 seasonal pitches. Caravan pitches. Motorhome pitches. 88 statics.

Open: all year **Last arrival:** 22.00hrs **Last departure:** noon

Pitches:

Leisure:

Facilities:

Services:

Within 3 miles:

Notes: No noise after 22.30hrs. Dogs must be kept on leads.

AA Pubs & Restaurants nearby: Farmers Arms Hotel, ULVERSTON, LA12 7BA, 01229 584469

LEISURE: Indoor swimming pool Outdoor swimming pool Children's playground Kid's club Tennis court Games room Separate TV room golf course Boats for hire Cinema Entertainment Fishing Mini golf Watersports Gym Sports field Spa Stables
FACILITIES: Bath Shower Electric shaver Hairdryer Ice Pack Facility Disabled facilities Public telephone Shop on site or within 200yds Mobile shop (calls at least 5 days a week) BBQ area Picnic area Wi-fi Internet access Recycling Tourist info Dog exercise area

WASDALE HEAD Map 18 NY10

Wasdale Head National Trust Campsite

►►► 78%

tel: 015394 63862 & 32733 **CA20 1EX**
email: campsite.bookings@nationaltrust.org.uk
dir: *From A595 N towards Whitehaven turn left at Gosforth; from Whitehaven S on A595 right at Holmrook for Santon Bridge, follow signs to Wasdale Head.* **grid ref:** *NY183076*

Set in a remote and beautiful spot at Wasdale Head, under the stunning Scafell peaks at the head of the deepest lake in England. Clean, well-kept facilities are set centrally amongst open grass pitches and trees, where seven camping pods and two tipis are also located. There are eight hardstandings for motorhomes and eight electric hook-ups for tents. The renowned Wasdale Head Inn is close by. 5 acre site. 120 touring pitches. 10 hardstandings. Motorhome pitches. Tent pitches. 2 tipis. 7 wooden pods.

Open: all year (rs Wknds Nov-Feb shop open) **Last arrival:** 20.00hrs
Last departure: 11.00hrs

Pitches: **Facilities:**

Services: **Within 3 miles:**

Notes: No cars by tents. No groups of more than 4 unless a family with children. Dogs must be kept on leads.

AA Pubs & Restaurants nearby: Wasdale Head Inn, WASDALE HEAD, CA20 1EX, 019467 26229

WATERMILLOCK Map 18 NY42

The Quiet Site

►►►► 88%

tel: 07768 727016 **Ullswater CA11 0LS**
email: info@thequietsite.co.uk
dir: *M6 junct 40, A592 towards Ullswater. Right at lake junct, then right at Brackenrigg Hotel. Site 1.5m on right.* **grid ref:** *NY431236*

A well-maintained site in a lovely, peaceful location, with good terraced pitches offering great fell views, very good toilet facilities including family bathrooms, and a charming 'olde-worlde' bar. Their policy of green sustainability is commendable, with solar panels and a biomass boiler delivering heat and hot water to the amenity blocks, even when the site is busy. There are wooden camping pods and self-catering stone cottages; plus new for 2015, The Hobbit Hole (underground accommodation for six people) available for hire. 10 acre site. 100 touring pitches. 60 hardstandings. 15 seasonal pitches. Caravan pitches. Motorhome pitches. Tent pitches. 23 statics. 14 wooden pods.

Open: all year (rs Low season bar closed some weekdays) **Last arrival:** 21.00hrs
Last departure: noon (or 11.00hrs for pods)

Pitches: * £15-£35 £15-£35 £15-£35

Leisure:

Facilities:

Services:

Within 3 miles:

Notes: Quiet from 22.00hrs. Pool table, soft play area for toddlers, caravan storage.

AA Pubs & Restaurants nearby: Macdonald Leeming House, WATERMILLOCK, CA11 0JJ, 01768 486674

Rampsbeck Country House Hotel, WATERMILLOCK, CA11 0LP, 017684 86442

Cove Caravan & Camping Park

►►►► 83%

tel: 017684 86549 **Ullswater CA11 0LS**
email: info@cove-park.co.uk
dir: *M6 junct 40, A592 for Ullswater. Right at lake junct, then right at Brackenrigg Inn. Site 1.5m on left.* **grid ref:** *NY431236*

A peaceful family site in an attractive and elevated position with extensive fell views and glimpses of Ullswater Lake. Extensive ground works have been carried out in order to provide spacious, mostly level pitches. Pretty, seasonal flowers are planted amid the wide variety of mature trees and shrubs. 3 acre site. 50 touring pitches. 27 hardstandings. 10 seasonal pitches. Caravan pitches. Motorhome pitches. Tent pitches. 39 statics.

Open: Mar-Oct **Last arrival:** 21.00hrs **Last departure:** noon

Pitches: * £20-£34 £20-£34 £15-£30

Leisure:

Facilities:

Services:

Within 3 miles:

Notes: No open fires, no noise after 22.30hrs. Dogs must be kept on leads.

AA Pubs & Restaurants nearby: Macdonald Leeming House, WATERMILLOCK, CA11 0JJ, 01768 486674

Rampsbeck Country House Hotel, WATERMILLOCK, CA11 0LP, 017684 86442

Ullswater Holiday Park

►►►► 83%

tel: 017684 86666 **High Longthwaite CA11 0LR**
email: info@ullswaterholidaypark.co.uk
dir: *M6 junct 40, A592, W towards Ullswater for 5m. Right, alongside Ullswater for 2m, right at phone box. Site 0.5m on right.* **grid ref:** *NY438232*

A pleasant rural site with its own nearby boat launching and marine storage facility, making it ideal for sailors. The family-owned and run park enjoys fell and lake views, and there is a bar, a stylish new café, a splendid undercover area for campers, and a shop on site. Many of the pitches are fully serviced and there are wooden cabins with barbecues. Please note that the Marine Park is one mile from the camping area. 12 acre site. 160 touring pitches. 58 hardstandings. Caravan pitches. Motorhome pitches. Tent pitches. 55 statics. 4 wooden pods.

Open: Mar-Nov (rs Low season bar open wknds only) **Last arrival:** 21.00hrs
Last departure: noon

Pitches: * £15-£28 £15-£28 £15-£28

Leisure:

Facilities:

Services:

Within 3 miles:

Notes: No open fires, no noise after 23.30hrs. Dogs must be kept on leads. Boat launching & moorings 1m.

AA Pubs & Restaurants nearby: Macdonald Leeming House, WATERMILLOCK, CA11 0JJ, 01768 486674

Rampsbeck Country House Hotel, WATERMILLOCK, CA11 0LP, 017684 86442

WINDERMERE — Map 18 SD49

Places to visit

Holehird Gardens, WINDERMERE, LA23 1NP, 015394 46008 www.holehirdgardens.org.uk

Blackwell The Arts & Crafts House, BOWNESS-ON-WINDERMERE, LA23 3JT, 015394 46139 www.blackwell.org.uk

Great for kids: Lake District Visitor Centre at Brockhole, WINDERMERE, LA23 1LJ, 015394 46601 www.brockhole.co.uk

PREMIER PARK

Park Cliffe Camping & Caravan Estate

90%

GOLD

tel: 015395 31344 **Birks Rd, Tower Wood LA23 3PG**
email: info@parkcliffe.co.uk **web:** www.parkcliffe.co.uk
dir: *M6 junct 36, A590. Right at Newby Bridge onto A592. 3.6m right into site. (NB due to difficult access from main road this is the only advised direction for approaching the site).* **grid ref:** *SD391912*

A lovely hillside park set in 25 secluded acres of fell land. The camping area is sloping and uneven in places, but well drained and sheltered; some pitches have spectacular views of Lake Windermere and the Langdales. The park offers a high level of customer care and is very well equipped for families (family bathrooms), and there is an attractive bar and brasserie restaurant serving quality food; wooden pods and three static holiday caravans are available for hire. 25 acre site. 60 touring pitches. 60 hardstandings. 25 seasonal pitches. Caravan pitches. Motorhome pitches. Tent pitches. 56 statics. 7 wooden pods.

Open: Mar-8 Nov (Wknds & school hols facilities open fully) **Last arrival:** 22.00hrs **Last departure:** noon

Pitches: * £26-£32 £26-£32 £20-£34

Leisure:

Facilities:

Services:

Within 3 miles:

Notes: No noise 23.00hrs-07.30hrs. Dogs must be kept on leads. Off-licence.

AA Pubs & Restaurants nearby: Eagle & Child Inn, WINDERMERE, LA8 9LP, 01539 821320

Beech Hill Hotel, WINDERMERE, LA23 3LR, 015394 42137

PREMIER PARK

Hill of Oaks & Blakeholme

84%

GOLD

tel: 015395 31578 **LA12 8NR**
email: enquiries@hillofoaks.co.uk **web:** www.hillofoaks.co.uk
dir: *M6 junct 36, A590 towards Barrow. At rdbt signed Bowness turn right onto A592. Site approx 3m on left.* **grid ref:** *SD386899*

A secluded, heavily wooded park on the shores of Lake Windermere. Pretty lakeside picnic areas, woodland walks and a play area make this a delightful park for families, with excellent serviced pitches, a licensed shop and a heated toilet block. Both ladies and gents amenities have been completely refurbished with quality decor and fittings and very good privacy options. Watersports include sailing and canoeing, with private jetties for boat launching. 31 acre site. 43 touring pitches. 43 hardstandings. Caravan pitches. Motorhome pitches. 215 statics.

Open: Mar-14 Nov **Last departure:** noon

Pitches: * £21-£37 £21-£37

Leisure:

Facilities:

Services:

Within 3 miles:

Notes: No tents (except trailer tents), no groups. Dogs must be kept on leads.

AA Pubs & Restaurants nearby: Eagle & Child Inn, WINDERMERE, LA8 9LP, 01539 821320

Beech Hill Hotel, WINDERMERE, LA23 3LR, 015394 42137

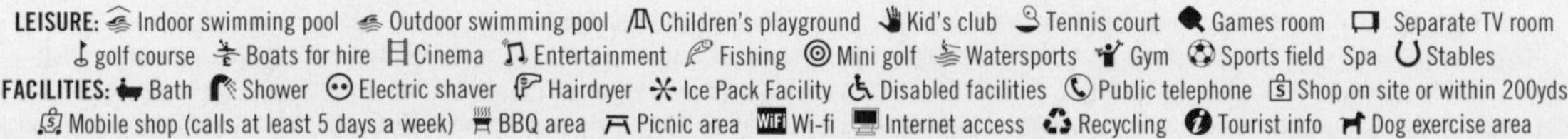

DERBYSHIRE

ASHBOURNE Map 10 SK14

Places to visit

Kedleston Hall, KEDLESTON HALL, DE22 5JH, 01332 842191 www.nationaltrust.org.uk

Carsington Fields Caravan Park

►►► 83%

tel: 01335 372872 **Millfields Ln, Nr Carsington Water DE6 3JS**
email: bookings@carsingtoncaravaning.co.uk
dir: *From Belper towards Ashbourne on A517, right approx 0.25m past Hulland Ward into Dog Ln. 0.75m right at x-rds signed Carsington. Site on right approx 0.75m.*
grid ref: *SK251493*

A very well-presented and spacious park with a good toilet block, open views and a large fenced pond that attracts plenty of wildlife. The popular tourist attraction of Carsington Water is a short stroll away, with its variety of leisure facilities including fishing, sailing, windsurfing and children's play area. The park is also a good base for walkers. 6 acre site. 58 touring pitches. 14 hardstandings. 14 seasonal pitches. Caravan pitches. Motorhome pitches. Tent pitches.

Open: Mar-Sep **Last arrival:** 21.00hrs **Last departure:** 14.00hrs

Pitches: * £24-£29 £24-£29 £24-£29

Facilities:

Services:

Within 3 miles:

Notes: No large groups or group bookings, no noise after 23.00hrs. Dogs must be kept on leads. Indian takeaway free delivery to site.

AA Pubs & Restaurants nearby: The Coach and Horses Inn, FENNY BENTLEY, DE6 1LB, 01335 350246

Bentley Brook Inn, FENNY BENTLEY, DE6 1LF, 01335 350278

BAKEWELL Map 16 SK26

Places to visit

Chatsworth, CHATSWORTH, DE45 1PP, 01246 565300 www.chatsworth.org

Greenhills Holiday Park

►►►► 78%

tel: 01629 813052 & 813467 **Crowhill Ln DE45 1PX**
email: info@greenhillsholidaypark.co.uk
dir: *1m NW of Bakewell on A6. Signed before Ashford-in-the-Water, onto unclassified road on right.* **grid ref:** *SK202693*

A well-established park set in lovely countryside within the Peak District National Park. Many pitches enjoy uninterrupted views, and there is easy accessibility to all facilities, including the spotlessly clean amenity blocks. The clubhouse, shop and children's playground are popular features. 8 acre site. 172 touring pitches. 30 hardstandings. Caravan pitches. Motorhome pitches. Tent pitches. 73 statics.

Open: Feb-Nov (rs Feb-Apr & Oct-Nov bar & shop closed) **Last arrival:** 22.00hrs
Last departure: noon

Pitches:

Leisure:

Facilities:

Services:

Within 3 miles:

AA Pubs & Restaurants nearby: The Monsal Head Hotel, BAKEWELL, DE45 1NL, 01629 640250

Piedaniel's, BAKEWELL, DE45 1BX, 01629 812687

BIRCHOVER Map 16 SK26

Places to visit

Haddon Hall, HADDON HALL, DE45 1LA, 01629 812855 www.haddonhall.co.uk

The Heights of Abraham Cable Cars, Caverns & Hilltop Park, MATLOCK BATH, DE4 3PD, 01629 582365 www.heightsofabraham.com

PREMIER PARK

Barn Farm Campsite

►►►►► 82%

tel: 01629 650245 **Barn Farm DE4 2BL**
email: gilberthh@msn.com
dir: *From A6 take B5056 towards Ashbourne. Follow brown signs to site.*
grid ref: *SK238621*

An interesting park on a former dairy farm with the many and varied facilities housed in high quality conversions of old farm buildings. The three large and well-maintained touring fields offer sweeping views across the Peak District National Park. There is an excellent choice of privacy cubicles, including shower and washbasin cubicles, a fully serviced family room, and even a shower and sauna.There are five stylish, self-catering camping barns for hire. 15 acre site. 62 touring pitches. 13 hardstandings. Caravan pitches. Motorhome pitches. Tent pitches.

Open: Apr-Oct **Last arrival:** 21.00hrs **Last departure:** 11.00hrs

Pitches: * £17-£22 £17-£22 £12-£20

Leisure:

Facilities:

Services:

Within 3 miles:

Notes: No music after 22.30hrs, minimum noise 22.30hrs-07.00hrs. Dogs must be kept on leads. Vending machines, sauna, sunbed.

AA Pubs & Restaurants nearby: The Druid Inn, BIRCHOVER, DE4 2BL, 01629 653836

The Peacock at Rowsley, ROWSLEY, DE4 2EB, 01629 733518

BUXTON

Map 16 SK07

Places to visit

Poole's Cavern (Buxton Country Park), BUXTON, SK17 9DH, 01298 26978 www.poolescavern.co.uk

Great for kids: Go Ape Buxton, BUXTON, SK17 9DH, 0845 643 9215 *(Calls cost 7p per minute plus your phone company's access charge)* www.goape.co.uk/buxton

Lime Tree Park

►►►► 89%

tel: 01298 22988 **Dukes Dr SK17 9RP**
email: info@limetreeparkbuxton.com
dir: *1m S of Buxton, between A515 & A6.* **grid ref:** *SK070725*

A most attractive and well-designed site, set on the side of a narrow valley in an elevated location, with separate, neatly landscaped areas for statics, tents, touring caravans and motorhomes. There's good attention to detail throughout including the clean toilets and showers, and WiFi is free of charge. Its backdrop of a magnificent old railway viaduct and views over Buxton and the surrounding hills, make this a sought-after destination. There are eight static caravans, a pine lodge and two apartments available for holiday lets. 10.5 acre site. 106 touring pitches. 22 hardstandings. Caravan pitches. Motorhome pitches. Tent pitches. 43 statics.

Open: Mar-Oct **Last arrival:** 18.00hrs **Last departure:** noon

Pitches:

Leisure:

Facilities: WiFi

Services:

Within 3 miles:

Notes: No noise after 22.00hrs, no fires. Dogs must be kept on leads.

AA Pubs & Restaurants nearby: The Queen Anne Inn, GREAT HUCKLOW, SK17 8RF, 01298 871246

Beech Croft Farm

►►►► 87%

DAVID BELLAMY CONSERVATION AWARD GOLD

tel: 01298 85330 **Beech Croft, Blackwell in the Peak SK17 9TQ**
email: mail@beechcroftfarm.co.uk **web:** www.beechcroftfarm.co.uk
dir: *Exit A6 midway between Buxton & Bakewell. Site signed.* **grid ref:** *SK122720*

A small terraced farm site with lovely Peak District views. There's a fine stone-built toilet block with ultra-modern fittings, under-floor heating and additional unisex facilities, fully-serviced hardstanding pitches, gravel roads, a campers' shelter, and a super tarmac pathway leading from the camping field to the toilet block. This makes an ideal site for those touring or walking in the Peak District. 3 acre site. 30 touring pitches. 30 hardstandings. Caravan pitches. Motorhome pitches. Tent pitches.

Open: all year (rs Nov-Feb not open for tents) **Last arrival:** 20.30hrs **Last departure:** noon

Pitches: * £20.50-£23 £20.50-£23 £14-£16

Leisure:

Facilities: WiFi

Services:

Notes: No noise after 22.00hrs. Dogs must be kept on leads. Breakfast & jacket potato van (high season).

AA Pubs & Restaurants nearby: The Queen Anne Inn, GREAT HUCKLOW, SK17 8RF, 01298 871246

**REGIONAL WINNER – HEART OF ENGLAND
AA CAMPSITE OF THE YEAR 2016**

Clover Fields Touring Caravan Park

►►► 95%

tel: 01298 78731 **1 Heath View, Harpur Hill SK17 9PU**
email: cloverfields@tiscali.co.uk
dir: *A515, B5053, then immediately right. Site 0.5m on left.* **grid ref:** *SK075704*

A developing and spacious adults-only park, just over a mile from the attractions of Buxton, with very good facilities, including an upmarket, timber chalet-style toilet block. All pitches are fully serviced and have individual barbecues, and are set out on terraces, each with extensive views over the countryside. Swathes of natural meadow grasses and flowers cloak the terraces and surrounding fields. The new Teapot Café serves a good range of meals. 12 acre site. 45 touring pitches. 39 hardstandings. Seasonal pitches. Caravan pitches. Motorhome pitches. Tent pitches.

Open: all year **Last arrival:** 20.00hrs **Last departure:** 18.00hrs

Pitches: £24-£28.50 £24-£28.50 £24

Facilities:

Services:

Within 3 miles:

Notes: Adults only. No commercial vehicles. Dogs must be kept on leads. Small fishing pond, boules area.

AA Pubs & Restaurants nearby: The Queen Anne Inn, GREAT HUCKLOW, SK17 8RF, 01298 871246

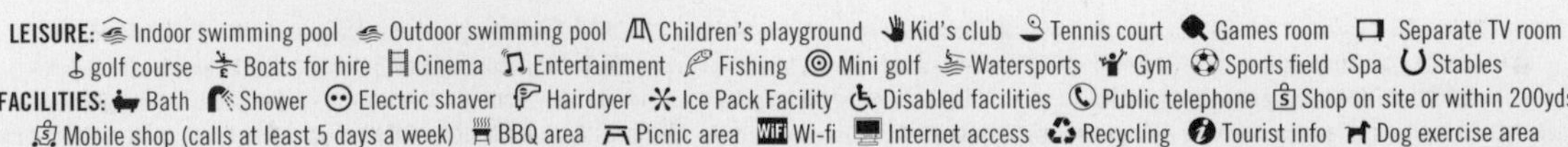

HOPE Map 16 SK18

Places to visit

Peveril Castle, CASTLETON, S33 8WQ, 01433 620613 www.english-heritage.org.uk/daysout/properties/peveril-castle

Speedwell Cavern, CASTLETON, S33 8WA, 01433 620512 www.speedwellcavern.co.uk

Pindale Farm Outdoor Centre

►►► 79%

tel: 01433 620111 **Pindale Rd S33 6RN**
email: pindalefarm@btconnect.com
dir: *From A6187 in Hope follow Pindale sign between church & Woodroffe Arms. Site 1m on left.* **grid ref:** *SK163825*

Set around a 13th-century farmhouse and a former lead mine pump house (now converted to a self-contained bunkhouse for up to 60 people), this simple, off-the-beaten-track site is an ideal base for walking, climbing, caving and various outdoor pursuits. Around the farm are several deeply wooded areas available for tents, and old stone buildings that have been converted to house modern toilet facilities. 4 acre site. 60 touring pitches. Tent pitches.

Open: Mar-Oct

Pitches: ⛺ **Facilities:** WiFi

Services: **Within 3 miles:**

Notes: No anti-social behaviour, noise must be kept to minimum after 21.00hrs, no fires. Dogs must be kept on leads. Charge for WiFi.

AA Pubs & Restaurants nearby: The Old Hall Hotel, HOPE, S33 6RH, 01433 620160

Ye Olde Nags Head, CASTLETON, S33 8WH, 01433 620248

The Yorkshire Bridge Inn, BAMFORD, S33 0AZ, 01433 651361

MATLOCK

Places to visit

Peak District Mining Museum, MATLOCK BATH, DE4 3NR, 01629 583834 www.peakmines.co.uk

Haddon Hall, HADDON HALL, DE45 1LA, 01629 812855 www.haddonhall.co.uk

Great for kids: The Heights of Abraham Cable Cars, Caverns & Hilltop Park, MATLOCK BATH, DE4 3PD, 01629 582365 www.heightsofabraham.com

MATLOCK Map 16 SK35

Lickpenny Caravan Site

►►►► 90%

tel: 01629 583040 **Lickpenny Ln, Tansley DE4 5GF**
email: enquiries@lickpennycaravanpark.co.uk
dir: *From Matlock take A615 towards Alfreton for 3m. Site signed to left, into Lickpenny Ln, right into site near end of road.* **grid ref:** *SK339597*

A picturesque site in the grounds of an old plant nursery with areas broken up and screened by a variety of shrubs, and with spectacular views, which are best enjoyed from the upper terraced areas. The pitches, several fully serviced, are spacious, well screened and well marked, and facilities are kept to a very good standard. The bistro/coffee shop is popular with visitors. 16 acre site. 80 touring pitches. 80 hardstandings. 20 seasonal pitches. Caravan pitches. Motorhome pitches.

Open: all year **Last arrival:** 20.00hrs **Last departure:** noon (late departure until 18.00hrs – charge applies).

Pitches: * £16-£28 £16-£28 **Leisure:**

Facilities: WiFi **Services:**

Within 3 miles:

Notes: No noise after 23.00hrs, 1 car per pitch, Dogs must be kept on leads. Child bath available.

AA Pubs & Restaurants nearby: The Red Lion, MATLOCK, DE4 3BT, 01629 584888

Stones Restaurant, MATLOCK, DE4 3LT, 01629 56061

NEWHAVEN Map 16 SK16

Places to visit

Middleton Top Engine House, MIDDLETON, DE4 4LS, 01629 823204 www.derbyshire.gov.uk/countryside

Peak District Mining Museum, MATLOCK BATH, DE4 3NR, 01629 583834 www.peakmines.co.uk

Newhaven Caravan & Camping Park

►►►► 83%

tel: 01298 84300 **SK17 0DT**
email: newhavencaravanpark@btconnect.com
dir: *Between Ashbourne & Buxton at A515 & A5012 junct.* **grid ref:** *SK167602*

Pleasantly situated within the Peak District National Park, this park has mature trees screening the three touring areas. Very good toilet facilities cater for touring vans and a large tent field, and there's a restaurant adjacent to the site. 30 acre site. 125 touring pitches. 95 hardstandings. 40 seasonal pitches. Caravan pitches. Motorhome pitches. Tent pitches. 73 statics.

Open: Mar-Oct **Last arrival:** 20.00hrs **Last departure:** 13.00hrs

Pitches: * £16.25-£21.25 £16.25-£21.25 ⛺ £12.50-£21.25

Leisure: **Facilities:**

Services: **Within 3 miles:**

Notes: No noise after 23.00hrs. Dogs must be kept on leads.

AA Pubs & Restaurants nearby: Red Lion Inn, BIRCHOVER, DE4 2BN, 01629 650363

The Druid Inn, BIRCHOVER, DE4 2BL, 01629 653836

RIDDINGS Map 16 SK45

Riddings Wood Caravan and Camping Park

NEW ►►►► 81%

tel: 01773 605160 & 07810 320506 **Bullock Ln DE55 4BP**
email: info@riddingswoodcaravanandcampingpark.co.uk
dir: *M1 junct 27, A608 signed Heanor. Right onto B600 signed Alfreton & Selston. Left onto B6016 signed Jacksdale. Through Jacksdale towards Ridding. Site on right.*
grid ref: *SK430524*

Located close to both Derby and Nottingham, this newly developed site can be described a sloping amphitheatre in layout. It is surrounded by the mature trees of Riddings Wood on all sides and has a fabulous panoramic view looking down towards Jacksdale. Beyond the sweeping driveway and security barrier, you'll find a smart chalet-style reception, neat gravel hardstandings, manicured grass tent pitches, and a modern and stylish amenity block with quality shower and toilet facilities. Picnic benches are scattered around the park for campers to use, and fully serviced pitches will be available for the 2016 season. A local bus service runs every nine minutes from the site entrance to both Derby and Nottingham. 11.5 acre site. 75 touring pitches. 25 hardstandings. Caravan pitches. Motorhome pitches. Tent pitches.

Open: Mar-Dec

Pitches: * £17-£23 £17-£23 £13-£23

Leisure:

Facilities:

Services:

Within 3 miles:

Notes: Children must be accompanied by an adult at all times. Rubbish must be placed in designated areas. Dogs must be kept on leads.

RIPLEY Map 16 SK35

Places to visit

Midland Railway Butterley, RIPLEY, DE5 3QZ, 01773 747674
www.midlandrailwaycentre.co.uk

Denby Pottery Visitor Centre, DENBY, DE5 8NX, 01773 740799
www.denbyvisitorcentre.co.uk

Golden Valley Caravan & Camping Park

►►►► 84%

tel: 01773 513881 & 746786 **Coach Rd DE55 4ES**
email: enquiries@goldenvalleycaravanpark.co.uk
web: www.goldenvalleycaravanpark.co.uk
dir: *M1 junct 26, A610 to Codnor. Right at lights. Right into Alfreton Rd. In 1m left into Coach Rd, park on left. (NB it is advised that Sat Nav is ignored for last few miles & guide directions are followed).* **grid ref:** *SK408513*

This superbly landscaped park is set within 30 acres of woodland in the Amber Valley. The fully serviced pitches are set out in informal groups in clearings amongst the trees. The park has a cosy bar and bistro with outside patio, a fully stocked fishing lake, an innovative and well-equipped play area, an on-site jacuzzi and fully equipped fitness suite. There is also a wildlife pond and a nature trail. 30 acre site. 45 touring pitches. 45 hardstandings. 12 seasonal pitches. Caravan pitches. Motorhome pitches. Tent pitches. 1 static.

Open: all year (rs Wknds only in low season bar & café open, children's activities)
Last arrival: 21.00hrs **Last departure:** noon

Pitches: * £22.50-£30 £22.50-£30 £15-£30

Leisure:

Facilities:

Services:

Within 3 miles:

Notes: No vehicles on grass, no open fires or disposable BBQs, no noise after 22.30hrs. Dogs must be kept on leads. Zip slide, donkey rides, tractor train, water walking balls, log flume ride.

AA Pubs & Restaurants nearby: Santo's Higham Farm Hotel, HIGHAM, DE55 6EH, 01773 833812

ROSLISTON Map 10 SK21

Places to visit

Ashby-de-la-Zouch Castle, ASHBY-DE-LA-ZOUCH, LE65 1BR, 01530 413343 www.english-heritage.org.uk/daysout/properties/ashby-de-la-zouch-castle

Great for kids: Conkers, MOIRA, DE12 6GA, 01283 216633 www.visitconkers.com

Beehive Woodland Lakes

84%

tel: 01283 763981 **DE12 8HZ**
email: info@beehivefarm-woodlandlakes.co.uk
dir: *From A444 in Castle Gresley into Mount Pleasant Rd, follow Rosliston signs for 3.5m through Linton to T-junct. Left signed Beehive Farms.* **grid ref:** *SK249161*

A small, informal and rapidly developing caravan area secluded from an extensive woodland park in the heart of the National Forest National Park. Toilet facilities include four family rooms. Young children will enjoy the on-site animal farm and playground, whilst anglers can pass many a happy hour fishing at the park's three lakes; bikes can be hired. There is an adults-only area and camping pods are available for hire. The Honey Pot tearoom provides snacks and is open most days. 2.5 acre site. 46 touring pitches. 46 hardstandings. Caravan pitches. Motorhome pitches. Tent pitches. 4 wooden pods.

Open: all year **Last arrival:** 20.00hrs **Last departure:** noon

Pitches:

Leisure:

Facilities:

Services:

Within 3 miles:

Notes: Last arrival time 18.00hrs low season. Dogs must be kept on leads. Takeaway food delivered to site.

AA Pubs & Restaurants nearby: The Waterfront, BARTON-UNDER-NEEDWOOD, DE13 8DZ, 01283 711500

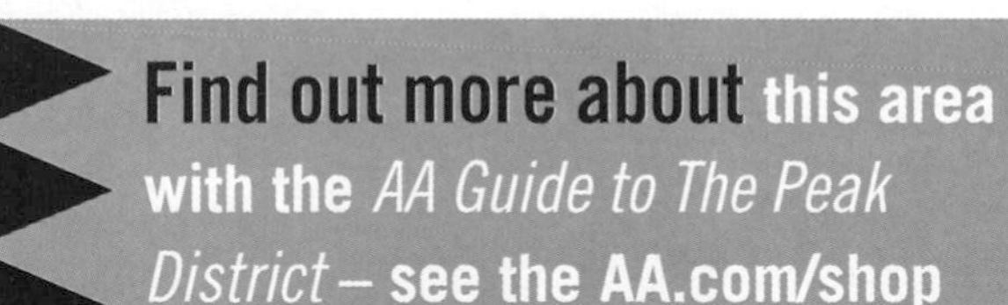

ROWSLEY

Places to visit

Temple Mine, MATLOCK BATH, DE4 3NR, 01629 583834 www.peakmines.co.uk

Great for kids: The Heights of Abraham Cable Cars, Caverns & Hilltop Park, MATLOCK BATH, DE4 3PD, 01629 582365 www.heightsofabraham.com

ROWSLEY Map 16 SK26

Grouse & Claret

►►►77%

tel: 01629 733233 **Station Rd DE4 2EB**
email: grouseandclaret.matlock@marstons.co.uk
dir: *M1 junct 29. Site on A6, 5m from Matlock & 3m from Bakewell.* **grid ref:** *SK258660*

A well-designed, purpose-built park at the rear of an eating house on the A6 between Bakewell and Chatsworth, and adjacent to the New Peak Shopping Village. The park comprises a level grassy area running down to the river, and all pitches have hardstandings and electric hook-ups. New TV sockets have been installed around site for improved reception. 2.5 acre site. 28 touring pitches. 28 hardstandings. Caravan pitches. Motorhome pitches.

Open: all year **Last arrival:** 22.00hrs **Last departure:** 11.00hrs

Pitches:

Leisure:

Facilities:

Services:

Within 3 miles:

Notes: Dogs must be kept on leads.

AA Pubs & Restaurants nearby: The Grouse & Claret, ROWSLEY, DE4 2EB, 01629 733233

The Peacock at Rowsley, ROWSLEY, DE4 2EB, 01629 733518

SHARDLOW Map 11 SK43

Places to visit

Melbourne Hall & Gardens, MELBOURNE, DE73 8EN, 01332 862502 www.melbournehall.com

Shardlow Marina Caravan Park

►►►72%

tel: 01332 792832 **London Rd DE72 2GL**
email: admin@shardlowmarina.co.uk
dir: *M1 junct 24a, A50 signed Derby. Exit from A50 junct 1 at rdbt signed Shardlow. Site 1m on right.* **grid ref:** *SK444303*

A large marina site with restaurant facilities, situated on the Trent and Merseyside Canal. Pitches are on grass surrounded by mature trees, and for the keen angler, the site offers fishing within the marina. The attractive grass touring area overlooks the marina. 25 acre site. 35 touring pitches. 26 hardstandings. 10 seasonal pitches. Caravan pitches. Motorhome pitches. Tent pitches. 73 statics.

Open: Mar-Jan **Last arrival:** 17.00hrs **Last departure:** noon

Pitches:

Facilities:

Services:

Within 3 miles:

Notes: Max 2 dogs per unit. Dogs must be kept on leads dogs, not be left unattended or tied up outside. Office closed between 13.00hrs-14.00hrs. .

AA Pubs & Restaurants nearby: The Old Crown Inn, SHARDLOW, DE72 2HL, 01332 792392

The Priest House Hotel, CASTLE DONINGTON, DE74 2RR, 01332 810649

Devon

With magnificent coastlines, two historic cities and the world-famous Dartmoor National Park, Devon sums up all that is best about the British landscape. For centuries it has been a fashionable and much loved holiday destination – especially south Devon's glorious English Riviera.

When the crime writer Agatha Christie was born in Torquay on Devon's glorious south coast, the town was a popular seaside resort. It was 1890, the start of Queen Victoria's last decade as monarch, and Torquay was a fashionable destination for all sorts of people; those looking for a permanent home by the sea as well as holidaymakers in search of long hours of sunshine and a mild climate. In many ways, Torquay remains much the same today and its impressive setting still evokes a sense of its Victorian heyday. A local steam train attraction adds to the atmosphere; you can travel from Paignton to Dartmouth, alighting on the way at the small station at Churston, just as Hercule Poirot does in Christie's 1930s detective novel *The ABC Murders*. The Queen of Crime herself used this station when she had a summer home nearby. The house, Greenway, overlooks a glorious sweep of the River Dart and is now managed as a popular visitor attraction by the National Trust.

Close to the English Riviera lies Dartmoor, one of the south-west's most spectacular landscapes. The contrast between the traditional attractions of the coast and this expanse of bleak, brooding moorland could not be greater. The National Park, which contains Dartmoor, covers 365 square miles and includes many fascinating geological features – isolated granite tors and two summits exceeding 2,000 feet among them. Dartmoor's waterfalls, including the tumbling Whitelady Waterfall at Lydford Gorge, can be seen in full spate even in the depths of winter. Everywhere you venture on Dartmoor, there are stone circles, burial chambers and mysterious clues to the distant past. The place oozes antiquity. Sir Arthur Conan Doyle set his classic Sherlock Holmes story *The Hound of the Baskervilles* on Dartmoor, and Agatha Christie stayed at a local hotel for two weeks at the height of the First World War in order to finish writing her first detective novel *The Mysterious Affair at Styles*, first published in 1920.

Not surprisingly, Dartmoor equates with walking and the opportunities are enormous. For something really adventurous, try the Two Moors Way. This long-distance route begins at Ivybridge and crosses the National Park to enter neighbouring Exmoor, which straddles the Devon/Somerset border. At Lynton and Lynmouth the trail connects with the South West Coast Path, which takes walkers on a breathtaking journey to explore north Devon's gloriously rugged coastline, renowned for its extraordinary collection of peaks and outcrops. Cycling in the two National Parks is also extremely popular and there is a good choice of off-road routes taking you to the heart of Dartmoor and Exmoor.

Devon's towns and cities offer a pleasing but stimulating alternative to the rigours of the countryside. There are scores of small market towns in the region – for example there is Tavistock with its popular farmers' market, one of many in the county. Plymouth lies in Devon's south-west corner and is a striking city and naval port. Much of its transformation over the years is a reminder of the devastation it suffered, together with Exeter, during the Second World War. The city places particular emphasis, of course, on the Spanish Armada and the voyage of the Pilgrim Fathers to America.

On the theme of sailing, Devon is synonymous with this most invigorating of boating activities. Salcombe, on the county's south coast, is a sailing playground. Situated on a tree-fringed estuary beneath lush rolling hills, the town thrives on boats – it hosts the week-long Salcombe Regatta in August. It's even suitable for swimming, with several sandy beaches and sheltered bays.

◁ East Dart River, Dartmoor National Park

DEVON

ASHBURTON

Map 3 SX77

Places to visit

Compton Castle, COMPTON, TQ3 1TA, 01803 842382
www.nationaltrust.org.uk/comptoncastle

Tuckers Maltings, NEWTON ABBOT, TQ12 4AA, 01626 334734
www.tuckersmaltings.com

Great for kids: Prickly Ball Farm and Hedgehog Hospital, NEWTON ABBOT, TQ12 6BZ, 01626 362319 www.pricklyballfarm.com

Parkers Farm Holiday Park

►►►► 85%

tel: 01364 654869 **Higher Mead Farm TQ13 7LJ**
email: parkersfarm@btconnect.com
dir: *From Exeter on A38, 2nd left after Plymouth (29m) sign, signed Woodland & Denbury. From Plymouth on A38 take A383 Newton Abbot exit, turn right across bridge, rejoin A38, then as above.* **grid ref:** *SX779713*

A well-developed site terraced into rising ground with stunning views across rolling countryside to the Dartmoor tors. Part of a working farm, this park offers excellent fully serviced hardstanding pitches, which make the most of the fine views; it is beautifully maintained and has good quality toilet facilities, a popular games room and a bar/restaurant that serves excellent meals. Large family rooms with two shower cubicles, a large sink and a toilet are especially appreciated by families with small children. There are regular farm walks when all the family can meet and feed the various animals. 25 acre site. 100 touring pitches. 20 hardstandings. Caravan pitches. Motorhome pitches. Tent pitches. 18 statics.

Open: Etr-end Oct (rs Out of season bar & restaurant open wknds only)
Last arrival: 22.00hrs **Last departure:** 10.00hrs

Pitches:

Leisure:

Facilities:

Services:

Within 3 miles:

Notes: Dogs must be kept on leads. Large field for dog walking.

AA Pubs & Restaurants nearby: The Rising Sun, ASHBURTON, TQ13 7JT, 01364 652544
Agaric, ASHBURTON, TQ13 7QD, 01364 654478

River Dart Country Park

►►►► 85%

tel: 01364 652511 **Holne Park TQ13 7NP**
email: info@riverdart.co.uk
dir: *M5 junct 31, A38 towards Plymouth. In Ashburton at Peartree junct follow brown site signs. Site 1m on left. (NB Peartree junct is 2nd exit at Ashburton; do not exit at Linhay junct as narrow roads are unsuitable for caravans).* **grid ref:** *SX734700*

Set in 90 acres of magnificent parkland that was once part of a Victorian estate, with many specimen and exotic trees, this peaceful, hidden-away touring park occupies several camping areas, all served with good quality toilet facilities. In spring the park is a blaze of colour from the many azaleas and rhododendrons. There are numerous outdoor activities for all ages including abseiling, caving and canoeing, plus high quality, well-maintained facilities. The open moorland of Dartmoor is only a few minutes away. 90 acre site. 170 touring pitches. 34 hardstandings. Caravan pitches. Motorhome pitches. Tent pitches.

Open: Apr-Sep (rs Low season café bar restricted opening hours) **Last arrival:** 21.00hrs
Last departure: 11.00hrs

Pitches: * £14-£33 £14-£33 £14-£33

Leisure:

Facilities:

Services:

Within 3 miles:

Notes: Dogs must be kept on leads. Adventure playground.

AA Pubs & Restaurants nearby: The Rising Sun, ASHBURTON, TQ13 7JT, 01364 652544

AXMINSTER Map 4 SY29

Places to visit

Branscombe - The Old Bakery, Manor Mill and Forge, BRANSCOMBE, EX12 3DB, 01752 346585 www.nationaltrust.org.uk

Allhallows Museum, HONITON, EX14 1PG, 01404 44966 www.honitonmuseum.co.uk

Great for kids: Pecorama Pleasure Gardens, BEER, EX12 3NA, 01297 21542 www.pecorama.info

Andrewshayes Holiday Park

►►►► 86%

GOLD

tel: 01404 831225 **Dalwood EX13 7DY**
email: info@andrewshayes.co.uk **web:** www.andrewshayes.co.uk
dir: *3m from Axminster (towards Honiton) on A35, right at Taunton Cross signed Dalwood & Stockland. Site 150mtrs on right.* **grid ref:** *ST248088*

An attractive family park within easy reach of Lyme Regis, Seaton, Branscombe and Sidmouth in an ideal touring location. This popular park offers modern toilet facilities, a quiet, cosy bar and takeaway service, and an excellent play area for children, set beside the swimming pool, bar and restaurant area. 12 acre site. 150 touring pitches. 105 hardstandings. 100 seasonal pitches. Caravan pitches. Motorhome pitches. Tent pitches. 80 statics.

Open: Apr-Nov (rs Off-peak shop, bar hours, takeaway limited) **Last arrival:** 22.00hrs **Last departure:** 11.00hrs

Pitches: £16-£24 £16-£24 £16-£24 **Leisure:** **Facilities:** **Services:**

Within 3 miles:

Notes: Children under 12 must be supervised by an adult in pool. Dogs must be on leads.

AA Pubs & Restaurants nearby: The Old Inn, KILMINGTON, EX13 7RB, 01297 32096

BICKINGTON (NEAR ASHBURTON) Map 3 SX87

Lemonford Caravan Park

►►►► 82%

tel: 01626 821242 **TQ12 6JR**
email: info@lemonford.co.uk **web:** www.lemonford.co.uk
dir: *From Exeter on A38 take A382, 3rd exit at rdbt, follow Bickington signs.*
grid ref: *SX793723*

Small, secluded and well-maintained park with a good mixture of attractively laid out pitches. The friendly owners pay a great deal of attention to detail, and the toilets in particular are kept spotlessly clean. This good touring base is only one mile from Dartmoor and 10 miles from the seaside at Torbay. The bus to Exeter, Plymouth and Torbay stops outside the park. 7 acre site. 82 touring pitches. 55 hardstandings. Caravan pitches. Motorhome pitches. Tent pitches. 44 statics.

Open: all year **Last arrival:** 22.00hrs **Last departure:** 11.00hrs

Pitches: **Leisure:** **Facilities:**

Services: **Within 3 miles:**

Notes: No noise after 23.00hrs. Dogs must be kept on leads. Clothes drying area.

AA Pubs & Restaurants nearby: The Wild Goose Inn, NEWTON ABBOT, TQ12 4RA, 01626 872241

See advert on opposite page

DAWLISH *continued*

PREMIER PARK

Lady's Mile Holiday Park

►►►►► 84%

GOLD

tel: 01626 863411 **EX7 0LX**
email: info@ladysmile.co.uk
dir: *1m N of Dawlish on A379.* **grid ref:** *SX968784*

A family owned and run touring park with a wide variety of pitches, including some that are fully serviced. There are plenty of activities for everyone, including two swimming pools with waterslides, a children's splash pool, a well-equipped gym, a sauna in the main season, a large adventure playground, extensive restaurant facilities, and a bar with entertainment in high season. Facilities are kept very clean, and the surrounding beaches are easily accessed. Holiday homes and two, high quality glamping pods are also available. 18 acre site. 570 touring pitches. 67 hardstandings. 200 seasonal pitches. Caravan pitches. Motorhome pitches. Tent pitches. 120 statics. 2 wooden pods.

Open: all year (rs Facilities open 23 Mar-Oct) **Last arrival:** 20.00hrs **Last departure:** 11.00hrs

Pitches:

Leisure: Spa

Facilities:

Services:

Within 3 miles:

Notes: No noise after mdnt. Dogs must be kept on leads. Bowling alley.

AA Pubs & Restaurants nearby: The Elizabethan, LUTON (NEAR CHUDLEIGH), TQ13 0BL, 01626 775425

The Anchor Inn, COCKWOOD, EX6 8RA, 01626 890203

Leadstone Camping

►►► 83%

tel: 01626 864411 **Warren Rd EX7 0NG**
email: info@leadstonecamping.co.uk **web:** www.leadstonecamping.co.uk
dir: *M5 junct 30, A379 to Dawlish. Before village turn left on brow of hill, signed Dawlish Warren. Site 0.5m on right.* **grid ref:** *SX974782*

A traditional, mainly level, grassy camping park approximately a half-mile walk from the sands and dunes at Dawlish Warren – a nature reserve and Blue Flag beach. This mainly tented park has been run by the same friendly family for many years, and is an ideal base for touring south Devon. A regular bus service from outside the gate takes in a wide area. The smart, well-equipped timber cabin toilet facility includes some privacy cubicles. There is a pub a short walk away. 8 acre site. 137 touring pitches. 14 seasonal pitches. Caravan pitches. Motorhome pitches. Tent pitches.

Open: 27 May-4 Sep **Last arrival:** 22.00hrs **Last departure:** noon

Pitches: * £24-£30 £20-£26 £16-£22

Leisure:

Facilities:

Services:

Within 3 miles:

Notes: No noise after 23.00hrs, only portable & disposable BBQs permitted. Dogs must be kept on leads.

AA Pubs & Restaurants nearby: The Elizabethan, LUTON (NEAR CHUDLEIGH), TQ13 0BL, 01626 775425

The Anchor Inn, COCKWOOD, EX6 8RA, 01626 890203

DREWSTEIGNTON — Map 3 SX79

Places to visit

Castle Drogo, DREWSTEIGNTON, EX6 6PB, 01647 433306
www.nationaltrust.org.uk/castle-drogo

Finch Foundry, STICKLEPATH, EX20 2NW, 01837 840046
www.nationaltrust.org.uk

PREMIER PARK

Woodland Springs Adult Touring Park

►►►►► 84%

tel: 01647 231695 **Venton EX6 6PG**
email: enquiries@woodlandsprings.co.uk
dir: *Exit A30 at Whiddon Down junct onto A382 towards Moretonhampstead. Site 1.5m on left.* **grid ref:** *SX695912*

An attractive park in a rural area within Dartmoor National Park. This site is surrounded by woodland and farmland, and is very peaceful. The toilet block offers superb facilities, including four fully serviced cubicles, some available for disabled visitors. Please note that children are not accepted. 4 acre site. 81 touring pitches. 48 hardstandings. 19 seasonal pitches. Caravan pitches. Motorhome pitches. Tent pitches.

Open: all year **Last arrival:** 20.00hrs **Last departure:** 11.00hrs

Pitches: * £20-£26 £20-£26 £17-£23

Facilities:

Services:

Within 3 miles:

Notes: Adults only. No fires, no noise 23.00hrs-08.00hrs. Dogs must be kept on leads. Day kennels, freezer, coffee vending machine.

AA Pubs & Restaurants nearby: The Old Inn, DREWSTEIGNTON, EX6 6QR, 01647 281276

Sandy Park Inn, CHAGFORD, TQ13 8JW, 01647 433267

EAST ALLINGTON
Map 3 SX74

Places to visit

Kingsbridge Cookworthy Museum, KINGSBRIDGE, TQ7 1AW, 01548 853235 www.kingsbridgemuseum.org.uk

Great for kids: Woodlands Family Theme Park, DARTMOUTH, TQ9 7DQ, 01803 712598 www.woodlandspark.com

Mounts Farm Touring Park

►►► 77%

tel: 01548 521591 **The Mounts TQ9 7QJ**
email: mounts.farm@lineone.net
dir: *A381 from Totnes towards Kingsbridge (NB ignore signs for East Allington). At 'Mounts', site 0.5m on left.* **grid ref:** *SX757488*

A neat, grassy park divided into four paddocks by mature natural hedges. Three of the paddocks are for the tourers and campers, and the fourth is a children's play area. The laundry, toilets and well-stocked little shop are in converted farm buildings. There's an on-site snack bar and Calor Gaz retailer. 7 acre site. 50 touring pitches. 10 seasonal pitches. Caravan pitches. Motorhome pitches. Tent pitches.

Open: Mar-Nov **Last arrival:** 22.00hrs **Last departure:** 16.00hrs

Pitches:

Leisure:

Facilities:

Services:

Within 3 miles:

Notes: Dogs must be kept on leads. Camping accessories shop on site.

AA Pubs & Restaurants nearby: The Fortescue Arms, EAST ALLINGTON, TQ9 7RA, 01548 521215

EAST ANSTEY
Map 3 SS82

Places to visit

Quince Honey Farm, SOUTH MOLTON, EX36 3AZ, 01769 572401 www.quincehoneyfarm.com

Tiverton Museum of Mid Devon Life, TIVERTON, EX16 6PJ, 01884 256295 www.tivertonmuseum.org.uk

Zeacombe House Caravan Park

►►►► 88%

tel: 01398 341279 **Blackerton Cross EX16 9JU**
email: enquiries@zeacombeadultretreat.co.uk
dir: *M5 junct 27, A361 signed Barnstaple, right at next rdbt onto A396 signed Dulverton & Minehead. In 5m at Exeter Inn left, 1.5m, at Black Cat junct left onto B3227 towards South Molton, site 7m on left.* **grid ref:** *SS860240*

Set on the southern fringes of Exmoor National Park, this sheltered, adult-only, 'garden' park is nicely landscaped in a tranquil location and enjoys panoramic views towards Exmoor. There is a choice of grass or hardstanding pitches and a unique restaurant-style meal service allows you to eat a home-cooked evening meal in the comfort of your own unit. 5 acre site. 50 touring pitches. 12 hardstandings. Caravan pitches. Motorhome pitches. Tent pitches.

Open: 7 Mar-Oct **Last arrival:** 21.00hrs **Last departure:** noon

Pitches: **Facilities:**

Services: **Within 3 miles:**

Notes: Adults only. No awning groundsheets. Dogs must be kept on leads. Caravan store & stay system.

AA Pubs & Restaurants nearby: The Masons Arms, KNOWSTONE, EX36 4RY, 01398 341231

EAST WORLINGTON
Map 3 SS71

Yeatheridge Farm Caravan Park

►►►► 84%

tel: 01884 860330 **EX17 4TN**
email: yeatheridge@talk21.com
dir: *M5 junct 27, A361, at 1st rdbt at Tiverton take B3137 for 9m towards Witheridge. Fork left 1m past Nomansland onto B3042. Site on left in 3.5m. (NB do not enter East Worlington).* **grid ref:** *SS768110*

A well-kept park in a remote woodland setting on the edge of the Tamar Valley. It is peacefully located at the end of a private, half-mile, tree-lined drive; it offers superb on-site facilities and high levels of customer care from the hands-on owners. The toilets are immaculate and well maintained, plus there is an indoor swimming pool, sauna and a good information and games room – all have a friendly atmosphere. Two fishing lakes are also available. 12 acre site. 103 touring pitches. 8 hardstandings. Caravan pitches. Motorhome pitches. Tent pitches. 19 statics.

Open: 15 Mar-end Sep **Last arrival:** 22.00hrs **Last departure:** 10.00hrs

Pitches: * £10-£21 £10-£21 £10-£21

Leisure: **Facilities:**

Services: **Within 3 miles:**

Notes: Dogs must be kept on leads.

AA Pubs & Restaurants nearby: The Grove Inn, KINGS NYMPTON, EX37 9ST, 01769 580406

EXETER

See Kennford and Kenn

EXMOUTH Map 3 SY08

Places to visit

A la Ronde, EXMOUTH, EX8 5BD, 01395 265514
www.nationaltrust.org.uk/alaronde

Bicton Park Botanical Gardens, BICTON, EX9 7BJ, 01395 568465
www.bictongardens.co.uk

Great for kids: The World of Country Life, EXMOUTH, EX8 5BU, 01395 274533
www.worldofcountrylife.co.uk

Devon Cliffs Holiday Park

HOLIDAY CENTRE 91%

GOLD

tel: 01395 226226 & 0871 230 2760 *(Calls cost 10p per minute plus your phone company's access charge)* **Sandy Bay EX8 5BT**
email: devoncliffs@haven.com **web:** www.haven.com/parks/devon/devon-cliffs
dir: *M5 junct 30, A376 towards Exmouth, follow brown signs to Sandy Bay.*
grid ref: *SY036807*

A large and exciting holiday park on a hillside setting close to Exmouth, with spectacular views across Sandy Bay. This all-action park offers a superb entertainment programme for all ages throughout the day, with very modern sports and leisure facilities available for everyone. An internet café is just one of the quality amenities, and though some visitors may enjoy relaxing and watching others play, the temptation to join in is overwhelming. South Beach Café, which overlooks the sea, is well worth a visit. Please note that this park does not accept tents. 163 acre site. 43 touring pitches. 43 hardstandings. Caravan pitches. Motorhome pitches. 1800 statics.

Devon Cliffs Holiday Park

Open: mid Mar-end Oct (rs mid Mar-May & Sep-Oct some facilities may be reduced) **Last arrival:** anytime **Last departure:** 10.00hrs

Pitches:

Leisure:

Facilities:

Services:

Within 3 miles:

Notes: No commercial vehicles, no bookings by persons under 21yrs unless a family booking, max 2 dogs per booking, certain dog breeds banned, no dogs on beach May-Sep. Dogs must be kept on leads. Crazy golf, fencing, archery, bungee trampoline, aqua jets.

AA Pubs & Restaurants nearby: Les Saveurs, EXMOUTH, EX8 1NT, 01395 269459

See advert on opposite page

HOLSWORTHY Map 3 SS30

Places to visit

Dartington Crystal, GREAT TORRINGTON, EX38 7AN, 01805 626242
www.dartington.co.uk

RHS Garden Rosemoor, GREAT TORRINGTON, EX38 8PH, 0845 265 8072 *(Calls cost 7p per minute plus your phone company's access charge)* www.rhs.org.uk/rosemoor

Great for kids: The Milky Way Adventure Park, CLOVELLY, EX39 5RY, 01237 431255 www.themilkyway.co.uk

Headon Farm Caravan Site

►►► 82%

tel: 01409 254477 **Headon Farm, Hollacombe EX22 6NN**
email: reader@headonfarm.co.uk
dir: *From Holsworthy A388 signed Launceston. 0.5m, at hill brow left into Staddon Rd. 1m (follow site signs) right signed Ashwater. 0.5m, left at hill brow. Site 25yds.*
grid ref: *SS367023*

Set on a working farm in a quiet rural location. All pitches have extensive views of the Devon countryside, yet the park is only two and a half miles from the market town of Holsworthy, and within easy reach of roads to the coast and beaches of north Cornwall. 2 acre site. 19 touring pitches. 11 hardstandings. Caravan pitches. Motorhome pitches. Tent pitches.

Open: all year **Last arrival:** 19.00hrs **Last departure:** noon

Pitches: * £15.50-£17.50 £15.50-£17.50

Leisure:

Facilities:

Services:

Within 3 miles:

Notes: Breathable groundsheets only. Dogs must be kept on leads. Caravan & motorhome storage (outside & undercover).

AA Pubs & Restaurants nearby: The Devil's Stone Inn, SHEBBEAR, EX21 5RU, 01409 281210

Noteworthy Farm Caravan and Campsite

►►77%

tel: 01409 253731 & 07811 000071 **Noteworthy, Bude Rd EX22 7JB**
email: enquiries@noteworthy-devon.co.uk
dir: *On A3072 between Holsworthy & Bude. 3m from Holsworthy on right.*
grid ref: *SS303052*

This campsite is owned by a friendly young couple with their own children. There are good views from the quiet rural location, and simple toilet facilities. The local bus stops outside the gate on request. 5 acre site. 5 touring pitches. 3 hardstandings. Caravan pitches. Motorhome pitches. Tent pitches. 5 statics.

Open: all year **Last departure:** 11.00hrs

Pitches: * £10-£15 £10-£15 £10-£15

Leisure:

Facilities:

Services:

Within 3 miles:

Notes: No open fires, no noise after 22.30hrs. Dogs must be kept on leads. Dog grooming available.

AA Pubs & Restaurants nearby: Bay View Inn, WIDEMOUTH BAY, EX23 0AW, 01288 361273

ILFRACOMBE — Map 3 SS54

Places to visit

Arlington Court, ARLINGTON, EX31 4LP, 01271 850296
www.nationaltrust.org.uk/arlington-court

Exmoor Zoological Park, BLACKMOOR GATE, EX31 4SG, 01598 763352
www.exmoorzoo.co.uk

Great for kids: Watermouth Castle & Family Theme Park, ILFRACOMBE, EX34 9SL, 01271 863879 www.watermouthcastle.com

Hele Valley Holiday Park

►►►►87%

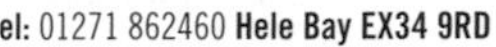

GOLD

tel: 01271 862460 **Hele Bay EX34 9RD**
email: holidays@helevalley.co.uk
dir: *M5 junct 27, A361, through Barnstaple & Braunton to Ilfracombe. Take A399 towards Combe Martin. Follow brown Hele Valley signs. In 400mtrs sharp right to T-junct. Park on left.* **grid ref:** *SS533472*

A deceptively spacious park set in a picturesque valley with glorious tree-lined hilly views from most pitches. High quality toilet facilities are provided, and the park is within walking distance of a lovely beach and on a regular bus route. Camping pods are available to hire. The harbour and other attractions of Ilfracombe are just a mile away. 17 acre site. 50 touring pitches. 15 hardstandings. Caravan pitches. Motorhome pitches. Tent pitches. 80 statics. 3 wooden pods.

Open: Etr-Oct **Last arrival:** 18.00hrs **Last departure:** 11.00hrs

Pitches: * £18-£38 £18-£38 £18-£38

Leisure: Spa **Facilities:**

Services: **Within 3 miles:**

Notes: Groups, motorhomes & tourers by arrangement only. Dogs must be kept on leads. Nature trail, postal collection.

AA Pubs & Restaurants nearby: The Quay Restaurant, ILFRACOMBE, EX34 9EQ, 01271 868090

PITCHES: Caravans Motorhomes Tents Glamping-style accommodation **SERVICES:** Electric hook up Launderette Licensed bar Calor Gas Camping Gaz Toilet fluid Café/Restaurant Fast Food/Takeaway Battery charging Baby care Motorvan service point
ABBREVIATIONS: BH/bank hols – bank holidays Etr – Easter Spring BH – Spring Bank Holiday fr – from hrs – hours m – mile mdnt – midnight rdbt – roundabout rs – restricted service wk – week wknd – weekend x-rds – cross roads No credit or debit cards No dogs Children of all ages accepted

KENN Map 3 SX98

Places to visit

Powderham Castle, POWDERHAM, EX6 8JQ, 01626 890243 www.powderham.co.uk

Great for kids: Go Ape Haldon Forest, KENNFORD, EX6 7XR, 0845 643 9215 *(Calls cost 7p per minute plus your phone company's access charge)* www.goape.co.uk/haldon

Glebe Farm Shepherd's Huts

NEW ►►►

tel: 07773 314240 **EX6 7XE**
email: mandy@glebefarm1.co.uk
dir: *From end of M5 onto A38 (S'bound) follow Kennford & Kenn signs. Right at T-junct signed Kenn. Left signed Kenn.* **grid ref:** *SX922853*

Developed for the 2015 season, the shepherd's huts on this farm occupy a peaceful location beside a babbling river. Both the new huts are very different, built to a high standard and kitted out with quality fixtures and fittings. Each has a well-equipped kitchen area, double bed with conveniently positioned TV, a wood-burning stove (one has under floor heating), and adjoining toilet and shower facilities. In addition each has an outside patio area with a picnic bench and barbecue. 4 acre site.

Open: all year **Last arrival:** 20.00hrs **Last departure:** 10.00hrs

Pitches: * £47-£86

Notes:

AA Pubs & Restaurants nearby: Cridford Inn, TRUSHAM, TQ13 0NR, 01626 853694

KENNFORD Map 3 SX98

Places to visit

St Nicholas Priory, EXETER, EX4 3BL, 01392 665858 www.exeter.gov.uk/priory

Quay House Visitor Centre, EXETER, EX2 4AN, 01392 271611 www.exeter.gov.uk/quayhouse

Great for kids: Devon's Crealy Great Adventure Park, CLYST ST MARY, EX5 1DR, 01395 233200 www.crealy.co.uk

Kennford International Caravan Park

►►►► 80%

tel: 01392 833046 **EX6 7YN**
email: ian@kennfordinternational.com
dir: *At end of M5 take A38, site signed at Kennford slip road.* **grid ref:** *SX912857*

Screened from the A38 by trees and shrubs, this park offers pitches divided by hedging for privacy. A high quality toilet block complements the park's facilities. A good, centrally-located base for exploring the coast and touring the countryside of Devon, and Exeter is easily accessible via buses that stop nearby. 15 acre site. 22 touring pitches. 4 hardstandings. Caravan pitches. Motorhome pitches. Tent pitches. 65 statics.

Open: all year **Last arrival:** 21.00hrs (Winter arrival times differ)
Last departure: 11.00hrs

Pitches: * £16-£19 £16-£19 £15-£19

Leisure:

Facilities:

Services:

Within 3 miles:

Notes: Dogs must be kept on leads.

AA Pubs & Restaurants nearby: Bridge Inn, TOPSHAM, EX3 0QQ, 01392 873862

KENTISBEARE Map 3 ST00

Places to visit

Killerton House & Garden, KILLERTON, EX5 3LE, 01392 881345 www.nationaltrust.org.uk

Allhallows Museum, HONITON, EX14 1PG, 01404 44966 www.honitonmuseum.co.uk

Great for kids: Diggerland, CULLOMPTON, EX15 2PE, 0871 227 7007 *(Calls cost 10p per minute plus your phone company's access charge)* www.diggerland.com

KENTISBEARE

Forest Glade Holiday Park

►►►► 80%

GOLD

tel: 01404 841381 **EX15 2DT**
email: enquiries@forest-glade.co.uk **web:** www.forest-glade.co.uk
dir: *Tent traffic: from A373 turn left past Keepers Cottage Inn (2.5m E of M5 junct 28). (NB due to narrow roads, touring caravans & larger motorhomes must approach from Honiton direction. Please phone for access details).* **grid ref:** *ST101073*

A quiet, attractive park in a forest clearing with well-kept gardens and beech hedge screening. One of the main attractions is the site's immediate proximity to the forest which offers magnificent hillside walks with surprising views over the valleys. Camping pods are available for hire. Please note that because the roads are narrow around the site, it is best to phone the site for suitable route details. 16 acre site. 80 touring pitches. 40 hardstandings. 28 seasonal pitches. Caravan pitches. Motorhome pitches. Tent pitches. 57 statics. 2 wooden pods.

Open: mid Mar-end Oct (rs Low season limited shop hours) **Last arrival:** 21.00hrs **Last departure:** noon

Pitches: £15-£23 £15-£23 £15-£22

Leisure:

Facilities: WiFi

Services:

Within 3 miles:

Notes: Families & couples only. Dogs must be kept on leads. Adventure & soft play area, wildlife information room, paddling pool.

AA Pubs & Restaurants nearby: The Blacksmiths Arms, PLYMTREE, EX15 2JU, 01884 277474

KINGSBRIDGE

Map 3 SX74

Places to visit

Kingsbridge Cookworthy Museum, KINGSBRIDGE, TQ7 1AW, 01548 853235 www.kingsbridgemuseum.org.uk

Overbeck's, SALCOMBE, TQ8 8LW, 01548 842893 www.nationaltrust.org.uk

PREMIER PARK

Parkland Caravan and Camping Site

►►►►► 80%

tel: 01548 852723 & 07968 222008 **Sorley Green Cross TQ7 4AF**
email: enquiries@parklandsite.co.uk
dir: *A384 to Totnes, A381 towards Kingsbridge. 12m, at Stumpy Post Cross rdbt turn right, 1m. Site 200yds on left after Sorley Green Cross.* **grid ref:** *SX728462*

Expect a high level of customer care at this family-run park set in the glorious South Hams countryside; it has panoramic views over Salcombe and the rolling countryside towards Dartmoor. The immaculately maintained grounds offer generous grass pitches, hardstandings and super pitches (RVs can be accommodated). The on-site shop sells seasonal produce, everyday provisions, pre-ordered hampers and camping supplies; the toilet facilities feature quality, fully serviced cubicles, family washrooms, a bathroom and a fully fitted disabled suite. Babysitting is available by arrangement. A bus stops close to the site entrance, which is handy for exploring the local towns and villages. 3 acre site. 50 touring pitches. 30 hardstandings. 15 seasonal pitches. Caravan pitches. Motorhome pitches. Tent pitches.

Open: all year **Last arrival:** 22.00hrs **Last departure:** 11.30hrs

Pitches: * £10-£30 £10-£30 £10-£30

Leisure:

Facilities: WiFi

Services:

Within 3 miles:

Notes: No camp fires, no noise after 23.00hrs, children must be accompanied by an adult when using facilities, site gates closed 22.00hrs-09.00hrs. Use of fridge freezers, campers' kitchen, coffee shop, short term caravan storage facility.

AA Pubs & Restaurants nearby: The Fortescue Arms, EAST ALLINGTON, TQ9 7RA, 01548 521215

The Crabshell Inn, KINGSBRIDGE, TQ7 1JZ, 01548 852345

KINGSBRIDGE *continued*

Island Lodge Caravan & Camping Site

►►►►► 78%

tel: 01548 852956 & 07968 222007 **Stumpy Post Cross TQ7 4BL**
email: enquiries@islandlodgesite.co.uk
dir: *Take A381 from Totnes towards Kingsbridge. In 12m, at rdbt (Stumpy Post Cross) right, 300mtrs left into lane, site signed. 200mtrs on left.* **grid ref:** *SX738470*

A small, peaceful and well-established park, with extensive views over the South Hams, which has been run by the same family for many years. Investment has seen several significant improvements, including a new security barrier, new low-level lighting around the park, refurbished hardstanding pitches, and an updated motorhome service point. The immaculate toilet facilities are of good quality. A scenic 35-minute walk will take you to Kingsbridge, or the Kingsbridge bus stops close to the site. There are several dog-friendly beaches nearby. 2 acre site. 30 touring pitches. 2 hardstandings. 20 seasonal pitches. Caravan pitches. Motorhome pitches. Tent pitches.

Open: all year (rs Nov-Etr shop closed) **Last arrival:** 20.30hrs **Last departure:** 11.30hrs

Pitches:

Leisure:

Facilities:

Services:

Within 3 miles:

Notes: No generators. Play area open 09.00hrs-21.00hrs. Electronic barrier closed overnight. Restrictions on certain dog breeds. Dogs must be kept on leads. Secure caravan storage yard, boat park, 24hr CCTV.

AA Pubs & Restaurants nearby: The Fortescue Arms, EAST ALLINGTON, TQ9 7RA, 01548 521215

The Crabshell Inn, KINGSBRIDGE, TQ7 1JZ, 01548 852345

LYNTON — Map 3 SS74

See also Oare (Somerset)

Places to visit

Arlington Court, ARLINGTON, EX31 4LP, 01271 850296
www.nationaltrust.org.uk/arlington-court

Great for kids: Exmoor Zoological Park, BLACKMOOR GATE, EX31 4SG, 01598 763352 www.exmoorzoo.co.uk

Channel View Caravan and Camping Park

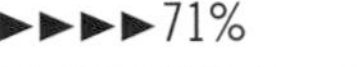

►►►► 71%

DAVID BELLAMY CONSERVATION AWARD GOLD

tel: 01598 753349 **Manor Farm EX35 6LD**
email: relax@channel-view.co.uk
dir: *A39 E for 0.5m on left past Barbrook.* **grid ref:** *SS724482*

On the top of the cliffs overlooking the Bristol Channel, this is a well-maintained park on the edge of Exmoor, and close to both Lynton and Lynmouth. Pitches can be selected from either those in a hidden hedged area or those with panoramic views over the coast. 6 acre site. 76 touring pitches. 15 hardstandings. Caravan pitches. Motorhome pitches. Tent pitches. 31 statics.

Open: 15 Mar-15 Nov **Last arrival:** 22.00hrs **Last departure:** noon

Pitches: * £13-£21 £13-£21 £13-£21

Leisure:

Facilities:

Services:

Within 3 miles:

Notes: Groups by prior arrangement only. Dogs must be kept on leads. Parent & baby room.

AA Pubs & Restaurants nearby: Rising Sun Hotel, LYNMOUTH, EX35 6EG, 01598 753223

Rockford Inn, BRENDON, EX35 6PT, 01598 741214

Sunny Lyn Holiday Park

►►► 77%

tel: 01598 753384 **Lynbridge EX35 6NS**
email: info@caravandevon.co.uk **web:** www.caravandevon.co.uk
dir: *M5 junct 27, A361 to South Molton. Right onto A399 to Blackmoor Gate, right onto A39, left onto B3234 towards Lynmouth. Site 1m on right.* **grid ref:** *SS719486*

Set in a sheltered riverside location in a wooded combe within a mile of the sea, in Exmoor National Park. This family-run park offers good facilities including an excellent café. 4.5 acre site. 9 touring pitches. 5 hardstandings. Caravan pitches. Motorhome pitches. Tent pitches. 7 statics.

Open: Mar-Oct **Last arrival:** 20.00hrs **Last departure:** 11.00hrs

Pitches: £15-£17.50 £15-£17.50 £12-£15

Facilities:

Services:

Within 3 miles:

Notes: No cars by tents. No wood fires, quiet after 22.30hrs. Dogs must be kept on leads.

AA Pubs & Restaurants nearby: Rising Sun Hotel, LYNMOUTH, EX35 6EG, 01598 753223

Rockford Inn, BRENDON, EX35 6PT, 01598 741214

MODBURY Map 3 SX65

Places to visit

Kingsbridge Cookworthy Museum, KINGSBRIDGE, TQ7 1AW, 01548 853235 www.kingsbridgemuseum.org.uk

Overbeck's, SALCOMBE, TQ8 8LW, 01548 842893 www.nationaltrust.org.uk

Great for kids: National Marine Aquarium, PLYMOUTH, PL4 0LF, 01752 275200 www.national-aquarium.co.uk

Pennymoor Camping & Caravan Park

►►► 83%

tel: 01548 830542 **PL21 0SB**
email: enquiries@pennymoor-camping.co.uk **web:** www.pennymoor-camping.co.uk
dir: *Exit A38 at Wrangaton Cross. Left & then right at x-rds. After by-passing Ermington, turn left onto A379. Turn left at Harraton Cross. Site on left.* **grid ref:** *SX685516*

A well-established rural park on part level, part gently sloping grass with good views over distant Dartmoor and the countryside in between. The park has been owned and run by the same family since 1935, and is very carefully tended, with clean, well-maintained toilets and a relaxing atmosphere. 12.5 acre site. 119 touring pitches. 3 hardstandings. Caravan pitches. Motorhome pitches. Tent pitches. 76 statics.

Open: 15 Mar-15 Nov (rs 15 Mar-mid May only one toilet & shower block open)
Last arrival: 20.00hrs **Last departure:** 11.00hrs

Pitches: * £14-£18 £14-£18 £14-£18

Leisure:

Facilities:

Services:

Within 3 miles:

Notes: No skateboards or scooters, no noise after 22.00hrs. Dogs must be kept on leads. Emergency phone.

AA Pubs & Restaurants nearby: California Country Inn, MODBURY, PL21 0SG, 01548 821449

Rose & Crown, YEALMPTON, PL8 2EB, 01752 880223

MORTEHOE Map 3 SS44

See also Woolacombe

Places to visit

Marwood Hill Gardens, BARNSTAPLE, EX31 4EB, 01271 342528 www.marwoodhillgarden.co.uk

Great for kids: Watermouth Castle & Family Theme Park, ILFRACOMBE, EX34 9SL, 01271 863879 www.watermouthcastle.com

North Morte Farm Caravan & Camping Park

►►►► 86%

tel: 01271 870381 **North Morte Rd EX34 7EG**
email: info@northmortefarm.co.uk **web:** www.northmortefarm.co.uk
dir: *From B3343 into Mortehoe, right at post office. Site 500yds on left.*
grid ref: *SS462455*

Set in spectacular coastal countryside close to National Trust land and 500 yards from Rockham Beach. This attractive park is very well run and maintained by friendly family owners, and the quaint village of Mortehoe with its cafés, shops and pubs, is just a five-minute walk away. 22 acre site. 180 touring pitches. 25 hardstandings. 13 seasonal pitches. Caravan pitches. Motorhome pitches. Tent pitches. 73 statics.

Open: Apr-Oct **Last arrival:** 22.00hrs **Last departure:** noon

Pitches:

Leisure:

Facilities:

Services:

Within 3 miles:

Notes: No large groups. Dogs must be kept on leads.

AA Pubs & Restaurants nearby: Watersmeet Hotel, WOOLACOMBE, EX34 7EB, 01271 870333

The Quay Restaurant, ILFRACOMBE, EX34 9EQ, 01271 868090

NEWTON ABBOT

Map 3 SX87

See also Bickington

Places to visit

Tuckers Maltings, NEWTON ABBOT, TQ12 4AA, 01626 334734 www.tuckersmaltings.com

Great for kids: Prickly Ball Farm and Hedgehog Hospital, NEWTON ABBOT, TQ12 6BZ, 01626 362319 www.pricklyballfarm.com

PREMIER PARK

Ross Park

►►►►► 97%

tel: 01803 812983 **Park Hill Farm, Ipplepen TQ12 5TT**
email: enquiries@rossparkcaravanpark.co.uk **web:** www.rossparkcaravanpark.co.uk
dir: *N of Ipplepen on A381 follow brown site signs & sign for Woodland opposite Texaco garage.* **grid ref:** *SX845671*

A top-class park in every way, with large secluded pitches, high quality toilet facilities (which include excellent family rooms) and colourful flower displays throughout – note the wonderful floral walk to the toilets. The beautiful tropical conservatory also offers a breathtaking show of colour. There's a conservation walk through glorious wild flower meadows, replete with nature trail, a dog shower/grooming area, and six fully serviced pitches. This very rural park enjoys superb views of Dartmoor, and good quality meals to suit all tastes and pockets are served in the restaurant. Expect high levels of customer care – this park gets better each year. Home-grown produce and honey are sold in the shop. A bus, which stops close to the entrance, runs to Totnes and Newton Abbot. 32 acre site. 110 touring pitches. 110 hardstandings. Caravan pitches. Motorhome pitches. Tent pitches.

Open: Mar-2 Jan (rs Nov-Jan & 1st 3 wks in Mar restaurant/bar closed (ex Xmas/New Year)) **Last arrival:** 21.00hrs **Last departure:** 11.00hrs

Pitches: * £16.25-£29.50 £16.25-£29.50 £15.25-£19.50

Leisure: **Facilities:**

Services: **Within 3 miles:**

Notes: Bikes, skateboards & scooters only permitted on leisure field. Dogs must be kept on leads. Snooker, table tennis, badminton.

AA Pubs & Restaurants nearby: The Church House Inn, MARLDON, TQ3 1SL, 01803 558279

The Union Inn, DENBURY, TQ12 6DQ, 01803 812595

REGIONAL WINNER – SOUTH WEST ENGLAND AA CAMPSITE OF THE YEAR 2016

PREMIER PARK

Dornafield

►►►►► 95%

tel: 01803 812732 **Dornafield Farm, Two Mile Oak TQ12 6DD**
email: enquiries@dornafield.com **web:** www.dornafield.com
dir: *From Newton Abbot take A381 signed Totnes for 2m. At Two Mile Oak Inn right, left at x-rds in 0.5m. Site on right.* **grid ref:** *SX838683*

An immaculately kept park in a tranquil wooded valley between Dartmoor and Torbay, divided into three areas. At the heart of the 30-acre site is Dornafield, a 14th-century farmhouse, adapted for campers' use but still retaining much charm. The friendly family owners are always available for help or to give advice. The site has superb facilities in two ultra modern toilet blocks. On-site there is the Quarry Café which provides takeaway fish and chips or jacket potatoes daily. This is a quiet and peaceful location convenient for Torbay, Dartmoor and the charming coastal villages of the South Hams. A bus service to Totnes or Newton Abbot runs nearby. 30 acre site. 135 touring pitches. 119 hardstandings. 26 seasonal pitches. Caravan pitches. Motorhome pitches. Tent pitches.

Open: 11 Mar-7 Nov **Last arrival:** 22.00hrs **Last departure:** 11.00hrs

Pitches: * £17-£33 £17-£33 £15-£27 **Leisure:**

Facilities:

Services: **Within 3 miles:**

Notes: No commercial vehicles; no sign-written vehicles. Dogs must be kept on leads. All year caravan storage.

Twelve Oaks Farm Caravan Park

►►► 80%

tel: 01626 335015 & 07976 440456 **Teigngrace TQ12 6QT**
email: info@twelveoaksfarm.co.uk **web:** www.twelveoaksfarm.co.uk
dir: *A38 from Exeter left signed Teigngrace (only), 0.25m before Drumbridges rdbt. 1.5m, through village, site on left. Or from Plymouth pass Drumbridges rdbt, take slip road for Chudleigh Knighton. Right over bridge, rejoin A38 towards Plymouth. Left for Teigngrace (only), then as above.* **grid ref:** *SX852737*

An attractive small park on a working farm close to Dartmoor National Park, and bordered by the River Teign. The tidy pitches are located amongst trees and shrubs, and the modern facilities are very well maintained. There are two well-stocked fishing lakes and children will enjoy visiting all the farm animals. Close by is Stover Country Park and also the popular Templar Way walking route. 2 acre site. 50 touring pitches. 25 hardstandings. 15 seasonal pitches. Caravan pitches. Motorhome pitches. Tent pitches.

Open: all year **Last arrival:** 21.00hrs **Last departure:** 10.30hrs

Pitches: * £14-£22 £14-£22 £14-£22

Leisure:

Facilities:

Services:

Within 3 miles:

Notes: No noise after 23.00hrs. Dogs must be kept on leads.

AA Pubs & Restaurants nearby: The Elizabethan, LUTON (NEAR CHUDLEIGH), TQ13 0BL, 01626 775425

The Union Inn, DENBURY, TQ12 6DQ, 01803 812595

OTTERY ST MARY Map 3 SY19

Cuckoo Down Farm Glamping

NEW ►►►►

tel: 01404 811714 **Lower Broad Oak Rd, West Hill EX11 1UE**
email: cuckoodownfarm@gmail.com
dir: *M5, A30 signed Honiton, after airport on left, left signed Daisymount & Ottery St Mary. At mini rdbt, last exit (under bridge). At next mini rdbt follow West Hill sign. 0.5m, left into Bendarroch Rd. 3rd right into School Ln, right at end, immediately left into Elsdon Ln. At end straight over onto track. 0.5m, fork right to site (bumpy road).* **grid ref:** *SY075938*

On arrival at Cuckoo Down Farm the first thing that strikes you is the peace and tranquillity and the far-reaching views from the very spacious, 6-acre glamping meadow. There are two safari tents (Daisy & Poppy) sleeping six and three yurts (Clover, Bluebell & Buttercup) sleeping four; all units are kitted out with style. Each has a wood-burning stove, rugs and scatter cushions to make them cosy and comfortable, and down duvets and quilts on the beds. Each unit has a decked outside area, a fully-equipped kitchen cabin and a compost toilet; showers, fridges, freezers, washing machine and tumble drier are located in a nearby barn, which also has a small 'honesty' shop of essentials.

Open: all year

SALCOMBE *continued*

Higher Rew Caravan & Camping Park

►►► 80%

tel: 01548 842681 **Higher Rew, Malborough TQ7 3BW**
email: enquiries@higherrew.co.uk
dir: *A381 to Malborough. Right at Townsend Cross, follow signs to Soar for 1m. Left at Rew Cross for 0.5m, site is on the right.* **grid ref:** *SX714383*

A long-established park in a remote location within sight of the sea. The spacious, open touring field has some tiered pitches in the sloping grass, and there are lovely countryside or sea views from every pitch. The friendly family owners are continually improving the facilities. 5 acre site. 90 touring pitches. Caravan pitches. Motorhome pitches. Tent pitches.

Open: Etr-Oct **Last arrival:** 22.00hrs **Last departure:** noon

Pitches: * £15-£22 £15-£22 £14-£21

Leisure:

Facilities:

Services:

Within 3 miles:

Notes: Minimum noise after 23.00hrs. Dogs must be kept on leads. Play barn.

AA Pubs & Restaurants nearby: The Victoria Inn, SALCOMBE, TQ8 8BU, 01548 842604

Soar Mill Cove Hotel, SALCOMBE, TQ7 3DS, 01548 561566

Alston Camping and Caravan Site

►► 69%

tel: 01548 561260 & 0780 803 0921 **Malborough, Kingsbridge TQ7 3BJ**
email: info@alstoncampsite.co.uk
dir: *From Salcombe on A381 towards Kingsbridge, through Malborough, site signed on right.* **grid ref:** *SX716406*

An established farm site in a rural location adjacent to the Kingsbridge/Salcombe estuary. The site is well sheltered and screened, and approached down a long, well-surfaced narrow farm lane with passing places. The toilet facilities are basic. 16 acre site. 90 touring pitches. Caravan pitches. Motorhome pitches. Tent pitches. 58 statics.

Open: 15 Mar-Oct

Pitches:

Leisure:

Facilities:

Services:

Within 3 miles:

Notes: Dogs must be kept on leads.

AA Pubs & Restaurants nearby: The Victoria Inn, SALCOMBE, TQ8 8BU, 01548 842604

Soar Mill Cove Hotel, SALCOMBE, TQ7 3DS, 01548 561566

SAMPFORD PEVERELL — Map 3 ST01

Places to visit

Tiverton Castle, TIVERTON, EX16 6RP, 01884 253200 www.tivertoncastle.com

Tiverton Museum of Mid Devon Life, TIVERTON, EX16 6PJ, 01884 256295 www.tivertonmuseum.org.uk

Great for kids: Diggerland, CULLOMPTON, EX15 2PE, 0871 227 7007 *(Calls cost 10p per minute plus your phone company's access charge)* www.diggerland.com

PREMIER PARK

Minnows Touring Park

►►►►► 84%

tel: 01884 821770 **Holbrook Ln EX16 7EN**
email: admin@minnowstouringpark.co.uk
dir: *M5 junct 27, A361 signed Tiverton & Barnstaple. In 600yds take 1st slip road, right over bridge, site ahead.* **grid ref:** *SS042148*

A small, well-sheltered park, peacefully located amidst fields and mature trees. The toilet facilities are of a high quality in keeping with the rest of the park, and there is a good laundry. The park has direct gated access to the canal towpath; a brisk 20-minute walk leads to a choice of pubs and a farm shop, and the bus stop is 15 minutes away. All pitches are hardstanding with some large enough for American RVs; fully serviced pitches are also available. The park has WiFi. 5.5 acre site. 59 touring pitches. 59 hardstandings. Caravan pitches. Motorhome pitches. Tent pitches. 1 static.

Open: 7 Mar-Oct **Last arrival:** 20.00hrs **Last departure:** noon

Pitches: * £15.50-£27 £15.50-£27 £13.60-£27

Leisure:

Facilities:

Services:

Within 3 miles:

Notes: No cycling, no groundsheets on grass. Dogs must be kept on leads. RVs welcome, caravan storage.

AA Pubs & Restaurants nearby: The Butterleigh Inn, BUTTERLEIGH, EX15 1PN, 01884 855433

SHALDON

Places to visit

'Bygones', TORQUAY, TQ1 4PR, 01803 326108 www.bygones.co.uk

Great for kids: Babbacombe Model Village, TORQUAY, TQ1 3LA, 01803 315315 www.model-village.co.uk

SHALDON Map 3 SX97

Coast View Holiday Park

HOLIDAY HOME PARK 82%

tel: 01626 818350 **Torquay Rd TQ14 0BG**
email: holidays@coastview.co.uk
dir: *M5 junct 31, A38 then A380 towards Torquay. A381 towards Teignmouth. Right in 4m at lights, over Shaldon Bridge. 0.75m, up hill, site on right.* **grid ref:** *SX935716*

This park has stunning sea views from its spacious pitches. The family-run park has a full entertainment programme every night for all the family, plus outdoor and indoor activities for children; this site will certainly appeal to lively families.

Open: mid Mar-end Oct

Dogs: on leads

Leisure:

Within 3 miles:

SIDMOUTH Map 3 SY18

Places to visit

Branscombe - The Old Bakery, Manor Mill and Forge, BRANSCOMBE, EX12 3DB, 01752 346585 www.nationaltrust.org.uk

Otterton Mill, OTTERTON, EX9 7HG, 01395 568521 www.ottertonmill.com

Great for kids: Pecorama Pleasure Gardens, BEER, EX12 3NA, 01297 21542 www.pecorama.info

PREMIER PARK

Oakdown Country Holiday Park

95%

Best of British GOLD

tel: 01297 680387 **Gatedown Ln, Weston EX10 0PT**
email: enquiries@oakdown.co.uk **web:** www.oakdown.co.uk
dir: *Exit A3052, 2.5m E of junct with A375.* **grid ref:** *SY167902*

A quality, friendly, well-maintained park with good landscaping and plenty of maturing trees that make it well screened from the A3052. Pitches are grouped in groves surrounded by shrubs, with a 50-pitch development replete with an upmarket toilet block. The park has excellent facilities including a 9-hole par 3 golf course and a good shop and café. New additions include a family room and undercover dishwashing sinks in Beech Grove, and three four-berth wooden pods. The park's conservation areas, with their natural flora and fauna, offer attractive walks, and there is a hide by the Victorian reed bed for both casual and dedicated bird watchers. A delightful park in every respect. 16 acre site. 150 touring pitches. 90 hardstandings. 35 seasonal pitches. Caravan pitches. Motorhome pitches. Tent pitches. 15 statics. 3 wooden pods.

Oakdown Country Holiday Park

Open: Apr-Oct **Last arrival:** 22.00hrs **Last departure:** 10.30hrs

Pitches: * £12.60-£31 £12.60-£31 £12.60-£24.80

Leisure: **Facilities:**

Services: **Within 3 miles:**

Notes: No bikes, skateboards or kite flying. Dogs must be kept on leads. Microwave available, field trail to donkey sanctuary.

AA Pubs & Restaurants nearby: Blue Ball Inn, SIDMOUTH, EX10 9QL, 01395 514062

The Salty Monk, SIDMOUTH, EX10 9QP, 01395 513174

Dukes, SIDMOUTH, EX10 8AR, 01395 513320

See advert on page 174

Kings Down Tail Caravan & Camping Park

►►►► 82%

tel: 01297 680313 & 07796 618668 **Salcombe Regis EX10 0PD**
email: info@kingsdowntail.co.uk **web:** www.kingsdowntail.co.uk
dir: *M5 junct 30, A3052 towards Sidmouth. Through Sidford, up hill for 2m, turn left just before Branscombe Cross.* **grid ref:** *SY173907*

This well managed family run park is well located near Sidmouth. There are new facilities, including a stunning reception building and well-appointed family rooms. There is also a play area for children including a pirate ship and den. The park is perfect for visiting south-east Devon, including Sidmouth, Beer, and Lyme Regis in Dorset. 5 acre site. 80 touring pitches. 68 hardstandings. 20 seasonal pitches. Caravan pitches. Motorhome pitches. Tent pitches. 5 wooden pods.

Open: 15 Mar-15 Nov **Last departure:** 11.00hrs

Pitches: **Leisure:**

Facilities:

Services:

Within 3 miles:

Notes: Dogs must be kept on leads.

AA Pubs & Restaurants nearby: Blue Ball Inn, SIDMOUTH, EX10 9QL, 01395 514062

The Salty Monk, SIDMOUTH, EX10 9QP, 01395 513174

Dukes, SIDMOUTH, EX10 8AR, 01395 513320

TAVISTOCK Map 3 SX47

Places to visit

Morwellham Quay, MORWELLHAM, PL19 8JL, 01822 832766
www.morwellham-quay.co.uk

PREMIER PARK

Woodovis Park

►►►►► 89%

tel: 01822 832968 **Gulworthy PL19 8NY**
email: info@woodovis.com
dir: *A390 from Tavistock signed Callington & Gunnislake. At hill top right at rdbt signed Lamerton & Chipshop. Site 1m on left.* **grid ref:** *SX431745*

A well-kept park in a remote woodland setting on the edge of the Tamar Valley. A peacefully located park at the end of a private, half-mile, tree-lined drive, it offers superb on-site facilities and high levels of customer care from hands-on owners. The toilets are immaculate and well maintained, plus there is an indoor swimming pool, sauna and a good information/games room, all creating a friendly atmosphere. New initiatives include electric bike hire, a charging point for electric cars, and a new bark path through the woods to the dog exercise field. 2-berth and 4-berth wooden pods are available for hire. 14.5 acre site. 50 touring pitches. 33 hardstandings. 8 seasonal pitches. Caravan pitches. Motorhome pitches. Tent pitches. 35 statics. 4 wooden pods.

Open: 22 Mar-1 Nov **Last arrival:** 20.00hrs **Last departure:** 11.00hrs

Pitches: * £19-£41 £19-£41 £19-£41

Leisure:

Facilities:

Services:

Within 3 miles:

Notes: No open fires. Dogs must be kept on leads. Petanque court, outdoor table tennis, archery, water-walking, infared therapy cabin, hot tub, circus skills workshops & story telling (in school hols).

AA Pubs & Restaurants nearby: The Cornish Arms, TAVISTOCK, PL19 8AN, 01822 612145

PREMIER PARK

Langstone Manor Camping & Caravan Park

►►►►► 80%

tel: 01822 613371 **Moortown PL19 9JZ**
email: jane@langstone-manor.co.uk **web:** www.langstone-manor.co.uk
dir: *Take B3357 from Tavistock to Princetown. Approx 1.5m turn right at x-rds, follow signs. Over bridge, cattle grid, up hill, left at sign, left again to park.*
grid ref: *SX524738*

A secluded and very peaceful site set in the well-maintained grounds of a manor house in Dartmoor National Park. Many attractive mature trees provide screening within the park, yet the west-facing terraced pitches on the main park enjoy the superb summer sunsets. There are excellent toilet facilities, a popular lounge bar with an excellent menu of reasonably priced evening meals. Plenty of activities and places of interest can be found within the surrounding moorland. Dogs are accepted. Wooden pods in a wooded setting are available for hire. 6.5 acre site. 40 touring pitches. 10 hardstandings. 4 seasonal pitches. Caravan pitches. Motorhome pitches. Tent pitches. 25 statics. 7 wooden pods.

Open: 15 Mar-15 Nov (rs 15 Mar-15 Nov bar & restaurant closed weekdays (excl BHs & school hols)) **Last arrival:** 21.00hrs **Last departure:** 11.00hrs

Pitches:

Leisure:

Facilities:

Services:

Within 3 miles:

Notes: Dogs must be kept on leads. Baguettes, croissants etc available.

AA Pubs & Restaurants nearby: The Cornish Arms, TAVISTOCK, PL19 8AN, 01822 612145

Harford Bridge Holiday Park

►►►► 82%

GOLD

tel: 01822 810349 & 07773 251457 **Peter Tavy PL19 9LS**
email: stay@harfordbridge.co.uk **web:** www.harfordbridge.co.uk
dir: *A386 from Tavistock towards Okehampton, 2m, right signed Peter Tavy, site 200yds on right.* **grid ref:** *SX504767*

This beautiful spacious park is set beside the River Tavy in the Dartmoor National Park. Pitches are located beside the river and around the copses, and the park is very well equipped for holidaymakers. An adventure playground and games room keep children entertained, and there is fly-fishing and a free tennis court. A lovely, authentic shepherd's hut complete with fridge and woodburner is available to let. 16 acre site. 125 touring pitches. 5 hardstandings. 5 seasonal pitches. Caravan pitches. Motorhome pitches. Tent pitches. 80 statics. 1 shepherd's hut.

Open: all year (rs 16 Nov-13 Mar no camping or touring, statics only)
Last arrival: 21.00hrs **Last departure:** noon

Pitches: **Leisure:**

Facilities:

Services:

Within 3 miles:

Notes: Expedition groups & rallies welcome by prior arrangement. Dogs must be kept on leads. Baguettes, croissants, snacks, sweets, cold drinks, ices & grocery basics available.

AA Pubs & Restaurants nearby: Peter Tavy Inn, TAVISTOCK, PL19 9NN, 01822 810348

TEDBURN ST MARY — Map 3 SX89

Places to visit

Finch Foundry, STICKLEPATH, EX20 2NW, 01837 840046 www.nationaltrust.org.uk

Castle Drogo, DREWSTEIGNTON, EX6 6PB, 01647 433306 www.nationaltrust.org.uk/castle-drogo

Springfield Holiday Park

►►►► 83%

tel: 01647 24242 **EX6 6EW**
email: info@springfield-park.co.uk
dir: *M5 junct 31, A30 towards Okehampton, exit at junct, signed to Cheriton Bishop. Follow brown tourist signs to site. (NB for Sat Nav use EX6 6JN).* **grid ref:** *SX788935*

Set in a quiet rural location with countryside views, this park continues to be upgraded to a smart standard. It has the advantage of being close to Dartmoor National Park, with village pubs and stores less than a mile away. There is a very inviting heated outdoor swimming pool. 9 acre site. 48 touring pitches. 38 hardstandings. 25 seasonal pitches. Caravan pitches. Motorhome pitches. Tent pitches. 49 statics.

Open: 15 Mar-Oct **Last arrival:** 21.00hrs **Last departure:** noon

Pitches: £15-£20 £15-£25 £10-£20

Leisure:

Facilities:

Services:

Within 3 miles:

Notes: Dogs must be kept on leads.

AA Pubs & Restaurants nearby: The Old Inn, DREWSTEIGNTON, EX6 6QR, 01647 281276

TIVERTON

See East Worlington

TORQUAY — Map 3 SX96

See also Newton Abbot

Places to visit

Torre Abbey, TORQUAY, TQ2 5JE, 01803 293593 www.torre-abbey.org.uk

'Bygones', TORQUAY, TQ1 4PR, 01803 326108 www.bygones.co.uk

Widdicombe Farm Touring Park

►►►► 86%

tel: 01803 558325 **Marldon TQ3 1ST**
email: info@widdicombefarm.co.uk **web:** www.widdicombefarm.co.uk
dir: *On A380, midway between Torquay & Paignton ring road.* **grid ref:** *SX876643*

A friendly family-run park on a working farm with good quality facilities, extensive views and easy access as there are no narrow roads. The level pitches are terraced to take advantage of the views towards the coast and Dartmoor. This is the only adult touring park within Torquay, and is also handy for Paignton and Brixham. There's a bus service from the park to the local shopping centre and Torquay's harbour. It has a small shop, a restaurant and a bar with entertainment from Easter to the end of September. Club WiFi is available throughout the park and The Nippy Chippy van calls regularly. 8 acre site. 180 touring pitches. 180 hardstandings. 20 seasonal pitches. Caravan pitches. Motorhome pitches. Tent pitches. 3 statics.

Open: mid Mar-end Oct **Last arrival:** 20.00hrs **Last departure:** 11.00hrs

Pitches: **Leisure:**

Facilities:

Services:

Within 3 miles:

Notes: Adults only. No groups. Most dog breeds accepted (contact site for details). Dogs must be kept on leads.

AA Pubs & Restaurants nearby: The Church House Inn, MARLDON, TQ3 1SL, 01803 558279

Cary Arms, TORQUAY, TQ1 3LX, 01803 327110

The Elephant Restaurant and Brasserie, TORQUAY, TQ1 2BH, 01803 200044

WHIDDON DOWN

Dartmoor View Holiday Park

NEW ►►► 81%

tel: 01647 231545 & 07585 301613 **EX20 2QL**
email: dartmoorviewtouring@haulfryn.co.uk
dir: *From M5 junct 31, take A30 to Okehampton. At Whiddon Down take left junct through village. Turn right at small rdbt. Park is 400mtrs on the right.* **grid ref:** *SX685925*

Located just off the A30 near Okehampton, on the northern edge of Dartmoor, this immaculate 20-acre park certainly lives up to its name, and more. Although predominantly a static park, the 27 designated super pitches, all hard standings with electric, water and waste drainage, for touring caravans and motorhomes are secluded away in a separate, well-landscaped field, replete with a spotlessly clean and well-equipped amenities block. Dogs and children are very welcome and there's an extensive children's play and a heated outdoor swimming pool, which has a newly refurbished sun-deck area. Dartmoor View is the ideal base for those keen to explore Dartmoor on foot or by bike. 20 acre site. 27 touring pitches. 27 hardstandings. 27 seasonal pitches. Caravan pitches. Motorhome pitches.

Open: Mar-Oct **Last arrival:** 18.00hrs **Last departure:** 11.00hrs

Pitches: * £18-£30 £18-£30

Leisure:

Facilities:

Services:

Within 3 miles:

Notes: Dogs must be kept on leads.

WOOLACOMBE

Map 3 SS44

See also Mortehoe

Twitchen House Holiday Park

HOLIDAY CENTRE 86%

tel: 0844 7700 365 *(Calls cost 5p per minute plus your phone company's access charge)*
Mortehoe Station Rd, Mortehoe EX34 7ES
email: goodtimes@woolacombe.com **web:** www.woolacombe.com/aac
dir: *M5 junct 27, A361 to Ilfracombe. From Mullacott Cross rdbt take B3343 (Woolacombe road) to Turnpike Cross junct. Take right fork, site 1.5m on left.* **grid ref:** *SS465447*

A very attractive, seaside park with excellent leisure facilities, all-weather activities and entertainment; visitors can use the amenities at all three of the group's holiday parks and a bus service connects them all with the beach. There's a show room, indoor soft play area, a 2D and 3D cinema and craft centre. The touring area features many fully serviced pitches and 80 that are available for tents; they have either sea views or a woodland countryside outlook. 45 acre site. 334 touring pitches. 110 hardstandings. Caravan pitches. Motorhome pitches. Tent pitches. 253 statics.

Open: Mar-Nov (rs Mar-mid May & mid Sep-Nov outdoor pool closed) **Last arrival:** mdnt **Last departure:** 10.00hrs

Pitches:

Leisure:

Facilities:

Services:

Within 3 miles:

Notes: Dogs must be kept on leads. Table tennis, sauna, swimming & surfing lessons, climbing wall, bungee trampoline.

AA Pubs & Restaurants nearby: Watersmeet Hotel, WOOLACOMBE, EX34 7EB, 01271 870333

See advert on opposite page

LEISURE: Indoor swimming pool Outdoor swimming pool Children's playground Kid's club Tennis court Games room Separate TV room golf course Boats for hire Cinema Entertainment Fishing Mini golf Watersports Gym Sports field Spa Stables
FACILITIES: Bath Shower Electric shaver Hairdryer Ice Pack Facility Disabled facilities Public telephone Shop on site or within 200yds Mobile shop (calls at least 5 days a week) BBQ area Picnic area Wi-fi Internet access Recycling Tourist info Dog exercise area

WOOLACOMBE *continued*

Woolacombe Bay Holiday Park

HOLIDAY CENTRE 85%

tel: 0844 7700 365 *(Calls cost 5p per minute plus your phone company's access charge)*
Sandy Ln EX34 7AH
email: goodtimes@woolacombe.com **web:** www.woolacombe.com/aac
dir: *M5 junct 27, A361 to Ilfracombe. At Mullacott rdbt take 1st exit to Woolacombe. Follow Mortehoe signs.* **grid ref:** *SS465442*

There's a well-developed touring section at this seaside holiday complex that offers a full entertainment and leisure programme. There are super pitches with TV aerial, water, drainage, electricity and a night light. The park has excellent amenities including a steam room and sauna, and an outdoor sports area with a circular Ocean Bar. For a small charge, a bus takes holidaymakers to the other Woolacombe Bay holiday centres where they can take part in any of the many activities offered, and there is also a bus to the beach. The sports complex features a surfing simulator, high ropes course and a climbing wall. 8.5 acre site. 171 touring pitches. Motorhome pitches. Tent pitches. 237 statics.

Open: May-Sep (rs Etr) **Last arrival:** mdnt **Last departure:** 10.00hrs

Pitches:

Leisure: Spa

Facilities:

Services:

Within 3 miles:

Notes: Max 21ft motorhomes, site not ideal for guests with mobility problems due to hills & stairs. Dogs must be kept on leads. Crazy golf, bungee trampoline.

AA Pubs & Restaurants nearby: Watersmeet Hotel, WOOLACOMBE, EX34 7EB, 01271 870333

See advert on page 179

Golden Coast Holiday Park

HOLIDAY CENTRE 80%

tel: 0844 7700 365 *(Calls cost 5p per minute plus your phone company's access charge)*
Station Rd EX34 7HW
email: goodtimes@woolacombe.com **web:** www.woolacombe.com/aac
dir: *M5 junct 27, A361 to Ilfracombe. At Mullacott rdbt 1st exit to Woolacombe.*
grid ref: *SS482436*

A seaside holiday village, set beside a three mile sandy beach, that offers excellent leisure facilities together with the amenities available at the other Woolacombe Bay holiday parks. There is a neat touring area with a unisex toilet block that has under-floor heating and individual cubicles – all maintained to a high standard; the super pitches have water, drainage, electricity, TV aerial and night light. The sports complex features ten-pin bowling, high ropes course, climbing wall, surfing simulator and adventure golf and much more; there are over 40 free activities available to try. 10 acre site. 93 touring pitches. 87 hardstandings. Caravan pitches. Motorhome pitches. Tent pitches. 324 statics.

Open: Feb-Nov (rs mid Sep-May outdoor pool closed) **Last arrival:** mdnt
Last departure: 10.00hrs

Pitches:

Leisure:

Facilities:

Services:

Within 3 miles:

Notes: No pets on touring pitches. Dogs must be kept on leads. Sauna, solarium, fishing, snooker, cinema, bungee trampoline, swimming & surfing lessons.

AA Pubs & Restaurants nearby: Watersmeet Hotel, WOOLACOMBE, EX34 7EB, 01271 870333

See advert on page 179

PREMIER PARK

Warcombe Farm Caravan & Camping Park

►►►►► 86%

tel: 01271 870690 **Station Rd, Mortehoe EX34 7EJ**
email: info@warcombefarm.co.uk **web:** www.warcombefarm.co.uk
dir: *On B3343 towards Woolacombe turn right towards Mortehoe. Site less than 1m on right.* **grid ref:** *SS478445*

Extensive views over the Bristol Channel can be enjoyed from the open areas of this attractive park, while other pitches are sheltered in paddocks with maturing trees. The site has 14 excellent super pitches with hardstandings. The superb sandy, Blue Flag beach at Woolacombe Bay is only a mile and a half away, and there is a fishing lake with direct access from some pitches. The local bus stops outside the park entrance. 35 acre site. 250 touring pitches. 82 hardstandings. 12 seasonal pitches. Caravan pitches. Motorhome pitches. Tent pitches.

Open: 15 Mar-Oct **Last arrival:** 21.00hrs **Last departure:** 11.00hrs

Pitches:

Leisure:

Facilities:

Services:

Within 3 miles:

Notes: No noise after 22.30hrs. Dogs must be kept on leads.

AA Pubs & Restaurants nearby: Watersmeet Hotel, WOOLACOMBE, EX34 7EB, 01271 870333

The Quay Restaurant, ILFRACOMBE, EX34 9EQ, 01271 868090

Easewell Farm Holiday Park

►►► 84%

tel: 0844 7700 365 *(Calls cost 5p per minute plus your phone company's access charge)*
Mortehoe Station Rd, Mortehoe EX34 7EH
email: goodtimes@woolacombe.com **web:** www.woolacombe.com/aac
dir: *M5 junct 27, A361 to Ilfracombe. At Mullacott rdbt 1st exit to Woolacombe. Follow Mortehoe signs.* **grid ref:** *SS465455*

A peaceful cliff-top park with superb views that offers full facility pitches for caravans and motorhomes. The shower rooms have under-floor heating and individual cubicles, plus there's a sauna, steam room, launderette, washing up area and chemical disposal facilities. The sports complex has a surfing simulator, high ropes course and climbing wall; the 40 activities available include indoor bowling, snooker and a 9-hole golf course. All the facilities at the three other nearby holiday centres within this group are open to everyone. 17 acre site. 318 touring pitches. 186 hardstandings. Caravan pitches. Motorhome pitches. Tent pitches. 1 static.

Open: Mar-Nov (rs Etr) **Last arrival:** 22.00hrs **Last departure:** 10.00hrs

Pitches:

Leisure:

Facilities:

Services:

Within 3 miles:

Notes: Dogs must be kept on leads.

AA Pubs & Restaurants nearby: Watersmeet Hotel, WOOLACOMBE, EX34 7EB, 01271 870333

See advert on page 179

Europa Park

►►► 77%

tel: 01271 871425 **Beach Rd EX34 7AN**
email: europaparkwoolacombe@yahoo.co.uk **web:** www.europapark.co.uk
dir: *M5 junct 27, A361 through Barnstaple to Mullacott Cross. Left onto B3343 signed Woolacombe. Site on right at Spa shop/garage.* **grid ref:** *SS475435*

A very lively family-run site handy for the beach at Woolacombe, and catering well for surfers but maybe not suitable for a quieter type of stay (please make sure the site is suitable for you before making your booking). Set in a stunning location high above the bay, it provides a wide range of accommodation including surf cabins, surf pods, a yurt and generous touring pitches. Visitors can enjoy the indoor pool and sauna, games room, restaurant/café/bar and clubhouse. 16 acre site. 200 touring pitches. 20 hardstandings. Caravan pitches. Motorhome pitches. Tent pitches. 22 statics. 1 yurt.

Open: all year **Last arrival:** 23.00hrs **Last departure:** 10.00hrs

Pitches:

Leisure:

Facilities:

Services:

Within 3 miles:

Notes: Beer deck, off licence, pub, big-screen TV.

AA Pubs & Restaurants nearby: Watersmeet Hotel, WOOLACOMBE, EX34 7EB, 01271 870333

The Quay Restaurant, ILFRACOMBE, EX34 9EQ, 01271 868090

The Williams Arms, BRAUNTON, EX33 2DE, 01271 812360

Dorset

Dorset means rugged varied coastlines and high chalk downlands with more than a hint of Thomas Hardy, its most famous son. Squeezed in among the cliffs and set amid some of Britain's most beautiful scenery is a chain of picturesque villages and seaside towns.

Along the coast you'll find the Lulworth Ranges, which run from Kimmeridge Bay in the east to Lulworth Cove in the west. Walking is the most obvious and rewarding recreational activity here, but the British Army firing ranges mean that access to this glorious landscape is restricted. This is Britain's Jurassic Coast, a UNESCO World Heritage Site and Area of Outstanding Natural Beauty, noted for its layers of shale and numerous fossils embedded in the rock. Among the best-known natural landmarks on this stretch of the Dorset coast is Durdle Door, a rocky arch that has been shaped and sculpted to perfection by the elements. The whole area has the unmistakable stamp of prehistory. The landscape and coastal views may be spectacular but the up-and-down nature of the walking here is often physically demanding.

This designated coastline stretches from Swanage and the Isle of Purbeck to east Devon, offering miles of breathtaking scenery. Beyond the seaside town of Weymouth is Chesil Beach, a long shingle reef running for 10 miles between Portland and Abbotsbury. The beach is covered by a vast wall of shingle left by centuries of dramatic weather-induced activity along the Devon and Dorset coast. Beyond Bridport and West Bay, where the hugely successful TV series *Broadchurch* is filmed, lies quaint Lyme Regis, with its sturdy breakwater, known as The Cobb. It's the sort of place where Georgian houses and pretty cottages jostle with historic pubs and independently run shops. With its blend of architectural styles and old world charm, Lyme Regis looks very much like a film set. Perhaps that is why film producers chose this setting as a location for the making of *The French Lieutenant's Woman* in 1981. Jeremy Irons and Meryl Streep starred in the film, based on the novel by John Fowles.

Away from Dorset's magical coastline lies a landscape with a very different character and atmosphere, but one that is no less appealing. Here, winding, hedge-lined country lanes lead beneath lush, green hilltops to snug, sleepy villages hidden from view and the wider world. The main roads lead to the country towns of Sherborne, Blandford Forum, Wareham and Shaftesbury and in September these routes fill with even more traffic as the county prepares to host the annual Dorset Steam Fair. This famous event draws many visitors who come to admire the various vintage and classic vehicles on display. The same month is also set aside for the two-day County Show, an eagerly anticipated annual fixture.

Inland there are further links with literature. Dorset is justifiably proud of the achievements of Thomas Hardy, and much of the county is immortalized in his writing. He was born at Higher Bockhampton, near Dorchester, and this quaint old cob-and-thatch cottage was where the writer lived until he was 34. As a child, Hardy spent much of his time here reading and writing poems about the countryside. The cottage contains the desk where he wrote *Far from the Madding Crowd*. In later years Hardy lived at Max Gate on the edge of Dorchester and here he was visited by many distinguished writers of the day, including Rudyard Kipling and Virginia Woolf. Even the Prince of Wales called on him one day in 1923. Both homes are now in the care of the National Trust.

One of Thomas Hardy's great friends was T. E. (Thomas Edward) Lawrence, better known as Lawrence of Arabia, who lived nearby in a modest cottage known as Clouds Hill. The cottage, also managed by the National Trust, was Lawrence's secluded retreat from the world, where he could read and play music.

◁ Durdle Door

DORSET

ALDERHOLT

Map 5 SU11

Places to visit

Breamore House & Countryside Museum, BREAMORE, SP6 2DF, 01725 512468 www.breamorehouse.com

Great for kids: Rockbourne Roman Villa, ROCKBOURNE, SP6 3PG, 01725 518541 (during opening times only) www.hants.gov.uk/rockbourne-roman-villa

PREMIER PARK

Hill Cottage Farm Camping and Caravan Park

80%

tel: 01425 650513 & 07714 648690 **Sandleheath Rd SP6 3EG**
email: hillcottagefarmcaravansite@supanet.com
dir: *Take B3078 W of Fordingbridge. Exit at Alderholt, site 0.25m on left after railway bridge.* **grid ref:** *SU119133*

Set within extensive grounds, this rural and beautifully landscaped park offers fully serviced pitches set in individual hardstanding bays with mature dividing hedges that give adequate pitch privacy. The modern toilet block is kept immaculately clean, and there's a good range of leisure facilities. In high season there is an area available for tents. Rallies are very welcome. A function room with skittle alley is available, and there is a fully-equipped shepherd's hut for hire. 40 acre site. 95 touring pitches. 35 hardstandings. Caravan pitches. Motorhome pitches. Tent pitches.

Open: Mar-Nov **Last arrival:** 20.00hrs **Last departure:** 11.00hrs

Pitches:

Leisure:

Facilities:

Services:

Within 3 miles:

Notes: No noise after 22.30hrs. Dogs must be kept on leads.

AA Pubs & Restaurants nearby: The Augustus John, FORDINGBRIDGE, SP6 1DG, 01425 652098

BERE REGIS

Map 4 SY89

Places to visit

Kingston Lacy, WIMBORNE, BH21 4EA, 01202 883402 (Mon-Fri) www.nationaltrust.org.uk/kingston-lacy

Priest's House Museum and Garden, WIMBORNE, BH21 1HR, 01202 882533 www.priest-house.co.uk

Great for kids: Monkey World-Ape Rescue Centre, WOOL, BH20 6HH, 01929 462537 www.monkeyworld.org

Rowlands Wait Touring Park

►►► 87%

tel: 01929 472727 **Rye Hill BH20 7LP**
email: enquiries@rowlandswait.co.uk **web:** www.rowlandswait.co.uk
dir: *From A35 or A31 to Bere Regis, follow Bovington Tank Museum signs. 0.75m, at top of Rye Hill turn right. 200yds to site.* **grid ref:** *SY842933*

This park lies in a really attractive setting overlooking Bere Regis and the Dorset countryside, and is set amongst undulating areas of trees and shrubs. It is located within a few miles of The Tank Museum (Bovingdon Camp) with its mock battles, and is also very convenient for visiting the Dorchester, Poole and Swanage areas. The toilet facilities include two family rooms. The park has for hire six fully-equipped bell tents (a pop-up Glampotel as they call them) each with a shower, toilet and wash basin, as well as a wood-burning stove. 8 acre site. 71 touring pitches. 2 hardstandings. 23 seasonal pitches. Caravan pitches. Motorhome pitches. Tent pitches. 6 bell tents.

Open: mid Mar-Oct (winter by arrangement) (rs Nov-Feb own facilities required)
Last arrival: 21.00hrs **Last departure:** noon

Pitches: * £17.50-£23 £17.50-£23 £15.50-£19.50

Leisure:

Facilities:

Services:

Within 3 miles:

Notes: No open fires. Dogs must be kept on leads.

AA Pubs & Restaurants nearby: The Cock & Bottle, EAST MORDEN, BH20 7DL, 01929 459238

BLANDFORD FORUM — Map 4 ST80

Places to visit

Kingston Lacy, WIMBORNE, BH21 4EA, 01202 883402 (Mon-Fri) www.nationaltrust.org.uk/kingston-lacy

Old Wardour Castle, TISBURY, SP3 6RR, 01747 870487 www.english-heritage.org.uk/daysout/properties/old-wardour-castle

Great for kids: Monkey World-Ape Rescue Centre, WOOL, BH20 6HH, 01929 462537 www.monkeyworld.org

The Inside Park

►►►► 84%

tel: 01258 453719 **Down House Estate DT11 9AD**
email: mail@theinsidepark.co.uk
dir: *From Blandford Forum follow Winterborne Stickland signs. Site in 1.5m.*
grid ref: *ST869046*

An attractive, well-sheltered and quiet park, half a mile along a country lane in a wooded valley. The spacious pitches are divided by mature trees and shrubs, and the amenities are housed in an 18th-century coach house and stables. There are some lovely woodland walks within the park, an excellent fenced play area for children and a dog-free area; four dog kennels are available for daily hire. This makes the perfect base for those visiting the Blandford Steam Fair in August. 12 acre site. 125 touring pitches. Caravan pitches. Motorhome pitches. Tent pitches.

Open: Etr-Oct **Last arrival:** 22.00hrs **Last departure:** noon

Pitches: * £18.50-£26.45 £18.50-£26.45 £18.50-£26.45

Leisure:

Facilities:

Services:

Within 3 miles:

Notes: Dogs must be kept on leads. Kennels (charges apply).

AA Pubs & Restaurants nearby: The Hambro Arms, MILTON ABBAS, DT11 0BP, 01258 880233

The Anchor Inn, SHAPWICK, DT11 9LB, 01258 857269

BRIDPORT

Places to visit

Dorset County Museum, DORCHESTER, DT1 1XA, 01305 262735 www.dorsetcountymuseum.org

Great for kids: Abbotsbury Swannery, ABBOTSBURY, DT3 4JG, 01305 871858 www.abbotsbury-tourism.co.uk

BRIDPORT — Map 4 SY49

Freshwater Beach Holiday Park

HOLIDAY CENTRE 91%

tel: 01308 897317 **Burton Bradstock DT6 4PT**
email: office@freshwaterbeach.co.uk **web:** www.freshwaterbeach.co.uk
dir: *Take B3157 from Bridport towards Burton Bradstock. Site 1.5m from Crown rdbt on right.* **grid ref:** *SY493892*

A family holiday centre sheltered by a sand bank and enjoying its own private beach. The park offers a wide variety of leisure and entertainment programmes for all the family, plus the Jurassic Fun Centre with indoor pool, gym, 6-lane bowling alley, restaurant and bar is excellent. There is a new adults-only Sunset Lounge Bar and Cellar function room. The park is well placed at one end of the Weymouth to Bridport coastal area with spectacular views of Chesil Beach. There are three immaculate toilet blocks with excellent private rooms. 40 acre site. 500 touring pitches. 25 hardstandings. Caravan pitches. Motorhome pitches. Tent pitches. 250 statics.

Open: mid Mar-mid Nov **Last arrival:** 22.00hrs **Last departure:** 10.00hrs

Pitches: * £20-£46 £20-£46 £20-£46

Leisure: Spa **Facilities:**

Services: **Within 3 miles:**

Notes: Families & couples only. Dogs must be kept on leads. Large TV, kids' club in high season & BHs.

AA Pubs & Restaurants nearby: The Shave Cross Inn, BRIDPORT, DT6 6HW, 01308 868358

Riverside Restaurant, BRIDPORT, DT6 4EZ, 01308 422011

The Anchor Inn, CHIDEOCK, DT6 6JU, 01297 489215

See advert on page 186

LEISURE: Indoor swimming pool · Outdoor swimming pool · Children's playground · Kid's club · Tennis court · Games room · Separate TV room · golf course · Boats for hire · Cinema · Entertainment · Fishing · Mini golf · Watersports · Gym · Sports field · Spa · Stables

FACILITIES: Bath · Shower · Electric shaver · Hairdryer · Ice Pack Facility · Disabled facilities · Public telephone · Shop on site or within 200yds · Mobile shop (calls at least 5 days a week) · BBQ area · Picnic area · Wi-fi · Internet access · Recycling · Tourist info · Dog exercise area

BRIDPORT *continued*

PREMIER PARK

Highlands End Holiday Park

92%

tel: 01308 422139 & 426947 **Eypes DT6 6AR**
email: holidays@wdlh.co.uk **web:** www.wdlh.co.uk
dir: *1m W of Bridport on A35, follow signs for Eype. Site signed.* **grid ref:** *SY454913*

A well-screened site with magnificent cliff-top views over the Channel and the Dorset coast, adjacent to National Trust land and overlooking Lyme Bay. The pitches are mostly sheltered by hedging and well spaced on hardstandings. The excellent facilities include a tasteful bar and restaurant, indoor pool, leisure centre and The Cowshed Café, a very good coffee shop. There is a mixture of statics and tourers, but the tourers enjoy the best cliff-top positions, including new gravel hardstanding pitches overlooking Lyme Bay. Six luxury lodges, and wooden pods that sleep four are available for hire. 9 acre site. 195 touring pitches. 45 hardstandings. Caravan pitches. Motorhome pitches. Tent pitches. 160 statics. 2 wooden pods.

Open: Mar-Nov **Last arrival:** 22.00hrs **Last departure:** 11.00hrs

Pitches: * £16.50-£37 £16.50-£37 £16.50-£33

Leisure:

Facilities:

Services:

Within 3 miles:

Notes: Dogs must be kept on leads. Steam room, sauna, pitch & putt.

AA Pubs & Restaurants nearby: The Shave Cross Inn, BRIDPORT, DT6 6HW, 01308 868358

Riverside Restaurant, BRIDPORT, DT6 4EZ, 01308 422011

The Anchor Inn, CHIDEOCK, DT6 6JU, 01297 489215

PREMIER PARK

Bingham Grange Touring & Camping Park

91%

tel: 01308 488234 **Melplash DT6 3TT**
email: enquiries@binghamgrange.co.uk
dir: *From A35 at Bridport take A3066 N towards Beaminster. Site on left in 3m.*
grid ref: *SY478963*

Set in a quiet rural location but only five miles from the Jurassic Coast, this adults-only park enjoys views over the west Dorset countryside. The mostly level pitches are attractively set amongst shrub beds and ornamental trees. There is an excellent restaurant with lounge bar and takeaway, and all facilities are of a high quality. This is a very dog-friendly site. 20 acre site. 150 touring pitches. 85 hardstandings. 50 seasonal pitches. Caravan pitches. Motorhome pitches. Tent pitches.

Open: 16 Mar-end Oct (approx) (rs Wed (all year), Tue (mid-low season) restaurant & bar closed) **Last arrival:** 19.00hrs (late arrival to 21.00hrs in high season can be arranged) **Last departure:** 11.00hrs

Pitches: * £20.50-£28.50 £19.50-£28.50 £17-£28.50

Facilities:

Services:

Within 3 miles:

Notes: Adults only. No children under 18yrs may stay or visit. No noise after 23.00hrs, Dogs must be kept on leads. Woodland walks.

AA Pubs & Restaurants nearby: The Shave Cross Inn, BRIDPORT, DT6 6HW, 01308 868358

Riverside Restaurant, BRIDPORT, DT6 4EZ, 01308 422011

Graston Copse Holiday Park

88%

tel: 01308 426912 & 422139 **Annings Ln, Burton Bradstock DT6 4QP**
email: holidays@wdlh.co.uk
dir: *From Dorchester take A35 to Bridport. In Bridport follow 'Westbound through traffic' sign at mini rdbt. At next rdbt left onto B3157 to Burton Bradstock.* **grid ref:** *SY491893*

This small, peaceful site offering good facilities for families, is located near the village of Burton Bradstock making it a perfect base for visiting the stunning cliffs and beaches along the Jurassic coastline. The facilities are modern and spotlessly clean. Wooden pods that sleep four are available to hire. Please note, care is needed if driving through Burton Bradstock to the site. 9 acre site. 26 touring pitches. Caravan pitches. Motorhome pitches. Tent pitches. 90 statics. 2 wooden pods.

Open: 17 Apr-7 Sep **Last arrival:** 22.00hrs **Last departure:** 11.00hrs

Pitches: * £15.50-£25 £15.50-£25 £13-£22.50

Facilities:

Services:

Within 3 miles:

Notes: Dogs must be kept on leads.

AA Pubs & Restaurants nearby: Riverside Restaurant, BRIDPORT, DT6 4EZ, 01308 422011

The Crown Inn, PUNCKNOWLE, DT2 9BN, 01308 897711

CERNE ABBAS Map 4 ST60

Places to visit

Athelhampton House & Gardens, ATHELHAMPTON, DT2 7LG, 01305 848363 www.athelhampton.co.uk

Hardy's Cottage, DORCHESTER, DT2 8QJ, 01305 262366 www.nationaltrust.org.uk

Great for kids: Maiden Castle, DORCHESTER, DT2 9PP, 0370 333 1181 www.english-heritage.org.uk/daysout/properties/maiden-castle

Lyons Gate Caravan and Camping Park

►►►► 79%

tel: 01300 345260 **Lyons Gate DT2 7AZ**
email: info@lyons-gate.co.uk
dir: *Direct access from A352, 3m N of Cerne Abbas, site signed.* **grid ref:** *ST660062*

A peaceful park with pitches set out around the four attractive coarse fishing lakes. It is surrounded by mature woodland, with many footpaths and bridleways. Other easily accessible attractions include the Cerne Giant carved into the hills, the old market town of Dorchester, and the superb sandy beach at Weymouth. Holiday homes are available for sale. 10 acre site. 90 touring pitches. 24 hardstandings. Caravan pitches. Motorhome pitches. Tent pitches. 14 statics.

Open: all year **Last arrival:** 20.00hrs **Last departure:** 11.30hrs

Pitches: 🚐 🚗 ⛺ **Leisure:** /A\ 🔍 ☐

Facilities: 🚿 ⊙ ✂ ✲ ♿ 🛍 ⊼ 🐕 WiFi ℹ

Services: 🍽 🗒 🔒 ⊘ **Within 3 miles:** ⛳ 🎣 🗒 U

Notes: Dogs must be kept on leads.

AA Pubs & Restaurants nearby: The New Inn, CERNE ABBAS, DT2 7JF, 01300 341274

The Poachers Inn, PIDDLETRENTHIDE, DT2 7QX, 01300 348358

Giants Head Caravan & Camping Park

►►► 78%

tel: 01300 341242 **Giants Head Farm, Old Sherborne Rd DT2 7TR**
email: holidays@giantshead.co.uk
dir: *From Dorchester into town avoiding by-pass, at Top O'Town rdbt take A352 (Sherborne road), in 500yds right fork at BP (Loder's) garage & Lidl store.* **grid ref:** *ST675029*

A pleasant, though rather basic, park set in Dorset downland near the Cerne Giant (the famous landmark figure cut into the chalk) with stunning views and a smart toilet block. This is a good stopover site especially for tenters and backpackers on The Ridgeway National Trail. Holiday chalets are available to let. 4 acre site. 50 touring pitches. Caravan pitches. Motorhome pitches. Tent pitches.

Open: Etr-Oct (rs Etr shop & bar closed) **Last arrival:** anytime **Last departure:** 13.00hrs

Pitches: 🚐 £12-£20 🚗 £12-£20 ⛺ £12-£20 **Facilities:** 🚿 ⊙ ✂ ✲ ⊼ 🐕 ♻ ℹ

Services: 🍽 🗒 🔒 ⊘ 🍴 **Within 3 miles:** 🎣 🛍 🗒

Notes: Dogs must be kept on leads.

AA Pubs & Restaurants nearby: The Greyhound Inn, SYDLING ST NICHOLAS, DT2 9PD, 01300 341303

CHARMOUTH Map 4 SY39

Places to visit

Forde Abbey, THORNCOMBE, TA20 4LU, 01460 221290 www.fordeabbey.co.uk

Great for kids: Abbotsbury Swannery, ABBOTSBURY, DT3 4JG, 01305 871858 www.abbotsbury-tourism.co.uk

PREMIER PARK

Wood Farm Caravan & Camping Park

Best of British

►►►►► 92%

tel: 01297 560697 **Axminster Rd DT6 6BT**
email: reception@woodfarm.co.uk **web:** www.woodfarm.co.uk
dir: *Accessed directly from A35 rdbt, on Axminster side of Charmouth.*
grid ref: *SY356940*

This top quality park, the perfect place to relax, is set amongst mature native trees with the various levels of the ground falling away into a beautiful valley below. The park offers excellent facilities including family rooms and fully serviced pitches. Everything throughout the park is spotless. At the bottom end of the park there is an indoor swimming pool and leisure complex, plus the licensed, conservatory-style Offshore Café. There's a very good children's play room and excellent new play area, in addition to tennis courts and a well-stocked, coarse-fishing lake. The park is well positioned on the Heritage Coast near Lyme Regis. Static holiday homes are also available for hire. 13 acre site. 175 touring pitches. 175 hardstandings. 20 seasonal pitches. Caravan pitches. Motorhome pitches. Tent pitches. 92 statics.

Open: Etr-Oct **Last arrival:** 19.00hrs **Last departure:** noon

Pitches: * 🚐 £11-£30 🚗 £11-£30 ⛺ £11-£30

Leisure: **Facilities:**

Services: **Within 3 miles:**

Notes: No bikes, skateboards, scooters or roller skates. Dogs must be kept on leads.

AA Pubs & Restaurants nearby: The Mariners, LYME REGIS, DT7 3HS, 01297 442753

See advert on page 190

PREMIER PARK

Newlands Caravan & Camping Park

►►►►► 81%

tel: 01297 560259 **DT6 6RB**
email: enq@newlandsholidays.co.uk **web:** www.newlandsholidays.co.uk
dir: *4m W of Bridport on A35.* **grid ref:** *SY374935*

A very smart site with excellent touring facilities, set on gently sloping ground in hilly countryside near the sea. The park offers a full cabaret and entertainment programme for all ages, and boasts an indoor swimming pool and an outdoor pool with water slide. Lodges, apartments and motel rooms are available, plus there are four new camping pods for hire. 23 acre site. 240 touring pitches. 52 hardstandings. 40 seasonal pitches. Caravan pitches. Motorhome pitches. Tent pitches. 86 statics. 4 wooden pods.

Open: 10 Mar-4 Nov **Last arrival:** 21.00hrs **Last departure:** 10.00hrs

Pitches: **Leisure:**

Facilities:

Services:

Within 3 miles:

Notes: Dogs must be kept on leads. Kids' club during school holidays.

AA Pubs & Restaurants nearby: The Mariners, LYME REGIS, DT7 3HS, 01297 442753

See advert on page 190

Manor Farm Holiday Centre

►►►► 81%

tel: 01297 560226 **Manor Farm Holiday Centre DT6 6QL**
email: enquiries@manorfarmholidaycentre.co.uk
dir: *From E: A35 into Charmouth, site 0.75m on right.* **grid ref:** *SY368937*

Set just a short walk from the safe sand and shingle beach at Charmouth, this popular family park offers a good range of facilities. There is an indoor/outdoor swimming pool plus café, a fully-equipped gym and sauna. Children enjoy the activity area and the park also offers a lively programme in the extensive bar and entertainment complex. In addition there are 16 luxury cottages available to let. 30 acre site. 400 touring pitches. 80 hardstandings. 100 seasonal pitches. Caravan pitches. Motorhome pitches. Tent pitches. 29 statics.

Open: all year (rs mid Mar-end Oct statics only) **Last arrival:** 20.00hrs
Last departure: 10.00hrs

Pitches: * £18-£36 £18-£36 £15-£32 **Leisure:** Spa

Facilities: **Services:**

Within 3 miles:

Notes: No skateboards. Dogs must be kept on leads.

AA Pubs & Restaurants nearby: The Mariners, LYME REGIS, DT7 3HS, 01297 442753

CHIDEOCK Map 4 SY49

Places to visit

Mapperton, BEAMINSTER, DT8 3NR, 01308 862645 www.mapperton.com

Golden Cap Holiday Park

►►►► 85%

tel: 01308 422139 & 426947 **Seatown DT6 6JX**
email: holidays@wdlh.co.uk
dir: *On A35, in Chideock follow Seatown signs, site signed.* **grid ref:** *SY422919*

A grassy site, overlooking the sea and beach and surrounded by National Trust parkland. This uniquely placed park slopes down to the sea, although pitches are generally level. A slight dip hides the view of the beach from the back of the park, but this area benefits from having trees, scrub and meadows, unlike the barer areas closer to the sea which do have a spectacular outlook. Wooden pods that sleep four are available to hire. This makes an ideal base for touring Dorset and Devon. Lake fishing is possible (a licence can be obtained locally). 11 acre site. 108 touring pitches. 24 hardstandings. 15 seasonal pitches. Caravan pitches. Motorhome pitches. Tent pitches. 234 statics. 3 wooden pods.

Open: Mar-Nov **Last arrival:** 22.00hrs **Last departure:** 11.00hrs

Pitches: * £16.50-£35 £16.50-£35 £16.50-£33

Leisure: **Facilities:**

Services: **Within 3 miles:**

Notes: Dogs must be kept on leads.

AA Pubs & Restaurants nearby: Riverside Restaurant, BRIDPORT, DT6 4EZ, 01308 422011

LEISURE: Indoor swimming pool · Outdoor swimming pool · Children's playground · Kid's club · Tennis court · Games room · Separate TV room · golf course · Boats for hire · Cinema · Entertainment · Fishing · Mini golf · Watersports · Gym · Sports field · Spa · Stables

FACILITIES: Bath · Shower · Electric shaver · Hairdryer · Ice Pack Facility · Disabled facilities · Public telephone · Shop on site or within 200yds · Mobile shop (calls at least 5 days a week) · BBQ area · Picnic area · Wi-fi · Internet access · Recycling · Tourist info · Dog exercise area

CHRISTCHURCH Map 5 SZ19

Places to visit

Red House Museum & Gardens, CHRISTCHURCH, BH23 1BU, 01202 482860 www3.hants.gov.uk/redhouse

Great for kids: Oceanarium, BOURNEMOUTH, BH2 5AA, 01202 311993 www.oceanarium.co.uk

PREMIER PARK

Meadowbank Holidays

►►►►► 85%

tel: 01202 483597 **Stour Way BH23 2PQ**
email: enquiries@meadowbank-holidays.co.uk
web: www.meadowbank-holidays.co.uk
dir: *A31 onto A338 towards Bournemouth. 5m, left towards Christchurch on B3073. Right at 1st rdbt into St Catherine's Way, becomes River Way. 3rd right into Stour Way to site.* **grid ref:** *SZ136946*

A very smart park on the banks of the River Stour, with a colourful display of hanging baskets and flower-filled tubs placed around the superb reception area. The facility block is excellent. Visitors can choose between the different pitch sizes, including luxury, fully serviced ones. There is also an excellent play area, a good shop on site and coarse fishing. Statics are available for hire. 2 acre site. 41 touring pitches. 22 hardstandings. Caravan pitches. Motorhome pitches. 180 statics.

Open: Mar-Oct **Last arrival:** 21.00hrs **Last departure:** noon

Pitches:

Leisure:

Facilities:

Services:

Within 3 miles:

Notes: No pets.

AA Pubs & Restaurants nearby: The Ship In Distress, CHRISTCHURCH, BH23 3NA, 01202 485123

Splinters Restaurant, CHRISTCHURCH, BH23 1BW, 01202 483454

CORFE CASTLE Map 4 SY98

Places to visit

Brownsea Island, BROWNSEA ISLAND, BH13 7EE, 01202 707744 www.nationaltrust.org.uk/brownsea

Great for kids: Swanage Railway, SWANAGE, BH19 1HB, 01929 425800 www.swanagerailway.co.uk

Corfe Castle Camping & Caravanning Club Site

►►►► 91%

tel: 01929 480280 & 0845 130 7633 *(Calls cost 7p per minute plus your phone company's access charge)* **Bucknowle BH20 5PQ**
dir: *A351 from Wareham towards Swanage for 4m. Right at foot of Corfe Castle signed Church Knowle. 0.75m, right to site on left.* **grid ref:** *SY950819*

This lovely campsite, where non-members are also very welcome, is set in woodland near the famous Corfe Castle at the foot of the Purbeck Hills. It has a stone reception building, on-site shop and modern toilet and shower facilities, which are spotless. Although the site is sloping, pitches are level and include spacious hardstandings. The site is perfect for visiting the many attractions of the Purbeck area, including the award-winning beaches at Studland and Swanage, and the seaside towns of Poole, Bournemouth and Weymouth. There is also a station at Corfe for the Swanage Steam Railway. The site is pet friendly. 6 acre site. 80 touring pitches. 33 hardstandings. Caravan pitches. Motorhome pitches. Tent pitches.

Open: Mar-Oct **Last arrival:** 20.00hrs **Last departure:** noon

Pitches:

Leisure:

Facilities:

Services:

Within 3 miles:

Notes: Site gates closed 23.00hrs-07.00hrs, later arrivals by prior arrangement only. Dogs must be kept on leads.

AA Pubs & Restaurants nearby: The New Inn, CHURCH KNOWLE, BH20 5NQ, 01929 480357

CORFE CASTLE *continued*

Woodyhyde Camp Site

►►► 80%

DAVID BELLAMY CONSERVATION AWARD SILVER

tel: 01929 480274 **Valley Rd BH20 5HT**
email: camp@woodyhyde.co.uk **web:** www.woodyhyde.co.uk
dir: *From Corfe Castle towards Swanage on A351, site approx 1m on right.*
grid ref: *SY974804*

A large grassy campsite in a sheltered location for tents and motorhomes only, divided into three paddocks – one is dog free. There is a well-stocked shop on site, a modern toilet and shower block, and a regular bus service that stops near the site entrance. Electric hook-ups and some hardstandings are available. This site offers traditional camping in a great location between Corfe Castle and Swanage. 13 acre site. 150 touring pitches. 25 hardstandings. Motorhome pitches. Tent pitches.

Open: Mar-Oct **Last departure:** noon

Pitches:

Facilities:

Services:

Within 3 miles:

Notes: No noise after 23.00hrs, no open fires. Dogs must be kept on leads.

AA Pubs & Restaurants nearby: The New Inn, CHURCH KNOWLE, BH20 5NQ, 01929 480357

DORCHESTER

See Cerne Abbas

DRIMPTON

Map 4 ST40

Places to visit

Forde Abbey, THORNCOMBE, TA20 4LU, 01460 221290 www.fordeabbey.co.uk

Mapperton, BEAMINSTER, DT8 3NR, 01308 862645 www.mapperton.com

Oathill Farm Touring and Camping Site

►►►► 83%

tel: 01460 30234 **Oathill TA18 8PZ**
email: oathillfarm@btconnect.com **web:** www.oathillfarmleisure.co.uk
dir: *From Crewkerne take B3165. Site on left just after Clapton.* **grid ref:** *ST404055*

This small peaceful park borders Somerset and Devon, with the Jurassic Coast at Lyme Regis, Charmouth and Bridport only a short drive away. The modern facilities are spotless and there are hardstandings and fully serviced pitches available. Lucy's Tea Room serves breakfast and meals. The well-stocked, landscaped fishing ponds prove a hit with anglers. Three luxury lodges are available for hire. 10 acre site. 13 touring pitches. 18 hardstandings. 8 seasonal pitches. Caravan pitches. Motorhome pitches. Tent pitches. 3 statics.

Open: all year (rs Winter shop not fully stocked) **Last arrival:** 20.00hrs
Last departure: noon

Pitches: * £18-£25 £18-£25 £15-£22.50

Leisure:

Facilities: WiFi

Services:

Within 3 miles:

Notes: No washing lines, no quad bikes, no noise after 23.00hrs. Separate recreational areas.

AA Pubs & Restaurants nearby: The George Inn, CREWKERNE, TA18 7LP, 01460 73650

FERNDOWN

Places to visit

Kingston Lacy, WIMBORNE, BH21 4EA, 01202 883402 (Mon-Fri) www.nationaltrust.org.uk/kingston-lacy

Great for kids: Oceanarium, BOURNEMOUTH, BH2 5AA, 01202 311993 www.oceanarium.co.uk

FERNDOWN Map 5 SU00

St Leonards Farm Caravan & Camping Park

►►► 83%

tel: 01202 872637 **Ringwood Rd, West Moors BH22 0AQ**
email: enquiries_stleonards@yahoo.co.uk **web:** www.stleonardsfarm.biz
dir: *From Ringwood on A31 (dual carriageway) towards Ferndown, exit left into slip road at site sign. From Wimborne Minster on A31 at rdbt (junct of A31 & A347) follow signs for Ringwood (A31)(pass Texaco garage on left) to next rdbt. 3rd exit (ie double back towards Ferndown) exit at slip road for site.* **grid ref:** *SU093014*

A private road accessed from the A31 leads to this well-screened park divided into paddocks that have spacious pitches; the site has an excellent secure children's play area, and is well located for visiting nearby Bournemouth and the New Forest National Park. A shepherd's hut is available for hire. 12 acre site. 151 touring pitches. 30 seasonal pitches. Caravan pitches. Motorhome pitches. Tent pitches. 6 statics. 1 shepherd's hut.

Open: Apr-Sep **Last departure:** 14.00hrs

Pitches: **Leisure:** **Facilities:**

Services: **Within 3 miles:**

Notes: No large groups, no noise after 23.00hrs, no disposable BBQs, no gazebos, no dogs Jul-Aug. Dogs must be kept on leads.

AA Pubs & Restaurants nearby: Les Bouviers Restaurant with Rooms, WIMBORNE MINSTER, BH21 3BD, 01202 889555

HURN Map 5 SZ19

Places to visit

Red House Museum & Gardens, CHRISTCHURCH, BH23 1BU, 01202 482860 www3.hants.gov.uk/redhouse

Oceanarium, BOURNEMOUTH, BH2 5AA, 01202 311993 www.oceanarium.co.uk

Fillybrook Farm Touring Park

►► 85%

tel: 01202 478266 **Matchams Ln BH23 6AW**
email: enquiries@fillybrookfarm.co.uk **web:** www.fillybrookfarm.co.uk
dir: *M27 junct 1, A31 to Ringwood, then Poole, left immediately after Texaco Garage signed Verwood & B3081, left into Hurn Ln signed Matchams. Site on right in 4m.*
grid ref: *SZ128997*

A small adults-only park well located on the edge of Hurn Forest, with Bournemouth, Christchurch, Poole and the New Forest within easy reach. Fillybrook provides a pleasant, peaceful camping environment, and the facilities are both modern and very clean. A dry-ski slope, with an adjoining restaurant and small bar, is a short walk from the site. There is also a separate rally field. 1 acre site. 18 touring pitches. Caravan pitches. Motorhome pitches. Tent pitches.

Open: Etr-Oct **Last arrival:** 20.00hrs **Last departure:** 11.00hrs

Pitches: **Facilities:**

Services: **Within 3 miles:**

Notes: Adults only. No large groups, no commercial vehicles, no campfires. Dogs must be kept on leads.

AA Pubs & Restaurants nearby: The Three Tuns, BRANSGORE, BH23 8JH, 01425 672232

LYME REGIS Map 4 SY39

See also Charmouth

Places to visit

Pecorama Pleasure Gardens, BEER, EX12 3NA, 01297 21542 www.pecorama.info

Shrubbery Touring Park

►►►► 87%

tel: 01297 442227 **Rousdon DT7 3XW**
email: info@shrubberypark.co.uk **web:** www.shrubberypark.co.uk
dir: *3m W of Lyme Regis on A3052 (coast road).* **grid ref:** *SY300914*

Mature trees enclose this peaceful park, which has distant views of the lovely countryside. The modern facilities are well kept, the hardstanding pitches are spacious, and there is plenty of space for children to play in the grounds. There is a small area set aside for adults only. Well located for visiting Lyme Regis, Sidmouth and Seaton, the park is right on the Jurassic Coast bus route, which is popular with visitors to this area. 10 acre site. 120 touring pitches. 28 hardstandings. Caravan pitches. Motorhome pitches. Tent pitches.

Open: Apr-1 Nov **Last arrival:** 21.00hrs **Last departure:** 11.00hrs

Pitches: * £12-£17.50 £12-£17.50 £12-£17.50

Leisure: **Facilities:**

Services: **Within 3 miles:**

Notes: No groups (except rallies), no motor scooters, roller skates or skateboards. Dogs must be kept on leads. Crazy golf.

AA Pubs & Restaurants nearby: The Mariners, LYME REGIS, DT7 3HS, 01297 442753

POOLE *continued*

ENGLAND & OVERALL WINNER OF THE AA CAMPSITE OF THE YEAR 2016

PREMIER PARK

South Lytchett Manor Caravan & Camping Park

►►►►► 96%

tel: 01202 622577 **Dorchester Rd, Lytchett Minster BH16 6JB**
email: info@southlytchettmanor.co.uk **web:** www.southlytchettmanor.co.uk
dir: *Exit A35 onto B3067, 1m E of Lytchett Minster, 600yds on right after village.*
grid ref: *SY954926*

Every year this site improves. Situated in the grounds of a historic manor house, the park has modern facilities that are spotless and well maintained. There's a TV hook-up on every pitch and access to free WiFi across the park. A warm and friendly welcome awaits at this lovely park which is well located for visiting Poole and Bournemouth; the Jurassic X53 bus route (Exeter to Poole) has a stop just outside the park. A new 'Twaggon' (a modern version of a gypsy caravan), replete with double bed and two singles plus kitchen and fridge, is available for hire. 22 acre site. 150 touring pitches. 85 hardstandings. 4 seasonal pitches. Caravan pitches. Motorhome pitches. Tent pitches.

Open: Mar-2 Jan **Last arrival:** 21.00hrs **Last departure:** 11.00hrs

Pitches: * £19.50-£33.25

Leisure:

Facilities:

Services:

Within 3 miles:

Notes: No camp fires or Chinese lanterns, no noise after 22.30hrs. Dogs must be kept on leads.

AA Pubs & Restaurants nearby: The Plantation, POOLE, BH13 7JF, 01202 701531

The Cock & Bottle, EAST MORDEN, BH20 7DL, 01929 459238

See advert on page 195

PORTESHAM Map 4 SY68

Places to visit

Tutankhamun Exhibition, DORCHESTER, DT1 1UW, 01305 269571
www.tutankhamun-exhibition.co.uk

Maiden Castle, DORCHESTER, DT2 9PP, 0370 333 1181
www.english-heritage.org.uk/daysout/properties/maiden-castle

Great for kids: Teddy Bear Museum, DORCHESTER, DT1 1JU, 01305 266040
www.teddybearmuseum.co.uk

Portesham Dairy Farm Campsite

►►►► 80%

tel: 01305 871297 **Weymouth DT3 4HG**
email: info@porteshamdairyfarm.co.uk
dir: *From Dorchester take A35 towards Bridport. In 5m left at Winterbourne Abbas, follow Portesham signs. Through village, left at Kings Arms pub, site 350yds on right.*
grid ref: *SY602854*

Located at the edge of the picturesque village of Portesham close to the Dorset coast. This family-run, level park is part of a small working farm in a quiet rural location. Fully serviced and seasonal pitches are available. Near the site entrance is a pub where meals are served, and it has a garden for children to play in. This quiet park is well postioned for visiting many areas of the West Dorset coast. 8 acre site. 90 touring pitches. 61 hardstandings. 60 seasonal pitches. Caravan pitches. Motorhome pitches. Tent pitches.

Open: Apr-Sep **Last arrival:** 18.00hrs **Last departure:** 11.00hrs

Pitches: * £14-£28 £14-£28 £12-£24

Leisure:

Facilities:

Services:

Within 3 miles:

Notes: No commercial vehicles, no groups, no camp fires, minimal noise after 22.00hrs. Dogs must be kept on leads. Caravan storage.

LEISURE: Indoor swimming pool · Outdoor swimming pool · Children's playground · Kid's club · Tennis court · Games room · Separate TV room · golf course · Boats for hire · Cinema · Entertainment · Fishing · Mini golf · Watersports · Gym · Sports field · Spa · Stables
FACILITIES: Bath · Shower · Electric shaver · Hairdryer · Ice Pack Facility · Disabled facilities · Public telephone · Shop on site or within 200yds · Mobile shop (calls at least 5 days a week) · BBQ area · Picnic area · Wi-fi · Internet access · Recycling · Tourist info · Dog exercise area

PUNCKNOWLE Map 4 SY58

Places to visit

Dinosaur Museum, DORCHESTER, DT1 1EW, 01305 269880 www.thedinosaurmuseum.com

Hardy's Cottage, DORCHESTER, DT2 8QJ, 01305 262366 www.nationaltrust.org.uk

Great for kids: Abbotsbury Swannery, ABBOTSBURY, DT3 4JG, 01305 871858 www.abbotsbury-tourism.co.uk

Home Farm Caravan and Campsite

►►► 79%

tel: 01308 897258 **Home Farm, Rectory Ln DT2 9BW**
dir: *From Dorchester towards Bridport on A35, left at start of dual carriageway, at hill bottom right to Litton Cheney. Through village, 2nd left to Puncknowle (Hazel Ln). Left at T-junct, left at phone box. Site 150mtrs on right. Caravan route: approach via A35 Bridport, then Swyre on B3157, continue to Swyre Ln & Rectory Ln.* **grid ref:** *SY535887*

This quiet site, hidden away on the edge of a little hamlet, has good facilities and is an excellent place to camp, with some hardstanding pitches now available. It offers sweeping views of the Dorset countryside from most pitches, and is just five miles from Abbotsbury, and one and a half miles from the South West Coast Path. A really good base from which to tour this attractive area. 6.5 acre site. 47 touring pitches. 14 seasonal pitches. Caravan pitches. Motorhome pitches. Tent pitches.

Open: Apr-Oct **Last arrival:** 21.00hrs (late arrivals by prior arrangement only; please check with campsite) **Last departure:** noon

Pitches:

Facilities:

Services:

Within 3 miles:

Notes: No cats, no wood-burning fires, skateboards, rollerblades, motorised toys or loud music. Dogs must be kept on leads. Calor gas exchange.

AA Pubs & Restaurants nearby: The Crown Inn, PUNCKNOWLE, DT2 9BN, 01308 897711

The Manor Hotel, WEST BEXINGTON, DT2 9DF, 01308 897660

ST LEONARDS

Places to visit

Rockbourne Roman Villa, ROCKBOURNE, SP6 3PG, 01725 518541 (during opening times only) www.hants.gov.uk/rockbourne-roman-villa

Red House Museum & Gardens, CHRISTCHURCH, BH23 1BU, 01202 482860 www3.hants.gov.uk/redhouse

Great for kids: Moors Valley Country Park and Forest, RINGWOOD, BH24 2ET, 01425 470721 www.moors-valley.co.uk

ST LEONARDS Map 5 SU10

PREMIER PARK

Shamba Holidays

►►►►► 85%

tel: 01202 873302 **Ringwood Rd, East Moors Ln BH24 2SB**
email: enquiries@shambaholidays.co.uk **web:** www.shambaholidays.co.uk
dir: *From Poole on A31, pass Woodman Pub on left, straight on at rdbt (keep in left lane), immediately left into East Moors Ln. Site 1m on right.* **grid ref:** *SU105029*

This top quality park has excellent modern facilities particularly suited to families, and you can be certain of a warm welcome from the friendly staff. There is a really good indoor/outdoor heated pool, plus a tasteful bar supplying a good range of meals. The park is well located for visiting the south coast, which is just a short drive away, and also for the New Forest National Park. 7 acre site. 150 touring pitches. 40 seasonal pitches. Caravan pitches. Motorhome pitches. Tent pitches.

Open: Mar-Oct (rs Low/mid season some facilities open only at wknds)
Last arrival: 20.00hrs (late arrivals by prior arrangement only)
Last departure: 11.00hrs

Pitches: **Leisure:**

Facilities: WiFi

Services: **Within 3 miles:**

Notes: No large groups or commercial vehicles, no noise after 23.00hrs. Dogs must be kept on leads. Phone card top-up facility.

AA Pubs & Restaurants nearby: The Kings Arms, FERNDOWN, BH22 9AA, 01202 577490

See advert on page 198

ST LEONARDS *continued*

Back of Beyond Touring Park

►►►► 88%

GOLD

tel: 01202 876968 **234 Ringwood Rd BH24 2SB**
email: info@backofbeyondtouringpark.co.uk
dir: *From E: on A31 over Little Chef rdbt, pass St Leonard's Hotel, at next rdbt U-turn into lane immediately left. Site at end of lane. From W: on A31 pass Texaco garage & Woodman Inn, immediately left to site.* **grid ref:** *SU103034*

This lovely adults-only park, a member of the Tranquil Parks group, is set in 30 acres of woodland and offers plenty of pleasant walks. Visitors are sure to receive a warm welcome from the owners and their team. In addition to good caravan and motorhome pitches there are some excellent areas for tents. The site has a fishing lake and a picnic area, and the whole area is a haven for wildlife. The facilities are well appointed and very clean. There are fish and chip and pizza nights as well as BBQ evenings. 30 acre site. 80 touring pitches. 40 seasonal pitches. Caravan pitches. Motorhome pitches. Tent pitches.

Open: Mar-Oct **Last arrival:** 18.30hrs **Last departure:** 11.00hrs

Pitches: * £25-£30 £25-£30 £20-£25

Leisure:

Facilities:

Services:

Within 3 miles:

Notes: Adults only. No commercial vehicles, no groups, no noise after 22.30hrs. Visiting food vans, coffee & tea available, morning bakery.

AA Pubs & Restaurants nearby: The Kings Arms, FERNDOWN, BH22 9AA, 01202 577490

Forest Edge Holiday Park

►►► 79%

tel: 01590 648331 **229 Ringwood Rd BH24 2SD**
email: holidays@shorefield.co.uk
dir: *From E: on A31 over 1st rdbt (Little Chef), pass St Leonards Hotel, left at next rdbt into Boundary Ln, site 100yds on left. From W: on A31 pass Texaco garage & Woodman Inn, right at rdbt into Boundary Ln.* **grid ref:** *SU104024*

A tree-lined park set in grassland with plenty of excellent amenities for all the family, including an outdoor heated swimming pool, a toddlers' pool and an adventure playground. Visitors are invited to use the superb leisure club plus all amenities and entertainment at the sister site of Oakdene Forest Park, which is less than a mile away. Holiday homes are available for hire. 9 acre site. 72 touring pitches. 29 seasonal pitches. Caravan pitches. Motorhome pitches. Tent pitches. 30 statics.

Open: Feb-3 Jan (rs School & summer hols pool open) **Last arrival:** 21.00hrs
Last departure: 10.00hrs

Pitches:

Leisure:

Facilities:

Services:

Within 3 miles:

Notes: Families & couples only, rallies welcome, 1 car & 1 dog per pitch, no gazebos, no noise after 22.00hrs. Dogs must be kept on leads.

AA Pubs & Restaurants nearby: The Kings Arms, FERNDOWN, BH22 9AA, 01202 577490

See advert on page 210

SHAFTESBURY

Places to visit

Shaftesbury Abbey Museum & Garden, SHAFTESBURY, SP7 8JR, 01747 852910 www.shaftesburyabbey.org.uk

PREMIER PARK

Dorset Country Holidays

NEW ►►►►►

tel: 01747 851523 & 01225 290924 **Sherborne Causeway SP7 9PX**
email: info@dche.co.uk
dir: *From Shaftesbury's Ivy Cross rdbt take A30 signed Sherborne. Site 2m on right.*
grid ref: *ST835233*

Blackmore Vale Caravan & Camping Park has a separate glamping area which is well screened from the main park and is run by its own 24/7, dedicated team. Two new-style luxury yurts of British design and manufacture offer excellent insulation, heating and lighting; they have king-size double beds, two singles, a fridge, a TV and are fully carpeted. Set on wooden decking, each comes with picnic benches and a BBQ and guests receive a welcome breakfast pack and towelling gowns. In addition there are two bell tents, one large family bell tent and a vintage caravan plus a 'country kabin' – all are fully equipped to a high standard. There's a modern and well-appointed toilet and shower room block. Customer service here is excellent and guests can be collected from the local railway station.

Open: all year **Facilities:**

AA Pubs & Restaurants nearby: The Kings Arms Inn, GILLINGHAM, SP8 5NB, 01747 838325

The Coppleridge Inn, MOTCOMBE, SP7 9HW, 01747 851980

Blackmore Vale Caravan & Camping Park

►►►► 86%

tel: 01747 851523 & 01225 290924 **Sherborne Causeway SP7 9PX**
email: info@dche.co.uk
dir: *From Shaftesbury's Ivy Cross rdbt take A30 signed Sherborne. Site 2m on right.*
grid ref: *ST835233*

This small park set in open countryside just outside Shaftesbury (famous for the steep, cobbled street known as Gold Hill) offers a wide range of camping opportunities, including touring pitches (some with large hardstandings), and an area for four luxury lodges. The facilities are modern and very clean, and a fully equipped gym is available to all customers. There is a separate glamping area with a dedicated team to look after guests. 3 acre site. 13 touring pitches. 7 hardstandings. Caravan pitches. Motorhome pitches. Tent pitches.

Open: all year **Last arrival:** 21.00hrs **Pitches:**

Leisure: **Facilities:**

Services:

Within 3 miles:

Notes: No noise after 23.00hrs. Dogs must be kept on leads. Caravan sales & accessories.

AA Pubs & Restaurants nearby: The Kings Arms Inn, GILLINGHAM, SP8 5NB, 01747 838325

The Coppleridge Inn, MOTCOMBE, SP7 9HW, 01747 851980

SIXPENNY HANDLEY Map 4 ST91

Places to visit

Larmer Tree Gardens, TOLLARD ROYAL, SP5 5PT, 01725 516971 www.larmertreegardens.co.uk

Shaftesbury Abbey Museum & Garden, SHAFTESBURY, SP7 8JR, 01747 852910 www.shaftesburyabbey.org.uk

Great for kids: Moors Valley Country Park and Forest, RINGWOOD, BH24 2ET, 01425 470721 www.moors-valley.co.uk

Church Farm Caravan & Camping Park

►►►► 85%

tel: 01725 552563 & 07766 677525 **The Bungalow, Church Farm, High St SP5 5ND**
email: churchfarmcandcpark@hotmail.co.uk **web:** www.churchfarmcandcpark.co.uk
dir: *1m S of Handley Hill rdbt. Exit for Sixpenny Handley, right by school, site 300yds by church.* **grid ref:** *ST994173*

A spacious park located within the Cranborne Chase Area of Outstanding Natural Beauty; the site is split into several camping areas including one for adults only. There is a first-class facility block with good private facilities and an excellent café/restaurant. The pretty village of Sixpenny Handley with all its amenities is just 200 yards away, and the site is well positioned for visiting the New Forest National Park, Bournemouth, Poole and Stonehenge. 10 acre site. 35 touring pitches. 4 hardstandings. 5 seasonal pitches. Caravan pitches. Motorhome pitches. Tent pitches. 2 statics.

Open: all year (rs Nov-Mar 10 vans max) **Last arrival:** 21.00hrs **Last departure:** 11.00hrs

Pitches: * £18-£20 £18-£20 £18-£20

Leisure:

Facilities:

Services:

Within 3 miles:

Notes: Quiet after 23.00hrs. Dogs must be kept on leads. Use of fridge/freezer & microwave.

AA Pubs & Restaurants nearby: The Museum Inn, FARNHAM, DT11 8DE, 01725 516261

The Drovers Inn, GUSSAGE ALL SAINTS, BH21 5ET, 01258 840084

SWANAGE

Map 5 SZ07

Places to visit

Corfe Castle, CORFE CASTLE, BH20 5EZ, 01929 481294
www.nationaltrust.org.uk/corfecastle

Brownsea Island, BROWNSEA ISLAND, BH13 7EE, 01202 707744
www.nationaltrust.org.uk/brownsea

Great for kids: Swanage Railway, SWANAGE, BH19 1HB, 01929 425800
www.swanagerailway.co.uk

PREMIER PARK

Ulwell Cottage Caravan Park

►►►►► 83%

tel: 01929 422823 **Ulwell Cottage, Ulwell BH19 3DG**
email: enq@ulwellcottagepark.co.uk **web:** www.ulwellcottagepark.co.uk
dir: *From Swanage N for 2m on unclassified road towards Studland.*
grid ref: *SZ019809*

Sitting under the Purbeck Hills and surrounded by scenic walks, this park is only two miles from the beach. It is a family-run and caters well for families and couples, and offers a toilet and shower block complete with good family rooms, all appointed to a high standard. There are fully serviced pitches, a good indoor swimming pool and the village inn offers a good range of meals. There is a camping pod for hire plus a new and stylish self-contained unit suitable for a couple; it comes complete with a decked area. 13 acre site. 77 touring pitches. 23 hardstandings. Caravan pitches. Motorhome pitches. Tent pitches. 140 statics. 1 wooden pod.

Open: Mar-7 Jan (rs Mar-Spring BH & mid Sep-early Jan takeaway closed, shop open variable hrs) **Last arrival:** 22.00hrs **Last departure:** 11.00hrs

Pitches: * £12-£50.50 £12-£50.50 £12-£47.50

Leisure:

Facilities:

Services:

Within 3 miles:

Notes: No bonfires or fireworks. Dogs must be kept on leads.

AA Pubs & Restaurants nearby: The Bankes Arms Hotel, STUDLAND, BH19 3AU, 01929 450225

The Square and Compass, WORTH MATRAVERS, BH19 3LF, 01929 439229

Herston Caravan & Camping Park

►►► 79%

tel: 01929 422932 **Washpond Ln BH19 3DJ**
email: office@herstonleisure.co.uk
dir: *From Wareham on A351 towards Swanage. Washpond Ln on left just after 'Welcome to Swanage' sign.* **grid ref:** *SZ018785*

Set in a rural area, with extensive views of the Purbecks, this tree-lined park has fully serviced pitches plus large camping areas. Herston Halt, a stop for the famous Swanage Steam Railway between the town centre and Corfe Castle, is within walking distance. There are also six yurts available for hire. 10 acre site. 100 touring pitches. 71 hardstandings. Caravan pitches. Motorhome pitches. Tent pitches. 5 statics. 6 yurts.

Open: all year

Pitches:

Leisure:

Facilities:

Services:

Within 3 miles:

Notes: No noise after 23.00hrs. Dogs must be kept on leads.

AA Pubs & Restaurants nearby: The Bankes Arms Hotel, STUDLAND, BH19 3AU, 01929 450225

The Square and Compass, WORTH MATRAVERS, BH19 3LF, 01929 439229

Acton Field Camping Site

►► 77%

tel: 01929 424184 & 439424 **Acton Field, Langton Matravers BH19 3HS**
email: enquiries@actonfieldcampsite.co.uk **web:** www.actonfieldcampsite.co.uk
dir: *From A351 right after Corfe Castle onto B3069 to Langton Matravers, 2nd right after village (bridleway sign).* **grid ref:** *SY991785*

The informal campsite, bordered by farmland on the outskirts of Langton Matravers, with good toilet facilities. There are superb views of the Purbeck Hills and towards

LEISURE: Indoor swimming pool Outdoor swimming pool Children's playground Kid's club Tennis court Games room Separate TV room golf course Boats for hire Cinema Entertainment Fishing Mini golf Watersports Gym Sports field Spa Stables
FACILITIES: Bath Shower Electric shaver Hairdryer Ice Pack Facility Disabled facilities Public telephone Shop on site or within 200yds Mobile shop (calls at least 5 days a week) BBQ area Picnic area Wi-fi Internet access Recycling Tourist info Dog exercise area

the Isle of Wight, and a footpath leads to the coastal path. The site occupies what was once a stone quarry so rock pegs may be required. 7 acre site. 80 touring pitches. Caravan pitches. Motorhome pitches. Tent pitches.

Acton Field Camping Site

Open: Early May BH wknd, Spring BH week, 10 Jul-8 Sep (rs Apr-Oct open for organised groups only) **Last arrival:** 22.00hrs **Last departure:** noon

Pitches:

Facilities:

Services:

Within 3 miles:

Notes: No open fires, no noise after 23.00hrs. Dogs must be kept on leads.

AA Pubs & Restaurants nearby: The Bankes Arms Hotel, STUDLAND, BH19 3AU, 01929 450225

The Square and Compass, WORTH MATRAVERS, BH19 3LF, 01929 439229

THREE LEGGED CROSS — Map 5 SU00

Places to visit

Moors Valley Country Park and Forest, RINGWOOD, BH24 2ET, 01425 470721 www.moors-valley.co.uk

Woolsbridge Manor Farm Caravan Park

 83%

tel: 01202 826369 **BH21 6RA**
email: woolsbridge@btconnect.com **web:** www.woolsbridgemanorcaravanpark.co.uk
dir: *From Ringwood take A31 towards Ferndown. Approx 1m, follow signs for Three Legged Cross & Horton. Site 2m on right.* **grid ref:** *SU099052*

A small farm site with spacious pitches on a level field. This quiet site is an excellent central base for touring the New Forest National Park, Salisbury and the

continued

PITCHES: Caravans Motorhomes Tents Glamping-style accommodation **SERVICES:** Electric hook up Launderette Licensed bar Calor Gas Camping Gaz Toilet fluid Café/Restaurant Fast Food/Takeaway Battery charging Baby care Motorvan service point
ABBREVIATIONS: BH/bank hols – bank holidays Etr – Easter Spring BH – Spring Bank Holiday fr – from hrs – hours m – mile mdnt – midnight rdbt – roundabout rs – restricted service wk – week wknd – weekend x-rds – cross roads No credit or debit cards No dogs Children of all ages accepted

THREE LEGGED CROSS *continued*

south coast, and is close to Moors Valley Country Park for outdoor family activities. Facilities are good and very clean and there are excellent family rooms available. A new camping pod is available for hire. 6.75 acre site. 60 touring pitches. Caravan pitches. Motorhome pitches. Tent pitches. 1 wooden pod.

Woolsbridge Manor Farm Caravan Park

Open: Mar-Oct **Last arrival:** 20.00hrs **Last departure:** 10.30hrs

Pitches: * £17.50-£24.50 £17.50-£24.50 £17.50-£24.50

Leisure:

Facilities:

Services:

Within 3 miles:

Notes: Dogs must be kept on leads.

AA Pubs & Restaurants nearby: The Star Inn, RINGWOOD, BH24 1AW, 01425 473105

See advert on page 201

WAREHAM — Map 4 SY98

Places to visit

Brownsea Island, BROWNSEA ISLAND, BH13 7EE, 01202 707744
www.nationaltrust.org.uk/brownsea

PREMIER PARK

Wareham Forest Tourist Park

96%

tel: 01929 551393 **North Trigon BH20 7NZ**
email: holiday@warehamforest.co.uk
dir: *From A35 between Bere Regis & Lytchett Minster follow Wareham sign into Sugar Hill. Site on left.* **grid ref:** *SY894912*

A woodland park within the tranquil Wareham Forest, with its many walks and proximity to Poole, Dorchester and the Purbeck coast. Two luxury blocks, with combined washbasin and toilets for total privacy, are maintained to a high standard of cleanliness. A heated outdoor swimming pool, off licence, shop and games room add to the pleasure of a stay on this top quality park. There is a new bike wash and a separate dog wash with hot water. 55 acre site. 200 touring pitches. 70 hardstandings. 70 seasonal pitches. Caravan pitches. Motorhome pitches. Tent pitches.

Open: all year (rs Off-peak season limited services) **Last arrival:** 21.00hrs
Last departure: 11.00hrs

Pitches:

Leisure:

Facilities:

Services:

Within 3 miles:

Notes: Families & couples only, no group bookings. Dogs must be kept on leads.

AA Pubs & Restaurants nearby: The New Inn, CHURCH KNOWLE, BH20 5NQ, 01929 480357

Birchwood Tourist Park

►►►► 81%

tel: 01929 554763 **Bere Rd, Coldharbour BH20 7PA**
email: birchwoodtouristpark@hotmail.com **web:** www.birchwoodtouristpark.co.uk
dir: *From Poole (A351) or Dorchester (A352) on N side of railway line at Wareham, follow Bere Regis signs. 2nd park after 2.25m.* **grid ref:** *SY896905*

Set in 50 acres of parkland located within Wareham Forest, this site offers direct access to ideal areas for walking, mountain biking, and horse and pony riding. This is a spacious open park with plenty of room for young people to play games including football. The modern facilities are in two central locations and are very clean. There is a good security barrier system. 25 acre site. 175 touring pitches. 25 hardstandings. Caravan pitches. Motorhome pitches. Tent pitches.

Birchwood Tourist Park

Open: all year **Last arrival:** 21.00hrs **Last departure:** 11.30hrs

Pitches: * £18.50-£31 £18.50-£31 £13.50-£26

Leisure:

Facilities:

Services:

Within 3 miles:

Notes: No groups on BH, no generators or camp fires. Dogs must be kept on leads. Pitch & putt, paddling pool.

AA Pubs & Restaurants nearby: The New Inn, CHURCH KNOWLE, BH20 5NQ, 01929 480357

See advert below

PITCHES: Caravans Motorhomes Tents Glamping-style accommodation **SERVICES:** Electric hook up Launderette Licensed bar Calor Gas Camping Gaz Toilet fluid Café/Restaurant Fast Food/Takeaway Battery charging Baby care Motorvan service point
ABBREVIATIONS: BH/bank hols – bank holidays Etr – Easter Spring BH – Spring Bank Holiday fr – from hrs – hours m – mile mdnt – midnight rdbt – roundabout rs – restricted service wk – week wknd – weekend x-rds – cross roads No credit or debit cards No dogs Children of all ages accepted

WAREHAM *continued*

Lookout Holiday Park

 80%

tel: 01929 552546 **Stoborough BH20 5AZ**
email: enquiries@caravan-sites.co.uk **web:** www.thelookoutholidaypark.co.uk
dir: *Take A351 through Wareham, cross River Frome, through Stoborough, site signed on left.* **grid ref:** *SY927858*

Divided into two paddocks and set well back from the Swanage road, this touring park is separated from the static part of the operation (32 static holiday homes are for hire). There are very good facilities including camping pods, while a superb children's playground and plenty of other attractions make this an ideal centre for families. The site is very convenient for visiting Corfe and Swanage. 15 acre site. 150 touring pitches. 99 hardstandings. Caravan pitches. Motorhome pitches. Tent pitches. 89 statics. 2 wooden pods.

Open: Mar-Jan – contact park for touring & camping opening dates
Last arrival: 22.00hrs **Last departure:** noon

Pitches: * £14-£28 £14-£28 £9-£24

Leisure:

Facilities:

Services:

Within 3 miles:

Notes: No pets.

AA Pubs & Restaurants nearby: The New Inn, CHURCH KNOWLE, BH20 5NQ, 01929 480357

Norden Farm Touring Caravan and Camping Site

►►►► 80%

tel: 01929 480098 **Norden Farm, Corfe Castle BH20 5DS**
email: campsite@nordenfarm.com
dir: *On A351 from Wareham towards Swanage, 3.5m to site on right.* **grid ref:** *SY950828*

This delightful farm site offers traditional camping but with excellent toilet and shower facilities. It is a very dog-friendly site and is ideally suited for those who enjoy country pursuits. Its location is very close to Corfe Castle so it's very convenient for visiting the Isle of Purbeck and Swanage (maybe by using the park and ride at Norden railway station and taking the train). There is a holiday cottage for hire plus a bed & breakfast operation with a restaurant that's open to all. 10 acre site. 140 touring pitches. Variable seasonal pitches. Caravan pitches. Motorhome pitches. Tent pitches.

Open: Mar-Oct (rs Early Mar or late Oct may close 1 shower block) **Last arrival:** 22.00hrs
Last departure: 11.00hrs (flexible departure times available in low season)

Pitches: * £8.50-£21 £8.50-£21 £8.50-£21

Leisure:

Facilities:

Services:

Within 3 miles:

Notes: Strict 5mph speed limit on site, no noise after 23.00hrs. Dogs must be kept on leads. Hot shower washroom for dogs.

AA Pubs & Restaurants nearby: The New Inn, CHURCH KNOWLE, BH20 5NQ, 01929 480357

East Creech Farm Campsite

►►► 82%

tel: 01929 480519 & 481312 **East Creech Farm, East Creech BH20 5AP**
email: east.creech@virgin.net
dir: *From Wareham on A351 S towards Swanage. On bypass at 3rd rdbt take Furzebrook/Blue Pool Rd exit, site approx 2m on right.* **grid ref:** *SY928827*

This grassy park set in a peaceful location beneath the Purbeck Hills, with extensive views towards Poole and Brownsea Island. The park boasts a woodland play area, bright, clean toilet facilities and a farm shop selling milk, eggs and bread. There are also four coarse fishing lakes teeming with fish. The park is close to Norden Station on the Swanage to Norden steam railway line, and is well located for visiting Corfe Castle, Swanage and the Purbeck coast. 4 acre site. 80 touring pitches. Caravan pitches. Motorhome pitches. Tent pitches.

Open: Apr-Oct **Last arrival:** 20.00hrs **Last departure:** noon

Pitches: * £12-£15.50 £12-£15.50 £12-£15.50

Leisure:

Facilities:

Services:

Within 3 miles:

Notes: No camp fires, no loud noise. Dogs must be kept on leads.

AA Pubs & Restaurants nearby: The New Inn, CHURCH KNOWLE, BH20 5NQ, 01929 480357

Ridge Farm Camping & Caravan Park

►►► 78%

tel: 01929 556444 & 07970 964672 **Barnhill Rd, Ridge BH20 5BG**
email: info@ridgefarm.co.uk
dir: *From Wareham take B3075 towards Corfe Castle, cross river, into Stoborough, left to Ridge. Follow site signs for 1.5m.* **grid ref:** *SY939868*

A quiet rural park, adjacent to a working farm and surrounded by trees and bushes. This away-from-it-all park is ideally located for touring this part of Dorset, and especially for birdwatchers, or those who enjoy walking and cycling. This site is perfect for visiting the Arne Nature Reserve, the Blue Pool and Corfe Castle. 3.47 acre site. 60 touring pitches. 2 hardstandings. Caravan pitches. Motorhome pitches. Tent pitches.

Open: Etr-Sep **Last arrival:** 21.00hrs **Last departure:** noon

Pitches:

Facilities:

Services:

Within 3 miles:

Notes: No dogs Jul-Aug. Dogs must be kept on leads.

AA Pubs & Restaurants nearby: The New Inn, CHURCH KNOWLE, BH20 5NQ, 01929 480357

WEYMOUTH Map 4 SY67

Places to visit

RSPB Nature Reserve Radipole Lake and Wild Weymouth Discovery Centre, WEYMOUTH, DT4 7TZ, 01305 778313 www.rspb.org.uk

Portland Castle, PORTLAND, DT5 1AZ, 01305 820539 www.english-heritage.org.uk/daysout/properties/portland-castle

Great for kids: Weymouth Sea Life Adventure Park & Marine Sanctuary, WEYMOUTH, DT4 7SX, 0871 423 2110 *(Calls cost 10p per minute plus your phone company's access charge)* www.sealifeweymouth.com

Littlesea Holiday Park

HOLIDAY CENTRE 87%

GOLD

tel: 0800 335 3677 **Lynch Ln DT4 9DT**
email: littlesea@haven.com **web:** www.haven.com/littlesea
dir: *A35 onto A354 signed Weymouth. Right at 1st rdbt, 3rd exit at 2nd rdbt towards Chickerell. Left into Lynch Lane after lights. Site at far end of road.* **grid ref:** *SY654783*

Just three miles from Weymouth with its lovely beaches and many attractions, Littlesea has a cheerful family atmosphere and fantastic facilities. Indoor and outdoor entertainment and activities are on offer for all the family, and the toilet facilities on the touring park are of a good quality. The touring section of this holiday complex is at the far end of the site adjacent to the South West Coast Path in a perfect location. 100 acre site. 155 touring pitches. Caravan pitches. Motorhome pitches. Tent pitches. 720 statics.

Littlesea Holiday Park

Open: end Mar-end Oct (rs end Mar-May & Sep-Oct facilities may be reduced)
Last arrival: mdnt **Last departure:** 10.00hrs

Pitches:

Leisure:

Facilities:

Services:

Within 3 miles:

Notes: No commercial vehicles, no bookings by persons under 21yrs unless a family booking, no boats, max 2 dogs per booking, certain dog breeds banned.

AA Pubs & Restaurants nearby: The Old Ship Inn, WEYMOUTH, DT3 5QQ, 01305 812522

See advert below

WEYMOUTH *continued*

Seaview Holiday Park

HOLIDAY CENTRE 84%

tel: 0871 230 2760 *(Calls cost 10p per minute plus your phone company's access charge)* **Preston DT3 6DZ**
email: seaview@haven.com **web:** www.haven.com/seaview
dir: *A354 to Weymouth, follow signs for Preston/Wareham onto A353. Site 3m on right just after Weymouth Bay Holiday Park.* **grid ref:** *SY707830*

A fun-packed holiday centre for all the family, with plenty of activities and entertainment during the day and evening. Terraced pitches are provided for caravans, and there is a separate field for tents. The park is close to Weymouth and other coastal attractions. There's a smart toilet and shower block, plus fully serviced hardstanding pitches. Holiday homes and six fully equipped safari tents are available for hire. 20 acre site. 87 touring pitches. 35 hardstandings. Caravan pitches. Motorhome pitches. Tent pitches. 259 statics. 6 safari tents.

Open: mid Mar-end Oct (rs mid Mar-May & Sep-Oct facilities may be reduced)
Last arrival: mdnt **Last departure:** 10.00hrs

Pitches: **Leisure:**

Facilities:

Services: **Within 3 miles:**

Notes: No commercial vehicles, no bookings by persons under 21yrs unless a family booking, max 2 dogs per booking, certain dog breeds banned. Dogs must be kept on leads.

AA Pubs & Restaurants nearby: The Old Ship Inn, WEYMOUTH, DT3 5QQ, 01305 812522

The Smugglers Inn, OSMINGTON MILLS, DT3 6HF, 01305 833125

See advert on opposite page

PREMIER PARK

East Fleet Farm Touring Park

90%

tel: 01305 785768 **Chickerell DT3 4DW**
email: enquiries@eastfleet.co.uk
dir: *On B3157 (Weymouth to Bridport road), 3m from Weymouth.* **grid ref:** *SY640797*

Set on a working organic farm and in a unique location on the shores of the Fleet Lagoon, overlooking Chesil Beach and the sea, with direct access to the South West Coast Path. There is a wide variety of pitches, including hardstandings and fully serviced pitches, and the largest family tents can be accommodated. This park offers excellent toilet and shower facilities with family rooms. There are good play facilities for children, including a fenced play area for younger ones and a separate play barn with table tennis and other activities. The Old Barn has a tasteful bar and lovely patio area, where customers are welcome to take their own food, or order locally and have the food delivered to the bar. In addition there is a pizza and fish and chip outlet near the Old Barn. Two high quality holiday cottages are available for hire. 21 acre site. 400 touring pitches. 90 hardstandings. 40 seasonal pitches. Caravan pitches. Motorhome pitches. Tent pitches.

Open: 16 Mar-Oct **Last arrival:** 22.00hrs **Last departure:** 10.30hrs

Pitches: * £19-£29 £19-£29 £19-£29

Leisure:

Facilities:

Services:

Within 3 miles:

Notes: Dogs must be kept on leads. Camping & caravan accessories shop.

AA Pubs & Restaurants nearby: The Old Ship Inn, WEYMOUTH, DT3 5QQ, 01305 812522

Bagwell Farm Touring Park

►►►► 86%

tel: 01305 782575 **Knights in the Bottom, Chickerell DT3 4EA**
email: aa@bagwellfarm.co.uk
dir: *From A354 follow signs for Weymouth town centre, then B3157 to Chickerell & Abbotsbury, 1m past Chickerell left into site 500yds after Victoria Inn.* **grid ref:** *SY627816*

This well located park is set in a small valley with access to the South West Coast Path and is very convenient for visiting Weymouth and Portland. It has excellent facilities including a good shop, pets' corner, children's play area plus the Red Barn bar and restaurant. A good range of hardstandings is available, including 25 super pitches. This is an excellent place to stay at any time of the year. 14 acre site. 320 touring pitches. 35 hardstandings. 70 seasonal pitches. Caravan pitches. Motorhome pitches. Tent pitches.

Open: all year (rs Winter bar closed) **Last arrival:** 21.00hrs **Last departure:** 11.00hrs

Pitches: **Leisure:**

Facilities:

Services:

Within 3 miles:

Notes: Families & couples only, no noise after 23.00hrs. Dogs must be kept on leads. Wet suit shower, campers' shelter.

AA Pubs & Restaurants nearby: The Old Ship Inn, WEYMOUTH, DT3 5QQ, 01305 812522

West Fleet Holiday Farm

90%

tel: 01305 782218 **Fleet DT3 4EF**
email: aa@westfleetholidays.co.uk
dir: *From Weymouth take B3157 towards Abbotsbury for 3m. Past Chickerell turn left at mini-rdbt to Fleet, site 1m on right.* **grid ref:** *SY625811*

A spacious farm site with both level and sloping pitches divided into paddocks and screened by hedges. This site has good views of the Dorset countryside, and is a relaxing place for a family holiday, particularly suited to tents, especially family-sized tents, and small motorhomes or campervans. The Barn Clubhouse has a bar, restaurant and entertainment area. WiFi is also available. 12 acre site. 250 touring pitches. Caravan pitches. Motorhome pitches. Tent pitches.

Open: Etr-Sep (rs May-Sep clubhouse & pool only during high season)
Last arrival: 21.00hrs **Last departure:** 11.00hrs

Pitches:

Leisure:

Facilities:

Services:

Within 3 miles:

Notes: Non-family groups by arrangement only, dogs restricted to certain areas. Dogs must be kept on leads.

AA Pubs & Restaurants nearby: The Old Ship Inn, WEYMOUTH, DT3 5QQ, 01305 812522

Pebble Bank Caravan Park

86%

tel: 01305 774844 **Camp Rd, Wyke Regis DT4 9HF**
email: info@pebblebank.co.uk
dir: *From Weymouth take Portland road. At last rdbt turn right, then 1st left to Army Tent Camp. Site opposite.* **grid ref:** *SY659775*

This site, although only one and a half miles from Weymouth, is in a peaceful location overlooking Chesil Beach and The Fleet, and is an excellent place to stay. There is a friendly little bar, which offers even better views. The toilet and shower block is very modern and spotlessly clean. The park is adjacent to the South West Coast Path making it a good base for walkers. 4 acre site. 40 touring pitches. Caravan pitches. Motorhome pitches. Tent pitches. 80 statics.

Open: Etr-mid Oct (rs High season & wknds only bar open) **Last arrival:** 18.00hrs
Last departure: 11.00hrs

Pitches: * £17.50-£29.50 £17.50-£29.50 £12-£26

Leisure:

Facilities: WiFi

Services:

Within 3 miles:

Notes: Dogs must be kept on leads.

AA Pubs & Restaurants nearby: The Old Ship Inn, WEYMOUTH, DT3 5QQ, 01305 812522

WEYMOUTH *continued*

Sea Barn Farm

►►► 82%

tel: 01305 782218 **Fleet DT3 4ED**
email: aa@seabarnfarm.co.uk
dir: *From Weymouth take B3157 towards Abbotsbury for 3m. Past Chickerell turn left at mini-rdbt into Fleet Rd, site 1m on left.* **grid ref:** *SY625807*

This site is set high on the Dorset coast and has spectacular views over Chesil Beach, The Fleet and Lyme Bay, and it is also on the South West Coast Path. Optional use of the clubhouse and swimming pool (in high season) at West Fleet Holiday Farm is available. The pitches are sheltered by hedging, and there is an excellent toilet facility block, and plenty of space for outdoor games. This site is suitable mainly for tents, especially large family tents, and small motorhomes or campervans. 12 acre site. 250 touring pitches. Motorhome pitches. Tent pitches. 1 static.

Open: 15 Mar-Oct (rs Mar-Jun & Sep-Oct Use of motor service point at West Fleet Holiday Park) **Last arrival:** 21.00hrs **Last departure:** 11.00hrs

Pitches: * £13-£24 £13-£24

Leisure:

Facilities:

Services:

Within 3 miles:

Notes: Non-family groups by prior arrangement only. Dogs must be kept on leads. Use of West Fleet facilities.

AA Pubs & Restaurants nearby: The Old Ship Inn, WEYMOUTH, DT3 5QQ, 01305 812522

Rosewall Camping

►►► 81%

tel: 01305 832248 **East Farm Dairy, Osmington Mills DT3 6HA**
email: holidays@weymouthcamping.com
dir: *Take A353 towards Weymouth. At Osmington Mills sign (opposite garage) turn left, 0.25m, site on 1st right.* **grid ref:** *SY736820*

This well positioned, sloping tent site is close to the coast and the South West Coast Path and has great views of Weymouth Bay. There are good toilet and shower blocks at the top and bottom of the site, and also a good shop. This site is a spacious place to camp and very suitable for families. 13 acre site. 225 touring pitches. Motorhome pitches. Tent pitches.

Open: Etr-Oct (rs Apr-May & Oct shop opening times vary) **Last arrival:** 22.00hrs **Last departure:** 10.00hrs

Pitches:

Leisure:

Facilities:

Services:

Within 3 miles:

Notes: Families & couples only, no noise after 23.00hrs. Dogs must be kept on leads. Riding stables & coarse fishing.

AA Pubs & Restaurants nearby: The Old Ship Inn, WEYMOUTH, DT3 5QQ, 01305 812522

The Smugglers Inn, OSMINGTON MILLS, DT3 6HF, 01305 833125

Weymouth Bay Holiday Park

HOLIDAY HOME PARK 92%

tel: 01305 832271 **Preston DT3 6BQ**
email: weymouthbay@haven.com **web:** www.haven.com/weymouthbay
dir: *From A35 towards Dorchester take A354 signed Weymouth. Follow towards Preston signs onto A353. At Chalbury rdbt 1st left into Preston Rd. Park on right.*
grid ref: *SY705830*

This well-located holiday park, just a short drive away from Weymouth beach, offers the complete holiday experience for the whole family. It has excellent indoor and outdoor pools complete with a 'Lazy River' attraction. There is an excellent choice of eating outlets as well as a full entertainment programme for all. The holiday homes are well appointed throughout. The park is conveniently placed for visiting Portland Bill, Lulworth Cove and Chesil Beach.

Open: Mar-Oct

Change over day: Mon, Fri, Sat

Arrival and departure times: Please contact the park

Statics: 83 Sleeps 6-8 Bedrms 2-3 Bathrms 1-2 Toilets 1-2 Microwave Freezer TV Sky/FTV Elec inc Gas inc Grass area

Children: Cots Highchair **Dogs:** 2 on leads No dangerous dogs

Leisure:

WIMBORNE MINSTER

Map 5 SZ09

Places to visit

Kingston Lacy, WIMBORNE, BH21 4EA, 01202 883402 (Mon-Fri) www.nationaltrust.org.uk/kingston-lacy

Priest's House Museum and Garden, WIMBORNE, BH21 1HR, 01202 882533 www.priest-house.co.uk

PREMIER PARK

Wilksworth Farm Caravan Park

Best of British

►►►►► 88%

tel: 01202 885467 **Cranborne Rd BH21 4HW**
email: info@wilksworthfarmcaravanpark.co.uk
dir: *1m N of Wimborne on B3078.* **grid ref:** *SU004018*

A popular and attractive park peacefully set in the grounds of a listed house in the heart of rural Dorset. This spacious site has much to offer visitors, including an excellent heated swimming pool, tennis courts, takeaway and café, a bar and restaurant plus a games room and an excellent Tiny Town play area for young children. The modern toilet facilities contain en suite rooms and good family rooms. 11 acre site. 85 touring pitches. 20 hardstandings. Caravan pitches. Motorhome pitches. Tent pitches. 77 statics.

Open: Apr-Oct (rs Oct no shop) **Last arrival:** 20.00hrs **Last departure:** 11.00hrs

Pitches: * £16-£33 £16-£33 £16-£33

Leisure:

Facilities: WiFi

Services:

Within 3 miles:

Notes: No cars by tents. Max 2 dogs per pitch, no noise 23.00hrs-07.00 hrs. Dogs must be kept on leads. Paddling pool, volley ball, mini football pitch.

AA Pubs & Restaurants nearby: Les Bouviers Restaurant with Rooms, WIMBORNE MINSTER, BH21 3BD, 01202 889555

Botany Bay Inne, WINTERBORNE ZELSTON, DT11 9ET, 01929 459227

PREMIER PARK

Merley Court Holiday Park

►►►►► 86%

tel: 01590 648331 **Merley BH21 3AA**
email: holidays@shorefield.co.uk **web:** www.shorefield.co.uk
dir: *Site signed on A31, Wimborne by-pass & Poole junct rdbt.* **grid ref:** *SZ008984*

A superb site in a quiet rural position on the edge of Wimborne, with woodland on two sides and good access roads. The park is well landscaped and offers generous individual pitches in sheltered grassland. There are plenty of amenities for all the family, including a heated outdoor pool, tennis court and adventure playground plus a tastefully appointed bar and restaurant. This park tends to get busy in summer, so prior booking is advised. 20 acre site. 160 touring pitches. 50 hardstandings. Caravan pitches. Motorhome pitches. Tent pitches. 6 statics.

Open: 6 Feb-2 Jan (rs Low season pool closed & bar, shop open limited hrs)
Last arrival: 21.00hrs **Last departure:** 10.00hrs

Pitches: **Leisure:**

Facilities:

Services: **Within 3 miles:**

Notes: Families & couples only, rallies welcome, no noise after 22.00hrs. Dogs must be kept on leads. Use of facilities at Oakdene Forest Park (7m).

AA Pubs & Restaurants nearby: Les Bouviers Restaurant with Rooms, WIMBORNE MINSTER, BH21 3BD, 01202 889555

Botany Bay Inne, WINTERBORNE ZELSTON, DT11 9ET, 01929 459227

See advert on page 210

LEISURE: Indoor swimming pool · Outdoor swimming pool · Children's playground · Kid's club · Tennis court · Games room · Separate TV room · golf course · Boats for hire · Cinema · Entertainment · Fishing · Mini golf · Watersports · Gym · Sports field · Spa · Stables
FACILITIES: Bath · Shower · Electric shaver · Hairdryer · Ice Pack Facility · Disabled facilities · Public telephone · Shop on site or within 200yds · Mobile shop (calls at least 5 days a week) · BBQ area · Picnic area · Wi-fi · Internet access · Recycling · Tourist info · Dog exercise area

WIMBORNE MINSTER *continued*

Charris Camping & Caravan Park

►►► 84%

tel: 01202 885970 **Candy's Ln, Corfe Mullen BH21 3EF**
email: bookings@charris.co.uk
dir: *From E, exit Wimborne bypass (A31) W end. 300yds after Caravan Sales, follow brown sign. From W on A31, over A350 rdbt, take next turn after B3074, follow brown signs.*
grid ref: *SY992988*

A sheltered park of grassland lined with trees on the edge of the Stour Valley, with Poole and the south coast resorts only a short drive away. Customers can be assured of a warm welcome at this well located park. The facilities are very clean, some hardstandings are available, and social get-togethers are held for customers including barbecues which prove very popular. Hardstandings were added for the 2015 season and a new toilet and shower block is planned for 2016. 3.5 acre site. 45 touring pitches. 12 hardstandings. 10 seasonal pitches. Caravan pitches. Motorhome pitches. Tent pitches.

Open: all year **Last arrival:** 21.00hrs (earliest arrival 11.00hrs) **Last departure:** 11.00hrs

Pitches:

Leisure:

Facilities:

Services:

Within 3 miles:

Notes: No noise after 23:00hrs. Dogs must be kept on leads.

AA Pubs & Restaurants nearby: Les Bouviers Restaurant with Rooms, WIMBORNE MINSTER, BH21 3BD, 01202 889555

Botany Bay Inne, WINTERBORNE ZELSTON, DT11 9ET, 01929 459227

Springfield Touring Park

►►► 84%

tel: 01202 881719 **Candys Ln, Corfe Mullen BH21 3EF**
email: john.clark18@btconnect.com
dir: *From Wimborne on Wimborne by-pass (A31) at W end turn left after Caravan Sales, follow brown sign.* **grid ref:** *SY987989*

A small touring park with extensive views over the Stour Valley and a quiet and friendly atmosphere. It is well positioned for visiting Poole, Bournemouth or the really lovely town of Wimborne. The park is maintained immaculately, has a well-stocked shop, and is a great place to stay. 3.5 acre site. 45 touring pitches. 38 hardstandings. Caravan pitches. Motorhome pitches. Tent pitches.

Open: Apr-14 Oct **Last arrival:** 21.00hrs **Last departure:** 11.00hrs

Pitches: £20-£25 £20-£25 £18-£25

Leisure:

Facilities:

Services:

Within 3 miles:

Notes: No skateboards. Dogs must be kept on leads.

AA Pubs & Restaurants nearby: Les Bouviers Restaurant with Rooms, WIMBORNE MINSTER, BH21 3BD, 01202 889555

Botany Bay Inne, WINTERBORNE ZELSTON, DT11 9ET, 01929 459227

COUNTY DURHAM

BARNARD CASTLE

Map 19 NZ01

Places to visit

Barnard Castle, BARNARD CASTLE, DL12 8PR, 01833 638212
www.english-heritage.org.uk/daysout/properties/barnard-castle

The Bowes Museum, BARNARD CASTLE, DL12 8NP, 01833 690606
www.thebowesmuseum.org.uk

Great for kids: Raby Castle, STAINDROP, DL2 3AH, 01833 660202
www.rabycastle.com

Pecknell Farm Caravan Park

►►► 81%

tel: 01833 638357 **Lartington DL12 9DF**
dir: *1.5m from Barnard Castle. From A66 take B6277. Site on right 1.5m from junct with A67.* **grid ref:** *NZ028178*

A small well laid out site on a working farm in beautiful rural meadowland, with spacious marked pitches on level ground. There are many walking opportunities that start directly from this friendly site. 1.5 acre site. 20 touring pitches. 5 hardstandings. Caravan pitches. Motorhome pitches.

Open: Apr-Oct **Last arrival:** 20.00hrs **Last departure:** noon

Pitches: * £13-£16 £13-£16

Facilities:

Services:

Within 3 miles:

Notes: No noise after 22.30hrs, maximum 2 dogs. Dogs must be kept on leads.

AA Pubs & Restaurants nearby: The Fox and Hounds, COTHERSTONE, DL12 9PF, 01833 650241

The Morritt Hotel, BARNARD CASTLE, DL12 9SE, 01833 627232

The Rose & Crown, ROMALDKIRK, DL12 9EB, 01833 650213

BEAMISH
Map 19 NZ25

Places to visit

Beamish Museum, BEAMISH, DH9 0RG, 0191 370 4000 www.beamish.org.uk

Great for kids: Diggerland, LANGLEY PARK, DH7 9TT, 0871 227 7007 *(Calls cost 10p per minute plus your phone company's access charge)* www.diggerland.com

Bobby Shafto Caravan Park

►►► 84%

tel: 0191 370 1776 **Cranberry Plantation DH9 0RY**
email: info@bobbyshaftocaravanpark.co.uk
dir: *From A693 signed Beamish to sign for Beamish Museum. Take approach road, turn right immediately before museum, left at pub to site 1m on right.* **grid ref:** *NZ232545*

A tranquil rural park surrounded by trees, with very clean and well organised facilities. The suntrap touring area has plenty of attractive hanging baskets, and there is a clubhouse with bar, TV and pool. The hardstandings, the 28 fully serviced pitches and the wooden pods for hire enhance the amenities. 9 acre site. 83 touring pitches. 47 hardstandings. Caravan pitches. Motorhome pitches. Tent pitches. 54 statics. 3 wooden pods.

Open: Mar-Oct **Last arrival:** 23.00hrs **Last departure:** 11.00hrs

Pitches: * £22-£27 £22-£27 £22-£27 **Leisure:**

Facilities: **Services:**

Within 3 miles: **Notes:** Dogs must be kept on leads.

AA Pubs & Restaurants nearby: The Stables Pub and Restaurant, STANLEY, DH9 0YB, 01207 288750

BLACKHALL COLLIERY
Map 19 NZ43

Places to visit

Hartlepool's Maritime Experience, HARTLEPOOL, TS24 0XZ, 01429 860077 www.hartlepoolsmaritimeexperience.com

Crimdon Dene

HOLIDAY CENTRE 80%

GOLD

tel: 0871 664 9737 *(Calls cost 5p per minute plus your phone company's access charge)*
Coast Rd TS27 4BN
email: crimdon.dene@park-resorts.com
dir: *From A19 just S of Peterlee, take B1281 signed Blackhall. Through Castle Eden, left in 0.5m signed Blackhall. Approx 3m right at T-junct onto A1086 towards Crimdon. Site in 1m signed on left, by Seagull pub.* **grid ref:** *NZ477378*

A large, popular coastal holiday park, handily placed for access to Teeside, Durham and Newcastle. The park contains a full range of holiday centre facilities for both children and their parents. Touring facilities are appointed to a very good standard. 44 touring pitches. 44 hardstandings. 12 seasonal pitches. Caravan pitches. Motorhome pitches. 586 statics.

Open: Apr-Oct **Last arrival:** 23.00hrs **Last departure:** 10.00hrs

Pitches: **Leisure:**

Facilities: **Services:**

Within 3 miles:

Notes: No cars by caravans. No quad bikes. Dogs must be kept on leads.

ESSEX

CLACTON-ON-SEA
Map 7 TM11

Places to visit

Harwich Redoubt Fort, HARWICH, CO12 3TE, 01255 503429 www.harwich-society.co.uk

The Beth Chatto Gardens, COLCHESTER, CO7 7DB, 01206 822007 www.bethchatto.co.uk

Great for kids: Colchester Zoo, COLCHESTER, CO3 0SL, 01206 331292 www.colchesterzoo.org

Martello Beach Holiday Park

HOLIDAY CENTRE 77%

tel: 0871 664 9782 *(Calls cost 10p per minute plus your phone company's access charge)* & 01442 830100 **Belsize Av, Jaywick CO15 2LF**
email: martello.beach@park-resorts.com
dir: *A133 towards Clacton-on-Sea. At rdbt right into St John's Rd, follow brown site signs. Left into Jaywick Ln (becomes Golf Green Rd, Broadway then Brooklands). Left into Belsize Ave to site.* **grid ref:** *TM136128*

Direct access to a seven-mile long Blue Flag beach is an undoubted attraction at this holiday park. The touring area is next to the leisure complex, where an indoor and outdoor swimming pool, shops, cafés and bars and evening entertainment are all provided. 40 acre site. 100 touring pitches. Caravan pitches. Motorhome pitches. Tent pitches. 294 statics.

Open: Apr-Oct **Last arrival:** 21.30hrs **Last departure:** 10.00hrs

Pitches:

Leisure:

Facilities:

Services:

Within 3 miles:

Notes: Watersports.

AA Pubs & Restaurants nearby: The Rose & Crown Hotel, COLCHESTER, CO1 2TZ, 01206 866677

The Whalebone, FINGRINGHOE, CO5 7BG, 01206 729307

Highfield Grange

HOLIDAY CENTRE 73%

tel: 0871 664 9746 *(Calls cost 5p per minute plus your phone company's access charge)*
London Rd CO16 9QY
email: highfield.grange@park-resorts.com
dir: *A12 to Colchester, A120 (Harwich), A133 to Clacton-on-Sea. Site on B1441 clearly signed on left.* **grid ref:** *TM173175*

The modern leisure facilities at this attractively planned park make it an ideal base for a lively family holiday. The swimming complex with both indoor and outdoor pools and a huge water shoot is especially popular. There are fully serviced touring pitches, each with its own hardstanding, located at the heart of the park. The nearby resorts of Walton on the Naze, Frinton and Clacton all offer excellent beaches and a wide range of popular seaside attractions. Please note, this site does not

accept tents. 30 acre site. 43 touring pitches. 43 hardstandings. Caravan pitches. Motorhome pitches. 700 statics.

Open: Apr-Oct **Last arrival:** mdnt **Last departure:** 10.00hrs

Pitches: * £7-£41 £7-£41

Leisure:

Facilities:

Services:

Within 3 miles:

Notes: No tents. Dogs must be kept on leads.

AA Pubs & Restaurants nearby: The Rose & Crown Hotel, COLCHESTER, CO1 2TZ, 01206 866677

The Whalebone, FINGRINGHOE, CO5 7BG, 01206 729307

MERSEA ISLAND — Map 7 TM01

Places to visit

Layer Marney Tower, LAYER MARNEY, CO5 9US, 01206 330784 www.layermarneytower.co.uk

Waldegraves Holiday Park

HOLIDAY CENTRE 82%

GOLD

tel: 01206 382898 **CO5 8SE**
email: holidays@waldegraves.co.uk **web:** www.waldegraves.co.uk
dir: *A12 junct 26, B1025 to Mersea Island across The Strood. Left to East Mersea, 2nd right, follow tourist signs to site.* **grid ref:** *TM033133*

A spacious and pleasant site located between farmland and its own private beach on the Blackwater Estuary. The facilities include two freshwater fishing lakes, a heated swimming pool, café, club, amusements and golf; there is generally good provision for families. Holiday static caravans are available for hire. 25 acre site. 60 touring pitches. 30 seasonal pitches. Caravan pitches. Motorhome pitches. Tent pitches. 250 statics.

Waldegraves Holiday Park

Open: Mar-Nov (rs Mar-Jun & Sep-Nov (excl BH & school half terms) pool, shop & club-house reduced opening hrs; pool open May-Sep weather permitting) **Last arrival:** 22.00hrs **Last departure:** 13.00hrs

Pitches:

Leisure:

Facilities:

Services:

Within 3 miles:

Notes: No groups of under 21s. Dogs must be kept on leads. Boating, slipway, pitch & putt, driving range, crazy golf, family games room, family entertainment.

AA Pubs & Restaurants nearby: The Peldon Rose, PELDON, CO5 7QJ, 01206 735248

Fen Farm Caravan Site

►►►► 81%

GOLD

tel: 01206 383275 **Moore Ln, East Mersea CO5 8FE**
email: havefun@fenfarm.co.uk
dir: *B1025 from Colchester to Mersea Island, left signed East Mersea. 1st right after Dog & Pheasant pub into Moore Lane. (NB road is tidal, please check tide times).*
grid ref: *TM059143*

The first tents were pitched at Fen Farm in 1923 and over the years the farm gave way entirely to becoming a caravan park. Enjoying an enviable location beside the Blackwater Estuary, it has unique atmosphere with a mixture of meadow, woodland and marine shore, and varied wildlife to match each environment. There are two excellent solar-heated toilet blocks, which include three family rooms and privacy cubicles, with the newest block constructed in the local style of black clapboard and a red tile roof. There is a woodland dog walk and two well-equipped play areas, while crabbing in the beach pools is also a popular pastime. 90 touring pitches. 3 hardstandings. 65 seasonal pitches. Caravan pitches. Motorhome pitches. Tent pitches. 90 statics.

Open: Mar-Oct **Last arrival:** dusk

Pitches: * £18-£30 £18-£30 £18-£30

Leisure:

Facilities:

Services:

Within 3 miles:

Notes: No open fires, no noise after 23.00hrs. Dogs must be kept on leads.

AA Pubs & Restaurants nearby: The Peldon Rose, PELDON, CO5 7QJ, 01206 735248

MERSEA ISLAND *continued*

Seaview Holiday Park

►►►79%

tel: 01206 382534 **Seaview Av, West Mersea CO5 8DA**
email: seaviewholidaypark@googlemail.com
dir: *From A12 (Colchester) onto B1025 (Mersea Island), cross causeway, left towards East Mersea, 1st right, follow signs.* **grid ref:** *TM025125*

With sweeping views across the Blackwater Estuary, this interesting, well-established park has its own private beach, complete with boat slipway and attractive beach cabins, a modern shop, café and a stylish clubhouse which offers evening meals and drinks in a quiet family atmosphere. The touring area is well maintained and has 40 fully serviced pitches. 30 acre site. 106 touring pitches. 40 hardstandings. 30 seasonal pitches. Caravan pitches. Motorhome pitches. 240 statics.

Open: Apr-Oct **Last arrival:** 18.00hrs (please phone site if late arrival expected) **Last departure:** noon

Pitches:

Facilities:

Services:

Within 3 miles:

Notes: No noise after mdnt, no boats or jet skis. Dogs must be kept on leads. Private beach.

AA Pubs & Restaurants nearby: The Peldon Rose, PELDON, CO5 7QJ, 01206 735248

ROCHFORD — Map 7 TQ89

Riverside Village Holiday Park

►►►81%

tel: 01702 258297 **Creeksea Ferry Rd, Wallasea Island, Canewdon SS4 2EY**
email: riversidevillage@tiscali.co.uk
dir: *M25 junct 29, A127 towards Southend-on-Sea. Take B1013 towards Rochford. Follow signs for Wallasea Island & Baltic Wharf.* **grid ref:** *TQ929951*

Situated adjacent to a nature reserve beside the River Crouch, this holiday park is surrounded by wetlands but only eight miles from Southend. A modern toilet block, with disabled facilities, is provided for tourers and there's a smart reception area. The park has several fishing lakes for site guests (permits available at reception). Several restaurants and pubs are within a short distance. 25 acre site. 60 touring pitches. Caravan pitches. Motorhome pitches. Tent pitches. 159 statics.

Open: Mar-Oct

Pitches:

Leisure:

Facilities: WiFi

Services:

Within 3 miles:

Notes: No dogs in tents. Dogs must be kept on leads.

ST LAWRENCE — Map 7 TL90

Waterside St Lawrence Bay

HOLIDAY CENTRE 74%

tel: 0871 664 9794 *(Calls cost 5p per minute plus your phone company's access charge)*
Main Rd CM0 7LY
email: waterside@park-resorts.com
dir: *A12 towards Chelmsford, A414 signed Maldon. Follow B1010 & signs to Latchingdon, then signs for Mayland/Steeple/St Lawrence. Left towards St Lawrence. Site on right.*
grid ref: *TL953056*

Waterside occupies a scenic location overlooking the Blackwater Estuary. In addition to the range of on-site leisure facilities there are opportunities for beautiful coastal walks and visits to the attractions of Southend. Tents are welcome on this expansive site, which has some touring pitches with electricity and good toilet facilities. The park has its own boat storage and slipway onto the Blackwater. 72 touring pitches. Caravan pitches. Motorhome pitches. Tent pitches. 271 statics.

Open: Apr-Oct (rs Wknds) **Last arrival:** 22.00hrs **Last departure:** 10.00hrs

Pitches:

Leisure:

Facilities: WiFi

Services:

Within 3 miles:

Notes: Sauna, spa pool.

AA Pubs & Restaurants nearby: Ye Olde White Harte Hotel, BURNHAM-ON-CROUCH, CM0 8AS, 01621 782106

The Ferry Boat Inn, NORTH FAMBRIDGE, CM3 6LR, 01621 740208

ST OSYTH

Places to visit

Colchester, St Botolph's Priory, COLCHESTER
www.english-heritage.org.uk/daysout/properties/colchester-st-botolphs-priory

Colchester Castle Museum, COLCHESTER, CO1 1TJ, 01206 282939
www.colchestermuseums.org.uk

Great for kids: Colchester Zoo, COLCHESTER, CO3 0SL, 01206 331292
www.colchesterzoo.org

ST OSYTH Map 7 TM11

The Orchards Holiday Park

HOLIDAY CENTRE 80%

DAVID BELLAMY CONSERVATION AWARD GOLD

tel: 0871 231 0861 *(Calls cost 10p per minute plus your phone company's access charge)*
CO16 8LJ
email: theorchards@haven.com **web:** www.haven.com/theorchards
dir: *From Clacton-on-Sea take B1027 towards Colchester. Left after petrol station, straight on at x-rds in St Osyth. Follow signs to Point Clear. Park in 3m.*
grid ref: *TM125155*

The Orchards offers good touring facilities with a quality toilet block which includes a laundry, play area and two very spacious family rooms. The touring pitches are generously sized. There's also direct access to all the leisure, entertainment and dining outlets available on this large popular holiday park on the Essex coast. 140 acre site. 63 touring pitches. Caravan pitches. Tent pitches. 1000 statics.

The Orchards Holiday Park

Open: end Mar-end Oct (rs end Mar-May & Sep-end Oct some facilities may be reduced) **Last arrival:** anytime **Last departure:** 10.00hrs

Pitches:

Leisure:

Facilities:

Services:

Within 3 miles:

Notes: No cars by tents. No commercial vehicles, no bookings by persons under 21yrs unless a family booking, max 2 dogs per booking, certain dog breeds banned.

AA Pubs & Restaurants nearby: The Rose & Crown Hotel, COLCHESTER, CO1 2TZ, 01206 866677

The Whalebone, FINGRINGHOE, CO5 7BG, 01206 729307

See advert below

WALTON ON THE NAZE Map 7 TM22

Naze Marine

HOLIDAY CENTRE 74%

tel: 0871 664 9755 *(Calls cost 5p per minute plus your phone company's access charge)*
Hall Ln CO14 8HL
email: naze.marine@park-resorts.com
dir: *A12 to Colchester. Then A120 (Harwich road), then A133 to Weeley. Take B1033 to Walton on the Naze seafront. Site on left.* **grid ref:** *TM255226*

With its modern indoor swimming pool, show bar, bar/restaurant and amusements, this park offers a variety of on-site attractions. The park is within easy access of the beaches and attractions of Walton on the Naze, Frinton and Clacton, and the more historic places of interest inland. Please note that this site does not accept tents. 46 acre site. 41 touring pitches. Caravan pitches. Motorhome pitches. 540 statics.

Open: Apr-Oct **Last arrival:** anytime **Last departure:** 10.00hrs

Pitches:

Leisure:

Facilities: WiFi

Services:

Within 3 miles:

Notes: Dogs must be kept on leads. Nature walk, natural meadowland.

GLOUCESTERSHIRE

BERKELEY Map 4 ST69

Places to visit

Dr Jenner's House, BERKELEY, GL13 9BN, 01453 810631 www.jennermuseum.com

WWT Slimbridge Wetland Centre, SLIMBRIDGE, GL2 7BT, 01453 891900 www.wwt.org.uk/slimbridge

Great for kids: Berkeley Castle & Butterfly House, BERKELEY, GL13 9BQ, 01453 810303 www.berkeley-castle.com

Hogsdown Farm Caravan & Camping Park

►►► 80%

tel: 01453 810224 **Hogsdown Farm, Lower Wick GL11 6DD**
web: www.hogsdownfarm.co.uk
dir: *M5 junct 14 (Falfield), A38 towards Gloucester. Through Stone & Woodford. After Newport turn right signed Lower Wick.* **grid ref:** *ST710974*

A pleasant site with good toilet facilities, located between Bristol and Gloucester. It is well positioned for visiting Berkeley Castle and the Cotswolds, and makes an excellent overnight stop when travelling to or from the West Country. 5 acre site. 45 touring pitches. 12 hardstandings. Caravan pitches. Motorhome pitches. Tent pitches.

Open: all year **Last arrival:** 21.00hrs **Last departure:** 16.00hrs

Pitches: * fr £13 fr £13 fr £11.50

Leisure:

Facilities:

Services:

Within 3 miles:

Notes: No skateboards or bikes. Dogs must be kept on leads.

AA Pubs & Restaurants nearby: The Malt House, BERKELEY, GL13 9BA, 01453 511177

The Anchor Inn, OLDBURY-ON-SEVERN, BS35 1QA, 01454 413331

CHELTENHAM — Map 10 SO92

Places to visit

Holst Birthplace Museum, CHELTENHAM, GL52 2AY, 01242 524846
www.holstmuseum.org.uk

Sudeley Castle, Gardens & Exhibitions, WINCHCOMBE, GL54 5JD, 01242 609485
www.sudeleycastle.co.uk

Briarfields Motel & Touring Park

 86%

GOLD

tel: 01242 235324 **Gloucester Rd GL51 0SX**
email: briarfields@hotmail.co.uk
dir: *M5 junct 11, A40 towards Cheltenham. At rdbt left onto B4063, site 200mtrs on left.* **grid ref:** *SO909218*

A well-designed level park, with a motel, where the facilities are modern and very clean. It is now for adults only. It is well positioned between Cheltenham and Gloucester, with easy access to the Cotswolds. And, being close to the M5, it makes a perfect overnight stopping point. 5 acre site. 72 touring pitches. 72 hardstandings. Caravan pitches. Motorhome pitches. Tent pitches.

Open: all year **Last arrival:** 21.00hrs **Last departure:** noon

Pitches: * £16-£20 £16-£20 £12-£20

Facilities:

Services:

Within 3 miles:

Notes: Adults only. No noise after 22.00hrs. Dogs must be kept on leads.

AA Pubs & Restaurants nearby: The Gloucester Old Spot, CHELTENHAM, GL51 9SY, 01242 680321

The Royal Oak Inn, CHELTENHAM, GL52 3DL, 01242 522344

GLOUCESTER

Places to visit

Gloucester Folk Museum, GLOUCESTER, GL1 2PG, 01452 396868
www.gloucester.gov.uk/folkmuseum

Nature in Art, GLOUCESTER, GL2 9PA, 01452 731422 www.nature-in-art.org.uk

Great for kids: The Gloucester Waterways Museum, GLOUCESTER, GL1 2EH, 01452 318200 www.canalrivertrust.org.uk/gloucester-waterways-museum

GLOUCESTER — Map 10 SO81

Red Lion Caravan & Camping Park

►►► 77%

tel: 01452 731810 & 01299 400787 **Wainlode Hill, Norton GL2 9LW**
email: redlion.loveri@btconnect.com
dir: *Exit A38 at Norton, follow road to river.* **grid ref:** *SO849258*

An attractive meadowland park, adjacent to a traditional pub, with the River Severn just across a country lane. There is a private lake for freshwater fishing. This makes an ideal touring base. 24 acre site. 60 touring pitches. 10 hardstandings. 60 seasonal pitches. Caravan pitches. Motorhome pitches. Tent pitches. 85 statics.

Open: all year **Last arrival:** 22.00hrs **Last departure:** 11.00hrs

Pitches: **Leisure:**

Facilities:

Services:

Within 3 miles: **Notes:**

AA Pubs & Restaurants nearby: Queens Head, GLOUCESTER, GL2 9EJ, 01452 301882

The Queens Arms, ASHLEWORTH, GL19 4HT, 01452 700395

NEWENT — Map 10 SO72

Places to visit

Odda's Chapel, DEERHURST, 0370 333 1181
www.english-heritage.org.uk/daysout/properties/oddas-chapel

Westbury Court Garden, WESTBURY-ON-SEVERN, GL14 1PD, 01452 760461
www.nationaltrust.org.uk

Great for kids: International Centre for Birds of Prey, NEWENT, GL18 1JJ, 01531 820286 www.icbp.org

Pelerine Caravan and Camping

►►► 84%

tel: 01531 822761 & 07909 914262 **Ford House Rd GL18 1LQ**
email: pelerine@hotmail.com
dir: *1m from Newent.* **grid ref:** *SO645183*

A pleasant, French-themed site divided into separate areas (Rue de Pelerine and Avenue des Familles), plus one for adults only; there are some hardstandings and electric hook-ups in each area. Facilities are very good, especially for families. It is close to several vineyards, and well positioned in the north of the Forest of Dean with Tewkesbury, Cheltenham and Ross-on-Wye within easy reach. 5 acre site. 35 touring pitches. 2 hardstandings. Caravan pitches. Motorhome pitches. Tent pitches.

Open: Mar-Nov **Last arrival:** 22.00hrs **Last departure:** 16.00hrs

Pitches: * fr £22 £20-£22 £15-£22

Facilities:

Services: **Within 3 miles:**

Notes: Dogs must be kept on leads. Woodburners, chimneas, burning pits available.

AA Pubs & Restaurants nearby: The Yew Tree, CLIFFORD'S MESNE, GL18 1JS, 01531 820719

Three Choirs Vineyards, NEWENT, GL18 1LS, 01531 890223

PITCHES: Caravans Motorhomes Tents Glamping-style accommodation **SERVICES:** Electric hook up Launderette Licensed bar Calor Gas Camping Gaz Toilet fluid Café/Restaurant Fast Food/Takeaway Battery charging Baby care Motorvan service point
ABBREVIATIONS: BH/bank hols – bank holidays Etr – Easter Spring BH – Spring Bank Holiday fr – from hrs – hours m – mile mdnt – midnight rdbt – roundabout rs – restricted service wk – week wknd – weekend x-rds – cross roads No credit or debit cards No dogs Children of all ages accepted

SLIMBRIDGE Map 4 SO70

Places to visit

Berkeley Castle & Butterfly House, BERKELEY, GL13 9BQ, 01453 810303 www.berkeley-castle.com

Great for kids: WWT Slimbridge Wetland Centre, SLIMBRIDGE, GL2 7BT, 01453 891900 www.wwt.org.uk/slimbridge

Tudor Caravan & Camping

►►►► 88%

GOLD

tel: 01453 890483 **Shepherds Patch GL2 7BP**
email: aa@tudorcaravanpark.co.uk **web:** www.tudorcaravanpark.com
dir: *M5 juncts 13 & 14, follow WWT Wetlands Wildlife Centre-Slimbridge signs. Site at rear of Tudor Arms pub.* **grid ref:** *SO728040*

This park benefits from one of the best locations in the county, situated right alongside the Sharpness to Gloucester canal and just a short walk from the famous Wildfowl & Wetlands Trust at Slimbridge. The site has two areas, one for adults only, and a more open area with a facility block. There are both grass and gravel pitches complete with electric hook-ups. Being beside the canal, there are excellent walks plus the National Cycle Network route 41 can be accessed from the site. There is a pub and restaurant adjacent to the site. 8 acre site. 75 touring pitches. 48 hardstandings. 4 seasonal pitches. Caravan pitches. Motorhome pitches. Tent pitches.

Open: all year **Last arrival:** 20.00hrs **Last departure:** 11.00hrs

Pitches: * £13-£24 £13-£24 £8-£24

Facilities:

Services:

Within 3 miles:

Notes: Debit cards accepted (no credit cards). Dogs must be kept on leads.

AA Pubs & Restaurants nearby: The Old Passage Inn, ARLINGHAM, GL2 7JR, 01452 740547

STONEHOUSE Map 4 SO80

Places to visit

Painswick Rococo Garden, PAINSWICK, GL6 6TH, 01452 813204 www.rococogarden.org.uk

WWT Slimbridge Wetland Centre, SLIMBRIDGE, GL2 7BT, 01453 891900 www.wwt.org.uk/slimbridge

Apple Tree Park Caravan and Camping Site

►►►► 88%

tel: 01452 742362 & 07708 221457 **A38, Claypits GL10 3AL**
email: appletreepark@hotmail.co.uk
dir: *M5 junct 13, A38. Take 1st exit at rdbt. Site 0.7m on left, 400mtrs beyond filling station.* **grid ref:** *SO766063*

This is a family-owned park conveniently located on the A38, not far from the M5. A peaceful site with glorious views of the Cotswolds, it offers modern and spotlessly clean toilet facilities with under-floor heating. The park is well located for visiting Slimbridge Wildfowl & Wetlands Trust and makes an excellent stopover for M5 travellers. There is a bus stop directly outside the park which is handy for those with motorhomes who wish to visit nearby Gloucester and Cheltenham. 6.5 acre site. 65 touring pitches. 14 hardstandings. 10 seasonal pitches. Caravan pitches. Motorhome pitches. Tent pitches.

Open: all year **Last arrival:** 21.00hrs **Last departure:** noon

Pitches: **Leisure:**

Facilities:

Services: **Within 3 miles:**

Notes: Minimum noise after 22.30hrs. Dogs must be kept on leads.

AA Pubs & Restaurants nearby: The Old Passage Inn, ARLINGHAM, GL2 7JR, 01452 740547

GREATER MANCHESTER

LITTLEBOROUGH Map 16 SD91

Hollingworth Lake Caravan Park

►►► 70%

tel: 01706 378661 & 373919 **Round House Farm, Rakewood Rd, Rakewood OL15 0AT**
email: info@hollingworthlakecaravanpark.com
dir: *From Littleborough or Milnrow (M62 junct 21), follow Hollingworth Lake Country Park signs to Fishermans Inn/The Wine Press. Take 'No Through Road' to Rakewood, then 2nd right.* **grid ref:** *SD943146*

A popular park adjacent to Hollingworth Lake, at the foot of the Pennines, within easy reach of many local attractions. Backpackers walking the Pennine Way are welcome at this family-run park, and there are also large rally fields. 5 acre site. 50 touring pitches. 25 hardstandings. Caravan pitches. Motorhome pitches. Tent pitches. 53 statics.

Open: all year **Last arrival:** 20.00hrs **Last departure:** noon

Pitches: * £15-£20 £15-£20 £10-£20

Facilities: **Services:**

Within 3 miles: **Notes:** Family groups only. Pony trekking.

AA Pubs & Restaurants nearby: The White House, LITTLEBOROUGH, OL15 0LG, 01706 378456

LEISURE: Indoor swimming pool · Outdoor swimming pool · Children's playground · Kid's club · Tennis court · Games room · Separate TV room · golf course · Boats for hire · Cinema · Entertainment · Fishing · Mini golf · Watersports · Gym · Sports field · Spa · Stables
FACILITIES: Bath · Shower · Electric shaver · Hairdryer · Ice Pack Facility · Disabled facilities · Public telephone · Shop on site or within 200yds · Mobile shop (calls at least 5 days a week) · BBQ area · Picnic area · Wi-fi · Internet access · Recycling · Tourist info · Dog exercise area

HAMPSHIRE

BRANSGORE Map 5 SZ19

Places to visit

Sammy Miller Motorcycle Museum, NEW MILTON, BH25 5SZ, 01425 620777 www.sammymiller.co.uk

Red House Museum & Gardens, CHRISTCHURCH, BH23 1BU, 01202 482860 www3.hants.gov.uk/redhouse

Great for kids: Moors Valley Country Park and Forest, RINGWOOD, BH24 2ET, 01425 470721 www.moors-valley.co.uk

Harrow Wood Farm Caravan Park

86%

SILVER

tel: 01425 672487 **Harrow Wood Farm, Poplar Ln BH23 8JE**
email: harrowwood@caravan-sites.co.uk **web:** www.caravan-sites.co.uk
dir: *From Ringwood take B3347 towards Christchurch. At Sopley, left for Bransgore, to T-junct. Turn right. Straight on at x-rds. Left in 400yds (just after garage) into Poplar Lane.* **grid ref:** *SZ194978*

A well laid-out, well-drained and spacious site in a pleasant rural position adjoining woodland and fields. Free on-site coarse fishing is available at this peaceful park. Well located for visiting Christchurch, the New Forest National Park and the south coast. 6 acre site. 60 touring pitches. 60 hardstandings. Caravan pitches. Motorhome pitches. Tent pitches. 14 bell tents/yurts.

Open: Mar-6 Jan **Last arrival:** 22.00hrs **Last departure:** noon

Pitches:

Facilities: WiFi

Services:

Within 3 miles:

Notes: No open fires.

AA Pubs & Restaurants nearby: The Three Tuns, BRANSGORE, BH23 8JH, 01425 672232

FORDINGBRIDGE Map 5 SU11

Places to visit

Rockbourne Roman Villa, ROCKBOURNE, SP6 3PG, 01725 518541 (during opening times only) www.hants.gov.uk/rockbourne-roman-villa

Breamore House & Countryside Museum, BREAMORE, SP6 2DF, 01725 512468 www.breamorehouse.com

Great for kids: Moors Valley Country Park and Forest, RINGWOOD, BH24 2ET, 01425 470721 www.moors-valley.co.uk

PREMIER PARK

Sandy Balls Holiday Village

90%

GOLD

tel: 0844 693 1336 *(Calls cost 7p per minute plus your phone company's access charge)*
Sandy Balls Estate Ltd, Godshill SP6 2JZ
email: post@sandyballs.co.uk
dir: *M27 junct 1, B3078, B3079, 8m to Godshill. Site 0.25m after cattle grid.*
grid ref: *SU167148*

A large, mostly wooded New Forest holiday complex with good provision of touring facilities on terraced, well laid-out fields. Pitches are fully serviced with shingle bases, and groups can be sited beside the river and away from the main site. There are excellent sporting, leisure and entertainment facilities for the whole family including a jacuzzi, sauna, beauty therapy, horse riding and children's activities. There's also a bistro, information centre and ready-erected tents, lodges and eight camping pods for hire. 120 acre site. 225 touring pitches. 225 hardstandings. Caravan pitches. Motorhome pitches. Tent pitches. 37 statics. 8 wooden pods.

Open: all year (rs Nov-Feb pitches reduced, limited activities, swimming pool & leisure centre open) **Last arrival:** 21.00hrs **Last departure:** 11.00hrs

Pitches: * £10-£60 £10-£60 £10-£60

Leisure: Spa

Facilities: WiFi

Services:

Within 3 miles:

Notes: Groups by prior arrangement only, no gazebos, no noise after 23.00hrs. Dogs must be kept on leads.

AA Pubs & Restaurants nearby: The Augustus John, FORDINGBRIDGE, SP6 1DG, 01425 652098

HAMBLE-LE-RICE Map 5 SU40

Riverside Holidays

►►►► 83%

tel: 023 8045 3220 **Satchell Ln SO31 4HR**
email: enquiries@riversideholidays.co.uk **web:** www.riversideholidays.co.uk
dir: *M27 junct 8, follow signs to Hamble on B3397. Left into Satchell Lane, site in 1m.*
grid ref: *SU481081*

A small, peaceful park beside the marina, and close to the pretty village of Hamble. The park is neatly kept, and there are two toilet and shower blocks, with the central facilities block having excellent private rooms. A pub and restaurant are very close by and there are good river walks alongside the Hamble. 6 acre site. 60 touring pitches. Caravan pitches. Motorhome pitches. Tent pitches. 15 statics.

Open: Mar-Oct **Last arrival:** 22.00hrs **Last departure:** 11.00hrs

Pitches: * £17-£46 £17-£46 £15-£30

Facilities:

Services:

Within 3 miles:

Notes: Dogs must be kept on leads. Bike hire, baby-changing facilities.

AA Pubs & Restaurants nearby: The Bugle, HAMBLE-LE-RICE, SO31 4HA, 023 8045 3000

See advert on opposite page

LINWOOD Map 5 SU10

Places to visit

The New Forest Centre, LYNDHURST, SO43 7NY, 023 8028 3444 www.newforestcentre.org.uk

Furzey Gardens, MINSTEAD, SO43 7GL, 023 8081 2464 www.furzey-gardens.org

Great for kids: Paultons Park, OWER, SO51 6AL, 023 8081 4442 www.paultonspark.co.uk

Red Shoot Camping Park

►►► 86%

tel: 01425 473789 **BH24 3QT**
email: enquiries@redshoot-campingpark.com
dir: *A31 onto A338 towards Fordingbridge & Salisbury. Right at brown signs for caravan park towards Linwood on unclassified roads, site signed.* **grid ref:** *SU187094*

Located behind the Red Shoot Inn in one of the most attractive parts of the New Forest, this park is in an ideal spot for nature lovers and walkers. It is personally supervised by friendly owners, and offers many amenities including a children's play area. There are modern and spotless facilities plus a smart reception and shop. 3.5 acre site. 110 touring pitches. Caravan pitches. Motorhome pitches. Tent pitches.

Open: Mar-Oct **Last arrival:** 19.00hrs **Last departure:** 13.00hrs

Pitches: * £17-£28 £17-£28 £17-£28

Leisure:

Facilities:

Services:

Within 3 miles:

Notes: Quiet after 22.30hrs. Dogs must be kept on leads.

AA Pubs & Restaurants nearby: The Star Inn, RINGWOOD, BH24 1AW, 01425 473105

The Augustus John, FORDINGBRIDGE, SP6 1DG, 01425 652098

MILFORD ON SEA Map 5 SZ29

Places to visit

Sammy Miller Motorcycle Museum, NEW MILTON, BH25 5SZ, 01425 620777 www.sammymiller.co.uk

Exbury Gardens & Railway, EXBURY, SO45 1AZ, 023 8089 1203 www.exbury.co.uk

Great for kids: Beaulieu, BEAULIEU, SO42 7ZN, 01590 612345 www.beaulieu.co.uk

Lytton Lawn Touring Park

►►►► 86%

tel: 01590 648331 **Lymore Ln SO41 0TX**
email: holidays@shorefield.co.uk
dir: *From Lymington A337 to Christchurch for 2.5m to Everton. Left onto B3058 to Milford on Sea. 0.25m, left into Lymore Lane.* **grid ref:** *SZ293937*

A pleasant well-run park with good facilities, located near the coast. The park is peaceful and quiet, but the facilities of a sister park 2.5 miles away are available to campers, including a swimming pool, tennis courts, bistro and bar/carvery, and large club with family entertainment. Fully serviced pitches provide good screening, and standard pitches are on gently sloping grass. 8 acre site. 136 touring pitches. 53 hardstandings. Caravan pitches. Motorhome pitches. Tent pitches.

Open: 6 Feb-2 Jan (rs Low season shop/reception limited hrs, no grass pitches)
Last arrival: 21.00hrs **Last departure:** 10.00hrs

Pitches:

Leisure:

Facilities:

Services:

Within 3 miles:

Notes: Families & couples only, no noise after 22.00hrs, rallies welcome. Dogs must be kept on leads.

AA Pubs & Restaurants nearby: Mayflower Inn, LYMINGTON, SO41 3QD, 01590 672160

See advert on page 210

RINGWOOD

See St Leonards (Dorset)

ROMSEY

Places to visit

The Sir Harold Hillier Gardens, AMPFIELD, SO51 0QA, 01794 369318
www.hilliergardens.org.uk

Mottisfont, MOTTISFONT, SO51 0LP, 01794 340757
www.nationaltrust.org.uk/mottisfont

Great for kids: Longdown Activity Farm, ASHURST, SO40 7EH, 023 8029 2837
www.longdownfarm.co.uk

ROMSEY

Map 5 SU32

PREMIER PARK

Hill Farm Caravan Park

►►►►► 88%

tel: 01794 340402 **Branches Ln, Sherfield English SO51 6FH**
email: gjb@hillfarmpark.com
dir: *Signed from A27 (Salisbury to Romsey road) in Sherfield English. 4m NW of Romsey & M27 junct 2.* **grid ref:** *SU287238*

A small, well-sheltered park peacefully located amidst mature trees and meadows. The two toilet blocks offer smart unisex showers as well as a fully en suite family/disabled room and plenty of privacy in the washrooms. The Garden Room, a good café/restaurant, with an outside patio, serves a wide range of snacks and meals. This attractive park is well placed for visiting Salisbury and the New Forest National Park, and the south coast is only a short drive away, making it an appealing holiday location. There is a separate caravan sales and full repair centre – South Coast Caravans. 10.5 acre site. 100 touring pitches. 60 hardstandings. Caravan pitches. Motorhome pitches. Tent pitches. 6 statics.

Open: Mar-Oct **Last arrival:** 20.00hrs **Last departure:** noon

Pitches:

Leisure:

Facilities:

Services:

Within 3 miles:

Notes: One unit per pitch. Site unsuitable for teenagers. Minimum noise at all times & no noise after 23.00hrs. 9-hole pitch & putt.

AA Pubs & Restaurants nearby: The Cromwell Arms, ROMSEY, SO51 8HG, 01794 519515

The Three Tuns, ROMSEY, SO51 8HL, 01794 512639

ROMSEY *continued*

Green Pastures Farm Camping & Touring Park

84%

tel: 023 8081 4444 **Ower SO51 6AJ**
email: enquiries@greenpasturesfarm.com
dir: *M27 junct 2. Follow Salisbury signs for 0.5m, then brown tourist signs for Green Pastures. Also signed from A36 & A3090 at Ower.* **grid ref:** *SU321158*

This pleasant site offers a variety of easily accessed pitches, including those with electric hook-up. There is a code access security barrier to the site. Green Pastures is well located for visiting Paultons Theme Park, Southampton and the New Forest National Park, and being close to the M27 it is convenient for overnight stops. There are kennels where dogs can be left while you visit the theme park or go shopping. 6 acre site. 53 touring pitches. 6 hardstandings. Caravan pitches. Motorhome pitches. Tent pitches.

Open: 13 Mar-Oct **Last arrival:** 20.30hrs **Last departure:** 11.00hrs

Pitches: * £19-£24 £19-£24 £14-£24 **Facilities:**

Services: **Within 3 miles:**

Notes: No water games, only off-ground BBQs permitted. Dogs must be kept on leads. Fish & chip van Friday nights.

AA Pubs & Restaurants nearby: Sir John Barleycorn, CADNAM, SO40 2NP, 023 8081 2236

WARSASH — Map 5 SU40

Places to visit

Explosion Museum of Naval Firepower, GOSPORT, PO12 4LE, 023 9250 5600 www.explosion.org.uk

Portchester Castle, PORTCHESTER, PO16 9QW, 023 9237 8291 www.english-heritage.org.uk/daysout/properties/portchester-castle

Great for kids: Blue Reef Aquarium, PORTSMOUTH, PO5 3PB, 023 9287 5222 www.bluereefaquarium.co.uk

Dibles Park

►►►► 84%

tel: 01489 575232 **Dibles Rd SO31 9SA**
email: dibles.park@btconnect.com
dir: *M27 junct 9, at rdbt 5th exit (Parkgate A27), 3rd rdbt 1st exit, 4th rdbt 2nd exit. Site 500yds on left. Or M27 junct 8, at rdbt 1st exit (Parkgate), next rdbt 3rd exit (Brook Ln), 4th rdbt 2nd exit. Site 500yds on left.* **grid ref:** *SU505060*

A small peaceful touring park adjacent to a private residential park. The facilities are excellent and spotlessly clean. A warm welcome awaits visitors to this well-managed park, which is very convenient for the Hamble, the Solent and the cross-Channel ferries. Excellent information on walks that start from the site is available. 0.75 acre site. 14 touring pitches. 14 hardstandings. Caravan pitches. Motorhome pitches. Tent pitches. 46 statics.

Open: all year **Last arrival:** 20.30hrs **Last departure:** 11.00hrs

Pitches: * £20-£23 £20-£23 £20-£23

Facilities: **Services:**

Within 3 miles: **Notes:** Dogs must be kept on leads.

AA Pubs & Restaurants nearby: Solent Hotel & Spa, FAREHAM, PO15 7AJ, 01489 880000

The Bun Penny, LEE-ON-THE-SOLENT, PO13 9JH, 023 9255 0214

HEREFORDSHIRE

EARDISLAND — Map 9 SO45

Places to visit

Berrington Hall, ASHTON, HR6 0DW, 01568 615721 www.nationaltrust.org.uk/berringtonhall

Hergest Croft Gardens, KINGTON, HR5 3EG, 01544 230160 www.hergest.co.uk

Great for kids: Croft Castle & Parkland, CROFT, HR6 9PW, 01568 780246 www.nationaltrust.org.uk/main/w-croftcastle

Arrow Bank Holiday Park

►►►► 87%

tel: 01544 388312 **Nun House Farm HR6 9BG**
email: info@arrowbank.co.uk
dir: *From Leominster A44 towards Rhayader. Right to Eardisland, follow signs.*
grid ref: *SO419588*

This peaceful park is set in the beautiful 'Black and White' village of Eardisland with its free exhibitions, tea rooms and heritage centre. The park is well positioned for visiting the many local attractions, as well as those further afield such as Ludlow Castle, Ross-on-Wye and Shrewsbury; the Welsh border is just down the road. The modern toilet facilities are spotlessly clean and there are 36 fully-serviced pitches. 65 acre site. 38 touring pitches. 38 hardstandings. 16 seasonal pitches. Caravan pitches. Motorhome pitches. Tent pitches. 60 statics.

Open: Mar-Nov **Last arrival:** 21.00hrs **Last departure:** 11.30hrs

Pitches:

Facilities:

Services:

Within 3 miles:

Notes: No rotary airers, ball games, skateboards or cycles. Dogs must be kept on leads.

AA Pubs & Restaurants nearby: New Inn, PEMBRIDGE, HR6 9DZ, 01544 388427

The Stagg Inn and Restaurant, KINGTON, HR5 3RL, 01544 230221

MORETON ON LUGG — Map 10 SO54

Places to visit

The Weir Gardens, SWAINSHILL, HR4 7QF, 01981 590509 www.nationaltrust.org.uk

Cuckoo's Corner Campsite

►►► 86%

tel: 01432 760234 **Cuckoo's Corner HR4 8AH**
email: cuckooscorner@gmail.com
dir: *Direct access from A49. From Hereford 2nd left after Moreton on Lugg sign. From Leominster 1st right (non gated road) after brown sign. Right just before island.*
grid ref: *SO501456*

This small adults-only site is well positioned just north of Hereford, with easy access to the city. The site has two areas and offers hardstandings and also some electric pitches. It is an ideal spot for an overnight stop or for a longer stay in order to visit the attractions of the area. The amenity blocks have unisex rooms with shower, washbasin and toilet. There's a bus stop just outside the site and a full

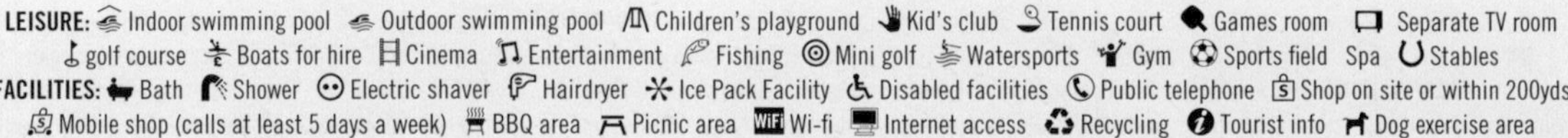

timetable is available from the reception. 3 acre site. 19 touring pitches. 15 hardstandings. Caravan pitches. Motorhome pitches. Tent pitches.

Open: all year **Last arrival:** 21.00hrs **Last departure:** 13.00hrs

Pitches: £16 £16 £11-£16

Facilities:

Services:

Within 3 miles:

Notes: Adults only. No large groups, no noise after 22.30hrs. Dogs must be kept on leads. DVD library, books & magazines.

AA Pubs & Restaurants nearby: The Bell, TILLINGTON, HR4 8LE, 01432 760395

The Wellington, WELLINGTON, HR4 8AT, 01432 830367

PEMBRIDGE — Map 9 SO35

PREMIER PARK

Townsend Touring Park

Best of British

90%

tel: 01544 388527 **Townsend Farm HR6 9HB**
email: info@townsend-farm.co.uk
dir: *A44 through Pembridge. Site 40mtrs from 30mph on E side of village.*
grid ref: *SO395583*

This outstanding park is spaciously located on the edge of one of Herefordshire's most beautiful Black and White villages. The park offers excellent facilities, and all hardstanding pitches are fully serviced, and it has its own award-winning farm shop and butchery. Coarse fishing is possible on the site's lake. It also makes an excellent base from which to explore the area, including Ludlow Castle and Ironbridge. There are camping pods available for hire. 12 acre site. 60 touring pitches. 23 hardstandings. 14 seasonal pitches. Caravan pitches. Motorhome pitches. Tent pitches. 4 wooden pods.

Open: Mar-mid Jan **Last arrival:** 22.00hrs **Last departure:** 11.00hrs

Pitches:

Leisure:

Facilities:

Services:

Within 3 miles:

Notes: Bike trails.

AA Pubs & Restaurants nearby: New Inn, PEMBRIDGE, HR6 9DZ, 01544 388427

The Stagg Inn and Restaurant, KINGTON, HR5 3RL, 01544 230221

SYMONDS YAT (WEST)

Places to visit

The Nelson Museum & Local History Centre, MONMOUTH, NP25 3XA, 01600 710630

Great for kids: Goodrich Castle, GOODRICH, HR9 6HY, 01600 890538 www.english-heritage.org.uk/daysout/properties/goodrich-castle

SYMONDS YAT (WEST) — Map 10 SO51

Doward Park Camp Site

►►► 86%

tel: 01600 890438 **Great Doward HR9 6BP**
email: enquiries@dowardpark.co.uk
dir: *A40 from Monmouth towards Ross-on-Wye. In 2m left signed Crockers Ash, Ganarew & The Doward. Cross over A40, 1st left at T-junct, in 0.5m 1st right signed The Doward. Follow park signs up hill. (NB it is advised that Sat Nav is not used for end of journey).*
grid ref: *SO539167*

This delightful little park is set in peaceful woodlands on the hillside above the Wye Valley. It is ideal for campers and motorhomes but not caravans due to the narrow, twisting approach roads. A warm welcome awaits and the facilities are kept spotless. The Bluebell Wood children's play area is a great place for imaginative games. 1.5 acre site. 28 touring pitches. 6 seasonal pitches. Motorhome pitches. Tent pitches.

Open: Mar-Oct **Last arrival:** 20.00hrs **Last departure:** 11.30hrs

Pitches:

Leisure:

Facilities:

Services:

Within 3 miles:

Notes: No cars by tents. No fires, quiet after 22.00hrs. Dogs must be kept on leads.

AA Pubs & Restaurants nearby: The Mill Race, WALFORD, HR9 5QS, 01989 562891

HERTFORDSHIRE

HODDESDON — Map 6 TL30

Lee Valley Caravan Park Dobbs Weir

►►► 82%

tel: 0845 677 0609 *(Calls cost 5p per minute plus your phone company's access charge)*
Charlton Meadows, Essex Rd EN11 0AS
email: dobbsweircampsite@leevalleypark.org.uk
dir: *From A10 follow Hoddesdon signs, at 2nd rdbt left signed Dobbs Weir. At next rdbt take 3rd exit. 1m to site on right.* **grid ref:** *TL382080*

This site provides much needed camping facilities close to London. Situated on level ground beside the River Lee, the smallest of the three London Authority parks has a modernised toilet block with good facilities, a large timber chalet housing the reception and shop, an extremely innovative motorhome service point, plus 12 wooden pods and pre-pitched tents for hire. On-site fishing is available. 11 acre site. 70 touring pitches. 15 hardstandings. Caravan pitches. Motorhome pitches. Tent pitches. 24 statics. 3 bell tents/yurts. 12 wooden pods.

Open: Mar-Jan **Last arrival:** 21.00hrs **Last departure:** noon

Pitches: * £14-£22 £14-£22 £14-£22

Leisure:

Facilities:

Services:

Within 3 miles:

Notes: No commercial vehicles. Dogs must be kept on leads. Cycle hire, fire pit area.

AA Pubs & Restaurants nearby: The Fox and Hounds, HUNSDON, SG12 8NH, 01279 843999

Isle of Wight

There is a timeless quality to the Isle of Wight. For many it embodies the spirit and atmosphere of English seaside holidays over the years, and being an island, it has a unique and highly distinctive identity. Small and intimate – it's just 23 miles by 13 miles – it's a great place to get away-from-it-all, and with its mild climate, long hours of sunshine and colourful architecture, it has something of a continental flavour.

The Isle of Wight is probably most famous for the world's premier sailing regatta. Cowes Week, which takes place at the height of summer, is a key annual fixture in the country's sporting calendar, with the regatta drawing more than 1,000 boats and around 100,000 spectators. It is a hugely colourful event attracting Olympic veterans, weekend sailors and top names from the worlds of sport and the media. Various spectator boats offer good views of the action, but for something less hectic and more sedate, take to the island's 65-mile Coast Path, which offers a continual, unfolding backdrop of magnificent coastal scenery and natural beauty. The sea is seen at numerous points along the route and during Cowes Week, you get constant views of the energetic sailing activity. The regatta is held in the first week of August.

The Isle of Wight Coast Path is a good way to explore the island's varied coastline at any time of the year. Even in the depths of winter, the weather conditions are often favourable for walking. Much of the trail in the southern half of the island represents a relatively undemanding walk over majestic chalk downs. Beyond Freshwater Bay the coast is largely uninhabited with a palpable air of isolation. It is on this stretch that walkers can appreciate how the elements have shaped and weathered the island over many centuries. Away from the coast an intricate network of paths offers the chance to discover a rich assortment of charming villages, hidden valleys and country houses. In all, the Isle of Wight has more than 500 miles of public rights of way and over half the island is acknowledged as an Area of Outstanding Natural Beauty. There is an annual walking festival in May and a weekend walking festival in October. Cycling is also extremely popular here, with the Round the Island Cycle Route attracting many enthusiasts. The route runs for 49 miles and there are starting points at Yarmouth, Cowes and Ryde.

Away from walking and cycling, the Isle of Wight offers numerous attractions and activities. You could plan a week's itinerary on the island and not set foot on the beach. The island's history is a fascinating and crucial aspect of its story. It was long considered as a convenient stepping stone for the French in their plan to invade the mainland, and various fortifications – including Fort Victoria and Yarmouth Castle – reflect its key strategic role in the defence of our coastline. Carisbrooke Castle at Newport – the island's capital – is where Charles I was held before his execution in 1649.

The Isle of Wight has been a fashionable destination for the rich and famous over the years, and members of royalty made their home here. Queen Victoria and Prince Albert boosted tourism hugely when they chose the island as the setting for their summer home, Osborne House, which is now open to the public. Elsewhere, there are echoes of the Isle of Wight's fascinating literary links. Charles Dickens is said to have written six chapters of *David Copperfield* in the village of Bonchurch, near Ventnor, and the Victorian Poet Laureate Alfred Lord Tennyson lived at Faringford House, near Freshwater Bay. He claimed that the air on the coast here was worth 'sixpence a pint.'

Tennyson Down ▷

ISLE OF WIGHT

BEMBRIDGE

See Whitecliff Bay

BRIGHSTONE Map 5 SZ48

Places to visit

Mottistone Gardens, MOTTISTONE, PO30 4ED, 01983 741302
www.nationaltrust.org.uk/isleofwight

Grange Farm

►►►► 79%

tel: 01983 740296 **Grange Chine PO30 4DA**
email: grangefarmholidays@gmail.com
dir: *From Freshwater Bay take A3055 towards Ventnor, 5m (pass Isle of Wight Pearl). Site approx 0.5m on right.* **grid ref:** *SZ421820*

This family-run site is set in a stunning location on the south-west coast of the island in Brighstone Bay. The facilities are very good. For children there is an imaginative play area and a wide range of animals to see including llamas and water buffalo. This site is right on the coastal path and ideally located for those who like walking and cycling. There are static homes and camping pods for hire. 8 acre site. 60 touring pitches. 8 hardstandings. Caravan pitches. Motorhome pitches. Tent pitches. 12 statics. 8 wooden pods.

Open: Mar-Oct **Last arrival:** noon **Last departure:** noon

Pitches:

Leisure:

Facilities:

Services:

Within 3 miles:

Notes: No fires. Dogs must be kept on leads. Bakery.

AA Pubs & Restaurants nearby: The Crown Inn, SHORWELL, PO30 3JZ, 01983 740293

COWES Map 5 SZ49

Places to visit

Osborne House, OSBORNE HOUSE, PO32 6JX, 01983 200022
www.english-heritage.org.uk/daysout/properties/osborne

Colemans Farm Park, PORCHFIELD, PO30 4LX, 01983 522831
www.colemansfarmpark.co.uk

Great for kids: Robin Hill Country Park, ARRETON, PO30 2NU, 01983 527352
www.robin-hill.com

Thorness Bay Holiday Park

HOLIDAY CENTRE 85%

tel: 01983 523109 **Thorness PO31 8NJ**
email: holidaysales.thornessbay@park-resorts.com **web:** www.park-resorts.com
dir: *On A3054 towards Yarmouth, 1st right after BMW garage, signed Thorness Bay.*
grid ref: *SZ448928*

Splendid views of The Solent can be enjoyed from this rural park located just outside Cowes. A footpath leads directly to the coast, while on site there is an all-weather sports court, entertainment clubs for children, cabaret shows, and a bar for all the family. There are 23 serviced pitches, with TV boosters, in the separate touring area. 130 holiday homes and fully-equipped safari tents are available for hire. 148 acre site. 124 touring pitches. 21 hardstandings. 8 seasonal pitches. Caravan pitches. Motorhome pitches. Tent pitches. 560 statics. Safari tents.

Open: Apr-1 Nov **Last arrival:** anytime **Last departure:** 10.00hrs

Pitches:

Leisure:

Facilities:

Services:

Within 3 miles:

Notes: Dogs must be kept on leads. Water slide.

AA Pubs & Restaurants nearby: The Fountain Inn, COWES, PO31 7AW, 01983 292397
Duke of York Inn, COWES, PO31 7BT, 01983 295171
The Folly, WHIPPINGHAM, PO32 6NB, 01983 297171

FRESHWATER Map 5 SZ38

Places to visit

Yarmouth Castle, YARMOUTH, PO41 0PB, 01983 760678
www.english-heritage.org.uk/daysout/properties/yarmouth-castle

Dimbola Lodge Museum, FRESHWATER, PO40 9QE, 01983 756814
www.dimbola.co.uk

Great for kids: The Needles Park, ALUM BAY, PO39 0JD, 0871 720 0022 *(Calls cost 13p per minute plus your phone company's access charge)* www.theneedles.co.uk

Heathfield Farm Camping

►►►► 87%

tel: 01983 407822 **Heathfield Rd PO40 9SH**
email: web@heathfieldcamping.co.uk **web:** www.heathfieldcamping.co.uk
dir: *2m W from Yarmouth ferry port on A3054, left to Heathfield Rd, entrance 200yds on right.* **grid ref:** *SZ335879*

A very good quality park with friendly and welcoming staff. There are lovely views across the Solent to Hurst Castle. The toilet facilities, the amenities, which include an excellent backpackers' area, and the very well maintained grounds, make this park one of the best on the island. 10 acre site. 75 touring pitches. Caravan pitches. Motorhome pitches. Tent pitches.

Open: May-Sep **Last arrival:** 20.00hrs **Last departure:** 11.00hrs

Pitches: * £14.50-£24 £14.50-£24 £12.50-£21

Leisure:

Facilities:

Services:

Within 3 miles:

Notes: Dogs must be kept on leads.

AA Pubs & Restaurants nearby: The Red Lion, FRESHWATER, PO40 9BP, 01983 754925

NEWBRIDGE Map 5 SZ48

Places to visit

Newtown Old Town Hall, NEWTOWN, PO30 4PA, 01983 531785
www.nationaltrust.org.uk/isleofwight

Great for kids: Yarmouth Castle, YARMOUTH, PO41 0PB, 01983 760678
www.english-heritage.org.uk/daysout/properties/yarmouth-castle

PREMIER PARK

The Orchards Holiday Caravan Park

►►►►► 94%

tel: 01983 531331 & 531350 **Main Rd PO41 0TS**
email: info@orchards-holiday-park.co.uk **web:** www.orchards-holiday-park.co.uk
dir: *A3054 from Yarmouth, right in 3m at Horse & Groom Inn. Follow signs to Newbridge. Entrance opposite post office. Or from Newport, 6m, via B3401.*
grid ref: *SZ411881*

A really excellent, well-managed park set in a peaceful village location amid downs and meadowland, with glorious downland views. The pitches are terraced and offer a good provision of hardstandings, including those that are water serviced. There is a high quality facility centre offering excellent, spacious showers and family rooms, plus there is access for less able visitors to all site facilities and disabled toilets. The park has indoor and outdoor swimming pools, a takeaway and licensed shop. Static homes are available for hire and 'ferry plus stay' packages are on offer. The site is just ten minutes from the Wightlink ferry terminal in Yarmouth and there are buses that stop at the entrance every hour. 15 acre site. 160 touring pitches. 52 hardstandings. Caravan pitches. Motorhome pitches. Tent pitches. 65 statics.

Open: 28 Mar-3 Nov (rs late May-early Sep outdoor pool open) **Last arrival:** 23.00hrs **Last departure:** 11.00hrs

Pitches: * £19.50-£35.50 £19.50-£35.50 £19.50-£35.50

Leisure:

Facilities:

Services:

Within 3 miles:

Notes: No cycling, no noise after mdnt. Dogs must be kept on leads. Table tennis room, poolside coffee shop.

AA Pubs & Restaurants nearby: The New Inn, SHALFLEET, PO30 4NS, 01983 531314

SHANKLIN Map 5 SZ58

Places to visit

Shanklin Chine, SHANKLIN, PO37 6PF, 01983 866432 www.shanklinchine.co.uk

Ventnor Botanic Garden, VENTNOR, PO38 1UL, 01983 855397 www.botanic.co.uk

Great for kids: Dinosaur Isle, SANDOWN, PO36 8QA, 01983 404344 www.dinosaurisle.com

Lower Hyde Holiday Park

HOLIDAY CENTRE 86%

tel: 01983 866131 **Landguard Rd PO37 7LL**
email: holidaysales.lowerhyde@park-resorts.com **web:** www.park-resorts.com
dir: *From Fishbourne ferry terminal follow A3055 to Shanklin. Site signed just past lake.*
grid ref: *SZ575819*

A popular holiday park on the outskirts of Shanklin, close to the sandy beaches. There is an outdoor swimming pool and plenty of organised activities for youngsters of all ages. In the evening there is a choice of family entertainment. The touring facilities are located in a quiet area away from the main complex, with good views over the downs. Holiday homes are available for hire or purchase. 65 acre site. 148 touring pitches. 24 hardstandings. Caravan pitches. Motorhome pitches. Tent pitches.

Open: Mar-end Oct **Last arrival:** 17.00hrs **Last departure:** noon

Pitches: * £9-£19 £14-£24 £7-£14

Leisure:

Facilities:

Services:

Within 3 miles:

Notes: Dogs must be kept on leads.

AA Pubs & Restaurants nearby: The Bonchurch Inn, BONCHURCH, PO38 1NU, 01983 852611

The Taverners, GODSHILL, PO38 3HZ, 01983 840707

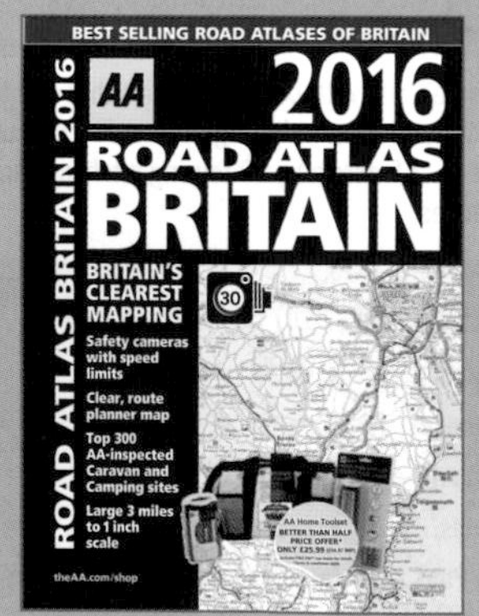

Ninham Country Holidays

►►►► 86%

tel: 01983 864243 **Ninham PO37 7PL**
email: office@ninham-holidays.co.uk **web:** www.ninham-holidays.co.uk
dir: *Signed from A3056 Newport to Sandown road.* **grid ref:** *SZ573825*

Enjoying a lofty rural location with fine country views, this delightful, spacious park occupies two separate, well-maintained areas in a country park setting near the sea and beach. It has an excellent toilet and shower block in The Orchards that has a good layout of pitches; there is also a good outdoor pool, a games room and an excellent children's play area. Willow Bank is a separate camping area that provides more basic, but adequate, facilities. There are also static holiday homes for hire. 12 acre site. 150 touring pitches. Caravan pitches. Motorhome pitches. Tent pitches. 6 statics.

Open: May-Sep **Last arrival:** 20.00hrs (late night arrival area available)
Last departure: 10.00hrs

Pitches: * £18.25-£25.75 £18.25-£25.75 £12.50-£17.50

Leisure:

Facilities:

Services:

Within 3 miles:

Notes: Swimming pool & coarse fishing rules apply. Dogs must be kept on leads.

AA Pubs & Restaurants nearby: The Bonchurch Inn, BONCHURCH, PO38 1NU, 01983 852611

The Taverners, GODSHILL, PO38 3HZ, 01983 840707

See advert on opposite page

Landguard Camping

►►► 80%

SILVER

tel: 01983 863100 **Manor Rd PO37 7PJ**
email: holidaysales.landguard@park-resorts.com
dir: *A3056 towards Sandown. After Morrisons on left, turn right into Whitecross Ln. Follow brown signs to site.* **grid ref:** *SZ580825*

Owned by Park Resorts, this peaceful and secluded park offers good touring facilities. Customers here also have the benefit of using the swimming pool and entertainment facilities at Lower Hyde Holiday Park nearby. Please note, this park will only open for six weeks in the main summer period. Please check with Park Resorts (Lower Hyde Holiday Park) for further details. 67 touring pitches. 2 hardstandings. Caravan pitches. Motorhome pitches. Tent pitches. 138 statics.

Open: Mar-end Sep **Last arrival:** 20.00hrs **Last departure:** noon

Pitches:

Leisure:

Facilities:

Services:

Within 3 miles:

Notes: Dogs must be kept on leads.

AA Pubs & Restaurants nearby: The Bonchurch Inn, BONCHURCH, PO38 1NU, 01983 852611

The Taverners, GODSHILL, PO38 3HZ, 01983 840707

TOTLAND BAY — Map 5 SZ38

Places to visit

Dimbola Lodge Museum, FRESHWATER, PO40 9QE, 01983 756814
www.dimbola.co.uk

Mottistone Gardens, MOTTISTONE, PO30 4ED, 01983 741302
www.nationaltrust.org.uk/isleofwight

Great for kids: Yarmouth Castle, YARMOUTH, PO41 0PB, 01983 760678
www.english-heritage.org.uk/daysout/properties/yarmouth-castle

Stoats Farm Caravan & Camping

►►► 77%

tel: 01983 755258 & 753416 **PO39 0HE**
email: bookings@stoats-farm.co.uk
dir: *0.75m S of Totland. NB It is advised for caravans & motorhomes to approach via Moons Hill (do not approach via Weston Ln which is narrow).* **grid ref:** *SZ324865*

A friendly, personally run site in a quiet country setting close to Alum Bay, Tennyson Down and The Needles. It has good laundry and shower facilities, and the shop, although small, is well stocked. Popular with families, walkers and cyclists, it makes the perfect base for campers wishing to explore this part of the island. 10 acre site. 100 touring pitches. Caravan pitches. Motorhome pitches. Tent pitches.

Open: Apr-Oct

Pitches: * £16-£21 £16-£21 £15-£20

Facilities:

Services:

Within 3 miles:

Notes: No loud noise after 23.00hrs, no camp fires. Dogs must be kept on leads. Campers' fridge available.

AA Pubs & Restaurants nearby: The Red Lion, FRESHWATER, PO40 9BP, 01983 754925

WHITECLIFF BAY Map 5 SZ68

Places to visit

Bembridge Windmill, BEMBRIDGE, PO35 5SQ, 01983 873945 www.nationaltrust.org.uk/isleofwight

Nunwell House & Gardens, BRADING, PO36 0JQ, 01983 407240

Great for kids: Lilliput Antique Doll & Toy Museum, BRADING, PO36 0DJ, 01983 407231 www.lilliputmuseum.co.uk

Whitecliff Bay Holiday Park

HOLIDAY CENTRE 86%

tel: 01983 872671 **Hillway Rd, Bembridge PO35 5PL**
email: holiday.sales@away-resorts.com
dir: *1m S of Bembridge, signed from B3395 in village.* **grid ref:** *SZ637862*

This is a large seaside complex on two sites, with camping on one and self-catering chalets and statics on the other. There is an indoor pool with flume and spa pool, and an outdoor pool with a kiddies' pool, a family entertainment club, and plenty of traditional on-site activities including crazy golf and table tennis, plus an indoor soft play area, a restaurant and a choice of bars. Activities include a My Active programme for all the family in partnership with Fit4Life. There is access to a secluded beach from the park. The glamping area offers fully-equipped Canvas Cottages (with heating and TV; two have a cedar barrel hot tub); equipped bell tents; and three vintage caravans for hire. Expect major improvements to the touring area for the 2016 season. 49 acre site. 400 touring pitches. 50 hardstandings. 400 seasonal pitches. Caravan pitches. Motorhome pitches. Tent pitches. 227 statics. 12 bell tents.

Open: all year (rs Off peak facilities restricted) **Last arrival:** flexible
Last departure: 10.00hrs

Pitches: £4-£45 £4-£45 £4-£45

Leisure:

Facilities:

Services:

Within 3 miles:

Notes: Adults & families only. Dogs must be kept on leads. Sauna, sports TV lounge, outdoor cinema.

AA Pubs & Restaurants nearby: The Crab & Lobster Inn, BEMBRIDGE, PO35 5TR, 01983 872244

WOOTTON BRIDGE Map 5 SZ59

Places to visit

Osborne House, OSBORNE HOUSE, PO32 6JX, 01983 200022 www.english-heritage.org.uk/daysout/properties/osborne

Carisbrooke Castle, CARISBROOKE, PO30 1XY, 01983 522107 www.english-heritage.org.uk/daysout/properties/carisbrooke-castle

Great for kids: Robin Hill Country Park, ARRETON, PO30 2NU, 01983 527352 www.robin-hill.com

Kite Hill Farm Caravan & Camping Park

►►► 87%

tel: 01983 883261 **Firestone Copse Rd PO33 4LE**
email: welcome@kitehillfarm.co.uk **web:** www.kitehillfarm.co.uk
dir: *Signed from A3054 at Wootton Bridge, between Ryde & Newport.* **grid ref:** *SZ549906*

The park, on a gently sloping field, is tucked away behind the owners' farm, just a short walk from the village and attractive river estuary. The facilities are excellent and very clean, and even include a defibrulator at reception. This park provides a pleasant relaxing atmosphere for a stay on the island. Rallies are welcome. 12.5 acre site. 50 touring pitches. Caravan pitches. Motorhome pitches. Tent pitches.

Open: all year **Last arrival:** anytime **Last departure:** noon

Pitches: £15-£18.50 £15-£18.50 £15-£18.50

Leisure:

Facilities:

Services:

Within 3 miles:

Notes: Owners must clean up after their pets. Dogs must be kept on leads.

AA Pubs & Restaurants nearby: The Folly, WHIPPINGHAM, PO32 6NB, 01983 297171

The Fountain Inn, COWES, PO31 7AW, 01983 292397

Duke of York Inn, COWES, PO31 7BT, 01983 295171

WROXALL Map 5 SZ57

Places to visit

Appuldurcombe House, WROXALL, PO38 3EW, 01983 852484 www.english-heritage.org.uk/daysout/properties/appuldurcombe-house

Great for kids: Blackgang Chine Fantasy Park, BLACKGANG, PO38 2HN, 01983 730330 www.blackgangchine.com

PREMIER PARK

Appuldurcombe Gardens Holiday Park

►►►►► 90%

tel: 01983 852597 **Appuldurcombe Rd PO38 3EP**
email: info@appuldurcombegardens.co.uk
dir: *From Newport take A3020 towards Shanklin & Ventnor. Through Rookley & Godshill. Right at Whiteley Bank rdbt towards Wroxall village, then follow brown signs.*
grid ref: *SZ546804*

This well-appointed park is set in a unique setting fairly close to the town of Ventnor. It has modern and smart facilities including a spotless toilet and shower block, and a very tasteful lounge bar and function room. There is an excellent, screened outdoor pool and paddling pool plus café and shop. The site is close to cycle routes and is only 150 yards from the bus stop, making it perfect for those with a motorhome or those not wanting to use their car. There is secure cycle storage plus a free-standing cycle work station, great for pumping tyres up or making adjustments to your bike. Static caravans and apartments are also available for hire. 14 acre site. 130 touring pitches. 40 hardstandings. Caravan pitches. Motorhome pitches. Tent pitches. 40 statics.

Open: Mar-Nov **Last arrival:** 21.00hrs **Last departure:** 11.00hrs

Pitches: * £16.95-£29.35 £16.95-£29.35 £16.95-£29.35

Leisure: **Facilities:**

Services:

Within 3 miles:

Notes: No skateboards. Dogs must be kept on leads. Entertainment in high season only.

AA Pubs & Restaurants nearby: The Pond Café, VENTNOR, PO38 1RG, 01983 855666

YARMOUTH

See Newbridge

KENT

ASHFORD Map 7 TR04

Places to visit

Kent & East Sussex Railway, TENTERDEN, TN30 6HE, 01580 765155 www.kesr.org.uk

Great for kids: Port Lympne Wild Animal Park, LYMPNE, CT21 4LR, 0844 842 4647 *(Calls cost 7p per minute plus your phone company's access charge)* www.aspinallfoundation.org/portlympne

PREMIER PARK

Broadhembury Caravan & Camping Park

►►►►► 88%

tel: 01233 620859 **Steeds Ln, Kingsnorth TN26 1NQ**
email: holidaypark@broadhembury.co.uk **web:** www.broadhembury.co.uk
dir: *M20 junct 10, A2070 towards Brenzett. Straight on at 1st rdbt. Left at 2nd rdbt (avoid left fork). Straight on at next rdbt. Left at 2nd x-rds in village.*
grid ref: *TR009387*

A well-run and well-maintained small family park surrounded by open pasture; it is neatly landscaped with pitches sheltered by mature hedges. There is a well-equipped campers' kitchen adjacent to the spotless toilet facilities and children will love the play areas, games room and football pitch. The adults-only area, close to the excellent reception building, includes popular fully serviced hardstanding pitches; this area has its own first-class, solar heated toilet block. 10 acre site. 110 touring pitches. 20 hardstandings. Caravan pitches. Motorhome pitches. Tent pitches. 25 statics.

Open: all year **Last arrival:** 21.00hrs (late arrivals to use designated area)
Last departure: noon

Pitches: * £20-£24 £20-£24 £20-£24

Leisure:

Facilities:

Services:

Within 3 miles:

Notes: No noise after 22.00hrs. Dogs must be kept on leads.

ST NICHOLAS AT WADE Map 7 TR26

Places to visit

Reculver Towers & Roman Fort, RECULVER, CT6 6SU, 01227 740676
www.english-heritage.org.uk/daysout/properties/reculver-towers-and-roman-fort

Great for kids: Richborough Roman Fort & Amphitheatre, RICHBOROUGH, CT13 9JW, 01304 612013
www.english-heritage.org.uk/daysout/properties/richborough-roman-fort-and-amphitheatre

St Nicholas Camping Site

►►78%

tel: 01843 847245 **Court Rd CT7 0NH**
web: www.stnicholascampingsite.co.uk
dir: *Signed from A299 & A28, site at W end of village near church.* **grid ref:** *TR254672*

A gently-sloping field with mature hedging, on the edge of the village close to the shop. This pretty site offers good facilities, including a family/disabled room, and is conveniently located close to primary routes and the north Kent coast. 3 acre site. 75 touring pitches. 6 seasonal pitches. Caravan pitches. Motorhome pitches. Tent pitches.

Open: Etr-Oct **Last arrival:** 22.00hrs **Last departure:** 14.00hrs

Pitches: **Leisure:**

Facilities: **Services:**

Within 3 miles:

Notes: No music after 22.30hrs. Dogs must be kept on leads. Baby changing area.

WHITSTABLE Map 7 TR16

Places to visit

Canterbury Westgate Towers Museum, CANTERBURY, CT1 2BZ, 07768 535766
www.canterburywestgatetowers.com

The Canterbury Tales, CANTERBURY, CT1 2TG, 01227 479227
www.canterburytales.org.uk

Great for kids: Druidstone Park, CANTERBURY, CT2 9JR, 01227 765168
www.druidstone.net

Homing Park

►►►►84%

tel: 01227 771777 **Church Ln, Seasalter CT5 4BU**
email: info@homingpark.co.uk
dir: *Exit A299 for Whitstable & Canterbury, left at brown camping-caravan sign into Church Ln. Site entrance has 2 large flag poles.* **grid ref:** *TR095645*

A small touring park close to Seasalter Beach and Whitstable, which is famous for its oysters. All pitches are generously sized and fully serviced, and most are separated by hedging and shrubs. A clubhouse and swimming pool are available on site with a small cost for the use of the swimming pool. Wooden camping pods, for four or six people are available for hire; their outwardly sloping walls adds to the internal space. 12.6 acre site. 43 touring pitches. Caravan pitches. Motorhome pitches. Tent pitches. 195 statics. 3 wooden pods.

Open: Etr-Oct **Last arrival:** 20.00hrs **Last departure:** 11.00hrs

Pitches: * £21-£28 £21-£28 £21-£28

Leisure:

Facilities:

Services:

Within 3 miles:

Notes: No commercial vehicles, no tents larger than 8 berths or 5mtrs wide, no unaccompanied minors, no cycles or scooters. Dogs must be kept on leads.

AA Pubs & Restaurants nearby: The Sportsman, WHITSTABLE, CT5 4BP, 01227 273370

WROTHAM HEATH
Map 6 TQ65

Places to visit

Ightham Mote, IGHTHAM, TN15 0NT, 01732 810378 www.nationaltrust.org.uk

St Leonard's Tower, WEST MALLING, ME19 6PE, 01732 870872 www.english-heritage.org.uk/daysout/properties/st-leonards-tower

Great for kids: Kent Life, MAIDSTONE, ME14 3AU, 01622 763936 www.kentlife.org.uk

Gate House Wood Touring Park

►►► 80%

tel: 01732 843062 **Ford Ln TN15 7SD**
email: contact@gatehousewoodtouringpark.com
web: www.gatehousewoodtouringpark.com
dir: *M26 junct 2a, A20 S towards Maidstone, through lights at Wrotham Heath. 1st left signed Trottiscliffe, left at next junct into Ford Ln. Site 100yds on left.* **grid ref:** *TQ635585*

A well-sheltered and mature site in a former quarry surrounded by tall deciduous trees and gorse banks. The well-designed facilities include a reception, shop and smart toilets, 11 new hardstandings, and there is good entrance security and high levels of customer care. The colourful flower beds and hanging baskets are impressive and give a positive first impression. Conveniently placed for the M20 and M25 and a fast rail link to central London. 3.5 acre site. 55 touring pitches. Caravan pitches. Motorhome pitches. Tent pitches.

Open: Mar-Oct **Last arrival:** 21.00hrs **Last departure:** noon

Pitches:

Leisure:

Facilities:

Services:

Within 3 miles:

Notes: No commercial vehicles, no noise after 23.00hrs.

AA Pubs & Restaurants nearby: The Bull, WROTHAM, TN15 7RF, 01732 789800

LANCASHIRE

See also sites under Greater Manchester & Merseyside

BLACKPOOL
Map 18 SD33

See also Lytham St Annes & Thornton

Places to visit

Blackpool Zoo, BLACKPOOL, FY3 8PP, 01253 830830 www.blackpoolzoo.org.uk

Marton Mere Holiday Village

HOLIDAY CENTRE 87%

GOLD

tel: 0800 197 2075 **Mythop Rd FY4 4XN**
email: martonmere@haven.com **web:** www.haven.com/martonmere
dir: *M55 junct 4, A583 towards Blackpool. Right at Clifton Arms lights into Mythop Rd. Site 150yds on left.* **grid ref:** *SD347349*

A very attractive holiday centre in an unusual setting on the edge of the mere, with plenty of birdlife to be spotted. The site has a stylish Mediterranean seaside-themed Boathouse Restaurant and the on-site entertainment is tailored for all ages, and includes a superb show bar. There's a regular bus service into Blackpool for those who want to explore further afield. The separate touring area is well equipped with hardstandings and electric pitches, and there are good quality facilities, including a superb amenities block. 30 acre site. 82 touring pitches. 82 hardstandings. Caravan pitches. Motorhome pitches. 700 statics.

Open: mid Mar-end Oct (rs Mar-end May & Sep-Oct reduced facilities, splash zone closed) **Last arrival:** 22.00hrs **Last departure:** 10.00hrs

Pitches:

continued

BLACKPOOL *continued*

Leisure:

Facilities:

Services:

Within 3 miles:

Notes: No commercial vehicles, no bookings by persons under 21yrs unless a family booking, max 2 dogs per booking, certain dog breeds banned. Dogs must be kept on leads.

See advert on this page

Manor House Caravan Park

►►►► 82%

tel: 01253 764723 **Kitty Ln, Marton Moss FY4 5EG**
email: info@manorhousecaravanpark.co.uk
dir: *At rdbt at end of M55 junct 4, take A5230 signed Sq Gate. At next rdbt take 3rd exit (Blackpool/Sq Gate/A5230). In 0.5m left at lights into Midgeland Rd. 500yds, straight on at x-rds. 250yds, right into Kitty Ln. 250yds site on right. (NB it is advised not to follow Sat Nav).* **grid ref:** *SD336318*

A sympathetically converted former small holding close to both Lytham St Annes and Blackpool, this peacefully located adults-only park is surrounded by high neat hedges and generous sized hardstanding pitches ensure optimum privacy. A warm welcome is assured by the resident owners and although there is no shop or launderette, both services are within a 10-minute drive. There are caravan pitches and motorhome pitches. Please note that tents are not accepted. 1 acre site. 10 touring pitches. 10 hardstandings. Caravan pitches. Motorhome pitches.

Open: Feb-Nov **Last arrival:** 20.00 (or dusk) **Last departure:** 11.30hrs

Pitches:

Facilities:

Services:

Within 3 miles:

Notes: Adults only. No ball games or loud music, pets accepted by prior arrangement only. Dogs must be kept on leads.

BOLTON-LE-SANDS — Map 18 SD46

Places to visit

Lancaster Maritime Museum, LANCASTER, LA1 1RB, 01524 382264
www.lancashire.gov.uk/museums

Lancaster City Museum, LANCASTER, LA1 1HT, 01524 64637
www.lancashire.gov.uk/museums

Great for kids: Lancaster Castle, LANCASTER, LA1 1YJ, 01524 64998
www.lancastercastle.com

Bay View Holiday Park

►►►► 86%

tel: 01524 732854 & 701508 **LA5 9TN**
email: info@holgatesleisureparks.co.uk **web:** www.holgates.co.uk
dir: *M6 junct 25, A6 through Carnforth to Bolton-le-Sands. Site on right.*
grid ref: *SD478683*

A high quality, family-oriented seaside destination with fully serviced all-weather pitches, many of which have views of Morecambe Bay and the Cumbrian hills. A stylish bar/restaurant is just one of the park's amenities, and there is a wide range of activities and attractions on offer within a few miles. This makes a good choice for a family holiday by the sea; two family pods are available to hire. 10 acre site. 100 touring pitches. 50 hardstandings. 127 seasonal pitches. Caravan pitches. Motorhome pitches. Tent pitches. 100 statics. 2 wooden pods.

Open: all year (rs Quiet periods restaurant & bar reduced hours) **Last arrival:** 20.00hrs **Last departure:** noon

Pitches: * £22-£27 £22-£27 £17-£25

Leisure:

Facilities:

Services:

Within 3 miles:

Notes: No noise after 23.00hrs. No dogs in pods. Dogs must be kept on leads.

AA Pubs & Restaurants nearby: The Longlands Inn and Restaurant, CARNFORTH, LA6 1JH, 01524 781256

Hest Bank Inn, HEST BANK, LA2 6DN, 01524 824339

See advert on page 243

Red Bank Farm

►►► 80%

tel: 01524 823196 **LA5 8JR**
email: mark.archer@hotmail.co.uk
dir: *From Morecambe take A5015 towards Carnforth. After Hest Bank left into Pastures Ln (follow brown site sign). Over rail bridge, right (follow site sign). At T-junct left into The Shore to site at end.* **grid ref:** *SD472681*

A gently sloping grassy field with mature hedges, close to the sea shore and a RSPB reserve. This farm site has smart toilet facilities, a superb view across Morecambe Bay to the distant Lake District hills, and is popular with tenters. Archers Café serves a good range of cooked food, including home-reared marsh lamb dishes. 3 acre site. 60 touring pitches. Motorhome pitches. Tent pitches.

Open: Mar-Oct

Pitches: * fr £14 fr £14

Facilities:

Services:

Within 3 miles:

Notes: No noise after 22.30hrs. Dogs must be kept on leads. Pets' corner.

AA Pubs & Restaurants nearby: The Longlands Inn and Restaurant, CARNFORTH, LA6 1JH, 01524 781256

Hest Bank Inn, HEST BANK, LA2 6DN, 01524 824339

CAPERNWRAY

Places to visit

Leighton Hall, CARNFORTH, LA5 9ST, 01524 734474 www.leightonhall.co.uk

RSPB Leighton Moss & Morecambe Bay Nature Reserve, SILVERDALE, LA5 0SW, 01524 701601 www.rspb.org.uk/leightonmoss

CAPERNWRAY — Map 18 SD57

Old Hall Caravan Park

►►►► 88%

tel: 01524 733276 **LA6 1AD**
email: info@oldhallcaravanpark.co.uk
dir: *M6 junct 35, A601(M) follow signs for Over Kellet, at T-junct left onto B6254. In Over Kellet left at village green signed Capernwray. Site 1.5m on right.* **grid ref:** *SD533716*

A lovely secluded park set in a clearing amongst trees at the end of a half-mile long drive. This peaceful park is home to a wide variety of wildlife, and there are marked walks in the woods. A pathway over a meandering brook through woodland separates the reception from the touring area. The facilities are well maintained by friendly owners, and booking is advisable. 3 acre site. 38 touring pitches. 38 hardstandings. 30 seasonal pitches. Caravan pitches. Motorhome pitches. 260 statics.

Open: Mar-Oct **Last departure:** noon

Pitches: * fr £20 fr £20 **Leisure:**

Facilities: **Services:**

Within 3 miles:

Notes: No skateboards, rollerblades or roller boots. Dogs must be kept on leads.

AA Pubs & Restaurants nearby: The Highwayman, BURROW, LA6 2RJ, 01524 273338

The Lunesdale Arms, TUNSTALL, LA6 2QN, 015242 74203

COCKERHAM — Map 18 SD45

Places to visit

Lancaster Maritime Museum, LANCASTER, LA1 1RB, 01524 382264 www.lancashire.gov.uk/museums

Lancaster City Museum, LANCASTER, LA1 1HT, 01524 64637 www.lancashire.gov.uk/museums

Great for kids: Blackpool Zoo, BLACKPOOL, FY3 8PP, 01253 830830 www.blackpoolzoo.org.uk

Moss Wood Caravan Park

GOLD

►►►► 84%

tel: 01524 791041 **Crimbles Ln LA2 0ES**
email: info@mosswood.co.uk
dir: *M6 junct 33, A6, approx 4m to site. From Cockerham take W A588. Left into Crimbles Lane to site.* **grid ref:** *SD456497*

A tree-lined grassy park with sheltered, level pitches, located on peaceful Cockerham Moss. The modern toilet block is attractively clad in stained wood, and the facilities include cubicled washing facilities and a launderette. 25 acre site. 25 touring pitches. 25 hardstandings. Caravan pitches. Motorhome pitches. Tent pitches. 143 statics.

Open: Mar-Oct **Last arrival:** 20.00hrs **Last departure:** 16.00hrs

Pitches: **Leisure:** **Facilities:**

Services: **Within 3 miles:**

Notes: Dogs must be kept on leads. Woodland walks.

AA Pubs & Restaurants nearby: The Bay Horse Inn, FORTON, LA2 0HR, 01524 791204

CROSTON Map 15 SD41

Places to visit

Harris Museum & Art Gallery, PRESTON, PR1 2PP, 01772 258248 www.harrismuseum.org.uk

Rufford Old Hall, RUFFORD, L40 1SG, 01704 821254 www.nationaltrust.org.uk/ruffordoldhall

Royal Umpire Caravan Park

►►► 84%

tel: 01772 600257 **Southport Rd PR26 9JB**
email: info@royalumpire.co.uk
dir: *From N: M6 junct 28 (from S: M6 junct 27), onto B5209, right onto B5250.*
grid ref: *SD504190*

A large park with tree- or hedge-lined bays for touring caravans and motorhomes, plus a large camping field in open countryside. There are many areas for children's activities and several pubs and restaurants within walking distance. Four camping pods are available for hire. 60 acre site. 195 touring pitches. 180 hardstandings. Caravan pitches. Motorhome pitches. Tent pitches. 4 wooden pods.

Open: all year **Last arrival:** 20.00hrs **Last departure:** 16.00hrs

Pitches: £15-£35 £18-£35 £15-£28

Leisure:

Facilities:

Services:

Within 3 miles:

Notes: Dogs must be kept on leads.

AA Pubs & Restaurants nearby: Farmers Arms, HESKIN GREEN, PR7 5NP, 01257 451276

Who are the AA's award-winning campsites this year? See pages 14-19

FAR ARNSIDE Map 18 SD47

Places to visit

Rufford Old Hall, RUFFORD, L40 1SG, 01704 821254 www.nationaltrust.org.uk/ruffordoldhall

RSPB Leighton Moss & Morecambe Bay Nature Reserve, SILVERDALE, LA5 0SW, 01524 701601 www.rspb.org.uk/leightonmoss

REGIONAL WINNER – NORTH WEST ENGLAND
AA CAMPSITE OF THE YEAR 2016

Hollins Farm Camping & Caravanning

►►►► 90%

tel: 01524 701767 & 701508 **LA5 0SL**
email: reception@holgates.co.uk **web:** www.holgates.co.uk
dir: *M6 junct 35, A601 (Carnforth). Left in 1m at rdbt to Carnforth. Right in 1m at lights signed Silverdale. Left in 1m into Sands Ln, signed Silverdale. 2.4m over auto-crossing, 0.3m to T-junct. Right, follow signs to site, in approx 3m take 2nd left after passing Holgates.* **grid ref:** *SD450764*

Hollins Farm is a long established park that continues to be upgraded by the owners. There are 50 fully serviced hardstanding pitches for tourers and 25 fully serviced tent pitches; the excellent amenities block provides very good facilities and privacy options. It has a traditional family camping feel and offers high standard facilities; most pitches offer views towards Morecambe Bay. Two family pods (Daisy and Buttercup) are available for hire. The leisure and recreation facilities of the nearby, much larger, sister park (Silverdale Caravan Park) can be accessed by guests here. 30 acre site. 12 touring pitches. 12 hardstandings. 38 seasonal pitches. Caravan pitches. Motorhome pitches. Tent pitches. 2 wooden pods.

Open: 14 Mar-7 Nov **Last arrival:** 20.00hrs **Last departure:** noon

Pitches: * fr £32 fr £32 fr £30

Leisure:

Facilities:

Services:

Within 3 miles:

Notes: No unaccompanied children. Dogs must be kept on leads.

FLEETWOOD Map 18 SD34

Places to visit

Blackpool Zoo, BLACKPOOL, FY3 8PP, 01253 830830 www.blackpoolzoo.org.uk

Cala Gran Holiday Park

HOLIDAY HOME PARK 84%

tel: 01253 872555 **Fleetwood Rd FY7 8JY**
email: calagran@haven.com **web:** www.haven.com/calagran
dir: *M55 junct 3, A585 signed Fleetwood. At 4th rdbt (Nautical College on left) take 3rd exit. Park 250yds on left.* **grid ref:** *SD330451*

Cala Gran is a lively holiday park close to Blackpool with a range of quality holiday caravans and apartments. The park is all about fun, and the entertainment includes live music, comedy shows and resident DJs, while for children there are swimming pools and SplashZone, and a new Pic 'n' Paint room.

Open: Mar-Oct **Change over day:** Mon, Fri, Sat

Arrival and departure times: Please contact the park.

Statics: 226 Sleeps 6-8 Bedrms 2-3 Bathrms 1-2 Toilets 1-2 Microwave Freezer TV Sky/FTV Elec inc Gas inc Grass area

Children: Cots Highchair **Dogs:** 2 on leads No dangerous dogs

Leisure: Cycle hire

GARSTANG Map 18 SD44

Places to visit

Lancaster Maritime Museum, LANCASTER, LA1 1RB, 01524 382264 www.lancashire.gov.uk/museums

Lancaster City Museum, LANCASTER, LA1 1HT, 01524 64637 www.lancashire.gov.uk/museums

Great for kids: Lancaster Castle, LANCASTER, LA1 1YJ, 01524 64998 www.lancastercastle.com

Claylands Caravan Park

►►►► 85%

tel: 01524 791242 **Cabus PR3 1AJ**
email: alan@claylands.com
dir: *From M6 junct 33, A6 towards Garstang, approx 6m, past Thorpy's chipshop, left into Weavers Lane.* **grid ref:** *SD496485*

Colourful seasonal floral displays create an excellent first impression. A well-maintained site with lovely river and woodland walks and good views over the River Wyre towards the village of Scorton. This friendly park is set in delightful countryside where guests can enjoy fishing, and the atmosphere is very relaxed. The quality facilities and amenities are of a high standard, and everything is immaculately maintained. 14 acre site. 30 touring pitches. 30 hardstandings. Caravan pitches. Motorhome pitches. Tent pitches. 68 statics.

Open: Mar-Jan **Last arrival:** 23.00hrs **Last departure:** noon

Pitches: **Leisure:** **Facilities:**

Services: **Within 3 miles:**

Notes: No rollerblades or skateboards. Dogs must be kept on leads.

AA Pubs & Restaurants nearby: Owd Nell's Tavern, BILSBORROW, PR3 0RS, 01995 640010

Bridge House Marina & Caravan Park

►►► 80%

tel: 01995 603207 **Nateby Crossing Ln, Nateby PR3 0JJ**
email: edwin@bridgehousemarina.co.uk
dir: *Exit A6 at pub & Knott End sign, immediately right into Nateby Crossing Ln, over canal bridge to site on left.* **grid ref:** *SD483457*

A well-maintained site in attractive countryside by the Lancaster Canal, with good views towards the Trough of Bowland. The boatyard atmosphere is interesting, and there is a good children's playground. 4 acre site. 50 touring pitches. 50 hardstandings. Caravan pitches. Motorhome pitches. 40 statics.

Open: Feb-Jan **Last arrival:** 22.00hrs **Last departure:** 13.00hrs

Pitches: * £22.50-£25 £22.50-£25

Leisure: **Facilities:**

Services: **Within 3 miles:**

Notes: Dogs must be kept on leads.

AA Pubs & Restaurants nearby: Owd Nell's Tavern, BILSBORROW, PR3 0RS, 01995 640010

LANCASTER Map 18 SD46

Places to visit

Lancaster Maritime Museum, LANCASTER, LA1 1RB, 01524 382264 www.lancashire.gov.uk/museums

Lancaster City Museum, LANCASTER, LA1 1HT, 01524 64637

www.lancashire.gov.uk/museums

Great for kids: Lancaster Castle, LANCASTER, LA1 1YJ, 01524 64998 www.lancastercastle.com

New Parkside Farm Caravan Park

►►► 83%

tel: 015247 70723 **Denny Beck, Caton Rd LA2 9HH**
email: enquiries@newparksidefarm.co.uk
dir: *M6 junct 34, A683 towards Caton/Kirkby Lonsdale. Site 1m on right.*
grid ref: *SD507633*

A peaceful, friendly, grassy park on a working farm convenient for exploring the historic City of Lancaster and the delights of the Lune Valley. 4 acre site. 40 touring pitches. 40 hardstandings. Caravan pitches. Motorhome pitches. Tent pitches. 16 statics.

Open: Mar-Oct **Last arrival:** 20.00hrs **Last departure:** 16.00hrs

Pitches: £15-£18 £15-£18 £8-£15 **Facilities:**

Services: **Within 3 miles:**

Notes: No football. Dogs must be kept on leads.

AA Pubs & Restaurants nearby: The Sun Hotel and Bar, LANCASTER, LA1 1ET, 01524 66006

The White Cross, LANCASTER, LA1 4XT, 01524 33999

The Stork Inn, LANCASTER, LA2 0AN, 01524 751234

LONGRIDGE Map 18 SD63

Places to visit

Brockholes Nature Reserve, SAMLESBURY, PR5 0AG, 01772 872000 www.brockholes.org

Beacon Fell View Holiday Park

NEW HOLIDAY CENTRE 79%

tel: 01772 783233 **110 Higher Rd PR3 2TF**
email: beacon@hagansleisure.co.uk
dir: *At junct of Dilworth Rd (B6243) & King St in Longridge into Higher Rd. Site on right.*
grid ref: *SD616380*

Located on the outskirts of Longridge with fine views of the surrounding fells, this long-established family holiday destination has a good range of all-weather attractions for both adults and children. In addition to holiday homes, the touring areas have good hardstanding pitches for caravans or motorhomes with electric hook-ups to all. 32 acre site. 79 touring pitches. Caravan pitches. Motorhome pitches. Tent pitches. 300 statics.

Open: Mar-11 Nov **Last arrival:** 22.00hrs **Last departure:** 11.00hrs

Pitches:

AA Pubs & Restaurants nearby: Derby Arms, LONGRIDGE, PR3 2NB, 01772 782370

LYTHAM Map 18 SD32

Places to visit

Blackpool Zoo, BLACKPOOL, FY3 8PP, 01253 830830 www.blackpoolzoo.org.uk

Little Orchard Caravan Park

►►► 80%

GOLD

tel: 01253 836658 **Shorrocks Barn, Back Ln, Weeton, Kirkham PR4 3HN**
email: info@littleorchardcaravanpark.com
dir: *M55 junct 3, A585 signed Fleetwood. Left in 0.5m opposite Ashiana Tandoori restaurant into Greenhalgh Ln in 0.75m, right at T-junct, site entrance 1st left.*
grid ref: *SD399355*

Set in a quiet rural location in an orchard, this attractive park welcomes mature visitors. The toilet facilities are to a very high standard. Two excellent fisheries are within easy walking distance. The site advises that bookings should be made by phone only, not on-line. 7 acre site. 45 touring pitches. 45 hardstandings. 20 seasonal pitches. Caravan pitches. Motorhome pitches. Tent pitches.

Open: 14 Feb-1 Jan **Last arrival:** 20.00hrs **Last departure:** noon

Pitches: £20-£25 £20-£25 £15-£20

Facilities:

Services:

Within 3 miles:

Notes: No cars by tents. No ball games or skateboards, no noise after 23.00hrs, children must be supervised when in toilet blocks,. No dangerous dog breeds. Dogs must be kept on leads. Winter caravan storage.

AA Pubs & Restaurants nearby: The Ship at Elswick, ELSWICK, PR4 3ZB, 01995 672777

LYTHAM ST ANNES Map 18 SD32

Places to visit

Blackpool Zoo, BLACKPOOL, FY3 8PP, 01253 830830 www.blackpoolzoo.org.uk

Eastham Hall Caravan Park

►►►► 82%

GOLD

tel: 01253 737907 **Saltcotes Rd FY8 4LS**
email: info@easthamhall.co.uk **web:** www.easthamhall.co.uk
dir: *M55 junct 3. Straight over 3 rdbts onto B5259. Through Wrea Green & Moss Side, site 1m after level crossing.* **grid ref:** *SD379291*

A large family-run park in a tranquil rural setting, surrounded by trees and mature shrubs. The pitch density is very good and some are fully serviced, plus the amenities blocks have been appointed to a high standard. Please note, this site does not accept tents. 15 acre site. 160 touring pitches. 99 hardstandings. 133 seasonal pitches. Caravan pitches. Motorhome pitches. 150 statics.

Open: Mar-Nov (rs Nov only hardstanding pitches available) **Last arrival:** 21.00hrs **Last departure:** noon

Pitches: **Leisure:** **Facilities:** WiFi

Services: **Within 3 miles:**

Notes: No tents. Only breathable groundsheets permitted in awnings. Dogs must be kept on leads. Football field, night touring pitches available.

AA Pubs & Restaurants nearby: Greens Bistro, LYTHAM ST ANNES, FY8 1SX, 01253 789990

See advert on opposite page

PITCHES: Caravans Motorhomes Tents Glamping-style accommodation **SERVICES:** Electric hook up Launderette Licensed bar Calor Gas Camping Gaz Toilet fluid Café/Restaurant Fast Food/Takeaway Battery charging Baby care Motorvan service point

ABBREVIATIONS: BH/bank hols – bank holidays Etr – Easter Spring BH – Spring Bank Holiday fr – from hrs – hours m – mile mdnt – midnight rdbt – roundabout rs – restricted service wk – week wknd – weekend x-rds – cross roads No credit or debit cards No dogs Children of all ages accepted

MERSEYSIDE

SOUTHPORT Map 15 SD31

Places to visit

The British Lawnmower Museum, SOUTHPORT, PR8 5AJ, 01704 501336 www.lawnmowerworld.com

Great for kids: Dunes Splash World, SOUTHPORT, PR8 1RX, 01704 537160 www.splashworldsouthport.com

Riverside Holiday Park

HOLIDAY CENTRE 86%

BRONZE

tel: 01704 228886 **Southport New Rd PR9 8DF**
email: reception@harrisonleisureuk.com
dir: *M6 junct 27, A5209 towards Parbold/Burscough, right onto A59. Left onto A565 at lights in Tarleton. Continue to dual carriageway. At rdbt straight across, site 1m on left.* **grid ref:** *SD405192*

A family friendly park north of Southport, with many indoor attractions, including a swimming pool, sauna, steam room and jacuzzi. The generously sized pitches are located on carefully landscaped grounds and served by two well-equipped, modern amenities blocks. Free WiFi is provided in an attractive café, and cycle hire is also available. 80 acre site. 260 touring pitches. 130 hardstandings. Caravan pitches. Motorhome pitches. 355 statics.

Open: 14 Feb-Jan **Last arrival:** 17.00hrs **Last departure:** 11.00hrs

Pitches:

Leisure:

Facilities:

Services: **Within 3 miles:**

Notes: One car per pitch. Dogs must be kept on leads.

AA Pubs & Restaurants nearby: Bistrot Vérité, SOUTHPORT, PR8 4AR, 01704 564199

Gusto Trattoria, SOUTHPORT, PR8 1QB, 01704 544255

Vincent Hotel, SOUTHPORT, PR8 1JR, 01704 883800

Hurlston Hall Country Caravan Park

►►►► 80%

tel: 01704 840400 & 842829 **Southport Rd L40 8HB**
email: enquiries@hurlstonhallcaravanpark.co.uk
dir: *On A570, 3m from Ormskirk towards Southport.* **grid ref:** *SD398107*

A peaceful tree-lined touring park next to a static site in attractive countryside about 10 minutes' drive from Southport. The park is maturing well, with growing trees and a coarse fishing lake, and the excellent on-site facilities include golf, a bistro, a well-equipped health centre, a bowling green and model boat lake. Please note that neither tents nor dogs are accepted at this site. 5 acre site. 60 touring pitches. Caravan pitches. Motorhome pitches. 68 statics.

Open: Etr-Oct **Last arrival:** 20.30hrs (18.30hrs at wknds & BHs)
Last departure: 17.00hrs

Pitches:

Leisure: Spa

Facilities:

Services:

Within 3 miles:

Notes:

AA Pubs & Restaurants nearby: Gusto Trattoria, SOUTHPORT, PR8 1QB, 01704 544255

Bistrot Vérité, SOUTHPORT, PR8 4AR, 01704 564199

Vincent Hotel, SOUTHPORT, PR8 1JR, 01704 883800

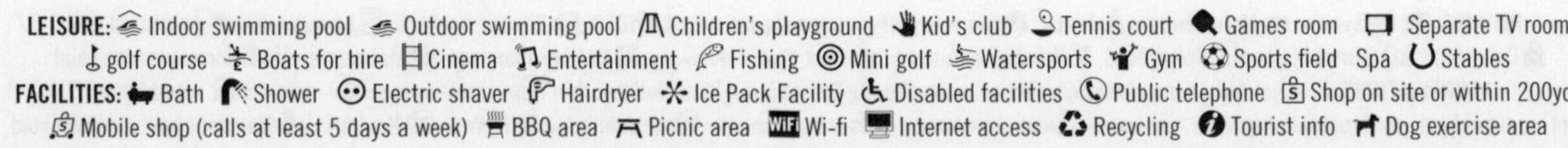

Willowbank Holiday Home & Touring Park

►►► 87%

GOLD

tel: 01704 571566 **Coastal Rd, Ainsdale PR8 3ST**
email: info@willowbankcp.co.uk **web:** www.willowbankcp.co.uk
dir: *From A565 between Formby & Ainsdale exit at Woodvale lights onto coast road, site 150mtrs on left. From N: M6 junct 31, A59 towards Preston, A565, through Southport & Ainsdale, right at Woodvale lights.* **grid ref:** *SD305110*

Set in woodland on a nature reserve next to sand dunes, this constantly improving park is a peaceful and relaxing holiday destination with mature trees, shrubs and colourful seasonal flowers surrounding neat pitches and modern amenities blocks. 8 acre site. 87 touring pitches. 61 hardstandings. Caravan pitches. Motorhome pitches. 228 statics.

Open: 14 Feb-31 Jan **Last arrival:** 21.00hrs **Last departure:** noon

Pitches: * £15.70-£20.80 £15.70-£20.80

Leisure:

Facilities:

Services:

Within 3 miles:

Notes: Cannot accommodate continental door entry units, no commercial vehicles, no dangerous dog breeds. Dogs must be kept on leads. Baby changing facility, bike hire.

AA Pubs & Restaurants nearby: Gusto Trattoria, SOUTHPORT, PR8 1QB, 01704 544255
Bistrot Vérité, SOUTHPORT, PR8 4AR, 01704 564199
Vincent Hotel, SOUTHPORT, PR8 1JR, 01704 883800

Norfolk

Think of Norfolk, and the theme of water – in particular the Norfolk Broads, a complex network of mostly navigable rivers and man-made waterways – usually springs to mind. This delightfully unspoiled region attracts thousands of visitors every year, as does the North Norfolk Coast, designated an Area of Outstanding Natural Beauty and probably the finest of its kind in Europe.

'A long way from anywhere' and 'a remote corner of England that has been able to hold on to its traditions and ancient secrets,' are two of the apt descriptions that apply to this spacious corner of the country that still seems a separate entity, as if it is strangely detached from the rest of the country.

The coastline here represents a world of lonely beaches, vast salt marshes and extensive sand dunes stretching to the far horizon. It remains essentially unchanged, a stark reminder of how this area has long been vulnerable to attack and enemy invasion.

The highly successful thriller writer Jack Higgins chose this theme as the subject of his hugely popular adventure yarn *The Eagle has Landed*, published in 1975. The book, about a wartime Nazi plot to kidnap and assassinate Winston Churchill while he is spending the weekend at a country house near the sea in this part of East Anglia, vividly conveys the strange, unsettling atmosphere of the North Norfolk Coast.

Walking is the best way to gain a flavour of that atmosphere and visit the story's memorable setting. The 93-mile Peddars Way and North Norfolk Coast Path is one of Britain's most popular national trails. Made up of two paths strung together to form one continuous route, the trail begins near Thetford on the Suffolk/Norfolk border and follows ancient tracks and sections of Roman road before reaching the coast near Hunstanton. Cycling is another popular pastime in this region and in places you can combine it with a local train ride. One option, for example, is to cycle beside the Bure Valley Railway on a 9-mile trail running from Aylsham to Wroxham, returning to the start by train. There is also the North Norfolk Coast Cycleway between King's Lynn and Cromer, among other routes.

Norfolk prides itself on its wealth of historic houses, the most famous being Sandringham, where Her Majesty the Queen and her family spend Christmas. The Grade II-listed house, which is surrounded by 20,000 acres, has been the private home of four generations of monarchs since 1862. 'Dear old Sandringham, the place I love better than anywhere in the world,' wrote King George V. The house and gardens are open to visitors. Among the other great houses in the region are Holkham Hall – the magnificent Palladian home of the Earls of Leicester – and the National Trust properties of Blickling Hall and Felbrigg Hall.

Many of Norfolk's towns have a particular charm and a strong sense of community. The quiet market towns of Fakenham and Swaffham are prime examples, and there is also Thetford, with its popular museum focusing on the iconic TV comedy series *Dad's Army*. Much of the filming for this cherished BBC production took place in the town and in nearby Thetford Forest. On the coast, you'll find a string of quaint villages and small towns. Wells-next-the-Sea is a popular destination for many visitors to Norfolk, as is Blakeney, renowned for its mudflats and medieval parish church, dedicated to the patron saint of seafarers, standing guard over the village and the estuary of the River Glaven. With its iconic pier, a key feature of coastal towns, Cromer is a classic example of a good old fashioned seaside resort where rather grand Victorian hotels look out to sea. Together with Sheringham, Cromer hosts a Crab and Lobster Festival in May.

◁ Horsey Mill, Horsey, Norfolk Broads National Park

NORFOLK

BARNEY — Map 13 TF93

Places to visit

Baconsthorpe Castle, BACONSTHORPE, NR25 6LN, 01799 322399
www.english-heritage.org.uk/daysout/properties/baconsthorpe-castle

Holkham Hall, HOLKHAM, NR23 1AB, 01328 710227 www.holkham.co.uk

Great for kids: Dinosaur Adventure Park, LENWADE, NR9 5JW, 01603 876310
www.dinosauradventure.co.uk

PREMIER PARK

The Old Brick Kilns

92%

tel: 01328 878305 **Little Barney Ln NR21 0NL**
email: enquiries@old-brick-kilns.co.uk **web:** www.old-brick-kilns.co.uk
dir: *From A148 Fakenham to Cromer road follow brown tourist signs to Barney, left into Little Barney Ln. Site at end of lane.* **grid ref:** *TG007328*

Under new ownership, this secluded and peaceful park is approached via a quiet, leafy country lane. The park is on two levels with its own boating and fishing pool and many mature trees. Excellent, well-planned toilet facilities can be found in two beautifully appointed blocks, and there is a short dog walk. Kate and David have already refurbished the bar and restaurant, upgraded eight hardstandings, and improved drainage across the park. Please note due to a narrow access road, no arrivals are accepted until after 1pm. There are four self-catering holiday cottages. 12.73 acre site. 65 touring pitches. 65 hardstandings. Caravan pitches. Motorhome pitches. Tent pitches.

Open: 15 Mar-15 Dec (rs Etr-Sep bar food & takeaway on selected nights only) **Last arrival:** 21.00hrs (no arrivals before 13.00hrs) **Last departure:** 11.00hrs

Pitches:

Leisure:

Facilities:

Services:

Within 3 miles:

Notes: No gazebos. Outdoor draughts, chess, family games, massages by appointment.

AA Pubs & Restaurants nearby: The Old Forge Seafood Restaurant, THURSFORD, NR21 0BD, 01328 878345

BELTON — Map 13 TG40

Places to visit

Burgh Castle, BURGH CASTLE, NR31 9PZ, 0370 333 1181
www.english-heritage.org.uk/daysout/properties/burgh-castle

Wild Duck Holiday Park

HOLIDAY CENTRE 74%

GOLD

tel: 0800 917 6394 **Howards Common NR31 9NE**
email: wildduck@haven.com **web:** www.haven.com/wildduck
dir: *A47 to Great Yarmouth, 3rd exit at Asda rdbt, straight on at next 2 rdbts. Left onto A143 signed Beccles. Right at lights, 2m to dual carriageway, right signed Belton. Straight on at mini rdbt. Right at T-junct. left at next T-junct. Park 200yds on right.* **grid ref:** *TG475028*

This a large holiday complex with plenty to do for all ages both indoors and out. This level grassy site has well laid-out facilities and is set in a forest with small, cleared areas for tourers. Clubs for children and teenagers, sporting activities and evening shows all add to the fun of a stay here. There are six new fully equipped safari tents for hire, each with their own stone-built barbecue and facility block. 97 acre site. 110 touring pitches. Caravan pitches. Motorhome pitches. Tent pitches. 560 statics. 6 safari tents.

Open: 16 Mar-5 Nov (rs mid Mar-May & Sep-early Nov some facilities may be reduced) **Last arrival:** 21.00hrs **Last departure:** 10.00hrs

Pitches:

Leisure:

Facilities:

Services:

LEISURE: Indoor swimming pool · Outdoor swimming pool · Children's playground · Kid's club · Tennis court · Games room · Separate TV room · golf course · Boats for hire · Cinema · Entertainment · Fishing · Mini golf · Watersports · Gym · Sports field · Spa · Stables
FACILITIES: Bath · Shower · Electric shaver · Hairdryer · Ice Pack Facility · Disabled facilities · Public telephone · Shop on site or within 200yds · Mobile shop (calls at least 5 days a week) · BBQ area · Picnic area · Wi-fi · Internet access · Recycling · Tourist info · Dog exercise area

Within 3 miles:

Notes: No commercial vehicles, no bookings by persons under 21yrs unless a family booking, max 2 dogs per booking, certain dog breeds banned. Dogs must be kept on leads.

AA Pubs & Restaurants nearby: Andover House, GREAT YARMOUTH, NR30 3JB, 01493 843490

See advert below

PREMIER PARK

Rose Farm Touring & Camping Park

►►►►► 85%

tel: 01493 780896 **Stepshort NR31 9JS**
email: myhra@rosefarmtouringpark.fsnet.co.uk
dir: *From A143 follow signs to Belton. In Belton, from mini rdbt on New Rd into Stepshort, site on right.* **grid ref:** *TG488033*

A former railway line is the setting for this very peaceful, beautifully presented site which enjoys rural views. It is brightened with many flower and herb beds. The toilet facilities are smart, spotlessly clean, inviting to use and include family rooms. The customer care here is truly exceptional and the quality café (open in peak season only) is very popular. 10 acre site. 145 touring pitches. 20 hardstandings. Caravan pitches. Motorhome pitches. Tent pitches.

Open: all year

Pitches:

Leisure:

Facilities: WiFi

Services:

Within 3 miles:

Notes: No dog fouling.

AA Pubs & Restaurants nearby: Andover House, GREAT YARMOUTH, NR30 3JB, 01493 843490

Swallow Park Leisure

NEW ►►►►

tel: 01493 601180 **Lawns Ln, Beccles Rd NR31 9JQ**
email: coll.colby@icloud.com
dir: *From A143 from Beccles towards Great Yarmouth, 0.5m after Cherry Lane Garden Centre left into Beccles Rd. In 400yds right into Lawns Ln.* **grid ref:** *TG486023*

This leisure park is located close to the village of Belton, only three miles from the beautiful beach at Gorleston, two miles from the Norfolk Broads and a short distance from Fritton Lake Outdoor Centre. This family owned park is a pleasant, quiet site and offers both fully-equipped safari tents with their own cooking, shower and toilet facilities, and bell tents with external cooking huts. These either have a wooden porch or decking areas, very good quality furnishings, and dining and cooking equipment. Heating in all glamping units is provided by log-burning stoves, and free fuel is provided. There are also five camping pitches. 3 acre site. Safari tents. Bell tents.

Open: Apr-Oct **Last arrival:** 22.00hrs **Last departure:** 10.30hrs

Pitches: Contact park for prices.

Leisure:

Facilities:

Services:

Within 3 miles:

Notes: No noise after mdnt. Dogs must be kept on leads.

BURGH CASTLE Map 13 TG40

Places to visit

Burgh Castle, BURGH CASTLE, NR31 9PZ, 0370 333 1181
www.english-heritage.org.uk/daysout/properties/burgh-castle

Breydon Water

HOLIDAY CENTRE 77%

BRONZE

tel: 0871 664 9710 *(Calls cost 5p per minute plus your phone company's access charge)*
Yare Holiday Park, Butt Ln NR31 9QB
email: breydon.water@park-resorts.com
dir: *From Gt Yarmouth take A12 towards Lowestoft. Right signed Diss & Beccles onto A143. Through Bradwell, right signed Burgh Castle & Belton. At mini rdbt right into Stepshort. Site on right.* **grid ref:** *TG479042*

This large park has two village areas just a short walk apart. Yare Village offers touring facilities, family fun and superb entertainment, while Bure Village, which is a quieter base, is now static caravans only. Although the villages are separated, guests are more than welcome to use facilities at both. Yare Village has modern, well maintained toilets, and tents are welcome. The park is just a short drive from the bright lights of Great Yarmouth and the unique Norfolk Broads. 189 touring pitches. Caravan pitches. Motorhome pitches. Tent pitches. 327 statics.

Open: Apr-Oct **Last arrival:** anytime **Last departure:** 10.00hrs

Pitches:

Leisure:

Facilities:

Services:

Within 3 miles:

AA Pubs & Restaurants nearby: Andover House, GREAT YARMOUTH, NR30 3JB, 01493 843490

CAISTER-ON-SEA

Places to visit

Caister Roman Fort, CAISTER-ON-SEA, 0370 333 1181
www.english-heritage.org.uk/daysout/properties/caister-roman-fort

Thrigby Hall Wildlife Gardens, FILBY, NR29 3DR, 01493 369477
www.thrigbyhall.co.uk

CAISTER-ON-SEA Map 13 TG51

Caister-on-Sea Holiday Park

HOLIDAY CENTRE 87%

GOLD

tel: 0800 587 2275 **Ormesby Rd NR30 5NH**
email: caister@haven.com **web:** www.haven.com/caister
dir: *A1064 signed Caister-on-Sea. At rdbt 2nd exit onto A149, at next rdbt 1st exit onto Caister by-pass, at 3rd rdbt 3rd exit to Caister-on-Sea. Park on left.* **grid ref:** *TG519132*

An all-action holiday park located beside the beach north of the resort of Great Yarmouth, yet close to the attractions of the Norfolk Broads. The touring area offers 46 fully serviced pitches and a modern purpose-built toilet block. Customer care is of an extremely high standard with a full time, experienced and caring warden. Please note that the park does not accept tents. 138 acre site. 46 touring pitches. 49 seasonal pitches. Caravan pitches. Motorhome pitches. 900 statics.

Open: mid Mar-end Oct **Last arrival:** anytime **Last departure:** 10.00hrs

Pitches:

Leisure:

Facilities:

Services:

Within 3 miles:

Notes: No tents, no commercial vehicles, no bookings by persons under 21yrs unless a family booking, no sleeping in awnings, max 2 dogs per booking, certain dog breeds banned. Dogs must be kept on leads.

AA Pubs & Restaurants nearby: Fishermans Return, WINTERTON-ON-SEA, NR29 4BN, 01493 393305

See advert on opposite page

CLIPPESBY Map 13 TG41

Places to visit

Fairhaven Woodland & Water Garden, SOUTH WALSHAM, NR13 6DZ, 01603 270449 www.fairhavengarden.co.uk

Great for kids: Caister Roman Fort, CAISTER-ON-SEA, 0370 333 1181 www.english-heritage.org.uk/daysout/properties/caister-roman-fort

PREMIER PARK

Clippesby Hall

93%

GOLD

tel: 01493 367800 **Hall Ln NR29 3BL**
email: holidays@clippesby.com **web:** www.clippesby.com
dir: *From A47 follow tourist signs for The Broads. At Acle rdbt take A1064, in 2m left onto B1152, 0.5m left opposite village sign, site 400yds on right.* **grid ref:** *TG423147*

A lovely country house estate with secluded pitches hidden among the trees or in sheltered sunny glades. The toilet facilities, appointed to a very good standard, provide a wide choice of cubicles. Amenities include a coffee shop with both WiFi and wired internet access, a family bar and restaurant and family golf. Excellent hardstanding pitches are available as the park is open all year. There are pine lodges and cottages for holiday lets. 30 acre site. 120 touring pitches. 41 hardstandings. Caravan pitches. Motorhome pitches. Tent pitches.

Open: all year (rs Nov-Mar coffee shop, bar & restaurant closed) **Last arrival:** 17.30hrs **Last departure:** 11.00hrs

Pitches: * £16.50-£40 £16.50-£40 £12.50-£40

Leisure:

Facilities:

Services:

Within 3 miles:

Notes: No groups, no noise after 23.00hrs, no camp fires. Dogs must be kept on leads. Bicycle hire, volley ball, table tennis, cycle trail.

AA Pubs & Restaurants nearby: Fishermans Return, WINTERTON-ON-SEA, NR29 4BN, 01493 393305

The Fur & Feather Inn, WOODBASTWICK, NR13 6HQ, 01603 720003

CROMER Map 13 TG24

Places to visit

RNLI Henry Blogg Museum, CROMER, NR27 9ET, 01263 511294 www.rnli.org/henryblogg

Felbrigg Hall, FELBRIGG, NR11 8PR, 01263 837444 www.nationaltrust.org.uk/main/w-felbrigghallgardenandpark

Forest Park

►►►► 81%

GOLD

tel: 01263 513290 **Northrepps Rd NR27 0JR**
email: info@forest-park.co.uk
dir: *A140 from Norwich, left at T-junct signed Cromer, right signed Northrepps, right then immediately left, left at T-junct, site on right.* **grid ref:** *TG233405*

Surrounded by forest, this gently sloping park offers a wide choice of pitches. Visitors have the use of a heated indoor swimming pool, and a large clubhouse with entertainment. 100 acre site. 262 touring pitches. Caravan pitches. Motorhome pitches. Tent pitches. 420 statics.

Open: 15 Mar-15 Jan **Last arrival:** 21.00hrs **Last departure:** 11.00hrs

Pitches:

Leisure:

Facilities:

Services:

Within 3 miles:

AA Pubs & Restaurants nearby: The Red Lion Food and Rooms, CROMER, NR27 9HD, 01263 514964

The White Horse Overstrand, CROMER, NR27 0AB, 01263 579237

Sea Marge Hotel, CROMER, NR27 0AB, 01263 579579

Manor Farm Caravan & Camping Site

►►►► 81%

tel: 01263 512858 **East Runton NR27 9PR**
email: stay@manorfarmcampsite.co.uk
dir: *1m W of Cromer, exit A148 or A149 (recommended towing route) at Manor Farm sign.*
grid ref: *TG198416*

A well-established family-run site on a working farm enjoying panoramic sea views. There are good modern facilities across the site, including three smart toilet blocks that include two quality family rooms and privacy cubicles, two good play areas and a large expanse of grass for games – the park is very popular with families. Care must be taken on approaching the site via the 0.5 mile farm track. 17 acre site. 250 touring pitches. Caravan pitches. Motorhome pitches. Tent pitches.

Open: Etr-Sep **Last arrival:** 20.30hrs **Last departure:** noon

Pitches: * £14.50-£23.50 £14.50-£23.50 £14.50-£23.50

Leisure:

Facilities:

Services:

Within 3 miles:

Notes: No groups, no noise after 23.00hrs. Dogs must be kept on leads. 2 dog-free fields available.

AA Pubs & Restaurants nearby: The Red Lion Food and Rooms, CROMER, NR27 9HD, 01263 514964

The White Horse Overstrand, CROMER, NR27 0AB, 01263 579237

Sea Marge Hotel, CROMER, NR27 0AB, 01263 579579

DOWNHAM MARKET Map 12 TF60

Lakeside Caravan Park & Fisheries

►►► 87%

tel: 01366 387074 & 07790 272978 **Sluice Rd, Denver PE38 0DZ**
email: richesflorido@aol.com **web:** www.westhallfarmholidays.co.uk
dir: *Exit A10 towards Denver, follow signs to Denver Windmill, site on right.*
grid ref: *TF608013*

A peaceful, rapidly improving park set around five pretty fishing lakes. There are several grassy touring areas which are sheltered by mature hedging and trees, a function room for social get togethers, shop, laundry and children's play area. Electric hook-up pitches are available. Rallies are welcome. 30 acre site. 100 touring pitches. Caravan pitches. Motorhome pitches. Tent pitches. 1 static.

Open: all year (rs Oct-Mar) **Last arrival:** 21.00hrs **Last departure:** 10.30hrs

Pitches:

Leisure:

Facilities:

Services:

Within 3 miles:

Notes: Dogs must be kept on leads. Pool table, fishing tackle & bait, caravan accessories, caravan storage.

AA Pubs & Restaurants nearby: The Hare Arms, STOW BARDOLPH, PE34 3HT, 01366 382229

FAKENHAM Map 13 TF92

Places to visit

Houghton Hall, HOUGHTON, PE31 6UE, 01485 528569 www.houghtonhall.com

Great for kids: Pensthorpe Nature Reserve & Gardens, FAKENHAM, NR21 0LN, 01328 851465 www.pensthorpe.co.uk

Fakenham Fairways Campsite

►►► 86%

tel: 01328 856614 **Burnham Market Rd, Sculthorpe NR21 9SA**
email: hello@fakenhamfairways.uk
dir: *From Fakenham take A148 towards King's Lynn then right onto B1355 towards Burnham Market. Site on right in 400yds.* **grid ref:** *TF907310*

Enthusiastic owners run this peaceful site that is surrounded by tranquil countryside and which is part of a 9-hole, par 3 golf complex and driving range. The toilet facilities are of good quality, and there is a golf shop and licensed bar. Please note there is no laundry. 4 acre site. 50 touring pitches. 13 hardstandings. Caravan pitches. Motorhome pitches. Tent pitches.

Open: all year **Last arrival:** 20.00hrs **Last departure:** noon

Pitches: * £12.50-£19 £12.50-£19 £12.50-£19

Leisure:

Facilities:

Services:

Within 3 miles:

Notes: No noise after 22.30hrs. Dogs must be kept on leads.

AA Pubs & Restaurants nearby: The Blue Boar Inn, GREAT RYBURGH, NR21 0DX, 01328 829212

The Wensum Lodge Hotel, FAKENHAM, NR21 9AY, 01328 862100

Caravan Club M.V.C. Site

►►► 83%

tel: 01328 862388 **Fakenham Racecourse NR21 7NY**
email: caravan@fakenhamracecourse.co.uk
dir: *From B1146, S of Fakenham follow brown Racecourse signs (with tent & caravan symbols) leads to site entrance.* **grid ref:** *TF926288*

A very well laid-out site set around the racecourse, with a grandstand offering smart, modern toilet facilities. Tourers move to the centre of the course on race days, and enjoy free racing, and there's a wide range of sporting activities in the club house. 11.4 acre site. 120 touring pitches. 25 hardstandings. 22 seasonal pitches. Caravan pitches. Motorhome pitches. Tent pitches.

Open: all year **Last arrival:** 21.00hrs **Last departure:** noon

Pitches:

Leisure:

Facilities:

Services:

Within 3 miles:

Notes: Max 2 dogs per unit. Dogs must be kept on leads. TV aerial hook-ups.

AA Pubs & Restaurants nearby: The Blue Boar Inn, GREAT RYBURGH, NR21 0DX, 01328 829212

The Wensum Lodge Hotel, FAKENHAM, NR21 9AY, 01328 862100

Crossways Caravan & Camping Park

►► 72%

tel: 01328 878335 **Crossways, Holt Rd, Little Snoring NR21 0AX**
email: joyholland@live.co.uk
dir: *From Fakenham take A148 towards Cromer. After 3m pass exit for Little Snoring. Site on A148 on left behind post office.* **grid ref:** *TF961321*

Set on the edge of the peaceful hamlet of Little Snoring, this level site enjoys views across the fields towards the north Norfolk coast some seven miles away. Visitors can use the health suite for a small charge, and there is a shop on site, and a village pub nearby. 2 acre site. 26 touring pitches. 10 hardstandings. 14 seasonal pitches. Caravan pitches. Motorhome pitches. Tent pitches. 1 static.

Open: all year **Last arrival:** 22.00hrs **Last departure:** noon

Pitches:

Leisure:

Facilities:

Services:

Within 3 miles:

Notes: Dogs must be kept on leads.

AA Pubs & Restaurants nearby: The Blue Boar Inn, GREAT RYBURGH, NR21 0DX, 01328 829212

The Wensum Lodge Hotel, FAKENHAM, NR21 9AY, 01328 862100

GREAT YARMOUTH Map 13 TG50

Places to visit

Yesterday's World Great Yarmouth, GREAT YARMOUTH, NR30 2EN, 01493 331148 www.yesterdaysworld.co.uk

Great for kids: Time and Tide Museum of Great Yarmouth Life, GREAT YARMOUTH, NR30 3BX, 01493 743930 www.museums.norfolk.gov.uk

Vauxhall Holiday Park

HOLIDAY CENTRE 89%

GOLD

tel: 01493 857231 **Acle New Rd NR30 1TB**
email: info@vauxhallholidays.co.uk **web:** www.vauxhallholidaypark.co.uk
dir: *On A47 approaching Great Yarmouth.* **grid ref:** *TG520083*

A very large holiday complex with plenty of entertainment and access to beach, river, estuary, lake and the A47. The touring pitches are laid out in four separate areas, each with its own amenity block, and all arranged around the main entertainment. 40 acre site. 220 touring pitches. Caravan pitches. Motorhome pitches. Tent pitches. 421 statics. 5 wooden pods.

Open: Etr, mid May-Sep & Oct half term **Last arrival:** 21.00hrs **Last departure:** 10.00hrs

Pitches: **Leisure:**

Facilities: **Services:**

Within 3 miles:

Notes: No pets. Children's pool, sauna, solarium.

AA Pubs & Restaurants nearby: Andover House, GREAT YARMOUTH, NR30 3JB, 01493 843490

See advert on opposite page

The Grange Touring Park

►►►► 81%

tel: 01493 730306 & 730023 **Yarmouth Rd, Ormesby St Margaret NR29 3QG**
email: info@grangetouring.co.uk
dir: *From A149, 3m N of Great Yarmouth. Site at junct of A149 & B1159, signed.*
grid ref: *TG510142*

A mature, ever improving park with plenty of trees, located just one mile from the sea, within easy reach of both coastal attractions and the Norfolk Broads. The level pitches have electric hook-ups and include 13 hardstanding pitches, and there are clean, modern toilets including three spacious family rooms. All pitches have WiFi. 3.5 acre site. 70 touring pitches. 7 hardstandings. Caravan pitches. Motorhome pitches. Tent pitches.

Open: Etr-Oct **Last arrival:** 21.00hrs **Last departure:** 14.00hrs

Pitches: * fr £13.50 fr £13.50 fr £12.50

Leisure:

Facilities:

Services:

Within 3 miles:

Notes: No football, no open fires. Dogs must be kept on leads.

AA Pubs & Restaurants nearby: Andover House, GREAT YARMOUTH, NR30 3JB, 01493 843490

Seashore Holiday Park

HOLIDAY HOME PARK 87%

tel: 01493 851131 **North Denes NR30 4HG**
email: seashore@haven.com **web:** www.haven.com/seashore
dir: *A149 from Great Yarmouth to Caister. Right at 2nd lights signed seafront & racecourse. Continue to sea, turn left. Park on left.* **grid ref:** *TG653103*

Bordered by sand dunes and with direct access to a sandy beach, Seashore Holiday Park is located in Great Yarmouth yet is close enough for day trips to the peaceful Norfolk Broads. Facilities include excellent water activities and bike hire for children and lively evening entertainment for adults. There is a good range of holiday caravans and apartments.

Open: Mar-Oct

Change over day: Mon, Fri, Sat

Arrival and departure times: Please contact the site

Statics: 285 Sleeps 6-8 Bedrms 2-3 Bathrms 1-2 Toilets 1-2 Microwave Freezer TV Sky/FTV Elec inc Gas inc

Children: Cots Highchair **Dogs:** 2 on leads No dangerous dogs

Leisure: Cycle hire

HOPTON ON SEA — Map 13 TM59

Places to visit

St Olave's Priory, ST OLAVES, 0370 333 1181
www.english-heritage.org.uk/daysout/properties/st-olaves-priory

Hopton Holiday Park

HOLIDAY HOME PARK 92%

tel: 01502 730214 **NR31 9BW**
email: hopton@haven.com **web:** www.haven.com/hopton
dir: *Site signed from A12 between Great Yarmouth & Lowestoft.* **grid ref:** *TG531002*

Located between Lowestoft and Great Yarmouth, close to beaches and the town attractions, this lively holiday park offers excellent sport activities, including golf on the 9-hole course and tennis coaching, plus popular evening entertainment in the form of shows, music and dancing. There is a good range of holiday caravans and apartments.

Open: Mar-Oct

Change over day: Mon, Fri, Sat

Arrival and departure times: Please contact the site

Statics: 216 Sleeps 6-8 Bedrms 2-3 Bathrms 1-2 Toilets 1-2 Microwave Freezer TV Sky/FTV Elec inc Gas inc Grass area

Children: Cots Highchair **Dogs:** 2 on leads No dangerous dogs

Leisure: Cycle hire

HUNSTANTON

Places to visit

Lynn Museum, KING'S LYNN, PE30 1NL, 01553 775001
www.museums.norfolk.gov.uk

Norfolk Lavender, HEACHAM, PE31 7JE, 01485 570384
www.norfolk-lavender.co.uk

Great for kids: Hunstanton Sea Life Sanctuary, HUNSTANTON, PE36 5BH, 01485 533576 www.sealife.co.uk

HUNSTANTON — Map 12 TF64

Searles Leisure Resort

HOLIDAY CENTRE 90%

tel: 01485 534211 **South Beach Rd PE36 5BB**
email: bookings@searles.co.uk
dir: *A149 from King's Lynn to Hunstanton. At rdbt follow signs for South Beach. Straight on at 2nd rdbt. Site on left.* **grid ref:** *TF671400*

A large seaside holiday complex with well managed facilities, adjacent to sea and beach. The tourers have their own areas, including two excellent toilet blocks, and pitches are individually marked by small maturing shrubs for privacy. The bars and entertainment, restaurant, bistro and takeaway, heated indoor and outdoor pools, golf, fishing and bowling green make this park popular throughout the year. 50 acre site. 255 touring pitches. 91 hardstandings. Caravan pitches. Motorhome pitches. Tent pitches. 158 statics.

Open: all year (rs Dec-Mar (ex Feb half term) limited facilities & use of indoor pool & country park only)

Pitches: * £12-£61 £12-£61 £12-£60

Leisure:

Facilities:

Services:

Within 3 miles:

Notes: Restrictions on certain dog breeds (contact site for details). Dogs must be kept on leads.

AA Pubs & Restaurants nearby: The King William IV Country Inn & Restaurant, HUNSTANTON, PE36 5LU, 01485 571765

The Neptune Restaurant with Rooms, HUNSTANTON, PE36 6HZ, 01485 532122

Marco Pierre White The Lifeboat Inn, THORNHAM, PE36 6LT, 01485 512236

HUNSTANTON *continued*

Manor Park Holiday Village

HOLIDAY CENTRE 80%

SILVER

tel: 01485 532300 **Manor Rd PE36 5AZ**
email: manor.park@park-resorts.com
dir: *Take A149 (King's Lynn Rd) to Hunstanton, left onto B1161 (Oasis Way).*
grid ref: *TF671399*

Situated just a few yards from the beach on the outskirts of the lively resort of Hunstanton, Manor Farm offers a range of leisure activities, including two heated outdoor swimming pools, children's playground, children's club, amusement arcade, restaurant, bar and cabaret. There are 64 electric, all-grass pitches set out in the heart of the park and adjacent to the leisure complex. Expect high standards of customer care. 64 touring pitches. 10 seasonal pitches. Caravan pitches. Motorhome pitches. 650 statics.

Open: Apr-Oct **Last arrival:** noon **Last departure:** 10.00hrs

Pitches:

Leisure:

Facilities:

Services:

Within 3 miles:

Notes: Dogs must be kept on leads. Bike hire.

AA Pubs & Restaurants nearby: The King William IV Country Inn & Restaurant, HUNSTANTON, PE36 5LU, 01485 571765

The Neptune Restaurant with Rooms, HUNSTANTON, PE36 6HZ, 01485 532122

KING'S LYNN — Map 12 TF62

See also Stanhoe

Places to visit

Bircham Windmill, GREAT BIRCHAM, PE31 6SJ, 01485 578393
www.birchamwindmill.co.uk

Castle Rising Castle, CASTLE RISING, PE31 6AH, 01553 631330
www.english-heritage.org.uk/daysout/properties/castle-rising-castle

PREMIER PARK

King's Lynn Caravan and Camping Park

►►►►► 84%

tel: 01553 840004 **New Rd, North Runcton PE33 0RA**
email: klcc@btconnect.com
dir: *From King's Lynn take A47 signed Swaffham & Norwich, in 1.5m turn right signed North Runcton. Site 100yds on left.* **grid ref:** *TF645160*

Set in approximately 10 acres of parkland, this developing camping park is situated on the edge of North Runcton, just a few miles south of the historic town of King's Lynn. The three very extensive touring fields are equipped with 150 electric hook-ups and one field is reserved for rallies. There is an eco-friendly toilet block which is powered by solar panels and an air-sourced heat pump which also recycles rainwater – this in itself proves a source of great interest to visitors. There are eight high quality camping pods and four new pine lodges for hire. 9 acre site. 150 touring pitches. 2 hardstandings. 54 seasonal pitches. Caravan pitches. Motorhome pitches. Tent pitches. 4 statics. 8 wooden pods.

Open: all year **Last arrival:** flexible **Last departure:** flexible

Pitches: * £15-£20 £15-£20 £12-£18

Facilities:

Services:

Within 3 miles:

Notes: No skateboards or fires. Dogs must be kept on leads.

AA Pubs & Restaurants nearby: The Stuart House Hotel, Bar & Restaurant, KING'S LYNN, PE30 5QX, 01553 772169

Bank House, KING'S LYNN, PE30 1RD, 01553 660492

NORTH WALSHAM — Map 13 TG23

Places to visit

Blickling Estate, BLICKLING, NR11 6NF, 01263 738030
www.nationaltrust.org.uk/blickling

Wolterton Park, ERPINGHAM, NR11 7LY, 01263 584175
www.manningtongardens.co.uk

PREMIER PARK

Two Mills Touring Park

►►►►► 85%

Best of British

tel: 01692 405829 **Yarmouth Rd NR28 9NA**
email: enquiries@twomills.co.uk
dir: *1m S of North Walsham on Old Yarmouth road past police station & hospital on left.* **grid ref:** *TG291286*

An intimate, beautifully presented park set in superb countryside in a peaceful, rural spot, which is also convenient for touring. The 'Top Acre' section is maturing and features fully serviced pitches, offering panoramic views over the site, an immaculate toilet block and good planting, plus the layout of pitches and facilities is excellent. The very friendly and helpful owners keep the park in immaculate condition. Please note this park is for adults only. 7 acre site. 81 touring pitches. 81 hardstandings. Caravan pitches. Motorhome pitches. Tent pitches.

Open: Mar-3 Jan **Last arrival:** 20.30hrs **Last departure:** noon

Pitches:

Leisure:

Facilities:

Services:

Within 3 miles:

Notes: Adults only. Max 2 dogs per pitch. Dogs must be kept on leads. Library.

AA Pubs & Restaurants nearby: The Butchers Arms, EAST RUSTON, NR12 9JG, 01692 650237

Beechwood Hotel, NORTH WALSHAM, NR28 0HD, 01692 403231

SCRATBY — Map 13 TG51

Places to visit

Time and Tide Museum of Great Yarmouth Life, GREAT YARMOUTH, NR30 3BX, 01493 743930 www.museums.norfolk.gov.uk

Great for kids: Caister Roman Fort, CAISTER-ON-SEA, 0370 333 1181 www.english-heritage.org.uk/daysout/properties/caister-roman-fort

Scratby Hall Caravan Park

►►► 86%

tel: 01493 730283 **NR29 3SR**
email: scratbyhall@aol.com **web:** www.scratbyhall.co.uk
dir: *5m N of Great Yarmouth. Exit A149 onto B1159, site signed.* **grid ref:** *TG501155*

A neatly-maintained site with a popular children's play area, well-equipped shop and outdoor swimming pool with sun terrace. The toilets are kept very clean. The beach and the Norfolk Broads are close by. 5 acre site. 85 touring pitches. Caravan pitches. Motorhome pitches. Tent pitches.

Open: Etr-end Sep (rs Etr-mid Jul & Sep pool closed) **Last arrival:** 21.00hrs **Last departure:** noon

Pitches:

Leisure:

Facilities:

Services:

Within 3 miles:

Notes: No commercial vehicles. Dogs must be kept on leads. Food preparation room.

AA Pubs & Restaurants nearby: Fishermans Return, WINTERTON-ON-SEA, NR29 4BN, 01493 393305

STANHOE — Map 13 TF83

Places to visit

Norfolk Lavender, HEACHAM, PE31 7JE, 01485 570384 www.norfolk-lavender.co.uk

Walsingham Abbey Grounds & Shirehall Museum, LITTLE WALSINGHAM, NR22 6BP, 01328 820510 www.walsinghamabbey.com

The Rickels Caravan & Camping Park

►►► 85%

tel: 01485 518671 **Bircham Rd PE31 8PU**
email: therickelscaravanandcampingpark@hotmail.co.uk
dir: *A148 from King's Lynn to Hillington. B1153 to Great Bircham. B1155 to x-rds, straight over, site on left.* **grid ref:** *TF794355*

Set in three acres of grassland, with sweeping country views and a pleasant, relaxing atmosphere fostered by being for adults only. The meticulously maintained grounds and facilities are part of the attraction, and the slightly sloping land has some level areas and sheltering for tents. A field is available to hire for rallies. 3 acre site. 30 touring pitches. Caravan pitches. Motorhome pitches. Tent pitches.

Open: all year **Last arrival:** 21.00hrs **Last departure:** 11.00hrs

Pitches: * £14-£16 £14-£16 £11-£13

Leisure:

Facilities:

Services:

Within 3 miles:

Notes: Adults only. No groundsheets. Dogs must be kept on leads.

AA Pubs & Restaurants nearby: The Lord Nelson, BURNHAM THORPE, PE31 8HN, 01328 738241

The Hoste, BURNHAM MARKET, PE31 8HD, 01328 738777

SWAFFHAM Map 13 TF80

Places to visit

Gressenhall Farm and Workhouse, GRESSENHALL, NR20 4DR, 01362 860563 www.museums.norfolk.gov.uk

Castle Acre Priory and Castle, CASTLE ACRE, PE32 2XD, 01760 755394 www.english-heritage.org.uk/daysout/properties/castle-acre-castle-acre-priory

Breckland Meadows Touring Park

►►►► 80%

tel: 01760 721246 **Lynn Rd PE37 7PT**
email: info@brecklandmeadows.co.uk
dir: *1m W of Swaffham on old A47.* **grid ref:** *TF809094*

An immaculate, well-landscaped little park on the edge of Swaffham. The toilet block is a very impressive facility, replete with quality fixtures and fittings, spacious cubicles, including a family/disabled room, a large, well-equipped laundry, and a high tech, and very efficient, hot water system. There are hardstandings with electricity, and the plentiful planting makes attractive screening. 3 acre site. 45 touring pitches. 35 hardstandings. 5 seasonal pitches. Caravan pitches. Motorhome pitches. Tent pitches.

Open: all year **Last arrival:** 21.00hrs **Last departure:** noon

Pitches: * £13.50-£15 £13.50-£15 £8-£11.50

Facilities:

Services: **Within 3 miles:**

Notes: Adults only. Dogs must be kept on leads. Newspaper deliveries.

SYDERSTONE Map 13 TF83

Places to visit

Creake Abbey, NORTH CREAKE, NR21 9LF, 0370 333 1181 www.english-heritage.org.uk/daysout/properties/creake-abbey

The Garden Caravan Site

►►► 78%

tel: 01485 578220 & 578178 **Barmer Hall Farm PE31 8SR**
email: nigel@gardencaravansite.co.uk
dir: *Signed from B1454 at Barmer between A148 & Docking, 1m W of Syderstone.*
grid ref: *TF812337*

In the tranquil setting of a former walled garden beside a large farmhouse, with mature trees and shrubs, a secluded site surrounded by woodland. The site is run mainly on trust, with a daily notice indicating which pitches are available, and an honesty box for basic foods. An ideal site for the discerning camper, and well placed for touring north Norfolk. 3.5 acre site. 30 touring pitches. Caravan pitches. Motorhome pitches. Tent pitches.

Open: Mar-Nov **Last arrival:** 21.00hrs **Last departure:** noon

Pitches: * £19-£21 £19-£21 £19-£21 **Facilities:**

Services: **Within 3 miles:**

Notes: Max 2 dogs per pitch, max tent width 5mtrs. Dogs must be kept on leads. Cold drinks, ice creams & eggs available.

AA Pubs & Restaurants nearby: The Lord Nelson, BURNHAM THORPE, PE31 8HN, 01328 738241

The Hoste, BURNHAM MARKET, PE31 8HD, 01328 738777

THREE HOLES Map 12 TF50

Places to visit

Oxburgh Hall, OXBOROUGH, PE33 9PS, 01366 328258 www.nationaltrust.org.uk/oxburgh-hall

Lode Hall Holiday Park

►►► 77%

tel: 01354 638133 **Lode Hall, Silt Rd PE14 9JW**
email: dick@lode-hall.co.uk
dir: *From Wisbech take A1101 towards Downham Market. At Outwell continue on A1101 signed Littleport. Site signed from Three Holes. Right onto B1094 to site.*
grid ref: *TF529989*

Peace and tranquillity is assured at this deeply rural park in the grounds of Lode Hall. The toilet facilities are located in an imaginative restoration of a former cricket pavilion and include combined toilet/wash basin cubicles and unisex showers. Please note that this is an adults-only site. 5 acre site. 20 touring pitches. 8 hardstandings. Caravan pitches. Motorhome pitches. Tent pitches.

Open: Apr-Oct **Pitches:**

Facilities: **Services:**

Within 3 miles: **Notes:** Adults only.

AA Pubs & Restaurants nearby: The Hare Arms, STOW BARDOLPH, PE34 3HT, 01366 382229

WORTWELL Map 13 TM28

Places to visit

Bressingham Steam Museum & Gardens, BRESSINGHAM, IP22 2AB, 01379 686900 www.bressingham.co.uk

Little Lakeland Caravan Park

►►►► 84%

tel: 01986 788646 **IP20 0EL**
email: information@littlelakeland.co.uk
dir: *From W: exit A143 at sign for Wortwell. In village turn right 300yds past garage. From E: on A143, left onto B1062, then right. After 800yds turn left.* **grid ref:** *TM279849*

A well-kept and pretty site built round a fishing lake, and accessed by a lake-lined drive. The individual pitches are sited in hedged enclosures for complete privacy, and the purpose-built toilet facilities are excellent. 4.5 acre site. 38 touring pitches. 6 hardstandings. 17 seasonal pitches. Caravan pitches. Motorhome pitches. Tent pitches. 21 statics.

Open: 15 Mar-Oct **Last arrival:** 22.00hrs **Last departure:** noon

Pitches: * £15.50-£22.50 **Leisure:**

Facilities:

Services: **Within 3 miles:**

Notes: No noise after 22.30hrs. Dogs must be kept on leads. Library.

AA Pubs & Restaurants nearby: Fox & Goose Inn, FRESSINGFIELD, IP21 5PB, 01379 586247

NORTHAMPTONSHIRE

BULWICK Map 11 SP99

Places to visit

Lyveden New Bield, LYVEDEN NEW BIELD, PE8 5AT, 01832 205358
www.nationaltrust.org.uk

New Lodge Farm Caravan & Camping Site

►►►► 85%

tel: 01780 450493 **New Lodge Farm NN17 3DU**
email: shop@newlodgefarm.com
dir: *On A43 between Corby (5m) & Stamford (10m) turn right at Laxton & Harringworth junct. Site signed.* **grid ref:** *SP959951*

Simon and Sarah Singlehurst have worked hard to create this beautiful adults-only site on their working farm in rural Northamptonshire. The result is impressive – large, fully serviced and level pitches (25 with hardstandings), all with views over the farm and rolling countryside. The heated toilet and amenity block is located in a beautifully restored stone barn, as is the site reception. There's an award-winning farm shop that sells home-reared meats, bread, cakes and locally grown fruit and vegetables. Attached to the shop is a cosy licensed café with a patio area overlooking the site – here breakfasts, lunches and afternoon teas are served. The site is situated in the heart of Rockingham Forest, making it a good base for visiting Stamford, Oundle and Uppingham. 4 acre site. 72 touring pitches. 25 hardstandings. Caravan pitches. Motorhome pitches. Tent pitches.

Open: 3 Apr-Oct **Last arrival:** 20.00hrs **Last departure:** noon

Pitches: * £21.50-£25 £21.50-£25 £17.50

Facilities:

Services:

Within 3 miles:

Notes: Adults only. No noise after 23.00hrs. Dogs must be kept on leads.

AA Pubs & Restaurants nearby: The Queen's Head, BULWICK, NN17 3DY, 01780 450272

NORTHUMBERLAND

BAMBURGH Map 21 NU13

Places to visit

Chillingham Wild Cattle Park, CHILLINGHAM, NE66 5NP, 01668 215250
www.chillinghamwildcattle.com

Great for kids: Bamburgh Castle, BAMBURGH, NE69 7DF, 01668 214515
www.bamburghcastle.com

Waren Caravan & Camping Park

►►►► 84%

tel: 01668 214366 **Waren Mill NE70 7EE**
email: waren@meadowhead.co.uk
dir: *2m E of town. From A1 onto B1342 signed Bamburgh. Take unclassified road past Waren Mill, signed Budle.* **grid ref:** *NU155343*

An attractive seaside site with footpath access to the beach, surrounded by a slightly sloping grassy embankment giving shelter to caravans. The park offers excellent facilities, including smartened up toilet/shower blocks, which have several family bathrooms, fully serviced pitches, and the on-site restaurant serves a good breakfast. There are also wooden wigwam pods for hire. 4 acre site. 150 touring pitches. 41 hardstandings. Caravan pitches. Motorhome pitches. Tent pitches. 300 statics. 8 wooden pods.

Open: Mar-Oct (rs Mar-Apr & Oct splash pool closed) **Last arrival:** 20.00hrs **Last departure:** noon

Pitches: * £12-£27 £12-£27 £12-£19

Leisure:

Facilities:

Services:

Within 3 miles:

Notes: No noise after 23.00hrs. Dogs must be kept on leads. 100 acres of private heathland, fire pits for hire, BBQ hut for hire.

AA Pubs & Restaurants nearby: The Olde Ship Inn, SEAHOUSES, NE68 7RD, 01665 720200

Blue Bell Hotel, BELFORD, NE70 7NE, 01668 213543

Waren House Hotel, BAMBURGH, NE70 7EE, 01668 214581

PITCHES: Caravans Motorhomes Tents Glamping-style accommodation **SERVICES:** Electric hook up Launderette Licensed bar Calor Gas Camping Gaz Toilet fluid Café/Restaurant Fast Food/Takeaway Battery charging Baby care Motorvan service point
ABBREVIATIONS: BH/bank hols – bank holidays Etr – Easter Spring BH – Spring Bank Holiday fr – from hrs – hours m – mile mdnt – midnight rdbt – roundabout rs – restricted service wk – week wknd – weekend x-rds – cross roads No credit or debit cards No dogs Children of all ages accepted

BAMBURGH *continued*

Glororum Caravan Park

►►►► 81%

tel: 01670 860256 **Glororum Farm NE69 7AW**
email: enquiries@northumbrianleisure.co.uk
dir: *Exit A1 at junct with B1341 (Purdy's Lodge). In 3.5m left onto unclassified road. Site 300yds on left.* **grid ref:** *NU166334*

A pleasantly situated site in an open countryside setting with good views of Bamburgh Castle. A popular holiday destination where tourers have their own separate area – 43 excellent, well-spaced, fully serviced pitches have a lush grass area in addition to the hardstanding. This field also has an excellent purpose-built amenities block with a smartly clad interior and modern, efficient fittings. 6 acre site. 43 touring pitches. 43 hardstandings. 30 seasonal pitches. Caravan pitches. Motorhome pitches. 170 statics.

Open: Mar-end Nov **Last arrival:** 18.00hrs **Last departure:** noon

Pitches: * fr £25 fr £25

Leisure:

Facilities:

Services:

Within 3 miles:

Notes: No commercial vehicles, no noise after 23.00hrs. Dogs must be kept on leads.

AA Pubs & Restaurants nearby: The Olde Ship Inn, SEAHOUSES, NE68 7RD, 01665 720200

The Bamburgh Castle Inn, SEAHOUSES, NE68 7SQ, 01665 720283

Blue Bell Hotel, BELFORD, NE70 7NE, 01668 213543

BELFORD

Map 21 NU13

Places to visit

Bamburgh Castle, BAMBURGH, NE69 7DF, 01668 214515
www.bamburghcastle.com

Lindisfarne Castle, HOLY ISLAND (LINDISFARNE), TD15 2SH, 01289 389244
www.nationaltrust.org.uk

PREMIER PARK

South Meadows Caravan Park

►►►►► 92%

tel: 01668 213326 **South Rd NE70 7DP**
email: info@southmeadows.co.uk
dir: *From A1 between Alnwick & Berwick-upon-Tweed take B6349 towards Belford, at right bend site signed, turn left, site on right.* **grid ref:** *NU115331*

South Meadows has become a top quality touring and holiday park. Set in open countryside, it is extremely spacious and no expense has been spared in its landscaping and redevelopment. Tree planting on a grand scale has been carried out, grassy areas are expertly mown and all pitches are fully serviced. The solar heated amenity block is ultra modern, with quality fittings and smart family rooms; everywhere is spotlessly clean and fresh. There's an adventure playground complete with a zip-wire and even dogs have two walking areas, one in a bluebell wood. 50 acre site. 120 touring pitches. 71 hardstandings. 67 seasonal pitches. Caravan pitches. Motorhome pitches. Tent pitches. 55 statics.

Open: all year **Last departure:** 16.00hrs

Pitches: * £19-£26 £19-£26 £19-£23

Leisure:

Facilities:

Services:

Within 3 miles:

Notes: Minimum noise after 23.00hrs, under 12s must be supervised in toilet blocks. Dogs must be kept on leads.

AA Pubs & Restaurants nearby: Blue Bell Hotel, BELFORD, NE70 7NE, 01668 213543

BELLINGHAM — Map 21 NY88

Places to visit

Wallington, CAMBO, NE61 4AR, 01670 773600
www.nationaltrust.org.uk/wallington

PREMIER PARK

Bellingham Camping & Caravanning Club Site

►►►►► 87%

tel: 01434 220175 & 0845 130 7633 *(Calls cost 7p per minute plus your phone company's access charge)* **Brown Rigg NE48 2JY**
dir: *From A69 take A6079 N to Chollerford & B6320 to Bellingham. Pass Forestry Commission land, site 0.5m S of Bellingham.* **grid ref:** *NY835826*

A beautiful and peaceful campsite set in the glorious Northumberland National Park. It is exceptionally well managed by the enthusiastic owners who offer high levels of customer care, maintenance and cleanliness. The excellent toilet facilities are spotlessly clean, and there are family washrooms, a recreation room, a campers' kitchen and a drying room. There are four camping pods for hire. This is a perfect base for exploring an undiscovered part of England, and it is handily placed for visiting the beautiful Northumberland coast. 5 acre site. 64 touring pitches. 42 hardstandings. Caravan pitches. Motorhome pitches. Tent pitches. 4 wooden pods.

Open: Mar-4 Jan **Last arrival:** 20.00hrs **Last departure:** noon

Pitches:

Leisure:

Facilities:

Services:

Within 3 miles:

Notes: Site gates closed & quiet time 23.00hrs-07.00hrs. Dogs must be kept on leads.

AA Pubs & Restaurants nearby: The Pheasant Inn, FALSTONE, NE48 1DD, 01434 240382

BERWICK-UPON-TWEED

Places to visit

Berwick-upon-Tweed Barracks, BERWICK-UPON-TWEED, TD15 1DF, 01289 304493
www.english-heritage.org.uk/daysout/properties/berwick-upon-tweed-barracks-and-main-guard

Paxton House, Gallery & Country Park, BERWICK-UPON-TWEED, TD15 1SZ, 01289 386291 www.paxtonhouse.com

Great for kids: Norham Castle, NORHAM, TD15 2JY, 01289 382329
www.english-heritage.org.uk/daysout/properties/norham-castle

BERWICK-UPON-TWEED — Map 21 NT95

Haggerston Castle Holiday Park

HOLIDAY CENTRE 80%

GOLD

tel: 0871 231 0865 *(Calls cost 10p per minute plus your phone company's access charge)* & 01289 381333 **Beal TD15 2PA**
email: haggerstoncastle@haven.com **web:** www.haven.com/haggerstoncastle
dir: *On A1, 7m S of Berwick-upon-Tweed, site signed.* **grid ref:** *NU041435*

A large holiday centre with a very well equipped touring park, offering comprehensive holiday activities. The entertainment complex contains amusements for the whole family, and there are several bars, an adventure playground, boating on the lake, a children's club, a 9-hole golf course, tennis courts, and various eating outlets. Please note that this site does not accept tents. 100 acre site. 132 touring pitches. 132 hardstandings. Caravan pitches. Motorhome pitches. 1200 statics.

Open: mid Mar-end Oct (rs mid Mar-May & Sep-Oct some facilities may be reduced) **Last arrival:** anytime **Last departure:** 10.00hrs

Pitches: **Leisure:**

Facilities:

Services: **Within 3 miles:**

Notes: No commercial vehicles, no bookings by persons under 21yrs unless a family booking, max 2 dogs per booking, certain dog breeds banned. Dogs must be kept on leads.

AA Pubs & Restaurants nearby: Blue Bell Hotel, BELFORD, NE70 7NE, 01668 213543

See advert on page 272

BERWICK-UPON-TWEED ***continued***

PREMIER PARK

Ord House Country Park

►►►►► 85%

Best of British · David Bellamy Conservation Award GOLD

tel: 01289 305288 **East Ord TD15 2NS**
email: enquiries@ordhouse.co.uk
dir: *At rdbt junct of A1 (Berwick bypass) & A698 take exit signed East Ord, follow brown camping signs.* **grid ref:** *NT982515*

A very well-run park set in the pleasant grounds of an 18th-century country house. Touring pitches are marked and well spaced – some are fully serviced. The very modern toilet facilities include family bath and shower suites, and first-class disabled rooms. There is an exceptional outdoor leisure shop that stocks a good range of camping and caravanning spares, as well as clothing and equipment, and an attractive licensed club selling bar meals. The provision for children is excellent, with a fantastic adventure playground, miniature golf, a football field and a soft play area in the clubhouse. Wooden pods (Wishbone Lodges) that sleep four are available for hire. 42 acre site. 79 touring pitches. 46 hardstandings. 30 seasonal pitches. Caravan pitches. Motorhome pitches. Tent pitches. 255 statics. 10 wooden pods.

Open: all year **Last arrival:** 23.00hrs **Last departure:** noon

Pitches:

Leisure:

Facilities:

Services:

Within 3 miles:

Notes: No noise after mdnt. Dogs must be kept on leads. Crazy golf, table tennis.

AA Pubs & Restaurants nearby: The Wheatsheaf at Swinton, SWINTON, TD11 3JJ, 01890 860257

Old Mill Caravan Site

►► 80%

tel: 01289 381279 & 07971 411625 **West Kyloe Farm, Fenwick TD15 2PG**
email: teresasmalley@westkyloe.demon.co.uk
dir: *A1 onto B6353, 9m S of Berwick-upon-Tweed. Road signed to Lowick/Fenwick. Site 1.5m signed on left.* **grid ref:** *NU055401*

Small, secluded site accessed through a farm complex, and overlooking a mill pond complete with resident ducks. Some pitches are in a walled garden, and the amenity block is simple but well kept. Delightful walks can be enjoyed on the 600-acre farm. A holiday cottage is also available. 2.5 acre site. 12 touring pitches. Caravan pitches. Motorhome pitches. Tent pitches.

Open: Apr-Oct **Last arrival:** 19.00hrs **Last departure:** 11.00hrs

Pitches: * £20 £15-£20 £15-£20

Facilities:

Services:

Within 3 miles:

Notes: No gazebos or open fires. Dogs must be kept on leads. Wet room.

AA Pubs & Restaurants nearby: Blue Bell Hotel, BELFORD, NE70 7NE, 01668 213543

Berwick Holiday Park

HOLIDAY HOME PARK 85%

David Bellamy Conservation Award GOLD

tel: 01289 307113 **Magdalene Fields TD15 1NE**
email: berwick@haven.com **web:** www.haven.com/berwick
dir: *From A1 follow Berwick-upon-Tweed signs. At Morrisons/McDonalds rdbt take 2nd exit. At mini rdbt straight on, into North Rd (pass Shell garage on left). At next mini rdbt 1st exit into Northumberland Ave. Park at end.* **grid ref:** *NT998535*

This all-happening, static-only holiday park has direct access to a beach on the edge of Berwick, and offers exciting family activities and entertainment including the FunWorks Amusement Centre and a multisports court.

Open: Mar-Oct

LEISURE: Indoor swimming pool · Outdoor swimming pool · Children's playground · Kid's club · Tennis court · Games room · Separate TV room · golf course · Boats for hire · Cinema · Entertainment · Fishing · Mini golf · Watersports · Gym · Sports field · Spa · Stables
FACILITIES: Bath · Shower · Electric shaver · Hairdryer · Ice Pack Facility · Disabled facilities · Public telephone · Shop on site or within 200yds · Mobile shop (calls at least 5 days a week) · BBQ area · Picnic area · Wi-fi · Internet access · Recycling · Tourist info · Dog exercise area

Change over day: Mon, Fri, Sat

Arrival and departure times: Please contact the site

Statics: 204 Sleeps 6-8 Bedrms 2-3 Bathrms 1-2 Toilets 1-2 Microwave Freezer TV Sky/FTV Elec inc Gas inc Grass area

Children: Cots Highchair **Dogs:** 2 on leads No dangerous dogs

Leisure: Cycle hire

HALTWHISTLE — Map 21 NY76

Places to visit

Corbridge Roman Site and Museum, CORBRIDGE, NE45 5NT, 01434 632349 www.english-heritage.org.uk/daysout/properties/corbridge-roman-town-hadrians-wall

Chesters Roman Fort, WALWICK, NE46 4EP, 01434 681379 www.english-heritage.org.uk/daysout/properties/chesters-roman-fort-and-museum-hadrians-wall

PREMIER PARK

Herding Hill Farm

►►►►► 87%

tel: 01434 320175 **Shield Hill NE49 9NW**
email: bookings@herdinghillfarm.co.uk
dir: *From W: exit A69 at Greenhead onto B6318 towards Chollerford. Follow brown campsite signs. From E: exit A69 at Corbridge onto A68 N, left onto B6318 towards Greenhead. Approx 12m, follow campsite signs.* **grid ref:** *NY712649*

In an idyllic moorland location above Haltwhistle, close to Hadrian's Wall, this beautifully developed working farm site is geared to families and offers a mix of accommodation – excellent tent pitches, quality hardstandings, a bunkhouse sleeping 28, a 6-berth lodge, and a community of tipis and wooden wigwams (eight with hot tubs). The upmarket amenity block is really ultra-modern – the internal red and grey partitioning really sets off the very high standard of fixtures and fittings, and the underfloor heating is very welcoming. A drying room, barbecues and firebaskets, a playground and petting farm, an excellent shop and café, and activities such as star-gazing, geo-caching, and walking along Hadrian's Wall complete the package. This is a top-class site developed over the last few years by the hands-on owners. 4.86 acre site. 44 touring pitches. 11 hardstandings. Caravan pitches. Motorhome pitches. Tent pitches. 4 tipis. 8 wooden pods.

Open: Feb-3 Jan **Last arrival:** 21.00hrs **Last departure:** 11.00hrs

Pitches:

Leisure:

Facilities: WiFi

Services: T

Notes: No noise after 23.00hrs. Dogs must be kept on leads. Unisex sauna.

HEXHAM — Map 21 NY96

Places to visit

Vindolanda (Chesterholm), BARDON MILL, NE47 7JN, 01434 344277 www.vindolanda.com

Temple of Mithras (Hadrian's Wall), CARRAWBROUGH, 0370 333 1181 www.english-heritage.org.uk/daysout/properties/temple-of-mithras-carrawburgh-hadrians-wall

Great for kids: Housesteads Roman Fort, HOUSESTEADS, NE47 6NN, 01434 344363 www.english-heritage.org.uk/daysout/properties/housesteads-roman-fort-hadrians-wall

Hexham Racecourse Caravan Site

►►► 72%

tel: 01434 606847 & 606881 **Hexham Racecourse NE46 2JP**
email: hexrace.caravan@btconnect.com
dir: *From Hexham take B6305 signed Allendale/Alston. Left in 3m signed to racecourse. Site 1.5m on right.* **grid ref:** *NY919623*

A part-level and part-sloping grassy site situated on a racecourse overlooking Hexhamshire Moors. The facilities, although clean, are of an older but functional type. 4 acre site. 50 touring pitches. Caravan pitches. Motorhome pitches. Tent pitches.

Open: May-Sep **Last arrival:** 20.00hrs **Last departure:** noon

Pitches: * £14-£17 £14-£17 fr £10

Leisure:

Facilities:

Services:

Within 3 miles:

Notes: No noise after 23.00hrs. Dogs must be kept on leads.

AA Pubs & Restaurants nearby: Miners Arms Inn, HEXHAM, NE46 4PW, 01434 603909

Dipton Mill Inn, HEXHAM, NE46 1YA, 01434 606577

Rat Inn, HEXHAM, NE46 4LN, 01434 602814

BLETCHINGDON *continued*

Diamond Farm Caravan & Camping Park

►►►► 84%

tel: 01869 350909 **Islip Rd OX5 3DR**
email: warden@diamondpark.co.uk
dir: *M40 junct 9, A34 S for 3m, B4027 to Bletchingdon. Site 1m on left.*
grid ref: *SP513170*

A well-run, quiet rural site in good level surroundings, and ideal for touring the Cotswolds, situated seven miles north of Oxford in the heart of the Thames Valley. This popular park has excellent facilities, and offers a heated outdoor swimming pool, a games room for children and a small bar. 3 acre site. 37 touring pitches. 20 hardstandings. Caravan pitches. Motorhome pitches. Tent pitches.

Open: Mar-Oct (rs Mar-Apr & Sep-Oct bar & swimming pool closed) **Last arrival:** dusk **Last departure:** 11.00hrs

Pitches:

Leisure:

Facilities:

Services:

Within 3 miles:

Notes: No gazebos or campfires, no groups occupying more than 3 pitches, no noise after 22.30hrs. Dogs must be kept on leads.

AA Pubs & Restaurants nearby: The Oxford Arms, KIRTLINGTON, OX5 3HA, 01869 350208

The Feathers Hotel, WOODSTOCK, OX20 1SX, 01993 812291

BURFORD — Map 5 SP21

Places to visit

Minster Lovell Hall & Dovecote, MINSTER LOVELL, OX29 0RR, 0370 333 1181 www.english-heritage.org.uk/daysout/properties/minster-lovell-hall-and-dovecote

Cotswold Wildlife Park and Gardens, BURFORD, OX18 4JP, 01993 823006 www.cotswoldwildlifepark.co.uk

Wysdom Touring Park

►► 85%

tel: 01993 823207 **Cheltenham Rd OX18 4PL**
email: geoffhayes@fsmail.net
dir: *On A40.* **grid ref:** *SP248117*

Owned by Burford School, this small adults-only park is very much a hidden gem being just a five-minute walk from Burford, one of prettiest towns in the Cotswolds. The pitches have good privacy; all have electricity and there are many hardstandings for caravans and motorhome. The unisex toilet facilities are very clean. This makes a good base from which to explore the Cotswolds. 25 touring pitches. 14 hardstandings. Caravan pitches. Motorhome pitches.

Open: all year **Last arrival:** 21.00hrs **Last departure:** noon

Pitches: * £13-£16 £13-£16

Facilities:

Services:

Within 3 miles:

Notes: Adults only. Dogs must be kept on leads.

AA Pubs & Restaurants nearby: The Lamb Inn, BURFORD, OX18 4LR, 01993 823155

The Highway Inn, BURFORD, OX18 4RG, 01993 823661

The Angel at Burford, BURFORD, OX18 4SN, 01993 822714

CHARLBURY — Map 11 SP31

Places to visit

Blenheim Palace, WOODSTOCK, OX20 1PP, 0800 849 6500 www.blenheimpalace.com

Minster Lovell Hall & Dovecote, MINSTER LOVELL, OX29 0RR, 0370 333 1181 www.english-heritage.org.uk/daysout/properties/minster-lovell-hall-and-dovecote

Great for kids: Cogges Witney, WITNEY, OX28 3LA, 01993 772602 www.cogges.org.uk

Cotswold View Touring Park

►►►► 85%

tel: 01608 810314 **Enstone Rd OX7 3JH**
email: bookings@gfwiddows.co.uk
dir: *From A44 in Enstone take B4022 towards Charlbury. Follow site signs. Site 1m from Charlbury.* **grid ref:** *SP365210*

A good Cotswold site, well screened and with attractive views across the countryside. The toilet facilities include fully-equipped family rooms and bathrooms, and there are spacious, sheltered pitches, some with hardstandings. Breakfasts and takeaway food are available from the shop. The site has camping pods for hire. This is the perfect location for exploring the Cotswolds and for anyone heading for the Charlbury Music Festival. 10 acre site. 125 touring pitches. Caravan pitches. Motorhome pitches. Tent pitches. 2 wooden pods.

Open: Etr or Apr-Oct **Last arrival:** 21.00hrs **Last departure:** noon

Pitches:

Leisure:

Facilities:

Services:

Within 3 miles:

Notes: Off licence, skittle alley, chess, boules.

AA Pubs & Restaurants nearby: The Bull Inn, CHARLBURY, OX7 3RR, 01608 810689

The Crown Inn, CHURCH ENSTONE, OX7 4NN, 01608 677262

FRINGFORD Map 11 SP62

Places to visit

Rousham House, ROUSHAM, OX25 4QX, 01869 347110 www.rousham.org

Buckinghamshire Railway Centre, QUAINTON, HP22 4BY, 01296 655720 www.bucksrailcentre.org

Glebe Leisure

NEW ►►► 77%

tel: 01869 277800 & 277410 **Stratton Ln OX27 8RJ**
email: ann.herring@btinternet.com
dir: *M40 junct 10, A43 (signed Northampton). At next rdbt take B4100 signed Bicester. 2nd right onto unclassified road signed Hethe & Stoke Lyne. Follow brown site signs.*
grid ref: *SP589273*

Glebe Leisure is a peaceful small park in a good countryside location just a few miles from Bicester and the M40, making it an ideal overnight stopover site. It is also very popular with fishing enthusiasts due to the well-stocked lake, and with keen shoppers wishing to spend time at the Bicester Village shopping outlet, three miles away. The park comprises two well-tended fields – one with new hardstandings and three newly installed camping pods, the other with neat grassy pitches. The main toilet block offers clean, well maintained facilities and there's a good motorhome service point. 5 acre site. 35 touring pitches. 15 hardstandings. Caravan pitches. Motorhome pitches. Tent pitches. 3 wooden pods.

Open: all year **Last arrival:** anytime **Last departure:** anytime

Pitches: * £15-£21 £15-£21 £15-£21

Facilities:

Services:

Within 3 miles:

Notes: No noise or taxis after 23.00hrs, no unaccompanied children in toilet block or around lakes. Dogs must be kept on leads. Dog walks.

AA Pubs & Restaurants nearby: The Butchers Arms, FRINGFORD, OX27 8EB, 01869 277363

The Muddy Duck, HETHE, OX27 8ES, 01869 278099

HENLEY-ON-THAMES

Map 5 SU78

Places to visit

Greys Court, HENLEY-ON-THAMES, RG9 4PG, 01491 628529 www.nationaltrust.org.uk

River & Rowing Museum, HENLEY-ON-THAMES, RG9 1BF, 01491 415600 www.rrm.co.uk

PREMIER PARK

Swiss Farm Touring & Camping

Best of British

92%

tel: 01491 573419 **Marlow Rd RG9 2HY**
email: info@swissfarmhenley.co.uk **web:** www.swissfarmcamping.co.uk
dir: *From Henley-on-Thames take A4155, towards Marlow. 1st left after rugby club.*
grid ref: *SU759837*

This park enjoys an excellent location within easy walking distance of the town and is perfect for those visiting the Henley Regatta (but booking is essential at that time). Pitches are spacious and well appointed, and include some that are fully serviced. There is a tasteful bar plus a nice outdoor swimming pool. Luxury lodge for hire. 6 acre site. 140 touring pitches. 100 hardstandings. Caravan pitches. Motorhome pitches. Tent pitches. 6 statics.

Open: Mar-Nov (rs Mar-May & Oct-Nov pool closed) **Last arrival:** 21.00hrs **Last departure:** noon

Pitches: * £19-£29 £19-£29 £16-£27 **Leisure:**

Facilities:

Services: **Within 3 miles:**

Notes: No groups, no dogs during high season. Dogs must be kept on leads.

AA Pubs & Restaurants nearby: The Little Angel, HENLEY-ON-THAMES, RG9 2LS, 01491 411008

Crooked Billet, STOKE ROW, RG9 5PU, 01491 681048

The Five Horseshoes, HENLEY-ON-THAMES, RG9 6EX, 01491 641282

See advert on page 279

STANDLAKE

Map 5 SP30

Places to visit

Buscot Park, BUSCOT, SN7 8BU, 01367 240786 www.buscotpark.com

Harcourt Arboretum, OXFORD, OX44 9PX, 01865 343501 www.botanic-garden.ox.ac.uk

Great for kids: Cotswold Wildlife Park and Gardens, BURFORD, OX18 4JP, 01993 823006 www.cotswoldwildlifepark.co.uk

PREMIER PARK

Lincoln Farm Park Oxfordshire

96%

tel: 01865 300239 **High St OX29 7RH**
email: info@lincolnfarmpark.co.uk **web:** www.lincolnfarmpark.co.uk
dir: *Exit A415 between Abingdon & Witney, 5m SE of Witney. Follow brown campsite sign in Standlake.* **grid ref:** *SP395028*

This attractively landscaped family-run park, located in a quiet village near the River Thames, offers a truly excellent camping or caravanning experience. There are top class facilities throughout the park. It has excellent leisure facilities in the Standlake Leisure Centre complete with two pools plus gym, sauna etc. This is the perfect base for visiting the many attractions in Oxfordshire and the Cotswolds. A warm welcome is assured from the friendly staff. 9 acre site. 90 touring pitches. 75 hardstandings. Caravan pitches. Motorhome pitches. Tent pitches.

Open: Feb-Nov **Last arrival:** 20.00hrs **Last departure:** noon

Pitches:

Leisure: Spa

Facilities:

Services:

Within 3 miles:

LEISURE: Indoor swimming pool Outdoor swimming pool Children's playground Kid's club Tennis court Games room Separate TV room golf course Boats for hire Cinema Entertainment Fishing Mini golf Watersports Gym Sports field Spa Stables
FACILITIES: Bath Shower Electric shaver Hairdryer Ice Pack Facility Disabled facilities Public telephone Shop on site or within 200yds Mobile shop (calls at least 5 days a week) BBQ area Picnic area Wi-fi Internet access Recycling Tourist info Dog exercise area

Notes: No gazebos, no noise after 23.00hrs. Dogs must be kept on leads. Putting green, outdoor chess.

AA Pubs & Restaurants nearby: Bear & Ragged Staff, CUMNOR, OX2 9QH, 01865 862329

The Vine Inn, CUMNOR, OX2 9QN, 01865 862567

RUTLAND

GREETHAM Map 11 SK91

Places to visit

Rutland County Museum & Visitor Centre, OAKHAM, LE15 6HW, 01572 758440 www.rutland.gov.uk/museum

Great for kids: Oakham Castle, OAKHAM, LE15 6HW, 01572 758440 www.rutland.gov.uk/castle

PREMIER PARK

Rutland Caravan & Camping

►►►►► 82%

tel: 01572 813520 **Park Ln LE15 7FN**
email: info@rutlandcaravanandcamping.co.uk
dir: *From A1 onto B668 towards Greetham. Before Greetham turn right at x-rds, left to site.* **grid ref:** *SK925148*

This pretty caravan park, built to a high specification and surrounded by well-planted banks, continues to improve due to the enthusiasm and vision of its owner. A swimming pool, six luxury lodges and 40 new fully serviced pitches were completed for the 2015 season, and there are plans to extend the toilet block and add family washrooms in time for 2016. From the spacious reception and the innovative play area to the toilet block, everything is of a very high standard. The spacious grassy site is close to the Viking Way and other footpath networks, and well situated for visiting Rutland Water and the many picturesque villages in the area. 5 acre site. 130 touring pitches. 65 hardstandings. Caravan pitches. Motorhome pitches. Tent pitches.

Open: all year **Last arrival:** 20.00hrs

Pitches:

Leisure:

Facilities:

Services:

Within 3 miles:

Notes: No noise after 23.00hrs. Dogs must be kept on leads. Dog shower.

AA Pubs & Restaurants nearby: The Wheatsheaf, GREETHAM, LE15 7NP, 01572 812325

The Olive Branch, CLIPSHAM, LE15 7SH, 01780 410355

OAKHAM

Places to visit

Oakham Castle, OAKHAM, LE15 6HW, 01572 758440 www.rutland.gov.uk/castle

Rutland County Museum & Visitor Centre, OAKHAM, LE15 6HW, 01572 758440 www.rutland.gov.uk/museum

OAKHAM Map 11 SK80

Louisa-Alice Campsite

►►► 80%

tel: 01572 722984 & 07794 949568 **Ranksborough Hall Estates, Langham LE15 7JR**
dir: *Take A606 from Oakham towards Melton Mowbray, through Langham, left at Ranksborough Hall sign.* **grid ref:** *SK838110*

This small, intimate, tranquil touring park is situated in the grounds of Ranksborough Hall. It occupies a level, secluded and mature tree fringed area with clean, well-maintained toilets, and a high priority is given to security. Several attractive and historic market towns are a short drive away through rolling and unspoilt countryside, plus there are opportunities for walking, sailing and cycling at nearby Rutland Water. 1.5 acre site. 33 touring pitches. 33 hardstandings. 10 seasonal pitches. Caravan pitches. Motorhome pitches. Tent pitches.

Open: all year **Last arrival:** 19.00hrs **Last departure:** anytime

Pitches: * £22 £22 £22-£30 **Facilities:**

Services: **Within 3 miles:**

Notes: No cars by caravans or tents. Quiet time after 22.30hrs, BBQs must be off the ground, no football games. Dogs must be kept on leads.

AA Pubs & Restaurants nearby: The Grainstore Brewery, OAKHAM, LE15 6RE, 01572 770065

The Fox & Hounds, KNOSSINGTON, LE15 8LY, 01664 452129

WING Map 11 SK80

Places to visit

Lyddington Bede House, LYDDINGTON, LE15 9LZ, 01572 822438 www.english-heritage.org.uk/daysout/properties/lyddington-bede-house

Great for kids: Oakham Castle, OAKHAM, LE15 6HW, 01572 758440 www.rutland.gov.uk/castle

Wing Hall Caravan & Camping

►►► 71%

tel: 01572 737283 & 737090 **Wing Hall LE15 8RQ**
email: winghall1891@aol.com
dir: *From A1 take A47 towards Leicester, 14m, follow Morcott signs. In Morcott follow Wing signs. 2.5m, follow site signs.* **grid ref:** *SK892031*

A deeply tranquil and rural park set in the grounds of an old manor house. The four grassy fields with attractive borders of mixed, mature deciduous trees have exceptional views across the Rutland countryside and are within one mile of Rutland Water. There's a good farm shop which specialises in locally sourced produce, a licensed café, and there are high quality showers and a fully-equipped laundry. Children and tents are very welcome in what is a safe environment where there is space to roam. 11 acre site. 250 touring pitches. 4 hardstandings. Caravan pitches. Motorhome pitches. Tent pitches.

Open: all year (rs Nov-Feb large motorhomes advised not to arrive if weather very wet) **Last arrival:** 21.00hrs **Last departure:** noon

Pitches: **Facilities:**

Services: **Within 3 miles:**

Notes: Dogs must be kept on leads. Coarse fishing.

AA Pubs & Restaurants nearby: King's Arms Inn, WING, LE15 8SE, 01572 737634

SHREWSBURY Map 15 SJ41

Places to visit

Attingham Park, ATCHAM, SY4 4TP, 01743 708123
www.nationaltrust.org.uk/attinghampark

Great for kids: Wroxeter Roman City, WROXETER, SY5 6PH, 01743 761330
www.english-heritage.org.uk/daysout/properties/wroxeter-roman-city

PREMIER PARK

Beaconsfield Farm Caravan Park

Best of British

90%

tel: 01939 210370 & 210399 **Battlefield SY4 4AA**
email: mail@beaconsfieldholidaypark.co.uk **web:** www.beaconsfieldholidaypark.co.uk
dir: *At Hadnall, 1.5m NE of Shrewsbury. Follow sign for Astley from A49.*
grid ref: *SJ522189*

A purpose-built family-run park on farmland in open countryside. This pleasant park offers quality in every area, including superior toilets, heated indoor swimming pool, luxury lodges for hire and attractive landscaping. Fly and coarse fishing are available from the park's own lake and The Bothy restaurant is excellent. Car hire is available directly from the site, and there's a steam room, plus free WiFi. 12 luxury lodges are available for hire or sale. Only adults over 21 years are accepted. 16 acre site. 60 touring pitches. 50 hardstandings. 10 seasonal pitches. Caravan pitches. Motorhome pitches. 35 statics.

Open: all year **Last arrival:** 19.00hrs **Last departure:** 11.00hrs

Pitches: * £20-£26 £23-£26

Leisure:

Facilities:

Services:

Within 3 miles:

Notes: Adults only. Dogs must be kept on leads. Cycle hire.

AA Pubs & Restaurants nearby: The Boat House, SHREWSBURY, SY3 8JQ, 01743 231658

The Prince of Wales, SHREWSBURY, SY3 7NZ, 01743 343301

Lion & Pheasant Hotel, SHREWSBURY, SY1 1XJ, 01743 770345

PREMIER PARK

Oxon Hall Touring Park

Best of British

88%

tel: 01743 340868 **Welshpool Rd SY3 5FB**
email: oxon@morris-leisure.co.uk
dir: *Exit A5 (ring road) at junct with A458. Site shares entrance with Oxon Park & Ride.*
grid ref: *SJ455138*

A delightful park with quality facilities and a choice of grass and fully serviced pitches. A warm welcome is assured from the friendly staff. The adults-only section proves very popular, and there is an inviting patio area next to reception and the shop, overlooking a small lake. This site is ideally located for a visit to Shrewsbury and the surrounding countryside, and the site also benefits from the Oxon Park & Ride, a short walk through the park. 15 acre site. 105 touring pitches. 72 hardstandings. Caravan pitches. Motorhome pitches. Tent pitches. 60 statics.

Open: all year **Last arrival:** 20.00hrs **Last departure:** noon

Pitches:

Leisure:

Facilities:

Services:

Within 3 miles:

Notes: Max 2 dogs per pitch. Dogs must be kept on leads.

AA Pubs & Restaurants nearby: The Mytton & Mermaid Hotel, SHREWSBURY, SY5 6QG, 01743 761220

Albright Hussey Manor Hotel & Restaurant, SHREWSBURY, SY4 3AF, 01939 290571

See which sites have been awarded Gold Pennants on page 34

LEISURE: Indoor swimming pool · Outdoor swimming pool · Children's playground · Kid's club · Tennis court · Games room · Separate TV room · golf course · Boats for hire · Cinema · Entertainment · Fishing · Mini golf · Watersports · Gym · Sports field · Spa · Stables
FACILITIES: Bath · Shower · Electric shaver · Hairdryer · Ice Pack Facility · Disabled facilities · Public telephone · Shop on site or within 200yds · Mobile shop (calls at least 5 days a week) · BBQ area · Picnic area · Wi-fi · Internet access · Recycling · Tourist info · Dog exercise area

TELFORD Map 10 SJ60

Places to visit

Lilleshall Abbey, LILLESHALL, TF10 9HW, 0121 625 6820 www.english-heritage.org.uk/daysout/properties/lilleshall-abbey

Ironbridge Gorge Museums, IRONBRIDGE, TF8 7DQ, 01952 433424 www.ironbridge.org.uk

PREMIER PARK

Severn Gorge Park

►►►►► 81%

tel: 01952 684789 **Bridgnorth Rd, Tweedale TF7 4JB**
email: info@severngorgepark.co.uk
dir: *S of Telford takeA442 towards Bridgnorth. Onto A4169 signed Telford Town Centre. Right at Cuckoo Oak rdbt into Bridgenorth Rd (follow site signs). Site on right.*
grid ref: *SJ705051*

A very pleasant wooded site in the heart of Telford, that is well screened and well maintained. The sanitary facilities are fresh and immaculate, and landscaping of the grounds is carefully managed. Although the touring section is small, this is a really delightful park to stay at, and it is also well positioned for visiting nearby Ironbridge and its museums. The Telford bus stops at the end of the drive. 6 acre site. 12 touring pitches. 12 hardstandings. Caravan pitches. Motorhome pitches. 120 statics.

Open: all year **Last arrival:** 20.00hrs **Last departure:** noon

Pitches:

Facilities:

Services:

Within 3 miles:

Notes: Adults only. Well behaved dogs only. Dogs must be kept on leads.

WEM Map 15 SJ52

Places to visit

Hawkstone Historic Park & Follies, WESTON-UNDER-REDCASTLE, SY4 5UY, 01948 841700 www.hawkstoneparkfollies.co.uk

Attingham Park, ATCHAM, SY4 4TP, 01743 708123 www.nationaltrust.org.uk/attinghampark

Great for kids: Shrewsbury Castle and Shropshire Regimental Museum, SHREWSBURY, SY1 2AT, 01743 358516 www.shropeshireregimentalmuseum.co.uk

Lower Lacon Caravan Park

►►► 79%

tel: 01939 232376 **SY4 5RP**
email: info@llcp.co.uk **web:** www.llcp.co.uk
dir: *A49 onto B5065. Site 3m on right.* **grid ref:** *SJ534304*

A large, spacious park with lively club facilities and an entertainments' barn, set safely away from the main road. The park is particularly suited to families, with an outdoor swimming pool and many farm animals including alpacas and kune kune pigs. Family-size wooden pods are available for hire. 57 acre site. 270 touring pitches. 30 hardstandings. 100 seasonal pitches. Caravan pitches. Motorhome pitches. Tent pitches. 50 statics. 2 wooden pods.

Open: all year (rs Winter entertainment barn & café closed) **Last arrival:** anytime
Last departure: 16.00hrs

Pitches:

Leisure:

Facilities:

Services:

Within 3 miles:

Notes: No skateboards, no commercial vehicles, no sign-written vehicles. Dogs must be kept on leads. Crazy golf.

WENTNOR Map 15 SO39

Places to visit

Montgomery Castle, MONTGOMERY, 01443 336000 www.cadw.wales.gov.uk

Great for kids: The Shropshire Hills Discovery Centre, CRAVEN ARMS, SY7 9RS, 01588 676000 www.shropshirehillsdiscoverycentre.co.uk

The Green Caravan Park

►►► 81%

tel: 01588 650605 **SY9 5EF**
email: lin@greencaravanpark.co.uk
dir: *1m NE of Bishop's Castle on A489. Right at brown tourist sign.* **grid ref:** *SO380932*

A pleasant site in a peaceful setting convenient for visiting Ludlow or Shrewsbury. Very family orientated, with good facilities. The grassy pitches are mainly level, and some hardstandings are available. 15 acre site. 140 touring pitches. 5 hardstandings. 42 seasonal pitches. Caravan pitches. Motorhome pitches. Tent pitches. 20 statics.

Open: Etr-Oct **Last arrival:** 21.00hrs **Last departure:** noon (fee charged for late departures)

Pitches: * fr £18.50 fr £18.50 fr £15.50

Leisure:

Facilities:

Services:

Within 3 miles:

Notes: No open fires, quiet from 22.00hrs-08.00 hrs, . Dogs must be kept on leads.

AA Pubs & Restaurants nearby: The Crown Inn, WENTNOR, SY9 5EE, 01588 650613

WHEATHILL Map 10 SO68

Places to visit

Ludlow Castle, LUDLOW, SY8 1AY, 01584 873355 www.ludlowcastle.com

PREMIER PARK

Wheathill Touring Park

►►►►► 82%

tel: 01584 823456 **WV16 6QT**
email: info@wheathillpark.co.uk
dir: *On B4364 between Ludlow & Bridgnorth. (NB Sat Nav may give directions to exit B4364, this should be ignored. Site entrance well signed from B4364).*
grid ref: *SO603805*

Ideally located in open countryside between the historic towns of Bridgnorth and Ludlow, this development, provides spacious, fully serviced pitches, most with stunning views and a top-notch amenities block with quality fittings and good privacy options. The park is situated adjacent to a pub serving a good range of ales and food. Please note that the on-site shop only sells caravan and camping spares but there's a licensed village shop within a 10-minute drive. 4 acre site. 25 touring pitches. 25 hardstandings. 5 seasonal pitches. Caravan pitches. Motorhome pitches.

Open: Mar-1 Jan **Last arrival:** 20.00hrs **Last departure:** noon

Pitches:

Facilities:

Services:

Within 3 miles:

Notes: Adults only. Dogs must be kept on leads.

AA Pubs & Restaurants nearby: Fighting Cocks, STOTTESDON, DY14 8TZ, 01746 718270

The Crown Inn, CLEOBURY MORTIMER, DY14 0NB, 01299 270372

Somerset

Somerset means 'summer pastures' – appropriate given that so much of this county remains rural and unspoiled. Ever popular areas to visit are the limestone and red sandstone Mendips Hills rising to over 1,000 feet, and by complete contrast, to the south and southwest, the flat landscape of the Somerset Levels.

At the heart of Somerset lies the city of Wells, one of the smallest in the country and surely one of the finest. The jewel in the city's crown is its splendid cathedral, with a magnificent Gothic interior; adorned with sculptures, the West Front is a masterpiece of medieval craftsmanship. Nearby are Vicar's Close, a delightful street of 14th-century houses, and the Bishop's Palace, which is 13th century and moated.

Radiating from Wells are numerous paths and tracks, offering walkers the chance to escape the noise and bustle of the city and discover Somerset's rural delights. Deep within the county are the Mendip Hills, 25 miles long by 5 miles wide, that have a distinctive character and identity.

One of Somerset's more adventurous routes, and a long-term favourite with walkers, is the West Mendip Way, running for 50 miles between the coast and the town of Frome. The starting point at Uphill is spectacular – a ruined hilltop church overlooking the coast near the classic seaside resort of Weston-Super-Mare. The town's famous pier replaces a previous structure destroyed by fire in 2008. Weston and Minehead, which lie on the edge of Exmoor National Park, are two traditional, much-loved holiday destinations on this stretch of coastline.

From Uphill, the West Mendip Way makes for Cheddar Caves and Gorge where stunning geological formations attract countless visitors who are left with a lasting impression of unique natural beauty. For almost a mile the gorge's limestone cliffs rise vertically above the road, in places giving Cheddar a somewhat sinister and oppressive air. Beyond Cheddar the trail heads for Wells. The choice of walks in Somerset is impressive, as is the range of cycle routes.

Descend to the Somerset Levels, an evocative lowland landscape that was the setting for the Battle of Sedgemoor in 1685. In the depths of winter this is a desolate place and famously prone to extensive flooding. There is also a palpable sense of the distant past among these fields and scattered communities. It is claimed that Alfred the Great retreated here after his defeat by the Danes.

One of Somerset's most famous features is the ancient, enigmatic Glastonbury Tor. Steeped in early Christian and Arthurian legend, the Isle of Avalon is one of a number of 'islands' rising above the Somerset Levels. This was once the site of the largest and richest monastery in medieval England and it is claimed that in this setting, Joseph of Arimathea founded the first Christian church in the country. Today, near this spot, modern-day pilgrims come for worship of a very different kind – every summer Glastonbury's legendary festival attracts big names from the world of music and large crowds who brave the elements to support them.

Away from the flat country are the Quantocks, once the haunt of poets. Samuel Taylor Coleridge wrote *The Ancient Mariner* while living in the area and William Wordsworth and his sister Dorothy visited on occasion and often accompanied their friend Coleridge on his country rambles among these hills. The Quantocks are noted for their gentle slopes, heather-covered moorland expanses and red deer. From the summit, the Bristol Channel is visible where it meets the Severn Estuary. So much of this hilly landscape has a timeless quality about it and large areas have hardly changed since Coleridge and William and Dorothy Wordsworth explored it on foot around the end of the 18th century.

◁ Glastonbury Tor

SOMERSET

BATH

See Bishop Sutton below

BISHOP SUTTON Map 4 ST55

Places to visit

Wookey Hole Caves & Papermill, WOOKEY HOLE, BA5 1BB, 01749 672243 www.wookey.co.uk

Roman Baths & Pump Room, BATH, BA1 1LZ, 01225 477785 www.romanbaths.co.uk

PREMIER PARK

Bath Chew Valley Caravan Park

94%

tel: 01275 332127 **Ham Ln BS39 5TZ**
email: enquiries@bathchewvalley.co.uk
dir: *From A4 towards Bath take A39 towards Weston-Super-Mare. Right onto A368. 6m, right opposite The Red Lion into Ham Ln, site 250mtrs on left.* **grid ref:** *ST586598*

This peaceful adults-only park can be described as 'a park in a garden', with caravan pitches set amidst lawns, shrubs and trees. There are excellent private facilities – rooms with showers, wash basins and toilets – all are spotlessly clean and well maintained. There is a good woodland walk on the park. WiFi is available throughout the site and there is a free internet workstation. This site is well situated for visiting Bath, Bristol, Wells, Cheddar and Wookey Hole, and for walking in the Mendip Hills. Chew Valley Lake, noted for its top quality fishing, is close by. 4.5 acre site. 45 touring pitches. 4 seasonal pitches. Caravan pitches. Motorhome pitches. Tent pitches.

Open: all year **Last arrival:** 19.00hrs **Last departure:** 11.00hrs

Pitches:

Facilities:

Services:

Within 3 miles:

Notes: Adults only. No cars by caravans or tents. Dogs must be kept on leads. Lending library. Pub/restaurant 200mtrs from site.

BREAN Map 4 ST25

Places to visit

King John's Hunting Lodge, AXBRIDGE, BS26 2AP, 01934 732012 www.kingjohnshuntinglodge.co.uk

Weston-Super-Mare Museum, WESTON-SUPER-MARE, BS23 1PR, 01934 621028 www.westonmuseum.org

Great for kids: The Helicopter Museum, WESTON-SUPER-MARE, BS24 8PP, 01934 635227 www.helicoptermuseum.co.uk

Warren Farm Holiday Centre

HOLIDAY CENTRE 92%

tel: 01278 751227 **Brean Sands TA8 2RP**
email: enquiries@warren-farm.co.uk **web:** www.warren-farm.co.uk
dir: *M5 junct 22 , B3140 through Burnham-on-Sea to Berrow & Brean. Site 1.5m past Brean Leisure Park.* **grid ref:** *ST297564*

A large family-run holiday park just a short walk from the beach and divided up into several fields each with its own designated facilities. Pitches are spacious and level (some hardstandings available), and there are good panoramic views of the Mendip Hills and Brean Down. The park has its own Beachcomber Inn with bar, restaurant and entertainment area. The site is perfect for families and has an indoor playbarn. Lake fishing is available on site and there is also a fishing tackle and bait shop. 100 acre site. 575 touring pitches. 70 hardstandings. 400 seasonal pitches. Caravan pitches. Motorhome pitches. Tent pitches. 400 statics.

Open: Apr-Oct **Last arrival:** 20.00hrs **Last departure:** noon

Pitches: * £9-£19 £9-£19 £9-£19

Leisure:

Facilities:

Services:

Within 3 miles:

Notes: No commercial vehicles.

See advert below

Holiday Resort Unity

HOLIDAY CENTRE 91%

tel: 01278 751235 **Coast Rd, Brean Sands TA8 2RB**
email: admin@hru.co.uk
dir: *M5 junct 22, B3140 through Burnham-on-Sea, through Berrow to Brean. Site on left just before Brean Leisure Park.* **grid ref:** *ST294539*

This is an excellent, family-run holiday park offering very good touring facilities plus a wide range of family oriented activities, including bowling, RJ's entertainment club plus good eating outlets etc. Brean Leisure Park and a swimming pool complex are available directly from the touring park at a discounted entry price. Wooden pods and ready-erected, fully-equipped safari tents are also available for hire. 200 acre site. 453 touring pitches. 158 hardstandings. 168 seasonal pitches. Caravan pitches. Motorhome pitches. Tent pitches. 650 statics. 3 wooden pods. Safari tents.

Open: Feb-Nov **Last arrival:** 21.00hrs **Last departure:** 10.00hrs (late departures available - charges apply)

Pitches:

Leisure:

Facilities:

Services:

Within 3 miles:

Notes: Family parties of 3 or more must be over 21yrs (young persons' policy applies). Dogs must be kept on leads. Fishing lake, indoor play centre.

AA Pubs & Restaurants nearby: Crossways Inn, WEST HUNTSPILL, TA9 3RA, 01278 783756

BREAN *continued*

Northam Farm Caravan & Touring Park

93%

tel: 01278 751244 **TA8 2SE**
email: stay@northamfarm.co.uk **web:** www.northamfarm.co.uk
dir: *M5 junct 22, B3140 to Burnham-on-Sea & Brean. Park on right 0.5m past Brean Leisure Park.* **grid ref:** *ST299556*

An attractive site that's just a short walk from the sea and a long sandy beach. This quality park also has lots of children's play areas, and also owns the Seagull Inn about 600 yards away, which includes a restaurant and entertainment. There is a top quality fishing lake on site, which is very popular and has been featured on TV. The facilities on this park are excellent. A DVD of the site is available on request, free of charge. 30 acre site. 350 touring pitches. 260 hardstandings. Caravan pitches. Motorhome pitches. Tent pitches.

Open: Mar-Oct (rs Mar & Oct shop, café, takeaway open limited hours)
Last arrival: 20.00hrs **Last departure:** 10.30hrs

Pitches: * £12-£27.50 £12-£27.50 £12-£23.50

Leisure:

Facilities: WiFi

Services:

Within 3 miles:

Notes: Families & couples only, no motorcycles or commercial vehicles. Dogs must be kept on leads.

See advert on opposite page

BRIDGETOWN Map 3 SS93

Places to visit

Dunster Castle, DUNSTER, TA24 6SL, 01643 821314
www.nationaltrust.org.uk/dunstercastle

Cleeve Abbey, WASHFORD, TA23 0PS, 01984 640377
www.english-heritage.org.uk/daysout/properties/cleeve-abbey

Exe Valley Caravan Site

92%

tel: 01643 851432 **Mill House TA22 9JR**
email: info@exevalleycamping.co.uk **web:** www.exevalleycamping.co.uk
dir: *From S: M5 junct 27, A361 signed Tiverton. 7m, right at rdbt signed Bampton. Left at Exeter Inn rdbt, 2m, take A396. Through Exebridge to Bridgetown, left after Badgers Holt Inn, site on right. (NB for Sat Nav use TA22 9JN).* **grid ref:** *SS923333*

Set in the Exmoor National Park, this adults-only park occupies an enchanting, peaceful spot in a wooded valley alongside the River Exe. There is free fly-fishing, an abundance of wildlife and excellent walks leading directly from the park. The site has good, spotlessly clean facilities. The inn opposite serves meals at lunchtime and in the evening. 4 acre site. 48 touring pitches. 13 hardstandings. Caravan pitches. Motorhome pitches. Tent pitches.

Open: 12 Mar-18 Oct **Last arrival:** 22.00hrs **Last departure:** 11.00hrs

Pitches: * £13-£19 £13-£19 £13-£22

Facilities: WiFi

Services:

Within 3 miles:

Notes: Adults only. 17th-century mill, cycle hire, TV sockets & cables.

AA Pubs & Restaurants nearby: The Rest and Be Thankful Inn, WHEDDON CROSS, TA24 7DR, 01643 841222

LEISURE: Indoor swimming pool Outdoor swimming pool Children's playground Kid's club Tennis court Games room Separate TV room golf course Boats for hire Cinema Entertainment Fishing Mini golf Watersports Gym Sports field Spa Stables
FACILITIES: Bath Shower Electric shaver Hairdryer Ice Pack Facility Disabled facilities Public telephone Shop on site or within 200yds Mobile shop (calls at least 5 days a week) BBQ area Picnic area WiFi Wi-fi Internet access Recycling Tourist info Dog exercise area

PITCHES: Caravans Motorhomes Tents Glamping-style accommodation **SERVICES:** Electric hook up Launderette Licensed bar Calor Gas Camping Gaz Toilet fluid Café/Restaurant Fast Food/Takeaway Battery charging Baby care Motorvan service point

ABBREVIATIONS: BH/bank hols – bank holidays Etr – Easter Spring BH – Spring Bank Holiday fr – from hrs – hours m – mile mdnt – midnight rdbt – roundabout rs – restricted service wk – week wknd – weekend x-rds – cross roads No credit or debit cards No dogs Children of all ages accepted

---

LEISURE: Indoor swimming pool · Outdoor swimming pool · Children's playground · Kid's club · Tennis court · Games room · Separate TV room · golf course · Boats for hire · Cinema · Entertainment · Fishing · Mini golf · Watersports · Gym · Sports field · Spa · Stables
FACILITIES: Bath · Shower · Electric shaver · Hairdryer · Ice Pack Facility · Disabled facilities · Public telephone · Shop on site or within 200yds · Mobile shop (calls at least 5 days a week) · BBQ area · Picnic area · Wi-fi · Internet access · Recycling · Tourist info · Dog exercise area

BRIDGWATER Map 4 ST23

Places to visit

Hestercombe Gardens, TAUNTON, TA2 8LG, 01823 413923 www.hestercombe.com

Coleridge Cottage, NETHER STOWEY, TA5 1NQ, 01278 732662 www.nationaltrust.org.uk/coleridgecottage

Great for kids: Tropiquaria Animal and Adventure Park, WASHFORD, TA23 0QB, 01984 640688 www.tropiquaria.co.uk

Mill Farm Caravan & Camping Park

HOLIDAY CENTRE 85%

tel: 01278 732286 **Fiddington TA5 1JQ**
web: www.millfarm.biz
dir: *From Bridgwater take A39 W, left at Cannington rdbt, 2m, right just beyond Apple Tree Inn towards Fiddington. Follow camping signs.* **grid ref:** *ST219410*

A large holiday park with plenty to interest all the family, including indoor and outdoor pools, a boating lake, a gym and horse riding. There is also a clubhouse with bar, and a full entertainment programme in the main season. Although lively and busy in the main season, the park also offers a much quieter environment at other times; out of season, some activities and entertainment may not be available. 6 acre site. 275 touring pitches. 10 hardstandings. 40 seasonal pitches. Caravan pitches. Motorhome pitches. Tent pitches.

Open: Mar-1 Dec **Last arrival:** 23.00hrs **Last departure:** 10.00hrs

Pitches: * £15-£24.50 £15-£24.50 £15-£24.50

Leisure: **Facilities:**

Services: **Within 3 miles:**

Notes: No noise after 23.00hrs. Dogs must be kept on leads. Canoeing, pool table, trampolines, fitness classes, saunas.

AA Pubs & Restaurants nearby: The Hood Arms, KILVE, TA5 1EA, 01278 741210

See advert on opposite page

BURNHAM-ON-SEA Map 4 ST34

Places to visit

The Helicopter Museum, WESTON-SUPER-MARE, BS24 8PP, 01934 635227 www.helicoptermuseum.co.uk

King John's Hunting Lodge, AXBRIDGE, BS26 2AP, 01934 732012 www.kingjohnshuntinglodge.co.uk

Burnham-on-Sea Holiday Village

HOLIDAY CENTRE 88%

GOLD

tel: 01278 783391 **Marine Dr TA8 1LA**
email: burnhamonsea@haven.com **web:** www.haven.com/burnhamonsea
dir: *M5 junct 22, A38 towards Highbridge. Over mini rdbt, right onto B3139 to Burnham. After petrol station, left into Marine Drive. Park 400yds on left.* **grid ref:** *ST305485*

A large, family-orientated holiday village complex with a separate touring park containing 43 super pitches. There is a wide range of activities, including excellent indoor and outdoor pools, plus bars, restaurants and entertainment for all the family. The coarse fishing lake is very popular, and the seafront at Burnham is only half a mile away. A wide range of well laid out holiday homes is available for hire and there's a Safari Village with fully-equipped safari tents for hire. 94 acre site. 75 touring pitches. 48 hardstandings. Caravan pitches. Motorhome pitches. Tent pitches. 700 statics. Safari tents.

Open: mid Mar-end Oct (rs mid Mar-May & Sep-Oct facilities may be reduced)

continued

MARTOCK
Map 4 ST41

Places to visit

Montacute House, MONTACUTE, TA15 6XP, 01935 823289 www.nationaltrust.org.uk

Great for kids: Fleet Air Arm Museum, YEOVILTON, BA22 8HT, 01935 840565 www.fleetairarm.com

Southfork Caravan Park

►►►► 82%

BRONZE

tel: 01935 825661 **Parrett Works TA12 6AE**
email: southforkcaravans@btconnect.com **web:** www.southforkcaravans.co.uk
dir: *From E: approx 2m after Cargate rdbt exit A303, signed Crewkerne. At T-junct right onto A356 signed Martock. Through Bower Hinton, left signed South Petherton. Site approx 1m. From W: at Hayes End rdbt left signed South Petherton. Through South Petherton, follow Martock signs. Site on left.* **grid ref:** *ST448188*

A neat, level mainly grass park in a quiet rural area, just outside the pretty village of Martock. Some excellent spacious hardstandings are available. The facilities are always spotless and the whole site is well cared for by the friendly owners, who will ensure your stay is a happy one, a fact borne out by the many repeat customers. The park is unique in that it also has a fully-approved caravan repair and servicing centre with accessory shop. There are also static caravans available for hire. 2 acre site. 27 touring pitches. 2 hardstandings. Caravan pitches. Motorhome pitches. Tent pitches. 3 statics.

Open: all year **Last arrival:** 22.30hrs **Last departure:** noon

Pitches: * £18-£26 £18-£26 £14-£19

Leisure:

Facilities:

Services:

Within 3 miles:

Notes: Dogs must be kept on leads.

AA Pubs & Restaurants nearby: The Nag's Head Inn, MARTOCK, TA12 6NF, 01935 823432

Ilchester Arms, ILCHESTER, BA22 8LN, 01935 840220

MINEHEAD
Map 3 SS94

Places to visit

West Somerset Railway, MINEHEAD, TA24 5BG, 01643 704996 www.west-somerset-railway.co.uk

Dunster Castle, DUNSTER, TA24 6SL, 01643 821314 www.nationaltrust.org.uk/dunstercastle

Great for kids: Tropiquaria Animal and Adventure Park, WASHFORD, TA23 0QB, 01984 640688 www.tropiquaria.co.uk

Minehead & Exmoor Caravan & Camping Park

►►► 78%

tel: 01643 703074 **Porlock Rd TA24 8SW**
email: enquiries@mineheadandexmoorcamping.co.uk
dir: *1m W of Minehead town centre, take A39 towards Porlock. Site on right.*
grid ref: *SS950457*

A small terraced park, on the edge of Exmoor, spread over five small paddocks and screened by the mature trees that surround it. The level pitches provide a comfortable space for each unit on this family-run park. The site is very conveniently placed for visiting Minehead and the Exmoor National Park. 3 acre site. 50 touring pitches. 9 hardstandings. 10 seasonal pitches. Caravan pitches. Motorhome pitches. Tent pitches.

Open: Mar-Oct (rs Nov-Feb open certain weeks only – please phone to check)
Last arrival: 21.00hrs **Last departure:** noon

Pitches: * £14-£20 £14-£20 £14-£20

Leisure:

Facilities:

Services:

Within 3 miles:

Notes: No open fires or loud music. Dogs must be kept on leads. Tumble dryer available.

AA Pubs & Restaurants nearby: The Luttrell Arms Hotel, DUNSTER, TA24 6SG, 01643 821555

The Stags Head Inn, DUNSTER, TA24 6SN, 01643 821229

OARE
Map 3 SS74

Places to visit

The Lyn & Exmoor Museum, LYNTON, EX35 6AF, 01598 753398 www.lyntonmuseum.org.uk

Great for kids: Exmoor Zoological Park, BLACKMOOR GATE, EX31 4SG, 01598 763352 www.exmoorzoo.co.uk

Cloud Farm

►►► 78%

tel: 01598 741278 **EX35 6NU**
email: stay@cloudfarmcamping.co.uk
dir: *M5 junct 24, A39 towards Minehead & Porlock then Lynton. Left in 6.5m, follow signs to Oare, right, site signed.* **grid ref:** *SS794467*

A traditional campsite set in a stunning location in Exmoor's Doone Valley – access is along narrow lanes that are unsuitable for large units. This quiet, sheltered campsite is arranged over four riverside fields with fairly basic but modern toilet and shower facilities. It offers a good shop and a café serving food all day, including breakfasts; there is a walled Tea Garden for alfresco eating. Several self-catering cottages are available for hire. Food is served all day at the pub that's only a 10-minute walk away. 110 acre site. 70 touring pitches. 6 hardstandings. Caravan pitches. Motorhome pitches. Tent pitches.

Open: all year **Last arrival:** anytime **Last departure:** anytime

Pitches: * fr £16 fr £16 fr £16

Facilities: WiFi

Services: T

Within 3 miles:

Notes: No noise after mdnt.

AA Pubs & Restaurants nearby: Rockford Inn, BRENDON, EX35 6PT, 01598 741214

PORLOCK — Map 3 SS84

Places to visit

West Somerset Railway, MINEHEAD, TA24 5BG, 01643 704996 www.west-somerset-railway.co.uk

Dunster Castle, DUNSTER, TA24 6SL, 01643 821314 www.nationaltrust.org.uk/dunstercastle

Great for kids: Tropiquaria Animal and Adventure Park, WASHFORD, TA23 0QB, 01984 640688 www.tropiquaria.co.uk

PREMIER PARK

Porlock Caravan Park

►►►►► 86%

DAVID BELLAMY CONSERVATION AWARD GOLD

tel: 01643 862269 **TA24 8ND**
email: info@porlockcaravanpark.co.uk **web:** www.porlockcaravanpark.co.uk
dir: *From A39 in Porlock follow Porlock Weir & Harbour signs, site on right.*
grid ref: *SS882469*

A sheltered touring park attractively laid out in the centre of lovely countryside on the edge of Porlock. The famous Porlock Hill, a few hundred yards from the site, leads to some spectacular areas of Exmoor and stunning views. The toilet facilities are superb, and there is a new dish washing room and kitchen with microwave and freezer. Rallies can be catered for in a separate rally field (without electricity) but with superb views over the coast. 3 acre site. 40 touring pitches. 14 hardstandings. Caravan pitches. Motorhome pitches. Tent pitches. 55 statics.

Open: 15 Mar-Oct **Last arrival:** 20.00hrs **Last departure:** 11.00hrs

Pitches:

Facilities: WiFi

Services:

Within 3 miles:

Notes: No fires, rollerblades or scooters. Dogs must be kept on leads.

AA Pubs & Restaurants nearby: The Ship Inn, PORLOCK, TA24 8QD, 01643 862507

The Bottom Ship, PORLOCK, TA24 8PB, 01643 863288

Burrowhayes Farm Caravan & Camping Site & Riding Stables

►►►► 91%

tel: 01643 862463 **West Luccombe TA24 8HT**
email: info@burrowhayes.co.uk **web:** www.burrowhayes.co.uk
dir: *A39 from Minehead towards Porlock for 5m. Left at Red Post to Horner & West Luccombe, site 0.25m on right, immediately before humpback bridge.* **grid ref:** *SS897460*

A delightful site on the edge of Exmoor that slopes gently down to Horner Water. The farm buildings have been converted into riding stables from where escorted rides onto the moors can be taken; the excellent toilet facilities are housed in timber-clad buildings. Hardstandings are available – some are fully serviced and many of the hook-ups have TV points. There is a popular, well-stocked shop and many countryside walks can be accessed directly from the site. 20 static holiday homes are for hire. 8 acre site. 120 touring pitches. 10 hardstandings. Caravan pitches. Motorhome pitches. Tent pitches. 20 statics.

Open: 15 Mar-Oct (rs Before Etr caravan hire & riding not available)
Last arrival: 22.00hrs **Last departure:** noon

Pitches: * £17.50-£21.50 £17.50-£21.50 £14-£21

Facilities: WiFi

Services: T

Within 3 miles:

Notes: Dogs must be kept on leads.

AA Pubs & Restaurants nearby: The Ship Inn, PORLOCK, TA24 8QD, 01643 862507

The Bottom Ship, PORLOCK, TA24 8PB, 01643 863288

WATCHET — Map 3 ST04

Places to visit

West Somerset Railway, MINEHEAD, TA24 5BG, 01643 704996 www.west-somerset-railway.co.uk

Dunster Castle, DUNSTER, TA24 6SL, 01643 821314 www.nationaltrust.org.uk/dunstercastle

Great for kids: Tropiquaria Animal and Adventure Park, WASHFORD, TA23 0QB, 01984 640688 www.tropiquaria.co.uk

Home Farm Holiday Centre

►►►► 81%

tel: 01984 632487 **St Audries Bay TA4 4DP**
email: dib@homefarmholidaycentre.co.uk
dir: *A39 for 17m to West Quantoxhead, B3191 after garage in village (signed Doniford), 1st right in 0.25m.* **grid ref:** *ST106432*

In a hidden valley beneath the Quantock Hills, this park overlooks its own private beach. The atmosphere is friendly and quiet, and there are lovely sea views from the level pitches. Flowerbeds, woodland walks and the Koi carp pond all enhance this very attractive site, along with a lovely indoor swimming pool, an excellent children's play area, and a beer garden. 45 acre site. 40 touring pitches. 35 hardstandings. Caravan pitches. Motorhome pitches. Tent pitches. 230 statics.

Open: all year (rs Nov-1 Mar no camping, shop & bar closed) **Last arrival:** dusk **Last departure:** noon

Pitches: * £12-£27.50 £12-£27.50 £12-£27.50

Leisure: **Facilities:**

Services:

Within 3 miles:

Notes: No cars by caravans or tents. No noise after 23.00hrs. Dogs must be kept on leads.

AA Pubs & Restaurants nearby: The Hood Arms, KILVE, TA5 1EA, 01278 741210

Doniford Bay Holiday Park

HOLIDAY HOME PARK 89%

GOLD

tel: 01984 632423 **TA23 0TJ**
email: donifordbay@haven.com **web:** www.haven.com/donifordbay
dir: *M5 junct 23, A38 towards Bridgwater, A39 towards Minehead. 15m, at West Quantoxhead, right after St Audries garage. Park 1m on right.* **grid ref:** *ST093432*

This well-appointed holiday park, situated adjacent to a shingle and sand beach, offers a wide range of activities for the whole family. The holiday homes are spacious and well-appointed and there is plenty to keep children (of all ages) interested, including great indoor and outdoor pools, a multi-sports centre, slides and archery. The park has good eating outlets including a nice café/restaurant. Being close to the Exmoor National Park, it offers visitors the chance to seek out some of the best scenery in the county.

Open: Mar-Oct **Change over day:** Mon, Fri, Sat

Arrival and departure times: Please contact the site

Statics: 143 Sleeps 6-8 Bedrms 2-3 Bathrms 1-2 Toilets 1-2 Microwave Freezer TV Sky/FTV Elec inc Gas inc Grass area

Children: Cots Highchair **Dogs:** 2 on leads No dangerous dogs

Leisure: Cycle hire

WELLINGTON — Map 3 ST12

Places to visit

Hestercombe Gardens, TAUNTON, TA2 8LG, 01823 413923 www.hestercombe.com

Great for kids: Diggerland, CULLOMPTON, EX15 2PE, 0871 227 7007 *(Calls cost 10p per minute plus your phone company's access charge)* www.diggerland.com

Greenacres Touring Park

►►►► 87%

tel: 01823 652844 **Haywards Ln, Chelston TA21 9PH**
email: enquiries@wellington.co.uk
dir: *M5 junct 26, A38 signed Wellington. Approx 1.5m, at Chelston rdbt take 1st left into West Buckland Rd signed A38. Straight on at next rdbt. Next left, follow sign for site.*
grid ref: *ST156001*

This attractively landscaped adults-only park is situated close to the Somerset/Devon border in a peaceful setting with great views of the Blackdown and Quantock Hills. It is in a very convenient location for overnight stays, being just one and half miles from the M5. This park is also well positioned for visiting both the north and south coasts, and it is also close to a local bus route. It has excellent facilities, which are spotlessly clean and well maintained. 2.5 acre site. 40 touring pitches. 30 hardstandings. Caravan pitches. Motorhome pitches.

Open: Apr-end Sep **Last arrival:** 19.00hrs **Last departure:** 11.00hrs

Pitches:

Facilities:

Services:

Within 3 miles:

Notes: Adults only. No RVs. Dogs must be kept on leads.

AA Pubs & Restaurants nearby: The Globe, MILVERTON, TA4 1JX, 01823 400534

Gamlins Farm Caravan Park

►►► 81%

tel: 01823 672859 & 07814 742462 & 07967 683738
Gamlins Farm House, Greenham TA21 0LZ
email: gamlinsfarmcaravanpark@hotmail.co.uk
dir: *M5 junct 26, A38 towards Tiverton & Exeter. 5m, right for Greenham, site 1m on right.*
grid ref: *ST083195*

This peaceful site (only two minutes from the A38) is set in a secluded valley with excellent views of the Quantock Hills; it is well placed for visiting both Devon and Somerset. The facilities are very good and spotlessly clean, and free coarse fishing is available. Static holiday homes for hire. 4 acre site. 30 touring pitches. 7 hardstandings. Caravan pitches. Motorhome pitches. Tent pitches. 4 statics.

Open: Mar-Oct

Pitches: * £15-£19 £15-£19 £12-£15

Leisure:

Facilities:

Services:

Within 3 miles:

Notes: Dogs not to be left unattended on site, no loud noise after 22.00hrs. Dogs must be kept on leads.

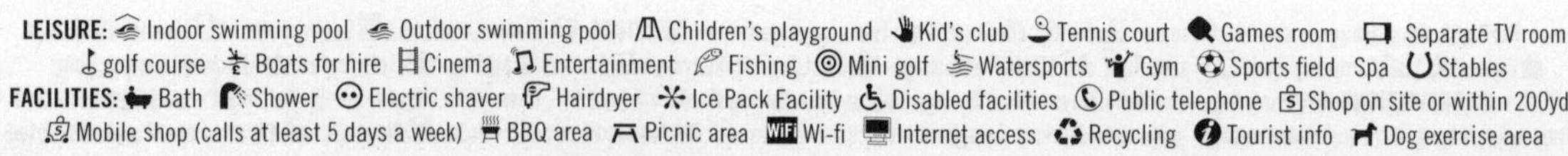

WELLS — Map 4 ST54

Places to visit

Glastonbury Abbey, GLASTONBURY, BA6 9EL, 01458 832267 www.glastonburyabbey.com

The Bishop's Palace, WELLS, BA5 2PD, 01749 988111 www.bishopspalace.org.uk

PREMIER PARK

Wells Touring Park

►►►►► 89%

tel: 01749 676869 **Haybridge BA5 1AJ**
email: jason@wellsholidaypark.co.uk
dir: *A38 then follow signs for Axbridge, Cheddar & Wells.* **grid ref:** *ST531459*

This well established, adults-only holiday park has first-class toilet facilities and many hardstandings, all with electricity. It is a restful park set in countryside on the outskirts of Wells, and is within easy walking distance of the city centre, with its spectacular cathedral and Bishop's Palace. Cheddar Gorge, Bath, Bristol, Weston-Super-Mare, Wookey Hole and Glastonbury are all within easy driving distance. The site has a function room and patio as well as a beauty salon. Holiday cottages are available for hire. 7.5 acre site. 72 touring pitches. 54 hardstandings. 20 seasonal pitches. Caravan pitches. Motorhome pitches. Tent pitches. 12 statics.

Open: all year **Last arrival:** 20.00hrs **Last departure:** noon

Pitches:

Facilities:

Services:

Within 3 miles:

Notes: Adults only. Dogs must be kept on leads. Pètanque.

AA Pubs & Restaurants nearby: The City Arms, WELLS, BA5 2AG, 01749 673916

The Fountain Inn, WELLS, BA5 2UU, 01749 672317

Goodfellows, WELLS, BA5 2RR, 01749 673866

The Old Spot, WELLS, BA5 2SE, 01749 689099

Homestead Park

►► 84%

tel: 01749 673022 **Wookey Hole BA5 1BW**
email: homesteadpark@onetel.com
dir: *0.5m NW from A371 (Wells to Cheddar road).* **grid ref:** *ST532474*

This attractive, small site for tents only is set on a wooded hillside and meadowland with access to the river and nearby Wookey Hole. This park is for adults only and the statics are residential caravans. 2 acre site. 30 touring pitches. Tent pitches. 28 statics.

Open: Etr-Sep **Last arrival:** 20.00hrs **Last departure:** noon

Pitches:

Facilities:

Services:

Within 3 miles:

Notes: Adults only. Dogs must be kept on leads.

AA Pubs & Restaurants nearby: The City Arms, WELLS, BA5 2AG, 01749 673916

The Fountain Inn, WELLS, BA5 2UU, 01749 672317

Goodfellows, WELLS, BA5 2RR, 01749 673866

The Old Spot, WELLS, BA5 2SE, 01749 689099

WESTON-SUPER-MARE — Map 4 ST36

Places to visit

Weston-Super-Mare Museum, WESTON-SUPER-MARE, BS23 1PR, 01934 621028 www.westonmuseum.org

Great for kids: The Helicopter Museum, WESTON-SUPER-MARE, BS24 8PP, 01934 635227 www.helicoptermuseum.co.uk

Country View Holiday Park

►►►► 85%

tel: 01934 627595 **Sand Rd, Sand Bay BS22 9UJ**
email: info@cvhp.co.uk **web:** www.cvhp.co.uk
dir: *M5 junct 21, A370 towards Weston-Super-Mare. Immediately into left lane, follow Kewstoke & Sand Bay signs. Straight over 3 rdbts onto Lower Norton Ln. At Sand Bay right into Sand Rd, site on right.* **grid ref:** *ST335647*

A pleasant open site in a rural area a few hundred yards from Sandy Bay and the beach. The park is also well placed for energetic walks along the coast at either end of the beach and is only a short drive away from Weston-Super-Mare. There is a touring section for tents, caravans and motorhomes with a toilet and shower block. There are 14 hardstanding pitches plus grass pitches all with electricity. The facilities are excellent and well maintained, including a nice outdoor swimming pool and small tasteful bar. 20 acre site. 190 touring pitches. 150 hardstandings. 90 seasonal pitches. Caravan pitches. Motorhome pitches. Tent pitches. 65 statics.

Open: Mar-Jan **Last arrival:** 20.00hrs **Last departure:** noon

Pitches: * £15-£25 £15-£25 £15-£25

Leisure:

Facilities:

Services:

Within 3 miles:

Notes: Dogs must be kept on leads.

AA Pubs & Restaurants nearby: The Cove, WESTON-SUPER-MARE, BS23 2BX, 01934 418217

PITCHES: Caravans Motorhomes Tents Glamping-style accommodation **SERVICES:** Electric hook up Launderette Licensed bar Calor Gas Camping Gaz Toilet fluid Café/Restaurant Fast Food/Takeaway Battery charging Baby care Motorvan service point
ABBREVIATIONS: BH/bank hols – bank holidays Etr – Easter Spring BH – Spring Bank Holiday fr – from hrs – hours m – mile mdnt – midnight rdbt – roundabout rs – restricted service wk – week wknd – weekend x-rds – cross roads No credit or debit cards No dogs Children of all ages accepted

WESTON-SUPER-MARE *continued*

West End Farm Caravan & Camping Park

►►► 84%

tel: 01934 822529 **Locking BS24 8RH**
email: robin@westendfarm.org
dir: *M5 junct 21 onto A370. Follow International Helicopter Museum signs. Right at rdbt, follow signs to site.* **grid ref:** *ST354600*

A spacious and well laid out park bordered by hedges, with good landscaping, and well-kept facilities. Fully serviced pitches are available. It is handily located next to a helicopter museum, and offers good access to Weston-Super-Mare and the Mendips. 10 acre site. 75 touring pitches. 10 hardstandings. 30 seasonal pitches. Caravan pitches. Motorhome pitches. Tent pitches. 11 statics.

Open: all year **Last arrival:** 21.00hrs **Last departure:** noon

Pitches: * £18-£24 £18-£24 £16-£20 **Leisure:**

Facilities: **Services:**

Within 3 miles:

Notes: No noise after 22.00hrs. Dogs must be kept on leads.

AA Pubs & Restaurants nearby: The Cove, WESTON-SUPER-MARE, BS23 2BX, 01934 418217

WINSFORD — Map 3 SS93

Places to visit

Dunster Castle, DUNSTER, TA24 6SL, 01643 821314 www.nationaltrust.org.uk/dunstercastle

Cleeve Abbey, WASHFORD, TA23 0PS, 01984 640377 www.english-heritage.org.uk/daysout/properties/cleeve-abbey

Great for kids: Tropiquaria Animal and Adventure Park, WASHFORD, TA23 0QB, 01984 640688 www.tropiquaria.co.uk

Halse Farm Caravan & Camping Park

►►►► 80%

GOLD

tel: 01643 851259 **TA24 7JL**
email: info@halsefarm.co.uk **web:** www.halsefarm.co.uk
dir: *Signed from A396 at Bridgetown. In Winsford turn left, bear left past pub. 1m up hill, entrance on left immediately after cattle grid.* **grid ref:** *SS894344*

A peaceful little site on Exmoor overlooking a wooded valley with glorious views. This moorland site is quite remote, but it provides good modern toilet facilities which are kept immaculately clean. This is a good base for exploring the Exmoor National Park, and Minehead, Porlock and Lynton are only a short drive away. 3 acre site. 44 touring pitches. Caravan pitches. Motorhome pitches. Tent pitches.

Open: 20 Mar-Oct **Last arrival:** 22.00hrs **Last departure:** noon

Pitches:

Leisure:

Facilities:

Services:

Within 3 miles:

Notes: Dogs must be kept on leads.

AA Pubs & Restaurants nearby: Crown Hotel, EXFORD, TA24 7PP, 01643 831554

Royal Oak Inn, WINSFORD, TA24 7JE, 01643 851455

WIVELISCOMBE — Map 3 ST02

Places to visit

Cleeve Abbey, WASHFORD, TA23 0PS, 01984 640377 www.english-heritage.org.uk/daysout/properties/cleeve-abbey

Hestercombe Gardens, TAUNTON, TA2 8LG, 01823 413923 www.hestercombe.com

PREMIER PARK

Waterrow Touring Park

Best of British

►►►►► 89%

tel: 01984 623464 **TA4 2AZ**
email: info@waterrowpark.co.uk **web:** www.waterrowpark.co.uk
dir: *M5 junct 25, A358 signed Minehead (bypassing Taunton), B3227 through Wiveliscombe. Site in 3m at Waterrow, 0.25m past Rock Inn.* **grid ref:** *ST053251*

Under pro-active ownership, this really delightful park for adults has spotless facilities, plenty of spacious hardstandings, including new fully serviced pitches and a new motorhome service point, alongside significant other improvements established during 2015. The River Tone runs along a valley beneath the park, accessed by steps to a nature area created by the owners, where fly-fishing is permitted. Watercolour painting workshops and other activities are available, and the local pub is a short walk away. There is also a bus stop just outside of the site. 8 acre site. 44 touring pitches. 40 hardstandings. Caravan pitches. Motorhome pitches. Tent pitches.

Open: all year **Last arrival:** 19.00hrs **Last departure:** 11.30hrs

Pitches:

Facilities:

Services:

Within 3 miles:

Notes: Adults only. No gazebos, max 3 dogs per unit. Dogs must be kept on leads. Caravan storage.

AA Pubs & Restaurants nearby: The Rock Inn, WATERROW, TA4 2AX, 01984 623293

The Three Horseshoes, LANGLEY MARSH, TA4 2UL, 01984 623763

YEOVIL — Map 4 ST51

Places to visit

Montacute House, MONTACUTE, TA15 6XP, 01935 823289 www.nationaltrust.org.uk

Lytes Cary Manor, KINGSDON, TA11 7HU, 01458 224471 www.nationaltrust.org.uk/lytes-cary-manor

Great for kids: Fleet Air Arm Museum, YEOVILTON, BA22 8HT, 01935 840565 www.fleetairarm.com

Halfway Caravan & Camping Park

►► 82%

tel: 01935 840342 **Trees Cottage, Halfway, Ilchester Rd BA22 8RE**
email: halfwaycaravanpark@earthlink.net
dir: *On A37 between Ilchester & Yeovil.* **grid ref:** *ST530195*

An attractive little park is near the Somerset and Dorset border, and adjacent to the Halfway House Inn which has a restaurant and AA-rated accommodation. It overlooks a fishing lake and is surrounded by attractive countryside. Friendly dogs are very welcome here. 2 acre site. 20 touring pitches. 10 hardstandings. Caravan pitches. Motorhome pitches. Tent pitches.

Open: Apr-Oct **Last arrival:** 19.00hrs (21.00hrs on Fri) **Last departure:** noon

Pitches:

Facilities:

Services:

Within 3 miles:

Notes: Earliest check-in noon. Dogs must be kept on leads.

AA Pubs & Restaurants nearby: The Masons Arms, YEOVIL, BA22 8TX, 01935 862591

The Helyar Arms, EAST COKER, BA22 9JR, 01935 862332

STAFFORDSHIRE

CHEADLE

Places to visit

Churnet Valley Railway, CHEDDLETON, ST13 7EE, 01538 750755 www.churnetvalleyrailway.co.uk

The Potteries Museum & Art Gallery, STOKE-ON-TRENT, ST1 3DW, 01782 232323 www.stoke.gov.uk/museum

Great for kids: Alton Towers Resort, ALTON, ST10 4DB, 0871 222 3330 *(Calls cost 10p per minute plus your phone company's access charge)* www.altontowers.com

Etruria Industrial Museum, STOKE-ON-TRENT, ST4 7AF, 01782 233144 www.stokemuseums.org.uk

CHEADLE — Map 10 SK04

Quarry Walk Park

►►► 75%

tel: 01538 723412 **Coppice Ln, Croxden Common, Freehay ST10 1RQ**
email: quarry@quarrywalkpark.co.uk
dir: *From A522 (Uttoxeter to Cheadle road) in Mobberley follow Freehay sign. In 1m at rdbt, 3rd exit signed Great Gate. 1.25m to site on right.* **grid ref:** *SK045405*

A pleasant park (for tents only), close to Alton Towers, that was developed in an old quarry; it has well-screened pitches, each with water and electricity, and surrounded by mature trees and shrubs which enhance the peaceful ambience of the park. There are seven glades of varying sizes used exclusively for tents, one with ten electric hook-ups. There are timber lodges for hire, each with its own hot tub. Please note caravans and motorhomes are not accepted. 46 acre site. Tent pitches.

Open: all year **Last arrival:** 18.00hrs **Last departure:** 11.00hrs

Pitches: **Leisure:** **Facilities:**

Services: **Within 3 miles:**

Notes: No cars by tents. No noise after 23.00hrs. Dogs must be kept on leads.

AA Pubs & Restaurants nearby: The Queens at Freehay, CHEADLE, ST10 1RF, 01538 722383

LONGNOR — Map 16 SK06

Places to visit

Poole's Cavern (Buxton Country Park), BUXTON, SK17 9DH, 01298 26978 www.poolescavern.co.uk

Haddon Hall, HADDON HALL, DE45 1LA, 01629 812855 www.haddonhall.co.uk

PREMIER PARK

Longnor Wood Holiday Park

►►►►► 91%

tel: 01298 83648 & 07866 016567 **Newtown SK17 0NG**
email: info@longnorwood.co.uk
dir: *From A53 follow Longnor sign. Site signed from village, 1.25m.* **grid ref:** *SK072640*

Enjoying a secluded and very peaceful setting in the heart of the Peak District National Park, this spacious adults-only park is a hidden gem, surrounded by beautiful rolling countryside and sheltered by woodland where there is a variety of wildlife to observe. Expect a warm welcome from the O'Neill family and excellent, well-maintained facilities, including spotlessly clean modern toilets, good hardstanding pitches, high levels of security, a putting green, badminton courts, a 4-acre dog walk (a new dog wash was installed for 2015) and super walks from the park gate. The reception building includes a small shop. There are lodges of different sizes and three equipped ready-erected tents for hire. 10.5 acre site. 47 touring pitches. 47 hardstandings. 13 seasonal pitches. Caravan pitches. Motorhome pitches. Tent pitches.

Open: Mar-10 Jan **Last arrival:** 19.00hrs **Last departure:** noon

Pitches: * £21.60-£25.20 £21.60-£25.20 £10-£21.60

Facilities:

Services: **Within 3 miles:**

Notes: Adults only. No fires, no noise after 23.00hrs. Dogs must be kept on leads.

AA Pubs & Restaurants nearby: The Queen Anne Inn, GREAT HUCKLOW, SK17 8RF, 01298 871246

The George, ALSTONEFIELD, DE6 2FX, 01335 310205

SHELLEY

Suffolk

Suffolk is Constable country, where the county's crumbling, time-ravaged coastline spreads itself under wide skies to convey a wonderful sense of remoteness and solitude. Highly evocative and atmospheric, this is where rivers wind lazily to the sea and notorious 18th-century smugglers hid from the excise men.

It was the artist John Constable who was responsible for raising the region's profile in the 18th century. Constable immortalised these expansive flatlands in his paintings and today the marketing brochures and websites usually refer to the area as Constable Country. Situated on the River Stour at Flatford, Constable's mill is now a major tourist attraction in the area but a close look at the surroundings confirms rural Suffolk is little changed since the family lived here. Constable himself maintained that the Suffolk countryside 'made me a painter and I am grateful.'

Facing the European mainland and with easy access by the various rivers, the county's open, often bleak, landscape made Suffolk vulnerable in early times to attack from waves of invaders. In the Middle Ages, however, it prospered under the wool merchants: it was their wealth that built the great churches which dominate the countryside.

Walking is one of Suffolk's most popular recreational activities. It may be flat but the county has much to discover on foot – not least the isolated Heritage Coast, which can be accessed via the Suffolk Coast Path. Running along the edge of the shore, between Felixstowe and Lowestoft, the trail is a fascinating blend of ecology and military history. Near its southerly start, the path passes close to one of the National Trust's most unusual acquisitions – Orford Ness. Acquired by the Trust in 1993, and officially opened in 1995, this spectacular stretch of coastline had previously been closed to the public since 1915 when the Royal Flying Corps chose Orford Ness as the setting for military research. These days, it is a Site of Special Scientific Interest, recognised in particular for its rare shingle habitats. Visitors to Orford Ness cross the River Ore by National Trust ferry from Orford Quay.

Beyond Orford, the Suffolk Coast Path parts company with the North Sea, albeit briefly, to visit Aldeburgh. Nearby are Snape Maltings, renowned internationally as the home of the Aldeburgh Festival that takes place in June. Benjamin Britten lived at Snape and wrote *Peter Grimes* here. The Suffolk coast is where both the sea and the natural landscape have influenced generations of writers, artists and musicians. An annual literary festival is staged at Aldeburgh on the first weekend in March.

Back on the Suffolk coast, the trail makes for Southwold, with its distinctive, white-walled lighthouse standing sentinel above the town and its colourful beach huts and attractive pier that feature on many a promotional brochure. The final section of the walk is one of the most spectacular, with low, sandy cliffs, several shallow Suffolk broads and the occasional church tower peeping through the trees. Much of Suffolk's coastal heathland is protected as a designated Area of Outstanding Natural Beauty and shelters several rare creatures including the adder, the heath butterfly and the nightjar.

In addition to walking, there is a good choice of cycling routes. There is the Heart of Suffolk Cycle Route, which extends for 78 miles, while the National Byway, a 4,000-mile cycle route around Britain takes in part of Suffolk and is a very enjoyable way to explore the county.

For something less demanding, visit some of Suffolk's best-known towns. Bury St Edmunds, Sudbury and Ipswich feature prominently on the tourist trail, while Lavenham, Kersey and Debenham are a reminder of the county's important role in the wool industry and the vast wealth it yielded the wool merchants. In these charming old towns look out for streets of handsome, period buildings and picturesque, timber-framed houses.

◁ Beach huts, Southwold

LOWESTOFT

See Kessingland

SAXMUNDHAM Map 13 TM36

Places to visit

Long Shop Museum, LEISTON, IP16 4ES, 01728 832189 www.longshopmuseum.co.uk

Leiston Abbey, LEISTON, IP16 4TD, 01728 831354 www.english-heritage.org.uk/daysout/properties/leiston-abbey

Great for kids: RSPB Nature Reserve Minsmere, WESTLETON, IP17 3BY, 01728 648281 www.rspb.org.uk/minsmere

PREMIER PARK

Carlton Meres Country Park

►►►►► 80%

tel: 01728 603344 **Rendham Rd, Carlton IP17 2QP**
email: enquiries@carlton-meres.co.uk
dir: *From A12 , W of Saxmundham, take B1119 towards Framlingham (site signed).*
grid ref: *TM372637*

With two large fishing lakes, a modern fitness suite, a beauty salon, sauna and steam rooms, tennis court, a bar, and a heated outdoor swimming pool, Carlton Meres offers a wealth of leisure facilities, and all for the exclusive use for those staying on the site (holiday statics and lodges for hire). The reception building and the modern heated toilet block have now been refurbished to a high standard, and security on the park is excellent. This site is well-placed for all the Suffolk coast attractions. 52 acre site. 160 touring pitches. 56 hardstandings. 25 seasonal pitches. Caravan pitches. Motorhome pitches. Tent pitches.

Open: Etr-Oct **Last arrival:** 17.00hrs **Last departure:** 10.00hrs

Pitches: * fr £10 **Leisure:** Spa

Facilities: **Services:**

Within 3 miles:

Notes: Dogs must be kept on leads.

AA Pubs & Restaurants nearby: Sibton White Horse Inn, SIBTON, IP17 2JJ, 01728 660337

Regatta Restaurant, ALDEBURGH, IP15 5AN, 01728 452011

Marsh Farm Caravan Site

►► 82%

tel: 01728 602168 **Sternfield IP17 1HW**
dir: *A12 onto A1094 (Aldeburgh road), at Snape x-rds left signed Sternfield, follow signs to site.* **grid ref:** *TM385608*

A very pretty site overlooking reed-fringed lakes which offer excellent coarse fishing. The facilities are very well maintained, and the park truly is a peaceful haven. 30 acre site. 45 touring pitches. Caravan pitches. Motorhome pitches. Tent pitches.

Open: all year **Last arrival:** 21.00hrs **Last departure:** 17.00hrs

Pitches:

Facilities:
Services:
Within 3 miles:
Notes: Campers must report to reception on arrival. Site closed when freezing temperatures are forecast. Dogs must be kept on leads.
AA Pubs & Restaurants nearby: The Parrot and Punchbowl Inn & Restaurant, ALDRINGHAM, IP16 4PY, 01728 830221

Regatta Restaurant, ALDEBURGH, IP15 5AN, 01728 452011

THEBERTON

Places to visit

Leiston Abbey, LEISTON, IP16 4TD, 01728 831354
www.english-heritage.org.uk/daysout/properties/leiston-abbey

RSPB Nature Reserve Minsmere, WESTLETON, IP17 3BY, 01728 648281
www.rspb.org.uk/minsmere

THEBERTON Map 13 TM46

Sycamore Park

►►►77%

tel: 01728 635830 & 830665 **Rearoff Pump Cottages, Main Rd IP16 4RA**
email: enquiries@sycamorepark.co.uk
dir: *From A12 at Yoxford take B1122 towards Theberton.* **grid ref:** *TM435660*

Sycamore Park is a very peaceful site in the village of Theberton, within easy reach of Southwold and Aldeburgh, and only three miles from RSPB Minsmere. There are 20 electric hook-ups on grass pitches set out in a compact field surrounded by mature trees. The small, but high quality and very stylish, toilet block contains combined cubicled facilities and has underfloor heating. 2 acre site. 20 touring pitches. Caravan pitches. Motorhome pitches. Tent pitches.

Open: 3 Mar-28 Jan **Last departure:** noon **Pitches:** £20 £20 £20
Facilities: **Services:** **Within 3 miles:**
Notes: Adults only. Dogs must be kept on leads.

WOODBRIDGE Map 13 TM24

Places to visit

Sutton Hoo, WOODBRIDGE, IP12 3DJ, 01394 389700
www.nationaltrust.org.uk/suttonhoo

Orford Castle, ORFORD, IP12 2ND, 01394 450472
www.english-heritage.org.uk/daysout/properties/orford-castle

Great for kids: Easton Farm Park, EASTON, IP13 0EQ, 01728 746475
www.eastonfarmpark.co.uk

PREMIER PARK

Moon & Sixpence

92%

tel: 01473 736650 **Newbourn Rd, Waldringfield IP12 4PP**
email: info@moonandsixpence.eu **web:** www.moonandsixpence.eu
dir: *From A12 rdbt, E of Ipswich, follow brown caravan & Moon & Sixpence signs (Waldringfield). 1.5m, left at x-rds, follow signs.* **grid ref:** *TM263454*

A well-planned site, with tourers occupying a sheltered valley position around an attractive boating lake with a sandy beach. Toilet facilities are housed in a smart Norwegian-style cabin, and there is a laundry and dish-washing area. Leisure facilities include two tennis courts, a bowling green, fishing, boating and a games room; there's also a lake, woodland trails, a cycle trail and 9-hole golf. The park has an adult-only area, and a strict 'no groups and no noise after 9pm' policy. 5 acre site. 50 touring pitches. 10 hardstandings. Caravan pitches. Motorhome pitches. 225 statics.

Open: Apr-Oct (rs Low season club, shop, reception open limited hours)

Last arrival: 20.00hrs **Last departure:** noon

Pitches: * £22-£34 £22-£34

Leisure:

Facilities:

Services:

Within 3 miles:

Notes: No tents. No group bookings or commercial vehicles, quiet 21.00hrs-08.00hrs. Dogs must be kept on leads. 10-acre sports area, 100-acre woods.

AA Pubs & Restaurants nearby: The Crown at Woodbridge, WOODBRIDGE, IP12 1AD, 01394 384242

Seckford Hall Hotel, WOODBRIDGE, IP13 6NU, 01394 385678

See advert on page 315

Moat Barn Touring Caravan Park

►►► 85%

tel: 01473 737520 **Dallinghoo Rd, Bredfield IP13 6BD**
dir: *Exit A12 at Bredfield, 1st right at village pump. Through village, 1m site on left.*
grid ref: *TM269530*

An attractive small park set in idyllic Suffolk countryside, perfectly located for touring the heritage coastline and for visiting the National Trust's Sutton Hoo. The modern toilet block is well equipped and maintained. There are 10 tent pitches and the park is located on the popular Hull to Harwich cycle route. Cycle hire is available, but there are no facilities for children. 2 acre site. 33 touring pitches. 10 seasonal pitches. Caravan pitches. Motorhome pitches. Tent pitches.

Open: Mar-15 Jan **Last arrival:** 22.00hrs **Last departure:** noon

Pitches: * £19 £19 £19

Facilities:

Services:

Within 3 miles:

Notes: Adults only. No ball games, only breathable groundsheets permitted. Dogs must be kept on leads.

AA Pubs & Restaurants nearby: The Crown at Woodbridge, WOODBRIDGE, IP12 1AD, 01394 384242

Seckford Hall Hotel, WOODBRIDGE, IP13 6NU, 01394 385678

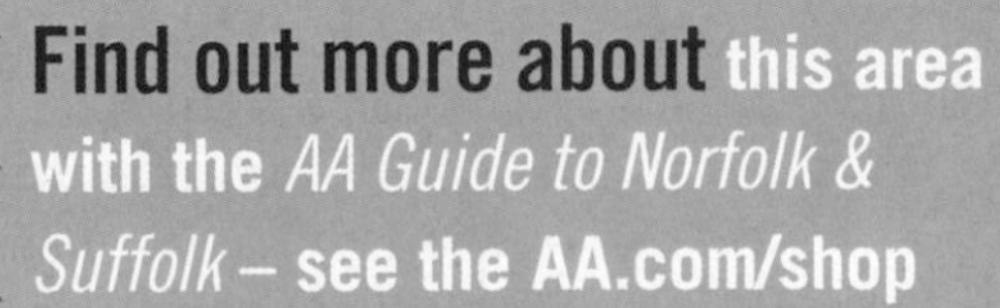

Sussex

East and West Sussex are adjoining counties packed with interest. This is a land of stately homes and castles, miles of breezy chalk cliffs overlooking the English Channel, pretty rivers, picturesque villages and links to our glorious past. Since 2011 it has been the home of Britain's newest national park – the South Downs

Mention Sussex to many people and images of the South Downs immediately spring to mind – 'vast, smooth, shaven, serene,' as the writer Virginia Woolf described them. She and her husband lived at Monk's House in the village of Rodmell, near Lewes, and today, her modest home is managed by the National Trust and open to the public.

Close by, on the downs, is Charleston Farmhouse where Woolf's sister, the artist Vanessa Bell, lived a bohemian life as part of the renowned Bloomsbury group, whose members were mainly notable writers, artists and thinkers. Rudyard Kipling resided at Bateman's, near Burwash, and described the house as 'a good and peaceable place,' after moving there in 1902. 'We have loved it ever since our first sight of it,' he wrote later. Bateman's is also in the care of the National Trust, as is Uppark House at South Harting, near Petersfield. The writer H. G. Wells stayed at Uppark as a boy while his mother was employed there as housekeeper. Away to the east, inland from Hastings, lies Great Dixter, an ancient house in a magical garden. This was the home of the pioneering gardening writer Christopher Lloyd and today both Great Dixter and its garden are open to visitors.

There are a great many historic landmarks within Sussex, but probably the most famous is the battlefield where William, Duke of Normandy defeated Harold and his Saxon army to become William the Conqueror of England. By visiting Battle, near Hastings, you can, with a little imagination, picture the bloody events that led to his defeat. Before the Battle of Hastings, William vowed that if God gave him victory that day, he would build an abbey on the site of the battle at Senlac Field. This he did, with the high altar set up on the spot where Harold died. The abbey was enlarged and improved over the years and today is maintained by English Heritage.

In terms of walking in Sussex, this county is spoilt for choice. Studying the map reveals a multitude of routes – many of them to be found within the boundaries of the South Downs National Park – and an assortment of scenic long-distance trails leading towards distant horizons; all of them offer a perfect way to get to the heart of 'Sussex by the sea,' as it has long been known. The Monarch's Way, one of the region's most popular trails, broadly follows Charles II's escape route in 1651, while the most famous of them, the South Downs Way, follows hill paths and cliff-top tracks all the way from Winchester to Eastbourne. As well as a good range of walks, Sussex offers exhilarating cycle rides through the High Weald, along the South Downs Way and via coastal routes between Worthing and Rye. There is also the Forest Way through East Grinstead to Groombridge. If you enjoy cycling with the salty tang of the sea for company, try the ride between Chichester and West Wittering. You can vary the return journey by taking the Itchenor ferry to Bosham.

Sussex is renowned for its many pretty towns, of course. There is Arundel, littered with period buildings and dominated by the castle, the family home of the Duke of Norfolk, that dates back nearly 1,000 years. Midhurst, Lewes, Rye and Uckfield also have their charms, while the cities of Chichester and Brighton offer countless museums and fascinating landmarks. Brighton's best-known and grandest feature is surely the Royal Pavilion, created as the seaside palace of the Prince Regent (later George IV). The town's genteel Regency terraces and graceful crescents reflect his influence on Brighton. Often referred to as 'London by the sea,' the city has long enjoyed a colourful reputation and has been used as a location in many high profile and highly successful films, including *Brighton Rock* and *Quadrophenia*.

Beachy Head ▷

EAST SUSSEX

BATTLE Map 7 TQ71

Places to visit

1066 Battle of Hastings Abbey & Battlefield, BATTLE, TN33 0AD, 01424 773792 www.english-heritage.org.uk/daysout/properties/1066-battle-of-hastings-abbey-and-battlefield

Yesterday's World, BATTLE, TN33 0AQ, 01424 777226 www.yesterdaysworld.co.uk

Great for kids: The Observatory Science Centre, HERSTMONCEUX, BN27 1RN, 01323 832731 www.the-observatory.org

Brakes Coppice Park

►►► 80%

tel: 01424 830322 **Forewood Ln TN33 9AB**
email: brakesco@btinternet.com
dir: *From Battle on A2100 towards Hastings. After 2m turn right for Crowhurst. Site 1m on left.* **grid ref:** *TQ765134*

A secluded farm site in a sunny meadow deep in woodland with a small stream and a coarse fishing lake. The toilet block has quality fittings and there's a good fully-serviced family/disabled room. Hardstanding pitches are neatly laid out on a terrace, and tents are pitched on grass edged by woodland. The hands-on owners offer high levels of customer care and this tucked-away gem proves a peaceful base for exploring Battle and the south coast. 3 acre site. 60 touring pitches. 10 hardstandings. Caravan pitches. Motorhome pitches. Tent pitches. 1 static.

Open: Mar-Oct **Last arrival:** 21.00hrs **Last departure:** noon

Pitches:

Leisure:

Facilities:

Services:

Within 3 miles:

Notes: No fires, footballs or kite flying. Dogs must be kept on leads.

AA Pubs & Restaurants nearby: Ash Tree Inn, ASHBURNHAM PLACE, TN33 9NX, 01424 892104

The Wild Mushroom Restaurant, WESTFIELD, TN35 4SB, 01424 751137

Senlac Wood

►►► 73%

tel: 01424 773969 **Catsfield Rd, Catsfield TN33 9LN**
email: senlacwood@xlninternet.co.uk
dir: *A271 from Battle onto B2204 signed Bexhill. Site on left.* **grid ref:** *TQ722153*

A woodland site with many secluded hardstanding bays and two peaceful grassy glades for tents. The functional toilet facilities are clean but there are plans to add new toilets in the tent area. The site is ideal for anyone looking for seclusion and shade and it is well placed for visiting nearby Battle and the south coast beaches. 20 acre site. 35 touring pitches. 16 hardstandings. Caravan pitches. Motorhome pitches. Tent pitches.

Open: Mar-Oct **Last arrival:** 22.00hrs **Last departure:** noon

Pitches:

Leisure:

Facilities:

Services:

Within 3 miles:

Notes: No camp fires, no noise after 23.00hrs. Dogs must be kept on leads. Caravan storage.

AA Pubs & Restaurants nearby: Ash Tree Inn, ASHBURNHAM PLACE, TN33 9NX, 01424 892104

The Wild Mushroom Restaurant, WESTFIELD, TN35 4SB, 01424 751137

BEXHILL Map 6 TQ70

Places to visit

Pevensey Castle, PEVENSEY, BN24 5LE, 01323 762604 www.english-heritage.org.uk/daysout/properties/pevensey-castle

1066 Battle of Hastings Abbey & Battlefield, BATTLE, TN33 0AD, 01424 773792 www.english-heritage.org.uk/daysout/properties/1066-battle-of-hastings-abbey-and-battlefield

Great for kids: The Observatory Science Centre, HERSTMONCEUX, BN27 1RN, 01323 832731 www.the-observatory.org

Cobbs Hill Farm Caravan & Camping Park

►►► 81%

tel: 01424 213460 & 07708 958910 **Watermill Ln TN39 5JA**
email: cobbshillfarmuk@hotmail.com
dir: *Exit A269 into Watermill Ln, park 1m on left. (NB it is advisable not to follow Sat Nav).* **grid ref:** *TQ736102*

A well-established farm site tucked away in pleasant rolling countryside close to Bexhill and a short drive from Battle, the South Downs and good beaches. Neat, well-maintained camping paddocks, one with eight hardstanding pitches, are sheltered by mature trees and hedging; the toilet block is clean and freshly painted. Children will love the menagerie of farm animals. 17 acre site. 55 touring pitches. 8 hardstandings. 20 seasonal pitches. Caravan pitches. Motorhome pitches. Tent pitches. 15 statics.

Open: Apr-Oct **Last arrival:** 20.00hrs **Last departure:** noon

Pitches:

Leisure:

Facilities:

Services:

Within 3 miles:

Notes: No camp fires. Dogs must be kept on leads.

AA Pubs & Restaurants nearby: Ash Tree Inn, ASHBURNHAM PLACE, TN33 9NX, 01424 892104

CAMBER Map 7 TQ91

Places to visit

Rye Castle Museum, RYE, TN31 7JY, 01797 226728 www.ryemuseum.co.uk

Lamb House, RYE, TN31 7ES, 01580 762334 www.nationaltrust.org.uk/main/w-lambhouse

CAMBER Map 7 TQ91

Camber Sands

HOLIDAY CENTRE 70%

tel: 0871 664 9719 *(Calls cost 5p per minute plus your phone company's access charge)* & 01797 222000 **New Lydd Rd TN31 7RT**
email: camber.sands@park-resorts.com
dir: *M20 junct 10 (Ashford International Station), A2070 signed Brenzett. Follow Hastings & Rye signs on A259. 1m before Rye, left signed Camber. Site in 3m.* **grid ref:** *TQ972184*

Located opposite Camber's vast sandy beach, this large holiday centre offers a good range of leisure and entertainment facilities. The touring area is positioned close to the reception and entrance, and is served by a clean and functional toilet block. 110 acre site. 55 touring pitches. 6 hardstandings. Caravan pitches. Motorhome pitches. Tent pitches. 921 statics.

Open: Mar-Nov **Last arrival:** anytime **Last departure:** 10.00hrs

Pitches:

Leisure: Spa

Facilities:

Services:

Within 3 miles:

Notes: Quiet from 23.00hrs-07.00hrs. Dogs must be kept on leads.

AA Pubs & Restaurants nearby: Mermaid Inn, RYE, TN31 7EY, 01797 223065

The Ypres Castle Inn, RYE, TN31 7HH, 01797 223248

The George in Rye, RYE, TN31 7JT, 01797 222114

FURNER'S GREEN Map 6 TQ42

Places to visit

Sheffield Park and Garden, SHEFFIELD PARK, TN22 3QX, 01825 790231 www.nationaltrust.org.uk/sheffieldpark

Nymans, HANDCROSS, RH17 6EB, 01444 405250 www.nationaltrust.org.uk/nymans

Great for kids: Bluebell Railway, SHEFFIELD PARK STATION, TN22 3QL, 01825 720800 www.bluebell-railway.co.uk

Heaven Farm

►► 83%

tel: 01825 790226 **TN22 3RG**
email: heavenfarmleisure@btinternet.com
dir: *On A275 between Lewes & East Grinstead, 1m N of Sheffield Park Garden.*
grid ref: *TQ403264*

A delightful, small, rural site on a popular farm complex incorporating a farm museum, craft shop, tea room and nature trail. The good, clean toilet facilities are housed in well-converted outbuildings and chickens and ducks roam freely around the site. Ashdown Forest, the Bluebell Railway and Sheffield Park Garden are nearby. 1.5 acre site. 25 touring pitches. 2 hardstandings. Caravan pitches. Motorhome pitches. Tent pitches. 3 statics.

Open: all year (rs Nov-Mar may close due to bad weather – please check with site) **Last arrival:** 21.00hrs **Last departure:** noon

Pitches:

Facilities:

Services:

Within 3 miles:

Notes: Credit & debit cards accepted only in shop & café. Dogs must be kept on leads. Fishing.

AA Pubs & Restaurants nearby: The Coach and Horses, DANEHILL, RH17 7JF, 01825 740369

The Griffin Inn, FLETCHING, TN22 3SS, 01825 722890

HASTINGS Map 7 TQ80

Places to visit

Old Town Hall Museum of Local History, HASTINGS & ST LEONARDS, TN34 3EW, 01424 451052 www.hmag.org.uk

Shipwreck Museum, HASTINGS & ST LEONARDS, TN34 3DW, 01424 437452 www.shipwreckmuseum.co.uk

Great for kids: Blue Reef Aquarium, HASTINGS & ST LEONARDS, TN34 3DW, 01424 718776 www.bluereefaquarium.co.uk

Smugglers Adventure, HASTINGS & ST LEONARDS, TN34 3HY, 01424 422964 www.discoverhastings.co.uk

Hastings Touring Park

NEW ►►► 82%

tel: 01424 423583 **Shearbarn Holiday Park, Barley Ln TN35 5DX**
email: touringwardens@shearbarn.co.uk
dir: *In Hastings from A259 into Ashburnham Rd. 1st right into Dudley Rd. At staggered x-rds straight over into Gurth Rd. At T-junct left into Barley Rd. Site on right.*
grid ref: *TQ838105*

This large, gently sloping site occupies a lofty position overlooking Hastings, and has great views, instant access to downland walks and provides a peaceful base for visiting this lovely area. The toilets are clean, tidy and well maintained; the two older blocks are freshly painted each year and appointed with modern fixtures and fittings, and the newer, bottom block offers privacy wash basins. There is an excellent children's play area and guests at this park have access to the bar, swimming pool, gym, shop and laundrette at the Shearbarn Holiday Park which is opposite and under the same ownership. Caravan pitches. Motorhome pitches. Tent pitches.

Open: Mar-Oct **Pitches:** **Leisure:**

Facilities: **Services:**

HASTINGS *continued*

Combe Haven Holiday Park

HOLIDAY HOME PARK 87%

GOLD

tel: 01424 427891 **Harley Shute Rd, St Leonards-on-Sea TN38 8BZ**
email: combehaven@haven.com **web:** www.haven.com/combehaven
dir: *A21 towards Hastings. In Hastings take A259 towards Bexhill. Park signed on right.*
grid ref: *TQ779091*

Close to a beach and the resort attractions of Hastings, this newly upgraded holiday park has been designed with families in mind. Activities include a pirates' adventure playground, heated swimming pools and a wealth of sports and outdoor activities.

Open: Mar-Oct **Change over day:** Mon, Fri, Sat

Arrival and departure times: Please contact the site

Statics: 296 Sleeps 6-8 Bedrms 2-3 Bathrms 1-2 Toilets 1-2 Microwave Freezer TV Sky/FTV Elec inc Gas inc Grass area

Children: Cots Highchair **Dogs:** 2 on leads No dangerous dogs

Leisure: Cycle hire

PEVENSEY BAY — Map 6 TQ60

Places to visit

"How We Lived Then" Museum of Shops & Social History, EASTBOURNE, BN21 4NS, 01323 737143 www.how-we-lived-then.co.uk

Alfriston Clergy House, ALFRISTON, BN26 5TL, 01323 871961 www.nationaltrust.org.uk/alfriston/

Great for kids: The Observatory Science Centre, HERSTMONCEUX, BN27 1RN, 01323 832731 www.the-observatory.org

Bay View Park

►►► 85%

tel: 01323 768688 **Old Martello Rd BN24 6DX**
email: holidays@bay-view.co.uk
dir: *Signed from A259 W of Pevensey Bay. On seaward side of A259 take private road towards beach.* **grid ref:** *TQ648028*

A pleasant well-run site just yards from the beach, in an area east of Eastbourne town centre known as 'The Crumbles'. The level grassy site is very well maintained and the toilet facilities feature fully-serviced cubicles. The seasonal tent field has marked pitches and toilet facilities with toilet and washbasins, and washbasins and shower cubicles. Adjacent there is a 9-hole par 4 golf course and clubhouse. 6 acre site. 94 touring pitches. 14 hardstandings. 27 seasonal pitches. Caravan pitches. Motorhome pitches. Tent pitches. 17 statics.

Open: Mar-Oct **Last arrival:** 20.00hrs **Last departure:** noon

Pitches: * £17-£26 £17-£26 £17-£26

Leisure: **Facilities:**

Services:

Within 3 miles:

Notes: Families & couples only, no commercial vehicles, no ball games, no noise after 23.00hrs. Dogs must be kept on leads.

AA Pubs & Restaurants nearby: The Farm @ Friday Street, LANGNEY, BN23 8AP, 01323 766049

WEST SUSSEX

ARUNDEL — Map 6 TQ00

Places to visit

Arundel Castle, ARUNDEL, BN18 9AB, 01903 882173 www.arundelcastle.org

Harbour Park, LITTLEHAMPTON, BN17 5LL, 01903 721200 www.harbourpark.com

Great for kids: Look & Sea! Visitor Centre, LITTLEHAMPTON, BN17 5AW, 01903 718984 www.lookandsea.co.uk

Ship & Anchor Marina

►► 79%

tel: 01243 551262 **Station Rd, Ford BN18 0BJ**

email: enquiries@shipandanchormarina.co.uk
dir: *From A27 at Arundel take road S signed Ford. Site 2m on left after level crossing.*
grid ref: *TQ002040*

Neatly maintained by the enthusiastic, hard working owner, this small, well located site has dated but spotlessly clean toilet facilities, a secluded tent area, and enjoys a pleasant position beside the Ship & Anchor pub and the tidal River Arun. There are good walks from the site to Arundel and the coast. 12 acre site. 120 touring pitches. 11 hardstandings. Caravan pitches. Motorhome pitches. Tent pitches.

Open: Mar-Oct **Last arrival:** 21.00hrs **Last departure:** noon

Pitches: * £16-£22 £16-£22 £16-£22

Leisure:

Facilities:

Services:

Within 3 miles:

Notes: No music audible to others. Dogs must be kept on leads. River fishing available from site.

AA Pubs & Restaurants nearby: The Town House, ARUNDEL, BN18 9AJ, 01903 883847

The George at Burpham, BURPHAM, BN18 9RR, 01903 883131

BARNS GREEN — Map 6 TQ12

Places to visit

Parham House & Gardens, PULBOROUGH, RH20 4HS, 01903 742021 www.parhaminsussex.co.uk

Great for kids: Bignor Roman Villa & Museum, BIGNOR, RH20 1PH, 01798 869259 www.bignorromanvilla.co.uk

Sumners Ponds Fishery & Campsite

►►►► 87%

GOLD

tel: 01403 732539 **Chapel Rd RH13 0PR**
email: bookings@sumnersponds.co.uk
dir: *From A272 at Coolham x-rds, N towards Barns Green. In 1.5m take 1st left at small x-rds. 1m, over level crossing. Site on left just after right bend.* **grid ref:** *TQ125268*

Dedication to provide high quality camping continues at this working farm set in attractive surroundings on the edge of the quiet village of Barns Green. There are three touring areas; one continues to develop and includes camping pods and extra hardstandings, and another, which has a stunning modern toilet block, has

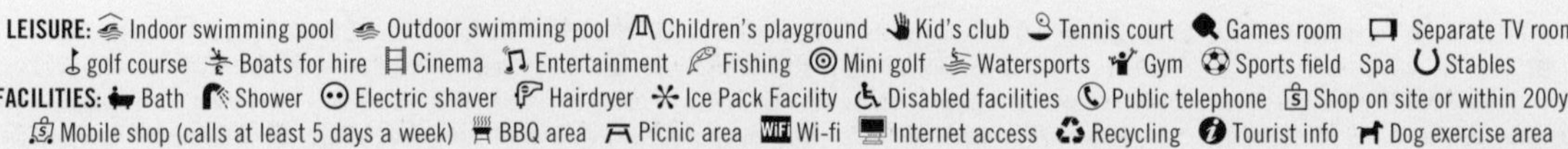

excellent pitches (and pods) on the banks of one of the well-stocked fishing lakes. There are many cycle paths on site and a woodland walk has direct access to miles of footpaths. The Café by the Lake serves meals from breakfast onwards. Horsham and Brighton are within easy reach. 40 acre site. 86 touring pitches. 45 hardstandings. Caravan pitches. Motorhome pitches. Tent pitches. 4 wooden pods.

Open: all year **Last arrival:** 20.00hrs **Last departure:** noon

Pitches: **Leisure:**

Facilities:

Services:

Within 3 miles:

Notes: Only one car per pitch. Easy/disabled access fishing platform.

AA Pubs & Restaurants nearby: The White Horse, MAPLEHURST, RH13 6LL, 01403 891208

BILLINGSHURST — Map 6 TQ02

Places to visit

Petworth House & Park, PETWORTH, GU28 0AE, 01798 342207 & 343929
www.nationaltrust.org.uk/petworth

Petworth Cottage Museum, PETWORTH, GU28 0AU, 01798 342100
www.petworthcottagemuseum.co.uk

Limeburners Arms Camp Site

►► 74%

tel: 01403 782311 **Lordings Rd, Newbridge RH14 9JA**
email: chippy.sawyer@virgin.net **web:** www.thelimeburners.com
dir: *From A29 take A272 towards Petworth for 1m, left onto B2133. Site 300yds on left.*
grid ref: *TQ072255*

A secluded site in rural West Sussex, at the rear of the Limeburners Arms public house, and surrounded by fields. It makes a pleasant base for touring the South Downs and the Arun Valley. The toilets are basic but very clean. 2.75 acre site. 40 touring pitches. Caravan pitches. Motorhome pitches. Tent pitches.

Open: Apr-Oct **Last arrival:** 22.00hrs **Last departure:** 14.00hrs

Pitches: **Leisure:** **Facilities:**

Services: **Within 3 miles:**

Notes: Dogs must be kept on leads.

AA Pubs & Restaurants nearby: The White Horse, MAPLEHURST, RH13 6LL, 01403 891208

CHICHESTER — Map 5 SU80

Places to visit

Chichester Cathedral, CHICHESTER, PO19 1PX, 01243 782595
www.chichestercathedral.org.uk

Pallant House Gallery, CHICHESTER, PO19 1TJ, 01243 774557
www.pallant.org.uk

REGIONAL WINNER – SOUTH EAST ENGLAND
AA CAMPSITE OF THE YEAR 2016

PREMIER PARK

Concierge Camping

NEW ►►►►► 87%

tel: 01243 573118 **Ratham Estate, Ratham Ln, West Ashling PO18 8DL**
email: service@conciergecamping.co.uk
dir: *From A27 onto A259 to Bosham, In Bosham at rdbt into Station Rd. Over railway line, over A27. At T-junct left onto B2146 signed West Ashling. 1st left into Ratham Lane.* **grid ref:** *SU811063*

Developing this stunning new park in a field adjoining their home has been a labour of love for Tracey and Guy. Major investment has created a first-class small park for 15 units (the larger ones are suitable for American RVs and cars towing caravans), and the attention to detail throughout is very impressive. Everything is high spec, from very spacious fully-serviced pitches and the new reception, complete with a shop that sells daily-delivered local produce, coffee, drinks, and late-arrival and breakfast hampers, to the state-of-the-art amenities block. Here you'll find full-length mirrors, ultra-efficient rain showers, an air-blade hand-drier, stylish wash basins and showers with temperature controls, piped radio and Ratham Estate toiletries plus an excellent family/disabled room. 4 acre site. 15 touring pitches. 15 hardstandings. Caravan pitches. Motorhome pitches.

Open: Mar-Jan **Last arrival:** 21.00hrs (late arrival times by prior arrangement)
Last departure: noon

Pitches: * £28-£60 £28-£60

Facilities:

Services:

Within 3 miles:

Notes: No bookings accepted by under 18yrs. No noise after 23.00hrs. Dogs must be kept on leads.

CHICHESTER *continued*

Ellscott Park

►►► 82%

tel: 01243 512003 **Sidlesham Ln, Birdham PO20 7QL**
email: camping@ellscottpark.co.uk
dir: *From Chichester take A286 for approx 4m, left at Butterfly Farm sign, site 500yds right.* **grid ref:** *SU829995*

A well-kept park set in sheltered meadowland behind the owners' nursery and van storage area. The park attracts a peace-loving clientele, has spotless, well maintained toilet facilities, and is handy for the beach, Chichester, Goodwood House, the racing at Goodwood and walking on the South Downs. Home-grown produce is for sale. 2.5 acre site. 50 touring pitches. 25 seasonal pitches. Caravan pitches. Motorhome pitches. Tent pitches.

Open: Apr-3rd wk in Oct **Last arrival:** daylight **Last departure:** variable

Pitches: * £14-£20 £14-£20 £11-£17

Leisure:

Facilities:

Services:

Within 3 miles:

Notes: Dogs must be kept on leads.

AA Pubs & Restaurants nearby: The Crab & Lobster, SIDLESHAM, PO20 7NB, 01243 641233

DIAL POST

Places to visit

Parham House & Gardens, PULBOROUGH, RH20 4HS, 01903 742021 www.parhaminsussex.co.uk

RSPB Pulborough Brooks Nature Reserve, PULBOROUGH, RH20 2EL, 01798 875851 www.rspb.org.uk/pulboroughbrooks

DIAL POST Map 6 TQ11

Honeybridge Park

►►►► 85%

tel: 01403 710923 **Honeybridge Ln RH13 8NX**
email: enquiries@honeybridgepark.co.uk
dir: *10m S of Horsham. Take A24 towards Ashington. S of Dial Post turn left signed Ashurst. Site on right behind Old Barn Nursery.* **grid ref:** *TQ152183*

An attractive and very popular park on gently-sloping ground surrounded by hedgerows and mature trees. A comprehensive amenities building houses upmarket toilet facilities including luxury family and disabled rooms, as well as a laundry, shop and off-licence. There are plenty of hardstandings and electric hook-ups, a games room, and an excellent children's play area. 15 acre site. 130 touring pitches. 70 hardstandings. 20 seasonal pitches. Caravan pitches. Motorhome pitches. Tent pitches. 50 statics.

Open: all year **Last arrival:** 19.00hrs **Last departure:** noon

Pitches:

Leisure:

Facilities:

Services:

Within 3 miles:

Notes: No open fires. Dogs must be kept on leads. Fridges available.

AA Pubs & Restaurants nearby: The Countryman Inn, SHIPLEY, RH13 8PZ, 01403 741383

The Crown Inn, DIAL POST, RH13 8NH, 01403 710902

The Queens Head, WEST CHILTINGTON, RH20 2JN, 01798 812244

HENFIELD

Places to visit

Bolney Wine Estate, BOLNEY, RH17 5NB, 01444 881575 www.bolneywineestate.com

LEISURE: Indoor swimming pool Outdoor swimming pool Children's playground Kid's club Tennis court Games room Separate TV room golf course Boats for hire Cinema Entertainment Fishing Mini golf Watersports Gym Sports field Spa Stables
FACILITIES: Bath Shower Electric shaver Hairdryer Ice Pack Facility Disabled facilities Public telephone Shop on site or within 200yds Mobile shop (calls at least 5 days a week) BBQ area Picnic area Wi-fi Internet access Recycling Tourist info Dog exercise area

HENFIELD Map 6 TQ21

Blacklands Farm Caravan & Camping

►► 72%

tel: 01273 493528 & 07773 792577 **Wheatsheaf Rd BN5 9AT**
email: info@blacklandsfarm.co.uk
dir: *A23, B2118, B2116 towards Henfield. Site approx 4m on right.* **grid ref:** *TQ231180*

Tucked away off the B2116, east of Henfield, and well placed for visiting Brighton and exploring the South Downs National Park, this simple, grassy site has great potential, and the owners plan improvements that will not spoil the traditional feel of the campsite. There are spacious pitches down by fishing lakes and the basic portaloos are clean and tidy and have been smartly clad in wood, but future plans do include building a new toilet block. 5 acre site. 75 touring pitches. Caravan pitches. Motorhome pitches. Tent pitches.

Open: Mar-Jan **Last arrival:** 20.00hrs **Last departure:** anytime

Pitches: **Leisure:** **Facilities:**

Services: **Within 3 miles:**

Notes: No commercial vehicles. Dogs must be kept on leads. Coffee machine.

AA Pubs & Restaurants nearby: The Fountain Inn, ASHURST, BN44 3AP, 01403 710219

Royal Oak, POYNINGS, BN45 7AQ, 01273 857389

HORSHAM

See Barns Green & Dial Post

PAGHAM Map 6 SZ89

Places to visit

Chichester Cathedral, CHICHESTER, PO19 1PX, 01243 782595
www.chichestercathedral.org.uk

Pallant House Gallery, CHICHESTER, PO19 1TJ, 01243 774557
www.pallant.org.uk

Church Farm Holiday Park

HOLIDAY HOME PARK 90%

tel: 01243 262635 **Church Ln PO21 4NR**
email: churchfarm@haven.com **web:** www.haven.com/churchfarm
dir: *At rdbt on A27 (S of Chichester) take B2145 signed Hunston & Selsey. At mini rdbt take 1st left signed North Mundham, Pagham & Bognor Regis. Site in approx 3m.*
grid ref: *SZ885974*

Close to Portsmouth, Chichester and south coast beaches, this relaxing and fun-packed holiday park is located close to Pagham Harbour Nature Reserve. On-site activities include golf on the 9-hole course, tennis coaching, shopping, kids' play areas and evening entertainment. There are a range of holiday caravans and apartments.

Open: Mar-Oct **Change over day:** Mon, Fri, Sat

Arrival and departure times: Please contact the site

Statics: 189 Sleeps 6-8 Bedrms 2-3 Bathrms 1-2 Toilets 1-2 Microwave Freezer TV Sky/FTV Elec inc Gas inc Grass area

Children: Cots Highchair **Dogs:** 2 on leads No dangerous dogs

Leisure: Cycle hire

SELSEY Map 5 SZ89

Places to visit

Chichester Cathedral, CHICHESTER, PO19 1PX, 01243 782595
www.chichestercathedral.org.uk

Pallant House Gallery, CHICHESTER, PO19 1TJ, 01243 774557
www.pallant.org.uk

Warner Farm Touring Park

HOLIDAY CENTRE 82%

tel: 01243 604499 **Warner Ln, Selsey PO20 9EL**
email: touring@bunnleisure.co.uk **web:** www.warnerfarm.co.uk
dir: *From B2145 in Selsey turn right into School Lane & follow signs.* **grid ref:** *SZ845939*

A well-screened touring site that adjoins the three static parks under the same ownership. A courtesy bus runs around the complex to entertainment areas and supermarkets. The park backs onto open grassland, and the leisure facilities with bar, amusements and bowling alley, and swimming pool/sauna complex are also accessible to tourers. 10 acre site. 250 touring pitches. 60 hardstandings. 25 seasonal pitches. Caravan pitches. Motorhome pitches. Tent pitches.

Open: Mar-Jan **Last arrival:** 17.30hrs **Last departure:** 10.00hrs

Pitches: **Leisure:**

Facilities:

Services: **Within 3 miles:**

Notes: Dogs must be kept on leads.

AA Pubs & Restaurants nearby: The Crab & Lobster, SIDLESHAM, PO20 7NB, 01243 641233

See advert on opposite page

PITCHES: Caravans Motorhomes Tents Glamping-style accommodation **SERVICES:** Electric hook up Launderette Licensed bar Calor Gas Camping Gaz Toilet fluid Café/Restaurant Fast Food/Takeaway Battery charging Baby care Motorvan service point
ABBREVIATIONS: BH/bank hols – bank holidays Etr – Easter Spring BH – Spring Bank Holiday fr – from hrs – hours m – mile mdnt – midnight rdbt – roundabout rs – restricted service wk – week wknd – weekend x-rds – cross roads No credit or debit cards No dogs Children of all ages accepted

WEST MIDLANDS

MERIDEN Map 10 SP28

Places to visit

Blakesley Hall, BIRMINGHAM, B25 8RN, 0121 348 8120 www.bmag.org.uk/blakesley-hall

Packwood House, PACKWOOD HOUSE, B94 6AT, 01564 782024 www.nationaltrust.org.uk/main/w-packwoodhouse

Somers Wood Caravan Park

Best of British

►►►► 92%

tel: 01676 522978 **Somers Rd CV7 7PL**
email: enquiries@somerswood.co.uk
dir: *M42 junct 6, A45 signed Coventry. Keep left, do not take flyover. Right onto A452 signed Meriden & Leamington. At next rdbt left onto B4102 Hampton Lane. Site in 0.5m on left.* **grid ref:** *SP225824*

A peaceful adults-only park set in the heart of England with spotless facilities. The park is well positioned for visiting the National Exhibition Centre (NEC), the NEC Arena and National Indoor Arena (NIA), and Birmingham is only 12 miles away. The park also makes an ideal touring base for Warwick, Coventry and Stratford-upon-Avon just 22 miles away. Please note that tents are not accepted. 4 acre site. 48 touring pitches. 48 hardstandings. Caravan pitches. Motorhome pitches.

Open: all year **Last arrival:** variable **Last departure:** variable

Pitches:

Facilities:

Services:

Within 3 miles:

Notes: Adults only. No noise 22.30hrs-08.00hrs. Dogs must be kept on leads.

AA Pubs & Restaurants nearby: The White Lion Inn, HAMPTON IN ARDEN, B92 0AA, 01675 442833

WILTSHIRE

AMESBURY Map 5 SU14

Places to visit

Stonehenge, STONEHENGE, SP4 7DE, 0370 333 1181 www.english-heritage.org.uk/daysout/properties/stonehenge

Heale Gardens, MIDDLE WOODFORD, SP4 6NT, 01722 782504 www.healegarden.co.uk

Great for kids: Wilton House, WILTON (NEAR SALISBURY), SP2 0BJ, 01722 746714 www.wiltonhouse.com

Stonehenge Touring Park

►►► 86%

tel: 01980 620304 **Orcheston SP3 4SH**
email: stay@stonehengetouringpark.com
dir: *From A360 towards Devizes turn right, follow lane, site at bottom of village on right.* **grid ref:** *SU061456*

A quiet site adjacent to the small village of Orcheston near the centre of Salisbury Plain. There are modern and very clean facilities which were upgraded for the 2015 season and there's an excellent on-site shop; some hardstandings are available. This is a well located site for visiting Stonehenge and nearby Salisbury plus its less that an hour's drive from the heart of the New Forest National Park. 2 acre site. 30 touring pitches. 13 hardstandings. Caravan pitches. Motorhome pitches. Tent pitches.

Open: all year **Last arrival:** 19.00hrs **Last departure:** 11.00hrs

Pitches: £11-£17 £11-£17 £11-£27

Leisure:

Facilities:

Services:

Within 3 miles:

Notes: No noise after 23.00hrs. Dogs must be kept on leads.

AA Pubs & Restaurants nearby: The Boot Inn, BERWICK ST JAMES, SP3 4TN, 01722 790243

BERWICK ST JAMES — Map 5 SU03

Places to visit

Stonehenge, STONEHENGE, SP4 7DE, 0370 333 1181
www.english-heritage.org.uk/daysout/properties/stonehenge

Heale Gardens, MIDDLE WOODFORD, SP4 6NT, 01722 782504
www.healegarden.co.uk

Stonehenge Campsite & Glamping Pods

►►► 86%

tel: 07786 734732 **SP3 4TQ**
email: stay@stonehengecampsite.co.uk
dir: *From Stonehenge Visitor Centre take A303 W, 2m. Through Winterbourne Stoke. Left onto B3083 towards Berwick St James. Site on left in 0.5m.* **grid ref:** *SU077405*

This small campsite is split into three areas and has good modern toilets and showers including a laundry facility. The lower end of the site has hardstandings for caravans and motorhomes plus five glamping pods, including the novel Festival Pod. The middle field is for tents, both for families and individuals, whilst the top area is for larger groups who can perhaps enjoy some of their holiday time sitting around open fires or fire pits. The site is close to Stonehenge and Longleat; there are plenty of excellent walks from the campsite and two good pubs nearby. 4 acre site. 35 touring pitches. 10 hardstandings. Caravan pitches. Motorhome pitches. Tent pitches. 5 wooden pods.

Open: all year **Last arrival:** 20.30hrs **Last departure:** 11.00hrs

Pitches: * £13-£24 £13-£22 £10-£25

Facilities:

Services:

Within 3 miles:

Notes: No noise after 22.00hrs. Dogs must be kept on leads. Fire pit & mobile fire pits.

CALNE — Map 4 ST97

Places to visit

Avebury Manor & Garden, AVEBURY, SN8 1RF, 01672 539250
www.english-heritage.org.uk/daysout/properties/avebury

Bowood House & Gardens, CALNE, SN11 0LZ, 01249 812102 www.bowood.org

Great for kids: Alexander Keiller Museum, AVEBURY, SN8 1RF, 01672 539250
www.nationaltrust.org.uk

Blackland Lakes Holiday & Leisure Centre

►►► 79%

tel: 01249 810943 **Stockley Ln SN11 0NQ**
email: enquiries@blacklandlakes.co.uk
dir: *From Calne take A4 E for 1.5m, right at camp sign. Site 1m on left.*
grid ref: *ST973687*

A rural site surrounded by the North and West Downs. The park is divided into several paddocks separated by hedges, trees and fences, and there are two well-stocked carp fisheries for the angling enthusiast. There are some excellent walks close by, and the interesting market town of Devizes is just a few miles away. 15 acre site. 180 touring pitches. 16 hardstandings. 25 seasonal pitches. Caravan pitches. Motorhome pitches. Tent pitches.

Open: all year (rs 30 Oct-1 Mar pre-paid bookings only) **Last arrival:** 22.00hrs
Last departure: noon

Pitches:

Leisure:

Facilities:

Services:

Within 3 miles:

Notes: No groups of under 25s. No noise after 22.30hrs, no loud music. Dogs must be kept on leads. Wildfowl sanctuary, cycle trail.

AA Pubs & Restaurants nearby: The White Horse, CALNE, SN11 8RG, 01249 813118

The Lansdowne, CALNE, SN11 0EH, 01249 812488

The George Inn, LACOCK, SN15 2LH, 01249 730263

LACOCK

Map 4 ST96

Places to visit

Lacock Abbey, Fox Talbot Museum & Village, LACOCK, SN15 2LG, 01249 730459 www.nationaltrust.org.uk/lacock

Corsham Court, CORSHAM, SN13 0BZ, 01249 701610 www.corsham-court.co.uk

Piccadilly Caravan Park

►►►► 83%

tel: 01249 730260 **Folly Lane West SN15 2LP**
email: info@piccadillylacock.co.uk **web:** www.piccadillylacock.co.uk
dir: *4m S of Chippenham just past Lacock. Exit A350 signed Gastard. Site 300yds on left.*
grid ref: *ST913683*

A peaceful, pleasant site, well established and beautifully laid-out, close to the village of Lacock and Lacock Abbey. Both the facilities and the grounds are immaculately maintained; there is very good screening. A section of the park has been developed to provide spacious pitches especially for tents, complete with its own toilet and shower block. 2.5 acre site. 41 touring pitches. 12 hardstandings. Caravan pitches. Motorhome pitches. Tent pitches.

Open: Etr & Apr-Oct **Last arrival:** 21.00hrs **Last departure:** noon

Pitches: * £19-£21 £19-£21 £19-£21

Leisure:

Facilities:

Services:

Within 3 miles:

Notes: Dogs must be kept on leads.

LANDFORD

Map 5 SU21

Places to visit

Furzey Gardens, MINSTEAD, SO43 7GL, 023 8081 2464 www.furzey-gardens.org

Mottisfont, MOTTISFONT, SO51 0LP, 01794 340757 www.nationaltrust.org.uk/mottisfont

Great for kids: Paultons Park, OWER, SO51 6AL, 023 8081 4442 www.paultonspark.co.uk

PREMIER PARK

Greenhill Farm Caravan & Camping Park

►►►►► 85%

tel: 01794 324117 **Greenhill Farm, New Rd SP5 2AZ**
email: info@greenhillfarm.co.uk
dir: *M27 junct 2, A36 towards Salisbury, approx 3m after Hampshire/Wiltshire border, pass Shoe Inn pub on right & BP garage on left, take next left into New Rd, signed Nomansland, 0.75m on left.* **grid ref:** *SU266183*

A tranquil, well-landscaped park hidden away in unspoilt countryside on the edge of the New Forest National Park. Pitches overlooking the fishing lake include hardstandings and are for adults only. The other section of the park is for families and includes a play area and games room. The site provides excellent toilet and shower blocks in both the family area and adults' only area. This site is also well placed for visiting Paultons Family Theme Park at Ower. 13 acre site. 160 touring pitches. 45 hardstandings. Caravan pitches. Motorhome pitches. Tent pitches.

Open: all year **Last arrival:** 21.30hrs **Last departure:** 11.00hrs

Pitches: * £18-£28 £18-£28 £16-£28

Leisure:

Facilities:

Services:

Within 3 miles:

Notes: No noise after 23.00hrs. Dogs must be kept on leads. Disposable BBQs.

SALISBURY — Map 5 SU12

See also Amesbury

Places to visit

The Salisbury Museum, SALISBURY, SP1 2EN, 01722 332151 www.salisburymuseum.org.com

Salisbury Cathedral, SALISBURY, SP1 2EJ, 01722 555120 www.salisburycathedral.org.uk

Great for kids: Wilton House, WILTON [NEAR SALISBURY], SP2 0BJ, 01722 746714 www.wiltonhouse.com

Coombe Touring Park

90%

tel: 01722 328451 **Race Plain, Netherhampton SP2 8PN**
email: enquiries@coombecaravanpark.co.uk **web:** www.coombecaravanpark.co.uk
dir: *A36 onto A3094, 2m SW, site adjacent to Salisbury Racecourse.* **grid ref:** *SU099282*

A very neat and attractive site adjacent to the racecourse with views over the downs. The park is well landscaped with shrubs and maturing trees, and the very colourful beds are stocked from the owner's own greenhouse. This is a lovely quiet and peaceful park to stay on with an excellent toilet and shower block, and a new heated function room and campers' retreat was added for the 2015 season. There are four static homes available for hire. 3 acre site. 50 touring pitches. 6 hardstandings. Caravan pitches. Motorhome pitches. Tent pitches. 6 statics.

Open: all year (rs Oct-Apr shop closed) **Last arrival:** 21.00hrs **Last departure:** noon

Pitches:

Leisure:

Facilities:

Services:

Within 3 miles:

Notes: No disposable BBQs or fires, no mini motorbikes, no noise between 23.00hrs-07.00hrs. Dogs must be kept on leads. Children's bathroom available.

AA Pubs & Restaurants nearby: The Wig and Quill, SALISBURY, SP1 2PH, 01722 335665

Alderbury Caravan & Camping Park

81%

tel: 01722 710125 **Southampton Rd, Whaddon SP5 3HB**
email: alderbury@aol.com
dir: *Follow Whaddon signs from A36, 3m from Salisbury. Site opposite The Three Crowns pub.* **grid ref:** *SU197259*

A pleasant, attractive park set in the village of Whaddon not far from Salisbury. The small site is well maintained by friendly owners, and is ideally positioned near the A36 for overnight stops to and from the Southampton ferry terminals. 2 acre site. 39 touring pitches. 12 hardstandings. Caravan pitches. Motorhome pitches. Tent pitches. 1 static.

Open: all year **Last arrival:** 21.00hrs **Last departure:** 12.30hrs

Pitches:

Facilities:

Services:

Within 3 miles:

Notes: No open fires. Dogs must be kept on leads. Microwave & electric kettle available.

AA Pubs & Restaurants nearby: Salisbury Seafood & Steakhouse, SALISBURY, SP1 3TE, 01722 417411

The Cloisters, SALISBURY, SP1 2DH, 01722 338102

TROWBRIDGE — Map 4 ST85

Places to visit

Great Chalfield Manor and Garden, BRADFORD-ON-AVON, SN12 8NH, 01225 782239 www.nationaltrust.org.uk

The Courts Garden, HOLT, BA14 6RR, 01225 782875 www.nationaltrust.org.uk

Great for kids: Longleat Safari & Adventure Park, LONGLEAT, BA12 7NW, 01985 844400 www.longleat.co.uk

Stowford Manor Farm

76%

tel: 01225 752253 **Stowford, Wingfield BA14 9LH**
email: stowford1@supanet.com
dir: *From Trowbridge take A366 W towards Radstock. Site on left in 3m.*
grid ref: *ST810577*

A very simple farm site set on the banks of the River Frome behind the farm courtyard. The owners are friendly and relaxed and the park enjoys a similarly comfortable ambience, with cream teas available at the farmhouse. Farleigh & District Swimming Club, one of the few remaining river swimming clubs, is just half a mile from the site. 1.5 acre site. 15 touring pitches. Caravan pitches. Motorhome pitches. Tent pitches.

Open: Etr-Oct **Last departure:** noon

Pitches: * fr £16 fr £16 fr £16

Facilities:

Services:

Within 3 miles:

Notes: No open fires, fire bowls for hire. Dogs must be kept on leads. Fishing, boating, river swimming.

AA Pubs & Restaurants nearby: George Inn, NORTON ST PHILIP, BA2 7LH, 01373 834224

WESTBURY Map 4 ST85

Places to visit

Great Chalfield Manor and Garden, BRADFORD-ON-AVON, SN12 8NH, 01225 782239 www.nationaltrust.org.uk

The Courts Garden, HOLT, BA14 6RR, 01225 782875 www.nationaltrust.org.uk

Brokerswood Country Park

►►►► 85%

GOLD

tel: 01373 822238 **Brokerswood BA13 4EH**
email: info@brokerswoodcountrypark.co.uk **web:** www.brokerswoodcountrypark.co.uk
dir: *M4 junct 17, S on A350. Right at Yarnbrook to Rising Sun pub at North Bradley, left at rdbt. Left on bend approaching Southwick, 2.5m, site on right.* **grid ref:** *ST836523*

A popular site on the edge of an 80-acre woodland park with nature trails, fishing lakes and a good range of activities including archery, tree tops high rope course and kayaking. The adventure playground offers plenty of fun for all ages, and there is a miniature railway, an undercover play area and a breakfast bar. There are high quality toilet facilities and fully-equipped, ready-erected tents are available for hire. 5 acre site. 69 touring pitches. 21 hardstandings. Caravan pitches. Motorhome pitches. Tent pitches.

Open: Apr-4 Nov **Last arrival:** 21.30hrs **Last departure:** 11.00hrs

Pitches: * £16-£32 £16-£32 £16-£32

Leisure:

Facilities:

Services:

Within 3 miles:

Notes: Families only. Dogs must be kept on leads.

WORCESTERSHIRE

HONEYBOURNE Map 10 SP14

Places to visit

Kiftsgate Court Garden, MICKLETON, GL55 6LN, 01386 438777 www.kiftsgate.co.uk

Hidcote Manor Garden, MICKLETON, GL55 6LR, 01386 438333 www.nationaltrust.org.uk/hidcote

Great for kids: Anne Hathaway's Cottage, SHOTTERY, CV37 9HH, 01789 201844 www.shakespeare.org.uk

PREMIER PARK

Ranch Caravan Park

►►►►► 84%

tel: 01386 830744 **Station Rd WR11 7PR**
email: enquiries@ranch.co.uk **web:** www.ranch.co.uk
dir: *From village x-rds towards Bidford, site 400mtrs on left.* **grid ref:** *SP113444*

An attractive and well-run park set amidst farmland in the Vale of Evesham and landscaped with trees and bushes. Tourers have their own excellent facilities in two locations, and the use of an outdoor heated swimming pool in peak season. There is also a licensed club serving meals. Please note that this site does not accept tents. 12 acre site. 120 touring pitches. 46 hardstandings. 23 seasonal pitches. Caravan pitches. Motorhome pitches. 218 statics.

Open: Mar-Nov (rs Mar-May & Sep-Nov swimming pool closed, shorter club hours) **Last arrival:** 20.00hrs **Last departure:** noon

Pitches: * £24.50-£29 £24.50-£29

Leisure:

Facilities:

Services:

Within 3 miles:

Notes: No unaccompanied minors. Dogs must be kept on leads.

AA Pubs & Restaurants nearby: The Fleece Inn, BRETFORTON, WR11 7JE, 01386 831173

The Ebrington Arms, EBRINGTON, GL55 6NH, 01386 593223

LEISURE: Indoor swimming pool · Outdoor swimming pool · Children's playground · Kid's club · Tennis court · Games room · Separate TV room · golf course · Boats for hire · Cinema · Entertainment · Fishing · Mini golf · Watersports · Gym · Sports field · Spa · Stables
FACILITIES: Bath · Shower · Electric shaver · Hairdryer · Ice Pack Facility · Disabled facilities · Public telephone · Shop on site or within 200yds · Mobile shop (calls at least 5 days a week) · BBQ area · Picnic area · Wi-fi · Internet access · Recycling · Tourist info · Dog exercise area

WORCESTER Map 10 SO85

Places to visit

City Museum & Art Gallery, WORCESTER, WR1 1DT, 01905 25371 www.museumsworcestershire.org.uk

The Greyfriars' House and Garden, WORCESTER, WR1 2LZ, 01905 23571 www.nationaltrust.org.uk

Great for kids: West Midland Safari & Leisure Park, BEWDLEY, DY12 1LF, 01299 402114 www.wmsp.co.uk

Peachley Leisure Touring Park

 87%

tel: 01905 641309 & 07764 540803 **Peachley Ln, Lower Broadheath WR2 6QX**
email: peachleyleisure@live.co.uk
dir: *M5 junct 7, A44 (Worcester ring road) towards Leominster. Exit at sign for Elgar's Birthplace Museum. Pass museum, at x-rds turn right. In 0.75m at T-junct turn left. Park signed on right.* **grid ref:** *SO807576*

The park is set in its own area in the grounds of Peachley Farm and has all hardstanding and fully serviced pitches. There are two fishing lakes, a really excellent quad bike course and outdoor giant draughts, chess and jenga. The park proves to be a peaceful haven, and is an excellent base from which to explore the area, which includes The Elgar Birthplace Museum, Worcester Racecourse and the Worcester Victorian Christmas Fayre (in late November); it is also convenient for Malvern's Three Counties Showground. 8 acre site. 82 touring pitches. 82 hardstandings. Caravan pitches. Motorhome pitches. Tent pitches.

Open: all year **Last arrival:** 21.30hrs **Last departure:** 15.00hrs

Pitches:

Leisure:

Facilities: WiFi

Services:

Within 3 miles:

Notes: No skateboards, no riding on motorbikes or scooters. Dogs must be kept on leads.

AA Pubs & Restaurants nearby: The Talbot, KNIGHTWICK, WR6 5PH, 01886 821235

The Bear & Ragged Staff, BRANSFORD, WR6 5JH, 01886 833399

Yorkshire

There is nowhere in the British Isles quite like Yorkshire. With such scenic and cultural diversity, it is almost a country within a country. For sheer scale, size and grandeur, there is nowhere to beat it. Much of it in the spectacular Pennines, Yorkshire is a land of glorious moors, gentle dales, ruined abbeys and picturesque market towns.

'My Yorkshire, a land of pure air, rocky streams and hidden waterfalls,' was how the celebrated vet Alf Wight described his adopted home. Wight was born in Sunderland but moved to the North Yorkshire market town of Thirsk soon after the outbreak of the Second World War. He fell in love with the place and in later years his affection for the beauty, spirit and character of this great county translated to the printed page when Wight, writing under the name of James Herriot, wrote eight best-selling volumes of memoirs about the life of a Yorkshire vet, which spawned two films and a long-running TV series. Today, thousands of visitors from near and far travel to the landscape he loved so dearly to see it all for themselves. His veterinary practice, and original home, in Thirsk is open to the public.

Not surprisingly, walking features prominently on the list of things to do in Yorkshire. There are countless footpaths and bridleways to explore and miles of long-distance trails across vast open moorland and through tranquil meandering valleys. The 81-mile Dales Way is a perfect way to discover the magnificent scenery of Wharfedale, Ribblesdale and Dentdale, while the Calderdale Way offers a fascinating insight into the Pennine heartland of industrial West Yorkshire. Most famous of all the region's longer routes is surely the Pennine Way, which opened 50 years ago in April 1965. Its inception was the most important achievement in the history of the Ramblers' Association, marking Britain's first national long-distance footpath.

The Pennine Way was the brainchild of Tom Stephenson, one-time secretary of the Association but his vision for a trail for everyone was a long time in the planning. Landowners regularly thwarted his attempts to make the landscape accessible to walkers and there were countless prosecutions for trespassing 'I could never understand how anyone could own a mountain,' Stephenson wrote. 'Surely it was there for everybody.'

One of the more surprising features to be found on the route of the Pennine Way is the ruined house known as Top Withins. This is thought to be the inspiration for *Wuthering Heights*, the Earnshaw home in Emily Brontë's stirring novel of the same name. The Brontë sisters knew the area well, and their home, now the Brontë Parsonage Museum, lies just a few miles from the ruins in the village of Haworth. The parsonage draws thousands of visitors every year; its atmospheric setting amid bleak moorland and gritstone houses vividly captures the spirit of this uniquely talented trio of writers.

An easier, more comfortable way of exploring much of Yorkshire's scenic landscape is by train. A ride on the famous Settle to Carlisle railway represents one of the region's most memorable train journeys. For a while during the late 1980s the future of this line was in serious doubt, when it seemed British Rail might close it because of soaring maintenance costs. Thanks to Michael Portillo, a noted railway enthusiast who was Secretary of State for Transport at the time, the line was saved. Essentially, the Settle to Carlisle railway is a lifeline for commuters and the people of the more remote communities of the western Dales, but it is also an extremely popular tourist attraction. Carriages are regularly filled with summer visitors in search of stunning scenery and they are not disappointed. Elsewhere in Yorkshire, a very different train recalls a very different age. In the National Railway Museum at York you'll find countless locomotives, including a replica of Stephenson's Rocket and the much-loved *Flying Scotsman*.

The Pennine Way near Stoodley Pike ▷

EAST RIDING OF YORKSHIRE

BRANDESBURTON Map 17 TA14

Places to visit

Beverley Guildhall, BEVERLEY, HU17 9AU, 01482 392783
www.eastriding.gov.uk/museums

Burton Constable Hall, SPROATLEY, HU11 4LN, 01964 562400
www.burtonconstable.com

Blue Rose Caravan Country Park

►►►► 90%

GOLD

tel: 01964 543366 & 07504 026899 **Star Carr Ln YO25 8RU**
email: info@bluerosepark.com
dir: *From A165 at rdbt into New Rd, signed Brandesburton, which becomes Star Carr Ln. Approx 1m, site on left.* **grid ref:** *TA110464*

A neat and well maintained adult-only site well placed for visiting Hornsea and the Yorkshire coastline. The park is within walking distance of Brandesburton and offers an idyllic stopover for caravanners wanting a peaceful break in the countryside. 12 acre site. 58 touring pitches. 58 hardstandings. 44 seasonal pitches. Caravan pitches. Motorhome pitches. 36 statics.

Open: all year **Last arrival:** 20.00hrs **Last departure:** noon

Pitches: * £17-£22 £17-£24

Facilities:

Services:

Within 3 miles:

Notes: Adults only. Dogs must be kept on leads.

Dacre Lakeside Park

►►► 87%

tel: 0800 180 4556 & 01964 543704 **YO25 8RT**
email: dacrepark@btconnect.com
dir: *From A165 (bypass) midway between Beverley & Hornsea, follow Brandesburton & brown site sign.* **grid ref:** *TA118468*

A large lake popular with watersports enthusiasts is the focal point of this grassy site, which offers predominantly seasonal pitches – only four touring pitches are available. The clubhouse offers indoor activities; there's a fish and chip shop, a pub and a Chinese takeaway in the village, which is within walking distance. The six-acre lake is used for windsurfing, sailing, kayaking, canoeing and fishing. Camping pods are available for hire. 8 acre site. 120 touring pitches. 110 seasonal pitches. Caravan pitches. Motorhome pitches. Tent pitches. 110 statics. 9 wooden pods.

Open: Mar-Oct **Last arrival:** 21.00hrs **Last departure:** noon

Pitches: **Leisure:**

Facilities: **Services:**

Within 3 miles:

Notes: No noise 23.00hrs-08.00hrs, no craft with engines permitted on lake.

BRIDLINGTON Map 17 TA16

See also Rudston

Places to visit

Sewerby Hall & Gardens, BRIDLINGTON, YO15 1EA, 01262 673769
www.eastriding.gov.uk/sewerby

RSPB Nature Reserve, BEMPTON, YO15 1JD, 01262 422212
www.rspb.org.uk/bemptoncliffs

Great for kids: Burton Agnes Hall, BURTON AGNES, YO25 4ND, 01262 490324
www.burtonagnes.com

Fir Tree Caravan Park

►►►► 81%

tel: 01262 676442 **Jewison Ln, Sewerby YO16 6YG**
email: info@flowerofmay.com
dir: *1.5m from centre of Bridlington. Left onto B1255 at Marton Corner. Site 600yds on left.* **grid ref:** *TA195702*

Fir Tree Park, a large, mainly static park, has a well laid out touring area (seasonal pitches only) with its own facilities. It has an excellent swimming pool complex and the adjacent bar-cum-conservatory serves meals. There is also a family bar, games room and outdoor children's play area. 22 acre site. 45 touring pitches. 45 hardstandings. 45 seasonal pitches. Caravan pitches. 400 statics.

Open: Mar-Oct (rs Early & late season bar & entertainment restrictions)

Pitches:

Leisure:

Facilities:

Services:

Within 3 miles:

Notes: No noise after mdnt, dogs accepted by prior arrangement only. Dogs must be kept on leads.

AA Pubs & Restaurants nearby: The Seabirds Inn, FLAMBOROUGH, YO15 1PD, 01262 850242

KINGSTON UPON HULL

See Sproatley

Prefer a child-free site?
See our list on page 39

RUDSTON Map 17 TA06

Places to visit

Sewerby Hall & Gardens, BRIDLINGTON, YO15 1EA, 01262 673769
www.eastriding.gov.uk/sewerby

Thorpe Hall Caravan & Camping Site

►►►► 80%

GOLD

tel: 01262 420393 & 420574 **Thorpe Hall YO25 4JE**
email: caravansite@thorpehall.co.uk **web:** www.thorpehall.co.uk
dir: *From Bridlington take B1253 W for 5m.* **grid ref:** *TA108677*

A delightful, peaceful small park within the walled gardens of Thorpe Hall yet within a few miles of the bustling seaside resort of Bridlington. The site offers a games field, its own coarse fishery, pitch and putt, and a games and TV lounge. There are numerous walks locally. 4.5 acre site. 92 touring pitches. Caravan pitches. Motorhome pitches. Tent pitches.

Open: Mar-Oct **Last arrival:** 22.00hrs **Last departure:** noon

Pitches:

Leisure:

Facilities:

Services:

Within 3 miles:

Notes: No ball games except in designated field, no noise 23.00hrs-08.00hrs, well behaved dogs only. Dogs must be kept on leads. 4.5-acre golf practice area.

AA Pubs & Restaurants nearby: The Seabirds Inn, FLAMBOROUGH, YO15 1PD, 01262 850242

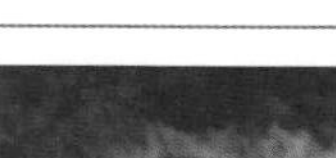

SKIPSEA Map 17 TA15

Places to visit

Hornsea Museum, HORNSEA, HU18 1AB, 01964 533443
www.hornseamuseum.com

Sewerby Hall & Gardens, BRIDLINGTON, YO15 1EA, 01262 673769
www.eastriding.gov.uk/sewerby

Skirlington Leisure Park

HOLIDAY CENTRE 89%

GOLD

tel: 01262 468213 & 468466 **YO25 8SY**
email: info@skirlington.com
dir: *From M62 towards Beverley then Hornsea. Between Skipsea & Hornsea on B1242.*
grid ref: *TA188528*

A large, well-run seaside park set close to the beach in partly-sloping meadowland with young trees and shrubs. The site has five toilet blocks, a supermarket and an amusement arcade, plus occasional entertainment in the clubhouse. The wide range of family amenities includes an indoor heated swimming pool complex with sauna, steam room and gym. A 10-pin bowling alley and indoor soft play area for children are added attractions. 140 acre site. 280 touring pitches. 15 hardstandings. 180 seasonal pitches. Caravan pitches. Motorhome pitches. 650 statics.

Open: Mar-Oct (rs Out of school hols & BH some facilities & diner only open Fri-Sun)
Last arrival: 20.00hrs **Last departure:** 11.00hrs

Pitches: * £11-£26 £11-£26

Leisure: Spa

Facilities:

Services:

Within 3 miles:

Notes: No noise after 22.00hrs. Dogs must be kept on leads. Putting green, fishing lake, arcade, mini bowling alley, Sunday market.

Skipsea Sands

HOLIDAY CENTRE 83%

tel: 01262 468210 **Mill Ln YO25 8TZ**
email: skipsea.sands@park-resorts.com
dir: *From A165 (Bridlington to Kingston upon Hull road) 8m S of Bridlington take B1242 to Skipsea. Follow Skipsea Sands signed to left just after sharp left bend.*
grid ref: *TA176563*

A busy and popular holiday park just a stone's throw from the beach, and offering an excellent range of leisure and entertainment facilities for families and couples. There's a good, well maintained touring area with clean toilets and neat grass pitches. A dedicated team ensure that standards are high across the park. 91 touring pitches. Caravan pitches. Motorhome pitches. Tent pitches.

Open: Apr-Oct **Last arrival:** noon **Last departure:** 10.00hrs

Pitches:

SPROATLEY — Map 17 TA13

Places to visit

Burton Constable Hall, SPROATLEY, HU11 4LN, 01964 562400
www.burtonconstable.com

Streetlife Museum Hull, KINGSTON UPON HULL, HU1 1PS, 01482 613902
www.hullcc.gov.uk

Great for kids: The Deep, KINGSTON UPON HULL, HU1 4DP, 01482 381000
www.thedeep.co.uk

Burton Constable Holiday Park & Arboretum

►►►► 89%

tel: 01964 562508 **Old Lodges HU11 4LJ**
email: info@burtonconstable.co.uk **web:** www.burtonconstable.co.uk
dir: *A165 onto B1238 to Sproatley. Follow signs to site.* **grid ref:** *TA186357*

Within the extensive estate of Constable Burton Hall, this large and secluded holiday destination provides a wide range of attractions including fishing and boating on the two 10-acre lakes, a snooker room, and a licensed bar with a designated family room. The grounds are immaculately maintained and generous pitch density offers good privacy. Camping pods are available for hire. 90 acre site. 135 touring pitches. 20 hardstandings. 14 seasonal pitches. Caravan pitches. Motorhome pitches. Tent pitches. 365 statics. 5 wooden pods.

Open: Mar-mid Feb (rs Mar-Nov tourers & tents) **Last arrival:** 22.00hrs
Last departure: noon

Pitches: * £18-£31 £18-£31 £18-£31

Leisure:

Facilities:

Services:

Within 3 miles:

Notes: No skateboards or rollerblades. Dogs must be kept on leads. Snooker, table tennis.

TUNSTALL

Places to visit

Burton Constable Hall, SPROATLEY, HU11 4LN, 01964 562400
www.burtonconstable.com

TUNSTALL — Map 17 TA33

Sand le Mere Holiday Village

HOLIDAY CENTRE 83%

GOLD

tel: 01964 670403 **Southfield Ln HU12 0JF**
email: info@sand-le-mere.co.uk **web:** www.sand-le-mere.co.uk
dir: *From Hull A1033 signed Withernsea, B1362 (Hull Rd) signed Hedon. In Hedon continue on B3162 towards Withernsea. Turn left signed Roos. In Roos take B1242. Turn left at brown sign for site. In Tunstall right at T-junct, right into Seaside Ln to site.*
grid ref: *TA305318*

Ideally located between Withernsea and Bridlington, this impressive development provides first-class indoor leisure facilities with swimming pool, entertainment and a kiddies' soft ball area. The touring pitches are level and surrounded by maturing trees and shrubs, and there are safari tents for hire. 135 acre site. 72 touring pitches. 51 hardstandings. 24 seasonal pitches. Caravan pitches. Motorhome pitches. Tent pitches. 14 statics. Safari tents.

Open: Mar-Nov **Last arrival:** 23.00hrs **Last departure:** 11.00hrs

Pitches:

Leisure: Spa

Facilities:

Services:

Within 3 miles:

Notes: No noise after 23.00hrs, speed limits around site, no camp fires. Dogs must be kept on leads.

See advert on opposite page

WITHERNSEA Map 17 TA32

Places to visit

Burton Constable Hall, SPROATLEY, HU11 4LN, 01964 562400
www.burtonconstable.com

Withernsea Sands Holiday Park

HOLIDAY CENTRE 82%

tel: 0871 664 9803 *(Calls cost 5p per minute plus your phone company's access charge)* & 01964 612189 **Waxholme Rd HU19 2BS**
email: withernsea.sands@park-resorts.com
dir: *M62 junct 38, A63 through Hull. At end of dual carriageway, right onto A1033, follow Withernsea signs. Through village, left at mini-rdbt onto B1242. 1st right at lighthouse. Site 0.5m on left.* **grid ref:** *TA335289*

Touring is very much at the heart of this holiday park's operation, with 100 all-electric pitches and additional space for tents. The owners, Park Resorts, continue to upgrade the facilities and attractions, and the leisure complex with its futuristic design is especially impressive. 115 touring pitches. Caravan pitches. Motorhome pitches. Tent pitches. 400 statics.

Open: Apr-Oct (rs BH & peak wknds sports available) **Last arrival:** 22.00hrs
Last departure: noon

Pitches:

Leisure:

Facilities:

Services:

Within 3 miles:

Notes: No noise between 23.00hrs-07.00hrs. Dogs must be kept on leads. Extension leads & utilities available from reception.

PITCHES: Caravans Motorhomes Tents Glamping-style accommodation **SERVICES:** Electric hook up Launderette Licensed bar Calor Gas Camping Gaz Toilet fluid Café/Restaurant Fast Food/Takeaway Battery charging Baby care Motorvan service point
ABBREVIATIONS: BH/bank hols – bank holidays Etr – Easter Spring BH – Spring Bank Holiday fr – from hrs – hours m – mile mdnt – midnight rdbt – roundabout rs – restricted service wk – week wknd – weekend x-rds – cross roads No credit or debit cards No dogs Children of all ages accepted

NORTH YORKSHIRE

ACASTER MALBIS — Map 16 SE54

Places to visit

National Railway Museum, YORK, YO26 4XJ, 01904 621261 www.nrm.org.uk

York Minster, YORK, YO1 7HH, 01904 557200 www.yorkminster.org

Great for kids: Jorvik Viking Centre, YORK, YO1 9WT, 01904 615505 www.jorvik-viking-centre.com

Moor End Farm

►► 75%

tel: 01904 706727 & 07860 405872 **YO23 2UQ**
email: moorendfarm@acaster99.fsnet.co.uk **web:** www.moor-end-farm.co.uk
dir: *Follow signs to Acaster Malbis from junct of A64 & A1237 at Copmanthorpe.*
grid ref: *SE589457*

A very pleasant farm site with modernised facilities including a heated family/disabled shower room. A river boat pickup to York is 150 yards from the site entrance, and the village inn and restaurant are a short stroll away. A very convenient site for visiting York Racecourse. 1 acre site. 12 touring pitches. Caravan pitches. Motorhome pitches. Tent pitches. 7 statics.

Open: Etr or Apr-Oct **Last arrival:** 22.00hrs **Last departure:** noon

Pitches: * £18-£22 £18-£22 £15-£25

Leisure:

Facilities:

Services:

Within 3 miles:

Notes: Dogs must be kept on leads. Fridge, freezer & microwave available.

AA Pubs & Restaurants nearby: Ye Old Sun Inn, COLTON, LS24 8EP, 01904 744261

ALLERSTON — Map 19 SE88

Places to visit

Scarborough Castle, SCARBOROUGH, YO11 1HY, 01723 372451 www.english-heritage.org.uk/daysout/properties/scarborough-castle

Pickering Castle, PICKERING, YO18 7AX, 01751 474989 www.english-heritage.org.uk/daysout/properties/pickering-castle

Great for kids: Flamingo Land Resort, KIRBY MISPERTON, YO17 6UX, 01653 668287 www.flamingoland.co.uk

PREMIER PARK

Vale of Pickering Caravan Park

►►►►► 90%

tel: 01723 859280 **Carr House Farm YO18 7PQ**
email: tony@valeofpickering.co.uk **web:** www.valeofpickering.co.uk
dir: *On B1415, 1.75m from A170 Pickering to Scarborough road.* **grid ref:** *SE879808*

A well-maintained, spacious family park with excellent facilities including a well-stocked shop and immaculate toilet facilities, and an interesting woodland walk. A new extension to the toilet block houses four family bathrooms and a wet room for less able visitors. Younger children will enjoy the attractive play area, while the large ball sports area will appeal to older ones. The park is set in open countryside bounded by hedges, has manicured grassland and stunning seasonal floral displays, and is handy for the North Yorkshire Moors and the attractions of Scarborough. 13 acre site. 120 touring pitches. 100 hardstandings. Caravan pitches. Motorhome pitches. Tent pitches.

Open: 5 Mar-3 Jan (rs Mar) **Last arrival:** 21.00hrs **Last departure:** 11.30hrs

Pitches:

Leisure:

Facilities:

Services:

Within 3 miles:

Notes: No open fires or Chinese lanterns, no noise after 23.00hrs. Microwave available.

AA Pubs & Restaurants nearby: The New Inn, THORNTON LE DALE, YO18 7LF, 01751 474226

The Coachman Inn, SNAINTON, YO13 9PL, 01723 859231

ALNE Map 19 SE46

Places to visit

Beningbrough Hall, Gallery & Gardens, BENINGBROUGH, YO30 1DD, 01904 472027 www.nationaltrust.org.uk/beningbrough

Sutton Park, SUTTON-ON-THE-FOREST, YO61 1DP, 01347 810249 www.statelyhome.co.uk

Great for kids: National Railway Museum, YORK, YO26 4XJ, 01904 621261 www.nrm.org.uk

PREMIER PARK

Alders Caravan Park

►►►►► 80%

tel: 01347 838722 **Home Farm YO61 1RY**
email: enquiries@homefarmalne.co.uk
dir: *From A19 exit at Alne sign, in 1.5m left at T-junct, 0.5m site on left in village centre.* **grid ref:** *SE497654*

A tastefully developed park on a working farm with screened pitches laid out in horseshoe-shaped areas. This well-designed park offers excellent toilet facilities including a bathroom and fully-serviced washing and toilet cubicles.
A woodland area and a water meadow are pleasant places to walk. Wooden pods are located in a separate landscaped area. 12 acre site. 87 touring pitches. 6 hardstandings. 71 seasonal pitches. Caravan pitches. Motorhome pitches. Tent pitches. 3 wooden pods.

Open: Mar-Oct **Last arrival:** 21.00hrs **Last departure:** 14.00hrs

Pitches:

Facilities:

Services:

Within 3 miles:

Notes: Max 2 dogs per pitch. Dogs must be kept on leads. Summer house, farm produce for sale.

AA Pubs & Restaurants nearby: The Black Bull Inn, BOROUGHBRIDGE, YO51 9AR, 01423 322413

The Dining Room Restaurant, BOROUGHBRIDGE, YO51 9AR, 01423 326426

BISHOP MONKTON

Places to visit

Newby Hall & Gardens, RIPON, HG4 5AE, 01423 322583 www.newbyhall.com

Fountains Abbey & Studley Royal, RIPON, HG4 3DY, 01765 608888 www.nationaltrust.org.uk/fountains-abbey

Great for kids: Lightwater Valley Theme Park, NORTH STAINLEY, HG4 3HT, 0871 720 0011 *(Calls cost 13p per minute plus your phone company's access charge)* www.lightwatervalley.co.uk

BISHOP MONKTON Map 19 SE36

Church Farm Caravan Park

►►► 75%

tel: 01765 676578 & 07861 770164 **Knaresborough Rd HG3 3QQ**
email: churchfarmcaravan@btinternet.com
dir: *From A61 at x-rds follow Bishop Monkton signs. 1.25m to village. At x-rds right into Knaresborough Rd, site approx 500mtrs on right.* **grid ref:** *SE328660*

A very pleasant rural site on a working farm, on the edge of the attractive village of Bishop Monkton with its well-stocked shop and pubs. Whilst very much a place to relax, there are many attractions close by, including Fountains Abbey, Newby Hall, Ripon and Harrogate. 4 acre site. 45 touring pitches. 1 hardstanding. Caravan pitches. Motorhome pitches. Tent pitches. 3 statics.

Open: Mar-Oct **Last arrival:** 22.30hrs **Last departure:** 15.30hrs

Pitches: £16-£18 £16-£18 £14-£18 **Facilities:**

Services: **Within 3 miles:**

Notes: No ball games. Dogs must be kept on leads.

AA Pubs & Restaurants nearby: The Black Bull Inn, BOROUGHBRIDGE, YO51 9AR, 01423 322413

The Dining Room Restaurant, BOROUGHBRIDGE, YO51 9AR, 01423 326426

BOLTON ABBEY Map 19 SE05

Places to visit

National Park Centre, GRASSINGTON, BD23 5LB, 01756 751690 www.yorkshiredales.org.uk

Parcevall Hall Gardens, GRASSINGTON, BD23 6DE, 01756 720311 www.parcevallhallgardens.co.uk

Great for kids: Stump Cross Caverns, PATELEY BRIDGE, HG3 5JL, 01756 752780 www.stumpcrosscaverns.co.uk

Howgill Lodge

►►►► 80%

tel: 01756 720655 **Barden BD23 6DJ**
email: info@howgill-lodge.co.uk
dir: *From Bolton Abbey take B6160 signed Burnsall. In 3m at Barden Tower right signed Appletreewick. 1.5m, at phone box right into lane to site.* **grid ref:** *SE064592*

A beautifully-maintained and secluded site offering panoramic views of Wharfedale. The spacious hardstanding pitches are mainly terraced, and there is a separate tenting area with numerous picnic tables. There are three toilet facilities spread throughout the site, with the main block (including private, cubicled wash facilities) is appointed to a high standard. There is also a well-stocked shop. 4 acre site. 40 touring pitches. 20 hardstandings. Caravan pitches. Motorhome pitches. Tent pitches.

Open: mid Mar-Oct **Last arrival:** 20.00hrs **Last departure:** noon

Pitches: * fr £21 fr £21 fr £21 **Leisure:**

Facilities: **Services:**

Within 3 miles: **Notes:** Dogs must be kept on leads.

AA Pubs & Restaurants nearby: The Devonshire Brasserie & Bar, BOLTON ABBEY, BD23 6AJ, 01756 710710

The Fleece, ADDINGHAM, LS29 0LY, 01943 830491

The Craven Arms, APPLETREEWICK, BD23 6DA, 01756 720270

LEISURE: Indoor swimming pool · Outdoor swimming pool · Children's playground · Kid's club · Tennis court · Games room · Separate TV room · golf course · Boats for hire · Cinema · Entertainment · Fishing · Mini golf · Watersports · Gym · Sports field · Spa · Stables

FACILITIES: Bath · Shower · Electric shaver · Hairdryer · Ice Pack Facility · Disabled facilities · Public telephone · Shop on site or within 200yds · Mobile shop (calls at least 5 days a week) · BBQ area · Picnic area · Wi-fi · Internet access · Recycling · Tourist info · Dog exercise area

CHOP GATE

Map 19 SE59

Lordstones Country Park

►►►► 82%

tel: 01642 778482 & 778000 **Carlton Bank TS9 7JH**
email: info@lordstones.com
dir: *From A172 between Stokesley & Osmotherly follow signs to Carlton-in-Cleveland. Through Carlton-in-Cleveland to Lordstones entrance.* **grid ref:** *NZ524030*

Situated in the North York Moors National Park and commanding one of the highest spots in the county, Lordstones has glorious views that extend over 40 miles. It is a privately owned country park that has been developed to become a distinctive visitor venue. Serious investment has resulted in a first-class café-restaurant, a quality farm shop selling local produce and a small camping-cum-glamping park. There are 20 pitches, some with electricity, enclosed by woodland, and two fully-equipped bell tents, two bothy tents, and five luxury wooden pods, each with a wood-burning stove, kitchenette, toilet and outside decking with barbecue and seating. Yurts are the latest additions to choose from. There is a new purpose-built amenity building housing showers and toilet facilities. The Cleveland Way national trail passes close to the site. 150 acre site. 21 touring pitches. Tent pitches. Bell tents. Wooden pods.

Open: all year **Last arrival:** 17.00hrs **Last departure:** 11.00hrs

Pitches: * £17-£24 **Facilities:**

Services: **Within 3 miles:**

Notes: Dogs must be kept on leads.

CONSTABLE BURTON

Map 19 SE19

Places to visit

Middleham Castle, MIDDLEHAM, DL8 4RJ, 01969 623899
www.english-heritage.org.uk/daysout/properties/middleham-castle

Great for kids: Bedale Museum, BEDALE, DL8 1AA, 01677 427516
www.bedalemuseum.org.uk

Constable Burton Hall Caravan Park

►►►► 83%

tel: 01677 450428 **DL8 5LJ**
email: caravanpark@constableburton.com
dir: *From Leyburn on A684 towards Bedale, approx 3m site on left.* **grid ref:** *SE158907*

A pretty site in the former deer park of the adjoining Constable Burton Hall, screened from the road by the park walls and surrounded by mature trees in a quiet rural location. The laundry is housed in a converted 18th-century deer barn and there is a pub and restaurant opposite; seasonal pitches are available. Please note that this site does not accept tents. 10 acre site. 120 touring pitches. Caravan pitches. Motorhome pitches.

Open: Apr-Oct **Last arrival:** 20.00hrs **Last departure:** noon

Pitches: * £20.50-£25.50 £20.50-£25.50

Facilities:

Services: **Within 3 miles:**

Notes: No commercial vehicles, no games. Dogs must be kept on leads.

AA Pubs & Restaurants nearby: Sandpiper Inn, LEYBURN, DL8 5AT, 01969 622206

The White Swan, MIDDLEHAM, DL8 4PE, 01969 622093

The Wensleydale Heifer, WEST WITTON, DL8 4LS, 01969 622322

FILEY

Map 17 TA18

Places to visit

Scarborough Castle, SCARBOROUGH, YO11 1HY, 01723 372451
www.english-heritage.org.uk/daysout/properties/scarborough-castle

Scarborough Sea Life Sanctuary, SCARBOROUGH, YO12 6RP, 01723 373414
www.sealife.co.uk

Flower of May Holiday Park

HOLIDAY CENTRE 91%

tel: 01723 584311 **Lebberston Cliff YO11 3NU**
email: info@flowerofmay.com **web:** www.flowerofmay.com
dir: *Take A165 from Scarborough towards Filey. Site signed.* **grid ref:** *TA085835*

A well-run, high quality family holiday park with top class facilities. This large landscaped park offers a full range of recreational activities, with plenty to occupy everyone. Grass and hard pitches are available – all are on level ground, and arranged in avenues screened by shrubs. Enjoy the 'Scarborough Fair' museum, with its collection of restored fairground attractions, including rides, organs and vintage cars. Introduced for hire in 2015 were 4-berth and 5-berth wooden camping pods, each with a decking area. 13 acre site. 300 touring pitches. 250 hardstandings. 100 seasonal pitches. Caravan pitches. Motorhome pitches. Tent pitches. 193 statics. 10 wooden pods.

Open: Etr-Oct (rs Early & late season restricted opening in café, shop & bars)
Last arrival: dusk **Last departure:** noon

Pitches: * £22-£28 £22-£28 £22-£28

Leisure:

continued

FILEY *continued*

Facilities: **Services:** **Within 3 miles:**

Notes: No noise after mdnt, 1 dog per pitch by prior arrangement only. Dogs must be kept on leads. Squash, bowling, basketball court, skate park.

See advert on page 342

Blue Dolphin Holiday Park

HOLIDAY CENTRE 82%

GOLD

tel: 0871 231 0893 *(Calls cost 10p per minute plus your phone company's access charge)*
Gristhorpe Bay YO14 9PU
email: bluedolphin@haven.com **web:** www.haven.com/bluedolphin
dir: *On A165, 2m N of Filey.* **grid ref:** *TA095829*

There are great cliff-top views to be enjoyed from this fun-filled holiday centre with an extensive and separate touring area. The emphasis is on non-stop entertainment, with organised sports and clubs, all-weather leisure facilities, heated swimming pools (with multi-slide), and plenty of well-planned amusements. Pitches are mainly on level or gently-sloping grass plus there are some fully serviced hardstandings. The beach is just two miles away. 85 acre site. 250 touring pitches. 42 hardstandings. 20 seasonal pitches. Caravan pitches. Motorhome pitches. Tent pitches. 850 statics.

Open: mid Mar-end Oct (rs mid Mar-May & Sep-Oct some facilities may be reduced & outdoor pool closed) **Last arrival:** mdnt **Last departure:** 10.00hrs

Pitches: **Leisure:**

Facilities: **Services:**

Within 3 miles:

Notes: No commercial vehicles, no bookings by persons under 21yrs unless a family booking, max 2 dogs per booking, certain dog breeds banned. Dogs must be kept on leads.

See advert on opposite page

Primrose Valley Holiday Park

HOLIDAY CENTRE 81%

GOLD

tel: 0800 316 0621 **YO14 9RF**
email: primrosevalley@haven.com **web:** www.haven.com/primrosevalley
dir: *Signed from A165 (Scarboroug to Bridlington road), 3m S of Filey.* **grid ref:** *TA123778*

A large all-action holiday centre with a wide range of sports and leisure activities to suit everyone from morning until late in the evening. The touring area is completely separate from the main park with its own high quality amenity block. All touring pitches are fully serviced hardstandings with grassed awning strips. The touring area has its own reception and designated warden. 160 acre site. 40 touring pitches. 50 hardstandings. Caravan pitches. Motorhome pitches. 1514 statics.

Open: mid Mar-end Oct **Last arrival:** anytime **Last departure:** 10.00hrs

Pitches: **Leisure:**

Facilities: **Services:**

Within 3 miles:

Notes: No commercial vehicles, no bookings by persons under 21yrs unless a family booking, max 2 dogs per booking, certain dog breeds banned. Dogs must be kept on leads.

See advert on opposite page

HUTTON-LE-HOLE Map 19 SE79

Places to visit

Nunnington Hall, NUNNINGTON, YO62 5UY, 01439 748283
www.nationaltrust.org.uk/nunnington-hall

Rievaulx Abbey, RIEVAULX, 01439 798228
www.english-heritage.org.uk/daysout/properties/rievaulx-abbey

Great for kids: Pickering Castle, PICKERING, YO18 7AX, 01751 474989
www.english-heritage.org.uk/daysout/properties/pickering-castle

Hutton-le-Hole Caravan Park

►►►► 81%

tel: 01751 417261 **Westfield Lodge YO62 6UG**
email: huttonleholecaravanpark@hotmail.com
dir: *From A170 at Keldholme follow Hutton-le-Hole signs. Approx 2m, over cattle grid, left in 500yds into Park Drive, site signed.* **grid ref:** *SE705895*

A small, high quality park on a working farm in the North York Moors National Park. The purpose-built toilet block offers en suite family rooms, and there is a choice of hardstanding or grass pitches within a well-tended area surrounded by hedges and shrubs. The village facilities are a 10-minute walk away. Please note that caravans are prohibited from the A170 at Sutton Bank between Thirsk and Helmsley. 5 acre site. 42 touring pitches. 4 hardstandings. Caravan pitches. Motorhome pitches. Tent pitches.

Open: Etr-Oct **Last arrival:** 21.00hrs **Last departure:** noon

Pitches: * £18-£25 £18-£25 £15-£22

Facilities:

Services:

Within 3 miles:

Notes: Boot, bike & dog washing area, farm walks.

AA Pubs & Restaurants nearby: Blacksmiths Arms, LASTINGHAM, YO62 6TN, 01751 417247

The Moors Inn, APPLETON-LE-MOORS, YO62 6TF, 01751 417435

KIRKLINGTON Map 16 SE38

Camp Kátur

NEW ►►►►

tel: 01845 202100 **The Camphill Estate DL8 2LS**
email: info@campkatur.com
dir: *A1(M) junct 50, A6055 towards Bedale. Left at 1st rdbt, 1st right to Kirklington. Through Kirklington, approx 1.5m to site on left.* **grid ref:** *SE311825*

Located within The Camp Estate, a popular centre for equestrian pursuits, quad biking, orienteering and corporate team building, Camp Kátur is a unique glamping destination with geo domes, safari tents, bell tents, hobbit pods and tipis set in meadowland or wooded areas that comprise a wide variety of indigenous and imported trees. All the glamping units are spaced well apart ensuring optimum privacy, and all have the benefit of fire pits, barbecues and outside seating areas. The safari tents and geo domes have en suite facilities and other units are serviced by a communal shower, toilet and wash basin facility. There is a great focus on upcycling materials here with fire pits created from washing machine drums and galvanised buckets for wash basins to name just two ideas. There's a campers' kitchen, a barbecue pod seating 16 around a central cooking area, and a rustic outdoor area ideal for gatherings such as a wedding reception or an anniversary or birthday celebration. The eco spa has a sauna and hot tub fuelled by wood-burning stoves. 20 acre site.

Open: Apr-Oct **Last arrival:** 22.00hrs **Last departure:** 11.00hrs

Pitches: * £35-£120

Leisure: Spa

Facilities:

Services:

Within 3 miles:

Notes: No noise after 22.00hrs, groups permitted only with management permission. Dogs must be kept on leads.

KNARESBOROUGH — Map 19 SE35

Places to visit

RHS Garden Harlow Carr, HARROGATE, HG3 1QB, 0845 265 8070 *(Calls cost 5p per minute plus your phone company's access charge)* www.rhs.org.uk/harlowcarr

Aldborough Roman Site, ALDBOROUGH, YO51 9ES, 01423 322768 www.english-heritage.org.uk/daysout/properties/aldborough-roman-site

Kingfisher Caravan Park

►►► 80%

tel: 01423 869411 **Low Moor Ln, Farnham HG5 9JB**
email: enquiries@kingfisher-caravanpark.co.uk
dir: *From Knaresborough take A6055. Left in 1m towards Farnham, left in village signed Scotton. Site 1m on left.* **grid ref:** *SE343603*

A large grassy site with open spaces set in a wooded area in rural countryside. Whilst Harrogate, Fountains Abbey and York are within easy reach, anglers will want to take advantage of on-site coarse and fly fishing lakes. The park has a separate, flat tenting field with electric hook-ups available. 14 acre site. 35 touring pitches. Caravan pitches. Motorhome pitches. Tent pitches. 80 statics.

Open: Mar-Oct **Last arrival:** 21.00hrs **Last departure:** 16.00hrs

Pitches:

Leisure:

Facilities:

Services:

Within 3 miles:

Notes: No football. Pets must be kept under strict adult control.

AA Pubs & Restaurants nearby: The General Tarleton Inn, KNARESBOROUGH, HG5 0PZ, 01423 340284

MARKINGTON — Map 19 SE26

Places to visit

Fountains Abbey & Studley Royal, RIPON, HG4 3DY, 01765 608888 www.nationaltrust.org.uk/fountains-abbey

Newby Hall & Gardens, RIPON, HG4 5AE, 01423 322583 www.newbyhall.com

Great for kids: Brimham Rocks, BRIMHAM, HG3 4DW, 01423 780688 www.nationaltrust.org.uk

Yorkshire Hussar Inn Holiday Caravan Park

►►► 84%

tel: 01765 677327 & 677715 **High St HG3 3NR**
email: yorkshirehussar@yahoo.co.uk
dir: *From A61 between Harrogate & Ripon at Wormald Green follow Markington signs, 1m, left past Post Office into High Street. Site signed on left behind The Yorkshire Hussar Inn.* **grid ref:** *SE288650*

A pleasant, terraced site behind the village inn with well-kept grass that offers spacious pitches (hardstanding and electric hook-up pitches are available) and a few holiday statics for hire. Although the Yorkshire Hussar Inn does not provide food, there is a pub within walking distance that does. 5 acre site. 20 touring pitches. 6 hardstandings. 12 seasonal pitches. Caravan pitches. Motorhome pitches. Tent pitches. 73 statics.

Open: Etr-Oct **Last arrival:** 19.00hrs **Last departure:** noon

Pitches: **Leisure:**

Facilities:

Services:

Within 3 miles:

Notes: Dogs must be kept on leads. Paddling pool.

MASHAM — Map 19 SE28

Places to visit

Theakston Brewery & Visitor Centre, MASHAM, HG4 4YD, 01765 680000 www.theakstons.co.uk

Norton Conyers, RIPON, HG4 5EQ, 01765 640333 www.weddingsatnortonconyers.co.uk

Great for kids: Lightwater Valley Theme Park, NORTH STAINLEY, HG4 3HT, 0871 720 0011 *(Calls cost 13p per minute plus your phone company's access charge)* www.lightwatervalley.co.uk

Old Station Holiday Park

►►►► 77%

tel: 01765 689569 **Old Station Yard, Low Burton HG4 4DF**
email: oldstation@tiscali.co.uk
dir: *From S: A1(M) junct 50, B6267, left in 8m; From N: A1(M) junct 51, A684 to Bedale, then B6268, 4m to site.* **grid ref:** *SE232812*

An interesting site at a former station that still retains a railway theme. The enthusiastic and caring family owners have created a park with high quality facilities. The reception and café are situated in a carefully restored wagon shed and here a range of meals using local produce is offered. The small town of Masham, with its Theakston and Black Sheep Breweries, is within easy walking distance of the park. Four BBQ log cabins (large and small) are available for hire. 3.75 acre site. 50 touring pitches. 12 hardstandings. 16 seasonal pitches. Caravan pitches. Motorhome pitches. Tent pitches.

Open: Mar-Nov (rs Mar-Nov café closed wkdays) **Last arrival:** 20.00hrs **Last departure:** 11.00hrs

Pitches: * fr £21 fr £21 fr £16

Facilities:

Services:

Within 3 miles:

Notes: No cars by tents. No cycling around site, no campfires. Dogs must be kept on leads.

AA Pubs & Restaurants nearby: The Black Sheep Brewery, MASHAM, HG4 4EN, 01765 680101

Vennell's, MASHAM, HG4 4DX, 01765 689000

PICKERING Map 19 SE78

Places to visit

Pickering Castle, PICKERING, YO18 7AX, 01751 474989 www.english-heritage.org.uk/daysout/properties/pickering-castle

North Yorkshire Moors Railway, PICKERING, YO18 7AJ, 01751 472508 www.nymr.co.uk

Great for kids: Flamingo Land Resort, KIRBY MISPERTON, YO17 6UX, 01653 668287 www.flamingoland.co.uk

Wayside Holiday Park

►►►► 78%

tel: 01751 472608 & 07940 938517 **Wrelton YO18 8PG**
email: wrelton@waysideholidaypark.co.uk
dir: *2.5m W of Pickering exit A170, follow signs at Wrelton.* **grid ref:** *SE764859*

Located in the village of Wrelton, this well-maintained seasonal touring and holiday home park is divided into small paddocks by mature hedging. The amenity block has smart, modern facilities. The village pub and restaurant are within a few minutes' walk of the park. Please note that this site has seasonal pitches only – caravans, motorhomes and tents are not accepted. 10 acre site. 40 seasonal pitches. 113 statics.

Open: Apr-Oct

Facilities:

Services:

Within 3 miles:

Notes: Dogs must be kept on leads.

AA Pubs & Restaurants nearby: Fox & Hounds Country Inn, PICKERING, YO62 6SQ, 01751 431577

The White Swan Inn, PICKERING, YO18 7AA, 01751 472288

The Fox & Rabbit Inn, PICKERING, YO18 7NQ, 01751 460213

RICHMOND Map 19 NZ10

Places to visit

Green Howards Museum, RICHMOND, DL10 4QN, 01748 826561 www.greenhowards.org.uk

Kiplin Hall, RICHMOND, DL10 6AT, 01748 818178 www.kiplinhall.co.uk

Great for kids: Richmond Castle, RICHMOND, DL10 4QW, 01748 822493 www.english-heritage.org.uk/daysout/properties/richmond-castle

Brompton Caravan Park

►►►► 83%

tel: 01748 824629 **Brompton-on-Swale DL10 7EZ**
email: brompton.caravanpark@btconnect.com **web:** www.bromptoncaravanpark.co.uk
dir: *Exit A1 signed Catterick. B6271 to Brompton-on-Swale, site 1m on left.*
grid ref: *NZ199002*

An attractive and well-managed family park where pitches have an open outlook across the River Swale. There is a good children's playground, an excellent family recreation room, a takeaway food service, and fishing is available on the river. Three river view camping pods and holiday apartments can also be hired. 14 acre site. 177 touring pitches. 25 hardstandings. 138 seasonal pitches. Caravan pitches. Motorhome pitches. Tent pitches. 22 statics. 3 wooden pods.

Open: mid Mar-Oct **Last arrival:** 21.00hrs **Last departure:** noon

Pitches: * fr £19 fr £19 fr £19

Leisure:

Facilities:

Services:

Within 3 miles:

Notes: No group bookings. No motor, electric cars or scooters, no gazebos, no open fires or woodburners, no electricity for tents, quiet from mdnt. Dogs must be kept on leads.

RIPON Map 19 SE37

See also North Stainley

Places to visit

Fountains Abbey & Studley Royal, RIPON, HG4 3DY, 01765 608888 www.nationaltrust.org.uk/fountains-abbey

Norton Conyers, RIPON, HG4 5EQ, 01765 640333 www.weddingsatnortonconyers.co.uk

Great for kids: Falconry UK - Birds of Prey Centre, THIRSK, YO7 4EU, 01845 587522 www.falconrycentre.co.uk

PREMIER PARK

Riverside Meadows Country Caravan Park

►►►►► 76%

tel: 01765 602964 **Ure Bank Top HG4 1JD**
email: info@flowerofmay.com
dir: *On A61 at N end of bridge from Ripon, W along river (do not cross river). Site in 400yds, signed.* **grid ref:** *SE317726*

This pleasant, well-maintained site stands on high ground overlooking the River Ure, one mile from the town centre. The site has an excellent club with family room and quiet lounge. There is no access to the river from the site. 28 acre site. 80 touring pitches. 40 hardstandings. 40 seasonal pitches. Caravan pitches. Motorhome pitches. Tent pitches. 269 statics.

Open: Etr-Oct (rs Early & late season bar open wknds only) **Last arrival:** dusk
Last departure: noon

Pitches: * £22-£28 £22-£28 £22-£28

Leisure:

Facilities:

Services:

Within 3 miles:

Notes: No noise after mdnt, dogs accepted by prior arrangement only. Dogs must be kept on leads.

AA Pubs & Restaurants nearby: The George at Wath, RIPON, HG4 5EN, 01765 641324

The Royal Oak, RIPON, HG4 1PB, 01765 602284

ROBIN HOOD'S BAY

See also Whitby

Places to visit

Whitby Abbey, WHITBY, YO22 4JT, 01947 603568 www.english-heritage.org.uk/daysout/properties/whitby-abbey

Scarborough Castle, SCARBOROUGH, YO11 1HY, 01723 372451 www.english-heritage.org.uk/daysout/properties/scarborough-castle

Great for kids: Scarborough Sea Life Sanctuary, SCARBOROUGH, YO12 6RP, 01723 373414 www.sealife.co.uk

ROBIN HOOD'S BAY Map 19 NZ90

Grouse Hill Caravan Park

►►►► 90%

tel: 01947 880543 & 880560 **Flask Bungalow Farm, Fylingdales YO22 4QH**
email: info@grousehill.co.uk **web:** www.grousehill.co.uk
dir: *From A171 (Whitby-Scarborough road), take loop road for Flask Inn (brown site sign).*
grid ref: *NZ928002*

A spacious family park on a south-facing slope with attractive, mostly level, terraced pitches overlooking the North Yorkshire National Park. The site has quality, solar-heated toilet blocks, a treatment plant to ensure excellent drinking water, security barriers, play areas (including a woodland adventure play area), CCTV and WiFi. Heated wooden wigwams are available for hire. Please note that there are no hardstandings for tourers, only grass pitches, and this sloping site is not suitable for disabled visitors (there are no disabled facilities). This is an ideal base for walking and touring. 14 acre site. 175 touring pitches. 30 hardstandings. Caravan pitches. Motorhome pitches. Tent pitches. 1 static. 12 wooden pods.

Open: Mar-Oct (rs Etr-May shop & reception restricted) **Last arrival:** 20.30hrs
Last departure: noon

Pitches: **Leisure:**

Facilities: **Services:**

Within 3 miles:

Notes: No noise after 22.30hrs. Dogs must be kept on leads.

AA Pubs & Restaurants nearby: Laurel Inn, ROBIN HOOD'S BAY, YO22 4SE, 01947 880400

The Magpie Café, WHITBY, YO21 3PU, 01947 602058

See advert on page 358

PITCHES: Caravans Motorhomes Tents Glamping-style accommodation **SERVICES:** Electric hook up Launderette Licensed bar Calor Gas Camping Gaz Toilet fluid Café/Restaurant Fast Food/Takeaway Battery charging Baby care Motorvan service point
ABBREVIATIONS: BH/bank hols – bank holidays Etr – Easter Spring BH – Spring Bank Holiday fr – from hrs – hours m – mile mdnt – midnight rdbt – roundabout rs – restricted service wk – week wknd – weekend x-rds – cross roads No credit or debit cards No dogs Children of all ages accepted

ROBIN HOOD'S BAY *continued*

Middlewood Farm Holiday Park

►►►► 88%

tel: 01947 880414 **Middlewood Ln, Fylingthorpe YO22 4UF**
email: info@middlewoodfarm.com **web:** www.middlewoodfarm.com
dir: *From A171 towards Robin Hood's Bay, into Fylingthorpe. Site signed from A171.*
grid ref: *NZ945045*

A peaceful, friendly family park enjoying panoramic views of Robin Hood's Bay in a picturesque fishing village. The park has two toilet blocks with private facilities. The village pub is a five-minute walk away, and the beach can be reached via a path leading directly from the site, which is also accessible for wheelchair users. Four 5-berth camping pods are available for hire. 7 acre site. 100 touring pitches. 21 hardstandings. Caravan pitches. Motorhome pitches. Tent pitches. 30 statics. 4 wooden pods.

Middlewood Farm Holiday Park

Open: 7 Feb-7 Jan (rs Nov-Feb no tents) **Last arrival:** 20.00hrs **Last departure:** 11.00hrs

Pitches:

Leisure:

Facilities:

Services:

Within 3 miles:

Notes: No radios or noise after 23.00hrs, dangerous dog breeds are not accepted. Dogs must be kept on leads.

AA Pubs & Restaurants nearby: Laurel Inn, ROBIN HOOD'S BAY, YO22 4SE, 01947 880400

The Magpie Café, WHITBY, YO21 3PU, 01947 602058

See advert on opposite page

LEISURE: Indoor swimming pool · Outdoor swimming pool · Children's playground · Kid's club · Tennis court · Games room · Separate TV room · golf course · Boats for hire · Cinema · Entertainment · Fishing · Mini golf · Watersports · Gym · Sports field · Spa · Stables
FACILITIES: Bath · Shower · Electric shaver · Hairdryer · Ice Pack Facility · Disabled facilities · Public telephone · Shop on site or within 200yds · Mobile shop (calls at least 5 days a week) · BBQ area · Picnic area · Wi-fi · Internet access · Recycling · Tourist info · Dog exercise area

ROSEDALE ABBEY

Map 19 SE79

Places to visit

Pickering Castle, PICKERING, YO18 7AX, 01751 474989
www.english-heritage.org.uk/daysout/properties/pickering-castle

North Yorkshire Moors Railway, PICKERING, YO18 7AJ, 01751 472508
www.nymr.co.uk

Great for kids: Flamingo Land Resort, KIRBY MISPERTON, YO17 6UX, 01653 668287 www.flamingoland.co.uk

Rosedale Caravan & Camping Park

►►►► 85%

tel: 01751 417272 **YO18 8SA**
email: info@flowerofmay.com
dir: *From Pickering take A170 towards Sinnington for 2.25m. At Wrelton right onto unclassified road signed Cropton & Rosedale, 7m. Site on left in village.*
grid ref: *SE725958*

Set in a sheltered valley in the centre of the North Yorkshire Moors National Park, this popular park is close to the pretty village of Rosedale Abbey. It is divided into separate areas for tents, tourers and statics. It has well-tended grounds, and is gradually being upgraded by the enthusiastic owners. Two toilet blocks offer private, combined facilities. There are camping pods (with or without electricity) situated by the river available for hire.
10 acre site. 100 touring pitches. 20 seasonal pitches. Caravan pitches. Motorhome pitches. Tent pitches. 35 statics. 6 wooden pods.

Open: Mar-Oct **Last arrival:** dusk **Last departure:** noon

Pitches: * £22-£28 £22-£28 £11-£28 **Leisure:**

Facilities:

Services: **Within 3 miles:**

Notes: No noise after mdnt, dogs accepted by prior arrangement only. Dogs must be kept on leads.

AA Pubs & Restaurants nearby: Blacksmiths Arms, LASTINGHAM, YO62 6TN, 01751 417247

The New Inn, CROPTON, YO18 8HH, 01751 417330

SCARBOROUGH

Map 17 TA08

See also Filey & Wykeham

Places to visit

Scarborough Castle, SCARBOROUGH, YO11 1HY, 01723 372451
www.english-heritage.org.uk/daysout/properties/scarborough-castle

Great for kids: Scarborough Sea Life Sanctuary, SCARBOROUGH, YO12 6RP, 01723 373414 www.sealife.co.uk

PREMIER PARK

Jacobs Mount Caravan Park

►►►►► 83%

tel: 01723 361178 **Jacobs Mount, Stepney Rd YO12 5NL**
email: jacobsmount@yahoo.co.uk **web:** www.jacobsmount.com
dir: *Direct access from A170.* **grid ref:** *TA021868*

An elevated family-run park surrounded by woodland and open countryside, yet only two miles from the beach. Touring pitches are terraced gravel stands with individual services. The Jacobs Tavern serves a wide range of appetising meals

continued

SCARBOROUGH *continued*

and snacks, and there is a separate well-equipped games room for teenagers. 18 acre site. 156 touring pitches. 131 hardstandings. Caravan pitches. Motorhome pitches. Tent pitches. 60 statics.

Open: Mar-Nov (rs Mar-May & Oct-Nov limited hours at shop & bar)
Last arrival: 22.00hrs **Last departure:** noon

Pitches: * £13.50-£24.50 £13.50-£24.50 £13.50-£24.50

Leisure:

Facilities:

Services:

Within 3 miles:

Notes: Dogs must be kept on leads. Food preparation area.

Cayton Village Caravan Park

►►►► 88%

tel: 01723 583171 **Mill Ln, Cayton Bay YO11 3NN**
email: info@caytontouring.co.uk
dir: *From Scarborough A64, B1261 signed Filey. In Cayton 2nd left after pedestrian crossing into Mill Ln. Site 150yds on left. Or from A165 from Scarborough towards Filey right at Cayton Bay rdbt into Mill Ln. Site 0.5m right. (NB it is advisable to follow guide directions not Sat Nav).* **grid ref:** *TA063838*

A long established, quietly located holiday destination close to all the major coastal attractions. The immaculately maintained grounds provide excellent pitch density and many areas are hedge-screened to create privacy. The newest touring field, The Laurels, is equipped with fully serviced hardstanding pitches that include TV hook-up and free WiFi. 30 acre site. 310 touring pitches. 239 hardstandings. 180 seasonal pitches. Caravan pitches. Motorhome pitches. Tent pitches.

Open: Mar-1 Nov **Last arrival:** 18.00hrs **Last departure:** noon (late arrivals & departures available if pre-booked; charges may apply)

Pitches: * £15-£35 £17-£35 £15-£28

Leisure:

Facilities:

Services:

Within 3 miles:

Notes: No noise after 23.00hrs, children must be supervised, no campfires. Dogs must be kept on leads. Dog walk, nature trail, maze.

AA Pubs & Restaurants nearby: Lanterna Ristorante, SCARBOROUGH, YO11 1HQ, 01723 363616

Scalby Close Park

►►►► 79%

tel: 01723 365908 **Burniston Rd YO13 0DA**
email: info@scalbyclosepark.co.uk
dir: *2m N of Scarborough on A615 (coast road), 1m from junct with A171.*
grid ref: *TA020925*

An attractive, well-landscaped park that is run by enthusiastic owners. The site has a shower block, laundry, fully serviced pitches and a motorhome service point. Just two miles from Scarborough, this makes an ideal base from which to explore both the coast and lovely countryside. 3 acre site. 42 touring pitches. 42 hardstandings. Caravan pitches. Motorhome pitches. 5 statics.

Open: Mar-Oct **Last arrival:** 22.00hrs **Last departure:** noon

Pitches: **Facilities:**

Services:

Within 3 miles:

Notes: Dogs must be kept on leads.

AA Pubs & Restaurants nearby: The Anvil Inn, SAWDON, YO13 9DY, 01723 859896

Lanterna Ristorante, SCARBOROUGH, YO11 1HQ, 01723 363616

Arosa Caravan & Camping Park

►►► 85%

tel: 01723 862166 & 07858 694077 **Ratten Row, Seamer YO12 4QB**
email: info@arosacamping.co.uk
dir: *A64 towards Scarborough onto B1261. On entering village 1st left at rdbt signed Seamer. From Pickering on A171 right at Seamer rdbt. Last right in village.*
grid ref: *TA014830*

A mature park in a secluded location, but with easy access to coastal attractions. Touring areas are hedge-screened to provide privacy, the toilet facilities are smart, and a well-stocked bar serving food is also available. Barbecues and hog roasts are a feature during the warmer months. 9 acre site. 118 touring pitches. 25 hardstandings. 40 seasonal pitches. Caravan pitches. Motorhome pitches. Tent pitches. 8 statics.

Open: Mar-4 Jan **Last arrival:** 21.00hrs **Last departure:** by arrangement

Pitches: * £14-£27 £14-£27 £5-£27 **Leisure:**

Facilities:

Services:

Within 3 miles:

Notes: No noise after 23.00hrs, no generators, no powered bikes or scooters. Dogs must be kept on leads.

AA Pubs & Restaurants nearby: Downe Arms Country Inn, SCARBOROUGH, YO13 9QB, 01723 862471

Killerby Old Hall

►►► 80%

tel: 01723 583799 **Killerby YO11 3TW**
email: killerbyhall@btconnect.com
dir: *From A165 between Scarborough & Filey at Cayton Bay rdbt into Mill Lane towards Cayton. At T-junct left onto B1261 signed Filey. Site on left.* **grid ref:** *TA063829*

A small secluded park, well sheltered by mature trees and shrubs, located at the rear of the old hall. Use of the small indoor swimming pool is shared by visitors to the hall's holiday accommodation. There is a children's play area. 2 acre site. 20 touring pitches. 20 hardstandings. Caravan pitches. Motorhome pitches.

Open: 14 Feb-4 Jan **Last arrival:** 20.00hrs **Last departure:** noon

Pitches: * £18-£30 £18-£30

Leisure:

Facilities:

Services: **Within 3 miles:**

Notes: Dogs must be kept on leads.

AA Pubs & Restaurants nearby: The Anvil Inn, SAWDON, YO13 9DY, 01723 859896

Lanterna Ristorante, SCARBOROUGH, YO11 1HQ, 01723 363616

LEISURE: Indoor swimming pool · Outdoor swimming pool · Children's playground · Kid's club · Tennis court · Games room · Separate TV room · golf course · Boats for hire · Cinema · Entertainment · Fishing · Mini golf · Watersports · Gym · Sports field · Spa · Stables
FACILITIES: Bath · Shower · Electric shaver · Hairdryer · Ice Pack Facility · Disabled facilities · Public telephone · Shop on site or within 200yds · Mobile shop (calls at least 5 days a week) · BBQ area · Picnic area · Wi-fi · Internet access · Recycling · Tourist info · Dog exercise area

SCOTCH CORNER Map 19 NZ20

Places to visit

Green Howards Museum, RICHMOND, DL10 4QN, 01748 826561
www.greenhowards.org.uk

Easby Abbey, EASBY, 0370 333 1181
www.english-heritage.org.uk/daysout/properties/easby-abbey

Scotch Corner Caravan Park

►►► 76%

tel: 01748 822530 & 07977 647722 **DL10 6NS**
email: marshallleisure@aol.com
dir: *From Scotch Corner junct of A1 & A66 take A6108 towards Richmond. 250mtrs, cross central reservation, return 200mtrs to site entrance.* **grid ref:** *NZ210054*

A well-maintained site with good facilities, ideally situated as a stopover, and an equally good location for touring. The Vintage Hotel, which serves food, can be accessed from the rear of the site. 7 acre site. 96 touring pitches. 4 hardstandings. Caravan pitches. Motorhome pitches. Tent pitches. 1 static.

Open: Etr or Apr-Oct **Last arrival:** 22.30hrs **Last departure:** noon

Pitches:

Facilities:

Services:

Within 3 miles:

Notes: Dogs must be kept on leads. Recreation area for children, soft ball.

AA Pubs & Restaurants nearby: The Frenchgate Restaurant, RICHMOND, DL10 7AE, 01748 822087

SELBY Map 16 SE63

Places to visit

The Yorkshire Waterways Museum, GOOLE, DN14 5TB, 01405 768730
www.waterwaysmuseum.org.uk

The Ranch Caravan Park

►►►► 84%

tel: 01757 638984 **Cliffe Common YO8 6PA**
email: contact@theranchcaravanpark.co.uk
dir: *Exit A63 at Cliffe signed Skipwith. Site 1m N on left.* **grid ref:** *SE664337*

A compact, sheltered park set in seven acres in a peaceful area of Cliffe Common. The enthusiastic and welcoming family owners have invested in the park over the past year, adding a superior wooden lodge development and a new smart wooden reception chalet close to the electronic gate at the park entrance. Of the 39 pitches, 14 are allocated to touring motorhomes and caravans and all are well spaced and neatly kept. Facilities include spotlessly clean toilets and showers and the welcoming and newly refurbished Sean's Bar. 7 acre site. 44 touring pitches. Caravan pitches. Motorhome pitches. Tent pitches.

Open: all year **Last arrival:** 21.00hrs **Last departure:** 13.00hrs

Pitches:

Notes:

SHERIFF HUTTON Map 19 SE66

Places to visit

Kirkham Priory, KIRKHAM, YO60 7JS, 01653 618768
www.english-heritage.org.uk/daysout/properties/kirkham-priory

Sutton Park, SUTTON-ON-THE-FOREST, YO61 1DP, 01347 810249
www.statelyhome.co.uk

Great for kids: Castle Howard, MALTON, YO60 7DA, 01653 648333
www.castlehoward.co.uk

York Meadows Caravan Park

►►►► 82%

tel: 01439 788269 & 788236 **York Rd YO60 6QP**
email: reception@yorkmeadowscaravanpark.com
web: www.yorkmeadowscaravanpark.com
dir: *From York take A64 towards Scarborough. Left signed Flaxton & Sheriff Hutton. At West Lilling left signed Strensall. Site opposite junct.* **grid ref:** *SE644653*

Peacefully located in open countryside and surrounded by mature trees, shrubs and wildlife areas, this park provides all level pitches and a modern, well-equipped amenities block. Outdoor games such as draughts and snakes and ladders are available. 12 acre site. 45 touring pitches. 45 hardstandings. 10 seasonal pitches. Caravan pitches. Motorhome pitches. Tent pitches. 15 statics.

Open: Mar-Oct **Last arrival:** 21.00hrs **Last departure:** noon

Pitches: * £17.50-£26 £17.50-£26 £17.50-£26

Leisure:

Facilities:

Services:

Within 3 miles:

Notes: No noise after 23.00hrs. Dogs must be kept on leads.

AA Pubs & Restaurants nearby: The Crown and Cushion, WELBURN, YO60 7DZ, 01653 618777

The Rose & Crown, SUTTON-ON-THE-FOREST, YO61 1DP, 01347 811333

PITCHES: Caravans Motorhomes Tents Glamping-style accommodation **SERVICES:** Electric hook up Launderette Licensed bar Calor Gas Camping Gaz Toilet fluid Café/Restaurant Fast Food/Takeaway Battery charging Baby care Motorvan service point
ABBREVIATIONS: BH/bank hols – bank holidays Etr – Easter Spring BH – Spring Bank Holiday fr – from hrs – hours m – mile mdnt – midnight rdbt – roundabout rs – restricted service wk – week wknd – weekend x-rds – cross roads No credit or debit cards No dogs Children of all ages accepted

SUTTON-ON-THE-FOREST Map 19 SE56

Places to visit

Sutton Park, SUTTON-ON-THE-FOREST, YO61 1DP, 01347 810249 www.statelyhome.co.uk

Treasurer's House, YORK, YO1 7JL, 01904 624247 www.nationaltrust.org.uk

Great for kids: Jorvik Viking Centre, YORK, YO1 9WT, 01904 615505 www.jorvik-viking-centre.com

PREMIER PARK

Goosewood Caravan Park

►►►►► 85%

tel: 01347 810829 **YO61 1ET**
email: enquiries@goosewood.co.uk
dir: *From A1237 take B1363. In 5m turn right. Right again in 0.5m, site on right.*
grid ref: *SE595636*

A relaxing and immaculately maintained park with its own lake and seasonal fishing. It is set in attractive woodland just six miles north of York. Mature shrubs and stunning seasonal floral displays at the entrance create an excellent first impression and the well-located toilet facilities are kept spotlessly clean. The generous patio pitches, providing optimum privacy, are randomly spaced throughout the site, and in addition to an excellent outdoor children's play area, you will find an indoor swimming pool, clubhouse, games room and bar/bistro. There are holiday homes for hire. 20 acre site. 100 touring pitches. 75 hardstandings. 50 seasonal pitches. Caravan pitches. Motorhome pitches. 35 statics.

Open: Mar-2 Jan (rs Low season shop, bar & pool reduced hours) **Last arrival:** dusk **Last departure:** noon

Pitches: * £22-£28 £22-£28

Leisure:

Facilities:

Services:

Within 3 miles:

Notes: No noise after mdnt. Dogs accepted by prior arrangement only & must be kept on leads.

AA Pubs & Restaurants nearby: The Rose & Crown, SUTTON-ON-THE-FOREST, YO61 1DP, 01347 811333

THIRSK

Places to visit

Monk Park Farm Visitor Centre, THIRSK, YO7 2AG, 01845 597730 www.monkparkfarm.co.uk

Byland Abbey, COXWOLD, YO61 4BD, 01347 868614 www.english-heritage.org.uk/daysout/properties/byland-abbey

Great for kids: Falconry UK - Birds of Prey Centre, THIRSK, YO7 4EU, 01845 587522 www.falconrycentre.co.uk

THIRSK Map 19 SE48

Hillside Caravan Park

►►►► 88%

tel: 01845 537349 & 07711 643652 **Canvas Farm, Moor Rd, Knayton YO7 4BR**
email: info@hillsidecaravanpark.co.uk
dir: *From Thirsk take A19 N exit at Knayton sign. In 0.25m right (cross bridge over A19), through village. Site on left in approx 1.5m.* **grid ref:** *SE447889*

A high quality, spacious park with first-class facilities, set in open countryside. A striking new sandstone amenity block was added in 2015 and houses the airy reception, shop and office, as well as a new kitchen and laundry, two excellent family rooms, a disabled room, a recreation room and two self-contained flats for hire. This is an excellent base for walkers and for those wishing to explore the Thirsk area. Please note that the park does not accept tents. 9 acre site. 50 touring pitches. 50 hardstandings. Caravan pitches. Motorhome pitches.

Open: 4 Feb-4 Jan **Last arrival:** 21.00hrs **Last departure:** noon

Pitches: * £21-£32.50 £21-£32.50

Leisure:

Facilities:

Services:

Within 3 miles:

Notes: Dogs must be kept on leads.

AA Pubs & Restaurants nearby: The Black Swan at Oldstead, OLDSTEAD, YO61 4BL, 01347 868387

Thirkleby Hall Caravan Park

►►► 75%

tel: 01845 501360 & 07799 641815 **Thirkleby YO7 3AR**
email: greenwood.parks@virgin.net **web:** www.greenwoodparks.com
dir: *3m S of Thirsk on A19. Turn left through arched gatehouse into site.*
grid ref: *SE472794*

A long-established site in the grounds of the old hall, with statics in wooded areas around a fishing lake and tourers based on slightly sloping grassy pitches. There is a quality amenities block and laundry. This well-screened park has superb views of the Hambledon Hills. 53 acre site. 50 touring pitches. 3 hardstandings. 20 seasonal pitches. Caravan pitches. Motorhome pitches. Tent pitches. 200 statics.

Open: Mar-Oct **Last arrival:** 17.30hrs **Last departure:** 14.30hrs

Pitches:

Leisure:

Facilities:

Services:

Within 3 miles:

Notes: No noise after 23.00hrs. Dogs must be kept on leads. Woodland walks.

AA Pubs & Restaurants nearby: The Black Swan at Oldstead, OLDSTEAD, YO61 4BL, 01347 868387

TOLLERTON Map 19 SE56

Places to visit

Beningbrough Hall, Gallery & Gardens, BENINGBROUGH, YO30 1DD, 01904 472027 www.nationaltrust.org.uk/beningbrough

Sutton Park, SUTTON-ON-THE-FOREST, YO61 1DP, 01347 810249 www.statelyhome.co.uk

Great for kids: Jorvik Viking Centre, YORK, YO1 9WT, 01904 615505 www.jorvik-viking-centre.com

Tollerton Holiday Park

►►►► 81%

tel: 01347 838313 **Station Rd YO61 1RD**
email: greenwood.parks@virgin.net **web:** www.greenwoodparks.com
dir: *From York take A19 towards Thirsk. At Cross Lanes left towards Tollerton. 1m to Chinese restaurant just before rail bridge. Site entrance through restaurant car park.* **grid ref:** *SE513643*

Set in open countryside within a few minutes' walk of Tollerton and just a short drive from the Park & Ride for York, this is a small park. There's an amenities block of real quality, which includes a family bathroom and laundry. There is little disturbance from the East Coast mainline which passes near to the park. 5 acre site. 50 touring pitches. 17 hardstandings. 25 seasonal pitches. Caravan pitches. Motorhome pitches. Tent pitches. 75 statics.

Open: Mar-Oct **Last arrival:** 20.00hrs **Last departure:** 15.00hrs

Pitches:

Leisure:

Facilities:

Services:

Within 3 miles:

Notes: No groups. Dogs must be kept on leads. Small fishing lake.

AA Pubs & Restaurants nearby: The Aldwark Arms, ALDWARK, YO61 1UB, 01347 838324

The Rose & Crown, SUTTON-ON-THE-FOREST, YO61 1DP, 01347 811333

TOWTHORPE Map 19 SE65

Places to visit

Barley Hall, YORK, YO1 8AR, 01904 615505 www.barleyhall.co.uk

York Castle Museum, YORK, YO1 9RY, 01904 687687 www.yorkcastlemuseum.org.uk

Great for kids: Jorvik Viking Centre, YORK, YO1 9WT, 01904 615505 www.jorvik-viking-centre.com

York Touring Caravan Site

►►►► 79%

tel: 01904 499275 **Greystones Farm, Towthorpe Moor Ln YO32 9ST**
email: info@yorkcaravansite.co.uk
dir: *From A64 follow Strensall & Haxby signs, site 1.5m on left.* **grid ref:** *SE648584*

This purpose-built golf complex and caravan park is situated just over five miles from York. There is a 9-hole golf course, crazy golf, driving range and golf shop with a coffee bar/café. The generously sized, level pitches are set within well-manicured grassland with a backdrop of trees and shrubs. 6 acre site. 44 touring pitches. 12 hardstandings. Caravan pitches. Motorhome pitches. Tent pitches.

Open: 8 Feb-3 Jan **Last arrival:** 21.00hrs **Last departure:** noon

Pitches: * £20-£25 £20-£25 £18-£22

Leisure:

Facilities: WiFi

Services:

Within 3 miles:

Notes: No noise after 23.00hrs, no commercial vehicles. Dogs must be kept on leads.

AA Pubs & Restaurants nearby: The Rose & Crown, SUTTON-ON-THE-FOREST, YO61 1DP, 01347 811333

WORSBROUGH Map 16 SE30

Places to visit

Monk Bretton Priory, BARNSLEY, S71 5QD, 0370 333 1181 www.english-heritage.org.uk/daysout/properties/monk-bretton-priory

Millennium Gallery, SHEFFIELD, S1 2PP, 0114 278 2600 www.museums-sheffield.org.uk

Great for kids: Magna Science Adventure Centre, ROTHERHAM, S60 1DX, 01709 720002 www.visitmagna.co.uk

Greensprings Touring Park

►► 80%

tel: 01226 288298 **Rockley Abbey Farm, Rockley Ln S75 3DS**
dir: *M1 junct 36, A61 to Barnsley. Left after 0.25m signed Pilley. Site 1m at bottom of hill.*
grid ref: *SE330020*

A secluded and attractive farm site set amidst woods and farmland, with access to the river and several good local walks. There are two touring areas, one gently sloping. Although not far from the M1, there is almost no traffic noise, and this site is convenient for exploring the area's industrial heritage, as well as the Peak District. 4 acre site. 65 touring pitches. 30 hardstandings. 22 seasonal pitches. Caravan pitches. Motorhome pitches. Tent pitches.

Open: Apr-30 Oct **Last arrival:** 21.00hrs **Last departure:** noon

Pitches: * fr £15 fr £15 fr £12

Leisure: **Facilities:**

Services: **Within 3 miles:**

Notes: Dogs must be kept on leads.

WEST YORKSHIRE

BARDSEY Map 16 SE34

Places to visit

Bramham Park, BRAMHAM, LS23 6ND, 01937 846000 www.bramhampark.co.uk

Thackray Medical Museum, LEEDS, LS9 7LN, 0113 244 4343 www.thackraymedicalmuseum.co.uk

Great for kids: Leeds Industrial Museum at Armley Mills, LEEDS, LS12 2QF, 0113 378 3173 www.leeds.gov.uk/armleymills

Glenfield Caravan Park

►►►► 83%

tel: 01937 574657 & 0776 1710862 **Blackmoor Ln LS17 9DZ**
email: glenfieldcp@aol.com **web:** www.glenfieldcaravanpark.co.uk
dir: *3m from A1 junct 45. From A58 at Bardsey into Church Ln, past church, up hill. 0.5m, site on right.* **grid ref:** *SE351421*

A quiet family-owned rural site in a well-screened, tree-lined meadow. The site has an excellent toilet block complete with family room. A convenient touring base for Leeds and the surrounding area. Discounted fees and food are both available at the local golf club. 4 acre site. 30 touring pitches. 30 hardstandings. 10 seasonal pitches. Caravan pitches. Motorhome pitches. Tent pitches. 1 static.

Open: all year **Last arrival:** 21.00hrs **Last departure:** noon

Pitches: £20-£24 £20-£24 £20-£24

Facilities: Wi-fi

Services:

Within 3 miles:

Notes: Children must be supervised. Dogs must be kept on leads. Walking maps.

AA Pubs & Restaurants nearby: The Windmill Inn, LINTON, LS22 4HT, 01937 582209

LEEDS Map 19 SE23

Places to visit

Leeds Art Gallery, LEEDS, LS1 3AA, 0113 247 8256 www.leeds.gov.uk/artgallery

Temple Newsam Estate, LEEDS, LS15 0AE, 0113 336 7460 (House) www.leeds.gov.uk/templenewsamhouse

Moor Lodge Park

►►►► 85%

tel: 01937 572424 **Blackmoor Ln, Bardsey LS17 9DZ**
email: moorlodgecp@aol.com **web:** www.moorlodgecaravanpark.co.uk
dir: *From A1(M) take A659 (S of Wetherby) signed Otley. Left onto A58 towards Leeds for 5m. Right after New Inn pub (Ling Lane), right at x-rds, 1m. Site on right.*
grid ref: *SE352423*

A warm welcome is assured at this well-kept site set in a peaceful and beautiful setting, close to Harewood House and only 25 minutes' drive from York and the Dales; the centre of Leeds is just 15 minutes away. The touring area is for adults only. Please note, this site does not accept tents. 7 acre site. 12 touring pitches. Caravan pitches. Motorhome pitches. 60 statics.

Open: all year **Last arrival:** 20.00hrs **Last departure:** noon

Pitches: * £16.50-£22 £16.50-£22

Facilities:

Services:

Within 3 miles:

Notes: Adults only. No large groups. Dogs must be kept on leads.

St Helena's Caravan Park

►►► 82%

tel: 0113 284 1142 **Otley Old Rd, Horsforth LS18 5HZ**
email: info@st-helenas.co.uk
dir: *From A658 follow signs for Leeds/Bradford Airport. Then follow site signs.*
grid ref: *SE240421*

A well-maintained parkland setting surrounded by woodland yet within easy reach of Leeds with its excellent shopping and cultural opportunities, Ilkley, and the attractive Wharfedale town of Otley. Some visitors may just want to relax in this adults-only park's spacious and pleasant surroundings. 25 acre site. 60 touring pitches. 31 hardstandings. Caravan pitches. Motorhome pitches. Tent pitches. 40 statics.

Open: Apr-Oct **Last arrival:** 19.30hrs **Last departure:** 14.00hrs

Pitches:

Facilities:

Services:

Within 3 miles:

Notes: Adults only.

CHANNEL ISLANDS

GUERNSEY

CASTEL Map 24

Places to visit

Sausmarez Manor, ST MARTIN, GY4 6SG, 01481 235571
www.sausmarezmanor.co.uk

Fort Grey Shipwreck Museum, ROCQUAINE BAY, GY7 9BY, 01481 265036
www.museums.gov.gg

PREMIER PARK

Fauxquets Valley Campsite

►►►►► 83%

tel: 01481 255460 & 07781 413333 **GY5 7QL**
email: info@fauxquets.co.uk
dir: *From pier take 2nd exit at rdbt. At top of hill left into Queens Rd. 2m. Right into Candie Rd. Site opposite sign for German Occupation Museum.*

A beautiful, quiet farm site in a hidden valley close to the sea. The friendly and helpful owners, who understand campers' needs, offer good quality facilities and amenities, including spacious pitches and an outdoor swimming pool. There are sports areas, a nature trail, pigs, sheep and chickens for the children to visit, plus BBQ food is available near the reception. There are fully serviced pitches and also four self-contained lodges for hire. Motorhomes up to 6.9 metres are allowed on Guernsey - contact the site for details and a permit. 3 acre site. 120 touring pitches. Motorhome pitches. Tent pitches.

Open: May-1 Sep

Pitches:

Leisure:

Facilities:

Services:

Within 3 miles:

Notes: Dogs must be kept on leads. Birdwatching.

AA Pubs & Restaurants nearby: Fleur du Jardin, CASTEL, GY5 7JT, 01481 257996

Cobo Bay Hotel, CASTEL, GY5 7HB, 01481 257102

ST SAMPSON Map 24

Places to visit

Sausmarez Manor, ST MARTIN, GY4 6SG, 01481 235571
www.sausmarezmanor.co.uk

Castle Cornet, ST PETER PORT, GY1 1AU, 01481 721657
www.museums.gov.gg

Le Vaugrat Camp Site

►►► 88%

tel: 01481 257468 **Route de Vaugrat GY2 4TA**
email: enquiries@vaugratcampsite.com **web:** www.vaugratcampsite.com
dir: *From main coast road on NW of island, site signed at Port Grat Bay into Route de Vaugrat, near Peninsula Hotel.*

Overlooking the sea and set within the grounds of a lovely 17th-century house, this level grassy park is backed by woodland, and is close to the lovely sandy beaches of Port Grat and Grand Havre. It is run by a welcoming family who pride themselves on creating magnificent floral displays. The facilities here are excellent and there are 18 electric hook ups. Motorhomes up to 6.9 metres are allowed on Guernsey – contact the site for details and permit. A 'round the island' bus stops very close to the site. 6 acre site. 150 touring pitches. Motorhome pitches. Tent pitches.

Open: May-mid Sep

Pitches:

Leisure:

Facilities:

Services:

Within 3 miles:

Notes: No pets.

AA Pubs & Restaurants nearby: The Pickled Pig, ST PETER PORT, GY1 2JP, 01481 721431

The Old Government House Hotel & Spa, ST PETER PORT, GY1 2NU, 01481 724921

The Absolute End, ST PETER PORT, GY1 2BG, 01481 723822

Mora Restaurant & Grill, ST PETER PORT, GY1 2LE, 01481 715053

VALE Map 24

Places to visit

Guernsey Museum & Art Gallery, ST PETER PORT, GY1 1UG, 01481 726518
www.museums.gov.gg

Great for kids: Castle Cornet, ST PETER PORT, GY1 1AU, 01481 721657
www.museums.gov.gg

La Bailloterie Camping

►►►► 82%

tel: 01481 243636 & 07781 103420 **Bailloterie Ln GY3 5HA**
email: info@campinginguernsey.com
dir: *3m N of St Peter Port into Vale Rd to Crossways, at x-rds right into Rue du Braye. Site 1st left at sign.*

A pretty rural site with one large touring field and a few small, well-screened paddocks. This delightful site has been privately run for over 50 years and offers good facilities in converted outbuildings. There are two log cabins for three, plus

LEISURE: Indoor swimming pool · Outdoor swimming pool · Children's playground · Kid's club · Tennis court · Games room · Separate TV room · golf course · Boats for hire · Cinema · Entertainment · Fishing · Mini golf · Watersports · Gym · Sports field · Spa · Stables
FACILITIES: Bath · Shower · Electric shaver · Hairdryer · Ice Pack Facility · Disabled facilities · Public telephone · Shop on site or within 200yds · Mobile shop (calls at least 5 days a week) · BBQ area · Picnic area · Wi-fi · Internet access · Recycling · Tourist info · Dog exercise area

top quality and very well equipped safari tents available for hire. The beaches and a supermarket are a short walk away. Motorhomes up to 6.9 metres are allowed on Guernsey – contact the site for detailed instructions. 10 acre site. 100 touring pitches. Motorhome pitches. Tent pitches.

Open: 15 May-15 Sep (rs 15-30 Sep motorhomes & cabins only) **Last arrival:** 23.00hrs **Last departure:** 11.00hrs

Pitches: **Leisure:**

Facilities:

Services:

Within 3 miles:

Notes: Dogs by prior arrangement only, no dogs in log cabins or safari tents. Dogs must be kept on leads. Volleyball net, boules pitch.

AA Pubs & Restaurants nearby: The Pickled Pig, ST PETER PORT, GY1 2JP, 01481 721431

The Old Government House Hotel & Spa, ST PETER PORT, GY1 2NU, 01481 724921

The Absolute End, ST PETER PORT, GY1 2BG, 01481 723822

Mora Restaurant & Grill, ST PETER PORT, GY1 2LE, 01481 715053

JERSEY

ST MARTIN — Map 24

Places to visit

Mont Orgueil Castle, GOREY, JE3 6ET, 01534 853292 www.jerseyheritage.org

Maritime Museum & Occupation Tapestry Gallery, ST HELIER, JE2 3ND, 01534 811043 www.jerseyheritage.org

Great for kids: Elizabeth Castle, ST HELIER, JE2 3WU, 01534 723971 www.jerseyheritage.org

PREMIER PARK

Beuvelande Camp Site

►►►►►86%

tel: 01534 853575 **Beuvelande JE3 6EZ**
email: info@campingjersey.com
dir: *Take A6 from St Helier to St Martin & follow signs to site before St Martins Church.*

A well-established site with excellent toilet facilities, accessed via narrow lanes in peaceful countryside close to St Martin. An attractive bar and restaurant is the focal point of the park, especially in the evenings, and there is a small swimming pool and playground. Motorhomes and towed caravans will be met at the ferry and escorted to the site if requested when booking. Two yurts, one safari tent, six bell tents and euro-style tents, all fully equipped, are available for hire. 6 acre site. 150 touring pitches. Caravan pitches. Motorhome pitches. Tent pitches. 75 statics. 6 bell tents 2 yurts.1 safari tent.

Open: Apr-Sep (rs Apr-May & Sep pool & restaurant closed, shop hours limited)

Pitches:

Leisure:

Facilities:

Services:

Within 3 miles:

Notes: Dogs must be kept on leads.

AA Pubs & Restaurants nearby: Royal Hotel, ST MARTIN, JE3 6UG, 01534 856289

Rozel Camping Park

►►►►91%

tel: 01534 855200 **Summerville Farm JE3 6AX**
email: enquiries@rozelcamping.com
dir: *Take A6 from St Helier through Five Oaks to St Martins Church, turn right onto A38 towards Rozel, site on right.*

Customers can be sure of a warm welcome at this delightful family-run park. Set in the north east of the island, it offers large spacious pitches, many with electric, for tents, caravans and motorhomes. The lovely Rozel Bay is just a short distance away and spectacular views of the French coast can be seen from one of the four fields on the park. The site also offers excellent facilities including a swimming pool. Motorhomes and caravans will be met at the ferry and escorted to the park if requested when booking. Fully equipped, ready-erected tents available for hire. 4 acre site. 100 touring pitches. Caravan pitches. Motorhome pitches. Tent pitches. 20 statics.

Open: May-mid Sep **Last departure:** noon

Pitches: **Leisure:**

Facilities: **Services:**

Within 3 miles:

Notes: No noise between 22.00hrs-07.30hrs. Dogs must be kept on leads. Free mini golf.

AA Pubs & Restaurants nearby: Royal Hotel, ST MARTIN, JE3 6UG, 01534 856289

ST OUEN — Map 24

Places to visit

Creux Baillot Cottage, ST OUEN, JE3 2FE, 01534 482191 www.judithqueree.com

The Channel Islands Military Museum, ST OUEN, JE3 2FN, 01534 483205

Great for kids: The Living Legend, ST PETER, JE3 7ET, 01534 485496 www.jerseyslivinglegend.co.je

Daisy Cottage Campsite

►►►►88%

tel: 01534 481700 **Route de Vinchelez JE3 2DB**
email: hello@daisycottagecampsite.com
dir: *From St Helier harbour, at 2nd rdbt, 1st exit onto A2 (Victoria Ave) (becomes A1). At 'filter-in-turn' mini rdbt in Beaumont, right into La Route de Beaumont (signed St Ouen & A12). In St Ouen right into Route de Vinchelez. Site on right.*

The only campsite on the west side of the island, this is a small quiet family site with a good choice of accommodation, including 10 luxury, well-appointed bell tents and a shepherd's hut. If you prefer, you can bring your own tent, caravan or motorhome. The campsite also has a unique Retreat offering a wide range of therapies, as well as its own on-site chiropractor. There is also a secluded decked area where you can relax or take part in yoga or relaxation classes. In addition, there is a small café and tasteful bar in keeping with the quiet and peaceful environment. The campsite is also very close to Greve de Lecq with its delightful beach. Caravan pitches. Motorhome pitches. Tent pitches. 12 bell tents. 1 shepherd's hut

Open: all year **Pitches:** **Leisure:** Spa

Facilities: **Services:**

Within 3 miles: **Notes:** No noise after 22.00hrs.

AA Pubs & Restaurants nearby: St Mary's Country Inn, ST MARY, JE3 3DS, 01534 482897

Mark Jordan at the Beach, ST PETER, JE3 7YD, 01534 780180

TRINITY Map 24

PREMIER PARK

Durrell Wildlife Camp

NEW ►►►►►

tel: 01534 860095 & 07797 832534 **Les Augres Manor, La Profonde Rue JE3 5BP**
email: ashley.mullins@durrell.org
dir: *From St Helier take A8 to Trinity. At T-junct right signed Rozel & Durrell Wildlife. Site on right.* **grid ref:** *SY161140*

Part of the Durrell Wildlife Park, the camp consists of 12 canvas geo pods set in a beautifully landscaped area. Each pod, named after different Lemur species, is sited in its own separate area offering good privacy. Inside is a king-size bed, two singles, a wood-burning stove and clothing storage space. Set on wooden decking, the pods have their own additional pod with high quality toilet, wash basin and shower plus a spacious fully-equipped kitchen. Table and chairs on the decking can be brought into the kitchen if the weather's not so good. Smaller tipis are available for extra children or guests.

Open: Mar-Oct **Last arrival:** 20.00hrs **Last departure:** 10.00hrs

Pitches: £170-£210

Leisure:

Facilities: WiFi

Services:

Within 3 miles:

Notes: No cars by pods. No pets. No noise after 23.00hrs. Free entry to Durrell Wildlife Park.

ISLE OF MAN

KIRK MICHAEL Map 24 SC39

Places to visit

Peel Castle, PEEL, IM5 1TB, 01624 648000 www.manxnationalheritage.im

House of Manannan, PEEL, IM5 1TA, 01624 648000 www.manxnationalheritage.im

Great for kids: Curraghs Wildlife Park, BALLAUGH, IM7 5EA, 01624 897323 www.gov.im/wildlife

Glen Wyllin Campsite

►►►72%

tel: 01624 878231 & 878836 **IM6 1AL**
email: michaelcommissioners@manx.net
dir: *From Douglas take A1 to Ballacraine, right at lights onto A3 to Kirk Michael. Left onto A4 signed Peel. Site 100yds on right.* **grid ref:** *SC302901*

Set in a beautiful wooded glen with bridges over a pretty stream dividing the camping areas. A gently-sloping tarmac road gives direct access to a good beach. Hire tents are available. 9 acre site. 90 touring pitches. Caravan pitches. Motorhome pitches. Tent pitches. 18 statics.

Open: mid Apr-mid Sep **Last departure:** noon

Pitches:

Leisure:

Facilities: WiFi

Services:

Within 3 miles:

Notes: No excess noise after mdnt, dogs must be kept under control. Dogs must be kept on leads.

AA Pubs & Restaurants nearby: The Creek Inn, PEEL, IM5 1AT, 01624 842216

Scotland

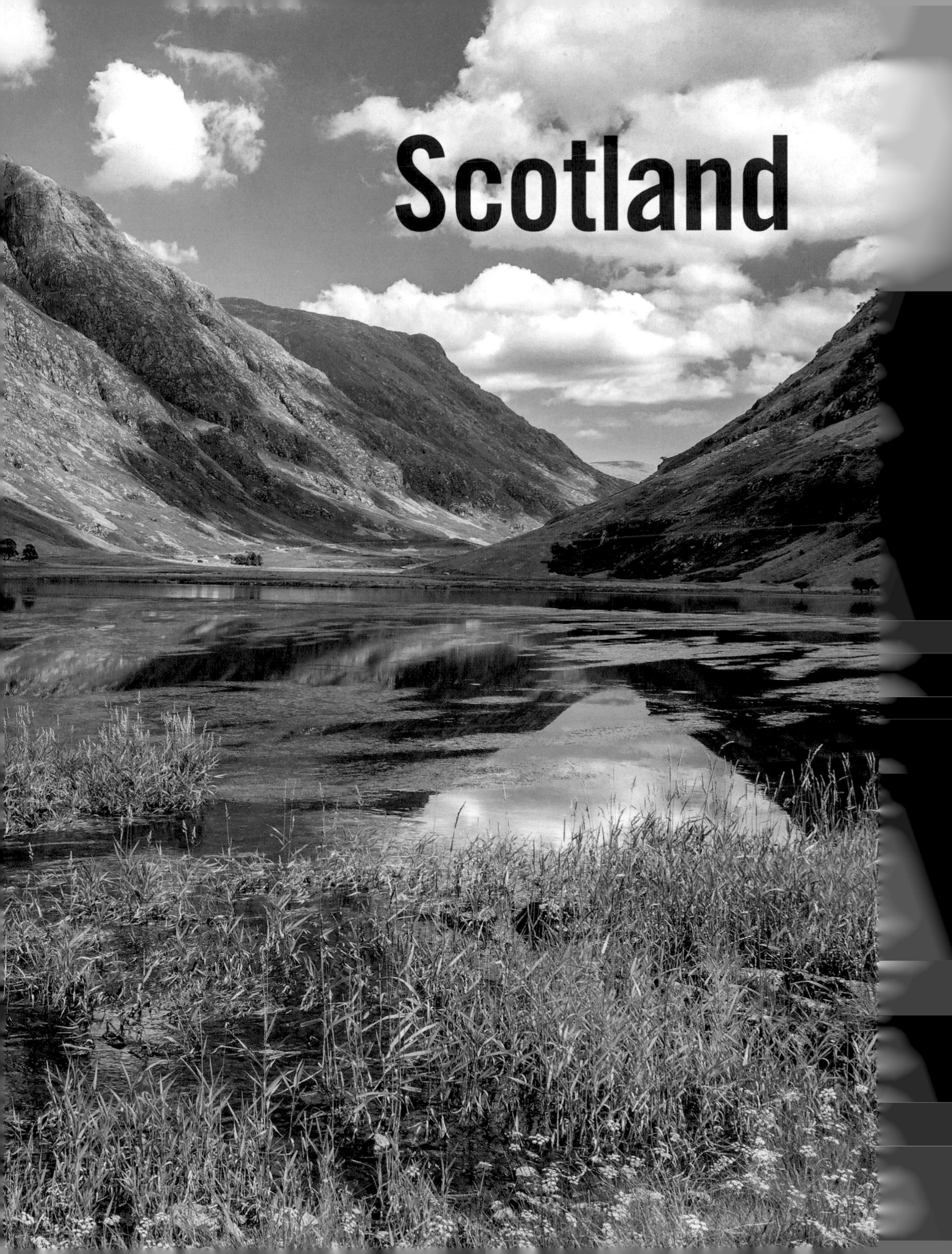

Scotland

With its remarkable, timeless beauty, jagged coastline and long and eventful history, Scotland is a country with something very special to offer. Around half the size of England, but with barely one fifth of its population and nearly 800 islands, the statistics alone are enough make you want to pack a suitcase and head north without hesitation.

The Scottish Borders region acts as a perfect introduction and is an obvious place to begin a tour of the country. The novelist and poet Sir Walter Scott was so moved by its remoteness and grandeur that he wrote: 'To my eye, these grey hills and all this wild border country have beauties peculiar to themselves. I like the very nakedness of the land; it has something bold and stern and solitary about it. If I did not see the heather at least once a year I think I should die.' Abbotsford, Scott's turreted mansion on the banks of the River Tweed near Melrose, was re-opened to the public in the summer of 2013 following a £12 million programme of major improvements.

Consisting of 1,800 square miles of dense forest, rolling green hills and the broad sweeps of heather that lifted Scott's spirits, this region is characterised by some of the country's most majestic landscapes. Adjacent to this region is Dumfries & Galloway, where, at Gretna Green on the border with England, eloping couples have tied the knot since Lord Hardwicke's Marriage Act came into force in 1754; it still can boast around 1,500 weddings a year. Travel north and you discover mile upon mile of open moorland and swathes of seemingly endless forest that stretch to the Ayrshire coast. At a crucial time in the country's history, it is fascinating to reflect on another momentous event in the story of Scotland when, following the signing of the Declaration of Arbroath in 1320, it became independent and was ruled by Robert the Bruce. Dumfries & Galloway is littered with the relics of his battles.

Not far from Dumfries is the cottage where Robert Burns, the Bard of Scotland, was born in 1759. This tiny white-washed dwelling, constructed of thatch and clay, was built by the poet's father two years earlier. In a 2009 poll, TV viewers voted Burns the 'Greatest ever Scot' and his song *Is there for Honest Poverty* opened the new Scottish Parliament in 1999. The cottage at Alloway is one of Scotland's most popular tourist attractions with a new museum allowing the poet's collection of precious manuscripts, correspondence and artefacts to be housed in one building.

Scotland's two greatest cities, Glasgow and Edinburgh, include innumerable historic sites, popular landmarks and innovative visitor attractions. Edinburgh is home to the annual, internationally famous Military Tattoo; Glasgow, once the second city of the British Empire and yet synonymous with the dreadful slums and the grime of industry, has, in places, been transformed beyond recognition. The city hosted the Great Exhibitions of 1888 and 1901, was designated European City of Culture in 1990 and in 2014 became the setting for the highly successful Commonwealth Games.

To the north of Glasgow and Edinburgh lies a sublime landscape of tranquil lochs, fishing rivers, wooded glens and the fine cities of Perth and Dundee. There is also the superb scenery of The Trossachs, Loch Lomond and Stirling, which, with its handsome castle perched on a rocky crag, is Scotland's heritage capital. Sooner or later the might and majesty of the Cairngorms and the Grampians beckon, drawing you into a breathtakingly beautiful landscape of mountains and remote, rugged terrain. Scotland's isolated far north is further from many parts of England than a good many European destinations. Cape Wrath is Britain's most northerly outpost.

For many visitors, the Western Highlands is the place to go, evoking a truly unique and breathtaking sense of adventure. The list of island names seems endless – Skye, Mull, Iona, Jura, Islay – each with their own individual character and identity, and the reward of everlasting and treasured memories.

Glenfinnan Viaduct, Lochaber ▷

ABERDEENSHIRE

ABOYNE — Map 23 NO59

Places to visit

Alford Valley Railway, ALFORD, AB33 8AD, 019755 63942 www.alfordvalleyrailway.org.uk

Crathes Castle Garden & Estate, CRATHES, AB31 5QJ, 01330 844525 www.nts.org.uk/Property/Crathes-Castle-Garden-and-Estate

Great for kids: Craigievar Castle, ALFORD, AB33 8JF, 01339 883635 www.nts.org.uk/Property/Craigievar-Castle

Aboyne Loch Caravan Park

►►► 76%

GOLD

tel: 01339 886244 & 882589 **AB34 5BR**
email: heatherreid24@yahoo.co.uk
dir: *On A93, 1m E of Aboyne.* **grid ref:** *NO538998*

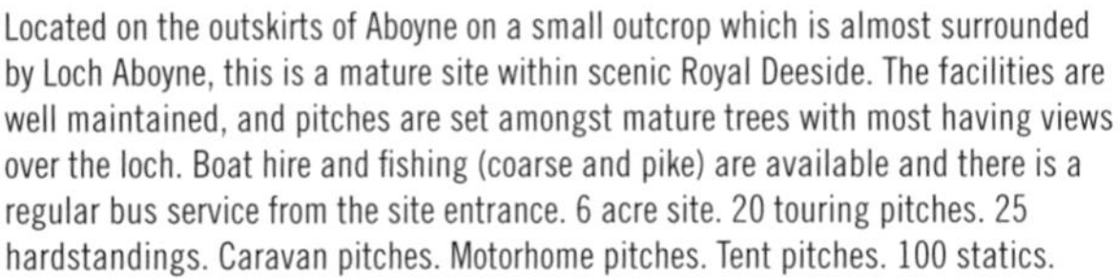

Located on the outskirts of Aboyne on a small outcrop which is almost surrounded by Loch Aboyne, this is a mature site within scenic Royal Deeside. The facilities are well maintained, and pitches are set amongst mature trees with most having views over the loch. Boat hire and fishing (coarse and pike) are available and there is a regular bus service from the site entrance. 6 acre site. 20 touring pitches. 25 hardstandings. Caravan pitches. Motorhome pitches. Tent pitches. 100 statics.

Open: 31 Mar-Oct **Last arrival:** 20.00hrs **Last departure:** 11.00hrs

Pitches: * £22-£25 £22-£25 £15-£25

Leisure:

Facilities:

Services:

Within 3 miles:

Notes: Dogs must be kept on leads.

AA Pubs & Restaurants nearby: The Milton Brasserie, CRATHES, AB31 5QH, 01330 844566

ALFORD

Places to visit

Alford Valley Railway, ALFORD, AB33 8AD, 019755 63942 www.alfordvalleyrailway.org.uk

Craigievar Castle, ALFORD, AB33 8JF, 01339 883635 www.nts.org.uk/Property/Craigievar-Castle

ALFORD — Map 23 NJ51

Haughton House Holiday Park

►►► 76%

tel: 01975 562107 **Montgarrie Rd AB33 8NA**
email: enquiries@haughtonhouse.co.uk
dir: *In Alford follow Haughton Country House signs.* **grid ref:** *NJ577168*

Located on the outskirts of Alford this site is set within a large country park with good countryside views. Now under the same ownership as Huntly Castle Caravan Park (Huntly), this park receives the same attention to detail to ensure facilities are of a high standard; the existing facilities are clean and well maintained. The pitches are set amid mature trees and the tenting area is within the old walled garden. There is plenty to do on site and within the country park which has various activities for children, including a narrow gauge railway that runs to the Grampian Transport Museum in nearby Alford. 22 acre site. 71 touring pitches. 71 hardstandings. 20 seasonal pitches. Caravan pitches. Motorhome pitches. Tent pitches. 70 statics.

Open: Mar-mid/end Oct **Last arrival:** 21.00hrs **Last departure:** noon

Pitches: * £18.25-£22 £18.25-£22 £11.25-£16

Leisure: **Facilities:**

Services:

Within 3 miles:

Notes: No noise after 22.30hrs. Dogs must be kept on leads. Putting green, fishing permits.

BANFF — Map 23 NJ66

Places to visit

Banff Museum, BANFF, AB45 1AE, 01261 812941

Duff House, BANFF, AB45 3SX, 01261 818181 www.historic-scotland.gov.uk

Banff Links Caravan Park

►►►► 82%

tel: 01261 812228 **Inverboyndie AB45 2JJ**
email: banfflinkscaravanpark@btconnect.com
dir: *From W: A98 onto B9038 signed Whitehills. 2nd right signed Inverboyndie. 4th left to site. From E (Banff): A98, right at brown 'Banff Links Beach' sign.* **grid ref:** *NJ668644*

This delightful small park, where the family owners are keen that their visitors enjoy their stay, is set beside the award-winning sandy beach at Banff Links with magnificent views over the Moray coast. Set at sea level, there is direct access to the beach and also a large grass esplanade and play area for children. A pleasant walk on good level paths by the sea will take you to either Banff or the small village of Whitehill, which has a leisure boat harbour. It is ideally located to explore this lovely coastline. Six static caravans are for hire. 5.78 acre site. 55 touring pitches. 10 hardstandings. 10 seasonal pitches. Caravan pitches. Motorhome pitches. Tent pitches. 38 statics.

Open: Apr-Oct

Pitches: **Leisure:**

Facilities:

Services: **Within 3 miles:**

Notes: Dogs must be kept on leads.

HUNTLY — Map 23 NJ53

Places to visit

Leith Hall, Garden & Estate, RHYNIE, AB54 4NQ, 01464 831 216 www.nts.org.uk/Property/Leith-Hall-Garden-and-Estate

Glenfiddich Distillery, DUFFTOWN, AB55 4DH, 01340 820373 www.glenfiddich.com

PREMIER PARK

Huntly Castle Caravan Park

►►►►► 90%

tel: 01466 794999 **The Meadow AB54 4UJ**
email: enquiries@huntlycastle.co.uk
dir: *From Aberdeen on A96 to Huntly. 0.75m after rdbt (on outskirts of Huntly) right towards town centre, left into Riverside Drive.* **grid ref:** *NJ525405*

A quality parkland site within striking distance of the Speyside Malt Whisky Trail, the beautiful Moray coast and the Cairngorm Mountains. The park provides exceptional toilet facilities, and there are some fully serviced pitches. The attractive town of Huntly is only a five-minute walk away, with its ruined castle plus a wide variety of restaurants and shops. 15 acre site. 90 touring pitches. 51 hardstandings. 10 seasonal pitches. Caravan pitches. Motorhome pitches. Tent pitches. 40 statics.

Open: Apr-Oct **Last arrival:** 20.00hrs **Last departure:** noon

Pitches: * £19.15-£24.95 £19.15-£24.95 £14.95-£19.10

Leisure:

Facilities:

Services:

Within 3 miles:

Notes: No noise after 23.00hrs. Dogs must be kept on leads.

KINTORE

Places to visit

Pitmedden Garden, PITMEDDEN, AB41 7PD, 01651 842352 www.nts.org.uk/Property/Pitmedden-Garden

Tolquhon Castle, PITMEDDEN, AB41 7LP, 01651 851286 www.historic-scotland.gov.uk

Great for kids: Castle Fraser, KEMNAY, AB51 7LD, 01330 833463 www.nts.org.uk/Property/Castle-Fraser-Garden-and-Estate

KINTORE — Map 23 NJ71

Hillhead Caravan Park

►►►► 77%

tel: 01467 632809 **AB51 0YX**
email: enquiries@hillheadcaravan.co.uk
dir: *1m from village & A96 (Aberdeen to Inverness road). From A96 follow signs to site on B994, then unclassified road.* **grid ref:** *NJ777163*

An attractive, nicely landscaped site, located on the outskirts of Kintore in the valley of the River Dee with excellent access to forest walks and within easy reach of the many attractions in rural Aberdeenshire. The toilet facilities are of a high standard. There are good play facilities for smaller children plus a small café with TV and internet access. 1.5 acre site. 29 touring pitches. 17 hardstandings. 10 seasonal pitches. Caravan pitches. Motorhome pitches. Tent pitches.

Open: all year **Last arrival:** 21.00hrs **Last departure:** 13.00hrs

Pitches: £20 £20 £15 **Leisure:**

Facilities:

Services: **Within 3 miles:**

Notes: Dogs must be kept on leads. Caravan storage, accessories shop.

AA Pubs & Restaurants nearby: The Cock & Bull Bar & Restaurant, BALMEDIE, AB23 8XY, 01358 743249

Old Blackfriars, ABERDEEN, AB11 5BB, 01224 581922

The Adelphi Kitchen, ABERDEEN, AB11 5BL, 01224 211414

The Silver Darling, ABERDEEN, AB11 5DQ, 01224 576229

MACDUFF — Map 23 NJ76

Places to visit

Duff House, BANFF, AB45 3SX, 01261 818181 www.historic-scotland.gov.uk

Banff Museum, BANFF, AB45 1AE, 01261 812941

Wester Bonnyton Farm Site

►► 68%

tel: 01261 832470 **Gamrie AB45 3EP**
email: westerbonnyton@fsmail.net
dir: *From A98 (1m S of Macduff) take B9031 signed Rosehearty. Site 1.25m on right.*
grid ref: *NJ741638*

A spacious farm site, with level touring pitches, overlooking the Moray Firth. The small, picturesque fishing villages of Gardenstown and Crovie and the larger town of Macduff, which has a marine aquarium, are all within easy reach. All the touring pitches have good views of the coastline. Families with children are welcome, and there is a play area and play barn. 8 acre site. 8 touring pitches. 5 hardstandings. Caravan pitches. Motorhome pitches. Tent pitches. 65 statics.

Open: Mar-Oct

Pitches: **Leisure:**

Facilities:

Services: **Within 3 miles:**

Notes: Dogs must be kept on leads.

MINTLAW Map 23 NJ94

Places to visit

Aberdeenshire Farming Museum, MINTLAW, AB42 5FQ, 01771 624590 www.aberdeenshire.gov.uk/museums

Deer Abbey, OLD DEER, 01667 460232 www.historic-scotland.gov.uk

Aden Caravan and Camping Park

►►► 82%

tel: 01771 623460 **Aden Country Park AB42 5FQ**
email: info@adencaravanandcamping.co.uk
dir: *From Mintlaw take A950 signed New Pitsligo & Aden Country Park. Park on left.*
grid ref: *NJ981479*

Situated in the heart of Buchan in Aberdeenshire and within Aden Country Park, this is a small tranquil site offering excellent facilities. It is ideally located for visiting the many tourist attractions in this beautiful north-east coastal area, not least of which is the 230-acre country park itself. The site is only a short drive from the busy fishing towns of Fraserburgh and Peterhead, and as it is only an hour from Aberdeen's centre; this is an ideal spot for a short stay or a longer holiday. The country park plays host to numerous events throughout the year, including pipe band championships, horse events and various ranger-run activities. 11.1 acre site. 66 touring pitches. 31 hardstandings. 10 seasonal pitches. Caravan pitches. Motorhome pitches. Tent pitches. 17 statics.

Open: Apr-Oct **Last arrival:** 20.00hrs **Last departure:** 14.00hrs

Pitches: * £20.49-£22.78 £10.26-£12.96

Leisure: **Facilities:**

Services: **Within 3 miles:**

Notes: Dogs must be kept on leads.

NORTH WATER BRIDGE Map 23 NO66

Places to visit

Edzell Castle and Garden, EDZELL, DD9 7UE, 01356 648631 www.historic-scotland.gov.uk

Pictavia Visitor Centre, BRECHIN, DD9 6RL, 01356 626241 www.pictavia.org.uk

Dovecot Caravan Park

►►► 77%

tel: 01674 840630 **AB30 1QL**
email: adele@dovecotcaravanpark.co.uk
dir: *From Laurencekirk on A90, 5m, at Edzell Woods sign turn left. Site 500yds on left.*
grid ref: *NO648663*

A level grassy site in a country area close to the A90, with mature trees screening one side and the River North Esk on the other. The immaculate toilet facilities make this a handy overnight stop in a good touring area. 6 acre site. 25 touring pitches. 8 hardstandings. 8 seasonal pitches. Caravan pitches. Motorhome pitches. Tent pitches. 44 statics.

Open: Apr-Oct **Last arrival:** 20.00hrs **Last departure:** noon

Pitches: * £15.50-£17.50 £15.50-£17.50 £12.50-£20.50

Leisure: **Facilities:**

Services: **Notes:** Dogs must be kept on leads.

PETERHEAD Map 23 NK14

Places to visit

Arbuthnot Museum, PETERHEAD, AB42 1QD, 01771 622807 www.aberdeenshire.gov.uk/museums

Aberdeenshire Farming Museum, MINTLAW, AB42 5FQ, 01771 624590 www.aberdeenshire.gov.uk/museums

Lido Caravan Park

►►► 76%

tel: 01779 478950 & 473358 **South Rd AB42 2YP**
email: admin@peterheadprojects.co.uk
dir: *From A90 (Aberdeen to Peterhead road) at Invernetty rdbt take A982.*
grid ref: *NK123452*

This small site is located on The Lido with direct access to a small sandy beach with a nice play area and sand dunes. Each of the all-electric pitches has a view over Peterhead's busy harbour and there is always some boating activity taking place to keep you interested. The site is under the management of the local enterprise company Peterhead Projects Limited. The Martine Heritage Centre, a few minutes' walk from the site, has an excellent café. 2 acre site. 25 touring pitches. Caravan pitches. Motorhome pitches. Tent pitches. 14 statics.

Open: Mar-Oct **Last departure:** noon

Pitches: **Facilities:** **Services:**

Within 3 miles:

Notes: No ball games, no nuisance noise after 22.00hrs. Dogs must be kept on leads.

PORTSOY Map 23 NJ56

Places to visit

Banff Museum, BANFF, AB45 1AE, 01261 812941

Duff House, BANFF, AB45 3SX, 01261 818181 www.historic-scotland.gov.uk

Great for kids: Macduff Marine Aquarium, MACDUFF, AB44 1SL, 01261 833369 www.macduff-aquarium.org.uk

Portsoy Links Caravan Park

►►► 74%

tel: 01261 842695 **Links Rd, Portsoy AB45 2RQ**
email: contact@portsoylinks.co.uk
dir: *At Portsoy from A98 into Church St. 2nd right into Institute St (follow brown camping sign). At T-junct right, down slope to site.* **grid ref:** *NJ591660*

Taken into community ownership under the auspices of the Scottish Traditional Boats Festival, this is a lovely links-type site with stunning views across the bay. There is a large, safe fenced play area for smaller children and the toilet facilities are kept clean and well maintained. Portsoy is a typical small fishing port and has various eateries and shops; it is very convenient for visiting the other small fishing villages on the North East Scotland's Coastal Trail. 0.8 acre site. 51 touring pitches. 2 hardstandings. 6 seasonal pitches. Caravan pitches. Motorhome pitches. Tent pitches. 16 statics.

Open: 30 Mar-Oct **Last arrival:** 20.00hrs **Last departure:** noon

Pitches: **Leisure:** **Facilities:**

Services: **Within 3 miles:**

STRACHAN Map 23 NO69

Places to visit

Banchory Museum, BANCHORY, AB31 5SX, 01771 622807 www.aberdeenshire.gov.uk/museums

Crathes Castle Garden & Estate, CRATHES, AB31 5QJ, 01330 844525 www.nts.org.uk/Property/Crathes-Castle-Garden-and-Estate

Great for kids: Go Ape Crathes Castle, CRATHES, AB31 5QJ, 0845 643 9215 *(Calls cost 7p per minute plus your phone company's access charge)* www.goape.co.uk/crathes-castle

Feughside Caravan Park

 82%

GOLD

tel: 01330 850669 **AB31 6NT**
email: info@feughsidecaravanpark.co.uk
dir: *From Banchory take B974 to Strachan, 3m, take B976, 2m to Feughside Inn, follow site signs.* **grid ref:** *NO636913*

A small, well maintained family-run site, set amongst mature trees and hedges and located five miles from Banchory. The site is ideally suited to those wishing for a peaceful location that is within easy reach of scenic Royal Deeside. 5.5 acre site. 27 touring pitches. 10 hardstandings. 12 seasonal pitches. Caravan pitches. Motorhome pitches. Tent pitches. 54 statics.

Open: Apr-Oct **Last arrival:** 22.00hrs **Last departure:** noon

Pitches: * fr £21 fr £21 £10-£21

Leisure:

Facilities:

Services:

Within 3 miles:

Notes: Quiet after 22.00hrs, no open fires. Dogs must be kept on leads & exercised off site.

AA Pubs & Restaurants nearby: Raemoir House Hotel, BANCHORY, AB31 4ED, 01330 824884

TURRIFF Map 23 NJ75

Places to visit

Fyvie Castle, TURRIFF, AB53 8JS, 01651 891266 www.nts.org.uk/Property/Fyvie-Castle

Turriff Caravan Park

77%

tel: 01888 562205 **Station Rd AB53 4ER**
email: turriffcaravanpark@btconnect.com
dir: *On A947, S of Turriff.* **grid ref:** *NJ727492*

Located on the outskirts of Turriff on the site of an old railway station, this site is owned by the local community. The pitches are level and the attractive landscaping is well maintained. The site also has a rally field. There is a large public park close to the site which has a boating pond and a large games park where the annual agricultural show is held. The town is only five minutes' walk through the park and has a good variety of shops. This is an ideal base for touring rural Aberdeenshire and the nearby Moray coastline with its traditional fishing villages. 5 acre site. 70 touring pitches. 4 hardstandings. Caravan pitches. Motorhome pitches. Tent pitches. 14 statics.

Open: Apr-Oct **Last arrival:** 18.00hrs **Last departure:** noon

Pitches:

Leisure:

Facilities:

Services:

Within 3 miles:

Notes: Dogs must be kept on leads.

AA Pubs & Restaurants nearby: The Redgarth, OLDMELDRUM, AB51 0DJ, 01651 872353

ANGUS

MONIFIETH Map 21 NO43

Places to visit

Barry Mill, BARRY, DD7 7RJ, 01241 856761 www.nts.org.uk/Property/Barry-Mill

HM Frigate Unicorn, DUNDEE, DD1 3BP, 01382 200900 www.frigateunicorn.org

Great for kids: Discovery Point & RRS Discovery, DUNDEE, DD1 4XA, 01382 309060 www.rrsdiscovery.com

Riverview Caravan Park

82%

Best of British

tel: 01382 535471 & 817979 **Marine Dr DD5 4NN**
email: info@riverview.co.uk
dir: *From Dundee on A930 follow signs to Monifieth, past supermarket, right signed golf course, left under rail bridge. Site signed on left.* **grid ref:** *NO502322*

A well-landscaped seaside site where the touring pitches are set in small areas; they are neatly divided by hedges and mature trees which are trimmed to allow light in; those on the beachfront enjoy excellent views. The site is a few minutes' walk from Monifieth and a pleasant stroll along the beachfront will take you to the nearby town of Broughty Ferry with its numerous boutique shops and other amenities. The site has good facilities, including a steam room and sauna and a gym. This is a good site for a traditional seaside holiday. 5.5 acre site. 49 touring pitches. 45 hardstandings. Caravan pitches. Motorhome pitches. 46 statics. 1 wooden pod.

Open: Mar-Jan **Last arrival:** 22.00hrs **Last departure:** 12.30hrs

Pitches:

Leisure:

Facilities:

Services:

Within 3 miles:

Notes: Dogs must be kept on leads.

AA Pubs & Restaurants nearby: The Royal Arch Bar, BROUGHTY FERRY, DD5 2DS, 01382 779741

ARGYLL & BUTE

CARRADALE — Map 20 NR83

Carradale Bay Caravan Park

►►► 90%

tel: 01583 431665 **PA28 6QG**
email: info@carradalebay.com
dir: *A83 from Tarbert towards Campbeltown, left onto B842 (Carradale road), right onto B879. Site 0.5m.* **grid ref:** *NR815385*

A beautiful, natural site on the sea's edge with superb views over Kilbrannan Sound to the Isle of Arran. Pitches are landscaped into small bays broken up by shrubs and bushes, and backed by dunes close to the long sandy beach. The toilet facilities are appointed to a very high standard. An environmentally-aware site that requires the use of green toilet chemicals (available on the site). Lodges and static caravans for holiday hire. 8 acre site. 74 touring pitches. Caravan pitches. Motorhome pitches. Tent pitches.
15 statics.

Open: Apr-Sep **Last arrival:** 22.00hrs **Last departure:** noon

Pitches:

Facilities:

Services:

Within 3 miles:

GLENDARUEL — Map 20 NR98

Places to visit

Benmore Botanic Garden, BENMORE, PA23 8QU, 01369 706261 www.rbge.org.uk

Glendaruel Caravan Park

►►► 82%

DAVID BELLAMY CONSERVATION AWARD GOLD

tel: 01369 820267 **PA22 3AB**
email: mail@glendaruelcaravanpark.com
dir: *A83 onto A815 to Strachur, 13m to site on A886. By ferry from Gourock to Dunoon take B836, then A886 for approx 4m N. (NB this route not recommended for towing vehicles – 1:5 uphill gradient on B836).* **grid ref:** *NR005865*

Glendaruel Gardens, with an arboretum, is the peaceful setting for this pleasant, well established wooded site in a valley surrounded by mountains. It is set back from the main road and screened by trees so that a peaceful stay is ensured. It has level grass and hardstanding pitches. A regular local bus service and a ferry at Portavadie (where there are retail outlets and eateries) make a day trip to the Mull of Kintyre a possibility. The Cowal Way, a long distance path, and a national cycle path pass the site. Static caravans and a 'little' camping lodge are available for hire. 6 acre site. 27 touring pitches. 15 hardstandings. 12 seasonal pitches. Caravan pitches. Motorhome pitches. Tent pitches. 32 statics.

Open: Apr-Oct **Last arrival:** 22.00hrs **Last departure:** noon

Pitches: * fr £19 fr £19 £16-£19

Leisure: **Facilities:**

Services:

Within 3 miles:

Notes: Dogs must be kept on leads. Sea trout & salmon fishing, woodland walks, 24-hour emergency phone.

OBAN — Map 20 NM82

Places to visit

Dunstaffnage Castle and Chapel, OBAN, PA37 1PZ, 01631 562465 www.historic-scotland.gov.uk

Bonawe Historic Iron Furnace, TAYNUILT, PA35 1JQ, 01866 822432 www.historic-scotland.gov.uk

Oban Caravan & Camping Park

►►► 80%

tel: 01631 562425 **Gallanachmore Farm, Gallanach Rd PA34 4QH**
email: info@obancaravanpark.com
dir: *From Oban centre follow signs for Mull Ferry. After terminal follow Gallanach signs. 2m to site.* **grid ref:** *NM831277*

Situated two miles from Oban this is a lovely site, with pleasant terraced areas that are separated by large swathes of well maintained grass and natural landscaping. Many pitches overlook the busy ferry route between Oban and the Isle of Colonsay. The site is convenient for the ferry terminal in Oban, and the train and bus stations provide easy access for public transport, making this an ideal site for both main holidays or for shorter stays. Three well-equipped camping pods are located in an area that offers privacy. 15 acre site. 120 touring pitches. 35 hardstandings. 10 seasonal pitches. Caravan pitches. Motorhome pitches. Tent pitches. 17 statics.
3 wooden pods.

Open: Etr & Apr-Oct (rs Etr-end May & Sep-Oct shop closed) **Last arrival:** 23.00hrs **Last departure:** noon

Pitches: * £17-£20 £17-£20 £15-£20

Leisure:

Facilities:

Services:

Within 3 miles:

Notes: No commercial vehicles, no noise after 23.00hrs. Dogs must be kept on leads. Indoor kitchen for tent campers.

AA Pubs & Restaurants nearby: Coast, OBAN, PA34 5NT, 01631 569900

NORTH AYRSHIRE

SALTCOATS Map 20 NS24

Places to visit

North Ayrshire Heritage Centre, SALTCOATS, KA21 5AA, 01294 464174 www.north-ayrshire.gov.uk/museums

Kelburn Castle and Country Centre, LARGS, KA29 0BE, 01475 568685 www.kelburnestate.com

Great for kids: Scottish Maritime Museum, IRVINE, KA12 8QE, 01294 278283 www.scottishmaritimemuseum.org

Sandylands

HOLIDAY CENTRE 80%

tel: 0871 664 9767 *(Calls cost 5p per minute plus your phone company's access charge)* & 01294 469411 **James Miller Crescent, Auchenharvie Park KA21 5JN**
email: sandylands@park-resorts.com
dir: *From Glasgow take M77 & A77 to Kilmarnock, A71 towards Irvine. Follow signs for Ardrossan. Take A78 follow Stevenston signs. Through Stevenston, past Auchenharvie Leisure Centre, 1st left follow signs to site on left.* **grid ref:** *NS258412*

A holiday centre with on-site recreational and entertainment facilities for all ages, including an indoor swimming pool. With good transport links and easy access to the ferry terminal in Ardrossan, day trips to the Isle of Arran are possible. The smart amenity block provides touring customers with modern facilities. There is a links golf course nearby. 55 acre site. 20 touring pitches. 20 hardstandings. Caravan pitches. Motorhome pitches. Tent pitches. 438 statics.

Open: Apr-Oct **Last arrival:** mdnt **Last departure:** 10.00hrs

Pitches:

Leisure:

Facilities:

Services:

Within 3 miles:

Notes: Dogs must be kept on leads.

SOUTH AYRSHIRE

AYR

Places to visit

Robert Burns Birthplace Museum, ALLOWAY, KA7 4PQ, 01292 443700 www.burnsmuseum.org.uk

Great for kids: Heads of Ayr Farm Park, ALLOWAY, KA7 4LD, 01292 441210 www.headsofayrfarmpark.co.uk

AYR Map 20 NS32

AA HOLIDAY CENTRE OF THE YEAR 2016

Craig Tara Holiday Park

HOLIDAY CENTRE 85%

tel: 0800 975 7579 & 01292 265141 **KA7 4LB**
email: craigtara@haven.com **web:** www.haven.com/craigtara
dir: *A77 towards Stranraer, 2nd right after Bankfield rdbt. Follow signs for A719 & to park.* **grid ref:** *NS300184*

This lovely holiday centre on the outskirts of Ayr is set in a sheltered spot on the coast, with direct access to a small beach. The park has a great family atmosphere with welcoming staff and entertainment for all ages. The touring area is in a secluded area, and has a new amenity block and 40 fully serviced hardstanding pitches. At the heart of the holiday centre are various large complexes with show bars, restaurants, takeaways, computer games and slot machines. There are also good shops, a supermarket with a bakery, and a large soft play area. In 2015 the pool complex was completely refurbished and the facilities are excellent with flumes, slides, splash zones and overhead viewing walkways. There is a regular service bus to Ayr. 213 acre site. 45 touring pitches. 45 hardstandings. Caravan pitches. Motorhome pitches. 1100 statics.

Open: mid Mar-end Oct (rs mid Mar-May & Sep-Oct some facilities may be limited) **Last arrival:** 20.00hrs **Last departure:** 10.00hrs

Pitches: **Leisure:** **Facilities:**

Services: **Within 3 miles:**

continued

AYR *continued*

Notes: No commercial vehicles, no bookings by persons under 21yrs unless a family booking. Max 2 dogs per booking, certain dog breeds banned. Dogs must be kept on leads.

AA Pubs & Restaurants nearby: Fairfield House Hotel, AYR, KA7 2AS, 01292 267461

The Kirkton Inn, DALRYMPLE, KA6 6DF, 01292 560241

See advert below

BARRHILL Map 20 NX28

Barrhill Holiday Park

►►►► 79%

tel: 01465 821355 **KA26 0PZ**
email: barrhillholidaypark@gmail.com
dir: *On A714 Newton Stewart to Girvan road. 1m N of Barrhill.* **grid ref:** *NX216835*

A small, friendly park in a tranquil rural location, screened from the A714 by trees. The park is terraced and well landscaped, and a high quality amenity block includes disabled facilities. The local bus to Girvan stops at the site entrance. 6 acre site. 30 touring pitches. 30 hardstandings. Caravan pitches. Motorhome pitches. Tent pitches. 49 statics.

Open: Mar-Jan **Last arrival:** 22.00hrs **Last departure:** 10.00hrs

Pitches: * £15 £15 £7-£15

Leisure:

Facilities:

Services:

Within 3 miles:

Notes: No noise after 23.00hrs. Dogs must be kept on leads.

GIRVAN Map 20 NX19

Turnberry Holiday Park

HOLIDAY HOME PARK 78%

BRONZE

tel: 01655 331288 **KA26 9JW**
email: enquiries@turnberryholidaypark.co.uk **web:** www.turnberryholidaypark.co.uk
dir: *Site signed from A77 between Turnberry & Girvan. 250mtrs to site adjacent to Dowhill Farm.* **grid ref:** *NS203033*

Situated in beautiful South Ayrshire with views of the Firth of Clyde and the iconic Ailsa Craig, this 26-acre park is between the busy seaside town of Ayr and the fishing town of Girvan. The many tourist attractions in the area include Turnberry Golf Course, The Burns Heritage Centre, Maidens and Culzean Castle and Country Park. The park is set in open farmland and continues to undergo major improvements. The Ailsa Bar provides family-centred entertainment as well as a café serving good food. There is a swimming pool, reception and sales office. There are 205 holiday homes, 9 statics, and a 3-bedroom chalet for hire.

Open: Mar-4 Jan

Change over day: Mon, Fri & Sat

Arrival and departure times: Please contact the site

Statics: 15 Sleeps 8 Bedrms 2-3 Bathrms 1-2 (inc en suite) Toilets 1-2 Microwave Freezer TV Sky/FTV DVD Modem/Wi-fi Linen inc Elec inc Gas inc Grass area
Low season £115-£398 High season £238-£573

Children: Cots Highchair **Dogs:** 2 on leads

Leisure: Cycle hire

Within 3 miles: Spa

DUMFRIES & GALLOWAY

ANNAN — Map 21 NY16

Places to visit

Ruthwell Cross, RUTHWELL, 0131 550 7612 www.historic-scotland.gov.uk

Great for kids: Caerlaverock Castle, CAERLAVEROCK, DG1 4RU, 01387 770244 www.historic-scotland.gov.uk

Galabank Caravan & Camping Group

►► 74%

tel: 01461 203539 & 07999 344520 **North St DG12 5DQ**
email: margaret.ramage@hotmail.com
dir: *Site access via North St.* **grid ref:** *NY192676*

A tidy, well-maintained grassy little park with spotless facilities close to the centre of town but with pleasant rural views, and skirted by the River Annan. 1 acre site. 30 touring pitches. Caravan pitches. Motorhome pitches. Tent pitches.

Open: Mar-Oct **Last departure:** noon

Pitches:

Facilities:

Services:

Within 3 miles:

Notes: Dogs must be kept on leads. Social club adjacent, washing machine & tumble dryer in ladies' block.

AA Pubs & Restaurants nearby: Smiths at Gretna Green, GRETNA, DG16 5EA, 01461 337007

BRIGHOUSE BAY — Map 20 NX64

Places to visit

MacLellan's Castle, KIRKCUDBRIGHT, DG6 4JD, 01557 331856 www.historic-scotland.gov.uk

Broughton House & Garden, KIRKCUDBRIGHT, DG6 4JX, 01557 330437 www.nts.org.uk/Property/Broughton-House-and-Garden

Great for kids: Galloway Wildlife Conservation Park, KIRKCUDBRIGHT, DG6 4XX, 01557 331645 www.gallowaywildlife.co.uk

PREMIER PARK

Brighouse Bay Holiday Park

►►►►► 88%

GOLD

tel: 01557 870267 **DG6 4TS**
email: info@gillespie-leisure.co.uk
dir: *From Gatehouse of Fleet take A755 towards Kirkcudbright, onto B727 (signed Borgue). Or from Kirkcudbright take A755 onto B727. Site signed in 3m.*
grid ref: *NX628453*

This top class park has a country club feel and enjoys a marvellous coastal setting adjacent to the beach and has superb views. Pitches have been imaginatively sculpted into the meadowland, where stone walls and hedges blend in with the site's mature trees. These features, together with the large range of leisure activities, make this an excellent park for families who enjoy an active holiday. Many of the facilities are at an extra charge. Wooden pods and self-catering units are available for hire. 120 acre site. 190 touring pitches. 100 hardstandings. 50 seasonal pitches. Caravan pitches. Motorhome pitches. Tent pitches. 225 statics. 3 wooden pods.

Open: all year (rs Outside school hols leisure club closed Mon-Wed inclusive; restricted services in winter months)
Last arrival: 20.00hrs **Last departure:** 11.30hrs

Pitches: * £19.50-£24 £19.50-£24 £15-£20.50

Leisure:

Facilities: WiFi

Services:

Within 3 miles:

Notes: No noise after 22.30hrs, no jet skis, 10mph speed limit on site. Dogs must be kept on leads. Mini golf, 18-hole golf, PGA professional on site, outdoor bowling green, jacuzzi, slipway, boating pond, coarse fishing, sea angling.

AA Pubs & Restaurants nearby: Selkirk Arms Hotel, KIRKCUDBRIGHT, DG6 4JG, 01557 330402

DALBEATTIE Map 21 NX86

Places to visit

Threave Garden & Estate, CASTLE DOUGLAS, DG7 1RX, 01556 502575 www.nts.org.uk/Property/Threave-Estate

Orchardton Tower, PALNACKIE www.historic-scotland.gov.uk

Glenearly Caravan Park

►►►► 86%

tel: 01556 611393 **DG5 4NE**
email: glenearlycaravan@btconnect.com **web:** www.glenearlycaravanpark.co.uk
dir: *From Dumfries take A711 towards Dalbeattie. Site entrance after Edingham Farm on right (200yds before boundary sign).* **grid ref:** *NX838628*

An excellent small park set in open countryside with good views of Long Fell, Maidenpap and Dalbeattie Forest. The park is located in 84 acres of farmland which has been carefully managed over the years to provide a peaceful and secluded location for a tranquil holiday. The attention to detail is excellent with neatly kept grass, well tended borders and an excellent amenity block. There's a fishing lochan and woodland plus a wildlife walk (created in 2015). Dalbeattie is a leisurely 10-minute walk away and the local bus service passes the end of the farm road. The beautiful Solway coast is just five minutes away by car with Rockcliffe, Colvend and Kippford interesting places to explore. For the more adventurous, the mountain bike trails are numerous. 10 acre site. 39 touring pitches. 33 hardstandings. 10 seasonal pitches. Caravan pitches. Motorhome pitches. Tent pitches. 74 statics.

Open: all year **Last arrival:** 19.00hrs **Last departure:** noon

Pitches: £16.50-£18.50 £16.50-£18.50 £16.50-£18.50

Leisure:

Facilities: WiFi

Services:

Within 3 miles:

Notes: No commercial vehicles. Dogs must be kept on leads.

ECCLEFECHAN Map 21 NY17

Places to visit

Robert Burns House, DUMFRIES, DG1 2PS, 01387 255297 www.dumgal.gov.uk

Old Bridge House Museum, DUMFRIES, DG2 7BE, 01387 256904 www.dumgal.gov.uk

Great for kids: Dumfries Museum & Camera Obscura, DUMFRIES, DG2 7SW, 01387 253374 www.dumgal.gov.uk/museums

PREMIER PARK

Hoddom Castle Caravan Park

►►►►► 82%

tel: 01576 300251 **Hoddom DG11 1AS**
email: hoddomcastle@aol.com
dir: *M74 junct 19, B725 signed Ecclefechan. At next rdbt left onto B7076. Right at x-roads in Ecclefechan, follow site signs. Left at T-junct onto B723. Right onto B725 to site. Or from Annan on B721 take B723 signed Lockerbie & follow site signs.*
grid ref: *NY154729*

A lovely, peaceful family park located close to Annan, with its large range of shops and eateries. The three amenity blocks, one adjacent to the reception, in part of the old castle buildings. The female showers have been updated to provide very good, modern amenities, and are indicative of the plans the owner has to modernise other facilities. There are extensive grounds, with many walks including the Annan Way which borders the River Annan. The park is neatly divided into statics, seasonal tourers and touring pitches with a large area for tents, plus seven attractive wooden 'chill' pods and four Kelo huts for hire. Fishing, a nine-hole golf course and a large children's play area are available; the small restaurant and café are open daily. 28 acre site. 200 touring pitches. 63 hardstandings. 94 seasonal pitches. Caravan pitches. Motorhome pitches. Tent pitches. 54 statics. 7 wooden pods. 4 Kelo lodges.

Open: Etr or Apr-Oct **Last arrival:** 21.00hrs **Last departure:** 13.00hrs

Pitches: * £17.50-£24.50 £17.50-£24.50 £17.50-£24.50

Leisure:

Facilities:

Services: T

Within 3 miles:

Notes: No electric scooters, no gazebos, no fires, no noise after mdnt, cash only accepted in bar/restaurant. Dogs must be kept on leads.

AA Pubs & Restaurants nearby: Smiths at Gretna Green, GRETNA, DG16 5EA, 01461 337007

GATEHOUSE OF FLEET Map 20 NX55

Places to visit

MacLellan's Castle, KIRKCUDBRIGHT, DG6 4JD, 01557 331856
www.historic-scotland.gov.uk

Great for kids: Galloway Wildlife Conservation Park, KIRKCUDBRIGHT, DG6 4XX, 01557 331645 www.gallowaywildlife.co.uk

Auchenlarie Holiday Park

HOLIDAY CENTRE 89%

tel: 01556 506200 & 206201 **DG7 2EX**
email: enquiries@auchenlarie.co.uk
dir: *Direct access from A75, 5m W of Gatehouse of Fleet.* **grid ref:** *NX536522*

A well-organised family park set on cliffs overlooking Wigtown Bay, with its own sandy beach. The tenting area, in sloping grassland surrounded by mature trees, has its own sanitary facilities, while the marked caravan pitches are in paddocks, with open views and the provision of high quality toilets. The leisure centre includes a swimming pool, gym, solarium and sports hall. There are six self-catering holiday apartments, with hot tubs, to rent. 32 acre site. 49 touring pitches. 52 hardstandings. Caravan pitches. Motorhome pitches. Tent pitches. 400 statics.

Open: Mar-Oct **Last arrival:** 20.00hrs **Last departure:** noon

Pitches: * £20-£25 £20-£25 £20-£25

Leisure:

Facilities:

Services:

Within 3 miles:

Notes: Dogs must be kept on leads. Crazy golf, teenagers' zone, baby-changing facilities.

AA Pubs & Restaurants nearby: Cally Palace Hotel, GATEHOUSE OF FLEET, DG7 2DL, 01557 814341

Anwoth Caravan Site

►►►► 79%

tel: 01557 814333 & 01556 506200 **DG7 2JU**
email: enquiries@auchenlarie.co.uk
dir: *From A75 into Gatehouse of Fleet, site on right towards Stranraer. Signed from town centre.* **grid ref:** *NX595563*

A very high quality park in a peaceful sheltered setting within easy walking distance of the village, ideally placed for exploring the scenic hills, valleys and coastline. Grass, hardstanding and fully serviced pitches are available and guests may use the leisure facilities at the sister site, Auchenlarie Holiday Park. 2 acre site. 28 touring pitches. 13 hardstandings. Caravan pitches. Motorhome pitches. Tent pitches. 44 statics.

Open: Mar-Oct **Last arrival:** 20.00hrs **Last departure:** noon

Pitches: * £17.50-£22.50 £17.50-£22.50 £17.50-£22.50

Facilities:

Services:

Within 3 miles:

Notes: Dogs must be kept on leads.

AA Pubs & Restaurants nearby: Cally Palace Hotel, GATEHOUSE OF FLEET, DG7 2DL, 01557 814341

GRETNA Map 21 NY36

Places to visit

Carlisle Cathedral, CARLISLE, CA3 8TZ, 01228 548071
www.carlislecathedral.org.uk

Tullie House Museum & Art Gallery Trust, CARLISLE, CA3 8TP, 01228 618718
www.tulliehouse.co.uk

Great for kids: Carlisle Castle, CARLISLE, CA3 8UR, 01228 591922
www.english-heritage.org.uk/daysout/properties/carlisle-castle

Braids Caravan Park

►►►► 78%

tel: 01461 337409 **Annan Rd DG16 5DQ**
email: enquiries@thebraidscaravanpark.co.uk
dir: *On B721, 0.5m from village on right, towards Annan.* **grid ref:** *NY313674*

A very well-maintained park conveniently located on the outskirts of Gretna village. Within walking distance is Gretna Gateway Outlet Village, and Gretna Green with the World Famous Old Blacksmith's Shop is nearby. It proves a convenient stop-over for anyone travelling to and from the north of Scotland or Northern Ireland (via the ferry at Stranraer). The park has first-class toilet facilities and generously-sized all-weather pitches. Please note that tents are not accepted. A rally field and a meeting room are available. 5 acre site. 50 touring pitches. 42 hardstandings. Caravan pitches. Motorhome pitches.

Open: all year **Last arrival:** 20.00hrs (19.00hrs in winter) **Last departure:** noon

Pitches: * £18-£22 £18-£22

Facilities:

Services:

Within 3 miles:

Notes: Dogs must be kept on leads.

AA Pubs & Restaurants nearby: Smiths at Gretna Green, GRETNA, DG16 5EA, 01461 337007

GRETNA *continued*

King Robert the Bruce's Cave Caravan & Camping Park

►►►► 76%

tel: 01461 800285 & 07779 138694 **Cove Estate, Kirkpatrick Fleming DG11 3AT**
email: enquiries@brucescave.co.uk **web:** www.brucescave.co.uk
dir: *Exit A74(M) junct 21, follow Kirkpatrick Fleming signs, N through village, pass Station Inn, left at Bruce's Court. Over rail crossing to site.* **grid ref:** *NY266705*

The lovely wooded grounds of an old castle and mansion are the setting for this pleasant park. The mature woodland is a haven for wildlife, there is a riverside walk to Robert the Bruce's Cave and on-site coarse fishing is available. A toilet block with en suite facilities is especially useful to families. The site is convenient for the M74 and there is a good local bus service available nearby; the site is on a National Cycle Route. 80 acre site. 75 touring pitches. 60 hardstandings. Caravan pitches. Motorhome pitches. Tent pitches. 35 statics.

Open: Apr-Nov (rs Nov shop closed, water restrictions) **Last arrival:** 22.00hrs
Last departure: 16.00hrs

Pitches:

Leisure:

Facilities:

Services:

Within 3 miles:

Notes: No noise after 23.00hrs. Dogs must be kept on leads. BMX bike hire, first aid available.

AA Pubs & Restaurants nearby: Smiths at Gretna Green, GRETNA, DG16 5EA, 01461 337007

KIPPFORD — Map 21 NX85

Places to visit

Orchardton Tower, PALNACKIE www.historic-scotland.gov.uk

Kippford Holiday Park

►►► 78%

GOLD

tel: 01556 620636 **DG5 4LF**
email: info@kippfordholidaypark.co.uk **web:** www.kippfordholidaypark.co.uk

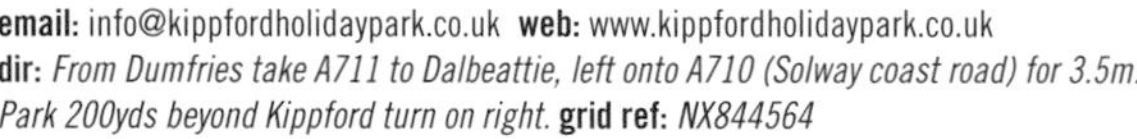

dir: *From Dumfries take A711 to Dalbeattie, left onto A710 (Solway coast road) for 3.5m. Park 200yds beyond Kippford turn on right.* **grid ref:** *NX844564*

An attractively landscaped park set in hilly countryside close to the Urr Water estuary and a sand and shingle beach, and with spectacular views. The level touring pitches are on grassed hardstands with private garden areas, and many are fully serviced; and there are attractive lodges for hire. The Doon Hill and woodland walks separate the park from the lovely village of Kippford. Red squirrels can be spotted in the woods, and opportunities to fish and to play golf are very close by. 18 acre site. 45 touring pitches. 35 hardstandings. 15 seasonal pitches. Caravan pitches. Motorhome pitches. Tent pitches. 119 statics.

Open: all year **Last arrival:** 21.30hrs **Last departure:** noon

Pitches:

Leisure:

Facilities:

Services:

Within 3 miles:

Notes: No camp fires. Dogs must be kept on leads.

AA Pubs & Restaurants nearby: Balcary Bay Hotel, AUCHENCAIRN, DG7 1QZ, 01556 640217

KIRKCUDBRIGHT — Map 20 NX65

Places to visit

The Stewartry Museum, KIRKCUDBRIGHT, DG6 4AQ, 01557 331643 www.dumgal.gov.uk/museums

Tolbooth Art Centre, KIRKCUDBRIGHT, DG6 4JL, 01557 331556 www.dumgal.gov.uk/museums

Great for kids: Broughton House & Garden, KIRKCUDBRIGHT, DG6 4JX, 01557 330437 www.nts.org.uk/Property/Broughton-House-and-Garden

KIRKCUDBRIGHT Map 20 NX65

PREMIER PARK

Seaward Caravan Park

►►►►► 84%

tel: 01557 870267 & 331079 **Dhoon Bay DG6 4TJ**
email: info@gillespie-leisure.co.uk
dir: *2m SW of Kirkcudbright take A755 W, then B727 signed Borgue.*
grid ref: *NX662492*

An attractive park with outstanding views over Kirkcudbright Bay which forms part of the Dee Estuary. Access to a sandy cove with rock pools is just across the road. Facilities are well organised and neatly kept, and the park offers a very peaceful atmosphere. The leisure facilities at the other Gillespie Parks are available to visitors to Seaward Caravan Park. There are five static homes, three wooden pods and two mini lodges for hire. 23 acre site. 25 touring pitches. 20 hardstandings. 6 seasonal pitches. Caravan pitches. Motorhome pitches. Tent pitches. 54 statics. 3 wooden pods.

Open: Mar-Oct (rs Mar-Spring BH & Sep-Oct swimming pool closed)
Last arrival: 20.00hrs **Last departure:** 11.30hrs

Pitches: * £18-£23 £18-£23 £14.50-£19.50

Leisure: **Facilities:**

Services: **Within 3 miles:**

Notes: No noise after 22.30hrs, 10mph speed limit on site. Dogs must be kept on leads. Mini golf, sea angling.

AA Pubs & Restaurants nearby: Selkirk Arms Hotel, KIRKCUDBRIGHT, DG6 4JG, 01557 330402

LANGHOLM Map 21 NY38

Places to visit

Hermitage Castle, HERMITAGE, TD9 0LU, 01387 376222
www.historic-scotland.gov.uk

Ewes Water Caravan & Camping Park

►► 67%

tel: 013873 80386 **Milntown DG13 0BG**
dir: *Access directly from A7 approx 0.5m N of Langholm. Site in Langholm Rugby Club.*
grid ref: *NY365855*

On the banks of the River Esk, this attractive park lies in a sheltered wooded valley close to an unspoilt Borders' town. 2 acre site. 24 touring pitches. Caravan pitches. Motorhome pitches. Tent pitches.

Open: Apr-Sep **Last departure:** noon

Pitches: **Facilities:**

Services: **Within 3 miles:**

Notes: Large playing area.

LOCKERBIE

See Ecclefechan

NEWTON STEWART Map 20 NX46

Places to visit

Kirroughtree Visitor Centre, NEWTON STEWART, DG8 7BE, 01671 402165
www.forestry.gov.uk/gallowayforestpark

Creebridge Caravan Park

►►► 69%

tel: 01671 402324 & 402432 **Minnigaff DG8 6AJ**
email: john_sharples@btconnect.com
dir: *From A75 (bypass) onto B7079 (signed Minnigaff & Newton Stewart) to Creebridge, site on left.* **grid ref:** *NX415656*

A small family-owned site a short walk from the town's amenities. The site is surrounded by mature trees, and the toilet facilities are clean and functional. 5.5 acre site. 26 touring pitches. 9 hardstandings. Caravan pitches. Motorhome pitches. Tent pitches. 60 statics.

Open: all year (rs Mar only one toilet block open) **Last arrival:** 20.00hrs
Last departure: 10.30hrs

Pitches: **Leisure:** **Facilities:**

Services: **Within 3 miles:**

Notes: Dogs must be kept on leads. Security lighting.

PALNACKIE Map 21 NX85

Places to visit

Orchardton Tower, PALNACKIE www.historic-scotland.gov.uk

Barlochan Caravan Park

►►► 79%

tel: 01557 870267 **DG7 1PF**
email: info@gillespie-leisure.co.uk
dir: *On A711 (Dalbeattie to Auchencairn road). Site signed before Palnackie.*
grid ref: *NX819572*

This is a lovely small caravan site situated within a short drive of the county town of Dalbeattie. It is ideally situated for exploring this particularly attractive corner of Dumfries & Galloway. The site has a number of static homes set on level terraces, with mature planting, whilst the caravan and camping area is located on the lower area, near the outdoor heated pool. There are hardstanding pitches, grass pitches with electricty for tents and new in the 2015 season, two wooden pods. The site is part of the Gillespie Group and customers can use the facilities of their other sites. 9 acre site. 20 touring pitches. 10 hardstandings. 2 seasonal pitches. Caravan pitches. Motorhome pitches. Tent pitches. 65 statics. 2 wooden pods.

Open: Apr-Oct (rs Apr-Spring BH & Sep-Oct swimming pool closed) **Last arrival:** 20.00hrs
Last departure: 11.30hrs

Pitches: * £17-£22 £17-£22 £13.50-£18.50

Leisure: **Facilities:**

Services: **Within 3 miles:**

Notes: Dogs must be kept on leads. Pitch & putt.

AA Pubs & Restaurants nearby: Balcary Bay Hotel, AUCHENCAIRN, DG7 1QZ, 01556 640217

PARTON Map 20 NX67

Places to visit

Threave Garden & Estate, CASTLE DOUGLAS, DG7 1RX, 01556 502575
www.nts.org.uk/Property/Threave-Estate

Threave Castle, CASTLE DOUGLAS, DG7 1TJ, 07711 223101
www.historic-scotland.gov.uk

Loch Ken Holiday Park

►►►► 86%

GOLD

tel: 01644 470282 **DG7 3NE**
email: office@lochkenholidaypark.co.uk
dir: *On A713, N of Parton. Site on main road (NB it is advisable not to use Sat Nav directions).* **grid ref:** *NX687702*

Run with energy, enthusiasm and commitment by the hands-on Bryson family, this busy and popular park, with a natural emphasis on water activities, is set on the eastern shores of Loch Ken. With superb views, it is in a peaceful and beautiful spot adjacent to the RSPB Ken Dee Marshes reserve, with direct access to the loch for fishing and boat launching. It is also on the Galloway Red Kite Trail. The park offers a variety of watersports (canoeing, sailing, water skiing) as well as farm visits and nature trails. There are now five Nordic-style tipis ('tentipis') for hire, each with a wood-burning stove, seating and wooden decking with stunning views across the loch, in addition to nine static homes also for hire. 15 acre site. 40 touring pitches. 20 hardstandings. 15 seasonal pitches. Caravan pitches. Motorhome pitches. Tent pitches. 35 statics. 5 tipis.

Open: Feb-mid Nov (rs Feb-Mar (ex Etr) & Nov restricted shop hours)
Last departure: noon

Pitches: * £18-£22 £18-£22 £12-£20

Leisure: **Facilities:**

Services: **Within 3 miles:**

Notes: No noise after 22.00hrs. Dogs must be kept on leads. Bike, boat & canoe hire.

AA Pubs & Restaurants nearby: Cross Keys Hotel, NEW GALLOWAY, DG7 3RN, 01644 420494

PORT WILLIAM Map 20 NX34

Places to visit

Glenluce Abbey, GLENLUCE, DG8 0AF, 01581 300541
www.historic-scotland.gov.uk

Whithorn Priory and Museum, WHITHORN, DG8 8PY, 01988 500508
www.historic-scotland.gov.uk

Kings Green Caravan Site

►►► 79%

tel: 01988 700489 **South St DG8 9SG**
dir: *Direct access from A747 at junct with B7085 towards Whithorn.* **grid ref:** *NX340430*

Located on the edge of Port William, with beautiful views across Luce Bay as far as the Isle of Man, this is a community run site which offers good facilities and large grass pitches with direct access to the pebble shore where otters have been seen. The road which runs along the coast is relatively traffic free so does not detract from the tranquillity of this small site. Two public boat launches are available. There are several good shops in the village and a local bus, with links to Whithorn, Garlieston and Newton Stewart, runs past the site. 3 acre site. 30 touring pitches. Caravan pitches. Motorhome pitches. Tent pitches.

Open: mid Mar-Oct **Last arrival:** 20.00hrs **Last departure:** noon

Pitches:

Facilities:

Services: **Within 3 miles:**

Notes: No golf, no fireworks. Dogs must be kept on leads. Free book lending.

AA Pubs & Restaurants nearby: The Steam Packet Inn, ISLE OF WHITHORN, DG8 8LL, 01988 500334

SANDHEAD Map 20 NX04

Places to visit

Glenwhan Gardens, STRANRAER, DG9 8PH, 01581 400222
www.glenwhangardens.co.uk

Ardwell House Gardens, ARDWELL, DG9 9LY, 01776 860227

Great for kids: Castle Kennedy Gardens, STRANRAER, DG9 8BX, 01776 702024
www.castlekennedygardens.com

Sands of Luce Holiday Park

►►►► 88%

tel: 01776 830456 & 830296 **Sands of Luce DG9 9JN**
email: info@sandsofluceholidaypark.co.uk
dir: *From S & E: left from A75 onto B7084 signed Drummore. Site signed at junct with A716. From N: A77 through Stranraer towards Portpatrick, 2m, follow A716 signed Drummore, site signed in 5m.* **grid ref:** *NX103510*

This is a large, well-managed holiday park overlooking Luce Bay. It has a private boat launch and direct access to a wide sandy beach, which proves popular with kite surfers. There is a small café providing snacks and light meals and the new 'StrEatery' facility, introduced in 2015, provides a wider range of meals for customers. Both are located near the touring area where seasonal and visiting customers have dedicated areas. While there are games' rooms and a large play area for children, adults may like to visit the Lighthouse Bar at the sites' entrance. A wide range of entertainment, listed on daily planners, is on offer including kite flying, kite surfing, foraging and cooking, and entertainers for both adults and children. There is a regular bus that passes the entrance, and Stranraer, the Mull of Galloway or Port Logan Botanical Gardens are not far away by car. 10 static caravans are available for hire. 30 acre site. 80 touring pitches. 20 hardstandings. 50 seasonal pitches. Caravan pitches. Motorhome pitches. Tent pitches. 270 statics.

Open: Mar-Jan (rs Nov-Jan toilet block & shower closed) **Last arrival:** 20.00hrs
Last departure: noon

Pitches: * £20-£25 £20-£25 £10-£25

Leisure:

Facilities:

Services:

Within 3 miles:

Notes: No quad bikes, Dogs must be kept on leads, owners must clear up their dogs. Boat launching & storage.

AA Pubs & Restaurants nearby: Tigh Na Mara Hotel, SANDHEAD, DG9 9JF, 01776 830210

Knockinaam Lodge, PORTPATRICK, DG9 9AD, 01776 810471

SANDYHILLS — Map 21 NX85

Places to visit

Threave Garden & Estate, CASTLE DOUGLAS, DG7 1RX, 01556 502575
www.nts.org.uk/Property/Threave-Estate

Orchardton Tower, PALNACKIE www.historic-scotland.gov.uk

Great for kids: Threave Castle, CASTLE DOUGLAS, DG7 1TJ, 07711 223101
www.historic-scotland.gov.uk

Sandyhills Bay Leisure Park

►►►► 75%

GOLD

tel: 01557 870267 **DG5 4NY**
email: info@gillespie-leisure.co.uk
dir: *On A710, 7m from Dalbeattie, 6.5m from Kirkbean.* **grid ref:** *NX892552*

A well-maintained park in a superb location beside a beach, and close to many attractive villages. The level, grassy site is sheltered by woodland, and the south-facing Sandyhills Bay and beach are a treasure trove for all the family, with their caves and rock pools. The leisure facilities at Brighouse Bay are available to visitors here. Two wooden wigwams with TV, fridge, kettle and microwave are available for hire. 15 acre site. 24 touring pitches. Caravan pitches. Motorhome pitches. Tent pitches. 32 statics. 2 wooden pods.

Open: Apr-Oct **Last arrival:** 20.00hrs **Last departure:** 11.30hrs

Pitches:

Leisure:

Facilities:

Services:

Within 3 miles:

Notes: No motorised scooters, jet skis or own quad bikes. Dogs must be kept on leads.

STRANRAER — Map 20 NX06

Places to visit

Glenwhan Gardens, STRANRAER, DG9 8PH, 01581 400222
www.glenwhangardens.co.uk

Great for kids: Castle Kennedy Gardens, STRANRAER, DG9 8BX, 01776 702024
www.castlekennedygardens.com

Aird Donald Caravan Park

 82%

tel: 01776 702025 **London Rd DG9 8RN**
email: enquiries@aird-donald.co.uk
dir: *From A75 left on entering Stranraer (signed). Opposite school, site 300yds.*
grid ref: *NX075605*

A spacious touring site set behind mature trees and within a five-minute walk of Stranraer town centre at the head of Loch Ryan. It is an ideal base to tour the 'Rinns of Galloway', to visit Port Logan Botanical Gardens or the lighthouse at the Mull of Galloway. It provides a very convenient stopover for the Cairnryan ferry to Ireland, but there's plenty to do in the area if staying longer. A 25-pitch rally field is available. 12 acre site. 50 touring pitches. 24 hardstandings. Caravan pitches. Motorhome pitches. Tent pitches.

Open: all year (rs Sep-Etr no tents) **Last arrival:** 22.00hrs **Last departure:** 16.00hrs

Pitches:

Leisure:

Facilities:

Services:

Within 3 miles:

Notes: Dogs must be kept on leads.

AA Pubs & Restaurants nearby: Knockinaam Lodge, PORTPATRICK, DG9 9AD, 01776 810471

Corsewall Lighthouse Hotel, STRANRAER, DG9 0QG, 01776 853220

WIGTOWN — Map 20 NX45

Drumroamin Farm Camping & Touring Site

►►► 90%

tel: 01988 840613 & 07752 471456 **1 South Balfern DG8 9DB**
email: enquiry@drumroamin.co.uk
dir: *A75 towards Newton Stewart, onto A714 for Wigtown. Left on B7005 through Bladnock, A746 through Kirkinner. Take B7004 signed Garlieston, 2nd left opposite Kilsture Forest, site 0.75m at end of lane.* **grid ref:** *NX444512*

An open, spacious site overlooking Wigtown Bay and the Galloway Hills. Located near Wigtown and Newton Stewart, this is an easily accessible site for those wishing to stay in a rural location. The toilet and other facilities are maintained in an exemplary manner. There is a large and separate tent field with a well-equipped day room, while the touring pitches can easily accommodate rally events. A new camp kitchen has been created to provide a sheltered spot for campers to prepare meals. The RSPB's Crook of Baldoon Reserve is located a 10-minute walk away. There is a good bus service at the top of the road which goes to Newton Stewart, Wigtown and Whithorn. Two of the three statics on site are for hire. 5 acre site. 48 touring pitches. Caravan pitches. Motorhome pitches. Tent pitches. 3 statics.

Open: all year **Last arrival:** 21.00hrs **Last departure:** noon

Pitches: * fr £18 fr £18 £14-£18

Leisure:

Facilities:

Services:

Within 3 miles:

Notes: No fires, no noise after 22.00hrs. Dogs must be kept on leads. Ball games area.

AA Pubs & Restaurants nearby: Kirroughtree House, NEWTON STEWART, DG8 6AN, 01671 402141

WEST DUNBARTONSHIRE

BALLOCH Map 20 NS38

Places to visit

Loch Lomond Bird of Prey Centre, BALLOCH, G83 8NB, 01389 729239 www.llbopc.co.uk

The Tall Ship at Riverside, GLASGOW, G3 8RS, 0141 357 3699 www.thetallship.com

PREMIER PARK

Lomond Woods Holiday Park

►►►►► 82%

tel: 01389 755000 **Old Luss Rd G83 8QP**
email: lomondwoods@holiday-parks.co.uk
dir: *From A82, 17m N of Glasgow, take A811 (Stirling to Balloch road). Left at 1st rdbt, follow holiday park signs, 150yds on left.* **grid ref:** *NS383816*

This site is ideally placed on the southern end of Loch Lomond, the UK's largest inland water and a designated National Park. This site has something to suit all tastes from the most energetic visitor to those who just wish to relax. Fully serviced pitches are available and there are three family rooms. There are loch cruises and boats to hire, plus retail outlets, superstores and eateries within easy walking distance. A drive or cycle ride along Loch Lomond reveals breathtaking views. There are two large boat storage areas. Please note that this site does not accept tents. Holiday caravans and lodges and three camping pods are available to let. 13 acre site. 117 touring pitches. 117 hardstandings. 55 seasonal pitches. Caravan pitches. Motorhome pitches. 35 statics. 3 wooden pods.

Open: all year **Last arrival:** 20.00hrs **Last departure:** noon

Pitches: * £21-£28 £21-£28

Leisure:

Facilities:

Services:

Within 3 miles:

Notes: No jet skis, no commercial vehicles. Dogs must be kept on leads.

AA Pubs & Restaurants nearby: The Cameron Grill, BALLOCH, G83 8QZ, 01389 722582

FIFE

ST ANDREWS

Places to visit

St Andrews Castle, ST ANDREWS, KY16 9AR, 01334 477196 www.historic-scotland.gov.uk

British Golf Museum, ST ANDREWS, KY16 9AB, 01334 460046 www.britishgolfmuseum.co.uk

Great for kids: St Andrews Aquarium, ST ANDREWS, KY16 9AS, 01334 474786 www.standrewsaquarium.co.uk

ST ANDREWS Map 21 NO51

PREMIER PARK

Cairnsmill Holiday Park

►►►►► 94%

tel: 01334 473604 **Largo Rd KY16 8NN**
email: cairnsmill@aol.com **web:** www.cairnsmill.co.uk
dir: *A915 from St Andrews towards Lathones. Approx 2m, site on right.*
grid ref: *NO502142*

Hidden behind mature trees and hedging in open countryside on the outskirts of St Andrews, this top quality park is ideally placed for visiting the town and exploring the Fife area. It is a family owned and run site providing high levels of customer care and excellent facilities, including a swimming pool, licensed bar and café, numerous play areas for children and a small fishing lochan, stocked annually with rainbow trout. Toilet facilities are first class, and the tent area has its own amenity block and outdoor kitchen area. Bunk house accommodation is available as well as five static homes for hire. The local bus to St Andrews stops at the site entrance. 27 acre site. 62 touring pitches. 33 hardstandings. 24 seasonal pitches. Caravan pitches. Motorhome pitches. Tent pitches. 194 statics.

Open: all year (rs Winter prior bookings only) **Last arrival:** flexible
Last departure: 11.00hrs

Pitches:

Leisure: Spa

Facilities:

Services:

Within 3 miles:

Notes: No noise after mdnt, 1 car per pitch. Dogs must be kept on leads.

AA Pubs & Restaurants nearby: The Inn at Lathones, ST ANDREWS, KY9 1JE, 01334 840494

AA CAMPSITE OF THE YEAR FOR SCOTLAND 2016

PREMIER PARK

Craigtoun Meadows Holiday Park

►►►►► 94%

GOLD

tel: 01334 475959 **Mount Melville KY16 8PQ**
email: info@craigtounmeadows.co.uk **web:** www.craigtounmeadows.co.uk
dir: *M90 junct 8, A91 to St Andrews. Just after Guardbridge right for Strathkinness. At 2nd x-rds left for Craigtoun.* **grid ref:** *NO482150*

An attractive site set unobtrusively in mature woodlands, with large pitches in spacious hedged paddocks. All pitches are fully serviced, and there are also some patio pitches and a summerhouse containing picnic tables and chairs. The modern toilet block provides cubicled en suite facilities as well as spacious showers, baths, disabled facilities and baby changing areas. The licensed restaurant and coffee shop are popular, and there is a takeaway, indoor and outdoor games areas and a launderette. Located one and half a mile from the centre of St Andrews which has sandy beaches, shops and restaurants, and being 'the home of golf', there are, of course, numerous golf courses including The Dukes, which borders the site. 32 acre site. 57 touring pitches. 57 hardstandings. 7 seasonal pitches. Caravan pitches. Motorhome pitches. Tent pitches. 199 statics.

Open: 15 Mar-Oct (rs Mar-Etr & Sep-Oct no shop & restaurant open shorter hours) **Last arrival:** 21.00hrs **Last departure:** 11.00hrs

Pitches: * £20-£25.50 £20-£25.50 £17-£23.50

Leisure:

Facilities:

Services:

Within 3 miles:

Notes: No groups of unaccompanied minors, no pets. Putting green, zip wire, all-weather football pitch.

AA Pubs & Restaurants nearby: Road Hole Restaurant, ST ANDREWS, KY16 9SP, 01334 474371

The Inn at Lathones, ST ANDREWS, KY9 1JE, 01334 840494

HIGHLAND

AVIEMORE Map 23 NH81

Aviemore Glamping

NEW ►►►►

tel: 01479 810717 **Eriskay, Craignagower Av PH22 1RW**
email: aviemoreglamping@outlook.com
dir: *From S: exit A9 onto B9152 signed Aviemore. Take 2nd exit at rdbt signed town centre. 2nd exit at next rdbt. 5th left into Craig Na Gower Ave (signed dental surgery). Site at end.* **grid ref:** *NH894130*

Aviemore is a well known outdoor enthusiasts' hotspot attracting tourists throughout the year for hillwalking and climbing in the Cairngorms, watersports at Loch Morlich and Loch Insch and skiing in the winter. Aviemore Glamping is a bit of a hidden secret located in the landscaped grounds of the owner's home yet is only a short walk from the town centre. The four eco-pods are beautifully built and luxuriously equipped with quality fittings and excellent en suite shower rooms; ideal for couples who are looking for something unique at a sensible price. The eco-pods are available all year and are heated to insulate against the chilly Scottish climate. 0.33 acre site. 4 wooden pods.

Open: all year **Last arrival:** 18.00hrs **Last departure:** 10.00hrs

Pitches: £60-£80 **Facilities:**

Within 3 miles:

Notes: No cars by pods. Min stay of 2 nights.

BALMACARA Map 22 NG82

Places to visit

Balmacara Estate & Lochalsh Woodland Garden, BALMACARA, IV40 8DN, 01599 566325 www.nts.org.uk/Property/Balmacara-Estate-Woodland-Walks

Eilean Donan Castle, DORNIE, IV40 8DX, 01599 555202 www.eileandonancastle.com

Reraig Caravan Site

►►► 79%

tel: 01599 566215 **IV40 8DH**
email: warden@reraig.com
dir: *On A87, 3.5m E of Kyle, 2m W of junct with A890.* **grid ref:** *NG815272*

A lovely site, on the saltwater Sound of Sleet, set back from the main road amongst mature trees in a garden-type environment. It is located near the Skye Bridge and very handy for exploring the surrounding area including Plockton. There is a regular bus that stops at the site entrance. 2 acre site. 40 touring pitches. 36 hardstandings. Caravan pitches. Motorhome pitches. Tent pitches.

Open: May-Sep **Last arrival:** 22.00hrs **Last departure:** noon

Pitches: * £16.40-£16.90 £16.40-£16.90 £13.50-£14

Facilities:

Services: **Within 3 miles:**

Notes: Pre-booking is not necessary. No awnings Jul & Aug. Dogs must be kept on leads. Charge for WiFi.

AA Pubs & Restaurants nearby: The Plockton Hotel, PLOCKTON, IV52 8TN, 01599 544274

Plockton Inn & Seafood Restaurant, PLOCKTON, IV52 8TW, 01599 544222

JOHN O'GROATS — Map 23 ND37

Places to visit

The Castle & Gardens of Mey, THURSO, KW14 8XH, 01847 851473
www.castleofmey.org.uk

John O'Groats Caravan Site

►►► 82%

tel: 01955 611329 & 07762 336359 **KW1 4YR**
email: info@johnogroatscampsite.co.uk
dir: *At end of A99.* **grid ref:** *ND382733*

An attractive site in an open position above the seashore and looking out towards the Orkney Islands. Nearby is the passenger ferry that makes day trips to the Orkneys, and there are grey seals to watch, and sea angling can be organised by the site owners. 4 acre site. 90 touring pitches. 30 hardstandings. Caravan pitches. Motorhome pitches. Tent pitches.

Open: Apr-Sep **Last arrival:** 22.00hrs **Last departure:** 11.00hrs

Pitches: * £17-£20 £17-£20 £15-£17

Facilities:

Services:

Within 3 miles:

Notes: No noise after 22.00hrs. Dogs must be kept on leads.

LAIDE — Map 22 NG89

Gruinard Bay Caravan Park

►►► 71%

tel: 01445 731225 **IV22 2ND**
email: gruinard@ecosse.net
dir: *From Inverness or Ullapool take A832 to Gairloch, follow signs to Laide. (NB on Inverness to Gairloch road – short stretch of single-track road with passing places just prior to Gairloch).* **grid ref:** *NG904919*

With views across Gruinard Bay to the Summer Isles and the mountains, this is a lovely, small park in a particularly peaceful location. There is direct access to a small sandy beach and a small hotel nearby with a restaurant and free WiFi access; the small post office provides basic groceries, while larger shops can be found in Aultbuie, Poolewe, Gairloch and Ullapool, where there are ferries to the Outer Hebrides. Being beside a beach the site has no hardstandings but the grass pitches are on well-compacted shingle. 3.5 acre site. 35 touring pitches. 2 seasonal pitches. Caravan pitches. Motorhome pitches. Tent pitches. 20 statics.

Open: Apr-Oct **Last arrival:** 22.00hrs **Last departure:** noon

Pitches: * fr £17 fr £17 fr £15

Facilities:

Services:

Within 3 miles:

Notes: No noise after 22.00hrs. Dogs must be kept on leads.

LAIRG — Map 23 NC50

Dunroamin Caravan and Camping Park

►►► 74%

tel: 01549 402447 **Main St IV27 4AR**
email: enquiries@lairgcaravanpark.co.uk
dir: *300mtrs from Lairg centre on S side of A839.* **grid ref:** *NC585062*

An attractive little park with clean and functional facilities, adjacent to a licensed restaurant. The park is close to the lower end of Loch Shin. 4 acre site. 20 touring pitches. 8 hardstandings. Caravan pitches. Motorhome pitches. Tent pitches. 9 statics.

Open: Apr-Oct **Last arrival:** 21.00hrs **Last departure:** noon

Pitches:

Facilities:

Services:

Within 3 miles:

Notes: No vehicles to be driven on site between 21.00hrs-07.00hrs. Dogs must be kept on leads.

Woodend Caravan & Camping Site

►►► 69%

tel: 01549 402248 **Achnairn IV27 4DN**
email: enquiries@woodendcampsite.co.uk
dir: *4m N of Lairg exit A836 onto A838, signed at Achnairn.* **grid ref:** *NC551127*

A clean, simple site set in hilly moors and woodland with access to Loch Shin. The area is popular with fishing and boating enthusiasts, and there is a choice of golf courses within a 30-mile radius. A spacious campers' kitchen is a useful amenity. There's also a holiday cottage to hire. 4 acre site. 55 touring pitches. 5 hardstandings. Caravan pitches. Motorhome pitches. Tent pitches.

Open: Apr-Sep **Last arrival:** 23.00hrs

Pitches:

Leisure:

Facilities:

Services:

Within 3 miles:

Notes: Dogs must be kept on leads.

ULLAPOOL Map 22 NH19

Broomfield Holiday Park

►►► 78%

tel: 01854 612020 & 612664 **West Shore St IV26 2UT**
email: sross@broomfieldhp.com **web:** www.broomfieldhp.com
dir: *Into Ullapool on A893, 2nd right past harbour.* **grid ref:** *NH123939*

Set right on the water's edge of Loch Broom and the open sea, with lovely views of the Summer Isles. This clean, well maintained and managed park is close to the harbour and town centre with their restaurants, bars and shops. The Ullapool ferry allows easy access to the Hebridian islands for day trips or longer visits. 12 acre site. 140 touring pitches. Caravan pitches. Motorhome pitches. Tent pitches.

Open: Etr or Apr-Sep **Last departure:** noon

Pitches:

Leisure:

Facilities: WiFi

Services:

Within 3 miles:

Notes: No noise at night. Dogs must be kept on leads.

SOUTH LANARKSHIRE

ABINGTON Map 21 NS92

Places to visit

Hidden Treasures Museum of Lead Mining, WANLOCKHEAD, ML12 6UT, 01659 74387 www.leadminingmuseum.co.uk

Mount View Caravan Park

►►► 79%

tel: 01864 502808 **ML12 6RW**
email: info@mountviewcaravanpark.co.uk **web:** www.mountviewcaravanpark.co.uk
dir: *M74 junct 13, A702 S into Abington. Left into Station Rd, over river & railway. Site on right.* **grid ref:** *NS935235*

A delightfully maturing family park, surrounded by the Southern Uplands and handily located between Carlisle and Glasgow. It is an excellent stopover site for those travelling between Scotland and the south, and the West Coast Railway passes beside the park. 5.5 acre site. 42 touring pitches. 42 hardstandings. 18 seasonal pitches. Caravan pitches. Motorhome pitches. Tent pitches. 28 statics.

Open: Mar-Oct **Last arrival:** 20.45hrs **Last departure:** 11.30hrs

Pitches: * £20-£25 £20-£25 fr £14

Leisure:

Facilities:

Services:

Within 3 miles:

Notes: 5mph speed limit, debit cards accepted (no credit cards). Dogs must be kept on leads & exercised off site. Emergency phone.

EAST LOTHIAN

ABERLADY Map 21 NT47

Places to visit

Dirleton Castle and Gardens, DIRLETON, EH39 5ER, 01620 850330 www.historic-scotland.gov.uk

Hailes Castle, EAST LINTON www.historic-scotland.gov.uk

Great for kids: Myreton Motor Museum, ABERLADY, EH32 0PZ, 01875 870288 www.myretonmotormuseum.co.uk

Aberlady Caravan Park

►►► 77%

tel: 01875 870666 **Haddington Rd EH32 0PZ**
email: aberladycaravanpark@hotmail.co.uk **web:** www.aberladycaravanpark.co.uk
dir: *From Aberlady take A6137 towards Haddington. Right in 0.25m, site on right.*
grid ref: *NT482797*

A small family-run site that is peacefully located within the grounds of the old Aberlady railway station, and is pleasantly landscaped with an open outlook towards the nearby hills; it is within easy reach of many seaside towns, beaches, golf courses and attractions including the National Museum of Flight at East Fortune. The A1 is nearby, making Edinburgh easily accessible. The park offers two-person wooden pods that have electricity. 4.5 acre site. 22 touring pitches. 12 hardstandings. Caravan pitches. Motorhome pitches. Tent pitches. 3 wooden pods.

Open: all year (rs Nov-Feb max of 5 caravans/motorhomes accepted at any one time) **Last arrival:** 21.00hrs **Last departure:** noon

Pitches:

Facilities:

Services:

Within 3 miles:

Notes: No ball games, no loud music. Dogs must be kept on leads.

AA Pubs & Restaurants nearby: La Potinière, GULLANE, EH31 2AA, 01620 843214

Macdonald Marine Hotel & Spa, NORTH BERWICK, EH39 4LZ, 01620 897300

DUNBAR Map 21 NT67

Places to visit

Preston Mill & Phantassie Doocot, EAST LINTON, EH40 3DS, 01620 860426 www.nts.org.uk/Property/Preston-Mill-Phantassie-Doocot

Great for kids: Tantallon Castle, NORTH BERWICK, EH39 5PN, 01620 892727 www.historic-scotland.gov.uk

PREMIER PARK

Thurston Manor Leisure Park

►►►►► 88%

tel: 01368 840643 **Innerwick EH42 1SA**
email: holidays@thurstonmanor.co.uk
dir: *4m S of Dunbar, signed from A1.* **grid ref:** *NT712745*

A pleasant park set in 250 acres of unspoilt countryside. The touring and static areas of this large park are in separate areas. The main touring area occupies an open, level position, and the toilet facilities are modern and exceptionally well maintained. The park boasts a well-stocked fishing loch, a heated indoor swimming pool, steam room, sauna, jacuzzi, mini-gym and fitness room plus seasonal entertainment. There is a superb family toilet block. 250 acre site. 120 touring pitches. 53 hardstandings. 52 seasonal pitches. Caravan pitches. Motorhome pitches. Tent pitches. 570 statics.

Open: 13 Feb-Jan **Last arrival:** 23.00hrs **Last departure:** 10.00hrs

Pitches: * £13.45-£28.95 £13.45-£28.95 £7.95-£13.65

Leisure: Spa

Facilities:

Services: **Within 3 miles:**

Notes: Quiet after 23.00hrs. Dogs must be kept on leads.

AA Pubs & Restaurants nearby: Macdonald Marine Hotel & Spa, NORTH BERWICK, EH39 4LZ, 01620 897300

Belhaven Bay Caravan & Camping Park

►►► 77%

tel: 01368 865956 **Belhaven Bay EH42 1TS**
email: belhaven@meadowhead.co.uk
dir: *A1 onto A1087 towards Dunbar. 1m to site in John Muir Park.* **grid ref:** *NT661781*

Located on the outskirts of Dunbar, this is a sheltered park within walking distance of the beach. There is a regular bus service to Dunbar where there is an East Coast Main Line railway station. The site is also convenient for the A1 and well placed for visiting the area's many seaside towns and various visitor attractions. There is a large children's play area. Six static caravans and three wooden wigwam pods are available for hire. 40 acre site. 52 touring pitches. 11 hardstandings. Caravan pitches. Motorhome pitches. Tent pitches. 64 statics. 3 wooden pods.

Open: Mar-13 Oct **Last arrival:** 20.00hrs **Last departure:** noon

Pitches: * £16.45-£29.80 £16.45-£29.80 £16.45-£28.30

Leisure:

Facilities:

Services:

Within 3 miles:

Notes: No rollerblades or skateboards, no open fires, no noise 23.00hrs-07.00hrs. Dogs must be kept on leads.

AA Pubs & Restaurants nearby: Macdonald Marine Hotel & Spa, NORTH BERWICK, EH39 4LZ, 01620 897300

LONGNIDDRY — Map 21 NT47

Places to visit

Prestongrange Museum, PRESTONPANS, EH32 9RX, 0131 653 2904 www.prestongrange.org

Great for kids: Myreton Motor Museum, ABERLADY, EH32 0PZ, 01875 870288 www.myretonmotormuseum.co.uk

Seton Sands Holiday Village

HOLIDAY CENTRE 84%

GOLD

tel: 0800 169 1129 **EH32 0QF**
email: setonsands@haven.com **web:** www.haven.com/setonsands
dir: *A1 to A198 exit, take B6371 to Cockenzie. Right onto B1348. Site 1m on right.*
grid ref: *NT420759*

A well-equipped holiday centre facing onto the Firth of Forth with mature landscaping. A dedicated entertainment team offers plenty of organised activities for children and there are pleasant bars, a show bar and a modern restaurant. It offers good sports and leisure facilities, including a multi-sports court, swimming pool and a variety of play areas, so ensuring there's always plenty without leaving the park. There is even a nine-hole golf course. A new touring area was created for the 2015 season offering fully serviced pitches set in lovely landscaping with a dedicated on-site warden . There is a regular bus from the site entrance, which makes day trips to Edinburgh easy. 150 holiday homes are available for hire. Please note this site does not accept tents. 1.75 acre site. 40 touring pitches. Caravan pitches. Motorhome pitches. 600 statics.

Seton Sands Holiday Village

Open: mid Mar-end Oct (rs mid Mar-May & Sep-Oct some facilities may be reduced) **Last arrival:** 22.00hrs **Last departure:** 10.00hrs

Pitches: **Leisure:** **Facilities:** WiFi

Services: **Within 3 miles:**

Notes: No commercial vehicles, no bookings by persons under 21yrs unless a family booking. Max 2 dogs per booking, certain dog breeds banned. Dogs must be kept on leads.

AA Pubs & Restaurants nearby: La Potinière, GULLANE, EH31 2AA, 01620 843214

The Longniddry Inn, LONGNIDDRY, EH32 0NF, 01875 852401

See advert below

MUSSELBURGH Map 21 NT37

Places to visit

Prestongrange Museum, PRESTONPANS, EH32 9RX, 0131 653 2904 www.prestongrange.org

Inveresk Lodge Garden, INVERESK, EH21 7TE, 0131 665 1855 www.nts.org.uk/Property/Inveresk-Lodge-Garden

Great for kids: Edinburgh Butterfly & Insect World, DALKEITH, EH18 1AZ, 0131 663 4932 www.edinburgh-butterfly-world.co.uk

Drum Mohr Caravan Park

 84%

tel: 0131 665 6867 **Levenhall EH21 8JS**
email: admin@drummohr.org
dir: *Exit A1 at A199 junct through Wallyford, at rdbt onto B1361 signed Prestonpans. 1st left, site 400yds.* **grid ref:** *NT373734*

This attractive park is carefully landscaped and sheltered by mature trees on all sides. It is divided into separate areas by mature hedging, trees and ornamental shrubs. The generously sized pitches include a number of fully serviced pitches, plus there are first-class amenities. The site is ideally located for exploring East Lothian area with its numerous seaside towns, and the National Museum of Flight at East Fortune is just 15 miles away. It's an easy drive on the nearby A1 to Edinburgh or alternatively, there is a regular bus service which stops near the site. There are camping pods and luxury lodges with hot tubs for hire. 9 acre site. 120 touring pitches. 50 hardstandings. Caravan pitches. Motorhome pitches. Tent pitches. 12 statics. 17 wooden pods.

Open: all year **Last arrival:** 18.00hrs (winter arrivals by prior arrangement) **Last departure:** noon

Pitches:

Leisure:

Facilities: WiFi

Services:

Within 3 miles:

Notes: Max 2 dogs per pitch. Dogs must be kept on leads. Freshly baked bread, croissants, tea & coffee in high season.

AA Pubs & Restaurants nearby: The Kitchin, EDINBURGH, EH6 6LX, 0131 555 1755

Plumed Horse, EDINBURGH, EH6 6DE, 0131 554 5556

WEST LOTHIAN

EAST CALDER Map 21 NT06

Places to visit

Almond Valley Heritage Trust, LIVINGSTON, EH54 7AR, 01506 414957 www.almondvalley.co.uk

Malleny Garden, BALERNO, EH14 7AF, 0131 449 2283 www.nts.org.uk/Property/Malleny-Garden

Linwater Caravan Park

 83%

tel: 0131 333 3326 **West Clifton EH53 0HT**
email: queries@linwater.co.uk
dir: *M9 junct 1, follow B7030 & Newbridge signs. Left after petrol station & Macdonalds onto B7030. 2m, after Edinburgh International Climbing Arena (EICA) right, follow site signs.* **grid ref:** *NT104696*

This is a farmland park in a peaceful rural area with access to good motorway and rail links enabling exploration of the heart of Scotland. The family who own the park are excellent hosts and offer a friendly service which is borne out by the many customers who return year after year. The grounds are very pleasant and the toilets are kept in an exemplary manner. It is a particularly popular park, especially with those wishing to visit the Royal Highland Show, the Edinburgh Festival and Military Tattoo. There are four wooden pods, and a self-catering lodge in a half acre for hire. 5 acre site. 60 touring pitches. 22 hardstandings. Caravan pitches. Motorhome pitches. Tent pitches. 4 wooden pods.

Open: mid Mar-late Oct **Last arrival:** 21.00hrs **Last departure:** noon

Pitches:

Leisure:

Facilities: WiFi

Services:

Within 3 miles:

Notes: No noise after 23.00hrs. Dogs must be kept on leads. Takeaway food can be ordered for delivery.

AA Pubs & Restaurants nearby: The Bridge Inn, RATHO, EH28 8RA, 0131 333 1320

LINLITHGOW

Map 21 NS97

Places to visit

Linlithgow Palace, LINLITHGOW, EH49 7AL, 01506 842896
www.historic-scotland.gov.uk

House of The Binns, LINLITHGOW, EH49 7NA, 01506 834255
www.nts.org.uk/Property/House-of-the-Binns

Great for kids: Blackness Castle, LINLITHGOW, EH49 7NH, 01506 834807
www.historic-scotland.gov.uk

Beecraigs Caravan & Camping Site

►►►► 86%

tel: 01506 844516 & 848943 **Beecraigs Country Park, The Visitor Centre EH49 6PL**
email: mail@beecraigs.com **web:** www.beecraigs.com
dir: *M9 junct 3 (from E) or junct 4 (from W), A803 to Linlithgow. From A803 into Preston Rd signed Beecraigs Country Park. Reception in visitor centre. (NB Preston Rd route is steep & winding).* **grid ref:** *NT006746*

Located on the hills above Linlithgow with unrivalled views towards the Forth Bridges, Beecraigs Country Park is an excellent caravan and camping site, with two modern washrooms, large hardstanding pitches and a secluded tenting area, together with the option of staying in a 6- or 4-person pod. This site has something for everyone. There are extensive walks and cycle trails, a fly-fishing loch, deer park, cattle fold and a very large play area for children. There is a lovely visitor centre, shop and café at the site entrance and there are good road and train links nearby making trips into Edinburgh easy. Boat trips are available. 6 acre site. 36 touring pitches. 36 hardstandings. Caravan pitches. Motorhome pitches. Tent pitches.

Open: all year (rs 25-26 Dec & 1-2 Jan no new arrivals) **Last arrival:** 20.00hrs
Last departure: noon

Pitches: * £18.80-£23.25 £18.80-£23.25 £15.50-£23.25

Leisure:

Facilities:

Services:

Within 3 miles:

Notes: No cars by tents. No ball games near caravans, no noise after 22.00hrs. Dogs must be kept on leads. Country park facilities including Ranger Service events. Child bath available.

AA Pubs & Restaurants nearby: Champany Inn, LINLITHGOW, EH49 7LU, 01506 834532

MORAY

ABERLOUR

Map 23 NJ24

Places to visit

Balvenie Castle, DUFFTOWN, AB55 4DH, 01340 820121
www.historic-scotland.gov.uk

Glenfiddich Distillery, DUFFTOWN, AB55 4DH, 01340 820373
www.glenfiddich.com

Aberlour Gardens Caravan Park

►►► 80%

tel: 01340 871586 **AB38 9LD**
email: info@aberlourgardens.co.uk
dir: *Midway between Aberlour & Craigellachie on A95 turn onto unclassified road. Site signed. (NB vehicles over 10' 6" should use A941, Dufftown to Craigellachie road).*
grid ref: *NJ282434*

This attractive parkland site is set in the five-acre walled garden of the Victorian Aberlour House, surrounded by the spectacular scenery of the Cairngorm National Park, through pine clad glens, to the famous Moray coastline; the park is also well placed for taking the world renowned Speyside Malt Whisky Trail. It offers a small, well-appointed toilet block, laundry and small licensed shop. 5 acre site. 34 touring pitches. 16 hardstandings. 10 seasonal pitches. Caravan pitches. Motorhome pitches. Tent pitches. 32 statics.

Open: Mar-27 Dec (rs Winter park opening dates weather dependant)
Last arrival: 19.00hrs **Last departure:** noon

Pitches: * £20.15-£25.10 £20.15-£25.10 £15.90-£25.10

Leisure:

Facilities: WiFi

Services:

Within 3 miles:

Notes: No ball games, max 5mph speed limit on site, no noise after 23.00hrs. Dogs must be kept on leads.

PITCHES: Caravans Motorhomes Tents Glamping-style accommodation **SERVICES:** Electric hook up Launderette Licensed bar Calor Gas Camping Gaz Toilet fluid Café/Restaurant Fast Food/Takeaway Battery charging Baby care Motorvan service point
ABBREVIATIONS: BH/bank hols – bank holidays Etr – Easter Spring BH – Spring Bank Holiday fr – from hrs – hours m – mile mdnt – midnight rdbt – roundabout rs – restricted service wk – week wknd – weekend x-rds – cross roads No credit or debit cards No dogs Children of all ages accepted

LOSSIEMOUTH

Map 23 NJ27

Places to visit

Elgin Cathedral, ELGIN, IV30 1HU, 01343 547171 www.historic-scotland.gov.uk

Duffus Castle, DUFFUS, IV30 5RH, 01667 460232 www.historic-scotland.gov.uk

PREMIER PARK

Silver Sands Holiday Park

►►►►► 82%

tel: 01343 813262 **Covesea, West Beach IV31 6SP**
email: holidays@silver-sands.co.uk
dir: *Take B9040 from Lossiemouth, 2m to site.* **grid ref:** *NJ205710*

This is an ideal family park located on the Moray coast two miles from the busy seaside town of Lossiemouth. There is direct access to a sandy beach and the entertainment complex caters for both children and adults, with a pool, sauna, steam room and a large gym. There is a well-stocked shop, takeaway food and a small bistro-style café on site. With a golf course adjacent to the park and several others within easy driving distance (including the world famous Nairn Golf Course), this site makes a perfect base for golfers and for those touring the area. There are fully serviced hardstandings and 15 static caravans for hire. 60 acre site. 140 touring pitches. 105 hardstandings. 35 seasonal pitches. Caravan pitches. Motorhome pitches. Tent pitches. 200 statics.

Open: 15 Feb-15 Jan (rs 15 Feb-Jun & Oct-15 Jan shops & entertainment restricted) **Last arrival:** 22.00hrs **Last departure:** noon

Pitches:

Leisure:

Facilities: WiFi

Services: **Within 3 miles:**

Notes: Dogs must be kept on leads.

See advert on opposite page

PERTH & KINROSS

BLAIR ATHOLL

Map 23 NN86

Places to visit

Blair Castle, BLAIR ATHOLL, PH18 5TL, 01796 481207 www.blair-castle.co.uk

Killiecrankie Visitor Centre, KILLIECRANKIE, PH16 5LG, 01796 473233 www.nts.org.uk/Property/Killiecrankie

PREMIER PARK

Blair Castle Caravan Park

►►►►► 90%

tel: 01796 481263 **PH18 5SR**
email: mail@blaircastlecaravanpark.co.uk
dir: *From A9 onto B8079 at Aldclune, follow to Blair Atholl. Site on right after crossing bridge in village.* **grid ref:** *NN874656*

An attractive site set in impressive seclusion within the Atholl Estate, surrounded by mature woodland and the River Tilt. Although a large park, the various groups of pitches are located throughout the extensive parkland, and each has its own sanitary block with all-cubicled facilities of a very high standard. There is a choice of grass pitches, hardstandings and fully serviced pitches. This park is particularly suitable for the larger type of motorhome. 32 acre site. 226 touring pitches. 155 hardstandings. 68 seasonal pitches. Caravan pitches. Motorhome pitches. Tent pitches. 97 statics.

Open: Mar-Nov **Last arrival:** 21.30hrs **Last departure:** noon

Pitches: £24-£35 £24-£35 £12-£29

Leisure:

Facilities: WiFi

Services: **Within 3 miles:**

Notes: Family park, no noise after 23.00hrs. Dogs must be kept on leads.

AA Pubs & Restaurants nearby: Killiecrankie Hotel, KILLIECRANKIE, PH16 5LG, 01796 473220

PREMIER PARK

River Tilt Caravan Park

►►►►► 84%

tel: 01796 481467 **PH18 5TE**
email: stuart@rivertilt.co.uk
dir: *7m N of Pitlochry on A9, take B8079 to Blair Atholl. Site at rear of Tilt Hotel.*
grid ref: *NN875653*

An attractive park with magnificent views of the surrounding mountains, idyllically set in hilly woodland country on the banks of the River Tilt, adjacent to the golf course. There is also a leisure complex with heated indoor swimming pool, sun lounge area, spa pool and multi-gym, all available for an extra charge; outdoors there is a short tennis court. The toilet facilities are very good. 2 acre site. 30 touring pitches. Caravan pitches. Motorhome pitches. Tent pitches. 69 statics.

Open: 16 Mar-12 Nov **Last arrival:** 21.00hrs **Last departure:** noon

Pitches: * fr £20 fr £18 fr £10

Leisure: Spa

Facilities:

Services:

Within 3 miles:

Notes: Dogs must be kept on leads. Sauna, solarium, steam room.

AA Pubs & Restaurants nearby: Killiecrankie Hotel, KILLIECRANKIE, PH16 5LG, 01796 473220

DUNKELD — Map 21 NO04

Places to visit

The Ell Shop & Little Houses, DUNKELD, PH8 0AN, 01350 728641
www.nts.org.uk/Property/Dunkeld

Loch of the Lowes Visitor Centre, DUNKELD, PH8 0HH, 01350 727337
www.swt.org.uk

Inver Mill Farm Caravan Park

►►►► 80%

tel: 01350 727477 **Inver PH8 0JR**
email: invermill@talk21.com
dir: *A9 onto A822 then immediately right to Inver.* **grid ref:** *NO015422*

A peaceful park on level former farmland, located on the banks of the River Braan and surrounded by mature trees and hills. The active resident owners keep the park in very good condition. 5 acre site. 65 touring pitches. 3 hardstandings. Caravan pitches. Motorhome pitches. Tent pitches.

Open: mid Mar-Oct **Last arrival:** 22.00hrs **Last departure:** noon

Pitches:

Facilities:

Services:

Within 3 miles:

Notes: Dogs must be kept on leads.

KINLOCH RANNOCH Map 23 NN65

Kilvrecht Campsite

►76%

tel: 01350 727284 **PH16 5QA**
email: tay.fd@forestry.gsi.gov.uk **web:** www.forestry.gov.uk
dir: *From north shore: B846 to Kinloch Rannoch. Follow South Loch Rannoch sign. Over river bridge, 1st right signed Kilvrecht. Approach via unclassified road along loch, with Forestry Commission signs.* **grid ref:** *NN623567*

Set within a large forest clearing, approximately half a mile from the road to Kinloch Rannoch which runs along the loch. This is a beautifully maintained site, with good clean facilities, for those who wish for a peaceful break. It also makes an ideal base for those who prefer the more active outdoor activities of hill walking (Schiehallion is within easy reach) or mountain biking; it is a great spot to observe the multitude of birds and wildlife in the area. Please note the site has no electricity. 17 acre site. 60 touring pitches. Caravan pitches. Motorhome pitches. Tent pitches.

Open: Apr-Oct **Last arrival:** 22.00hrs **Last departure:** 10.00hrs

Pitches:

Facilities:

Within 3 miles:

Notes: No fires. Dogs must be kept on leads.

PITLOCHRY

Places to visit

Edradour Distillery, PITLOCHRY, PH16 5JP, 01796 472095 www.edradour.com

Great for kids: Scottish Hydro Electric Visitor Centre, Dam & Fish Pass, PITLOCHRY, PH16 5ND, 01796 473152 www.scottish-hydro-centre.co.uk

PITLOCHRY Map 23 NN95

Milton of Fonab Caravan Park

►►►►89%

tel: 01796 472882 **Bridge Rd PH16 5NA**
email: info@fonab.co.uk
dir: *From S on A924, pass petrol station on left, next left opposite Bell's Distillery into Bridge Rd. Cross river, site on left. From N (& Pitlochry centre) on A924, under rail bridge, turn right opposite Bell's Distillery into Bridge Rd.* **grid ref:** *NN945573*

Set on the banks of River Tummel on the outskirts of the picturesque town of Pitlochry, this is a family-owned site with excellent toilet facilities and large spacious pitches. The town, with various tourist attractions – Bells Distillery and the Pitlochry Festival Theatre to name but two – has a wide variety of shops and eateries to suit all tastes. The site makes a great base for touring this beautiful area. 15 acre site. 154 touring pitches. Caravan pitches. Motorhome pitches. Tent pitches. 34 statics.

Open: Apr-Oct **Last arrival:** 21.00hrs **Last departure:** 13.00hrs

Pitches:

Facilities: WiFi

Services:

Within 3 miles:

Notes: Couples & families only, no motor cycles. Dogs must be kept on leads.

AA Pubs & Restaurants nearby: Moulin Hotel, PITLOCHRY, PH16 5EH, 01796 472196

Killiecrankie Hotel, KILLIECRANKIE, PH16 5LG, 01796 473220

Faskally Caravan Park

►►►►82%

tel: 01796 472007 **PH16 5LA**
email: info@faskally.co.uk
dir: *1.5m N of Pitlochry on B8019.* **grid ref:** *NN916603*

A large park near Pitlochry, which is divided into smaller areas by mature trees and set within well-tended grounds. This family-owned site has two large amenity blocks and an entertainment complex with a heated swimming pool, bar, restaurant and indoor games area. There are numerous walks from the site and it is ideal for either a longer stay to explore the area or as a convenient stopover. A regular bus service is available at the site entrance. 27 acre site. 300 touring pitches. 45 hardstandings. Caravan pitches. Motorhome pitches. Tent pitches. 130 statics.

Open: 15 Mar-Oct **Last arrival:** 23.00hrs **Last departure:** 11.00hrs

Pitches:

Leisure: Spa

Facilities: WiFi

Services:

Within 3 miles:

Notes: Dogs must be kept on leads.

AA Pubs & Restaurants nearby: Moulin Hotel, PITLOCHRY, PH16 5EH, 01796 472196

Killiecrankie Hotel, KILLIECRANKIE, PH16 5LG, 01796 473220

SCOTTISH BORDERS

EYEMOUTH — Map 21 NT96

Places to visit

Berwick-upon-Tweed Barracks, BERWICK-UPON-TWEED, TD15 1DF, 01289 304493 www.english-heritage.org.uk/daysout/properties/berwick-upon-tweed-barracks-and-main-guard

Great for kids: Eyemouth Museum, EYEMOUTH, TD14 5JE, 018907 50678

Eyemouth

HOLIDAY CENTRE 75%

tel: 0871 664 9740 *(Calls cost 5p per minute plus your phone company's access charge)*
Fort Rd TD14 5BE
email: eyemouth@park-resorts.com
dir: *From A1, approx 6m N of Berwick-upon-Tweed take A1107 to Eyemouth. On entering town, site signed. Right after petrol station, left at bottom of hill into Fort Rd.*
grid ref: *NT941646*

A cliff-top holiday park on the outskirts of the small fishing village of Eyemouth, within easy reach of Edinburgh and Newcastle. The site is handily placed for exploring the beautiful Scottish Borders and the magnificent coastline and countryside of north Northumberland. 22 acre site. 17 touring pitches. 7 hardstandings. 17 seasonal pitches. Caravan pitches. Motorhome pitches. 276 statics.

Open: Apr-Oct **Last arrival:** mdnt **Last departure:** 10.00hrs

Pitches: **Leisure:**

Facilities:

Services:

Within 3 miles:

Notes: Dogs must be kept on leads.

LAUDER — Map 21 NT54

Thirlestane Castle Caravan & Camping Site

►►► 78%

tel: 01578 718884 & 07976 231032 **Thirlestane Castle TD2 6RU**
email: info@thirlestanecastlepark.co.uk
dir: *Signed from A68 & A697, just S of Lauder.* **grid ref:** *NT536473*

Located on the outskirts of Lauder, close to the A68 and within the grounds of Thirlestane Castle, this is an ideal site from which to explore the many attractions in the Scottish Borders. The amenity block is immaculately maintained and the pitches are behind the estate boundary wall to provide a secluded and peaceful location. There is a regular service bus near the site entrance. 5 acre site. 60 touring pitches. 22 hardstandings. 30 seasonal pitches. Caravan pitches. Motorhome pitches. Tent pitches. 27 statics.

Open: Apr-4 Oct **Last arrival:** 20.00hrs **Last departure:** noon

Pitches: * £16-£18 £18-£21 £12-£19

Facilities:

Services: **Within 3 miles:**

Notes: Dogs must be kept on leads. Tourer storage facilities, discounted access to castle & grounds during opening hours.

PEEBLES — Map 21 NT24

Places to visit

Kailzie Gardens, PEEBLES, EH45 9HT, 01721 720007 www.kailziegardens.com

Robert Smail's Printing Works, INNERLEITHEN, EH44 6HA, 01896 830206 www.nts.org.uk/Property/Robert-Smails-Printing-Works

Crossburn Caravan Park

►►►► 81%

tel: 01721 720501 **Edinburgh Rd EH45 8ED**
email: enquiries@crossburncaravans.co.uk **web:** www.crossburn-caravans.com

dir: *0.5m N of Peebles on A703.* **grid ref:** *NT248417*

A peaceful, family-run park, on the edge of Peebles and within easy driving distance for Edinburgh and the Scottish Borders. The park is divided by well-maintained landscaping and mature trees, and has good views over the countryside. There is a regular bus service at the site entrance and Peebles has a wide range of shops and attractions. The facilities are maintained to a high standard. Four-person wooden pods are available for hire. There is also a main caravan dealership on site and a large stock of spares and accessories are available. 6 acre site. 45 touring pitches. 15 hardstandings. Caravan pitches. Motorhome pitches. Tent pitches. 85 statics. 2 wooden pods.

Open: Apr-Oct **Last arrival:** 21.00hrs **Last departure:** 14.00hrs

Pitches: * £25-£27 £25-£27 £21-£25

Leisure:

Facilities:

Services:

Within 3 miles:

Notes: Dogs must be kept on leads.

STIRLING

ABERFOYLE
Map 20 NN50

Places to visit

Inchmahome Priory, PORT OF MENTEITH, FK8 3RA, 01877 385294
www.historic-scotland.gov.uk

PREMIER PARK

Trossachs Holiday Park

►►►►► 88%

GOLD

tel: 01877 382614 **FK8 3SA**
email: info@trossachsholidays.co.uk **web:** www.trossachsholidays.co.uk
dir: *Access on E side of A81, 1m S of junct A821 & 3m S of Aberfoyle.*
grid ref: *NS544976*

An attractively landscaped and peaceful park with outstanding views towards the hills, including the Munro, Ben Lomond. Set within the Loch Lomond National Park, boating, walking, cycling and beautiful drives over the Dukes Pass through the Trossachs are just some of the attractions within easy reach. Bikes can be hired from the reception and there is an internet café that sells home baked items. There are lodges for hire. 40 acre site. 66 touring pitches. 46 hardstandings. 24 seasonal pitches. Caravan pitches. Motorhome pitches. Tent pitches. 84 statics.

Open: Mar-Oct **Last arrival:** 21.00hrs **Last departure:** noon

Pitches: * £19-£25 £19-£25 £15-£21

Leisure:

Facilities:

Services: **Within 3 miles:**

Notes: Groups by prior arrangement only.

AA Pubs & Restaurants nearby: The Clachan Inn, DRYMEN, G63 0BG, 01360 660824

See advert on opposite page

BLAIRLOGIE
Map 21 NS89

Places to visit

Alloa Tower, ALLOA, FK10 1PP, 01259 211701
www.nts.org.uk/Property/Alloa-Tower

The National Wallace Monument, STIRLING, FK9 5LF, 01786 472140
www.nationalwallacemonument.com

Witches Craig Caravan & Camping Park

►►►► 90%

GOLD

tel: 01786 474947 **FK9 5PX**
email: info@witchescraig.co.uk
dir: *3m NE of Stirling on A91 (Hillfoots to St Andrews road).* **grid ref:** *NS821968*

In an attractive setting with direct access to the lower slopes of the dramatic Ochil Hills, this is a well-maintained family-run park. It is in the centre of 'Braveheart' country, with easy access to historical sites and many popular attractions. 5 acre site. 60 touring pitches. 60 hardstandings. 6 seasonal pitches. Caravan pitches. Motorhome pitches. Tent pitches.

Open: Apr-Oct **Last arrival:** 20.00hrs **Last departure:** noon

Pitches: * £17.50-£24 £17.50-£24 £17-£19.50

Leisure: **Facilities:**

Services: **Within 3 miles:**

Notes: Dogs must be kept on leads. Food preparation area, cooking shelters, baby bath & changing area.

CALLANDER
Map 20 NN60

Places to visit

Doune Castle, DOUNE, FK16 6EA, 01786 841742 www.historic-scotland.gov.uk

Gart Caravan Park

►►►► 87%

tel: 01877 330002 **The Gart FK17 8LE**
email: enquiries@theholidaypark.co.uk
dir: *1m E of Callander on A84.* **grid ref:** *NN643070*

A very well appointed and spacious parkland site within easy walking distance of the tourist and outdoor activity-friendly town of Callander. The site is in an excellent location for touring the area – The Trossachs, Loch Katrine (where there are trips on the SS *Sir Walter Scott*) and the Rob Roy Centre are only a few of the many nearby attractions. Free fishing is available on the River Teith which runs along the edge of the site. The statics vans are in a separate area. Please note that tents are not accepted. 26 acre site. 128 touring pitches. 45 hardstandings. Caravan pitches. Motorhome pitches. 66 statics.

Open: Etr or Apr-15 Oct **Last arrival:** 22.00hrs **Last departure:** 18.00hrs

Pitches: * £24-£30 £24-£30 **Leisure:**

Facilities:

Services: **Within 3 miles:**

Notes: No commercial vehicles. Dogs must be kept on leads.

AA Pubs & Restaurants nearby: Roman Camp Country House Hotel, CALLANDER, FK17 8BG, 01877 330003

The Lade Inn, CALLANDER, FK17 8HD, 01877 330152

LUIB — Map 20 NN42

Glendochart Holiday Park

►►►► 74%

tel: 01567 820637 **FK20 8QT**
email: info@glendochart-caravanpark.co.uk
dir: *On A85 Oban to Stirling road, midway between Killin & Crianlarich.*
grid ref: *NN477278*

A small site located on the A85 some eight miles from Killin, with boating and fishing available on Loch Tay. It is also convenient for Oban, Fort William and Loch Lomond. Hill walkers have direct access to numerous walks to suit all levels including the nearby Munro of Ben More. There is a regular bus service at the site entrance and nearby Crianlarich provides access to the West Highland Railway known as Britain's most scenic rail route, and also the West Highland Way. An ideal site as a stopover to the west coast or for a longer holiday. 15 acre site. 35 touring pitches. 28 hardstandings. Caravan pitches. Motorhome pitches. Tent pitches. 60 statics.

Open: Mar-Nov **Last arrival:** 21.00hrs **Last departure:** noon

Pitches: * £18.50-£20 £18.50-£20 £12.50-£15

Facilities: **Services:**

Within 3 miles:

Notes: Dogs must be kept on leads.

AA Pubs & Restaurants nearby: The Lade Inn, CALLANDER, FK17 8HD, 01877 330152

STIRLING

See Blairlogie

STRATHYRE — Map 20 NN51

Immervoulin Caravan and Camping Park

►►► 78%

tel: 01877 384285 **FK18 8NJ**
email: immervoulin@freenetname.co.uk
dir: *On A84, approx 1m S of Strathyre.* **grid ref:** *NN560164*

A family-run park on open meadowland beside the River Balvaig, where fishing, canoeing and other water sports can be enjoyed. A riverside walk leads to Loch Lubnaig, and the small village of Strathyre has various pubs offering food. Located on the A84, the site is ideally located for exploring this lovely area. The park has a modern well-appointed amenity block. 5 acre site. 50 touring pitches. Caravan pitches. Motorhome pitches. Tent pitches.

Open: Mar-Oct **Last arrival:** 22.00hrs

Pitches:

Facilities:

Services:

Within 3 miles:

Notes: No noise after 23.00hrs.

AA Pubs & Restaurants nearby: Creagan House, STRATHYRE, FK18 8ND, 01877 384638

PITCHES: Caravans Motorhomes Tents Glamping-style accommodation **SERVICES:** Electric hook up Launderette Licensed bar Calor Gas Camping Gaz Toilet fluid Café/Restaurant Fast Food/Takeaway Battery charging Baby care Motorvan service point
ABBREVIATIONS: BH/bank hols – bank holidays Etr – Easter Spring BH – Spring Bank Holiday fr – from hrs – hours m – mile mdnt – midnight rdbt – roundabout rs – restricted service wk – week wknd – weekend x-rds – cross roads No credit or debit cards No dogs Children of all ages accepted

TYNDRUM Map 20 NN33

PREMIER PARK

Strathfillan Wigwam Village

NEW 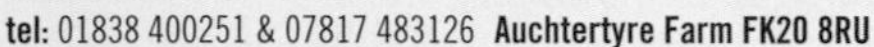

tel: 01838 400251 & 07817 483126 **Auchtertyre Farm FK20 8RU**
email: enquiries@wigwamholidays.com
dir: *From A82 (3m N of Crianarich) site on right. Follow signs for Strathfillan Wigwams & farm shop.* **grid ref:** *NN362273*

The hand-crafted wooden wigwams provide good accommodation, especially for walkers as this site is on the West Highland Way. Available all year, each unit is well insulated, has electric panel heaters and an external wood-burner (wood is available at the Trading Post shop). They are kept spotlessly clean and well maintained. The wigwams have been grouped in small clusters, some have outstanding mountain views and others benefit from the seclusion of a woodland setting. The lodges, with kitchen, shower and toilet, cater for up to eight, and a small yurt is also available for hire. The surrounding area offers many walking and mountain bike opportunities, and various eateries can be found in Tyndrum not far away. There is a local bus service at the end of the farm road. The site offers touring pitches as well. 6 acre site. 1 yurt. 24 wooden pods.

Open: all year **Last arrival:** 20.00hrs **Last departure:** 10.30hrs

Pitches: * £46-£90

Leisure:

Facilities:

Services:

Within 3 miles:

Notes: No noise or music after 23.00hrs.

SCOTTISH ISLANDS

ISLE OF ARRAN

KILDONAN Map 20 NS02

Places to visit

Brodick Castle, Garden & Country Park, BRODICK, KA27 8HY, 01770 302202
www.nts.org.uk/Property/Brodick-Castle-Garden-and-Country-Park

Isle of Arran Heritage Museum, BRODICK, KA27 8DP, 01770 302636
www.arranmuseum.co.uk

Sealshore Camping and Touring Site

83%

tel: 01770 820320 **KA27 8SE**
email: enquiries@campingarran.com
dir: *From ferry terminal in Brodick turn left, 12m, through Lamlash & Whiting Bay. Left to Kildonan, site on left.* **grid ref:** *NS024210*

On the south coast of Arran and only 12 miles from the ferry at Brodick, this is a peaceful, family-run site with direct access to a sandy beach. There are fabulous views across the water to Pladda Island and Ailsa Craig, and an abundance of wildlife. The site is suited for all types of touring vehicles but caters very well for non-motorised campers. The resident owner, also a registered fisherman, sells fresh lobster and crab, and on request will give fishing lessons on a small, privately owned lochan. There is an undercover BBQ, campers' kitchen and day room with TV. A bus, which stops on request, travels around the island. 3 acre site. 43 touring pitches. 8 hardstandings. Caravan pitches. Motorhome pitches. Tent pitches. 2 wooden pods.

Open: Mar-Oct **Last arrival:** 21.00hrs **Last departure:** noon

Pitches:

Leisure:

Facilities:

Services:

Within 3 miles:

Notes: No cars by tents. No fires, no noise after 22.00hrs. Dogs must be kept on leads.

ISLE OF MULL

CRAIGNURE — Map 20 NM73

Places to visit

Duart Castle, CRAIGNURE, PA64 6AP, 01680 812309 www.duartcastle.com

Shieling Holidays

►►►► 86%

tel: 01680 812496 & 0131 556 0068 **PA65 6AY**
email: sales@shielingholidays.co.uk
dir: *From ferry left onto A849 to Iona. 400mtrs left at church, follow site signs towards sea.* **grid ref:** *NM724369*

A lovely site on the water's edge with spectacular views, and less than one mile from the ferry landing. Hardstandings and service points are provided for motorhomes, and there are astro-turf pitches for tents. The park also offers unique, en suite Shieling cottage tents for hire and bunkhouse accommodation for families. There is also a wildlife trail on site. 7 acre site. 90 touring pitches. 30 hardstandings. Caravan pitches. Motorhome pitches. Tent pitches.

Open: 6 Mar-2 Nov **Last arrival:** 22.00hrs **Last departure:** noon

Pitches: * fr £18 fr £18 fr £17

Leisure:

Facilities:

Services:

Within 3 miles:

Notes: Dogs must be kept on leads. Bikes available.

ISLE OF SKYE

EDINBANE — Map 22 NG35

Places to visit

Dunvegan Castle and Gardens, DUNVEGAN, IV55 8WF, 01470 521206 www.dunvegancastle.com

Skye Camping & Caravanning Club Site

►►►► 90%

tel: 01470 582230 **Loch Greshornish, Borve, Arnisort IV51 9PS**
email: skye.site@thefriendlyclub.co.uk
dir: *Approx 12m from Portree on A850, Dunvegan road. Site by loch shore.*
grid ref: *NG345527*

Situated on the beautiful Isle of Skye, this campsite stands out for its stunning waterside location and glorious views, the generous pitch density, the overall range of facilities, and the impressive ongoing improvements under enthusiastic franchisee owners. The layout maximises the beauty of the scenery and genuine customer care is very evident with an excellent tourist information room and campers' shelter being just two examples. The amenities block has smart, modern fittings, including excellent showers, a generously proportioned disabled room and a family bathroom. This is a green site that uses only eco-friendly toilet fluids, which are available on site. There is an on-site shop, two camping pods to let, plus car hire is available on the site. Non-members are very welcome too. 7.5 acre site. 105 touring pitches. 36 hardstandings. Caravan pitches. Motorhome pitches. Tent pitches. 2 wooden pods.

Open: Apr-Oct **Last arrival:** 22.00hrs **Last departure:** noon

Pitches: *

Facilities:

Services:

Within 3 miles:

Notes: Barrier locked 23.00hrs-07.00hrs. Dogs must be kept on leads. Fresh fish van visits weekly.

AA Pubs & Restaurants nearby: Stein Inn, STEIN, IV55 8GA, 01470 592362

Loch Bay Seafood Restaurant, STEIN, IV55 8GA, 01470 592235

The Three Chimneys & The House Over-By, COLBOST, IV55 8ZT, 01470 511258

STAFFIN — Map 22 NG46

Staffin Camping & Caravanning

►►► 80%

tel: 01470 562213 **IV51 9JX**
email: staffincampsite@btinternet.com
dir: *On A855, 16m N of Portree. Turn right before 40mph signs.* **grid ref:** *NG492670*

A large sloping grassy site with level hardstandings for motorhomes and caravans, close to the village of Staffin. The toilet block is appointed to a very good standard and the park has a laundry. Mountain bikes are available for hire. 2.5 acre site. 50 touring pitches. 18 hardstandings. Caravan pitches. Motorhome pitches. Tent pitches.

Open: Apr-Oct **Last arrival:** 22.00hrs **Last departure:** 11.00hrs

Pitches: * fr £16 fr £16 fr £15

Facilities:

Services:

Within 3 miles:

Notes: No music after 22.00hrs. Dogs must be kept on leads. Picnic tables, kitchen area, campers' bothy.

AA Pubs & Restaurants nearby: Cuillin Hills Hotel, PORTREE, IV51 9QU, 01478 612003

Wales

Wales

Wales – a place of myth and legend, a country loved passionately by actors and poets and male voice choirs, a land of rugged mountain grandeur and craggy, meandering coastline. Crossing the Severn Bridge, you sense at once you are entering a completely different country. The culture is different, so are the traditions and so are the physical characteristics. With its lush hills and dramatic headlands, it has echoes of other Celtic lands – most notably, Ireland and Scotland.

Wales's legacy of famous names from the world of the arts is truly impressive. Richard Burton hailed from the valleys in South Wales, Anthony Hopkins originates from Port Talbot and Dylan Thomas was born a century ago in a house on a hilltop street in Swansea. His birthplace in Cwmdonkin Drive can be hired for self-catering breaks and holidays and there is even the chance to sleep in the poet's tiny bedroom. Thomas described the house as 'a provincial villa...a small, not very well painted gateless house...very nice, very respective.'

Further west is the house where he lived in his final years. Thomas and his wife Caitlin moved to the Boat House at Laugharne, 40 miles from Swansea, in the spring of 1949. With its magnificent views across an expansive estuary, this was Dylan Thomas's perfect retreat and much of his creative writing was completed in the modest wooden shed on a bluff above the house. The Boat House is open to visitors and nearby Brown's Hotel, his favourite watering hole, offers the chance to relax and enjoy something to eat and drink.

On the Pembrokeshire coast, renowned for its beautiful beaches, is another, less familiar link with Dylan Thomas. The old fishing village of Lower Fishguard was home to a film unit of almost 100 people in the early months of 1971. Presided over by the film director Andrew Sinclair, filming of Thomas's classic play *Under Milk Wood* began, with Richard Burton and Peter O'Toole among the many film stars seen around the village. A young, virtually unknown David Jason, also appeared in the film. Sinclair and his team built false fronts on the dock cottages and created an undertaker's parlour – among other work. The National Eisteddfod in Llangollen is one of the most important events in the Welsh cultural calendar, celebrating the country's long heritage of storytelling, music and poetry.

Think of Wales and you often think of castles. The formidable Caernarfon Castle, the setting for the investure of the Prince of Wales in 1969, stands in the northwest corner of the country. Harlech Castle was built around 1283 by Edward I and from it are seen the peaks of Snowdonia. This glorious region of towering summits and crags, which has the highest range of mountains in England and Wales and is now a National Park, has long attracted walkers and climbers. Edmund Hillary and his team rehearsed here for the first successful assault on Everest in 1953. However, Snowdonia is not just about mountain peaks. There are plenty of gentler alternatives, including an extensive network of lowland routes, forest trails and waymarked walks. Below Snowdon lies the historic village of Llanberis, one of the region's most popular attractions and ideally placed for touring Snowdonia. Betws-y-Coed is another mountain resort with a range of delightful walks exploring picturesque river scenery and pretty, pastoral uplands.

For the buzz and vibrancy of the city, Swansea and Cardiff cannot be beaten, the latter boasting a lively café culture, docklands-style apartments, a science discovery centre that's fun for all the family, and the internationally renowned Wales Millennium Centre (Canolfan Mileniwm Cymru). However, in terms of Welsh scenery, there is so much waiting to be discovered and explored; the grand, immensely varied landscape of the Brecon Beacons, and the gentler, pastoral acres of the Welsh Borders – among a host of famed beauty spots throughout Wales.

◁ Mumbles Head lighthouse

ISLE OF ANGLESEY

BEAUMARIS — Map 14 SH67

Places to visit

Beaumaris Castle, BEAUMARIS, LL58 8AP, 01248 810361 www.cadw.wales.gov.uk

Kingsbridge Caravan Park

►►►► 82%

tel: 01248 490636 & 07774 842199 **Camp Rd, Llanfaes LL58 8LR**
email: info@kingsbridgecaravanpark.co.uk
dir: *From either Menai Bridge or Britannia Bridge follow signs for Beaumaris & A545. In Beaumaris (castle on left) take B5109 towards Llangoed, 2m to x-rds, turn left signed Kingsbridge.* **grid ref:** *SH605784*

Peacefully located two miles from historic Beaumaris, this long-established park has been transformed by its caring owners into a must-stay destination for lovers of walking and wildlife. The generously sized pitches are located in two separate touring areas – one for families and one for adults only – each has its own modern, well-equipped amenities block that are smartly presented with quality decor and fittings. Please note that a laundry is not provided but modern facilities are available in nearby Beaumaris. 14 acre site. 90 touring pitches. 21 hardstandings. 15 seasonal pitches. Caravan pitches. Motorhome pitches. Tent pitches. 29 statics.

Open: Mar-Oct **Last arrival:** 21.00hrs **Last departure:** noon

Pitches: * £20-£30 £20-£28 £18-£34

Leisure: **Facilities:**

Services: **Within 3 miles:**

Notes: No noise after 23.00hrs, no camp fires. Dogs must be kept on leads.

AA Pubs & Restaurants nearby: Ye Olde Bulls Head Inn, BEAUMARIS, LL58 8AP, 01248 810329

The Ship Inn, RED WHARF BAY, LL75 8RJ, 01248 852568

DULAS — Map 14 SH48

Places to visit

Din Lligwy Hut Group, LLANALLGO, 01443 336000 www.cadw.wales.gov.uk

PREMIER PARK

Tyddyn Isaf Caravan Park

►►►►► 91%

tel: 01248 410203 & 410667 **Lligwy Bay LL70 9PQ**
email: mail@tyddynisaf.co.uk **web:** www.tyddynisaf.co.uk
dir: *Take A5025 through Benllech to Moelfre rdbt, left towards Amlwch to Brynrefail. Turn right to Lligwy at phone box. Site 0.5m down lane on right.* **grid ref:** *SH486873*

A beautifully situated, and very spacious family park on rising ground adjacent to a sandy beach, with magnificent views overlooking Lligwy Bay. A private footpath leads directly to the beach and there is an excellent nature trail around the park. The site has very good toilet facilities, including a block with underfloor heating and excellent unisex privacy cubicles, a well-stocked shop, and bar/restaurant serving meals, which are best enjoyed on the terrace with its magnificent coast and sea views. Dogs are welcome in the two superb sea-view Mediterranean beach huts, located beside the terrace at the bar. 16 acre site. 80 touring pitches. 60 hardstandings. 50 seasonal pitches. Caravan pitches. Motorhome pitches. Tent pitches. 56 statics.

Open: Mar-Oct (rs Mar-Jul & Sep-Oct bar & shop opening limited)
Last arrival: 21.30hrs **Last departure:** 11.00hrs

Pitches:

Leisure:

Facilities:

Services:

Within 3 miles:

Notes: No groups, loud music or open fires, max 3 units can be booked together. Dogs must be kept on leads. Baby changing unit.

AA Pubs & Restaurants nearby: The Ship Inn, RED WHARF BAY, LL75 8RJ, 01248 852568

Ye Olde Bulls Head Inn, BEAUMARIS, LL58 8AP, 01248 810329

Bishopsgate House Hotel, BEAUMARIS, LL58 8BB, 01248 810302

MARIAN-GLAS Map 14 SH58

Places to visit

Din Lligwy Hut Group, LLANALLGO, 01443 336000 www.cadw.wales.gov.uk

PREMIER PARK

Home Farm Caravan Park

►►►►► 94%

Best of British — David Bellamy Conservation Award GOLD

tel: 01248 410614 **LL73 8PH**
email: enq@homefarm-anglesey.co.uk **web:** www.homefarm-anglesey.co.uk
dir: *On A5025, 2m N of Benllech. Site 300mtrs beyond church.* **grid ref:** *SH498850*

A first-class park run with passion and enthusiasm, set in an elevated and secluded position sheltered by trees, and with good planting and landscaping. The peaceful rural setting affords views of farmland, the sea and the mountains of Snowdonia. The modern toilet blocks are spotlessly clean and well maintained, and there are excellent play facilities for children both indoors and out. Facilities also include a visitors' parking area and a smart reception and shop. The area is blessed with sandy beaches, and the local pubs and shops cater for everyday needs. 12 acre site. 102 touring pitches. 65 hardstandings. Caravan pitches. Motorhome pitches. Tent pitches. 84 statics.

Open: Apr-Oct **Last arrival:** 21.00hrs **Last departure:** noon

Pitches:

Leisure:

Facilities:

Services:

Within 3 miles:

Notes: No roller blades, skateboards or scooters.

AA Pubs & Restaurants nearby: The Ship Inn, RED WHARF BAY, LL75 8RJ, 01248 852568

Ye Olde Bulls Head Inn, BEAUMARIS, LL58 8AP, 01248 810329

Bishopsgate House Hotel, BEAUMARIS, LL58 8BB, 01248 810302

RED WHARF BAY Map 14 SH58

St David's Park

►►►► 88%

tel: 01248 852341 & 852702 **LL75 8RJ**
email: info@stdavidspark.com
dir: *A55 junct 8, A5025 towards Benllech. Approx 8m, right towards Red Wharf Bay, site 0.5m on left.* **grid ref:** *SH529811*

In a stunning location with panoramic coastal and mountain views and direct access to sandy beaches, this long-established holiday village has been transformed in recent years to provide touring pitches, 44 of which are allocated to seasonal customers. A haven for campers, the all-tent pitches have electric hook-up facilities and a stylish modern amenities block with hi-spec facilities. The Tavern Bistro and Bar offers a wide range of imaginative food and beverages. 47 acre site. 45 touring pitches. 44 seasonal pitches. Caravan pitches. Motorhome pitches. Tent pitches. 180 statics.

Open: 15 Mar-end Sep **Last arrival:** 21.00hrs **Last departure:** noon

Pitches: * £25-£36 £25-£36 £25-£36

Leisure:

Facilities:

Services:

Within 3 miles:

Notes: No group bookings, no jet skis, gazebos or disposable BBQs, no noise after 23.00hrs.

RHOS LLIGWY Map 14 SH48

Places to visit

Din Lligwy Hut Group, LLANALLGO, 01443 336000 www.cadw.wales.gov.uk

Ty'n Rhos Caravan Park

►►► 68%

tel: 01248 852417 **Lligwy Bay, Moelfre LL72 8NL**
email: robert@bodafonpark.co.uk
dir: *Take A5025 from Benllech to Moelfre rdbt, right to T-junct in Moelfre. Left, approx 2m, pass x-rds leading to beach, site 50mtrs on right.* **grid ref:** *SH495867*

A family park close to the beautiful beach at Lligwy Bay, and cliff walks along the Heritage Coast. Historic Din Lligwy, and the shops at picturesque Moelfre are nearby. All the touring pitches have water, electric hook-up and TV connection. Please note that guests should register at Bodafon Caravan Park in Benllech where detailed directions will be given and pitches allocated. 10 acre site. 30 touring pitches. 4 hardstandings. 48 seasonal pitches. Caravan pitches. Motorhome pitches. Tent pitches. 80 statics.

Open: Mar-Oct **Last arrival:** 20.00hrs **Last departure:** 11.00hrs

Pitches: * £22-£30 £22-£30 £20-£27

Facilities:

Services: **Within 3 miles:**

Notes: No campfires, no noise after 23.00hrs. Dogs must be kept on leads.

AA Pubs & Restaurants nearby: The Ship Inn, RED WHARF BAY, LL75 8RJ, 01248 852568

Ye Olde Bulls Head Inn, BEAUMARIS, LL58 8AP, 01248 810329

Bishopsgate House Hotel, BEAUMARIS, LL58 8BB, 01248 810302

RHOSNEIGR Map 14 SH37

Ty Hen

►►► 77%

GOLD

tel: 01407 810331 **Station Rd LL64 5QZ**
email: info@tyhen.com
dir: *From A55 junct 5 follow signs to Rhosneigr, at clock turn right (red gate post) entrance 50mtrs before Rhosneigr railway station.* **grid ref:** *SH327738*

This site is in an attractive seaside location near a large fishing lake and riding stables. Surrounded by lovely countryside, this former working farm is close to RAF Valley, which is great for plane spotters, but expect some aircraft noise during the day. The friendly owners are always on hand. 7.5 acre site. 38 touring pitches. 5 hardstandings. 33 seasonal pitches. Caravan pitches. Motorhome pitches. Tent pitches. 42 statics.

Open: mid Mar-Oct **Last arrival:** 21.00hrs **Last departure:** noon

Pitches: **Leisure:**

Facilities:

Services:

Within 3 miles:

Notes: 1 motor vehicle per pitch, children must not be out after 22.00hrs. Dogs must be kept on leads. Family room, walks.

BRIDGEND

PORTHCAWL Map 9 SS87

Places to visit

Newcastle Castle, BRIDGEND, 01443 336000 www.cadw.wales.gov.uk

Coity Castle, COITY, CF35 6BG, 01443 336000 www.cadw.wales.gov.uk

Brodawel Camping & Caravan Park

►►► 82%

tel: 01656 783231 **Moor Ln, Nottage CF36 3EJ**
email: info@brodawelcamping.co.uk
dir: *M4 junct 37, A4229 towards Porthcawl. After Grove Golf Club right into Moor Ln, follow site signs.* **grid ref:** *SS816789*

A lovely family park close to sea and other attractions, with a lush grass touring field that provides generously sized pitches; most have electric hook-up. There is a smart amenities block appointed to a high standard, a well-stocked shop and WiFi. 4 acre site. 100 touring pitches. 4 hardstandings. 40 seasonal pitches. Caravan pitches. Motorhome pitches. Tent pitches.

Open: Apr-mid Oct **Last arrival:** 19.00hrs **Last departure:** 11.00hrs

Pitches: * £14-£26 £14-£26 £14-£26

Leisure:

Facilities:

Services:

Within 3 miles:

Notes: Dogs must be kept on leads. Free electrical sockets, undercover picnic area, baby changing facility.

AA Pubs & Restaurants nearby: Prince of Wales Inn, KENFIG, CF33 4PR, 01656 740356

CARMARTHENSHIRE

LLANDOVERY Map 9 SN73

Places to visit

Dolaucothi Gold Mines, PUMSAINT, SA19 8US, 01558 650177 www.nationaltrust.org.uk/main/w-dolaucothigoldmines

PREMIER PARK

Erwlon Caravan & Camping Park

►►►►► 85%

tel: 01550 721021 & 720332 **Brecon Rd SA20 0RD**
email: peter@erwlon.co.uk **web:** www.erwlon.co.uk
dir: *0.5m E of Llandovery on A40.* **grid ref:** *SN776343*

A long-established, family-run site set beside a brook in the Brecon Beacons foothills. The town of Llandovery and the hills overlooking the Towy Valley are a short walk away. The superb, Scandinavian-style facilities block has cubicled washrooms, family and disabled rooms and is an impressive feature. 8 acre site. 75 touring pitches. 15 hardstandings. Caravan pitches. Motorhome pitches. Tent pitches.

Open: all year **Last arrival:** anytime **Last departure:** noon

Pitches:

Leisure:

Facilities:

Services:

Within 3 miles:

Notes: Quiet after 22.30hrs. Dogs must be kept on leads. Fishing, cycle storage & hire.

AA Pubs & Restaurants nearby: The Kings Head, LLANDOVERY, SA20 0AB, 01550 720393

LEISURE: Indoor swimming pool Outdoor swimming pool Children's playground Kid's club Tennis court Games room Separate TV room golf course Boats for hire Cinema Entertainment Fishing Mini golf Watersports Gym Sports field Spa Stables
FACILITIES: Bath Shower Electric shaver Hairdryer Ice Pack Facility Disabled facilities Public telephone Shop on site or within 200yds Mobile shop (calls at least 5 days a week) BBQ area Picnic area Wi-fi Internet access Recycling Tourist info Dog exercise area

Llandovery Caravan Park

►►► 77%

tel: 01550 721065 & 07970 650606 **Church Bank SA20 0DT**
email: llandoverycaravanpark@gmail.com
dir: *A40 from Carmarthen, over rail crossing, past junct with A483 (Builth Wells). Turn right for Llangadog, past church, 1st right signed Rugby Club & Camping.*
grid ref: *SN762342*

Within easy walking distance of the town centre and adjacent to the notable Llandovery Dragons Rugby Club, this constantly improving park is an ideal base for touring the Brecon Beacons and many local attractions. Most pitches have both water and a hardstanding, and guests are welcome to use the popular on-site rugby club lounge bar. Please note a laundry is not provided but there is one in the town. 8 acre site. 100 touring pitches. 10 hardstandings. 60 seasonal pitches. Caravan pitches. Motorhome pitches. Tent pitches.

Open: all year **Last arrival:** 20.00hrs **Last departure:** 20.00hrs

Pitches: **Leisure:**

Facilities:

Services:

Within 3 miles:

Notes: Dogs must be kept on leads.

AA Pubs & Restaurants nearby: The Kings Head, LLANDOVERY, SA20 0AB, 01550 720393

LLANGADOG — Map 9 SN72

Places to visit

Dinefwr Park and Castle, LLANDEILO, SA19 6RT, 01558 823902
www.nationaltrust.org.uk/dinefwrpark

Carreg Cennen Castle, CARREG CENNEN CASTLE, SA19 6UA, 01558 822291
www.cadw.wales.gov.uk

Abermarlais Caravan Park

►►► 78%

tel: 01550 777868 & 777797 **SA19 9NG**
dir: *On A40 midway between Llandovery & Llandeilo, 1.5m NW of Llangadog.*
grid ref: *SN695298*

An attractive, well-run site with a welcoming atmosphere. This part-level, part-sloping park is in a wooded valley on the edge of the Brecon Beacons National Park, beside the River Marlais. 17 acre site. 88 touring pitches. 2 hardstandings. Caravan pitches. Motorhome pitches. Tent pitches.

Open: 15 Mar-15 Nov (rs Mar & Nov 1 toilet block, water point - no hot water)
Last arrival: 23.00hrs **Last departure:** noon

Pitches: * fr £8 fr £8 fr £8

Leisure:

Facilities:

Services:

Within 3 miles:

Notes: No open fires, quiet from 23.00hrs-08.00hrs. Dogs must be kept on leads. Volleyball, badminton court, softball tennis net.

AA Pubs & Restaurants nearby: The Angel Hotel, LLANDEILO, SA19 6EN, 01558 822765
The Kings Head, LLANDOVERY, SA20 0AB, 01550 720393

LLANGENNECH — Map 8 SN50

Places to visit

WWT LLanelli Wetland Centre, LLANELLI, SA14 9SH, 01554 741087
www.wwt.org.uk/wetland-centres/llanelli/

South Wales Caravan Park

►►► 91%

tel: 01554 820420 **Llwynifan Farm SA14 8AX**
email: info@southwalescaravanpark.com
dir: *M4 junct 48, A4138 signed Llanelli. In 11.5m right at rdbt. In 425yds left between bungalows into farm road.* **grid ref:** *SN554027*

This site is located in an elevated position close to Llanelli. The touring pitches, including 10 that are fully serviced, are on three terraced levels providing stunning countryside views. The grounds are immaculately maintained with a wide variety of trees, shrubs and pretty seasonal flowers, and a very well-equipped gym is also available. A same-day laundry service is provided too. Excellent customer care is assured; hands-on management from owners Cathrin and Hywel Davies means that visitors will have a memorable stay. 5 acre site. 27 touring pitches. 27 hardstandings. Caravan pitches. Motorhome pitches.

Open: Feb-Nov **Last arrival:** 19.00hrs **Last departure:** noon

Pitches: £15.50-£23 £15.50-£23

Leisure:

Facilities:

Services:

Within 3 miles:

Notes: Adults only. No noise after 22.00hrs. Dogs must be kept on leads.

NEWCASTLE EMLYN Map 8 SN34

Places to visit

Cilgerran Castle, CILGERRAN, SA43 2SF, 01239 621339 www.cadw.wales.gov.uk

Castell Henllys Iron Age Fort, CRYMYCH, SA41 3UT, 01239 891319 www.castellhenllys.com

PREMIER PARK

Cenarth Falls Holiday Park

►►►►► 88%

Best of British

tel: 01239 710345 **Cenarth SA38 9JS**
email: enquiries@cenarth-holipark.co.uk **web:** www.cenarth-holipark.co.uk
dir: *From Newcastle Emlyn on A484 towards Cardigan. Through Cenarth, site on right.*
grid ref: *SN265421*

Located close to the village of Cenarth where the River Teifi, famous for its salmon and trout fishing, cascades through the Cenarth Falls Gorge. With beautifully landscaped grounds and spotless amenities, the park also benefits from an indoor heated swimming pool, sauna, fitness suite and a restaurant with bar. 2 acre site. 30 touring pitches. 30 hardstandings. Caravan pitches. Motorhome pitches. Tent pitches. 89 statics.

Open: Mar-Nov (rs Off peak bar & meals restricted to wknds only)
Last arrival: 20.00hrs **Last departure:** 11.00hrs

Pitches: * £18-£28 £18-£28 £18-£28

Leisure:

Facilities:

Services:

Within 3 miles:

Notes: No skateboards. Dogs must be kept on leads. Pool table.

AA Pubs & Restaurants nearby: Nags Head Inn, ABERCYCH, SA37 0HJ, 01239 841200

Moelfryn Caravan & Camping Park

►►►► 86%

tel: 01559 371231 **Ty-Cefn, Pant-y-Bwlch SA38 9JE**
email: info@moelfryncaravanpark.co.uk
dir: *A484 from Carmarthen towards Cynwyl Elfed. Pass the shops on right, 200yds take left fork onto B4333 towards Hermon. In 7m follow brown sign on left. Turn left, site on right.* **grid ref:** *SN321370*

A small, beautifully maintained, family-run park in a glorious elevated location overlooking the valley of the River Teifi. Pitches are level and spacious, and well screened by hedging and mature trees. The centrally located amenities block has stylish decor, smart cladding, provision of good privacy options and excellent fixtures and fittings. 3 acre site. 25 touring pitches. 18 hardstandings. 12 seasonal pitches. Caravan pitches. Motorhome pitches. Tent pitches.

Open: Mar-10 Jan **Last arrival:** 22.00hrs **Last departure:** noon

Pitches: * £14-£18 £14-£18 £13-£16

Leisure:

Facilities:

Services:

Within 3 miles:

Notes: Games to be played in designated area only. Dogs must be kept on leads. Caravan storage.

AA Pubs & Restaurants nearby: Nags Head Inn, ABERCYCH, SA37 0HJ, 01239 841200

Webley Waterfront Inn & Hotel, ST DOGMAELS, SA43 3LN, 01239 612085

Argoed Meadow Caravan and Camping Site

►►►► 82%

tel: 01239 710690 **Argoed Farm SA38 9JL**
email: argoedfarm@btinternet.com **web:** www.cenarthcampsite.co.uk
dir: *From Newcastle Emlyn on A484 towards Cenarth, take B4332. Site 300yds on right.*
grid ref: *SN268415*

A warm welcome is assured at this attractive and immaculately maintained site, situated on the banks of the River Teifi and close to Cenarth Falls Gorge. The spotlessly clean amenities block provides very good privacy options for the less able visitors. 3 acre site. 30 touring pitches. 5 hardstandings. Caravan pitches. Motorhome pitches. Tent pitches. 5 statics.

Open: all year **Last arrival:** anytime **Last departure:** noon

Pitches:

Facilities:

Services:

Within 3 miles:

Notes: No bikes or skateboards. Dogs must be kept on leads.

AA Pubs & Restaurants nearby: Nags Head Inn, ABERCYCH, SA37 0HJ, 01239 841200

Webley Waterfront Inn & Hotel, ST DOGMAELS, SA43 3LN, 01239 612085

Afon Teifi Caravan & Camping Park

►►►► 80%

tel: 01559 370532 **Pentrecagal SA38 9HT**
email: afonteifi@btinternet.com **web:** www.afonteifi.co.uk
dir: *Signed from A484, 2m E of Newcastle Emlyn.* **grid ref:** *SN338405*

Set on the banks of the River Teifi, a famous salmon and sea trout river, this secluded, family-owned and run park has good views. It is only two miles from the market town of Newcastle Emlyn. The smart amenities block is appointed to a high standard. 6 acre site. 110 touring pitches. 22 hardstandings. 25 seasonal pitches. Caravan pitches. Motorhome pitches. Tent pitches. 15 statics.

Open: Apr-Oct **Last arrival:** 23.00hrs

Pitches: * £20-£22 £20-£22 £10-£22

Leisure:

Facilities:

Services:

Within 3 miles:

Notes: No noise after mdnt, no bikes or scooters after dark. Dogs must be kept on leads.

AA Pubs & Restaurants nearby: Nags Head Inn, ABERCYCH, SA37 0HJ, 01239 841200

Webley Waterfront Inn & Hotel, ST DOGMAELS, SA43 3LN, 01239 612085

CEREDIGION

ABERAERON — Map 8 SN46

Places to visit

Llanerchaeron, ABERAERON, SA48 8DG, 01545 570200 www.nationaltrust.org.uk

Aeron Coast Caravan Park

►►► 90%

tel: 01545 570349 **North Rd SA46 0JF**
email: enquiries@aeroncoast.co.uk
dir: *On A487 (coast road), N outskirts of Aberaeron, signed. Filling station at entrance.*
grid ref: *SN460631*

A well-managed family holiday park on the edge of the attractive resort of Aberaeron, with direct access to the beach. The spacious pitches are all level. On-site facilities include an extensive outdoor pool complex, a multi-activity outdoor sports area, an indoor children's play area, a small lounge bar which serves food, a games room and an entertainment suite. 22 acre site. 100 touring pitches. 30 hardstandings. Caravan pitches. Motorhome pitches. Tent pitches. 200 statics.

Open: Mar-Oct **Last arrival:** 23.00hrs **Last departure:** 11.00hrs

Pitches:

Leisure:

Facilities:

Services:

Within 3 miles:

Notes: Families only, no motorcycles. Dogs must be kept on leads.

AA Pubs & Restaurants nearby: The Harbourmaster, ABERAERON, SA46 0BT, 01545 570755

Ty Mawr Mansion, ABERAERON, SA48 8DB, 01570 470033

Who has won Campsite of the Year for Wales?
See page 15

ABERYSTWYTH Map 8 SN58

Places to visit

The National Library of Wales, ABERYSTWYTH, SY23 3BU, 01970 632565 www.llgc.org.uk

Vale of Rheidol Railway, ABERYSTWYTH, SY23 1PG, 01970 625819 www.rheidolrailway.co.uk

Ocean View Caravan Park

►►► 82%

tel: 01970 828425 & 623361 **North Beach, Clarach Bay SY23 3DT**
email: enquiries@oceanviewholidays.com
dir: *In Bow Street village on A487 follow Clarach sign. In Llangorwen Clarach straight on at next x-rds. Site 2nd on right.* **grid ref:** *SN592842*

This site is in a sheltered valley on gently sloping ground, with wonderful views of both the sea and the countryside. The beach of Clarach Bay is just 200 yards away, and this welcoming park is ideal for all the family. There is a children's football field and dog walking area. Campers may use the pool, gym, restaurant and bar at Clarach Bay which is within walking distance of the site. 9 acre site. 24 touring pitches. 15 hardstandings. 20 seasonal pitches. Caravan pitches. Motorhome pitches. Tent pitches. 56 statics.

Open: Mar-Oct **Last arrival:** 20.00hrs **Last departure:** noon

Pitches: * £18-£23 £18-£23 **Leisure:**

Facilities:

Services: **Within 3 miles:**

Notes: Dogs must be kept on leads.

BORTH Map 14 SN69

Places to visit

The National Library of Wales, ABERYSTWYTH, SY23 3BU, 01970 632565 www.llgc.org.uk

Brynowen Holiday Park

HOLIDAY CENTRE 77%

tel: 01970 871366 **SY24 5LS**
email: brynowen@park-resorts.com
dir: *Signed from B4353, S of Borth.* **grid ref:** *SN608893*

Enjoying spectacular views across Cardigan Bay and the Cambrian Mountains, this is a small touring park in a large and well-equipped holiday centre. The well-run park offers a wide range of organised activities and entertainment for all the family from morning until late in the evening. The Boathouse Bar & Restaurant was refurbished for the 2015 season. A long sandy beach is a few minutes' drive away. 52 acre site. 16 touring pitches. 16 hardstandings. 4 seasonal pitches. Caravan pitches. Motorhome pitches. 480 statics.

Open: Apr-Oct **Last arrival:** mdnt **Last departure:** 10.00hrs

Pitches: **Leisure:**

Facilities:

Services: **Within 3 miles:**

Notes: No cars by caravans. Dogs must be kept on leads. Mini ten-pin bowling.

NEW QUAY Map 8 SN35

Places to visit

Llanerchaeron, ABERAERON, SA48 8DG, 01545 570200 www.nationaltrust.org.uk

Quay West Holiday Park

HOLIDAY HOME PARK 86%

tel: 01545 560477 **SA45 9SE**
email: quaywest@haven.com **web:** www.haven.com/quaywest
dir: *From Cardigan on A487 left onto A486 into New Quay. Or from Aberystwyth on A487 right onto B4342 into New Quay.* **grid ref:** *SN397591*

This holiday park enjoys a stunning clifftop position overlooking picturesque New Quay and Cardigan Bay. It's an easy walk to a glorious sandy beach, and the all-action on-site activities include heated swimming pools, SplashZone, football, archery and fencing (with professional tuition), the Aqua Bar and terrace, and a new kiddies' Pic 'n' Paint room was added in 2015. There is a good range of holiday caravans.

Open: Mar-Oct

Change over day: Mon, Fri, Sat

Arrival and departure times: Please contact the site

Statics: 125 Sleeps 6-8 Bedrms 2-3 Bathrms 1-2 Toilets 1-2 Microwave Freezer TV Sky/FTV Elec inc Gas inc Grass area

Children: Cots Highchair **Dogs:** 2 on leads No dangerous dogs

Leisure: Cycle hire

CONWY

BETWS-YN-RHOS Map 14 SH97

Places to visit

Bodelwyddan Castle, BODELWYDDAN, LL18 5YA, 01745 584060 www.bodelwyddan-castle.co.uk

Bodnant Garden, TAL-Y-CAFN, LL28 5RE, 01492 650460 www.nationaltrust.org.uk/bodnant-garden

Hunters Hamlet Caravan Park

►►►► 85%

tel: 01745 832237 & 07721 552106 **Sirior Goch Farm LL22 8PL**
email: huntershamlet@aol.com
dir: *From A55 W'bound, A547 junct 24 into Abergele. At 2nd lights turn left by George & Dragon pub, onto A548. 2.75m right at x-rds onto B5381. Site 0.5m on left.*
grid ref: *SH928736*

A warm welcome is assured at this long established, family-run working farm park adjacent to the owners' Georgian farmhouse. Well-spaced pitches, including 15 with water, electricity and TV hook-up, are within two attractive hedge-screened grassy paddocks. The well-maintained amenities block, includes unisex bathrooms. Please note that this site does not accept tents. 2 acre site. 30 touring pitches. 30 hardstandings. Caravan pitches. Motorhome pitches.

Open: Mar-Oct **Last arrival:** 22.00hrs **Last departure:** noon

Pitches: * £18-£29 £18-£29

Leisure:

LEISURE: Indoor swimming pool Outdoor swimming pool Children's playground Kid's club Tennis court Games room Separate TV room golf course Boats for hire Cinema Entertainment Fishing Mini golf Watersports Gym Sports field Spa Stables **FACILITIES:** Bath Shower Electric shaver Hairdryer Ice Pack Facility Disabled facilities Public telephone Shop on site or within 200yds Mobile shop (calls at least 5 days a week) BBQ area Picnic area Wi-fi Internet access Recycling Tourist info Dog exercise area

Facilities:

Services:

Within 3 miles:

Notes: No football, dogs must not be left unattended. Dogs must be kept on leads. Baby bath & changing facilities.

AA Pubs & Restaurants nearby: The Hawk & Buckle Inn, LLANNEFYDD, LL16 5ED, 01745 540249

The Kinmel Arms, ABERGELE, LL22 9BP, 01745 832207

Plas Farm Caravan Park

►►►► 85%

DAVID BELLAMY CONSERVATION AWARD GOLD

tel: 01492 680254 & 07831 482176 **LL22 8AU**
email: info@plasfarmcaravanpark.co.uk **web:** www.plasfarmcaravanpark.co.uk
dir: *A55 junct 24, A547 through Abergele, straight on at 2 mini rdbts, follow Rhyd-Y-Foel signs, 3m. Left, follow signs.* **grid ref:** *SH897744*

Ideally located for exploring the many attractions of north Wales and within easy travelling distance of historic Chester, this beautifully landscaped park, adjacent to a 16th-century farmhouse, is certainly a popular choice. Major investment within recent years has resulted in superb pitches, many fully serviced on terraced area; the camping area sited in woodland ensures tranquillity and relaxation, with only birdsong to disturb the peace. There are two modern amenities blocks, a good laundry and a well-equipped campers' kitchen. 10 acre site. 54 touring pitches. 54 hardstandings. Caravan pitches. Motorhome pitches. Tent pitches.

Open: Mar-Oct **Last arrival:** 19.00hrs **Last departure:** 11.00hrs

Pitches: £19.50-£29.50 £19.50-£29.50 £10-£25

Leisure:

Facilities:

Services:

Within 3 miles:

Notes: Quiet after 23.00hrs, no campfires, no large groups. Dogs must be kept on leads. Woodland walk.

AA Pubs & Restaurants nearby: The Kinmel Arms, ABERGELE, LL22 9BP, 01745 832207

LLANDDULAS

Map 14 SH97

Places to visit

Rhuddlan Castle, RHUDDLAN, LL18 5AD, 01745 590777 www.cadw.wales.gov.uk

Bodelwyddan Castle, BODELWYDDAN, LL18 5YA, 01745 584060 www.bodelwyddan-castle.co.uk

PREMIER PARK

Bron-Y-Wendon Caravan Park

►►►►► 86%

tel: 01492 512903 **Wern Rd LL22 8HG**
email: stay@northwales-holidays.co.uk
dir: *Take A55 W. Right at Llanddulas & A547 junct 23 sign, sharp right. 200yds, under A55 bridge. Park on left.* **grid ref:** *SH903785*

A top quality site in a stunning location, with panoramic sea views from every pitch and excellent purpose-built toilet facilities including heated shower blocks. Pitch density is excellent, offering a high degree of privacy, and the grounds are beautifully landscaped and immaculately maintained. Super pitches are available. Staff are helpful and friendly, and everything from landscaping to maintenance has a stamp of excellence. An ideal seaside base for touring Snowdonia and visiting Colwyn Bay, Llandudno and Conwy. 8 acre site. 130 touring pitches. 110 hardstandings. Caravan pitches. Motorhome pitches.

Open: all year **Last arrival:** anytime **Last departure:** 11.00hrs

Pitches: * £21-£25 £21-£25

Leisure:

Facilities:

Services:

Within 3 miles:

Notes: Dogs must be kept on leads.

AA Pubs & Restaurants nearby: Pen-y-Bryn, COLWYN BAY, LL29 6DD, 01492 533360

Find out about the AA's Pennant rating scheme on pages 10-11

LLANRWST Map 14 SH86

Places to visit

Gwydir Uchaf Chapel, LLANRWST, 01443 336000 www.cadw.wales.gov.uk

Trefriw Woollen Mills, TREFRIW, LL27 0NQ, 01492 640462 www.t-w-m.co.uk

Great for kids: Conwy Valley Railway Museum, BETWS-Y-COED, LL24 0AL, 01690 710568 www.conwyrailwaymuseum.co.uk

PREMIER PARK

Bron Derw Touring Caravan Park

►►►►► 85%

tel: 01492 640494 **LL26 0YT**
email: bronderw@aol.com **web:** www.bronderw-wales.co.uk
dir: *A55 onto A470 for Betws-y-Coed & Llanrwst. In Llanrwst left into Parry Rd signed Llanddoged. Left at T-junct, site signed at 1st farm entrance on right.*
grid ref: *SH798628*

A previous AA campsite award winner, Bron Derw, once a dairy farm, is beautifully landscaped with stunning floral displays and surrounded by hills. The park has been built to a very high standard and is fully matured. All pitches are fully serviced, and there is a heated, stone-built toilet block with excellent and immaculately maintained facilities. The Parc Derwen adults-only field has 28 fully serviced pitches and its own designated amenities block. CCTV security cameras cover the whole park. 4.5 acre site. 48 touring pitches. 48 hardstandings. 17 seasonal pitches. Caravan pitches. Motorhome pitches.

Open: Mar-Oct **Last arrival:** 22.00hrs **Last departure:** 11.00hrs

Pitches: * £21-£23 £21-£23

Facilities:

Services:

Within 3 miles:

Notes: Children must be supervised, no bikes, scooters or skateboards. Dogs must be kept on leads.

AA Pubs & Restaurants nearby: Ty Gwyn Inn, BETWS-Y-COED, LL24 0SG, 01690 710383

The Old Ship, TREFRIW, LL27 0JH, 01492 640013

Bodnant Caravan Park

►►►► 84%

tel: 01492 640248 **Nebo Rd LL26 0SD**
email: ermin@bodnant-caravan-park.co.uk
dir: *S in Llanrwst, at lights exit A470 opposite Birmingham garage onto B5427 signed Nebo. Site 300yds on right, opposite leisure centre.* **grid ref:** *SH805609*

This well maintained and stunningly attractive park is filled with flower beds, and the landscape includes shrubberies and trees. The statics are unobtrusively sited and the quality, spotlessly clean toilet blocks have fully serviced private cubicles. All caravan pitches are multi-service, and the tent pitches serviced. There is a separate playing field and rally field, and there are lots of farm animals on the park to keep children entertained, and Victorian farming implements are on display around the touring fields. 5 acre site. 54 touring pitches. 20 hardstandings. Caravan pitches. Motorhome pitches. Tent pitches. 2 statics.

Open: Mar-end Oct **Last arrival:** 21.00hrs **Last departure:** 11.00hrs

Pitches: * £19.50-£20.50 £19.50-£20.50 £15.50-£18.50

Facilities:

Services:

Within 3 miles:

Notes: No bikes, skateboards or camp fires, main gates locked 23.00hrs-08.00hrs, no noise after 23.00hrs. Dogs must be kept on leads.

AA Pubs & Restaurants nearby: Ty Gwyn Inn, BETWS-Y-COED, LL24 0SG, 01690 710383

The Old Ship, TREFRIW, LL27 0JH, 01492 640013

TAL-Y-BONT (NEAR CONWY) Map 14 SH76

Places to visit

Bodnant Garden, TAL-Y-CAFN, LL28 5RE, 01492 650460 www.nationaltrust.org.uk/bodnant-garden

Great for kids: Smallest House, CONWY, LL32 8BB, 07925 049786 www.thesmallesthouseingreatbritain.co.uk

Tynterfyn Touring Caravan Park

► 89%

tel: 01492 660525 **LL32 8YX**
email: info@tynterfyn.co.uk
dir: *5m S of Conwy on B5106, signed Tal-y-Bont, 1st on left.* **grid ref:** *SH768695*

A quiet, secluded little park set in the beautiful Conwy Valley, and run by family owners. The grounds are tended with care, and the older-style toilet facilities sparkle. There is lots of room for children and dogs to run around. 2 acre site. 15 touring pitches. 4 hardstandings. Caravan pitches. Motorhome pitches. Tent pitches.

Open: Mar-Oct (rs 28 days in year tent pitches only) **Last arrival:** 22.00hrs
Last departure: noon

Pitches: **Leisure:**

Facilities:

Services:

Within 3 miles:

Notes: Dogs must be kept on leads.

AA Pubs & Restaurants nearby: The Old Ship, TREFRIW, LL27 0JH, 01492 640013

TOWYN (NEAR ABERGELE) Map 14 SH97

Places to visit

Rhuddlan Castle, RHUDDLAN, LL18 5AD, 01745 590777 www.cadw.wales.gov.uk

Bodelwyddan Castle, BODELWYDDAN, LL18 5YA, 01745 584060 www.bodelwyddan-castle.co.uk

Great for kids: Welsh Mountain Zoo, COLWYN BAY, LL28 5UY, 01492 532938 www.welshmountainzoo.org

Ty Mawr Holiday Park

HOLIDAY CENTRE 76%

tel: 01745 832079 **Towyn Rd LL22 9HG**
email: holiday.sales@park-resorts.com **web:** www.park-resorts.com
dir: *On A548, 0.25m W of Towyn.* **grid ref:** *SH965792*

Located between Chester and the Isle of Anglesey and close to many attractions including the lively resort of Rhyl. This is a very large coastal holiday park with extensive leisure facilities including sports and recreational amenities. The touring areas are on two level, grassy fields and all amenities blocks are centrally located. The entertainment facilities are ideal for both adults and families, and a choice of eating outlets is available, including the stylish Boathouse Bar & Restaurant. 18 acre site. 406 touring pitches. Caravan pitches. Motorhome pitches. Tent pitches. 464 statics.

Open: Apr-Oct (rs Apr (excl Etr)) **Last arrival:** mdnt **Last departure:** 10.00hrs

Pitches:

Leisure:

Facilities:

Services:

Within 3 miles:

Notes: Newcomers not accepted after 18:00hrs unless pre-booked. Dogs must be kept on leads.

DENBIGHSHIRE

PRESTATYN

Places to visit

Basingwerk Abbey, HOLYWELL, CH8 7GH, 01443 336000 www.cadw.wales.gov.uk

Great for kids: Rhuddlan Castle, RHUDDLAN, LL18 5AD, 01745 590777 www.cadw.wales.gov.uk

PRESTATYN Map 15 SJ08

Presthaven Sands Holiday Park

HOLIDAY CENTRE 83%

David Bellamy Conservation Award GOLD

tel: 0800 389 0396 **Gronant LL19 9TT**
email: presthavensands@haven.com **web:** www.haven.com/presthavensands
dir: *A548 from Prestatyn towards Gronant. Site signed. (NB for Sat Nav use LL19 9ST).*
grid ref: *SJ091842*

Set beside two miles of superb sandy beaches and dunes (with donkeys on site at weekends) this constantly improving holiday park provides a wide range of both indoor and outdoor attractions. The site can boast happy returning visitors. The small touring field at the park entrance offers good electric pitches – the majority are hardstandings and include five super pitches. The centrally located entertainment area includes two indoor swimming pools, excellent children's activities and a choice of eating outlets. 21 acre site. 34 touring pitches. 33 hardstandings. Caravan pitches. Motorhome pitches. 1052 statics.

Open: mid Mar-end Oct (rs mid Mar-May & Sep-Oct facilities may be reduced)
Last arrival: 20.00hrs **Last departure:** 10.00hrs

Pitches: **Leisure:**

Facilities:

Services:

Within 3 miles:

Notes: No commercial vehicles, no bookings by persons under 21yrs unless a family booking, max 2 dogs per booking, certain dog breeds banned. Dogs must be kept on leads.

See advert on page 424

RHUALLT Map 15 SJ07

Places to visit

Rhuddlan Castle, RHUDDLAN, LL18 5AD, 01745 590777 www.cadw.wales.gov.uk

Bodelwyddan Castle, BODELWYDDAN, LL18 5YA, 01745 584060 www.bodelwyddan-castle.co.uk

Great for kids: Denbigh Castle, DENBIGH, LL16 3NB, 01745 813385 www.cadw.wales.gov.uk

Penisar Mynydd Caravan Park

►►►► 90%

tel: 01745 582227 & 07831 408017 **Caerwys Rd LL17 0TY**
email: contact@penisarmynydd.co.uk
dir: *From A55 junct 29 follow Dyserth & brown caravan signs. Site 500yds on right.*
grid ref: *SJ093770*

A very tranquil, attractively laid-out park set in three grassy paddocks with superb facilities block including a disabled room and dishwashing area. The majority of pitches are super pitches. Immaculately maintained throughout, the park is within easy reach of historic Chester and the seaside resort of Rhyl. 6.6 acre site. 71 touring pitches. 71 hardstandings. Caravan pitches. Motorhome pitches. Tent pitches.

Open: Mar-15 Jan **Last arrival:** 21.00hrs **Last departure:** 21.00hrs

Pitches: * £15-£17 £15-£17 fr £12

Leisure:

Facilities:

Services:

Within 3 miles:

Notes: No cycling, no fires. Dogs must be kept on leads. Rally area.

AA Pubs & Restaurants nearby: The Plough Inn, ST ASAPH, LL17 0LU, 01745 585080

RUABON Map 15 SJ34

Places to visit

Plas Newydd, LLANGOLLEN, LL20 8AW, 01978 861314 www.denbighshire.gov.uk

Valle Crucis Abbey, LLANGOLLEN, LL20 8DD, 01978 860326 www.cadw.wales.gov.uk

Great for kids: Horse Drawn Boats Centre, LLANGOLLEN, LL20 8TA, 01978 860702 www.horsedrawnboats.co.uk

James' Caravan Park

►►► 75%

tel: 01978 820148 **LL14 6DW**
email: ray@carastay.demon.co.uk
dir: *From Oswestry on A483 take slip road signed Llangollen & A539. At rdbt left onto A539 towards Llangollen. Site 500yds on left. Or from Wrexham on A483 follow Llangollen & A539 signs. Right at rdbt onto A539, at next rdbt straight on, site on left.*
grid ref: *SJ300434*

A well-landscaped park on a former farm, with modern heated toilet facilities. Old farm buildings house a collection of restored original farm machinery, and the village shop, four pubs, takeaway and launderette are a 10-minute walk away. 6 acre site. 40 touring pitches. 4 hardstandings. Caravan pitches. Motorhome pitches.

Open: all year **Last arrival:** 21.00hrs **Last departure:** 11.00hrs

Pitches:

Facilities:

Services:

Within 3 miles:

Notes: No fires. Dogs must be kept on leads. Chest freezer available.

AA Pubs & Restaurants nearby: The Boat Inn, ERBISTOCK, LL13 0DL, 01978 780666

GWYNEDD

ABERSOCH — Map 14 SH32

Places to visit

Plas-yn-Rhiw, PLAS YN RHIW, LL53 8AB, 01758 780219 www.nationaltrust.org.uk

Penarth Fawr, PENARTH FAWR, 01443 336000 www.cadw.wales.gov.uk

Deucoch Touring & Camping Park

►►►► 85%

tel: 01758 713293 & 07740 281770 **Sarn Bach LL53 7LD**
email: info@deucoch.com
dir: *From Abersoch take Sarn Bach road, at x-rds turn right, site on right in 800yds.*
grid ref: *SH301269*

A colourful, sheltered site with stunning views of Cardigan Bay and the mountains, and situated just a mile from Abersoch and a long sandy beach. The friendly, enthusiastic, hands-on proprietors make year-on-year improvements to enhance their visitors' experience. Facilities include outside hot showers, a superb dish-washing facility, housed in an attractive log cabin, and caravan repairs. 5 acre site. 70 touring pitches. 10 hardstandings. Caravan pitches. Motorhome pitches. Tent pitches.

Open: Mar-Oct **Last arrival:** 20.00hrs **Last departure:** 11.00hrs

Pitches: **Leisure:**

Facilities:

Services:

Within 3 miles:

Notes: Families only. Dogs must be kept on leads.

AA Pubs & Restaurants nearby: Porth Tocyn Hotel, ABERSOCH, LL53 7BU, 01758 713303

Beach View Caravan Park

►►►► 83%

tel: 01758 712956 **Bwlchtocyn LL53 7BT**
email: enquiries@beachviewholidaypark.co.uk
dir: *A499 to Abersoch. Through Abersoch, through Sarn Bach. Straight on at x-rds, next left signed Porth Tocyn Hotel. Pass chapel. Left at next Porth Tocyn Hotel sign. Site on left.*
grid ref: *SH316262*

A compact family park run by a very enthusiastic owner who makes continual improvements. Just a six-minute walk from the beach, the site's immaculately maintained grounds, good hardstanding pitches (mostly seasonal) and excellent facilities are matched by great sea and country views. 4 acre site. 47 touring pitches. 47 hardstandings. 40 seasonal pitches. Caravan pitches. Motorhome pitches. Tent pitches.

Open: mid Mar-mid Oct **Last arrival:** 19.00hrs **Last departure:** 11.00hrs

Pitches:

Facilities:

Services:

Within 3 miles:

Notes: Dogs must be kept on leads.

AA Pubs & Restaurants nearby: Porth Tocyn Hotel, ABERSOCH, LL53 7BU, 01758 713303

Tyn-y-Mur Touring & Camping

►►► 86%

tel: 01758 712328 **Lon Garmon LL53 7UL**
email: info@tyn-y-mur.co.uk **web:** www.tyn-y-mur.co.uk
dir: *From Pwllheli into Abersoch on A499, sharp right at Land & Sea Garage. Site approx 0.5m on left.* **grid ref:** *SH304290*

A family-only park in a glorious hill-top location overlooking a lush valley and with views extending across Abersoch to the mountains beyond Cardigan Bay. Good, clean, modern toilet facilities and spacious tent pitches in a level grassy field are on offer. A pretty shrub and flower display at the entrance surrounds a ship's anchor recovered from a Royal Navy frigate, which was lost it in the bay in 1948. There is a pathway from the site to private river fishing, and the beach at Abersoch is just a short walk away. The park offers boat storage facilities. 22 acre site. 90 touring pitches. 42 hardstandings. 42 seasonal pitches. Caravan pitches. Motorhome pitches. Tent pitches.

Open: Apr-Oct **Last arrival:** 22.00hrs **Last departure:** 11.00hrs

Pitches:

Leisure:

Facilities:

Services:

Within 3 miles:

Notes: No open fires, no motorcycles, no noisy activity after 23.00hrs, 1 dog per unit. Dogs must be kept on leads.

AA Pubs & Restaurants nearby: Porth Tocyn Hotel, ABERSOCH, LL53 7BU, 01758 713303

Bryn Bach Caravan & Camping Site

►►► 81%

tel: 01758 712285 & 07789 390808 **Tyddyn Talgoch Uchaf, Bwlchtocyn LL53 7BT**
email: brynbach@abersochcamping.co.uk
dir: *From Abersoch take Sarn Bach road for approx 1m, left at sign for Bwlchtocyn. Site approx 1m on left.* **grid ref:** *SH315258*

This well-run, elevated park overlooks Abersoch Bay, with lovely sea views towards the Snowdonia mountain range. Pitches are well laid out in sheltered paddocks, with well-placed modern facilities. Fishing, watersports and golf are all nearby. The site has a private shortcut to the beach. 4 acre site. 34 touring pitches. 1 hardstanding. 30 seasonal pitches. Caravan pitches. Motorhome pitches. Tent pitches. 2 statics.

Open: Mar-Oct **Last arrival:** 20.00hrs **Last departure:** 11.00hrs

Pitches:

Leisure:

Facilities:

Services:

Within 3 miles:

Notes: Families & couples only. Dogs must be kept on leads. Boat & caravan storage.

AA Pubs & Restaurants nearby: Porth Tocyn Hotel, ABERSOCH, LL53 7BU, 01758 713303

ABERSOCH *continued*

Rhydolion

►►► 71%

tel: 01758 712342 **Llangian LL53 7LR**
email: enquiries@rhydolion.co.uk
dir: *From A499 take unclassified road to Llangian for 1m, left, through Llangian. Site 1.5m after road forks towards Hell's Mouth & Porth Neigwl.* **grid ref:** *SH283276*

A peaceful small site with good views, on a working farm close to the long sandy surfers beach at Hell's Mouth. The simple toilet facilities are kept to a high standard by the friendly owners, and nearby Abersoch is a mecca for boat owners and water sports enthusiasts. 1.5 acre site. 28 touring pitches. Caravan pitches. Motorhome pitches. Tent pitches.

Open: Mar-Oct **Last arrival:** 22.00hrs **Last departure:** noon

Pitches: * fr £25 fr £25 fr £16

Leisure:

Facilities:

Services:

Within 3 miles:

Notes: Families & couples only. Dogs only accepted by prior arrangement & must be kept on leads. 3 fridge freezers available.

AA Pubs & Restaurants nearby: Porth Tocyn Hotel, ABERSOCH, LL53 7BU, 01758 713303

BALA — Map 14 SH93

Places to visit

Bala Lake Railway, LLANUWCHLLYN, LL23 7DD, 01678 540666
www.bala-lake-railway.co.uk

Pen-y-Bont Touring Park

►►►► 83%

tel: 01678 520549 **Llangynog Rd LL23 7PH**
email: penybont-bala@btconnect.com
dir: *From A494 take B4391. Site 0.75m on right.* **grid ref:** *SH932350*

A family-run, attractively landscaped park in a woodland country setting. It is set close to Bala Lake and the River Dee with plenty of opportunities for watersports including kayaking and white-water rafting. The park offers good facilities including a motorhome service point, and many pitches have water and electricity. Around the park are superb, large wood carvings of birds and mythical creatures depicting local legends. Two reproduction Romany caravans are available for hire. 6 acre site. 95 touring pitches. 47 hardstandings. 20 seasonal pitches. Caravan pitches. Motorhome pitches. Tent pitches. 2 Romany caravans.

Open: Mar-Oct **Last arrival:** 21.00hrs **Last departure:** noon

Pitches:

Facilities:

Services:

Within 3 miles:

Notes: No camp fires, BBQs must be kept off ground, quiet after 22.30hrs. Dogs must be kept on leads.

Tyn Cornel Camping & Caravan Park

►►►► 80%

tel: 01678 520759 **Frongoch LL23 7NU**
email: tyncornel@mail.com
dir: *From Bala take A4212 Porthmadog road for 4m. Site on left before National White Water Centre.* **grid ref:** *SH895400*

A delightful riverside park with mountain views that is popular with those seeking a base for river kayaking and canoeing – The National White Water Centre is adjacent, and there's a pleasant riverside walk to reach its café. The resident owners are always improving the already very well maintained and colourful grounds. 10 acre site. 67 touring pitches. 12 hardstandings. 14 seasonal pitches. Caravan pitches. Motorhome pitches. Tent pitches.

Open: Etr-Oct **Last arrival:** 20.00hrs **Last departure:** 11.00hrs

Pitches: * £20-£23 £20-£23 £15-£32

Leisure:

Facilities:

Services:

Within 3 miles:

Notes: Quiet after 23.00hrs, no cycling, no camp fires or wood burning. Dogs must be kept on leads. Fridge, freezer & tumble dryer available.

BANGOR — Map 14 SH57

Places to visit

Penrhyn Castle, BANGOR, LL57 4HN, 01248 353084
www.nationaltrust.org.uk/penrhyncastle

Gwynedd Museum, BANGOR, LL57 1DT, 01248 353368
www.gwynedd.gov.uk/museums

Great for kids: GreenWood Forest Park, Y FELINHELI, LL56 4QN, 01248 671493
www.greenwoodforestpark.co.uk

Treborth Hall Farm Caravan Park

►►► 74%

tel: 01248 364399 **The Old Barn, Treborth Hall Farm LL57 2RX**
email: enquiries@treborthleisure.co.uk
dir: *A55 junct 9, 1st left at rdbt, straight over 2nd rdbt, site approx 800yds on left.*
grid ref: *SH554707*

Set in eight acres of beautiful parkland with its own trout fishing lake and golf course, this park offers serviced pitches in a sheltered, walled orchard. Tents have a separate grass area, and there is a good clean toilet block. This is a useful base for families, with easy access for the Menai Straits, Anglesey beaches, Snowdon and the Lleyn peninsula. 8 acre site. 34 touring pitches. 34 hardstandings. Caravan pitches. Motorhome pitches. Tent pitches. 4 statics.

Open: Etr-end Oct **Last arrival:** 22.30hrs **Last departure:** 10.30hrs

Pitches: * £20-£24 £20-£24 £12-£24

Leisure: **Facilities:**

Services: **Within 3 miles:**

Notes: Dogs must be kept on leads.

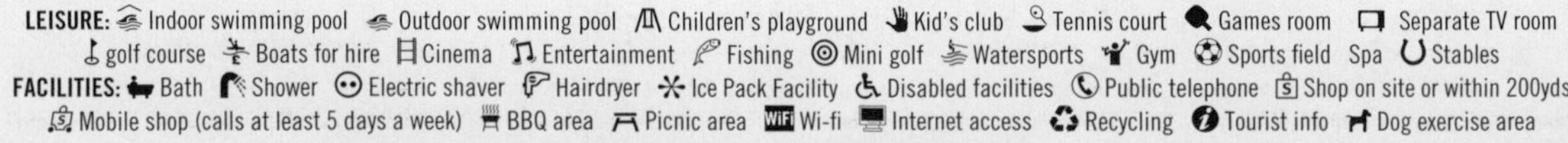

BARMOUTH

Map 14 SH61

Places to visit

Harlech Castle, HARLECH, LL46 2YH, 01766 780552 www.cadw.wales.gov.uk

Cymer Abbey, CYMER ABBEY, LL40 2HE, 01443 336000 www.cadw.wales.gov.uk

PREMIER PARK

Trawsdir Touring Caravans & Camping Park

►►►►► 93%

tel: 01341 280999 **Llanaber LL42 1RR**
email: enquiries@barmouthholidays.co.uk
dir: *3m N of Barmouth on A496, just past Wayside pub on right.* **grid ref:** *SH596198*

Well run by the owners, this quality park enjoys spectacular views to the sea and hills, and is very accessible for motor traffic. The facilities are appointed to a very high standard, and include spacious cubicles containing showers and washbasins, individual showers, smart toilets with sensor-operated flush and under-floor heating. Tents and caravans have their own designated areas divided by dry-stone walls (both have spacious fully serviced pitches), the site is very convenient for large recreational vehicles, and there are eight camping pods for hire. There is an excellent children's play area, plus glorious seasonal floral displays and an illuminated dog walk that leads directly to the nearby pub! 15 acre site. 70 touring pitches. 70 hardstandings. 30 seasonal pitches. Caravan pitches. Motorhome pitches. Tent pitches. 8 wooden pods.

Open: Mar-Jan **Last arrival:** 17.00hrs **Last departure:** 11.00hrs

Pitches: * £18-£35 £18-£35 £12-£30

Leisure:

Facilities:

Services:

Within 3 miles:

Notes: Families & couples only. Dogs must be kept on leads. Milk, bread etc available from reception, takeaway food can be delivered from sister site.

AA Pubs & Restaurants nearby: Victoria Inn, LLANBEDR, LL45 2LD, 01341 241213

PREMIER PARK

Hendre Mynach Touring Caravan & Camping Park

►►►►► 86%

tel: 01341 280262 **Llanaber Rd LL42 1YR**
email: info@hendremynach.co.uk **web:** www.hendremynach.co.uk
dir: *0.75m N of Barmouth on A496.* **grid ref:** *SH605170*

A constantly improving site where the enthusiastic owners invest year on year to enhance the customer experience. Although there is a steep decent to the arrivals' area, staff are always on hand to assist. The beautifully maintained touring areas benefit from attractive hedge screening around the large well-spaced pitches that are equipped with water and TV hook-ups. There is direct access to the seafront which leads to the town centre and its many attractions. 10 acre site. 240 touring pitches. 75 hardstandings. 23 seasonal pitches. Caravan pitches. Motorhome pitches. Tent pitches. 1 static.

Open: Mar-9 Jan (rs Winter months shop closed) **Last arrival:** 22.00hrs
Last departure: 11.30hrs

Pitches: * £19-£32 £19-£32 £10-£31

Leisure:

Facilities:

Services:

Within 3 miles:

Notes: No open fires. Dogs must be kept on leads.

AA Pubs & Restaurants nearby: Victoria Inn, LLANBEDR, LL45 2LD, 01341 241213

BETWS GARMON

Map 14 SH55

Places to visit

Snowdon Mountain Railway, LLANBERIS, LL55 4TY, 01286 870223
www.snowdonrailway.co.uk

Great for kids: Dolbadarn Castle, LLANBERIS, LL55 4UD, 01443 336000
www.cadw.wales.gov.uk

Bryn Gloch Caravan & Camping Park

►►►► 84%

tel: 01286 650216 **LL54 7YY**
email: eurig@bryngloch.co.uk **web:** www.campwales.co.uk
dir: *On A4085, 5m SE of Caernarfon.* **grid ref:** *SH534574*

An excellent family-run site with immaculate modern facilities, and all level pitches in beautiful surroundings. The park offers the best of two worlds, with its bustling holiday atmosphere and the peaceful natural surroundings; there are plenty of walks in the area. The 28 acres of level fields are separated by mature hedges and trees, guaranteeing sufficient space for families wishing to spread themselves out. There are some excellent fully serviced camping pitches and static holiday caravans for hire. 28 acre site. 160 touring pitches. 80 hardstandings. 80 seasonal pitches. Caravan pitches. Motorhome pitches. Tent pitches. 17 statics.

Open: all year **Last arrival:** 23.00hrs **Last departure:** 17.00hrs

Pitches: * £16-£26 £16-£26 £16-£26

Leisure:

Facilities:

Services:

Within 3 miles:

Notes: Dogs must be kept on leads. Heated family bathroom, mother & baby room.

CAERNARFON

Map 14 SH46

See also Dinas Dinlle & Llandwrog

Places to visit

Welsh Highland Railway, CAERNARFON, LL55 2YD, 01766 516024
www.festrail.co.uk

Great for kids: Caernarfon Castle, CAERNARFON, LL55 2AY, 01286 677617
www.cadw.wales.gov.uk

Llys Derwen Caravan & Camping Site

►►►► 86%

tel: 01286 673322 **Ffordd Bryngwyn, Llanrug LL55 4RD**
email: llysderwen@aol.com
dir: *Exit A55 junct 11 (follow Bangor (A5) & Llanberis signs). At rdbt left signed Betwys y Coed (A5) & Llanberis (A4244). At next rdbt right signed Llanberis. Right at T-junct signed Caernarfon onto A4086. Through Llanrug, left at Y Glyntwrog pub, site 500mtrs on right.* **grid ref:** *SH539629*

On the outskirts of the village of Llanrug, three miles from Caernarfon on the way to Llanberis and Snowdon. A beautifully maintained site with enthusiastic owners who are constantly making investments to improve the facilities. The amenities block is appointed to a high standard and the immaculately maintained grounds are planted with an abundance of colourful shrubs and seasonal flowers. 5 acre site. 20 touring pitches. Caravan pitches. Motorhome pitches. Tent pitches. 2 statics.

Open: Mar-Oct **Last arrival:** 22.00hrs **Last departure:** noon

Pitches: * £16-£18 £16-£18 £16-£18

Facilities:

Services:

Within 3 miles:

Notes: No open fires, no noise after 22.00hrs, no ball games. Dogs must be kept on leads.

AA Pubs & Restaurants nearby: Seiont Manor Hotel, CAERNARFON, LL55 2AQ, 01286 673366

Riverside Camping

►►►► 86%

tel: 01286 678781 **Seiont Nurseries, Pont Rug LL55 2BB**
email: info@riversidecamping.co.uk
dir: *2m from Caernarfon on right of A4086 towards Llanberis, follow signs at entrance.* **grid ref:** *SH505630*

Set in the grounds of a former garden centre and enjoying a superb location along the River Seiont, this park is approached by an impressive tree-lined drive. Immaculately maintained by the owners, there is a mixture of riverside grassy pitches and fully serviced pitches for caravans and motorhomes. Hardstanding pitches have electric hook-up, water, drainage and TV connection (especially suitable for motorhomes). In addition to the smart amenities blocks, other facilities include an excellent café/restaurant, a volleyball court and boules pitch; river fishing permits are also available. Two superb chalets for hire were added for the 2015 season, each for six people, with a wood-burning stove, a picnic garden and Japanese hot tub. This is a haven of peace close to Caernarfon, Snowdonia and some great walking opportunities. 5 acre site. 73 touring pitches. 16

hardstandings. 10 seasonal pitches. Caravan pitches. Motorhome pitches. Tent pitches.

Open: 14 Mar-Oct **Last arrival:** anytime **Last departure:** noon

Pitches: * £21-£27 £22-£27 £15-£24

Leisure:

Facilities:

Services:

Within 3 miles:

Notes: No fires, no loud music, debit cards accepted (no credit cards). Dogs must be kept on leads. Family shower room, baby-changing facilities, undercover picnic area.

AA Pubs & Restaurants nearby: Seiont Manor Hotel, CAERNARFON, LL55 2AQ, 01286 673366

Plas Gwyn Caravan & Camping Park

►►►► 81%

tel: 01286 672619 **Llanrug LL55 2AQ**
email: info@plasgwyn.co.uk
dir: *A4086, 3m E of Caernarfon, site on right. Between River Seiont & Llanrug.*
grid ref: *SH520633*

A secluded park in an ideal location for visiting the glorious nearby beaches, historic Caernarfon, the attractions of Snowdonia and for walking opportunities. The site is set within the grounds of Plas Gwyn House, a Georgian property with colonial additions; the friendly owners constantly improve the facilities, including the well-equipped amenities block, introduced for the 2015 season. A 'breakfast butty' service with fresh tea or coffee is available for delivery to individual pitches. The all-electric pitches include hardstandings and five that are fully serviced. Three wooden 'tents' and five statics are available for hire. 3 acre site. 42 touring pitches. 8 hardstandings. 8 seasonal pitches. Caravan pitches. Motorhome pitches. Tent pitches. 18 statics. 3 wooden pods.

Open: Mar-Oct **Last arrival:** 22.00hrs **Last departure:** 11.30hrs

Pitches: * £17.50-£21 £17.50-£21 £10.50-£25

Facilities:

Services:

Within 3 miles:

Notes: Minimal noise between 22.00hrs-mdnt, complete quiet between mdnt-08.00hrs.

AA Pubs & Restaurants nearby: Seiont Manor Hotel, CAERNARFON, LL55 2AQ, 01286 673366

Ty'n yr Onnen Caravan Park

►►► 81%

tel: 01286 650281 & 07976 529428 **Waunfawr LL55 4AX**
email: tynronnen.farm@btconnect.com
dir: *At Waunfawr on A4085, onto unclassified road opposite church. Site signed.*
grid ref: *SH533588*

A gently sloping site on a 200-acre sheep farm set in magnificent surroundings close to Snowdon and enjoying stunning mountain views. This secluded park is well equipped and the amenity blocks have been appointed to a high standard. Added for the 2015 season – a mountain facing camping pod and a static caravan converted to a family-friendly holiday home. Access is via a narrow, unclassified road. 3.5 acre site. 20 touring pitches. 25 seasonal pitches. Caravan pitches. Motorhome pitches. Tent pitches. 1 wooden pod.

Open: Apr-Oct **Last arrival:** 22.00hrs **Last departure:** noon

Pitches:

Leisure:

Facilities:

Services:

Within 3 miles:

Notes: No music after 23.00hrs. Dogs must be kept on leads.

AA Pubs & Restaurants nearby: Snowdonia Parc Brewpub & Campsite, WAUNFAWR, LL55 4AQ, 01286 650409

Cwm Cadnant Valley

►►► 80%

tel: 01286 673196 **Llanberis Rd LL55 2DF**
email: aa@cwmcadnant.co.uk **web:** www.cwmcadnant.co.uk
dir: *On outskirts of Caernarfon on A4086 towards Llanberis, adjacent to fire station.*
grid ref: *SH487628*

Set in an attractive wooded valley with a stream is this terraced site with secluded pitches, a good camping area for backpackers and clean, modern toilet facilities. It is located on the outskirts of Caernarfon in a rural location, close to the main Caernarfon-Llanberis road and just a 10-minute walk from the castle and town centre. 4.5 acre site. 60 touring pitches. 9 hardstandings. 5 seasonal pitches. Caravan pitches. Motorhome pitches. Tent pitches.

Open: 14 Mar-3 Nov **Last arrival:** 22.00hrs **Last departure:** 11.00hrs

Pitches: * £14-£22 £14-£22 £10-£22

Leisure:

Facilities:

Services:

Within 3 miles:

Notes: No noise after 23.00hrs, no wood fires. Dogs must be kept on leads. Family room with baby-changing facilities.

AA Pubs & Restaurants nearby: Seiont Manor Hotel, CAERNARFON, LL55 2AQ, 01286 673366

CRICCIETH

Map 14 SH43

Places to visit

Criccieth Castle, CRICCIETH, LL52 0DP, 01766 522227 www.cadw.wales.gov.uk

Portmeirion, PORTMEIRION, LL48 6ER, 01766 772306 www.portmeirion-village.com

Great for kids: Ffestiniog Railway, PORTHMADOG, LL49 9NF, 01766 516024 www.festrail.co.uk

Eisteddfa

►►►► 83%

tel: 01766 522696 **Eisteddfa Lodge, Pentrefelin LL52 0PT**
email: info@eisteddfapark.co.uk
dir: *From Porthmadog take A497 towards Criccieth. Approx 3.5m, through Pentrefelin, site signed 1st right after Plas Gwyn Nursing Home.* **grid ref:** *SH518394*

A quiet, secluded park on elevated ground, sheltered by the Snowdonia Mountains and with lovely views of Cardigan Bay; Criccieth is nearby. The owners continue to steadily improve the park without diminishing its unspoilt beauty, and are keen to welcome families, who will appreciate the cubicled facilities. There's a field and play area, woodland walks, six superb slate-based hardstandings, a 'cocoon' pod, two tipis and three static holiday caravans for hire, plus a three-acre coarse fishing lake adjacent to the park. Free WiFi is available across the park. 24 acre site. 100 touring pitches. 17 hardstandings. 20 seasonal pitches. Caravan pitches. Motorhome pitches. Tent pitches. 13 statics. 2 tipis. 1 wooden pod.

Open: Mar-Oct **Last arrival:** 22.30hrs **Last departure:** 11.00hrs

Pitches: * £15.50-£23 £15.50-£23 £13.50-£23

Leisure:

Facilities:

Services:

Within 3 miles:

Notes: No noise after 22.30hrs. Dogs must be kept on leads. Baby bath available.

AA Pubs & Restaurants nearby: Bron Eifion Country House Hotel, CRICCIETH, LL52 0SA, 01766 522385

Plas Bodegroes, PWLLHELI, LL53 5TH, 01758 612363

Llwyn-Bugeilydd Caravan & Camping Site

►►► 79%

tel: 01766 522235 & 07714 196137 **LL52 0PN**
email: cazzyanne1@hotmail.com
dir: *From Porthmadog on A497, 1m N of Criccieth on B4411. Site 1st on right. From A55 take A487 through Caernarfon. After Bryncir right onto B4411, site on left in 3.5m.*
grid ref: *SH498398*

A quiet rural site, convenient for touring Snowdonia and coastal areas. It is set amid stunning scenery and has well-tended grass pitches enhanced by shrubs and seasonal flowers. The smartly presented amenities block is kept spotlessly clean. 6 acre site. 40 touring pitches. 2 hardstandings. Caravan pitches. Motorhome pitches. Tent pitches.

Open: Mar-Oct **Last arrival:** anytime **Last departure:** 11.00hrs

Pitches: £14-£22 £14-£22 £12-£18

Leisure:

Facilities:

Services:

Within 3 miles:

Notes: No skateboards, no noise between 22.30hrs-08.00hrs. Dogs must be kept on leads.

AA Pubs & Restaurants nearby: Bron Eifion Country House Hotel, CRICCIETH, LL52 0SA, 01766 522385

Plas Bodegroes, PWLLHELI, LL53 5TH, 01758 612363

DINAS DINLLE

Map 14 SH45

Places to visit

Inigo Jones Slateworks, GROESLON, LL54 7UE, 01286 830242 www.inigojones.co.uk

Caernarfon Castle, CAERNARFON, LL55 2AY, 01286 677617 www.cadw.wales.gov.uk

Great for kids: Welsh Highland Railway, CAERNARFON, LL55 2YD, 01766 516024 www.festrail.co.uk

PREMIER PARK

Dinlle Caravan Park

►►►►► 85%

tel: 01286 830324 **LL54 5TW**
email: enq@thornleyleisure.co.uk
dir: *From A487 at rdbt onto A499 (signed Pwllheli). Right at sign for Caernarfon Airport (& brown camping sign).* **grid ref:** *SH438568*

A very accessible, well-kept, grassy site adjacent to a sandy beach and with good views towards Snowdonia. The park is situated in acres of flat grassland that provides plenty of space for large groups. The man-made dunes offer campers additional protection from sea breezes. The lounge bar and family room are comfortable places in which to relax, and children will enjoy the exciting adventure playground. A superb new landscaped entrance and reception was added in 2015 and there are now camping pods with decking and barbecue areas. A golf club, a nature reserve and the Airworld Aviation Museum at Caernarfon Airport can all be accessed from the beach road. 20 acre site. 175 touring pitches. 20 hardstandings. Caravan pitches. Motorhome pitches. Tent pitches. 167 statics. 7 wooden pods.

Open: Mar-Nov **Last arrival:** 23.00hrs **Last departure:** noon

Pitches:

Leisure:

Facilities:

Services:

Within 3 miles:

Notes: No skateboards. Dogs must be kept on leads.

DYFFRYN ARDUDWY

Map 14 SH52

Places to visit

Cymer Abbey, CYMER ABBEY, LL40 2HE, 01443 336000 www.cadw.wales.gov.uk

Great for kids: Harlech Castle, HARLECH, LL46 2YH, 01766 780552 www.cadw.wales.gov.uk

Murmur-yr-Afon Touring Park

►►► 81%

tel: 01341 247353 **LL44 2BE**
email: murmuryrafon1@btinternet.com
dir: *On A496 N of village.* **grid ref:** *SH586236*

A pleasant family-run park alongside a wooded stream on the edge of the village, and handy for large sandy beaches. Expect good, clean facilities, and lovely views of rolling hills and mountains. 7.5 acre site. 78 touring pitches. 37 hardstandings. Caravan pitches. Motorhome pitches. Tent pitches.

Open: Mar-Oct **Last arrival:** 22.00hrs **Last departure:** 11.00hrs

Pitches: * £14-£25 £14-£25 £10-£23

Leisure:

Facilities:

Services:

Within 3 miles:

Notes: Dogs must be kept on leads.

AA Pubs & Restaurants nearby: Victoria Inn, LLANBEDR, LL45 2LD, 01341 241213

LLANDWROG

Map 14 SH45

Places to visit

Welsh Highland Railway, CAERNARFON, LL55 2YD, 01766 516024 www.festrail.co.uk

Great for kids: Caernarfon Castle, CAERNARFON, LL55 2AY, 01286 677617 www.cadw.wales.gov.uk

White Tower Caravan Park

►►►► 84%

tel: 01286 830649 & 07802 562785 **LL54 5UH**
email: whitetower@supanet.com
dir: *From Caernarfon take A487 Porthmadog road. 1st right into Pant Rd signed Llanfaglan & Saron. Site 3m on right.* **grid ref:** *SH453582*

There are lovely views of Snowdonia from this park located just two miles from the nearest beach at Dinas Dinlle. A well-maintained toilet block has key access, and the hardstanding pitches have water and electricity. Popular amenities include an outdoor heated swimming pool, a lounge bar with family room, and a games and TV room. 6 acre site. 60 touring pitches. 60 hardstandings. 58 seasonal pitches. Caravan pitches. Motorhome pitches. Tent pitches. 71 statics.

Open: Mar-10 Jan (rs Mar-mid May & Sep-Nov bar open wknds only)
Last arrival: 23.00hrs **Last departure:** noon

Pitches: £20-£30 £20-£30 £20-£30

Leisure:

Facilities:

Services:

Within 3 miles:

Notes: Dogs must be kept on leads.

AA Pubs & Restaurants nearby: Black Boy Inn, CAERNARFON, LL55 1RW, 01286 673604

PONT-RUG

See Caernarfon

PORTHMADOG

Map 14 SH53

Places to visit

Portmeirion, PORTMEIRION, LL48 6ER, 01766 772306
www.portmeirion-village.com

Great for kids: Ffestiniog Railway, PORTHMADOG, LL49 9NF, 01766 516024
www.festrail.co.uk

Greenacres Holiday Park

HOLIDAY CENTRE 87%

tel: 0871 231 0886 *(Calls cost 13p per minute plus your phone company's access charge)*
Black Rock Sands, Morfa Bychan LL49 9YF
email: greenacres@haven.com **web:** www.haven.com/greenacres
dir: *From Porthmadog High Street follow Black Rock Sands signs between The Factory Shop & Post Office. Park 2m on left at end of Morfa Bychan.* **grid ref:** *SH539374*

A quality holiday park on level ground just a short walk from Black Rock Sands, and set against a backdrop of Snowdonia National Park. All touring pitches are on hardstandings surrounded by closely-mown grass, and near the entertainment complex. A full programme of entertainment, organised clubs, indoor and outdoor sports and leisure, pubs, shows and cabarets all add to a holiday experience here. A bowling alley and a large shop with bakery are useful amenities. A superb new touring field was opened in 2015 that has excellent fully serviced Euro pitches, extensive, colourful planting and a smart, well-equipped amenities block. Six fully-equipped safari tents are also available for a glamping experience. 121 acre site. 46 touring pitches. 39 hardstandings. Caravan pitches. Motorhome pitches. 900 statics. 6 safari tents.

Greenacres Holiday Park

Open: mid Mar-end Oct (rs mid Mar-May & Sep-Oct some facilities may be reduced) **Last arrival:** anytime **Last departure:** 10.00hrs

Pitches:

Leisure:

Facilities:

Services:

Within 3 miles:

Notes: No commercial vehicles, no bookings by persons under 21yrs unless a family booking, max 2 dogs per booking, certain dog breeds banned. Dogs must be kept on leads.

AA Pubs & Restaurants nearby: Royal Sportsman Hotel, PORTHMADOG, LL49 9HB, 01766 512015

The Hotel Portmeirion, PORTMEIRION, LL48 6ET, 01766 770000

See advert on page 431

PWLLHELI

Places to visit

Penarth Fawr, PENARTH FAWR, 01443 336000 www.cadw.wales.gov.uk

Lloyd George Museum, LLANYSTUMDWY, LL52 0SH, 01766 522071
www.gwynedd.gov.uk/museums

Great for kids: Criccieth Castle, CRICCIETH, LL52 0DP, 01766 522227
www.cadw.wales.gov.uk

PWLLHELI Map 14 SH33

Hafan y Mor Holiday Park

HOLIDAY CENTRE 89%

GOLD

tel: 0800 917 3267 **LL53 6HJ**
email: hafanymor@haven.com **web:** www.haven.com/hafanymor
dir: *From Caernarfon take A499 to Pwllheli. A497 to Porthmadog. Park on right, approx 3m from Pwllheli. Or from Telford, A5, A494 to Bala. Right for Porthmadog. Left at rdbt in Porthmadog signed Criccieth & Pwllheli. Park on left 3m from Criccieth.*
grid ref: *SH431368*

Located between Pwllheli and Criccieth, and surrounded by mature trees that attract wildlife, this popular holiday centre provides a wide range of all-weather attractions. Activities include a sports hall, an ornamental boating lake, a large indoor swimming pool, a show bar and a high-ropes activity plus Segways are available. There are also great eating options – the Mash and Barrel bar and bistro, Traditional Fish and Chips, Burger King, Papa John's and a Starbucks coffeehouse. The touring area includes 75 fully serviced all-weather pitches and a top notch, air-conditioned amenities block. 500 acre site. 75 touring pitches. 75 hardstandings. Caravan pitches. Motorhome pitches. 800 statics.

Hafan y Mor Holiday Park

Open: mid Mar-end Oct (rs mid Mar-May & Sep-Oct reduced facilities)
Last arrival: 21.00hrs **Last departure:** 10.00hrs

Pitches:

Leisure:

Facilities: WiFi

Services:

Within 3 miles:

Notes: No commercial vehicles, no bookings by persons under 21yrs unless a family booking, max 2 dogs per booking, certain dog breeds banned. Dogs must be kept on leads.

See advert below

PWLLHELI *continued*

Abererch Sands Holiday Centre

►►► 73%

tel: 01758 612327 **LL53 6PJ**
email: enquiries@abererch-sands.co.uk **web:** www.abererch-sands.co.uk
dir: *On A497 (Porthmadog to Pwllheli road), 1m from Pwllheli.* **grid ref:** *SH403359*

Glorious views of Snowdonia and Cardigan Bay can be enjoyed from this very secure, family-run site adjacent to a railway station and a four-mile stretch of sandy beach. A large heated indoor swimming pool, snooker room, pool room, fitness centre and children's play area make this an ideal holiday venue. 85 acre site. 70 touring pitches. 70 hardstandings. Caravan pitches. Motorhome pitches. Tent pitches. 90 statics.

Open: Mar-Oct **Last arrival:** 21.00hrs **Last departure:** 21.00hrs

Pitches:

Leisure:

Facilities:

Services:

Within 3 miles:

Notes: Dogs must be kept on leads.

AA Pubs & Restaurants nearby: Plas Bodegroes, PWLLHELI, LL53 5TH, 01758 612363

TALSARNAU Map 14 SH63

Places to visit

Portmeirion, PORTMEIRION, LL48 6ER, 01766 772306 www.portmeirion-village.com

Harlech Castle, HARLECH, LL46 2YH, 01766 780552 www.cadw.wales.gov.uk

Great for kids: Ffestiniog Railway, PORTHMADOG, LL49 9NF, 01766 516024 www.festrail.co.uk

Barcdy Touring Caravan & Camping Park

►►►► 84%

tel: 01766 770736 **LL47 6YG**
email: anwen@barcdy.co.uk **web:** www.barcdy.co.uk
dir: *From Maentwrog take A496 for Harlech. Site 4m on left.* **grid ref:** *SH620375*

A quiet picturesque park on the edge of the Vale of Ffestiniog near the Dwryd estuary. Two touring areas serve the park, one near the park entrance, and the other with improved and more secluded terraced pitches beside a narrow valley. The tent area is secluded and peaceful, and the toilet facilities are clean and tidy. Footpaths through adjacent woodland lead to small lakes and an established nature trail. 12 acre site. 80 touring pitches. 40 hardstandings. 15 seasonal pitches. Caravan pitches. Motorhome pitches. Tent pitches. 30 statics.

Open: Apr-Oct (rs Selected dates (excl high season & school hols) 2nd facility building closed) **Last arrival:** 21.00hrs **Last departure:** noon

Pitches:

Facilities:

Services:

Within 3 miles:

Notes: Quiet families & couples only (no noisy parties), no groups except Duke of Edinburgh Award participants.

AA Pubs & Restaurants nearby: The Hotel Portmeirion, PORTMEIRION, LL48 6ET, 01766 770000

PITCHES: Caravans Motorhomes Tents Glamping-style accommodation **SERVICES:** Electric hook up Launderette Licensed bar Calor Gas Camping Gaz Toilet fluid Café/Restaurant Fast Food/Takeaway Battery charging Baby care Motorvan service point

ABBREVIATIONS: BH/bank hols – bank holidays Etr – Easter Spring BH – Spring Bank Holiday fr – from hrs – hours m – mile mdnt – midnight rdbt – roundabout rs – restricted service wk – week wknd – weekend x-rds – cross roads No credit or debit cards No dogs Children of all ages accepted

TAL-Y-BONT Map 14 SH52

Places to visit

Cymer Abbey, CYMER ABBEY, LL40 2HE, 01443 336000 www.cadw.wales.gov.uk

Harlech Castle, HARLECH, LL46 2YH, 01766 780552 www.cadw.wales.gov.uk

PREMIER PARK

Islawrffordd Caravan Park

91%

tel: 01341 247269 **LL43 2AQ**
email: info@islawrffordd.co.uk **web:** www.islawrffordd.co.uk
dir: *From A496 into Ffordd Glan-Mor towards sea, follow brown campsite sign. Over rail line, site on left.* **grid ref:** *SH584215*

Situated on the coast between Barmouth and Harlech, and within the Snowdonia National Park, with clear views of Cardigan Bay, the Lleyn Peninsula and the Snowdonia and Cader Idris mountain ranges, this excellent, family-run and family-friendly park has seen considerable investment over recent years. Fully matured, the touring area boasts fully serviced pitches, a superb toilet block with underfloor heating and top-quality fittings; the park has private access to miles of sandy beach. The superb restaurant and Bar Nineteen57 opened in 2015, and offers both formal and and relaxed areas for enjoying locally sourced food. 25 acre site. 105 touring pitches. 75 hardstandings. 50 seasonal pitches. Caravan pitches. Motorhome pitches. Tent pitches. 201 statics.

Open: Mar-1 Nov **Last arrival:** 20.00hrs **Last departure:** noon

Pitches: * £36 £36 £29.50-£36

Leisure:

Facilities:

Services:

Within 3 miles:

Notes: Strictly families & couples only. Dogs must be kept on leads.

AA Pubs & Restaurants nearby: Victoria Inn, LLANBEDR, LL45 2LD, 01341 241213

See advert on page 435

TYWYN Map 14 SH50

Places to visit

Talyllyn Railway, TYWYN, LL36 9EY, 01654 710472 www.talyllyn.co.uk

Castell-y-Bere, LLANFIHANGEL-Y-PENNANT, 01443 336000 www.cadw.wales.gov.uk

Great for kids: King Arthur's Labyrinth, CORRIS, SY20 9RF, 01654 761584 www.kingarthurslabyrinth.co.uk

Ynysymaengwyn Caravan Park

81%

tel: 01654 710684 **LL36 9RY**
email: rita@ynysy.co.uk
dir: *On A493, 1m N of Tywyn, towards Dolgellau.* **grid ref:** *SH602021*

A lovely park set in the wooded grounds of a former manor house, with designated nature trails through 13 acres of wildlife-rich woodland, scenic river walks, fishing and a sandy beach nearby. The attractive stone amenity block is clean and well kept, and this smart municipal park is ideal for families. 4 acre site. 80 touring pitches. Caravan pitches. Motorhome pitches. Tent pitches. 115 statics.

Open: Etr or Apr-Oct **Last arrival:** 23.00hrs **Last departure:** noon

Pitches:

Leisure:

Facilities:

Services:

Within 3 miles:

Notes: Dogs must be kept on leads.

MONMOUTHSHIRE

ABERGAVENNY Map 9 SO21

Places to visit

Big Pit National Coal Museum, BLAENAVON, NP4 9XP, 029 20573650 www.museumwales.ac.uk

Hen Gwrt, LLANTILIO CROSSENNY, 01443 336000 www.cadw.wales.gov.uk

Great for kids: Raglan Castle, RAGLAN, NP15 2BT, 01291 690228 www.cadw.wales.gov.uk

Wernddu Caravan Park

►►►► 83%

tel: 01873 856223 **Old Ross Rd NP7 8NG**
email: info@wernddu-golf-club.co.uk
dir: *From A465, N of Abergavenny, take B4521 signed Skenfrith. Site on right in 0.25m.*
grid ref: *SO321153*

Located north of the town centre, this former fruit farm, adjacent to a golf club and driving range, is managed by three generations of the same family, and has been transformed into an ideal base for those visiting the many nearby attractions. The well-spaced touring pitches have water, electricity and waste water disposal, and the smart modern amenities block provides very good privacy options. Site guests are welcome to use the golf club bar which also serves meals during the busy months; they are also eligible for half-price green fees. There is no shop on site but a daily newspaper service is provided, and a mini-market is less than a mile away. 6 acre site. 70 touring pitches. 20 hardstandings. 30 seasonal pitches. Caravan pitches. Motorhome pitches. Tent pitches.

Open: Mar-Oct **Last arrival:** 21.00hrs **Last departure:** noon

Pitches:

Leisure:

Facilities:

Services:

Within 3 miles:

Notes: Adults only. Dogs must be kept on leads. 9-hole pitch & putt, driving range, bar with sports TV.

AA Pubs & Restaurants nearby: Walnut Tree Inn, ABERGAVENNY, NP7 8AW, 01873 852797

Angel Hotel, ABERGAVENNY, NP7 5EN, 01873 857121

Pyscodlyn Farm Caravan & Camping Site

►►►► 81%

tel: 01873 853271 & 07816 447942 **Llanwenarth Citra NP7 7ER**
email: info@pyscodlyncaravanpark.com
dir: *From Abergavenny take A40 Brecon road, site 1.5m from entrance of Nevill Hall Hospital, on left 50yds past phone box.* **grid ref:** *SO266155*

With its outstanding views of the mountains, this quiet park in the Brecon Beacons National Park makes a pleasant holiday venue for country lovers. The Sugarloaf Mountain and the River Usk are within easy walking distance and, despite being a working farm, dogs are welcome but must be under strict control of course. The separate ladies' and gents' amenities blocks are appointed to a high standard. Please note that credit and debit cards are not accepted at this site. 4.5 acre site. 60 touring pitches. Caravan pitches. Motorhome pitches. Tent pitches. 6 statics.

Open: Apr-Oct

Pitches:

Facilities:

Services:

Within 3 miles:

Notes: No noise after 23.00 hrs. Dogs must be kept on leads.

AA Pubs & Restaurants nearby: Angel Hotel, ABERGAVENNY, NP7 5EN, 01873 857121

Walnut Tree Inn, ABERGAVENNY, NP7 8AW, 01873 852797

DINGESTOW Map 9 SO41

Places to visit

Raglan Castle, RAGLAN, NP15 2BT, 01291 690228 www.cadw.wales.gov.uk

Tintern Abbey, TINTERN PARVA, NP16 6SE, 01291 689251 www.cadw.wales.gov.uk

Great for kids: The Nelson Museum & Local History Centre, MONMOUTH, NP25 3XA, 01600 710630

Bridge Caravan Park & Camping Site

►►► 85%

tel: 01600 740241 **Bridge Farm NP25 4DY**
email: info@bridgecaravanpark.co.uk
dir: *M4 junct 24, A449 towards Monmouth. Left onto A40 towards Abergavenny. Turn right (across dual carriageway) signed Dinglestow (& brown caravan sign).* **grid ref:** *SO459104*

The River Trothy runs along the edge of this quiet village park, which has been owned by the same family for many years. Touring pitches are both grass and hardstanding and have a woodland backdrop. The quality facilities are enhanced by good laundry equipment. River fishing is available on site, and there is a dog walking area. The village shop is within 100 yards and a play field within 200 yards. 4 acre site. 94 touring pitches. 15 hardstandings. 50 seasonal pitches. Caravan pitches. Motorhome pitches. Tent pitches. 3 statics.

Open: Etr-Oct **Last arrival:** 22.00hrs **Last departure:** 16.00hrs

Pitches: * £15-£18 £15-£18 £15-£17

Facilities:

Services:

Within 3 miles:

Notes: Dogs must be kept on leads.

AA Pubs & Restaurants nearby: The Beaufort Arms Coaching Inn & Brasserie, RAGLAN, NP15 2DY, 01291 690412

LLANVAIR DISCOED Map 9 ST49

PREMIER PARK

Penhein Glamping

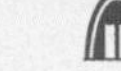

NEW ►►►►►

tel: 01633 400581 **Penhein NP16 6RB**
email: enquiries@penhein.co.uk
dir: *M48 junct 2, A446 towards Chepstow. 1st exit at rdbt onto A48 signed Caerwent. Approx 8m, through Caerwent, right signed Llanvair Discoed. 1st right at village sign, immediately left into private drive. Site 1.5m.* **grid ref:** *ST449932*

Travel along a narrow lane and through two grazing fields to reach a small wood where there are large yurts (alachighs) and an Iranian communal yurt. The sumptuous yurt interiors have superb beds (a double, two truckle beds and a sofa bed for children), quality dining furniture, lanterns, a cold water sink, a large cool box and a wood-burning stove (wood provided), plus an en suite modern, low-level toilet. Outside each yurt there is a fire pit and carved tree-trunk seating. There are level bark pathways between the units, and a lean-to with kettle, microwave and freezer as there is no electricity in the yurts. The separate shower block has a drying room and unisex rooms with underfloor heating, monsoon showers and a roll-top bath. The communal yurt has a wood-burning stove, bespoke oak tables, benches and electricity to power 13 amp sockets and lighting. On arrival visitors are provided with a welcome pack, and there is a wild meadow for archery, bike riding and orienteering. 11 acre site. 6 yurts.

Open: Mar-Nov **Last arrival:** 19.00hrs **Last departure:** 11.00hrs

Pitches: £85-£181

Leisure:

Facilities:

Services:

Within 3 miles:

Notes: No pets. No cars by yurts. Xmas & New Year bookings possible (contact site). 8-acre private wildflower & hay meadow.

USK

Places to visit

Caerleon Roman Fortress and Baths, CAERLEON, NP18 1AE, 01663 422518 www.cadw.wales.gov.uk

Big Pit National Coal Museum, BLAENAVON, NP4 9XP, 029 20573650 www.museumwales.ac.uk

Great for kids: Greenmeadow Community Farm, CWMBRAN, NP44 5AJ, 01633 647662 www.greenmeadowcommunityfarm.org.uk

USK Map 9 SO30

AA CAMPSITE OF THE YEAR FOR WALES 2016

PREMIER PARK

Pont Kemys Caravan & Camping Park

►►►►► 86%

tel: 01873 880688 **Chainbridge NP7 9DS**
email: info@pontkemys.com **web:** www.pontkemys.com
dir: *From Usk take B4598 towards Abergavenny. Approx 4m, over river bridge, bear right, 300yds to site. For other routes contact site for detailed directions.*
grid ref: *SO348058*

A peaceful park next to the River Usk, offering an excellent standard of toilet facilities with family rooms. A section of the park has fully serviced pitches. The park is in a rural area with mature trees and country views, and attracts quiet visitors who enjoy the many attractions of this area. The local golf club is open during the day and serves breakfast and lunches. 8 acre site. 65 touring pitches. 29 hardstandings. 25 seasonal pitches. Caravan pitches. Motorhome pitches. Tent pitches.

Open: Mar-Oct **Last arrival:** 21.00hrs **Last departure:** noon

Pitches: * £18-£22 £18-£22 £18-£22

Leisure:

Facilities:

Services:

Within 3 miles:

Notes: No music. Dogs must be kept on leads. Mother & baby room, kitchen facilities for groups.

AA Pubs & Restaurants nearby: The Nags Head Inn, USK, NP15 1BH, 01291 672820

The Raglan Arms, USK, NP15 1DL, 01291 690800

PEMBROKESHIRE

BROAD HAVEN — Map 8 SM81

Places to visit

Llawhaden Castle, LLAWHADEN, 01443 336000 www.cadw.wales.gov.uk

Great for kids: Scolton Manor Museum & Country Park, SCOLTON, SA62 5QL, 01437 731328 (Museum) www.pembrokeshirevirtualmuseum.co.uk

Creampots Touring Caravan & Camping Park

►►► 86%

tel: 01437 781776 **Broadway SA62 3TU**
email: creampots@btconnect.com
dir: *From Haverfordwest take B4341 to Broadway. Turn left, follow brown tourist signs to site.* **grid ref:** *SM882131*

Set just outside the Pembrokeshire National Park, this quiet site is just one and a half miles from a safe sandy beach at Broad Haven, and the coastal footpath. The park is well laid out and carefully maintained, and the toilet block offers a good standard of facilities. The owners welcome families. 8 acre site. 72 touring pitches. 32 hardstandings. Caravan pitches. Motorhome pitches. Tent pitches. 1 static.

Open: Mar-Nov **Last arrival:** 21.00hrs **Last departure:** 11.00hrs

Pitches:

Facilities:

Services:

Within 3 miles:

Notes: Dogs must be kept on leads.

AA Pubs & Restaurants nearby: The Swan Inn, LITTLE HAVEN, SA62 3UL, 01437 781880

South Cockett Caravan & Camping Park

►►► 78%

tel: 01437 781296 & 781760 & 07774 782572 **South Cockett SA62 3TU**
email: esmejames@hotmail.co.uk
dir: *From Haverfordwest take B4341 to Broad Haven, at Broadway turn left, site 300yds.* **grid ref:** *SM878136*

A warm welcome is assured at this small site on a working farm. The touring areas are divided into neat paddocks by high, well-trimmed hedges, and there are good toilet facilities. The lovely beach at Broad Haven is only about two miles away. 6 acre site. 73 touring pitches. 25 seasonal pitches. Caravan pitches. Motorhome pitches. Tent pitches.

Open: Etr-Oct **Last arrival:** 22.30hrs

Pitches: * £13-£16 £13-£16 £12-£15

Leisure:

Facilities:

Services:

Within 3 miles:

Notes: Dogs must be kept on leads.

AA Pubs & Restaurants nearby: The Swan Inn, LITTLE HAVEN, SA62 3UL, 01437 781880

FISHGUARD — Map 8 SM93

Places to visit

Pentre Ifan Burial Chamber, NEWPORT, 01443 336000 www.cadw.wales.gov.uk

Great for kids: OceanLab, FISHGUARD, SA64 0DE, 01348 874737 www.ocean-lab.co.uk

Fishguard Bay Resort

►►► 92%

tel: 01348 811415 **Garn Gelli SA65 9ET**
email: enquiries@fishguardbay.com **web:** www.fishguardbay.com
dir: *Accessed from A487. Turn at park sign onto single track road. (NB if approaching Fishguard from Cardigan on A487 ignore Sat Nav to turn right).* **grid ref:** *SM984383*

Set high up on cliffs with outstanding views of Fishguard Bay, this site (under new ownership in 2015) has the Pembrokeshire Coastal Path running right through its centre, so affording many opportunities for wonderful walks. The park is extremely well kept, with a good toilet block, a common room with TV, a lounge with library, laundry and a well-stocked shop. Two camping pods with stunning sea views were installed for the 2015 season. 7 acre site. 50 touring pitches. 6 hardstandings. Caravan pitches. Motorhome pitches. Tent pitches. 50 statics. 2 wooden pods.

Open: Mar-9 Jan **Last arrival:** anytime **Last departure:** noon

Pitches: * £19.50-£23.50 £19.50-£23.50 £15-£23.50

Leisure:

Facilities:

Services:

Within 3 miles:

Notes: Dogs must be kept on leads.

AA Pubs & Restaurants nearby: The Sloop Inn, PORTHGAIN, SA62 5BN, 01348 831449

The Shed, PORTHGAIN, SA62 5BN, 01348 831518

Salutation Inn, NEWPORT, SA41 3UY, 01239 820564

FISHGUARD *continued*

Gwaun Vale Touring Park

►►► 80%

tel: 01348 874698 **Llanychaer SA65 9TA**
email: margaret.harries@talk21.com
dir: *B4313 from Fishguard. Site 1.5m on right.* **grid ref:** *SM977356*

Located in the beautiful Gwaun Valley, this carefully landscaped park, with colourful, seasonal flowers, is set on the hillside with generously sized, tiered pitches on two levels that provide superb views of the surrounding countryside. 1.6 acre site. 29 touring pitches. 5 hardstandings. Caravan pitches. Motorhome pitches. Tent pitches. 1 static.

Open: Apr-Oct **Last arrival:** anytime **Last departure:** 11.00hrs

Pitches: * £18-£21 £18-£21 £16-£23

Leisure:

Facilities:

Services:

Within 3 miles:

Notes: No skateboards. Dogs must be kept on leads. Guidebooks available.

AA Pubs & Restaurants nearby: The Sloop Inn, PORTHGAIN, SA62 5BN, 01348 831449

The Shed, PORTHGAIN, SA62 5BN, 01348 831518

Salutation Inn, NEWPORT, SA41 3UY, 01239 820564

HASGUARD CROSS — Map 8 SM80

Hasguard Cross Caravan Park

►►► 85%

tel: 01437 781443 **SA62 3SL**
email: hasguard@aol.com
dir: *From Haverfordwest take B4327 towards Dale. In 7m right at x-rds. Site 1st right.*
grid ref: *SM850108*

A very clean, efficient and well-run site in the Pembrokeshire National Park, just one and a half miles from the sea and beach at Little Haven, and with views of the surrounding hills. The toilet and shower facilities are immaculately clean, and there is a licensed bar (evenings only) serving a good choice of food. 4.5 acre site. 12 touring pitches. 3 hardstandings. Caravan pitches. Motorhome pitches. Tent pitches. 42 statics.

Open: all year (rs Aug tent field for 28 days) **Last arrival:** 21.00hrs
Last departure: 10.00hrs

Pitches: * £15 £15 £15

Leisure:

Facilities:

Services:

Within 3 miles:

Notes: No noise after 22.30hrs, no fires or open BBQs. Dogs must be kept on leads.

AA Pubs & Restaurants nearby: The Swan Inn, LITTLE HAVEN, SA62 3UL, 01437 781880

HAVERFORDWEST — Map 8 SM91

Places to visit

Llawhaden Castle, LLAWHADEN, 01443 336000 www.cadw.wales.gov.uk

Great for kids: Oakwood Theme Park, NARBERTH, SA67 8DE, 01834 815170 www.oakwoodthemepark.co.uk

Nolton Cross Caravan Park

►► 83%

tel: 01437 710701 **Nolton SA62 3NP**
email: info@noltoncross-holidays.co.uk
dir: *1m from A487 (Haverfordwest to St Davids road) at Simpson Cross, towards Nolton & Broadhaven.* **grid ref:** *SM879177*

High grassy banks surround the touring area of this park next to the owners' working farm. It is located on open ground above the sea and St Bride's Bay (within one and a half miles), and there is a coarse fishing lake close by – equipment for hire and reduced permit rates for campers are available. 4 acre site. 15 touring pitches. Caravan pitches. Motorhome pitches. Tent pitches. 30 statics.

Open: Mar-Dec **Last arrival:** 22.00hrs **Last departure:** noon

Pitches:

Leisure:

Facilities:

Services:

Within 3 miles:

Notes: No youth groups. Dogs must be kept on leads.

AA Pubs & Restaurants nearby: The Swan Inn, LITTLE HAVEN, SA62 3UL, 01437 781880

LITTLE HAVEN

See Hasguard Cross

ST DAVIDS

Places to visit

St Davids Bishop's Palace, ST DAVIDS, SA62 6PE, 01437 720517 www.cadw.wales.gov.uk

St Davids Cathedral, ST DAVID'S, SA62 6PE, 01437 720202 www.stdavidscathedral.org.uk

ST DAVIDS Map 8 SM72

PREMIER PARK

Caerfai Bay Caravan & Tent Park

►►►►► 90%

tel: 01437 720274 **Caerfai Bay SA62 6QT**
email: info@caerfaibay.co.uk **web:** www.caerfaibay.co.uk
dir: *From E on A487 towards St Davids left into Caerfai Rd (Ffordd Caerfai) signed Caerfai & parking. Right at end of road.* **grid ref:** *SM759244*

Magnificent coastal scenery and an outlook over St Bride's Bay can be enjoyed from this delightful site, located just 300 yards from a bathing beach. The park offers good roadways, modern water points, solar-heated wet suit shower rooms and excellent toilet facilities which include four family rooms. There is a very good farm shop just across the road. 10 acre site. 106 touring pitches. 26 hardstandings. Caravan pitches. Motorhome pitches. Tent pitches. 30 statics.

Open: Mar-mid Nov **Last arrival:** 21.00hrs **Last departure:** 11.00hrs

Pitches: * £19-£24 £13-£24 £13-£17.50

Facilities:

Services:

Within 3 miles:

Notes: No dogs in tent field mid Jul-Aug, no skateboards or rollerblades. Dogs must be kept on leads.

AA Pubs & Restaurants nearby: Cwtch, ST DAVIDS, SA62 6SD, 01437 720491

The Sloop Inn, PORTHGAIN, SA62 5BN, 01348 831449

The Shed, PORTHGAIN, SA62 5BN, 01348 831518

Tretio Caravan & Camping Park

►►► 82%

tel: 01437 781600 & 07814 588289 **SA62 6DE**
email: info@tretio.com
dir: *From St Davids take A487 towards Fishguard, left at Rugby Football Club, straight on for 3m. Site signed, left to site.* **grid ref:** *SM787292*

An attractive site in a very rural spot with distant country views, and close to beautiful beaches; the tiny cathedral city of St Davids is only three miles away. A mobile shop calls daily at peak periods, and orienteering advice and maps are available. 6.5 acre site. 40 touring pitches. 8 seasonal pitches. Caravan pitches. Motorhome pitches. Tent pitches. 30 statics.

Open: Mar-Oct **Last arrival:** 20.00hrs **Last departure:** 10.00hrs

Pitches: * £12-£31 £12-£31 £12-£31

Leisure:

Facilities:

Services:

Within 3 miles:

Notes: Dogs must be kept on leads. Pitch & putt, climbing wall, play area.

AA Pubs & Restaurants nearby: Cwtch, ST DAVIDS, SA62 6SD, 01437 720491

The Sloop Inn, PORTHGAIN, SA62 5BN, 01348 831449

The Shed, PORTHGAIN, SA62 5BN, 01348 831518

Hendre Eynon Camping & Caravan Site

►►► 81%

tel: 01437 720474 **SA62 6DB**
email: hendreeynoninfo@gmail.com **web:** www.hendreeynon.co.uk
dir: *Take A487 from St Davids towards Fishguard. Left at rugby club signed Llanrhian. Site 2m on right (NB do no take turn to Whitesands).* **grid ref:** *SM771284*

A peaceful, level site on a working farm, with a modern toilet block including family rooms. Within easy reach of many lovely sandy beaches, and just two miles from the cathedral city of St Davids. The National Cycle Network's Celtic Trail (Route 4) passes the site. 7 acre site. 50 touring pitches. 20 seasonal pitches. Caravan pitches. Motorhome pitches. Tent pitches.

Open: Apr-Sep **Last arrival:** 21.00hrs **Last departure:** noon

Pitches: * £14-£21 £14-£21 £14-£21

Facilities:

Services:

Within 3 miles:

Notes: Maximum 2 dogs per unit. Dogs must be kept on leads.

AA Pubs & Restaurants nearby: Cwtch, ST DAVIDS, SA62 6SD, 01437 720491

The Sloop Inn, PORTHGAIN, SA62 5BN, 01348 831449

The Shed, PORTHGAIN, SA62 5BN, 01348 831518

TENBY Map 8 SN10

Places to visit

Tudor Merchant's House, TENBY, SA70 7BX, 01834 842279 www.nationaltrust.org.uk/tudormerchantshouse

Tenby Museum & Art Gallery, TENBY, SA70 7BP, 01834 842809 www.tenbymuseum.org.uk

Great for kids: Colby Woodland Garden, AMROTH, SA67 8PP, 01834 811885 www.nationaltrust.org.uk/main

Kiln Park Holiday Centre

HOLIDAY CENTRE 86%

GOLD

tel: 0800 820000 **Marsh Rd SA70 8RB**
email: kilnpark@haven.com **web:** www.haven.com/kilnpark
dir: *Follow A477, A478 to Tenby for 6m. Then follow signs to Penally, site 0.5m on left.*
grid ref: *SN119002*

A large holiday complex complete with leisure and sports facilities and lots of entertainment for all the family. There are bars and cafés and plenty of security. This touring, camping and static site is on the outskirts of town, and it's only a short walk through dunes to the sandy beach. The modern amenities block provides a stylish interior with under-floor heating and superb fixtures and fittings. Well-equipped safari tents are also available. 103 acre site. 130 touring pitches. 60 hardstandings. Caravan pitches. Motorhome pitches. Tent pitches. 703 statics. Safari tents.

Kiln Park Holiday Centre

Open: mid Mar-end Oct (rs mid Mar-May & Sep-Oct some facilities may be reduced) **Last arrival:** dusk **Last departure:** 10.00hrs

Pitches: **Leisure:**

Facilities:

Services:

Within 3 miles:

Notes: No commercial vehicles, no bookings by persons under 21yrs unless a family booking, max 2 dogs per booking, certain dog breeds banned. Dogs must be kept on leads. Entertainment complex, bowling & putting green.

AA Pubs & Restaurants nearby: Hope and Anchor, TENBY, SA70 7AX, 01834 842131

See advert below

Trefalun Park

►►►► 87%

tel: 01646 651514 **Devonshire Dr, St Florence SA70 8RD**
email: trefalun@aol.com **web:** www.trefalunpark.co.uk
dir: *1.5m NW of St Florence & 0.5m N of B4318.* **grid ref:** *SN093027*

Set within 12 acres of sheltered, well-kept grounds, this quiet country park offers well-maintained level grass pitches separated by bushes and trees, with plenty of space to relax in. Children can feed the park's friendly pets. Plenty of activities are available at the nearby Heatherton Country Sports Park, including go-karting, indoor bowls, golf and bumper boating. 12 acre site. 90 touring pitches. 54 hardstandings. 45 seasonal pitches. Caravan pitches. Motorhome pitches. Tent pitches. 10 statics.

Trefalun Park

Open: Etr-Oct **Last arrival:** 19.00hrs **Last departure:** noon

Pitches: * £15-£27 £15-£24 £15-£24

Leisure:

Facilities:

Services:

Within 3 miles:

Notes: No motorised scooters, no gazebos. Dogs must be kept on leads.

AA Pubs & Restaurants nearby: Hope and Anchor, TENBY, SA70 7AX, 01834 842131

See advert below

TENBY *continued*

Well Park Caravan & Camping Site

►►►► 82%

tel: 01834 842179 **SA70 8TL**
email: enquiries@wellparkcaravans.co.uk
dir: *A478 towards Tenby. At rdbt at Kilgetty follow Tenby/A478 signs. 3m to next rdbt, take 2nd exit, site 2nd right.* **grid ref:** *SN128028*

An attractive, well-maintained park with good landscaping from trees, ornamental shrubs and flower borders. The amenities include a launderette and indoor dishwashing, games room with table tennis, and an enclosed play area. The park is ideally situated between Tenby and Saundersfoot; Tenby just a 15-minute walk away, or the town can be reached via a traffic-free cycle track. 10 acre site. 100 touring pitches. 16 hardstandings. Caravan pitches. Motorhome pitches. Tent pitches. 42 statics.

Open: Mar-Oct (rs Mar-mid Jun & mid Sep-Oct bar may be closed) **Last arrival:** 22.00hrs **Last departure:** 11.00hrs

Pitches: * £15-£28 £15-£28 £14-£20

Leisure:

Facilities:

Services:

Within 3 miles:

Notes: Family groups only. Dogs must be kept on leads. TV hook-ups.

AA Pubs & Restaurants nearby: Hope and Anchor, TENBY, SA70 7AX, 01834 842131

Wood Park Caravans

►►► 80%

tel: 01834 843414 **New Hedges SA70 8TL**
email: info@woodpark.co.uk
dir: *At rdbt 2m N of Tenby follow A478 towards Tenby, take 2nd right & right again.* **grid ref:** *SN128025*

Situated in beautiful countryside between the popular seaside resorts of Tenby and Saundersfoot, and with Waterwynch Bay just a 15-minute walk away, this peaceful site provides a spacious and relaxing atmosphere for holidays. The slightly sloping touring area is divided by shrubs and hedge-screened paddocks and a licensed bar and games room are also available. 10 acre site. 60 touring pitches. 40 hardstandings. 10 seasonal pitches. Caravan pitches. Motorhome pitches. Tent pitches. 90 statics.

Open: Spring BH-Sep (rs Etr-Spring BH & Sep bar, laundrette & games room may not be open) **Last arrival:** 22.00hrs **Last departure:** 10.00hrs

Pitches: * £15-£25 £15-£25 £14-£23

Leisure:

Facilities:

Services:

Within 3 miles:

Notes: No groups, 1 car per unit. Only small dogs accepted, no dogs Jul-Aug & BH. Dogs must be kept on leads.

AA Pubs & Restaurants nearby: Hope and Anchor, TENBY, SA70 7AX, 01834 842131

POWYS

BRECON

Map 9 SO02

Places to visit

Regimental Museum of The Royal Welsh, BRECON, LD3 7EB, 01874 613310
www.royalwelsh.org.uk

Tretower Court & Castle, TRETOWER, NP8 1RD, 01874 730279
www.cadw.wales.gov.uk

PREMIER PARK

Pencelli Castle Caravan & Camping Park

►►►►► 90%

tel: 01874 665451 **Pencelli LD3 7LX**
email: pencelli@tiscali.co.uk
dir: *Exit A40 2m E of Brecon onto B4558, follow signs to Pencelli.* **grid ref:** *SO096248*

Lying in the heart of the Brecon Beacons National Park, this charming park offers peace, beautiful scenery and high quality facilities. It is bordered by the Brecon and Monmouth Canal. The attention to detail is superb, and the well-equipped heated toilets with en suite cubicles are matched by a drying room for clothes and boots, full laundry, and a shop. Regular buses stop just outside the gate and go to Brecon, Abergavenny and Swansea. 10 acre site. 80 touring pitches. 40 hardstandings. Caravan pitches. Motorhome pitches. Tent pitches.

Open: 15 Feb-30 Nov (rs 30 Oct-Etr shop closed) **Last arrival:** 22.00hrs **Last departure:** noon

Pitches: * £18-£28.80 £18-£28.80 £13-£25

Leisure:

Facilities:

Services:

Within 3 miles:

Notes: Assistance dogs only. No radios, music or camp fires. Cycle hire.

AA Pubs & Restaurants nearby: Star Inn, TALYBONT-ON-USK, LD3 7YX, 01874 676635
The Usk Inn, BRECON, LD3 7JE, 01874 676251

BRONLLYS Map 9 SO13

Places to visit

Regimental Museum of The Royal Welsh, BRECON, LD3 7EB, 01874 613310 www.royalwelsh.org.uk

Anchorage Caravan Park

►►►► 82%

tel: 01874 711246 & 711230 **LD3 OLD**
web: www.anchoragecp.co.uk
dir: *8m NE of Brecon in village centre.* **grid ref:** *SO142351*

A well-maintained site with a choice of south-facing, sloping grass pitches and superb views of the Black Mountains, or a more sheltered lower area with a number of excellent super pitches. The site is a short distance from the water sports centre at Llangorse Lake. 8 acre site. 110 touring pitches. 8 hardstandings. 60 seasonal pitches. Caravan pitches. Motorhome pitches. Tent pitches. 101 statics.

Open: all year (rs Nov-Mar TV room closed) **Last arrival:** 23.00hrs
Last departure: 18.00hrs

Pitches: fr £13 fr £13 fr £13

Leisure:

Facilities:

Services:

Within 3 miles:

Notes: Dogs must be kept on leads. Post office, hairdresser.

AA Pubs & Restaurants nearby: The Harp Inn, GLASBURY, HR3 5NR, 01497 847373

The Old Black Lion, HAY-ON-WYE, HR3 5AD, 01497 820841

BUILTH WELLS Map 9 SO05

PREMIER PARK

Fforest Fields Caravan & Camping Park

►►►►► 85%

GOLD

tel: 01982 570406 **Hundred House LD1 5RT**
email: office@fforestfields.co.uk **web:** www.fforestfields.co.uk
dir: *From town centre follow New Radnor signs on A481. 4m to signed entrance on right, 0.5m before Hundred House village.* **grid ref:** *SO100535*

This is a constantly improving, sheltered park surrounded by magnificent scenery and an abundance of wildlife. The spacious pitches are well spaced to create optimum privacy, and the superb eco-friendly amenities block is fuelled by a bio-mass boiler and solar panels. Two bell tents with character shed kitchens and the Fforest Café, specialising in cream teas, were introduced for the 2015 season. The historic town of Builth Wells and The Royal Welsh Showground are just four miles away. 12 acre site. 80 touring pitches. 17 hardstandings. 12 seasonal pitches. Caravan pitches. Motorhome pitches. Tent pitches. 2 bell tents.

Open: all year (rs 4 Jan-end Mar small shop) **Last arrival:** 21.00hrs
Last departure: 18.00hrs

Pitches: £18-£24 £18-£24 £15-£21

Leisure:

Facilities:

Services:

Within 3 miles:

Notes: No loud music. Fridges, microwave, phone charging available.

AA Pubs & Restaurants nearby: The Laughing Dog, LLANDRINDOD WELLS, LD1 5PT, 01597 822406

CHURCHSTOKE

Map 15 SO29

Places to visit

Montgomery Castle, MONTGOMERY, 01443 336000 www.cadw.wales.gov.uk

PREMIER PARK

Daisy Bank Caravan Park

►►►►► 84%

tel: 01588 620471 & 07918 680712 **Snead SY15 6EB**
email: enquiries@daisy-bank.co.uk
dir: *On A489, 2m E of Churchstoke.* **grid ref:** *SO309926*

Peacefully located between Craven Arms and Churchstoke and surrounded by rolling hills, this idyllic, adults-only park offers generously sized, fully serviced pitches; all are situated in attractive hedged areas, surrounded by lush grass and pretty seasonal flowers. The immaculately maintained amenity blocks provide smart, modern fittings and excellent privacy options. Camping pods, a pitch and putt course and free WiFi are also available. 7 acre site. 80 touring pitches. 75 hardstandings. 30 seasonal pitches. Caravan pitches. Motorhome pitches. Tent pitches. 2 wooden pods.

Open: all year **Last arrival:** 20.00hrs **Last departure:** 13.00hrs

Pitches: * £19-£28 £19-£28 £20-£24

Facilities:

Services:

Within 3 miles:

Notes: Adults only. Dogs must be kept on leads. Caravan storage.

AA Pubs & Restaurants nearby: The Three Tuns Inn, BISHOP'S CASTLE, SY9 5BW, 01588 638797

CRICKHOWELL

Map 9 SO21

Places to visit

Tretower Court & Castle, TRETOWER, NP8 1RD, 01874 730279 www.cadw.wales.gov.uk

Big Pit National Coal Museum, BLAENAVON, NP4 9XP, 029 20573650 www.museumwales.ac.uk

Riverside Caravan & Camping Park

►►► 81%

tel: 01873 810397 **New Rd NP8 1AY**
email: riversideccp@btopenworld.com
dir: *On A4077, well signed from A40.* **grid ref:** *SO215184*

A very well tended adults-only park in delightful countryside on the edge of the small country town of Crickhowell. The adjacent riverside park is an excellent facility for all, including dog-walkers. Crickhowell has numerous specialist shops including a first-class delicatessen. Within a few minutes' walk of the park are several friendly pubs with good restaurants. 3.5 acre site. 35 touring pitches. Caravan pitches. Motorhome pitches. Tent pitches. 20 statics.

Open: Mar-Oct **Last arrival:** 21.00hrs

Pitches: * fr £18 fr £18 fr £12

Facilities:

Services:

Within 3 miles:

Notes: Adults only. No hang gliders or paragliders. Dogs must be kept on leads. Large canopied area for drying clothes, cooking etc.

AA Pubs & Restaurants nearby: The Bear, CRICKHOWELL, NP8 1BW, 01873 810408

LLANDRINDOD WELLS

Map 9 SO06

Disserth Caravan & Camping Park

►►►► 83%

tel: 01597 860277 **Disserth, Howey LD1 6NL**
email: disserthcaravan@btconnect.com
dir: *1m from A483, between Newbridge-on-Wye & Howey, by church. Follow brown signs from A483 or A470.* **grid ref:** *SO035583*

By a 13th-century church, this is a delightfully secluded and predominantly adult park that sits in a beautiful valley on the banks of the River Ithon, a tributary of the River Wye. It has a small bar which is open at weekends and during busy periods. The amenities block and laundry are appointed to a high standard and provide good privacy options. The site now offers a shepherd's hut and a wooden 'morphPod' for hire. 4 acre site. 30 touring pitches. 6 hardstandings. Caravan pitches. Motorhome pitches. Tent pitches. 25 statics. 1 wooden pod. 1 shepherd's hut.

Open: Mar-Oct **Last arrival:** sunset **Last departure:** noon

Pitches: * £15-£20 £15-£20 £8-£20

Facilities:

Services:

Within 3 miles:

Notes: Dogs must be kept on leads. Private trout fishing.

AA Pubs & Restaurants nearby: The Laughing Dog, LLANDRINDOD WELLS, LD1 5PT, 01597 822406

Dalmore Camping & Caravanning Park

►► 82%

tel: 01597 822483 **Howey LD1 5RG**
email: brianthorpe@tiscali.co.uk
dir: *From A438 between Llandrindod Wells & Builth Wells follow site signs at hill top. (3m from Llandrindod Wells; 4m from Builth Wells).* **grid ref:** *SO045575*

An intimate and well laid out adults-only park. Pitches are attractively terraced to ensure that all enjoy the wonderful views from this splendidly landscaped little park. 3 acre site. 20 touring pitches. 12 hardstandings. 6 seasonal pitches. Caravan pitches. Motorhome pitches. Tent pitches. 20 statics.

Open: Mar-Oct **Last arrival:** 22.00hrs **Last departure:** noon

Pitches: * £9-£12 £9-£12 £9-£12

Facilities:

Services:

Within 3 miles:

Notes: Adults only. Gates closed 23.00hrs-07.00hrs, no ball games. Dogs must be kept on leads. Separate male & female washing areas, no cubicles.

AA Pubs & Restaurants nearby: The Laughing Dog, LLANDRINDOD WELLS, LD1 5PT, 01597 822406

LLANGORS Map 9 SO12

Places to visit

Regimental Museum of The Royal Welsh, BRECON, LD3 7EB, 01874 613310 www.royalwelsh.org.uk

Great for kids: Tretower Court & Castle, TRETOWER, NP8 1RD, 01874 730279 www.cadw.wales.gov.uk

Lakeside Caravan Park

►►► 78%

tel: 01874 658226 **LD3 7TR**
email: holidays@llangorselake.co.uk
dir: *Exit A40 at Bwlch onto B4560 towards Llangorse. Site signed towards lake in Llangorse village.* **grid ref:** *SO128272*

Surrounded by spectacular mountains and set alongside Llangorse Lake, with mooring and launching facilities, this is a must-do holiday destination for lovers of outdoor pursuits, from walking to watersports and even pike fishing for which the lake is renowned. The hedge- or tree-screened touring areas provide generously sized pitches. There's a well-stocked shop, bar and café, with takeaway, under the same ownership. 2 acre site. 40 touring pitches. 8 hardstandings. Caravan pitches. Motorhome pitches. Tent pitches. 72 statics.

Open: Etr or Apr-Oct (rs Mar-May & Oct clubhouse, restaurant) **Last arrival:** 21.30hrs **Last departure:** 10.00hrs

Pitches: * £13.50-£19.75 £13.50-£19.75 £13.50-£19.75

Leisure:

Facilities:

Services:

Within 3 miles:

Notes: No open fires, no dogs in hire caravans. Dogs must be kept on leads. Boat hire in summer.

AA Pubs & Restaurants nearby: The Usk Inn, BRECON, LD3 7JE, 01874 676251
Star Inn, TALYBONT-ON-USK, LD3 7YX, 01874 676635

MIDDLETOWN Map 15 SJ31

Places to visit

Powis Castle & Garden, WELSHPOOL, SY21 8RF, 01938 551929 www.nationaltrust.org.uk

Bank Farm Caravan Park

►►► 80%

tel: 01938 570526 **SY21 8EJ**
email: bankfarmcaravans@yahoo.co.uk
dir: *13m W of Shrewsbury, 5m E of Welshpool on A458.* **grid ref:** *SJ293123*

An attractive park on a small farm, maintained to a high standard. There are two touring areas, one on either side of the A458, and each with its own amenity block, and immediate access to hills, mountains and woodland. A pub serving good food, and a large play area are nearby. 2 acre site. 40 touring pitches. Caravan pitches. Motorhome pitches. Tent pitches. 33 statics.

Open: Mar-Oct **Last arrival:** 20.00hrs

Pitches: * fr £16 fr £16 fr £13

Leisure:

Facilities:

Services:

Within 3 miles:

Notes: Dogs must be kept on leads. Coarse fishing, jacuzzi, snooker room.

AA Pubs & Restaurants nearby: The Old Hand and Diamond Inn, COEDWAY, SY5 9AR, 01743 884379

RHAYADER Map 9 SN96

Places to visit

Great for kids: Gilfach Nature Reserve & Visitor Centre, RHAYADER, LD6 5LF, 01597 823298 www.rwtwales.org

Wyeside Caravan & Camping Park

►►► 76%

tel: 01597 810183 **Llangurig Rd LD6 5LB**
email: wyesidecc@powys.gov.uk
dir: *400mtrs N of Rhayader town centre on A470.* **grid ref:** *SO967690*

With direct access from the A470, the park sits on the banks of the River Wye. Situated just 400 metres from the centre of the market town of Rhayader, and next to a recreation park with tennis courts, bowling green and children's playground. There are good riverside walks from here, though the river is fast flowing and unfenced, and care is especially needed when walking with children. 6 acre site. 120 touring pitches. 22 hardstandings. 21 seasonal pitches. Caravan pitches. Motorhome pitches. Tent pitches. 39 statics.

Open: Mar-Oct **Last arrival:** 20.00hrs **Last departure:** noon

Pitches: * £17-£21 £17-£21 fr £15

Facilities:

Services:

Within 3 miles:

Notes: No noise after 23.00hrs. Dogs must be kept on leads.

SWANSEA

OLDWALLS Map 8 SS49

Oldwalls Gower Glamping NEW ►►►►

tel: 01792 391468 **SA3 1HA**
email: info@oldwallsgower.com
dir: *M4 junct, A483 towards Swansea. At rdbt take A484 signed Llanelli & The Gower. In Gowerton follow B4295 signs. Through Llanrhidian to Oldwalls.* **grid ref:** *SS488918*

Head down the winding and well-maintained approach road, with rare breed sheep and llamas to admire on the way, to find this excellent new glamping operation. It's a memorable destination – everything is immaculately presented with stone walling, lush neat grass, well-trimmed hedging and a stunning display of seasonal flowers. The glamping area is set beside an ornamental lake with abundant wild flowers; tarmac pathways lead to each of the 10 well-spaced bell tents. Each unit is on a level artificial grass hardstanding and the beautifully styled interiors have rattan flooring, oil-heated radiators, smart furnishings and quality double beds. Just a stroll away is a modern, bright centrally-heated amenities block with five unisex shower, wash basin and toilet rooms.

Open: Apr-Oct **Last arrival:** 20.00hrs **Last departure:** 10.30hrs

Pitches: * £79-£95

PORT EYNON Map 8 SS48

Places to visit

Weobley Castle, LLANRHIDIAN, SA3 1HB, 01792 390012 www.cadw.wales.gov.uk

Gower Heritage Centre, PARKMILL, SA3 2EH, 01792 371206 www.gowerheritagecentre.co.uk

Great for kids: Oxwich Castle, OXWICH, SA3 1ND, 01792 390359 www.cadw.wales.gov.uk

Carreglwyd Camping & Caravan Park ►►►► 83%

tel: 01792 390795 **SA3 1NL**
email: booking@porteynon.com
dir: *A4118 to Port Eynon, site adjacent to beach.* **grid ref:** *SS465863*

Set in an unrivalled location alongside the safe sandy beach of Port Eynon on the Gower Peninsula, this popular park is an ideal family holiday spot; it is also close to an attractive village with pubs and shops. The sloping ground has been partly terraced and most pitches have sea views; the excellent toilet facilities include three superb family bathrooms. 12 acre site. 150 touring pitches. Caravan pitches. Motorhome pitches. Tent pitches.

Open: all year **Last arrival:** 22.00hrs **Last departure:** 15.00hrs

Pitches: **Facilities:**

Services:

Within 3 miles:

Notes: Dogs must be kept on leads.

AA Pubs & Restaurants nearby: Fairyhill, REYNOLDSTON, SA3 1BS, 01792 390139

King Arthur Hotel, REYNOLDSTON, SA3 1AD, 01792 390775

RHOSSILI Map 8 SS48

Places to visit

Weobley Castle, LLANRHIDIAN, SA3 1HB, 01792 390012 www.cadw.wales.gov.uk

Gower Heritage Centre, PARKMILL, SA3 2EH, 01792 371206 www.gowerheritagecentre.co.uk

Great for kids: Oxwich Castle, OXWICH, SA3 1ND, 01792 390359 www.cadw.wales.gov.uk

Pitton Cross Caravan & Camping Park ►►► 90%

tel: 01792 390593 **SA3 1PT**
email: admin@pittoncross.co.uk **web:** www.pittoncross.co.uk
dir: *2m W of Scurlage on B4247.* **grid ref:** *SS434877*

Surrounded by farmland close to sandy Mewslade Bay, which is within walking distance across the fields, this grassy park is divided by hedging into paddocks; hardstandings for motorhomes are available. Some areas are deliberately left uncultivated, resulting in colourful displays of wild flowers including roses and orchids. Rhossili Beach, which is popular with surfers, and the Wales Coastal Path are nearby. Both children's kites and power kites are sold on site, and instruction is available. Geocaching and paragliding are possible too. 6 acre site. 100 touring pitches. 27 hardstandings. Caravan pitches. Motorhome pitches. Tent pitches.

Open: all year (rs Nov-Mar no bread, milk or newspapers) **Last arrival:** 20.00hrs **Last departure:** 11.00hrs

Pitches: * £20-£27.50 £20-£27.50 £11-£35

Leisure:

Facilities:

Services:

Within 3 miles:

Notes: Quiet at all times, charcoal BBQs must be off ground, no fire pits or log burning. Dogs must be kept on leads. Baby bath available.

AA Pubs & Restaurants nearby: Fairyhill, REYNOLDSTON, SA3 1BS, 01792 390139

King Arthur Hotel, REYNOLDSTON, SA3 1AD, 01792 390775

Kings Head, LLANGENNITH, SA3 1HX, 01792 386212

SWANSEA
Map 9 SS69

Places to visit

Swansea Museum, SWANSEA, SA1 1SN, 01792 653763 www.swanseamuseum.co.uk

Great for kids: Plantasia, SWANSEA, SA1 2AL, 01792 474555 www.plantasia.org

Riverside Caravan Park

HOLIDAY CENTRE 77%

tel: 01792 775587 **Ynys Forgan Farm, Morriston SA6 6QL**
email: reception@riversideswansea.com
dir: *At M4 junct 45 follow Swansea signs. Before joining A4067 turn left into private road signed to site.* **grid ref:** *SS679991*

A large and busy park close to the M4 but in a quiet location beside the River Taw. This friendly, family orientated park has a licensed club and bar with a full high-season entertainment programme. There is a choice of eating outlets – the clubhouse restaurant, takeaway and chip shop. The park has a good indoor pool. 5 acre site. 90 touring pitches. Caravan pitches. Motorhome pitches. Tent pitches. 256 statics.

Open: all year (rs Winter months pool & club closed) **Last arrival:** mdnt
Last departure: noon

Pitches: **Leisure:**

Facilities: **Services:**

Within 3 miles:

Notes: Dogs by prior arrangement only, no aggressive breeds permitted. Fishing on site by arrangement.

WREXHAM

BRONINGTON
Map 15 SJ43

Places to visit

Erddig, WREXHAM, LL13 0YT, 01978 355314 www.nationaltrust.org.uk/erddig

The Little Yurt Meadow

►►►►

tel: 01948 780136 & 07984 400134 **Bay Tree Barns, Mill Rd SY13 3HJ**
email: info@thelittleyurtmeadow.co.uk
dir: *A525 from Whitchurch to Redbrook. In Redbrook left onto A495 (Oswestry). Right to Bronington. At staggered x-rds right into Mill Rd.* **grid ref:** *SJ483397*

Located in a former meadow on the Shropshire/Welsh border this site has become a luxury glamping destination for those wishing to escape from the pressures of everyday life. Three spacious yurts with stylishly furnished interiors are equipped with sumptuous beds, two settees (one converts to a sofa bed), a wood-burning stove, mini-cooker and lots of quality extras. Each yurt has its own luxury shower room and there are areas for communal outdoor and indoor relaxation. 3 acre site. 3 yurts.

Open: all year **Last arrival:** 23.00hrs **Last departure:** 11.00hrs

Leisure: **Facilities:**

Services: **Within 3 miles:**

Notes: No cars by yurts. No noise after 23.00hrs. No credit or debit cards, PayPal accepted. Self-catering kitchen area, wet rooms.

EYTON

Map 15 SJ34

Places to visit

Erddig, WREXHAM, LL13 0YT, 01978 355314 www.nationaltrust.org.uk/erddig

Chirk Castle, CHIRK, LL14 5AF, 01691 777701
www.nationaltrust.org.uk/main/w-chirkcastle

PREMIER PARK

Plassey Holiday Park

94%

Best of British — David Bellamy Conservation Award GOLD

tel: 01978 780277 **The Plassey LL13 0SP**
email: enquiries@plassey.com **web:** www.plassey.com
dir: *From A483 at Bangor-on-Dee exit onto B5426 for 2.5m. Site entrance signed on left.* **grid ref:** *SJ353452*

A lovely park set in several hundred acres of quiet farm and meadowland in the Dee Valley. The superb toilet facilities include individual cubicles for total privacy and security, while the Edwardian farm buildings have been converted into a restaurant, coffee shop, beauty studio and various craft outlets. There is plenty here to entertain the whole family, from scenic walks and a swimming pool to free fishing, and use of the 9-hole golf course. 10 acre site. 90 touring pitches. 60 hardstandings. 60 seasonal pitches. Caravan pitches. Motorhome pitches. Tent pitches. 15 statics.

Plassey Holiday Park

Open: Feb-Nov **Last arrival:** 20.30hrs **Last departure:** noon

Pitches:

Leisure:

Facilities:

Services:

Within 3 miles:

Notes: No footballs or skateboards. Dogs must be kept on leads. Sauna, badminton, table tennis, driving range.

AA Pubs & Restaurants nearby: The Boat Inn, ERBISTOCK, LL13 0DL, 01978 780666

See advert below

LEISURE: Indoor swimming pool Outdoor swimming pool Children's playground Kid's club Tennis court Games room Separate TV room golf course Boats for hire Cinema Entertainment Fishing Mini golf Watersports Gym Sports field Spa Stables
FACILITIES: Bath Shower Electric shaver Hairdryer Ice Pack Facility Disabled facilities Public telephone Shop on site or within 200yds Mobile shop (calls at least 5 days a week) BBQ area Picnic area Wi-fi Internet access Recycling Tourist info Dog exercise area

OVERTON

Map 15 SJ34

The Trotting Mare Caravan Park

►►►► 83%

tel: 01978 711963 **LL13 0LE**
email: info@thetrottingmare.co.uk
dir: *From Oswestry towards Whitchurch take A495. In Ellesmere take A528 towards Overton. Site on left. Or from Wrexham take A525 signed Whitchurch. In Marchwiel turn right onto A528 towards Overton. Through Overton to Ellesmere A528, site on right.*
grid ref: *SJ374396*

Located between Overton-on-Dee and Ellesmere, this adults-only touring park is quietly located behind The Trotting Mare pub. The majority of pitches are fully serviced, and creative landscaping and a free coarse-fishing lake are additional benefits. Please note that there is no laundry on this site but facilities are available at either Ellesmere or Overton. 4.2 acre site. 53 touring pitches. 50 hardstandings. Caravan pitches. Motorhome pitches. Tent pitches. 11 statics.

Open: all year **Last arrival:** 20.00hrs **Last departure:** noon

Pitches:

Facilities:

Services: T

Within 3 miles:

Notes: Adults only. No commercial vehicles, no open fires, no gas bottles outside caravan or awning, no bikes, no ball games, no noise after 23.00 hrs. Dogs must be kept on leads.

AA Pubs & Restaurants nearby: The Boat Inn, ERBISTOCK, LL13 0DL, 01978 780666

Readers' Report Form

Please send this form to:–
The Editor, AA Caravan & Camping Guide,
AA Lifestyle Guides,
13th Floor,
Fanum House,
Basingstoke RG21 4EA

email: lifestyleguides@theAA.com

Please use this form to tell us about any site that you have visited, whether it is in the guide or not currently listed. Feedback from readers helps us to keep our guide accurate and up to date. However, if you have a complaint during your visit, we recommend that you discuss the matter with the management there and then, so that they have a chance to put things right before your visit is spoilt.

Please note that the AA does not undertake to arbitrate between you and the establishment, or to obtain compensation or engage in protracted correspondence.

Date

Your name (BLOCK CAPITALS)

Your address (BLOCK CAPITALS)

Post code

E-mail address

Name of site/park

Location

Comments

(please attach a separate sheet if necessary)

Please tick here ☐ if you DO NOT wish to receive details of AA offers or products

PTO

Readers' Report Form *continued*

Have you bought this guide before? ☐ YES ☐ NO

How often do you visit a caravan park or camp site? (tick one choice)
Once a year ☐ Twice a year ☐ Three times a year ☐
More than three times a year ☐

How long do you generally stay at a park or site? (tick one choice)
One night ☐ Up to a week ☐ 1 week ☐
2 weeks ☐ Over 2 weeks ☐

Do you have a: (tick all that apply)
Tent ☐ Caravan ☐ Motorhome ☐

Please answer these questions to help us make improvements to the guide:
Which of these factors are the most important when choosing a site? (tick one choice)
Location ☐ Toilet/washing facilities ☐ Personal Recommendation ☐
Leisure facilities ☐
Other (please state)

Do you read the editorial features in the guide? ☐ YES ☐ NO

Do you use the location atlas? ☐ YES ☐ NO

What elements of the guide do you find most useful when choosing a site/park? (tick all that apply)
Description ☐ Photo ☐ Advertisement ☐

Is there any other information you would like to see added to this guide?

Readers' Report Form

Please send this form to:–
The Editor, AA Caravan & Camping Guide,
AA Lifestyle Guides,
13th Floor,
Fanum House,
Basingstoke RG21 4EA

email: lifestyleguides@theAA.com

Please use this form to tell us about any site that you have visited, whether it is in the guide or not currently listed. Feedback from readers helps us to keep our guide accurate and up to date. However, if you have a complaint during your visit, we recommend that you discuss the matter with the management there and then, so that they have a chance to put things right before your visit is spoilt.

Please note that the AA does not undertake to arbitrate between you and the establishment, or to obtain compensation or engage in protracted correspondence.

Date ....

Your name (BLOCK CAPITALS) ....

Your address (BLOCK CAPITALS) ....

....

....

Post code ....

E-mail address ....

Name of site/park ....

Location ....

Comments ....

....

....

....

....

....

....

....

(please attach a separate sheet if necessary)

Please tick here ☐ if you DO NOT wish to receive details of AA offers or products

PTO

Readers' Report Form *continued*

Have you bought this guide before? ☐ YES ☐ NO

How often do you visit a caravan park or camp site? (tick one choice)

Once a year ☐ Twice a year ☐ Three times a year ☐

More than three times a year ☐

How long do you generally stay at a park or site? (tick one choice)

One night ☐ Up to a week ☐ 1 week ☐

2 weeks ☐ Over 2 weeks ☐

Do you have a: (tick all that apply)

Tent ☐ Caravan ☐ Motorhome ☐

Please answer these questions to help us make improvements to the guide:

Which of these factors are the most important when choosing a site? (tick one choice)

Location ☐ Toilet/washing facilities ☐ Personal Recommendation ☐

Leisure facilities ☐

Other (please state)

Do you read the editorial features in the guide? ☐ YES ☐ NO

Do you use the location atlas? ☐ YES ☐ NO

What elements of the guide do you find most useful when choosing a site/park? (tick all that apply)

Description ☐ Photo ☐ Advertisement ☐

Is there any other information you would like to see added to this guide?